The Complete Guide to

# Family Photography

# The Complete Guide to Family Photography

A Simple Approach to Lighting and Posing for Family, Maternity, and Newborn Photographers

Sandra Coan

The Complete Guide to Family Photography
Sandra Coan
www.sandracoan.com

Project editor: Maggie Yates
Project manager: Lisa Brazieal
Marketing manager: Koryn Olage
Copyeditor: Maggie Yates
Interior design and layout: Kim Scott, Bumpy Design
Cover design: Aren Straiger

ISBN: 979-8-88814-371-1

1st Edition (1st printing)


Rocky Nook Inc.
1010 B Street, Suite 350
San Rafael, CA 94901
USA
www.rockynook.com
info@rockynook.com
(415) 747-8756

Represented in the E.U. by:
Rheinwerk Verlag GmbH
Rheinwerkallee 4
53227 Bonn
Germany
service@rheinwerk-verlag.de

Distributed in the UK and Europe by Publishers Group UK
Distributed in the U.S. and all other territories by Publishers Group West

Library of Congress Control Number: 2025936513



Printed in China.

# Dedication

One of my very first memories is sitting in the darkroom my dad built in our basement, watching him develop photos he'd taken of me and my brother playing at an amusement park. Seeing the images slowly emerge on paper felt like magic. I think I fell in love with photography then, and that passion has stayed with me my entire life.

My dad bought me my first camera when I was nine—a little point-and-shoot that I treasured for years. He later gave me my first "real" camera—a Minolta SLR—as a graduation gift when I finished college.

He was an avid photographer himself and even tried to make a career of it briefly in his twenties. He had a true gift for seeing light, and he captured some truly beautiful images of me and my brothers when we were little. Many of them hang on my walls today.

He was always my biggest cheerleader. As my photography career began to grow, he encouraged me to write a book—to share what I'd learned with others. And this was *years* before I ever believed that was even remotely possible.

Well . . . here's that book.

Thank you, Dad. I love you. I miss you.

This is for you.

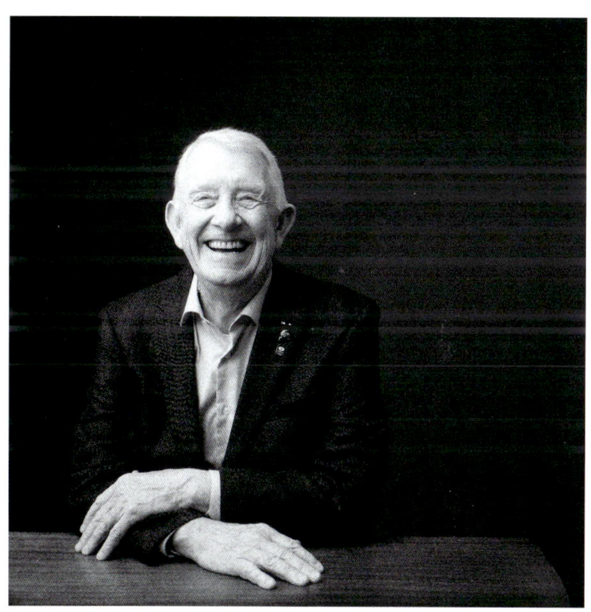

James A. Coan. My dad.

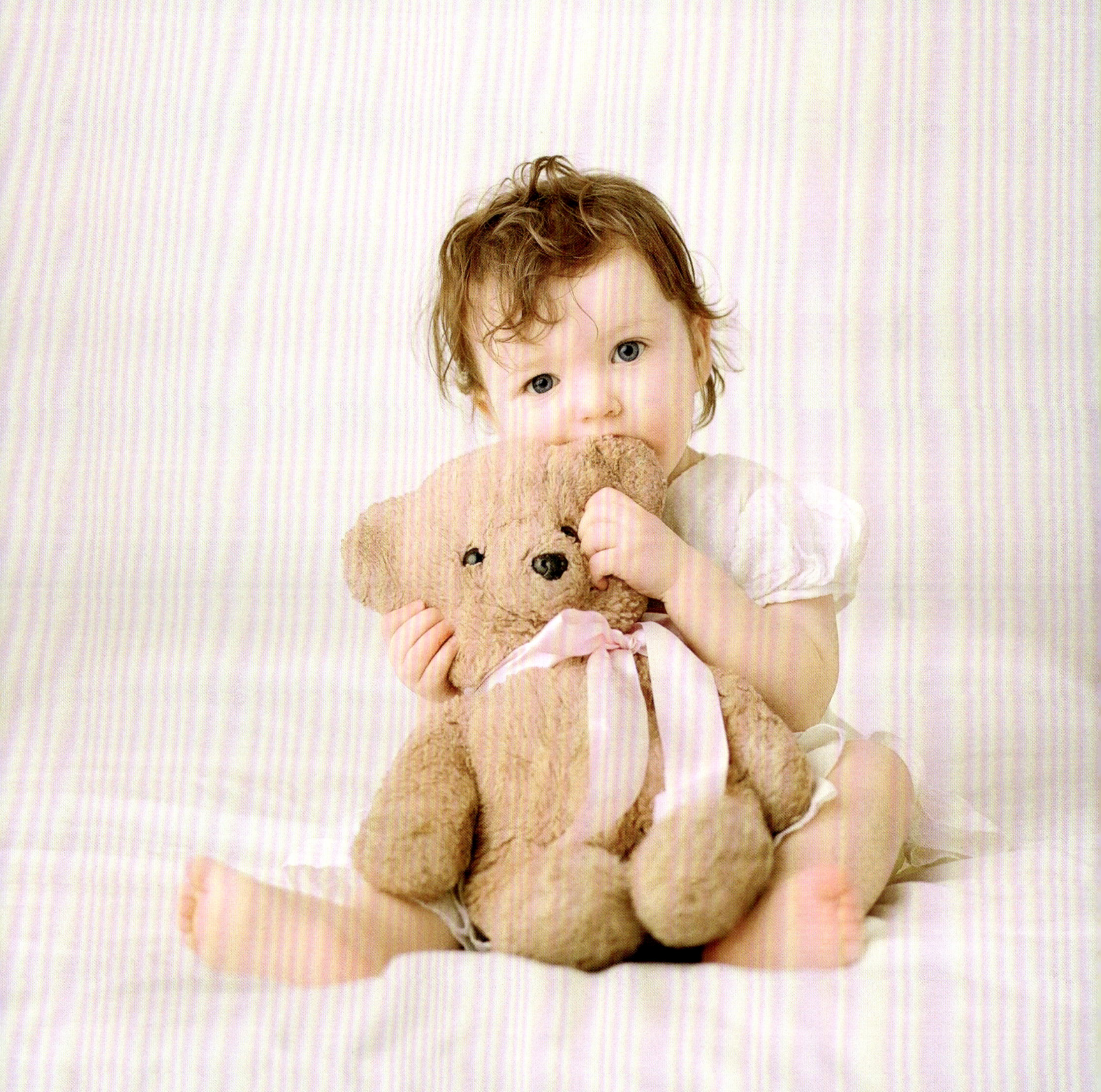

# Contents

Introduction . . . 1

LIGHTING . . . 5

My Posing Doll . . . 6
This Is a Life-Changing Skill . . . 7

1 Lighting Fundamentals . . . 9
Quality . . . 10
Intensity . . . 13
Temperature . . . 18
Patterns . . . 19
Putting It All Together . . . 32
Finding Your Own Style . . . 32

2 Working with Natural Light . . . 35
The Technicals . . . 36
Wrapping It All Up . . . 65

3 Working with Artificial Light . . . 67
Equipment . . . 68
Know the Rules to Break the Rules . . . 92
Putting It All Together . . . 94

4 Lighting on Location . . . 97
Common Problems When on Location . . . 98
Assessing Your Environment . . . 102
Bouncing Light . . . 116
Don't Be Afraid to Experiment . . . 121
A Real-World Example . . . 123
Next Steps . . . 125

POSING . . . 127

My Approach to Posing . . . 128
What You'll Learn . . . 129
Patience and Practice . . . 129

5 Posing Fundamentals . . . 131
What Posing Is and Isn't, Specific to Family Photography . . . 132
Hands . . . 133
Eyes . . . 139
Chins and Jawlines . . . 148
Heads and Faces . . . 149
The Takeaway . . . 155

6 Composition . . . 157
Creating Triangles . . . 158
Rule of Thirds . . . 169
Negative Space . . . 171
Fill the Frame . . . 171
Leading Lines . . . 172
Putting It All Together . . . 174

7 Posing Flow . . . 177
Consistent, Predictable Routines . . . 178

8 Posing Newborns, Babies, and Small Children ... 193

My Approach to Posing Children ... 194
Maximizing Each Pose ... 195
Newborns ... 195
Three Months ... 208
Sitters ... 214
One Year ... 220
Toddlers ... 228
School-Age and Beyond ... 231
Next Steps ... 235

9 Posing Siblings and Families ... 237

Working with Siblings ... 238
Adding the Parents ... 250
Make These Poses Your Own ... 267

10 Maternity Posing ... 271

When to Schedule ... 272
How to Prepare ... 273
Safety ... 276
Body Position ... 276
Posing with Partners ... 291
Posing with Older Children ... 294
Final Thoughts ... 295

IN REAL LIFE ... 297

11 Newborn, Sitter, and Family ... 301

Backstory: The Rosellini Family ... 302
Session Flow ... 303
Standing Poses ... 313
The Takeaway ... 317

12 Shooting on Location ... 319

Session Prep ... 320
Who ... 320
Where ... 321
What and How ... 321
Fresh 48 (Hospital) Session ... 336
The Takeaway ... 345

13 Maternity Session ... 347

My Philosophy ... 348
My Look ... 349
Full Disclosure ... 349
The Session ... 350
One Last Look ... 362
Final Thoughts ... 362

Conclusion ... 365
Index ... 367

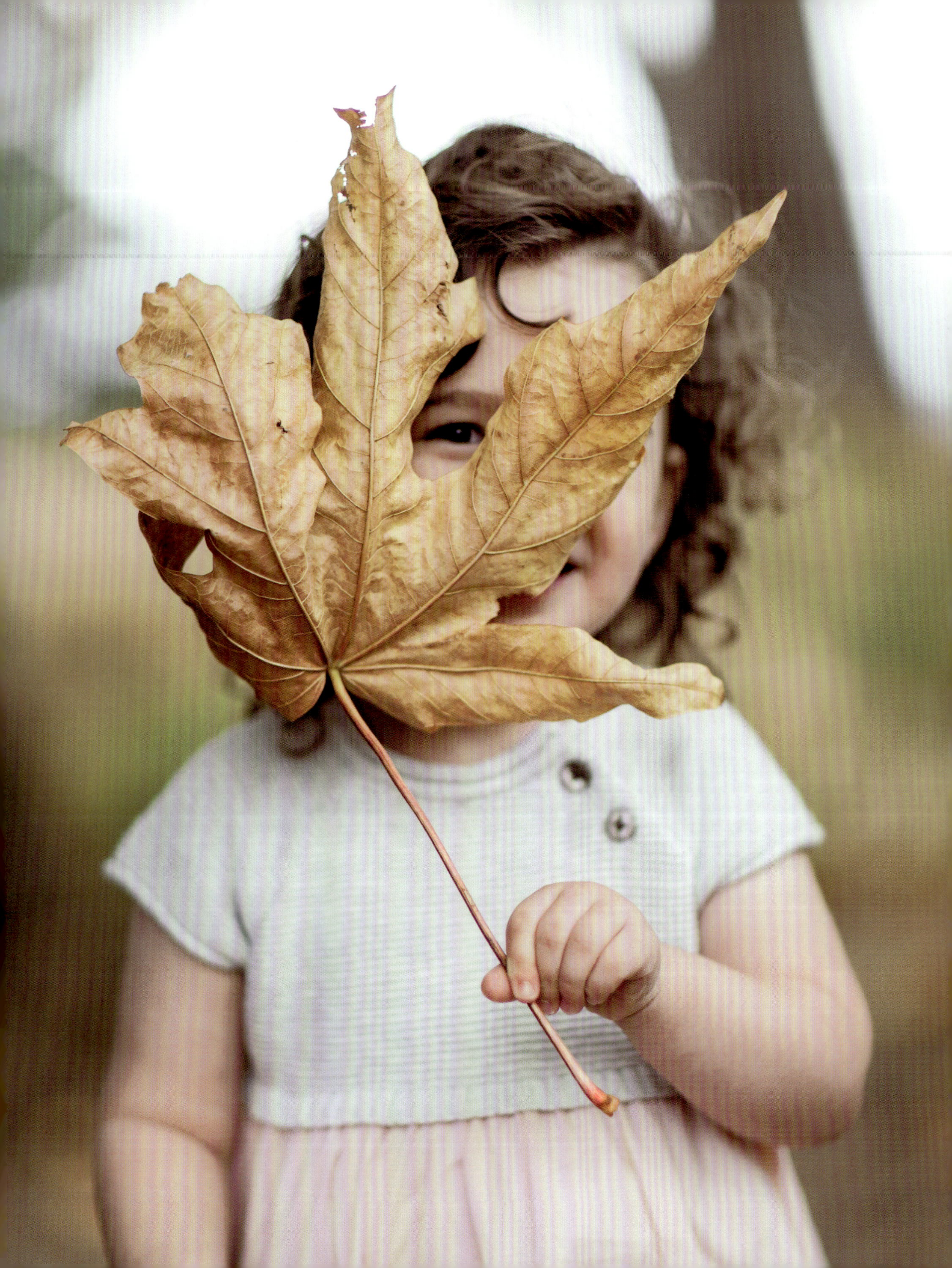

# Introduction

I started my photography career in 1999 with a maternity photo of my friend Ginger (**FIGURE 0.1**).

At the time, I was teaching kindergarten and struggling to get by on my teacher's salary. Money was tight, and I was looking for a way to supplement my income. Ginger was expecting her first child, and we thought it would be fun to recreate the iconic image Annie Leibovitz had taken of Demi Moore for a 1991 cover of *Vanity Fair*. We loved the photos we created, and Ginger—along with a few other friends—encouraged me to offer this kind of photography to other pregnant women in our community. Just like that, my side hustle was born.

I turned my favorite portrait of Ginger into a postcard printed with my name and phone number and dropped a stack of them off at every maternity shop, coffeehouse, and yoga studio I could find. To my surprise, women began to call.

Maternity clients became newborn clients, then family clients. Within three years I quit my teaching job, and my side hustle became my career. I've been working as a maternity, newborn, and family photographer ever since.

Photography has been good to me. I get to do what I love every day while supporting my family financially. I have the freedom to shape my work life around my personal life—not the other way around. I've had the privilege of watching countless children grow up before my lens. I've seen families evolve from one baby to two, three, and sometimes more. I've even photographed the babies of adults I once captured as small children.

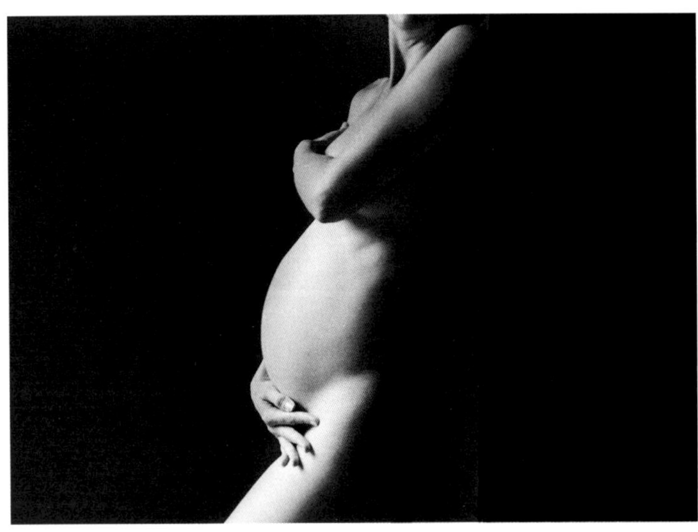

**FIGURE 0.1** Ginger. The photograph that launched my career!

Being a professional family photographer truly is a fantastic job. But mastering your craft takes time—especially when you're trying to figure it all out on your own. I know that struggle firsthand.

Like many photographers, I'm self-taught. I spent years learning and perfecting my skills. My hope is that this book will fast-track your journey so you can skip some of the trial and error I had to endure.

## What Family Photography Means to Me

To me, *family photography* is an umbrella term that encapsulates the entire family journey—from pregnancy and newborns to small children, high school seniors, and even grown children with their parents or caregivers.

Families are formed in many ways. They can include blood relatives and people who took on important roles in our lives. They may consist of one parent or two, grandparents instead of parents, biological parents, adoptive parents, two dads, or two moms. However your family is formed, I see my job the same: to honor and document the love I see in front of my camera.

Throughout this book, I use the terms *Mother* and *Father* when describing setups, but please note that everything I share applies to any family configuration. While I focus primarily on maternity, newborns, and families with young children, the techniques in this book can be adapted to families of all shapes and ages.

## My Approach to Family Photography

My photography style is very minimal. I stay away from props, elaborate backdrops, and settings. I use mostly artificial light, but favor lighting techniques that result in a natural light look. My posing strategy is simple. I practice a baby-led approach with my newborns, and strive to create relaxed, almost candid-looking images for my maternity and family clients. I'll share detailed instructions on how I achieve this look—my true hope is that you take what resonates with you and make it your own. Use this information to develop your own distinct style.

## How to Use This Book

This book is divided into three sections: *Lighting*, *Posing*, and *In Real Life*, where I'll share entire sessions from start to finish to illustrate how my lighting and posing techniques work together in real-life situations. Each section builds upon the previous one. I highly recommend following the order of the book on your first read and save skipping around for subsequent readings.

Take the time to practice(!) what you learn. This book is designed to be a resource, a manual, and a guide that you can come back to again. Use #SCfamilyphotography when posting on social media so I can see what you are creating!

This book is the culmination of over two decades of experience working as a maternity, newborn, and family photographer. I hope you find it inspiring, supportive, and truly helpful.

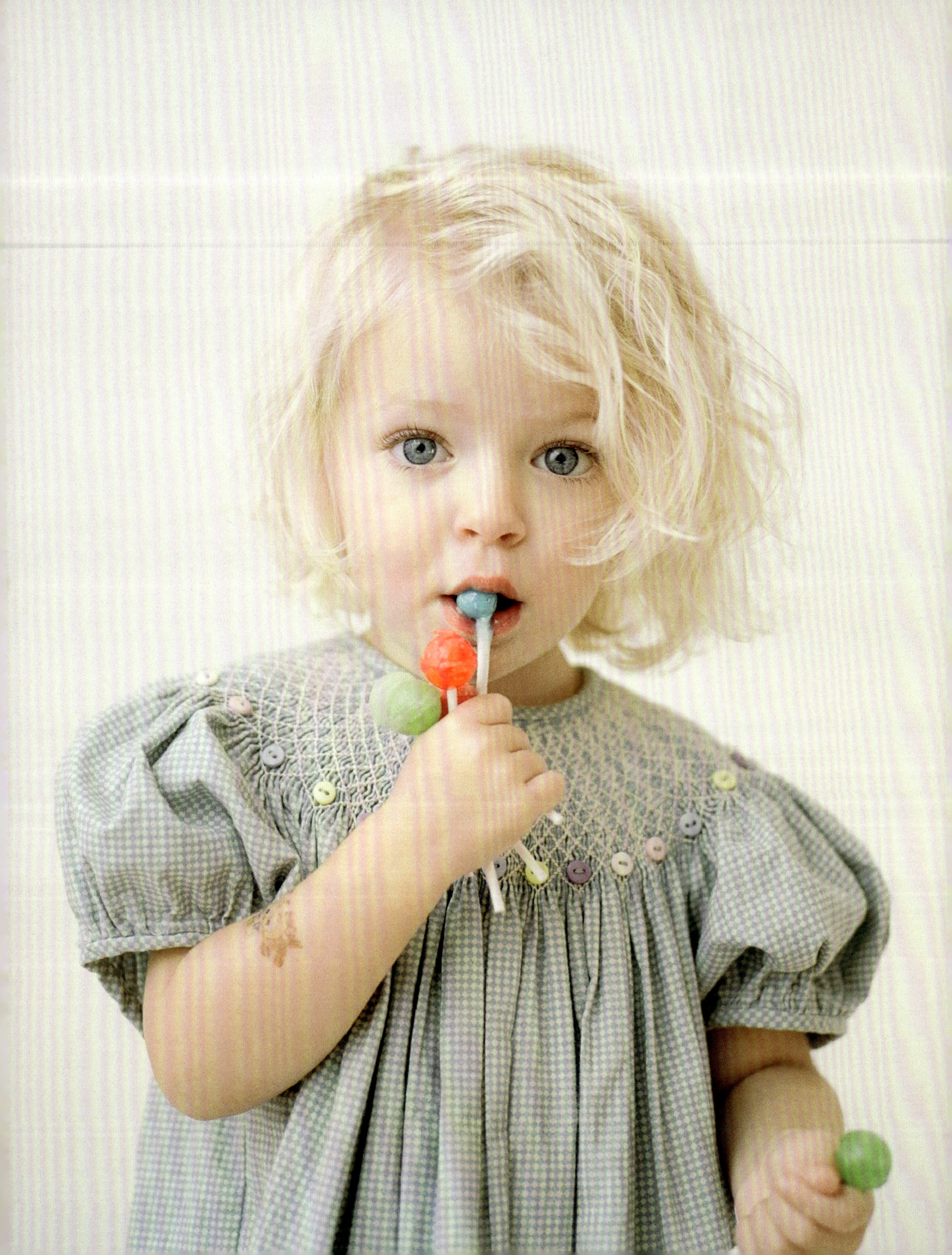

# Lighting

Whether you're working with natural or artificial light, truly understanding your light is *essential* to mastering your craft as a photographer.

Because of its importance, entire books have been written on the subject—including one by me! My book, *Crafting the Natural Light Look*, teaches photographers how to create soft, natural-looking light with strobes and flash. It's a wonderful resource, and the techniques inside can be applied to almost any genre of photography, which I'm very proud of.

After specializing in family photography for over two decades, I know the unique challenges this specific genre presents. I also know that most lighting resources out there were *not* written with family photographers in mind.

That, my friend, is why I'm so excited about the book you're holding in your hands.

Some family photographers, like me, do most of their work in a studio. But many do not. They're working in client homes, small apartments, and dim hospital rooms. As someone who spent the first half of my career working entirely on location, I know how hard that can be! That's why I've included an entire chapter (see Chapter 4) on using lighting on location.

Before we dive into that juicy topic, we're going to cover the lighting fundamentals: quality, intensity, color, and direction. You'll learn how to see light, how to understand it, and how to shape it to create the look you want. I'll walk you through natural-light techniques and show you how to replicate that same soft, natural feel using strobes, flash, and continuous lighting.

We'll also go over what equipment you need to get started with artificial light, including how to set it up and, most importantly, how to assess the environment you're working in and know exactly *where* to place your lights to get your desired look.

By the end of this section, my goal is for you to feel like a lighting expert—confident in your ability to work with any kind of light in any kind of space.

## My Posing Doll

Throughout this section, you'll see images of Betty, my posing doll (**FIGURE L.1**). I found Betty at a garage sale years ago and used her to practice lighting techniques when I was first learning. Now she travels with me to conferences and workshops as my teaching assistant. She'll feature prominently in this part of the book.

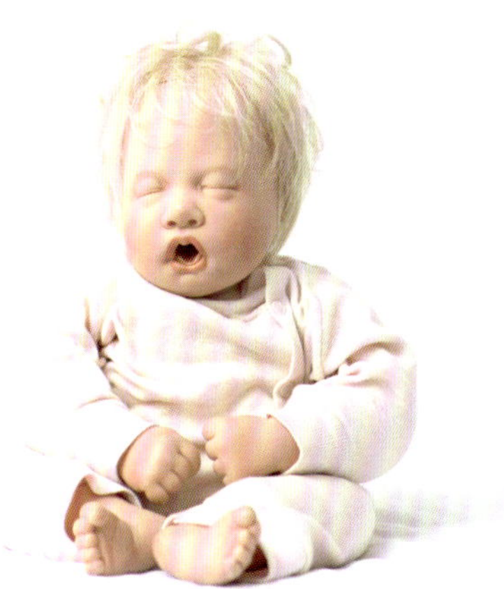

**FIGURE: L.1** Betty the posing doll. Find a doll or stuffed animal to practice the techniques you are learning throughout this book. Practice makes perfect, after all!

Having a Betty (or Betty-equivalent!) will help you practice and refine your lighting skills without the pressure of working with a real client. Practice makes perfect, as they say, and I believe it's better to practice on dolls than on paying clients! Find yourself a doll or stuffed animal to practice with.

## This Is a Life-Changing Skill

Knowing how to work with natural light *and* artificial light is life-changing for any photographer, but especially for family photographers. This knowledge allows you to walk into any situation, no matter how challenging, with confidence!

Beautiful day, perfect window light? No problem. You know how to work with that. But it feels amazing to know you can walk into a windowless room or a bad lighting situation and know how to work with that as well.

I cannot wait to share everything I know with you.

There is a lot to cover! Let's dive in!

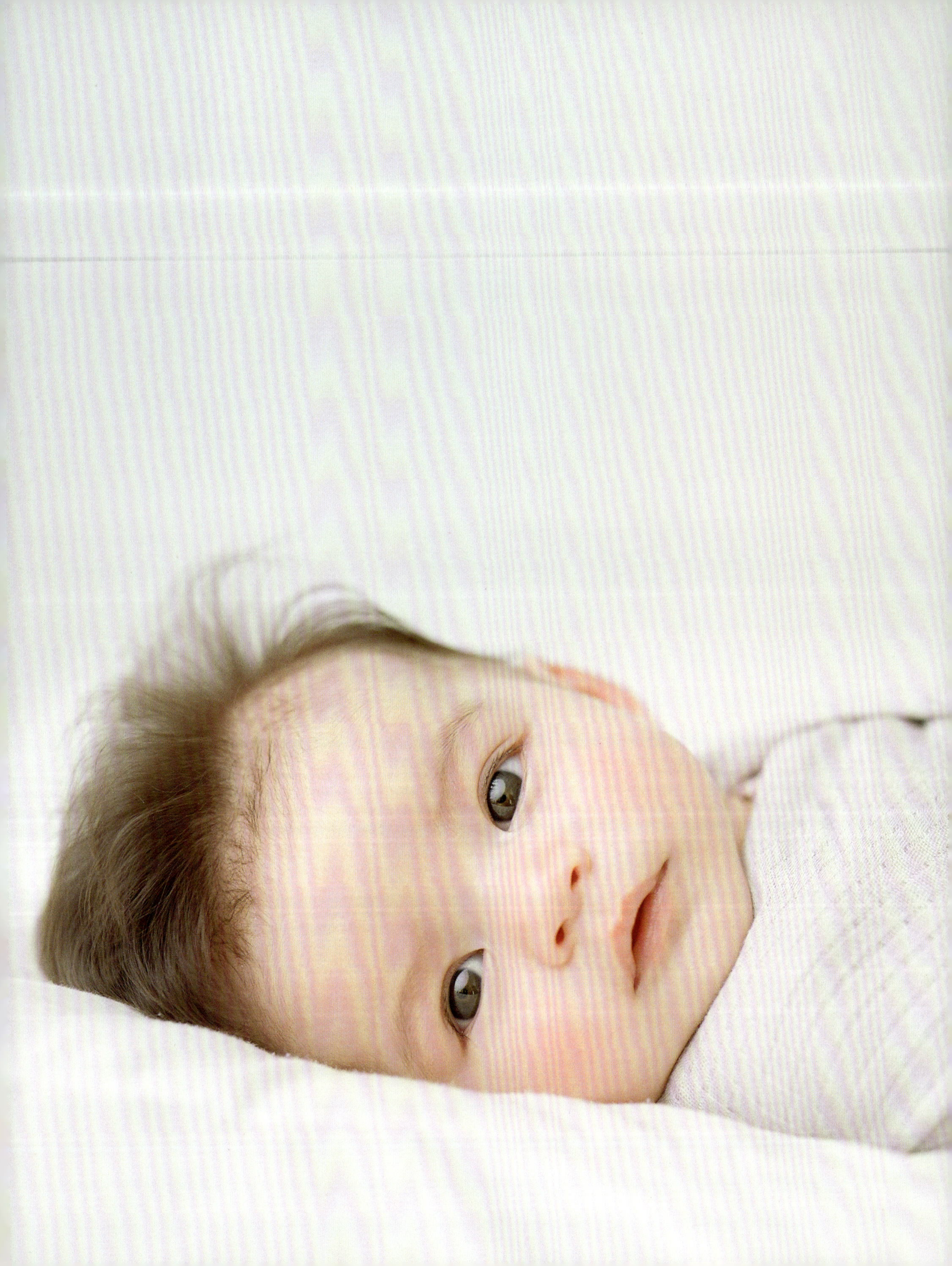

CHAPTER

# 1

# Lighting Fundamentals

Understanding the fundamentals of light is essential for any photographer. The word photography literally means "drawing with light," after all. The quality, intensity, temperature, and direction of the light all have individual roles to play in creating a final image. When used with intention, each of those elements will help you develop a signature style. And as a family photographer, having a signature style is key to standing out.

As we explore these fundamental elements of light, I'll be sharing photos that were captured in my studio to highlight each example, but please note that all these principles apply to working on location, as well.

## Quality

Light quality is often described as being either hard or soft. I think of light quality as living on a spectrum, with hard light on one end and soft light on the other. *How* hard or soft you like your light is a matter of personal taste.

### Hard Light

Hard light is the kind of light we're used to seeing on bright sunny days. This kind of light is very contrasty and is characterized by having sharp, well-defined shadows. Hard light accentuates detail and highlights texture, which is something to keep in mind when using it in portraiture (**FIGURE 1.1A**).

### Soft Light

Soft light, on the other hand, is the kind of light we see on overcast days or in open shade. Soft light can still have contrast, but the transition from highlight to shadow is more gradual and less defined than with hard light (**FIGURE 1.1B**). Details and textures will be less noticeable when using soft light, as well—an important fact to remember when photographing someone with textured skin. Soft light will minimize the texture, whereas hard light will accentuate it.

I personally prefer soft light for my work, but I have seen many beautiful family photos captured in hard light. Again, light quality is a matter of personal taste, but it's important to know which you prefer so you can learn how to consistently create it.

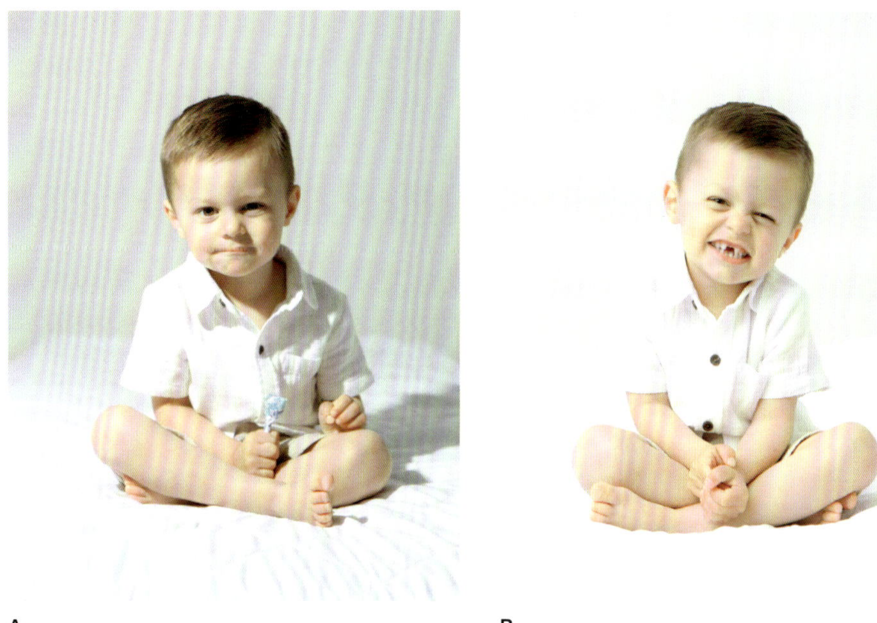


**FIGURE 1.1** Figure 1.1A shows hard light. Notice the sharp, distinct shadows on the subject's face and on the bed. Figure 1.1B shows soft light. Notice the gradual transition from highlight to shadow on the subject's face and on the bed.

## Controlling Light Quality

Whether using natural light or artificial light, we can control the quality of the light we are working with to achieve a desired look and feel.

### Diffusion

One of the simplest ways to control the light quality is by adding or removing diffusion. Diffusion is the act of spreading out light from a single light source evenly across a larger surface, resulting in light that is softer in quality.

Clouds diffuse the sunlight. When working inside, curtains, sheers, blinds, and frosted glass diffuse natural light from windows. Light modifiers, like softboxes and umbrellas, diffuse light when working with strobes, flash, and continuous lights.

### Relative Size

The size of the light source you're working with will also impact the quality of your light. Small light sources, such as small windows and small light modifiers, result in harder light. Large light sources, such as large windows and large light modifiers, produce light that is softer in appearance.

What makes a light source "small" or "large" is relative to the size of the subject you're photographing and how close to the light source that subject is. A three-foot window, for example, can be considered either small or large depending on what you're placing in front of it. This is an important fact to remember when working with newborns and families. A three-foot window is large relative to a newborn baby who is sleeping alone on a bed. That same window, however, is small relative to a family of four gathered on a sofa. The same size window will result in softer light on the newborn, and harder light on the family.

How close a subject is to a light source will also impact the relative size, and, therefore, the quality of the light it produces. Let's revisit our three-foot window example. That window will appear larger, relative to the newborn, if the newborn is positioned close to it. If the newborn is positioned on the other side of the room, however, the window will appear small relative to the newborn and therefore produce harder light.

Using this information will help you control your light quality. If you want soft light, add diffusion, use a large light source (relative to your subject), and move your subject closer to the light (**FIGURE 1.2A**). If you want hard light, remove diffusion, use a small light source (relative to your subject), and move your subject away from the light (**FIGURE 1.2B**). These rules are the same whether you are working with natural light or artificial light.

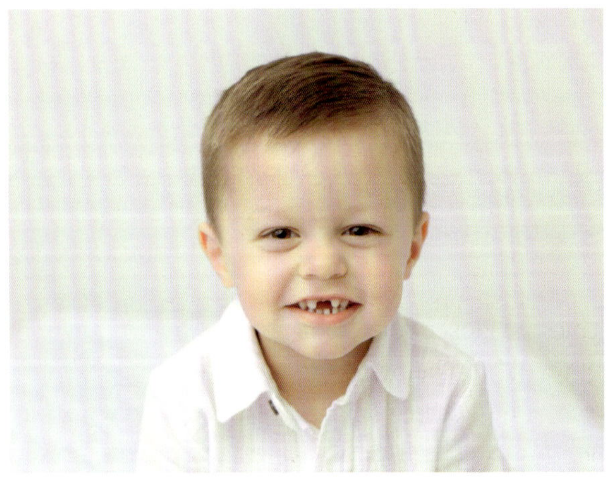

A

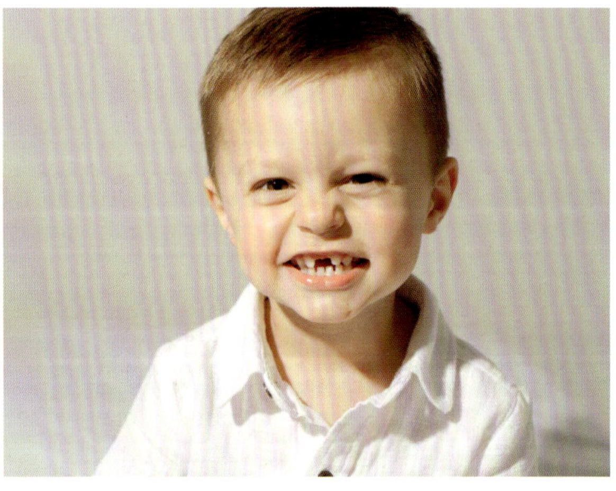

B

**FIGURE 1.2** Both images were captured using a Westcott FJ200 strobe placed 45 degrees to the subject at f/4, 1/125 sec., ISO 100. Figure 1.2A was captured using a 7-foot umbrella with a diffusion panel. The relatively large size of the light modifier, combined with the level of diffusion, resulted in soft light. Figure 1.2B was captured with the bare strobe, a relatively small light source. The small size of the light source combined with the absence of any diffusion resulted in hard light.

# Intensity

Light intensity is sometimes confused with light quality, but they are two very different things!

Light quality, as you will recall, is defined by the shadows the light produces. Hard light is characterized by sharp, defined shadows and soft light is defined by softer, less defined shadows. Light intensity, however, is about the brightness of the light we are working with. Bright light can be either hard or soft.

Light intensity is impacted by the amount of light coming from your light source that falls on your subject. This will affect what settings you can use to capture an image. Controlling light intensity is easy when working with artificial light, as you can simply turn the power of your light up or down as needed. It's a little trickier to control when working with natural light. Paying attention to the proximity of your light source to your subject will help.

## Proximity

The closer your subject is to your light source, the more intense the light will be. The farther away your subject is from your light source, the less intense your light will be. Proximity, as we learned, also impacts the relative size of your light source, and, therefore, its quality. So even though light intensity and light quality are different, they are closely linked.

And that brings us to the Inverse Square Law.

## The Inverse Square Law

The Inverse Square Law is a law in physics that states that the intensity of the light, its brightness, spread, and falloff are inversely proportional to the square of its distance. Whew! That's a mouthful!

The Inverse Square Law is just a fancy way of saying that the closer your light source is to the subject, the softer and brighter the light will be. The proximity of the light source to the subject also impacts the spread of light, so the closer the light is, the more narrow the spread of light will be. Conversely, the farther away the light is from the subject, the harder and dimmer the light will be, and the spread of the light will be wider.

You can observe all these properties by looking at **FIGURE 1.3**.

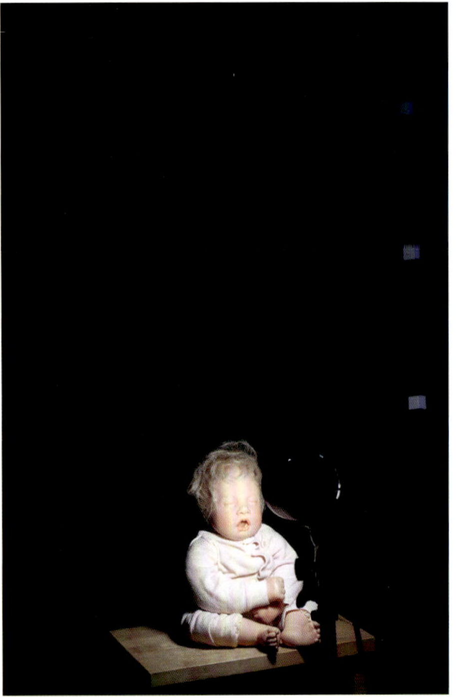

A

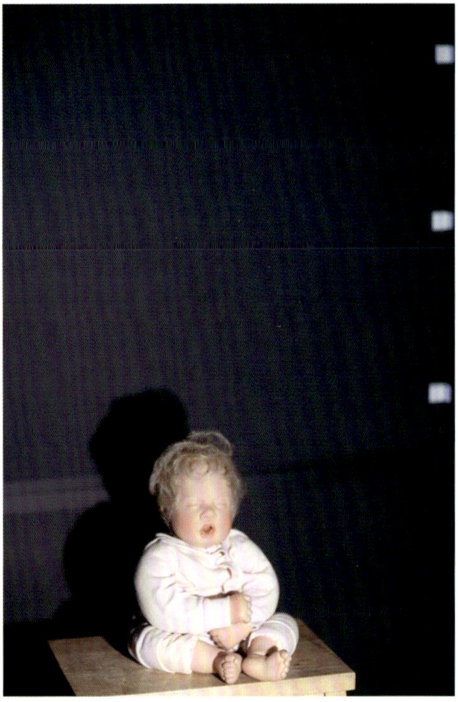

B

**FIGURE 1.3** In Figure 1.3A, the light is positioned very close to Betty (just one foot away). At this distance, the light intensity is strong and bright, requiring an aperture of f/8 for proper exposure, but it is soft in quality. The light is focused on Betty with very little spill onto the stool and the backdrop. In Figure 1.3B, the light is positioned four feet away from Betty. At this distance, the light is much harder in quality, but it also has less intensity and is much dimmer, requiring an aperture of f/2 for proper exposure. At this distance, the light is also less focused, covering a wider surface (including the stool and all the backdrop).

Both images in Figure 1.3 were captured using a bare strobe head, at ISO 100 with a shutter speed of 1/125 sec. I did not adjust the power of the light between taking the photos, and I metered each exposure using a handheld light meter. Betty was set one foot away from the backdrop.

In **FIGURE 1.3A**, the light was positioned just one foot away from Betty. At this distance, the light is soft but bright, requiring an aperture of f/8. The majority of light is focused on the doll, with very little spill onto the stool and the backdrop.

In **FIGURE 1.3B**, the light was positioned four feet away from Betty. At this distance, the light is harder (notice the sharp shadows, especially on the backdrop) but dimmer, requiring an aperture of f/2. The spread of light is wider, illuminating all of the doll, the stool, and the backdrop.

As we pull the light back from the subject, the intensity and quality of the light changes. The farther the light source is from the subject, the harder and dimmer the light becomes.

The proximity of the light influences its spread, as well. The farther we pull the light back, the wider the spread. You can see this by looking at **FIGURE 1.4**.

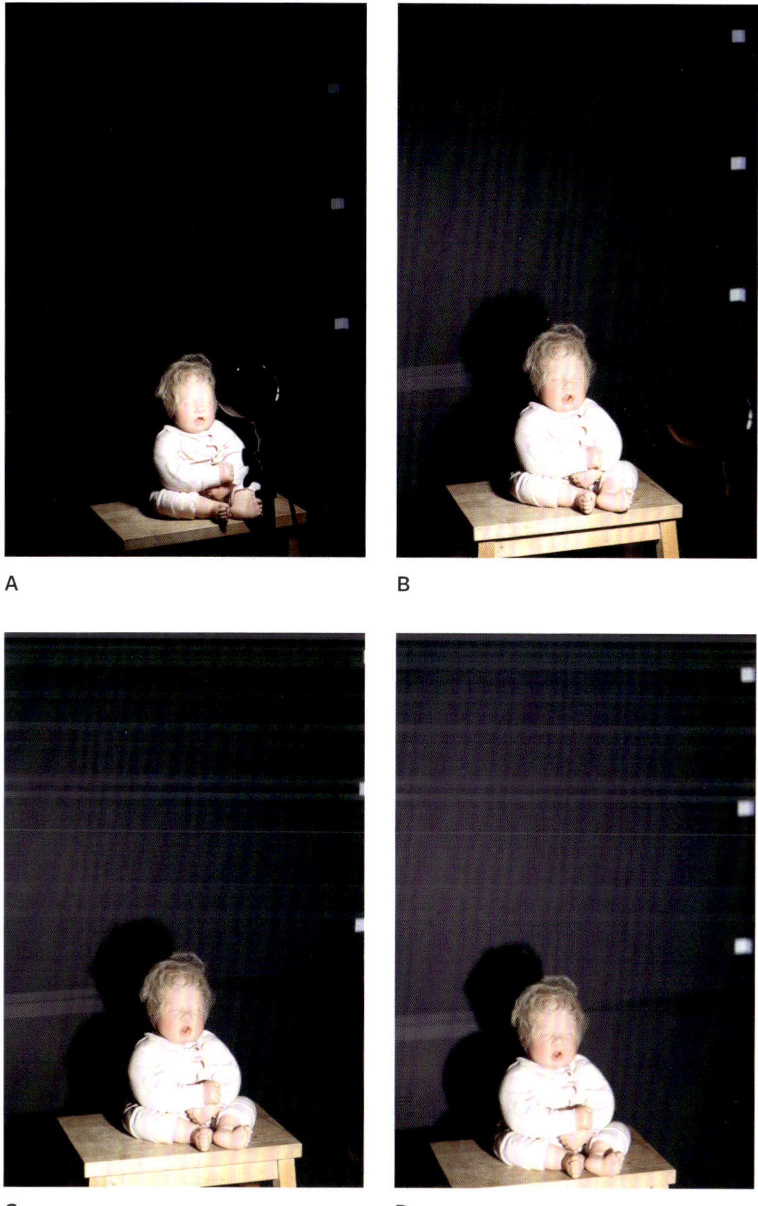


**FIGURE 1.4** In this series, I started with the light positioned one foot away from Betty and moved it back in one-foot increments. Notice how the quality, intensity, and spread of light changes as we move the light farther away from the subject.

## Relative Size and The Inverse Square Law

While the Inverse Square Law tells us that light quality and light intensity will change relative to the proximity of the light, it's important to note that the relative size of your light source will also have an impact on the quality of the light, regardless of its proximity to the subject.

In **FIGURE 1.5**, both images were captured with the light source six feet from Betty. Both images show a wide spread of light at this distance (notice how the backdrop is evenly lit). But, as you can see, the quality of the light in each photo is different due to the size of the light source I was using. **FIGURE 1.5A** was captured using a bare strobe head (a relatively small light source), resulting in hard light. **FIGURE 1.5B** was captured using a 5-foot softbox (a relatively large light source), resulting in softer light, even at this distance.

A

B

**FIGURE 1.5** Both images were taken with the light positioned six feet away from Betty, resulting in an even spread of light across the backdrop. In Figure 1.5A, a bare strobe head was used, creating a relatively small light source that produced hard, defined shadows. In contrast, Figure 1.5B was captured using a 5-foot softbox, creating a much larger apparent light source and resulting in soft, gradual transitions between light and shadow—even at the same distance.

## Having Fun with the Inverse Square Law

Now that you understand the Inverse Square Law, you know that the farther away your light source is from your subject, the dimmer the light will be. You can use that knowledge to achieve different looks with your background.

The images in **FIGURE 1.6** were all captured at f/2.8, 1/125 sec, ISO 100. The light, a Westcott FJ200 strobe, coupled with a 53-inch Deep Umbrella and diffusion panel, was approximately three feet from my subject in each photo. The only thing that changed was the distance of the light from the white wall in the background.

As we move the light away from the backdrop, the light hitting the backdrop will dim. By keeping the model at an equal distance from the light as we move the light away from the backdrop, we achieve consistent light intensity on the model but change the appearance of the backdrop.

This is a great way to get different looks out of the same location!

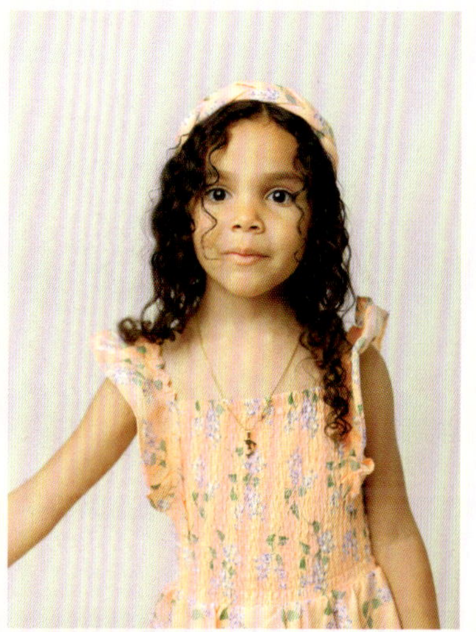

**FIGURE 1.6A** The light is six feet from the wall.

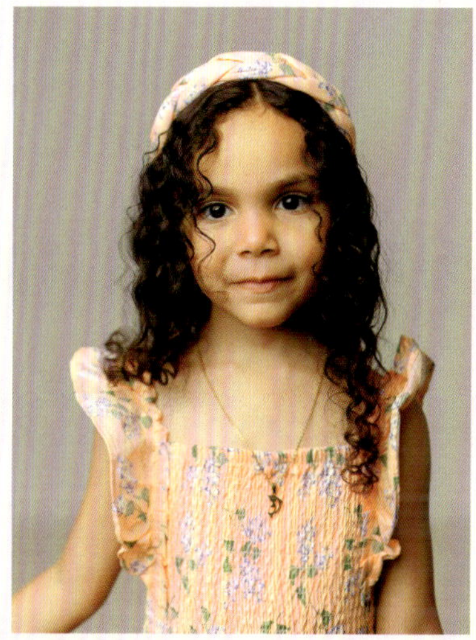

**FIGURE 1.6B** The light is nine feet from the wall.

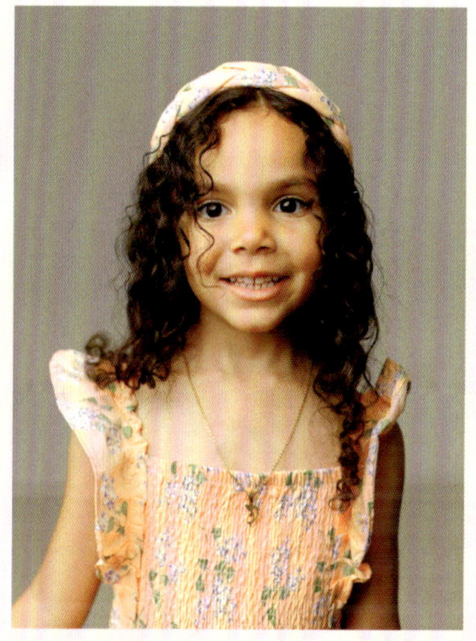

**FIGURE 1.6C** The light is twelve feet from the wall.

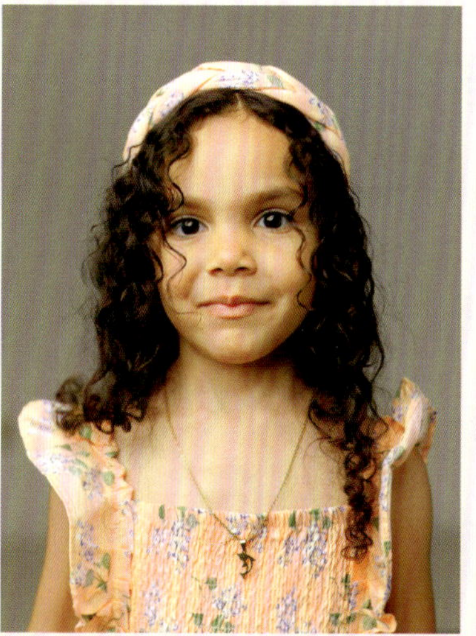

**FIGURE 1.6D** The light is fifteen feet from the wall. Notice how the color of the wall changes as we pull the light away, changing the white wall to a dark gray.

## Temperature

Another factor that must be considered when discussing the fundamentals of light is temperature. Simply put, all light has color. Some light is warm, resulting in orange/yellow tones, and some light is cool, resulting in a blue quality. This color is referred to as light temperature and is measured in degrees of Kelvin (**FIGURE 1.7**). Lower Kelvin numbers refer to warmer light, or light that looks orange or yellow, and higher Kelvin numbers refer to cooler light, or light that looks blue.

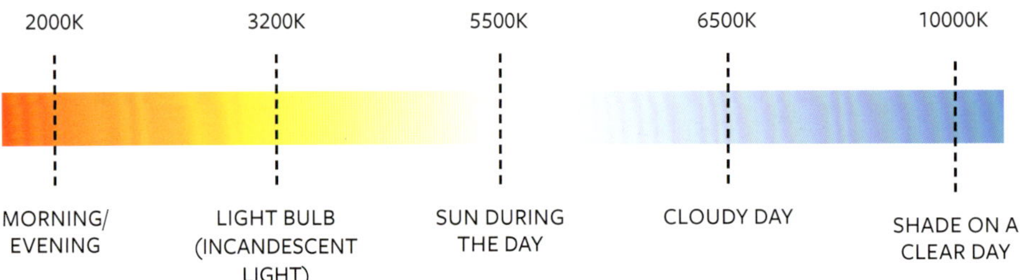


**FIGURE 1.7** Light temperature is measured in degrees Kelvin (K) and affects the color quality of light. Lower Kelvin values, such as 2000K to 3200K, produce warm tones with an orange or yellow appearance. Higher Kelvin values, like 6500K to 10,000K, create cooler, blue-toned light.

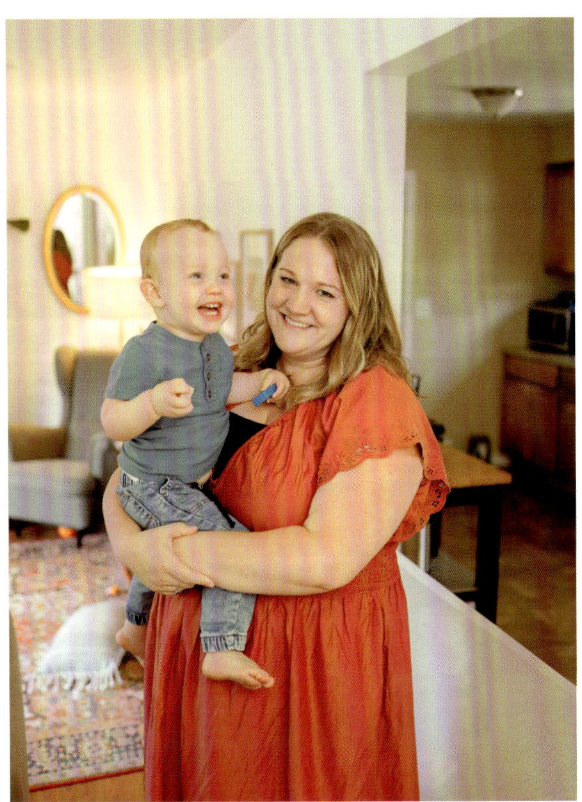

Our brains are very good at filtering out slight differences in color temperature, so to our eyes, most light looks neutral. Our cameras, on the other hand, are very sensitive to light temperature, which is why the light of a tungsten light bulb looks perfectly fine to us in real life, but very orange in a photo (**FIGURE 1.8**).

Daylight is generally considered to be a neutral, white light. However, true daylight will fluctuate in temperature depending on the time of day and the amount of cloud cover.

Strobes and flash are "daylight" balanced, meaning they have a Kelvin number of around 5500, making them a consistent and reliable source of neutral white light.

**FIGURE 1.8** Notice the warm yellow glow of the tungsten light coming from the lamp in the background.

# Patterns

The quality, intensity, and temperature of your light will all make a huge impact on the look and feel of your photographs. You can also significantly impact the look of an image by paying attention to the direction of the light and how it falls on your subject.

**FIGURE 1.9**, for example, shows two images captured moments apart at f/4, 1/125 sec., ISO 100. The child I was working with was seated on a stool and didn't move. The only thing that changed was the direction of the light and where the subject was looking.

For this reason, learning to see, create, and name lighting patterns is an incredibly useful skill to have as a family photographer, since lighting patterns like catchlights and shadows play such an important role in the look and feel of an image.

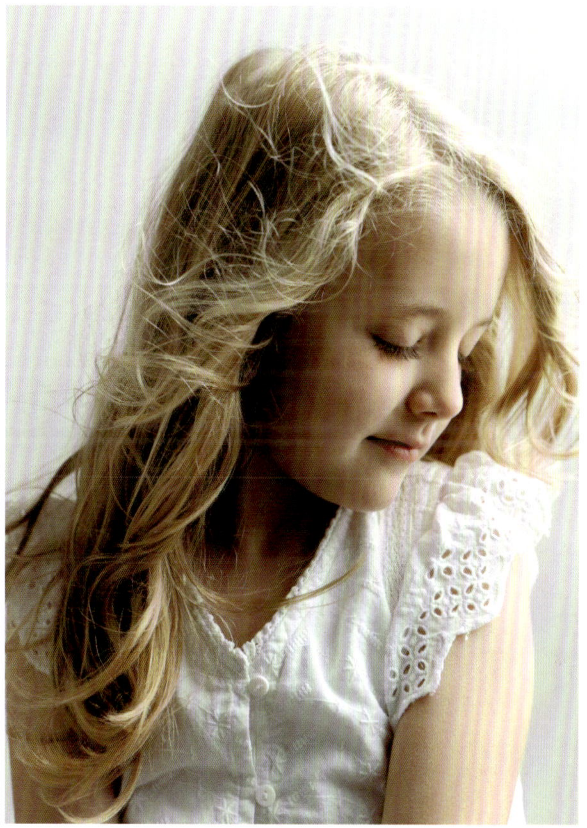

A

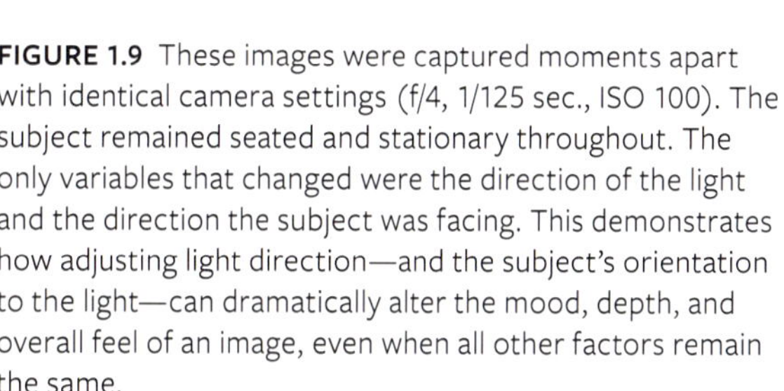

B

**FIGURE 1.9** These images were captured moments apart with identical camera settings (f/4, 1/125 sec., ISO 100). The subject remained seated and stationary throughout. The only variables that changed were the direction of the light and the direction the subject was facing. This demonstrates how adjusting light direction—and the subject's orientation to the light—can dramatically alter the mood, depth, and overall feel of an image, even when all other factors remain the same.

## Catchlights

Catchlights are the specular patches of light reflected in your subject's eyes (**FIGURE 1.10**). These lights brighten up portraits by adding dimension and depth and create a sense of connection between the viewer and the subject.

In addition to brightening up a portrait, catchlights communicate valuable information about how an image was created. Round light sources like the sun, or round light modifiers like umbrellas, produce round catchlights; likewise, square and rectangle light sources like windows or softboxes produce catchlights with a straight edge. Relatively large light sources produce large catchlights and relatively small light sources produce small catchlights. And, because proximity impacts the relative size of the light, the closer your subject is to the light source, the larger your catchlights will be.

**FIGURE 1.11** was captured in my studio using a strobe and seven-foot umbrella placed about three feet from my subject. The relatively large size of the modifier, its proximity, and its round shape resulted in a large, round catchlight in the baby's eye. The light was positioned to my left, resulting in a catchlight on the left side of the baby's eyes.

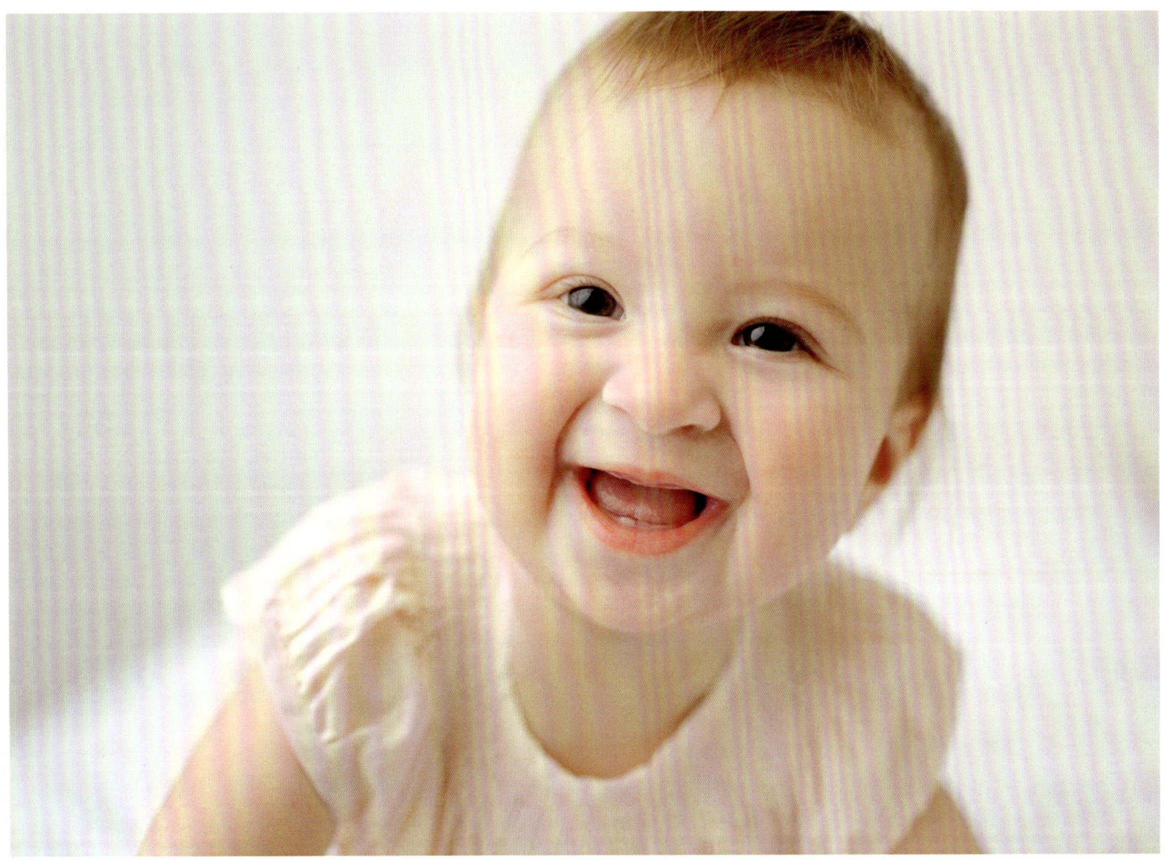

**FIGURE 1.10** Catchlights are the specular patch of light reflected in your subject's eyes. Their appearance can tell us a lot about the lighting pattern being used to create the image.

**FIGURE 1.12** was captured in the nursery at my client's home. For this image, my light source was coming from a flash that I bounced into a relatively large window to my right (more on that technique in Chapter 4). The size of the window and its square shape resulted in a large catchlight with a straight edge in the right half of her eyes.

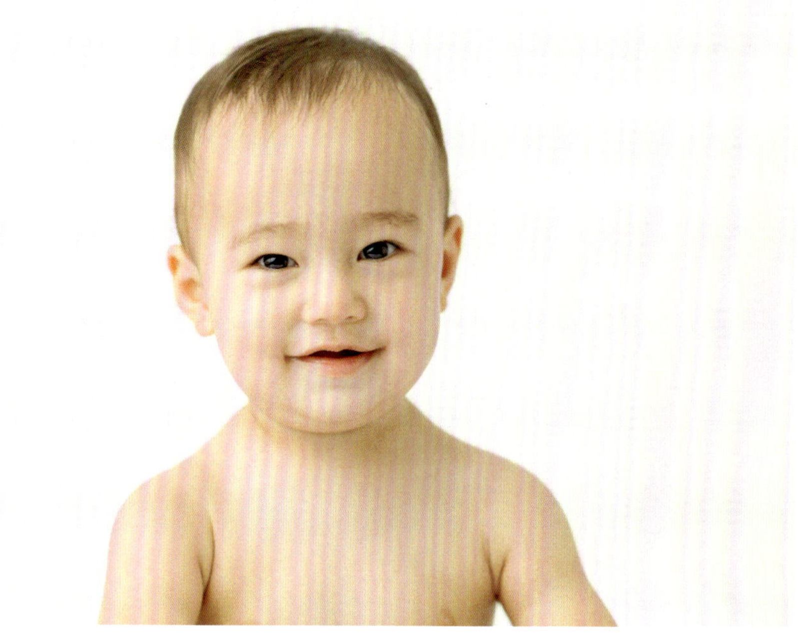

A

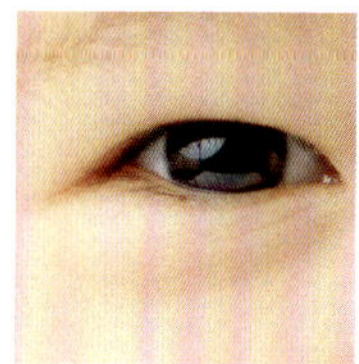

B

**FIGURE 1.11** Figure 1.11A was captured in studio with a Westcott FJ200 Strobe and a Westcott seven-foot Umbrella. The size of the modifier and its round shape resulted in a large, round catchlight in the baby's eye (Figure 1.11B).

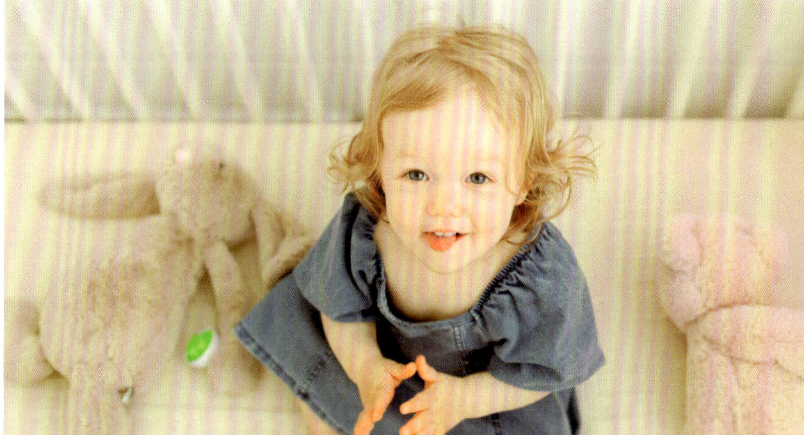

A

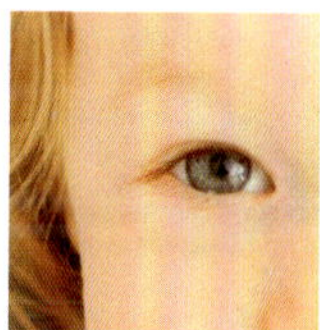

B

**FIGURE 1.12** Figure 1.12A was captured in my client's home by bouncing the light from my Westcott FJ80 off a large window, resulting in a catchlight with a straight edge, as you can see in Figure 1.12B.

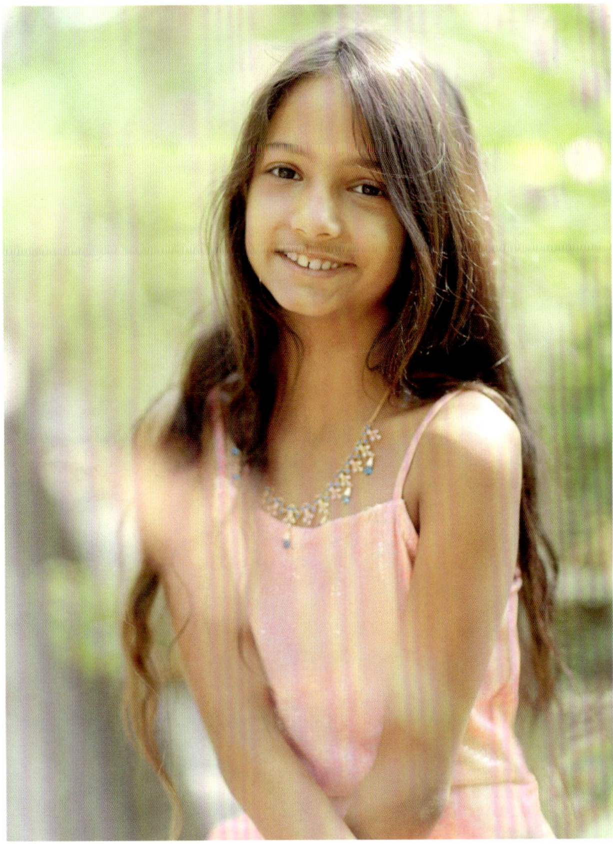

A

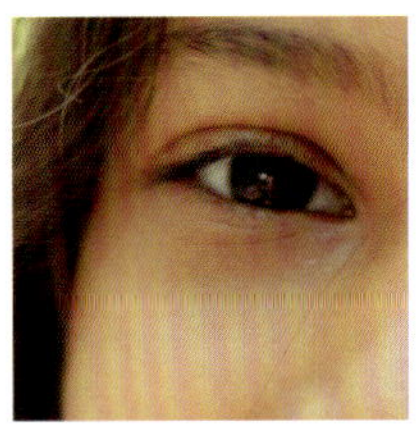

B

**FIGURE 1.13** The light source in this image was the sun. Its small, round size resulted in a small round catchlight in my client's eyes.

**FIGURE 1.13** was captured outside at a local park and my light source was the sun. The sun is very large, but because it is so far away from us, it appears small in the sky. Its relatively small size and round shape resulted in a small round catchlight in my client's eye (**FIGURE 1.13B**).

## Shadows

Like catchlights, shadows reveal valuable information about the light we are working with. They can tell you if your light is soft or hard, give you information about how your light is falling on your subject, and help you create a mood or convey emotion in your portrait.

In **FIGURE 1.14**, you can see the soft shadow on the right side of this baby's face. That shadow pattern tells us that the light used to capture this image was positioned to the left. Knowing what you now know about light quality and catchlights, you might also guess that this image was created with a relatively large light source—and you would be right! The large light source produced beautiful, soft light and a prominent catchlight in the child's eyes.

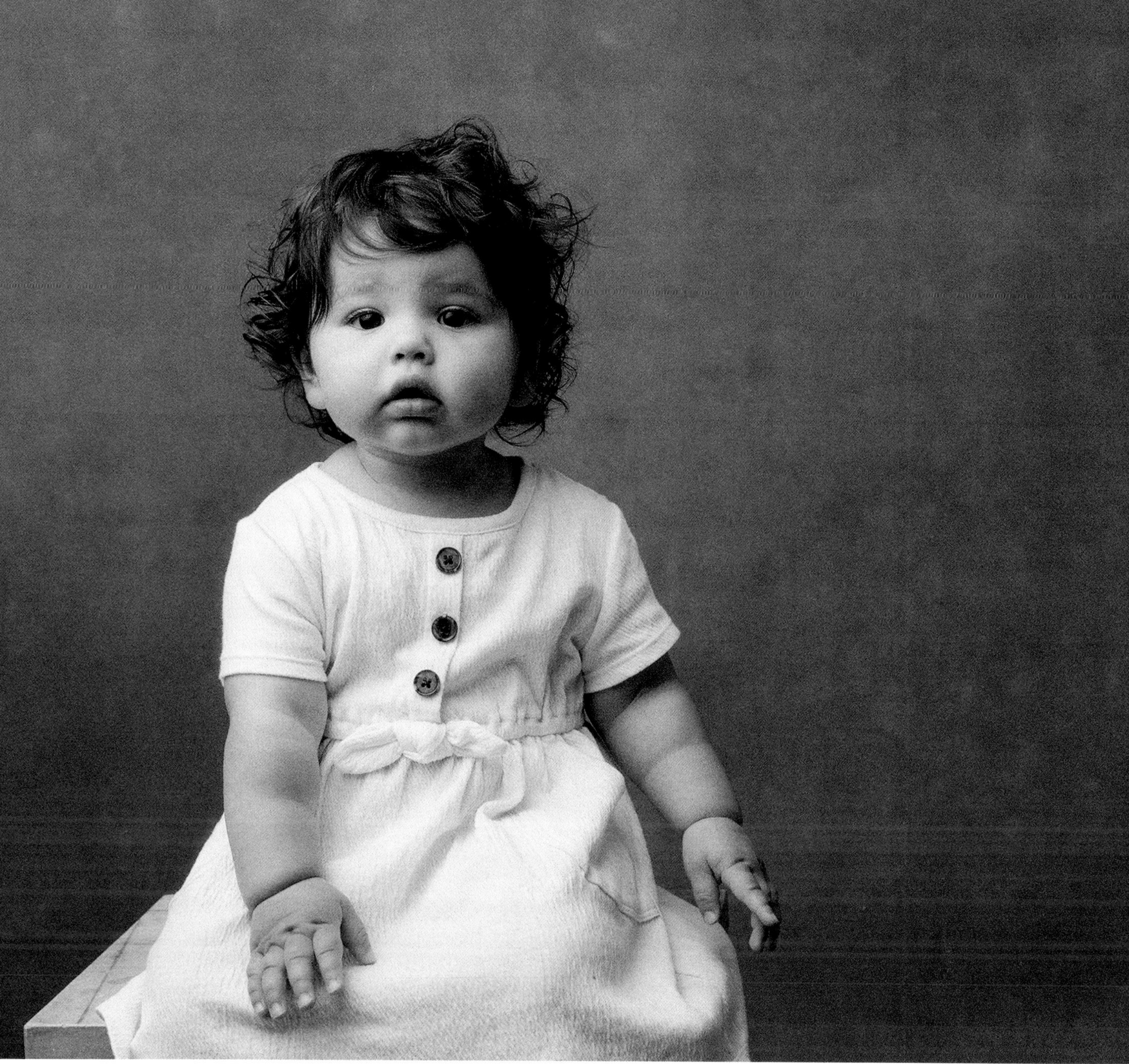

**FIGURE 1.14** The soft quality of these shadows and their placement on my little client indicated that this image was captured with a relatively large light source to my left.

Now that you're beginning to recognize how light direction, quality, catchlights, and shadows work together to shape an image, it's helpful to have a common language to describe these effects. That's where named lighting patterns come in. Lighting patterns provide a simple, consistent way to describe how light is falling on a subject based on the shape and placement of shadows and catchlights.

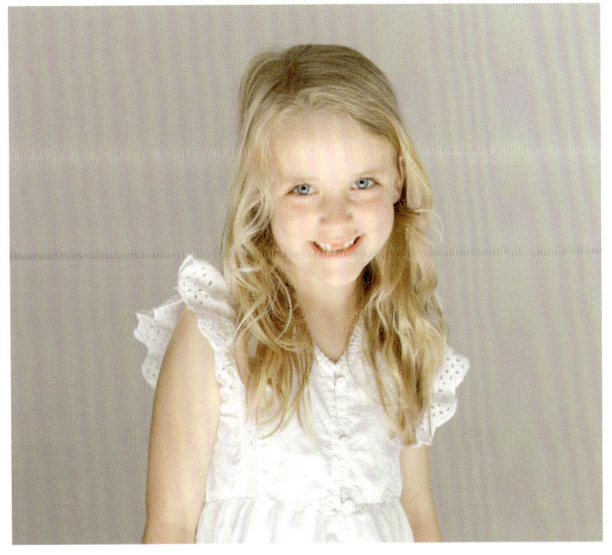

A

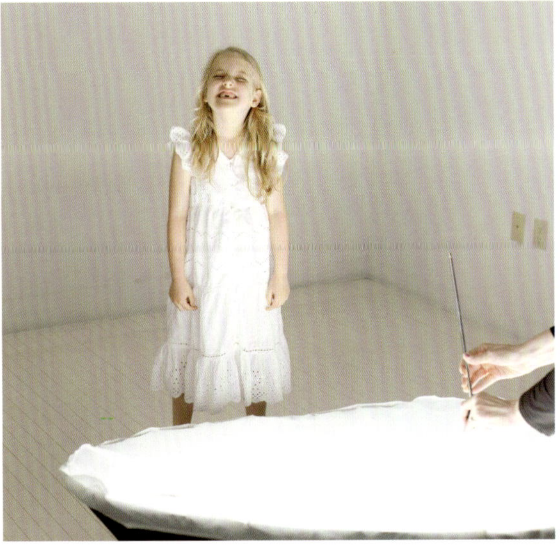

B

**FIGURE 1.15** Ghoul light. Notice the catchlights in the bottom half of the eye, and the unsettling shadows that are falling up the face. Ghoul light is created by placing your light source below your subject (Figure 1.15B) and is not recommended for portrait work.

## Ghoul Light/Uplight

*Ghoul light*, or *uplight*, is a lighting pattern that is created by placing your light source below your subject. It results in shadows that fall up the face at the chin, nose, and cheeks, and catchlight in the bottom half of the eyes (**FIGURE 1.15**).

In the natural world, we're used to seeing light coming from above—like the sun shining down from the sky—so light that falls from above tends to feel natural and flattering to us. On the other hand, we're not used to seeing light coming from below in our everyday lives, and when we do, it can feel unsettling without us even realizing why. That's why ghoul light is often used in horror and suspense movies to make scenes feel creepy or uncomfortable. Because of that, ghoul light isn't something we want to use in family photography. It's just not a flattering look!

## Butterfly Light/Paramount Light

The opposite of ghoul light is *butterfly light*, or what is sometimes known as *Paramount light*. This kind of light is created by placing the light source in front of and above your subject so that the shadows fall down the face, resulting in a small shadow under the nose and chin, and catchlights in the upper-middle part of the eyes (**FIGURE 1.19**).

This pattern looks good on everyone, which is why it was so often used in the glamor portraits created by the old Hollywood studios, like Paramount Pictures (hence the name "Paramount" light). It's also beautiful when used to photograph small children and babies (**FIGURE 1.20**).

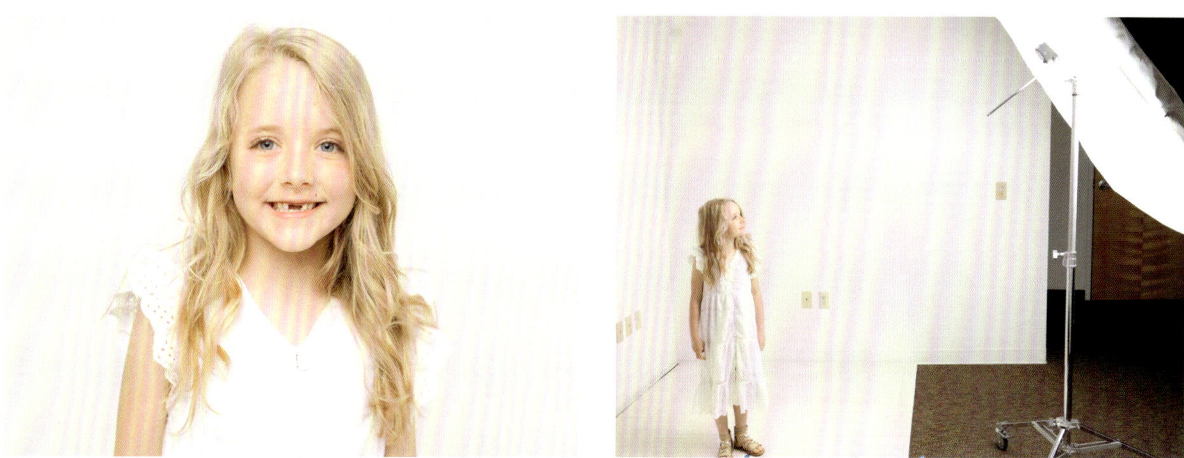

**FIGURE 1.19** Butterfly light, also known as Paramount light. You create this lighting pattern by placing your light directly in front of and slightly above the subject. This placement results in a small shadow under the nose and chin, and catchlights in the upper-middle part of the eyes.

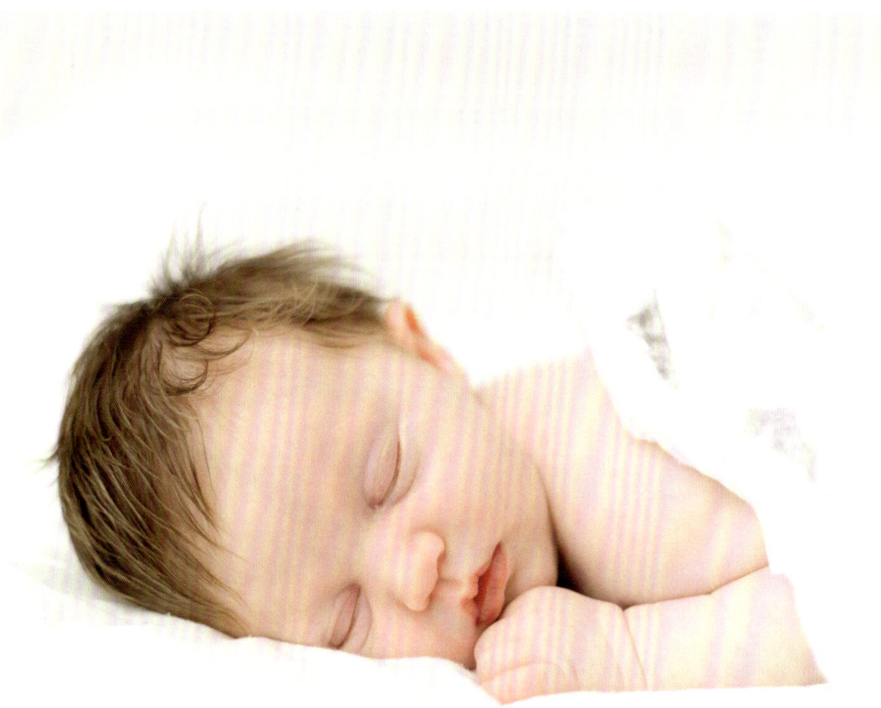

**FIGURE 1.20** Butterfly light on a sleeping newborn. Notice the small, butterfly-shaped shadow under the baby's nose—this shadow pattern is what gives butterfly light its name.

## How to Avoid Accidental Uplighting

As mentioned previously, ghoul lighting results in unflattering images that can leave the viewer feeling unsettled.

While most photographers know that this is not a great way to light a portrait, accidental ghoul lighting can happen, especially when working with newborns and small children who are lying down on a bed or being held in their parent's arms.

To avoid accidental uplighting, always point your subjects head toward the light source. This will ensure that the person in your photo is captured in the most flattering light possible!

If you notice that you have accidentally used uplighting in a photo, take a moment to slow down and reposition your subject into a more flattering light pattern.

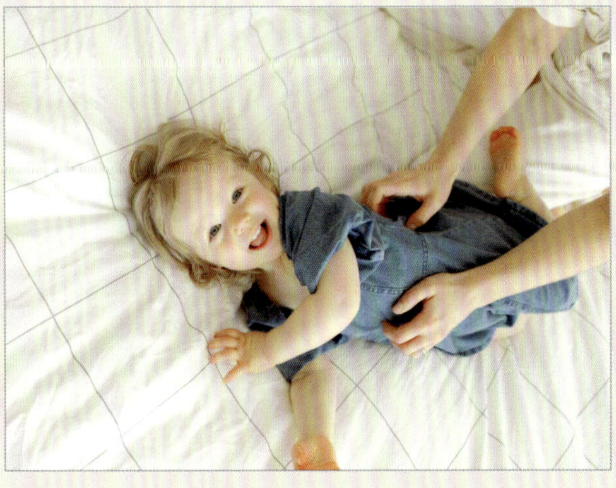

**FIGURE 1.16** Accidental uplighting at a lifestyle family session.

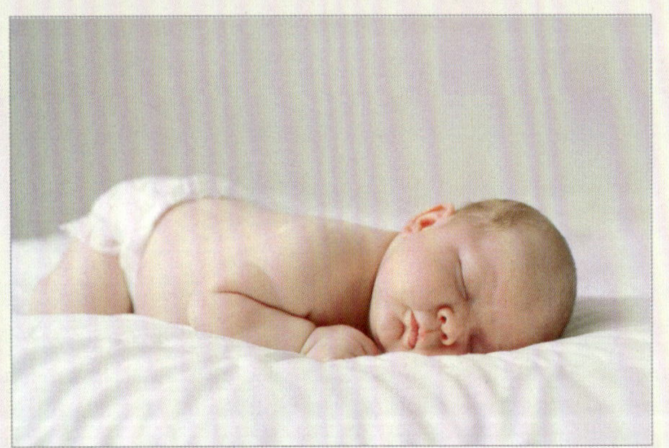

A

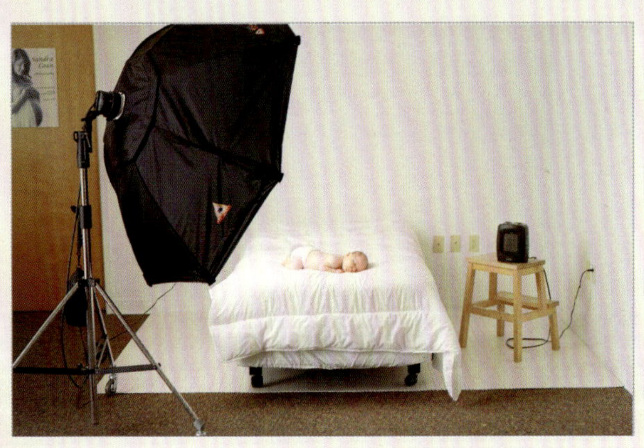

B

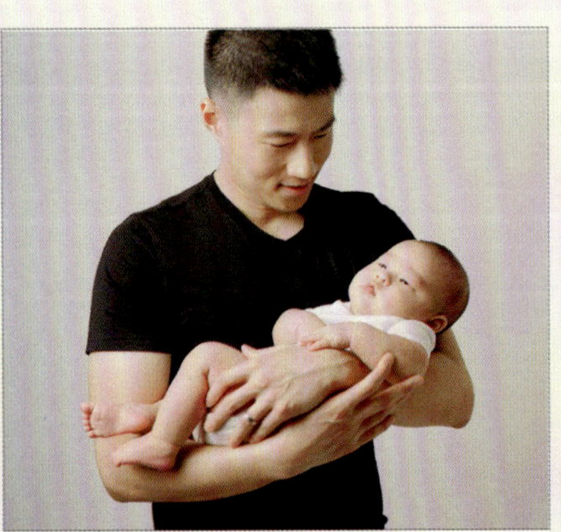

C

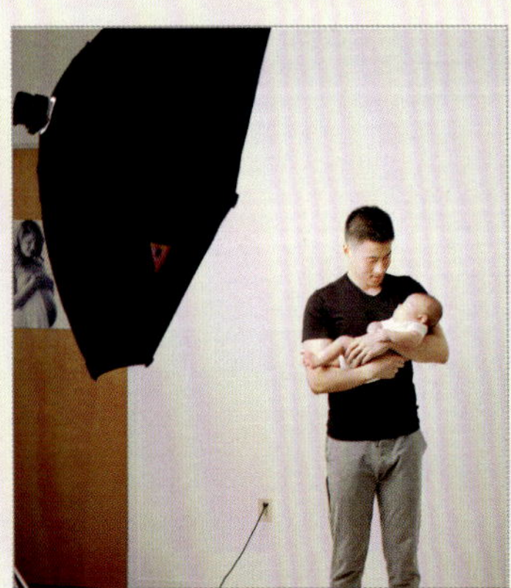

D

**FIGURES 1.17** The baby in Figures 1.17A and 17.C is being lit in the ghoul light pattern. This happened because their feet are pointing toward the light source (Figures 1.17B and 1.17D), causing the light to fall up the face from below.

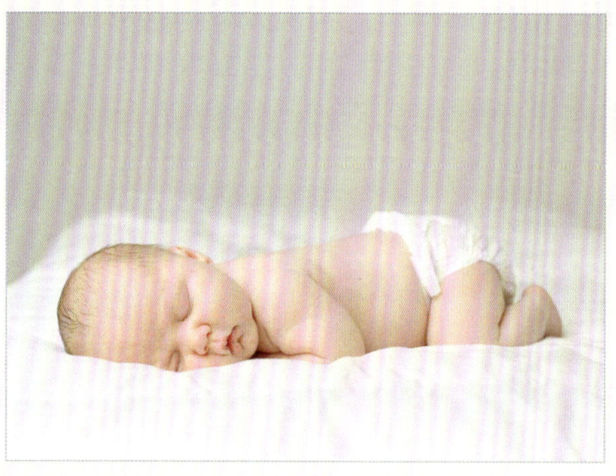

A

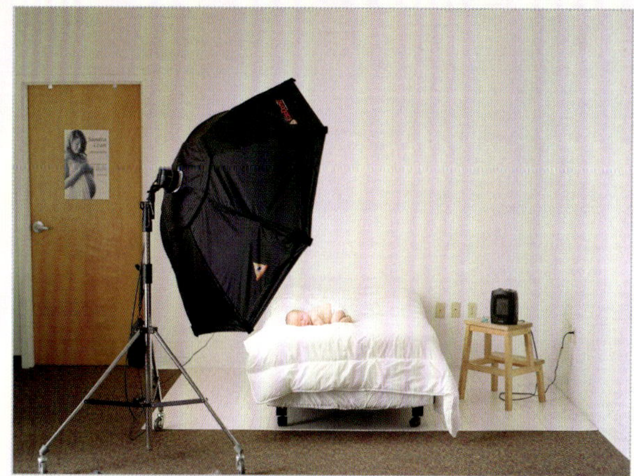

B

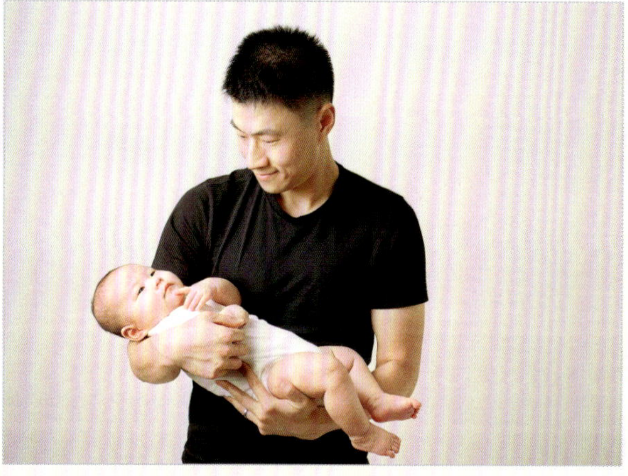

C

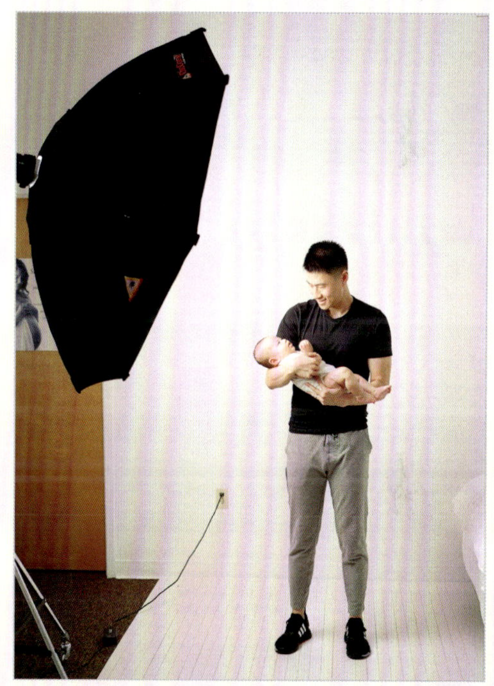

D

**FIGURE 1.18** In Figures 1.18A and 1.18C, I fixed the ghoul light problem by turning the baby around so that their head is pointed toward the light, as you can see in Figures 1.18B and 1.18D.

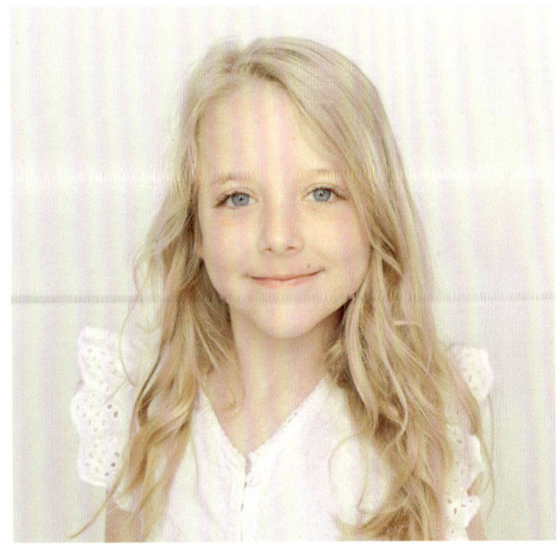

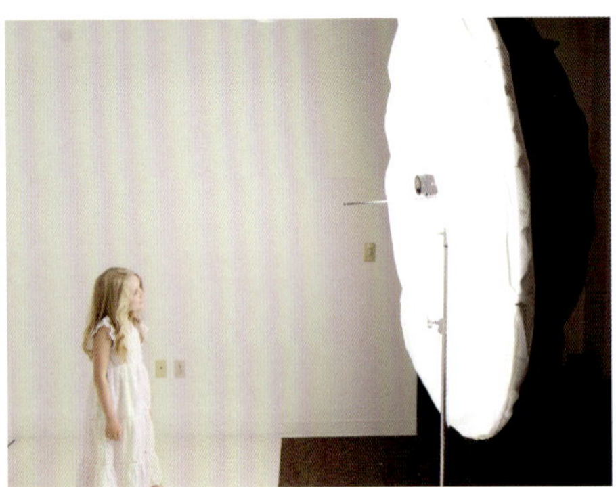

FIGURE 1.21 Flat light. Notice the catchlights in the middle of the eye, and the lack of shadows on the face.

## Flat Light

*Flat light* has no definition between highlights and shadows, resulting in even light across the face. This kind of light is sometimes poo pooed by photographers due to its low contrast, but I personally love it.

Flat light is incredibly kind to skin. Its lack of contrast smooths texture, like bumps and wrinkles, and helps hide the tired eyes I so often see on the parents of the newborn babies I work with.

To produce flat light, place your light source directly in front of and level to the subject. Flat light will produce catchlights in the middle of the eye (**FIGURE 1.21**).

## Loop Light/45-Degree Light

*Loop light*, sometimes called *45-degree light*, is created by placing your light at a 45-degree angle to your subject. This pattern produces catchlights in both eyes at the two o'clock or ten o'clock position, depending on which direction your light is coming from. It also results in a shadow pattern that "loops" slightly around the face (**FIGURE 1.22**).

Like flat light, loop light is extremely flattering and looks good on just about everyone, young and old alike. It is my favorite lighting pattern when working in a studio.

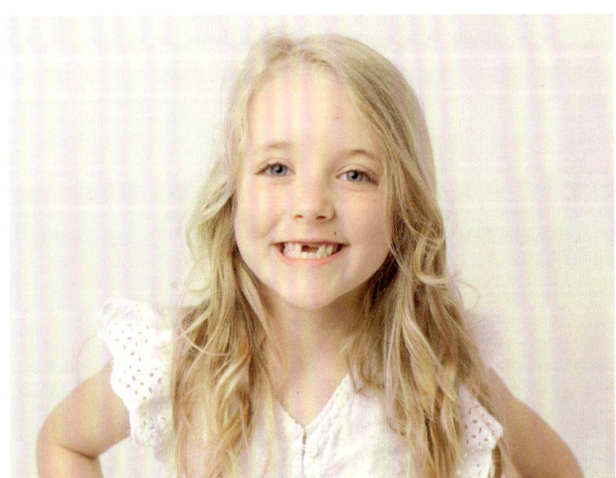

FIGURE 1.22 Loop light. Notice the catchlight in the upper-left corner of the eye at 10 o'clock, and the soft shadow looping around the face at the nose and chin. Loop light is a classic lighting pattern and one I use in every portrait session.

## Split Light/90-Degree Light

*Split light*, or *90-degree light*, is achieved when the light source is placed at 90 degrees to the subject. This creates a shadow pattern that splits the face into two halves, one in highlight and one in shadow, and results in a catchlight that is larger on the highlight side of the face (**FIGURE 1.23**).

Split light can be very dramatic and beautiful, but it will also emphasize texture. For this reason, I stay away from split light when photographing faces and use it mostly in my maternity work (**FIGURE 1.24**).

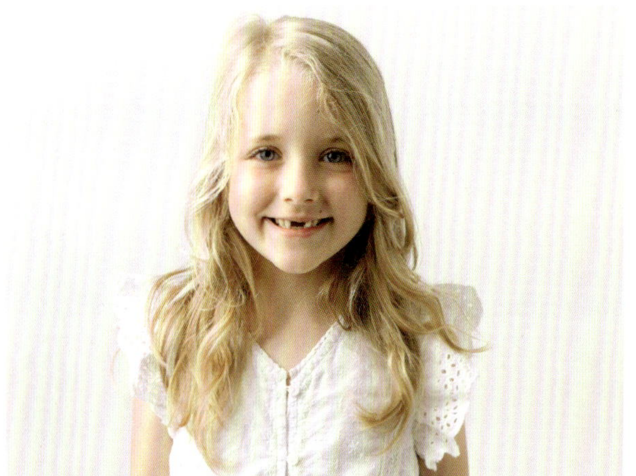

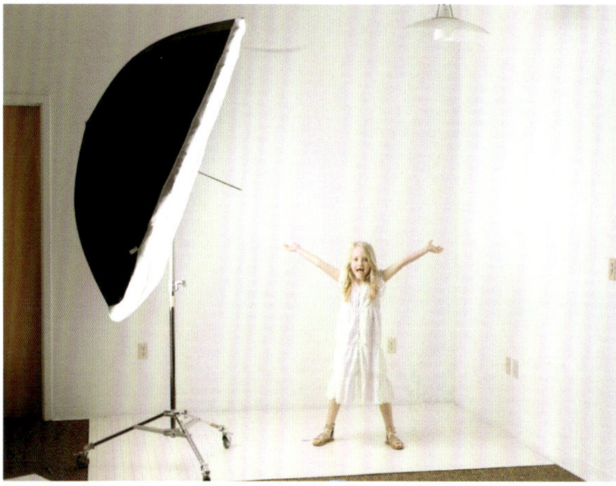

**FIGURE 1.23** Split light. Notice how the shadow splits the face in two.

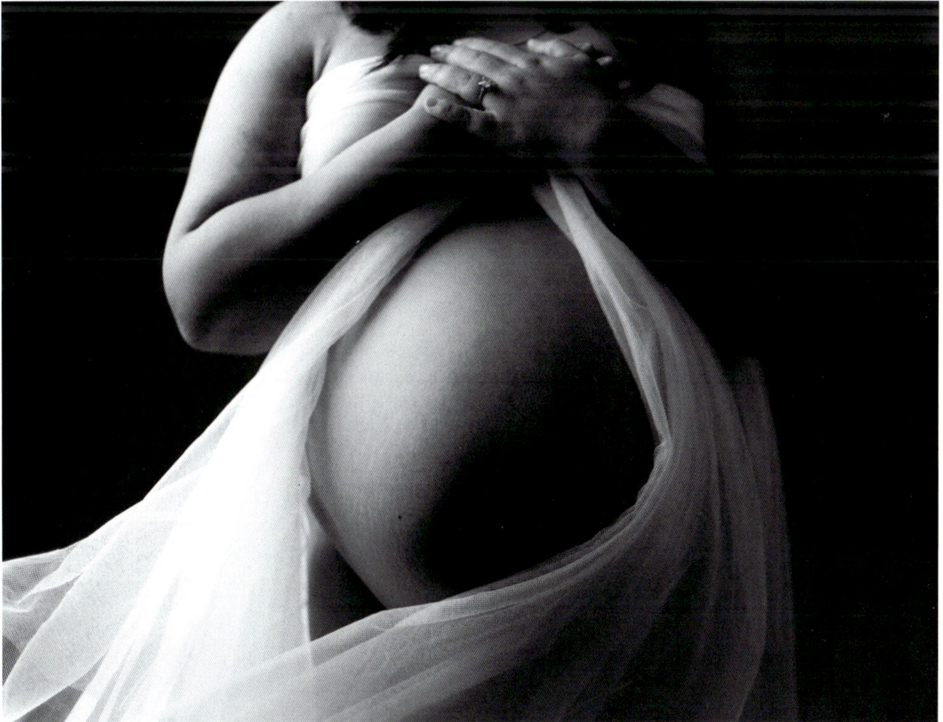

**FIGURE 1.24** Split light is beautiful when used for maternity portraits.

## Rim Light

*Rim light* is a lighting pattern that produces a small rim of light along the edge of your subject, leaving most of your subject in shadow. To create rim light, place your light slightly behind your subject at 30 to 45 degrees and look for the rim of light on the edge of their skin (**FIGURE 1.25**).

Like split light, rim light is a lighting pattern that I use a lot in my maternity work to emphasize the roundness of the baby bump. It's very dramatic and is the perfect lighting pattern for showing off curves (**FIGURE 1.26**)!

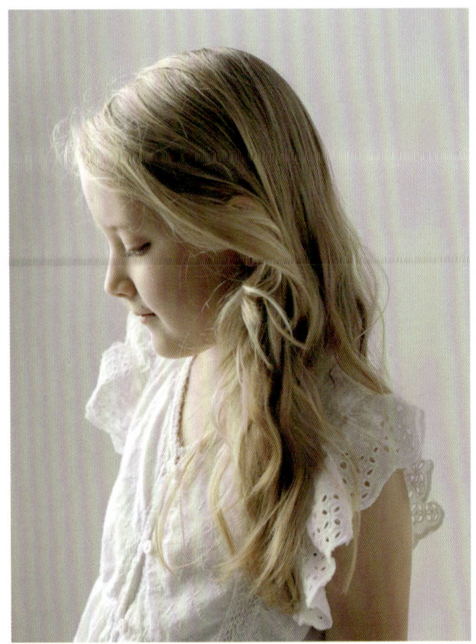

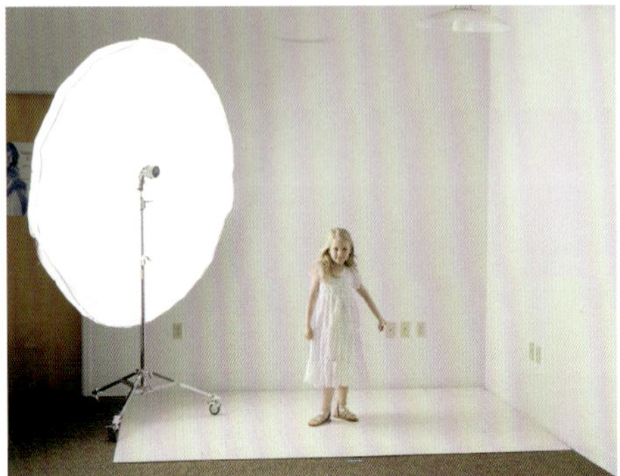

**FIGURE 1.25** Rim light. Notice the thin line of light outlining the subject's hair and shoulder, while the rest of her face falls into soft shadow. In the setup image, you can see how the light was placed slightly behind and off to the side of the subject to create this beautiful, dramatic effect.

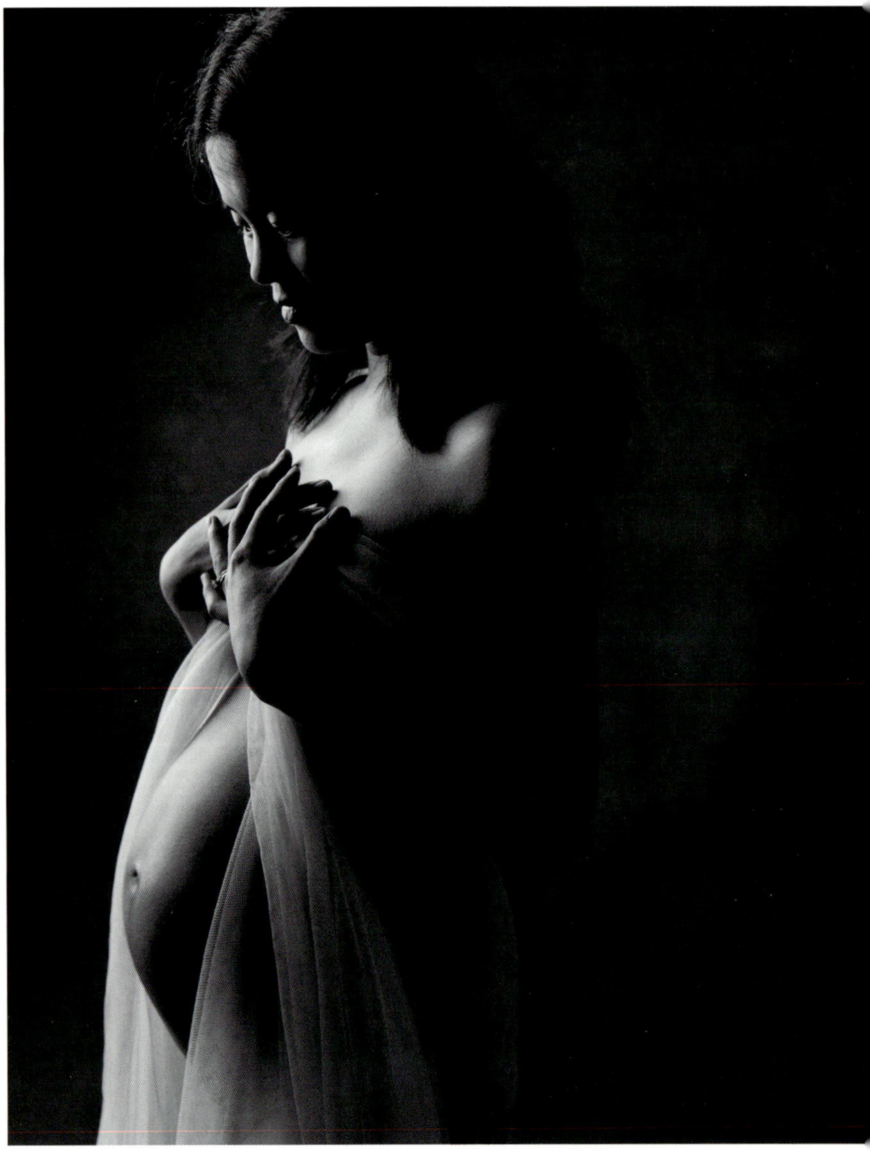

**FIGURE 1.26** Rim light is a great lighting pattern to use when taking maternity portraits as it emphasizes curves.

## Backlight

*Backlight* refers to light that is hitting a subject from behind, giving them a subtle glow. This kind of light is very versatile. Metering for your highlights with backlight results in a silhouette look. Meter for your shadows and you'll get a bright glow around the subject, as you can see in **FIGURE 1.27** (I'll go into detail on how to meter in Chapters 2 and 3).

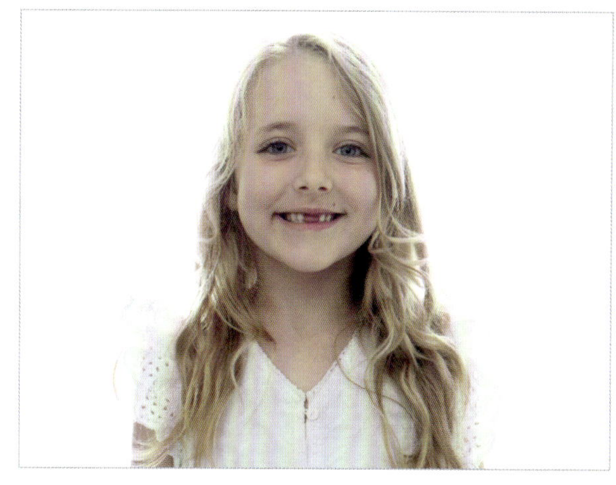

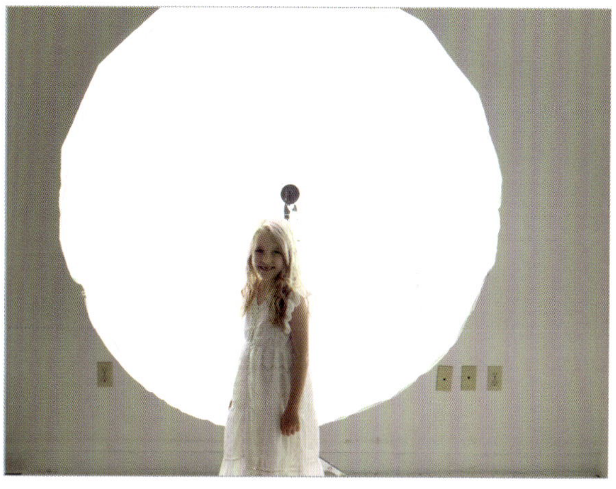

**FIGURE 1.27** Backlight creates a lovely glow around your client when metered for the shadows.

## Light Quality Will Affect the Look of These Lighting Patterns

These patterns can be created with natural light or with artificial light, inside or out, but it's important to note that the quality of your light will have an impact on the appearance of these lighting patterns in a photo.

Small light sources, for example, produce harder light, and hard light will amplify the look of your lighting pattern (see **FIGURE 1.28A**). Large light sources produce softer light, and soft light will result in softer shadows, and therefore, a more subtle look to your lighting pattern (**FIGURE 1.28B**).

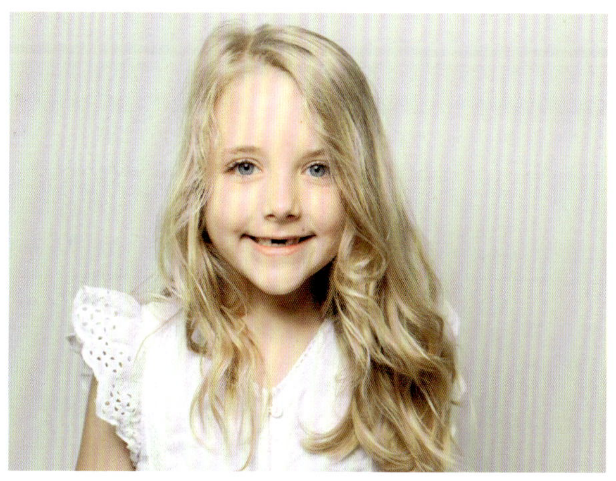

A

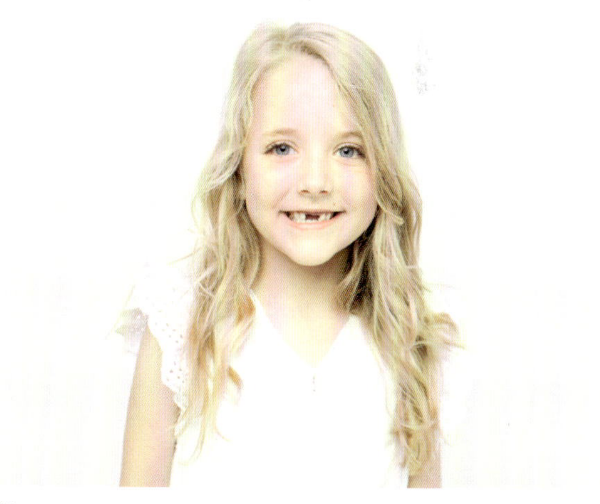

B

**FIGURE 1.28** Both of these images were captured using the butterfly light pattern. Figure 1.28A was created with a relatively small light source (a two-foot softbox), while Figure 1.28B was created with a relatively large light source (a seven-foot umbrella). Notice how the difference in light quality impacts the look of the lighting pattern.

## Putting It All Together

My studio work has a very distinct look. I love soft light, subtle shadows, and a shallow depth of field. Over time, that look has become my signature style—it's what my clients expect when they hire me. So, achieving "my look" at every session is important.

Here's how I do it, based on everything we've covered in this chapter.

- Whether I'm using natural or artificial light, I choose relatively large light sources to produce softer light.
- I add at least one layer of diffusion to my light source to soften it even further.
- I use strobes and flash to bring consistency to my light temperature.
- I keep my light intensity low, allowing me to work with a wide-open aperture (more on that in Chapters 2 and 3).
- I use 45-degree light for the majority of my sessions.

## Finding Your Own Style

I encourage you to start thinking about the kind of light you love most. Do you prefer hard light or soft light? Warm tones or cool tones? Are there certain lighting patterns you find yourself drawn to?

Taking the time to answer these questions will help you develop your own signature style—a style that feels like you and supports the work you want to create.

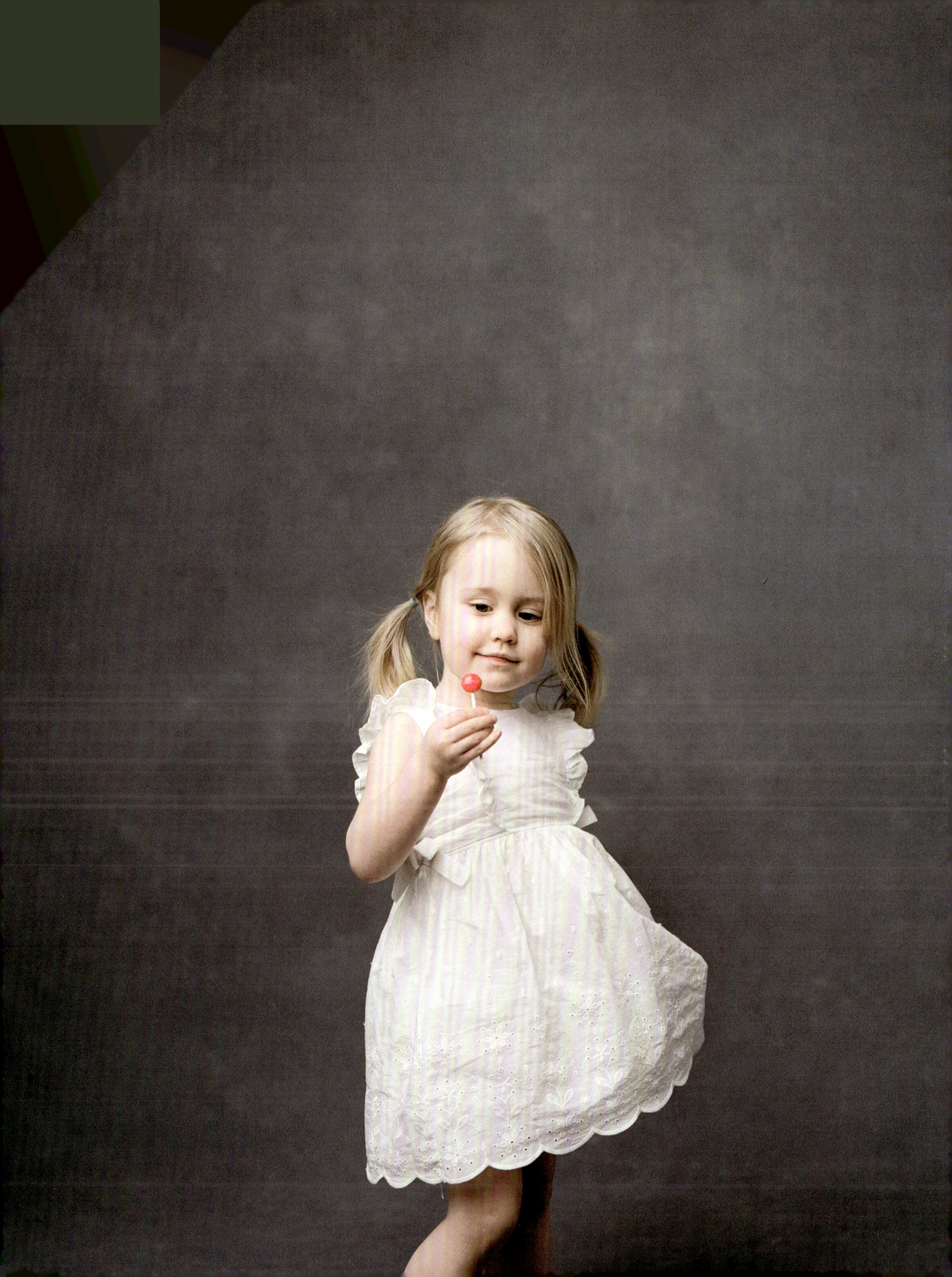

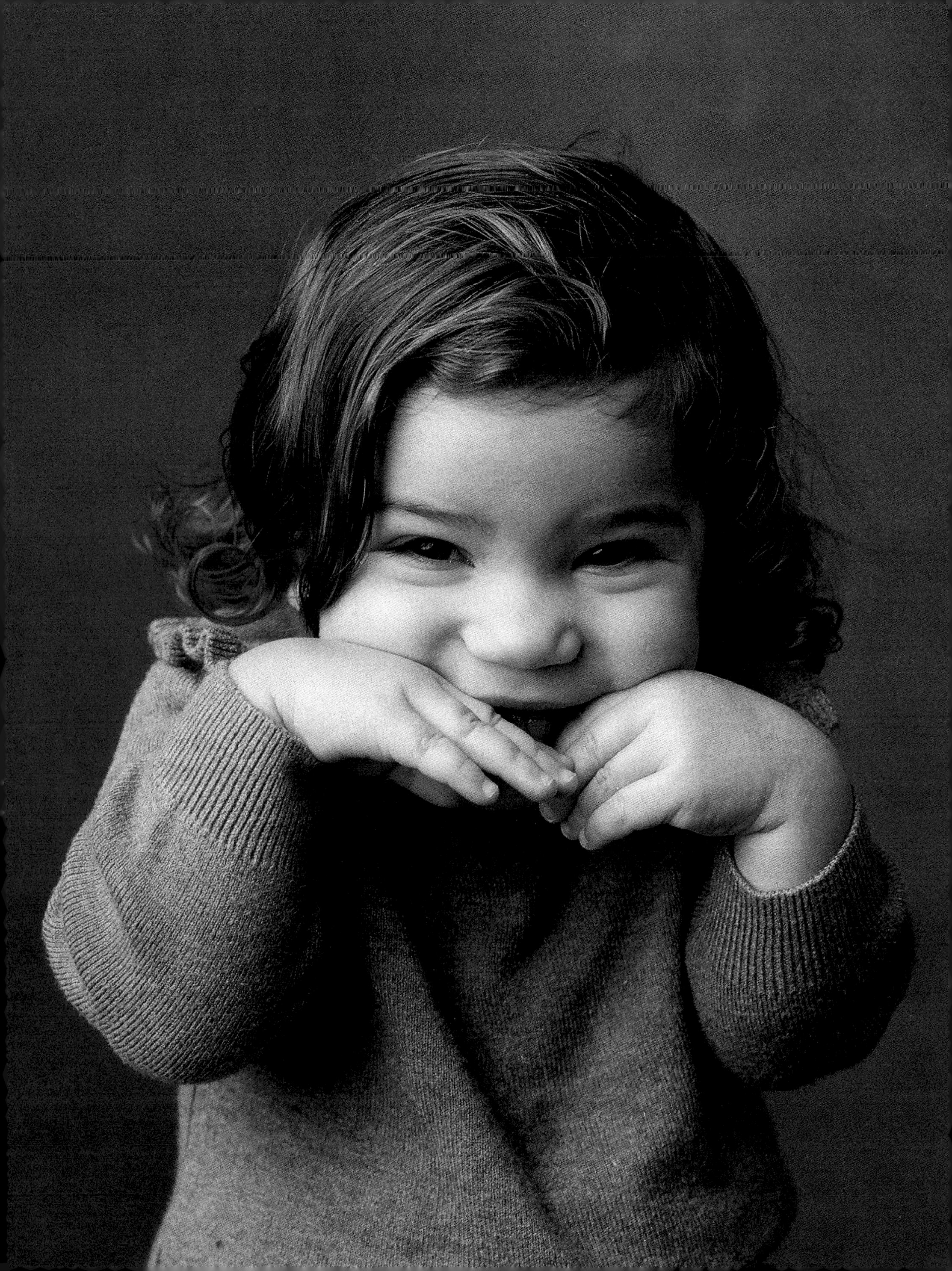

CHAPTER

# 2

# Working with Natural Light

I'm obsessed with light. Even when I don't have my camera on hand, I study it: I watch the way it falls through windows, or how it reflects off of objects outside and inside my home. I notice light temperature and how it changes depending on the time of day and the weather. I love to watch light filter through trees on sunny days, and the soft, romantic feel it creates when it's overcast.

I've made a career out of teaching other photographers how to create natural-looking light with strobes and flash, and I'll be teaching you how to do that in Chapters 3 and 4. But in order to get really good with artificial light, you need a solid understanding of natural light, which we'll cover in this chapter.

Let's begin with the technicals.

## The Technicals

I know most people don't enjoy talking about the technical aspects of photography. And I get it! When discussing photography, we want to talk about light and emotion and how photos make us feel, not what settings the photographer used to capture the image. The truth is, understanding the technical side of photography is how you take the "art" side of it to the next level!

Knowing about settings, what they do, and how to manipulate them for artistic effect is empowering! Yes, modern cameras are really smart, and your camera will probably take good photos in auto mode or in aperture or shutter priority mode. But the settings photographers use to take a photo are instrumental in all aspects of the final image. Exposure matters and balancing your settings will result in a properly exposed image. Settings also have a role to play in how an image makes a viewer feel. Does the photo depict movement? Do we feel connected to the subject? What pulls your gaze? All of that is controlled by the creative use of settings.

Knowing what your settings do and how to use them to achieve proper exposure and a desired look is how you go from creating good photos to creating great photos. And we all want to create great photos!

### The Exposure Triangle

Photography is all about light. Knowing how to expose it correctly is a fundamental skill for any photographer, regardless of genre. To do that, you need to balance your setting.

There are three settings in your camera that work in unison to create perfect exposure: ISO, aperture, and shutter speed. Together, they create what is known as the exposure triangle (**FIGURE 2.1**).

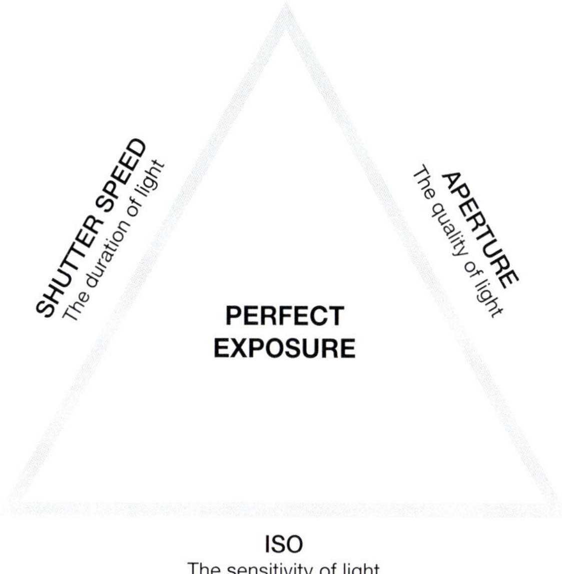


**FIGURE 2.1** The exposure triangle

## ISO

ISO tells you how sensitive to light your sensor or film stock is. The bigger the number, the more sensitive to light your sensor or film stock is (**FIGURE 2.2**).

Low ISO numbers, like 100 or 200, are less sensitive to light and are generally best on bright days or in situations where light is plentiful. Higher numbers, like 400, 800, 1600, and 3200, are more sensitive to light and are generally used in low-light situations, like when shooting indoors or in the evening.

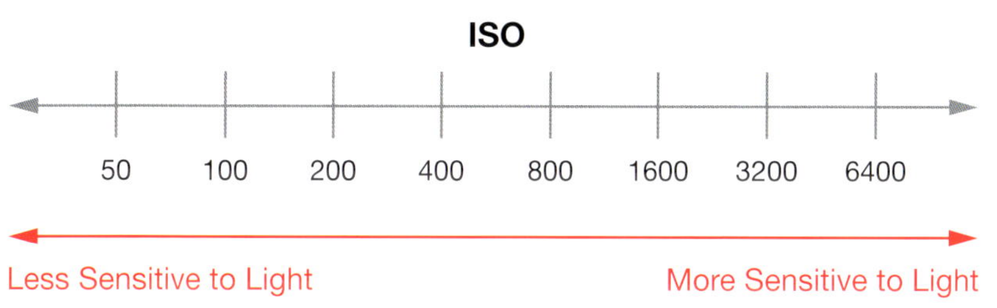


**FIGURE 2.2** Low ISO numbers indicate a sensor or film stock that is less sensitive to light. Higher ISO numbers indicate a sensor or film stock that is more sensitive to light.

With film, ISO (formerly known as ASA) is determined by the manufacturer and printed on the box. For example, Kodak Portra 400 has an ISO rating of 400. While many film photographers choose to shoot their film at different speeds than what the manufacturer recommends, the printed ISO is a good baseline. Personally, when working with film, I always shoot at box speed (the ISO number printed on the box).

With digital cameras, you have a lot more flexibility. You can change your ISO setting based on the lighting conditions you're working in. In bright light, stick with a lower ISO. In dim light, raise your ISO to help achieve proper exposure.

### Aperture

Aperture controls the amount of light that enters your camera through the lens. It does this by adjusting the size of the opening inside your lens.

In photography, light is measured in units called stops. Full stops for aperture include: f/1, f/1.4, f/2, f/2.8, f/4, f/5.6, f/8, f/11, f/16, and so on. Each full stop lets in half as much light as the previous one.

Modern digital cameras (and lighting equipment) often allow you to adjust your aperture in 1/2-stop or 1/3-stop increments, which gives you more precise control over your exposure. So don't worry if your camera shows values like f/3.2 or f/3.5 between f/2.8 and f/4—that's completely normal. Older cameras, like most film cameras, will only show full stop measurements.

When the opening in your lens is wide, it's letting in a lot of light, and your aperture numbers will be low, like f/2 and f/2.8. When the opening in your lens is narrow, it's letting in less light, and your aperture numbers will be high, like f/8 and f/11.

With aperture, low numbers (f/2, f/2.8) let in more light and high numbers (f/5.6, f/8) let in less light.

### Shutter Speed

Shutter speed is another way to control the amount of light that enters your camera.

Think of your shutter like a door. When it's open, light comes in. Your shutter speed determines how long that "door" stays open, and, therefore, how much light reaches your camera's sensor (or film).

Just like aperture, shutter speed is measured in stops of light. But with shutter speed, these stops refer to time—specifically, how long the shutter stays open. Full-stop increments typically follow this pattern: 1 second, ½ sec., ¼ sec., 1/8 sec., 1/15 sec., 1/30 sec., 1/60 sec., 1/125 sec., 1/250 sec., 1/500 sec., 1/1000 sec., 1/2000 sec., and so on.

You can also set your shutter speed for longer than 1 second, such as 2 seconds, 4 seconds, or more, which is useful when photographing low-light scenes like starry skies or nighttime cityscapes. However, for family photography, especially when working with moving subjects like a toddler, such long exposures are rarely used.

For the purposes of this book, you need to know that the lower your shutter speed (1/60 sec., 1/30 sec., 1/15 sec.), the longer your shutter is open, and the more light will be let in. The higher your shutter speed (1/125 sec., 1/500 sec., 1/1000 sec.), the shorter amount of time your shutter is open, and less light gets in.

To create a perfectly exposed image, you want your ISO, aperture, and shutter speed to be in balance. You balance them by metering (more on that later).

## Visual Interest Triangle

Balancing ISO, aperture, and shutter speed is essential for achieving correct exposure—but these settings also have a huge impact on the look and feel of your images. That's why I refer to these settings as the Visual Interest Triangle (see **FIGURE 2.3**). Each setting influences your image creatively—not just technically.

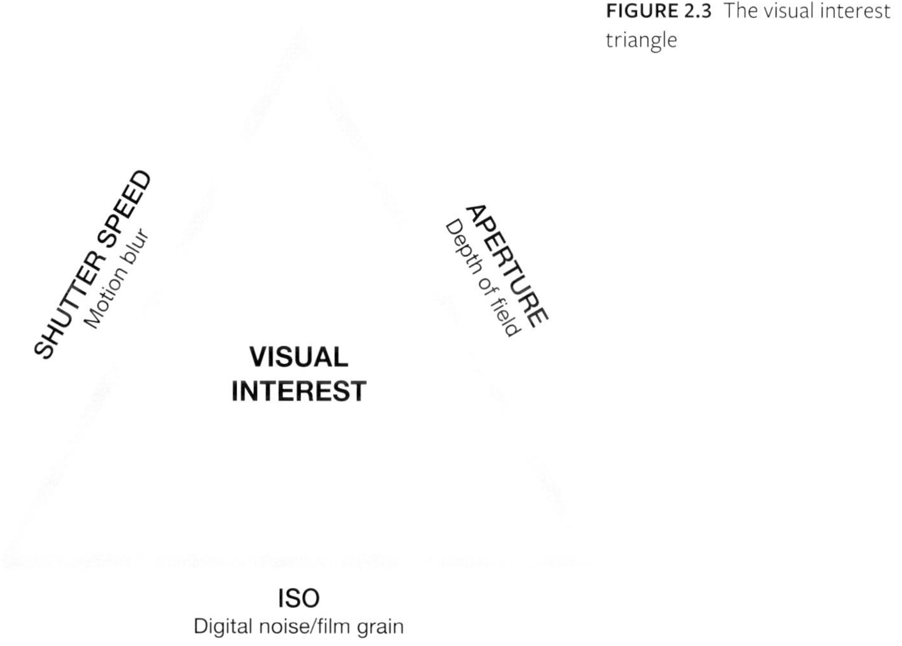


**FIGURE 2.3** The visual interest triangle

### ISO

In addition to telling us about our film or sensor sensitivity to light, ISO also has an effect on the amount of digital noise or film grain we see in an image. The lower the number (ISO 100 or 200), the less noise or grain. The higher the number (ISO 800 or 3200), the more noise or grain (**FIGURE 2.4**).

You can use this to your creative advantage.

For example, I love the look of film grain. When I'm working in the studio, I'll often choose high-speed film stocks—like Ilford Delta 3200—not because I need the extra sensitivity to light (I'm using strobes, after all), but because I love the texture the grain adds (**FIGURE 2.5**).

I don't like the look of digital noise however, so when working with digital cameras, I work at lower ISOs to keep my images clean and crisp.

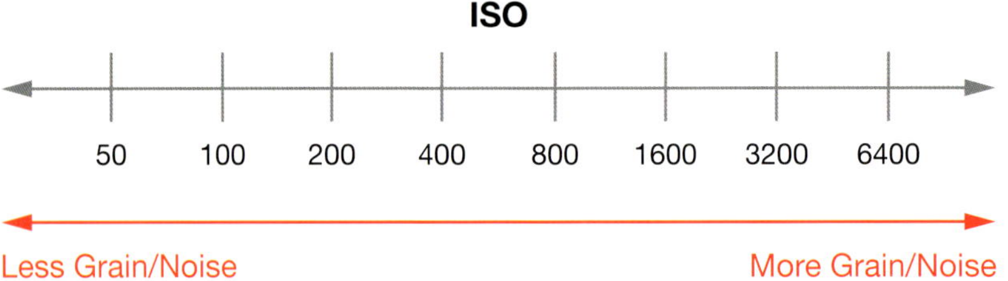


**FIGURE 2.4** Low ISO numbers result in less grain and digital noise. High ISO numbers result in more grain and digital noise.

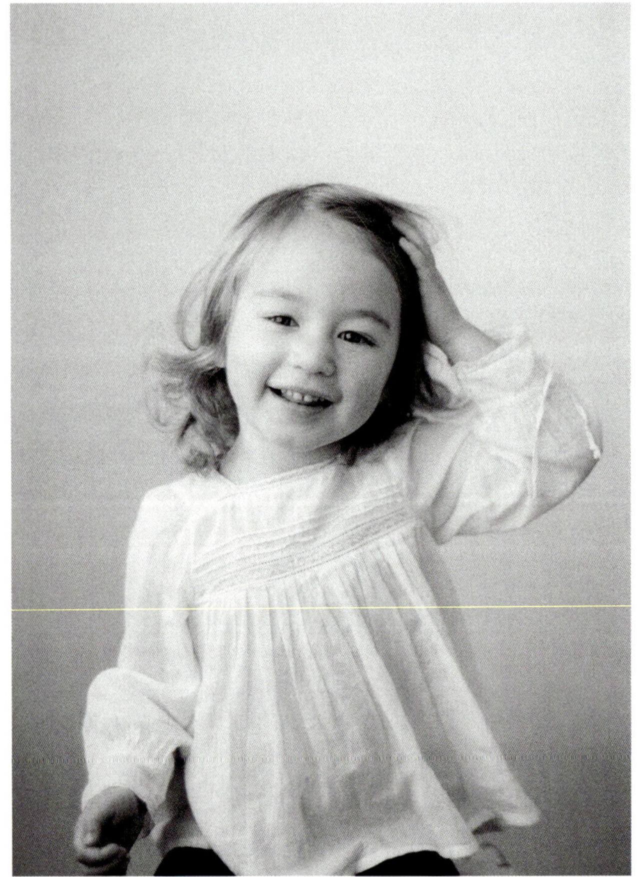

**FIGURE 2.5** This image was captured on Ilford Delta 3200—my favorite black-and-white film stock. I choose this high ISO film for its grain texture, not for its light sensitivity.

### Aperture

Aperture affects more than just exposure. It also determines how much of your image appears in focus—a concept known as depth of field. Depth of field refers to how much of your image looks sharp from front to back.

#### *Deep Depth of Field*

The higher your aperture number, the more in-focus everything in your image will be, resulting in what is known as a deep depth of field. Working with a deep depth of field is important when you want everything (or everyone) in your image to be in focus, such as when taking group portraits.

In **FIGURE 2.6**, for example, it was important that every person in the frame be in focus. To achieve that goal, I intentionally created a relatively deep depth of field by closing my aperture down to f/5.6.

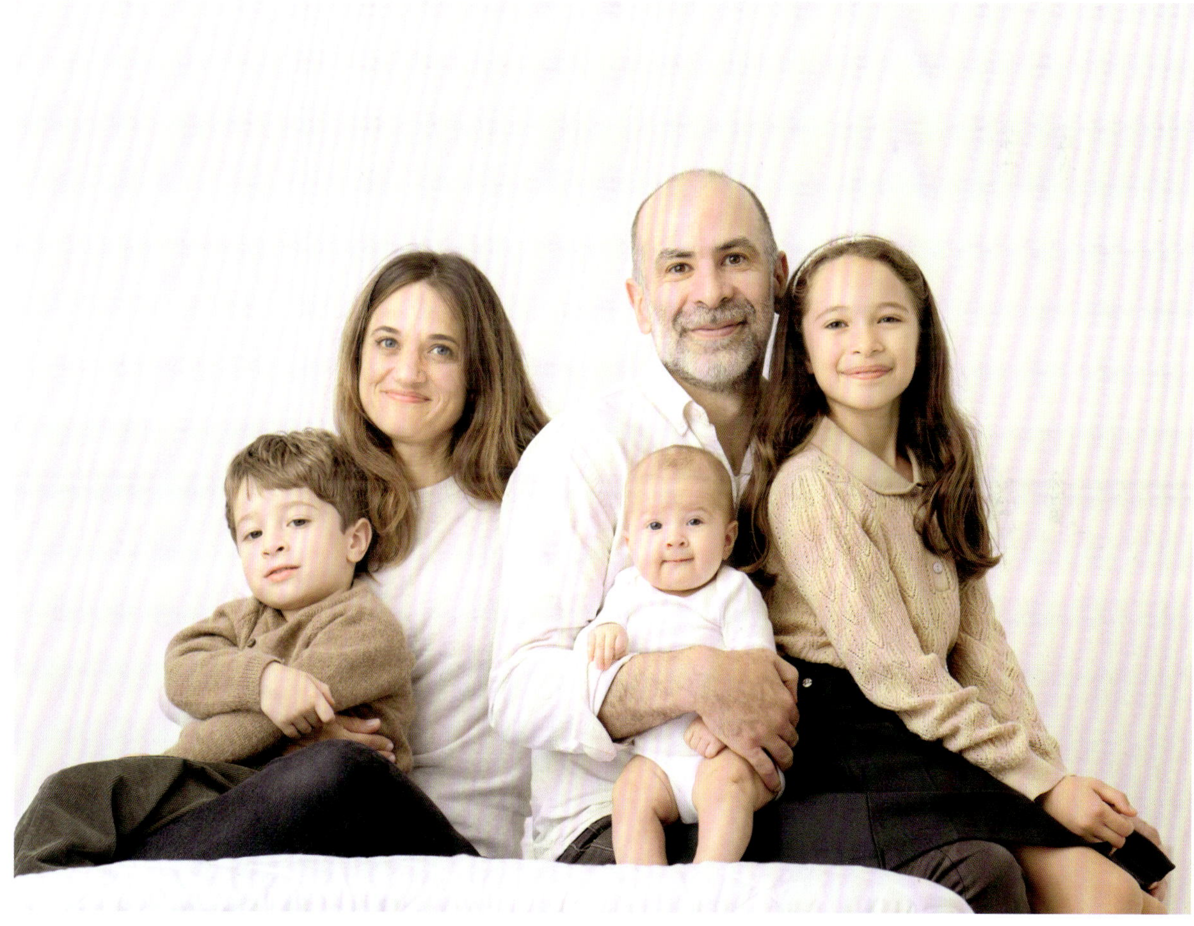

**FIGURE 2.6** Deep depth of field. For this image, I stopped down to f/5.6 to ensure that everyone in the photo was in focus.

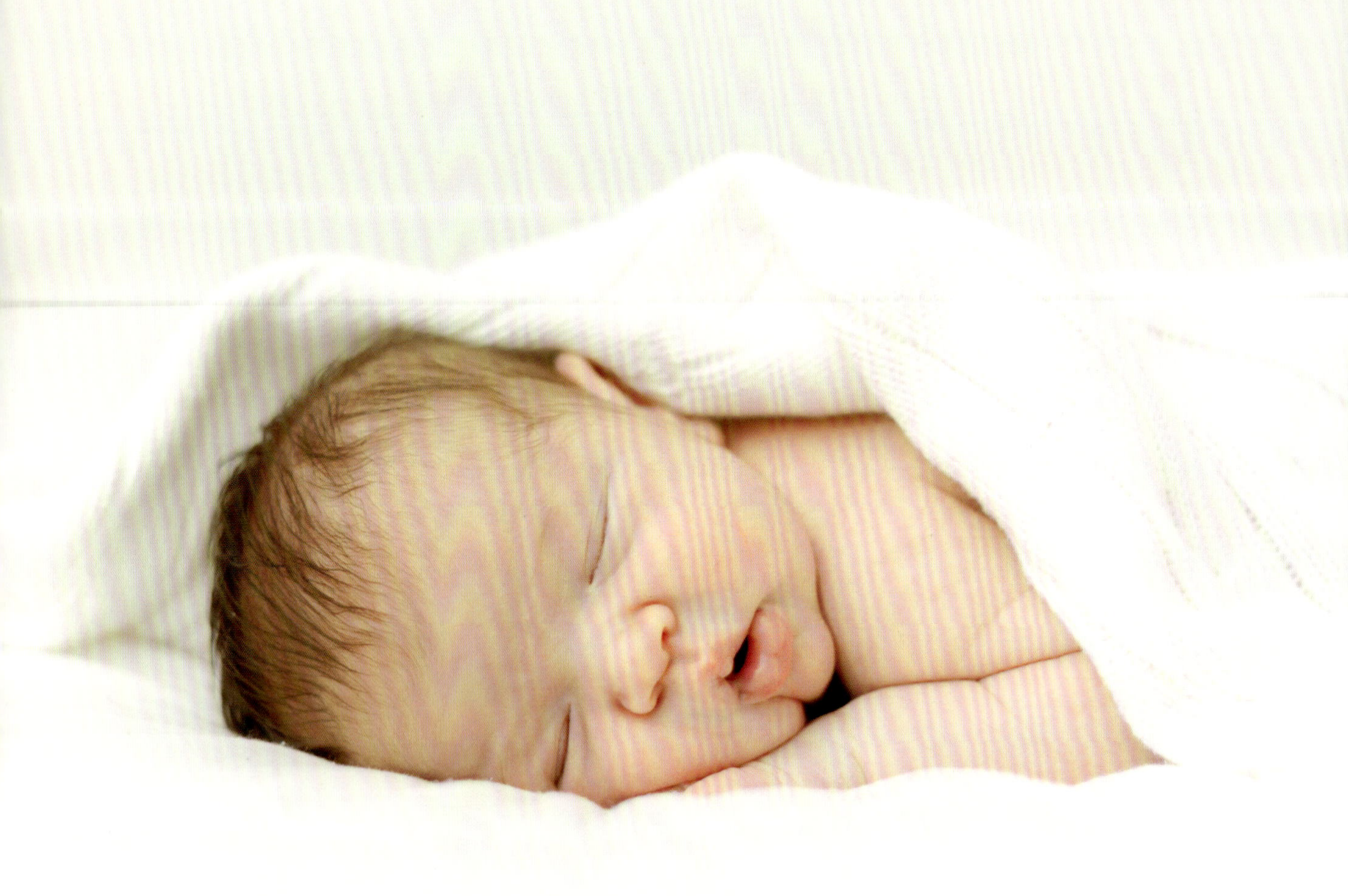

**FIGURE 2.7** I personally love shallow depth of field and frequently shoot wide open to achieve this effect. This image was captured at f/1.8.

*Shallow Depth of Field*

The lower your aperture, the less of your image will be in focus. This is called having a shallow depth of field. With a shallow depth of field, the part of the image you focus on will be crisp while everything else fades from focus. Create this look by using a wide aperture. The wider the aperture, the shallower the depth of field (**FIGURE 2.7**).

I personally love a shallow depth of field and frequently work at f/1.8 or f/2 to create this effect.

### Shutter Speed

Like ISO and aperture, shutter speed has an important role outside of exposure, as well. When working with natural light, you can use your shutter speed to help freeze motion in an image or allow motion blur, depending on the look you are trying to create.

If you want to freeze motion, set your shutter to a high speed, like 1/250 sec. or 1/500 sec. If you want to allow some motion blur into your photo, set your shutter to a low speed, like 1/15 or 1/30.

In **FIGURE 2.8**, I asked the model to play with her dress, swishing it back and forth to create movement, and then shot each frame at a different shutter speed.

**FIGURE 2.8A** was captured at ISO 100, f/2.8, 1/30 sec. Notice there is a fair amount of motion blur. **FIGURE 2.8B** was captured at ISO 100, f/2.8, 1/125 sec. In this image, there is still motion blur, but much less than in Figure 2.8A because of the faster shutter speed. **FIGURE 2.8C** was captured at ISO 100, f/2.8, 1/500 sec., and the high shutter speed completely froze the movement in the frame, resulting in no motion blur.

As you can see, the slower the shutter speed, the more motion blur; the faster the shutter speed, the less motion blur.

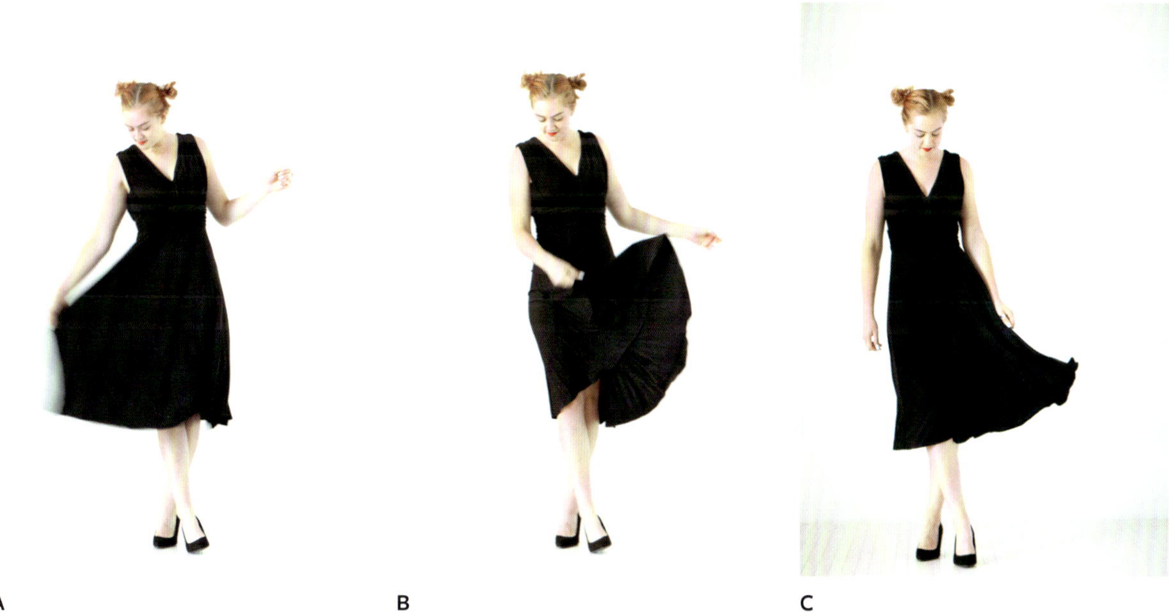

A B C

**FIGURE 2.8** Slower shutter speeds allow motion blur. Faster shutter speeds freeze motion. Figure 2.8A was captured at ISO 100, f/2.8, 1/30 sec. Figure 2.8B was captured at ISO 100, f/2.8, 1/125 sec. Figure 2.8C was captured at ISO 100, f/2.8, 1/500 sec.

### Manual Mode

When you're working in auto mode, your camera evaluates the available light and selects the settings for you to achieve proper exposure. While this can be helpful when you're just starting out, auto mode limits your creative control because your camera is only concerned with exposure, not style.

There are semi-auto modes that will give you a little more control. Aperture priority allows you to choose your aperture, and shutter priority allows you to choose your shutter speed. But for full creative freedom, you'll want to work in manual mode.

Manual mode allows you to control all three settings—ISO, shutter speed, and aperture—based on the look you're going for. You can choose your ISO depending on your available light and the amount of grain or digital noise you want to introduce or eliminate in your image. If you are working with small children who are running around in a natural-light setting, you can choose a shutter speed of 1/200 sec. or higher to freeze the movement and cut down on motion blur. Or, if you want to show motion, you can set your shutter to a low speed to capture that movement. If your goal is to create a portrait with a shallow depth of field, you can open your aperture, and if you are photographing a large family and want everyone in focus, you can choose to stop down. The point is, you get to decide, not your camera!

In manual mode, you can adjust any of the three exposure settings at any time to match your lighting conditions and creative goals. Personally, I usually set my aperture and shutter speed first, then adjust my ISO as needed to achieve proper exposure.

Just remember: All three settings need to work together—that's where metering comes in.

### Metering

All meters are designed to find the perfect balance between absolute black and absolute white, or what is known in the photography world as "middle gray."

Middle gray is a term coined by Ansel Adams in his Zone System (**FIGURE 2.9**). There are entire books written on how to use and understand the Zone System, including books written by Ansel Adams himself. For this book, all you need to know is how middle gray relates to metering.

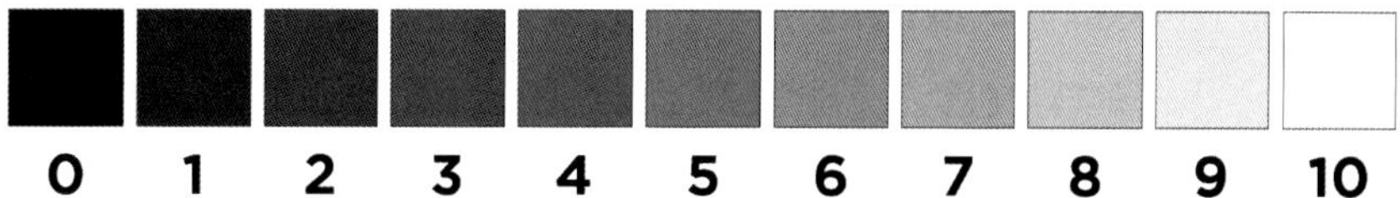


**FIGURE 2.9** The Zone System. The Zone System is made up of eleven zones that represent the gradation of tones between absolute black (Zone 0) and absolute white (Zone 10). Middle gray (Zone 5) is the perfect mid-point between total black and total white.

The Zone System is made up of eleven zones that represent the gradation of tones between absolute black (Zone 0) and absolute white (Zone 10). Middle gray (Zone 5) is the perfect mid-point between total black and total white.

The job of your meter is to place the details you want to photograph at Zone 5: perfect exposure. It's your job as the artist to decide where within your photograph you want that middle gray reading to be.

When it comes to metering, there are two types of readings to take: reflective and incident.

### Reflective Metering

Reflective metering measures the light that is reflecting off your subject (**FIGURE 2.10**). This is the method used by in-camera meters, or when in Spot Meter mode on your handheld meter. This is the method I use when working with natural light in manual mode.

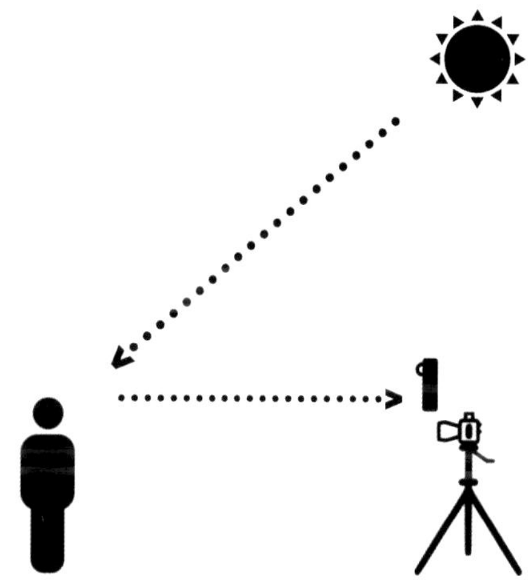

There are many benefits to reflective metering, including speed and convenience. You do not need to physically place your meter next to your subject to get a reading, which makes it easy to meter a family when they are far away from you.

**FIGURE 2.10** Reflective metering reads the light that is reflecting off your subject.

The problem with reflective metering, however, is that it can be inconsistent. Because it reads the light that is bouncing off your subject, the reading you get will be affected by the brightness and colors your subjects are wearing, as well as the tones of their skin. For example, if you are photographing a family and one of the family members is wearing white while everyone else is wearing black, the white clothing will reflect more light than the black clothing. Therefore, the reflective meter reading you'll get off the white clothing will be different than the reading you will get off the black clothing, even if they are all standing in the same light. This would result in one or the other of them being under- or overexposed.

# Reflective Metering: Using Your Camera's Internal Meter

Modern cameras make working in manual mode super easy, as most of them have great internal meters. Most cameras have a built-in exposure indicator that shows you whether your image is underexposed (–), overexposed (+), or just right (centered).

At f/2.8, 1/125 sec., ISO 100, the camera's internal meter shows that the image is 3 stops underexposed (indicated by the marker under the –3 on the exposure indicator). The resulting image verifies that (**FIGURES 2.11A** and **2.11D**).

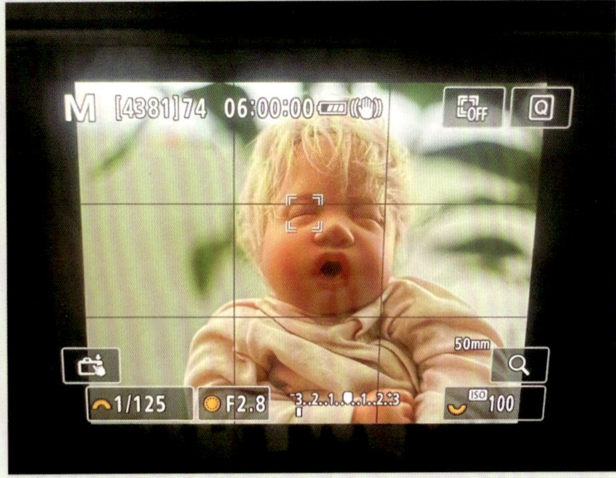


A

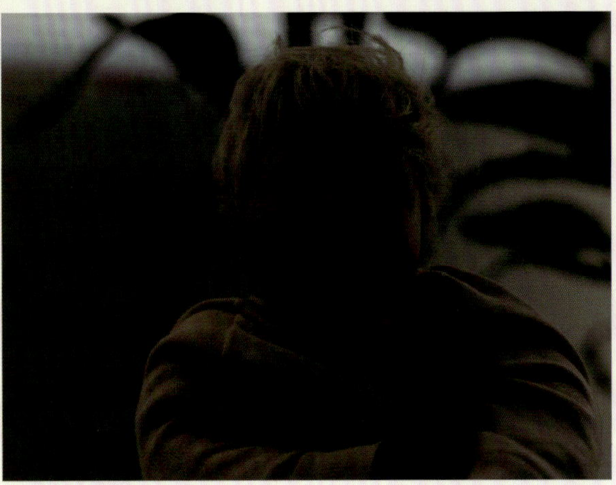

B

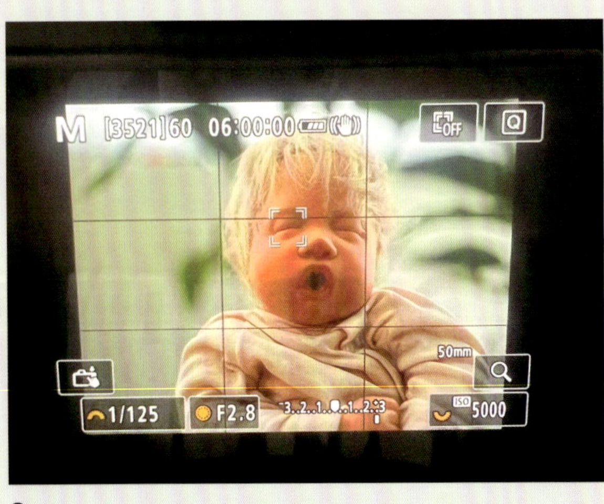


C

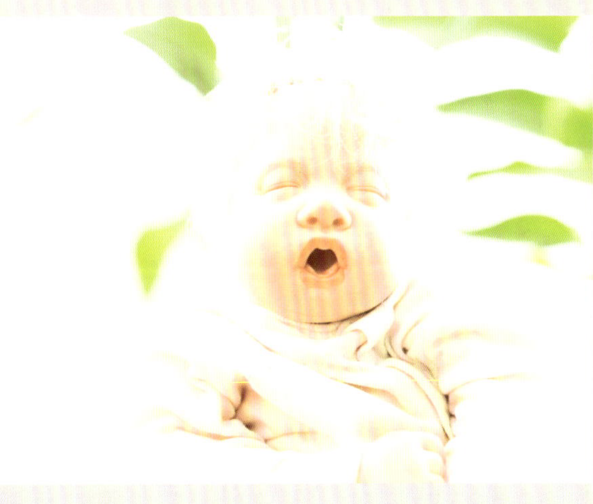

D

**FIGURE 2.11** Figures 2.11 A, B, and C show the back of my Canon R6 in manual mode. This view allows me to see my aperture, shutter speed, and ISO, as well as an exposure indicator line that goes from –3 to +3. The exposure indicator lets me know if my exposure is under, over, or just right! Figure 2.11 D, E, and F show the results.

At f/2.8, 1/125 sec., ISO 5000, the camera's internal meter shows that the image is 3 stops overexposed (**FIGURE 2.11B**), as shown in **FIGURE 2.11E**.

At f/2.8, 1/125 sec., ISO 800, the exposure indicator is reporting a perfectly exposed image (**FIGURE 2.11C**), and after seeing **FIGURE 2.11F**, I agree!

Knowing what you know about the exposure triangle, you can decide which setting (or settings) to change to reach perfect exposure. I personally find setting my aperture and shutter speed to my desired speed and adjusting the ISO to be the easiest. Using the camera's meter and exposure indicator makes finding perfect exposure simple!

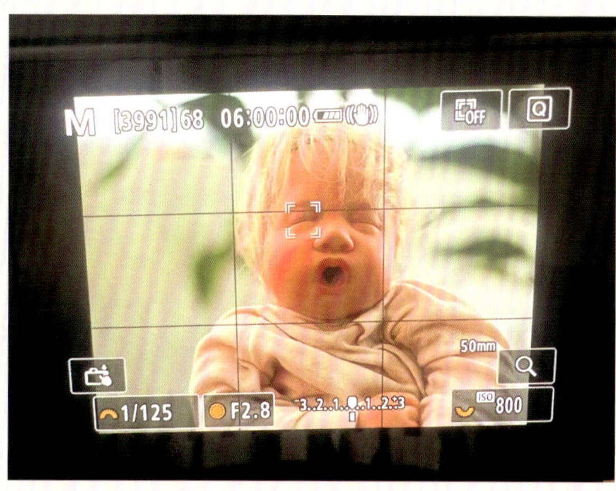

E

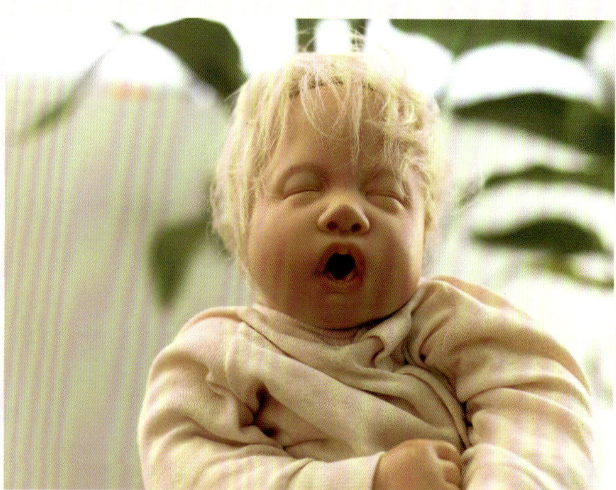
F

To get around this problem, many photographers use a gray card when metering this way. A gray card is a small card that has been printed to be a perfect "middle gray" tone.

To use a gray card, place your card in the front of the subject you are photographing and read the light that is bouncing off it.

Using a gray card works well in most natural-light settings, but it does require an extra piece of equipment (the card). It also requires that you are close enough to your subject to walk up and place your card in front of them, which can be inconvenient or not possible if your subject is far away.

Also, reflective metering can only be used when working with natural light. When metering for strobes and flash, you will meter using the incident metering method.

### Incident Metering

Incident metering measures the light that is falling onto your subject rather than the light that is reflecting off your subject (**FIGURE 2.12**).

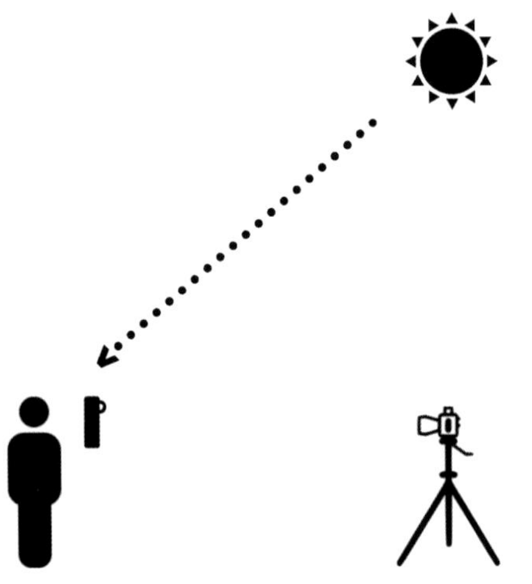

**FIGURE 2.12** Incident metering measures the light that is falling on your subject. Use incident metering with artificial light.

This is my preferred method of metering. It's easy, accurate, and consistent in all lighting situations. You don't need to worry about having a gray card on hand, and it doesn't matter what your subject is wearing or the tone of their skin; the only thing the meter reads is the light that is falling on them.

To better illustrate how incident metering works, let's again consider the example of our family in black and white clothing. With incident metering, you will get the same reading metering in front of the person in white as you will metering in front of the people in black. Because you are only measuring the light that is falling on them, as long as they are all standing in the same light, your readings will be the same.

The drawback to incident metering is that it requires you to be close enough to your subject to walk over and take a reading. It also requires an extra piece of equipment: a handheld light meter.

## Incident Metering: Using a Handheld Light Meter

When metering for natural light using a handheld light meter, make sure your meter is set to "natural light mode." Every meter is different, so check your meter's manual, but on the Sekonics, natural light mode is indicated by a sunshine icon (**FIGURE 2.13**). Once your meter is in the proper mode, enter two of the three components that make up the exposure triangle into the meter. When triggered, the meter will give you the third value.

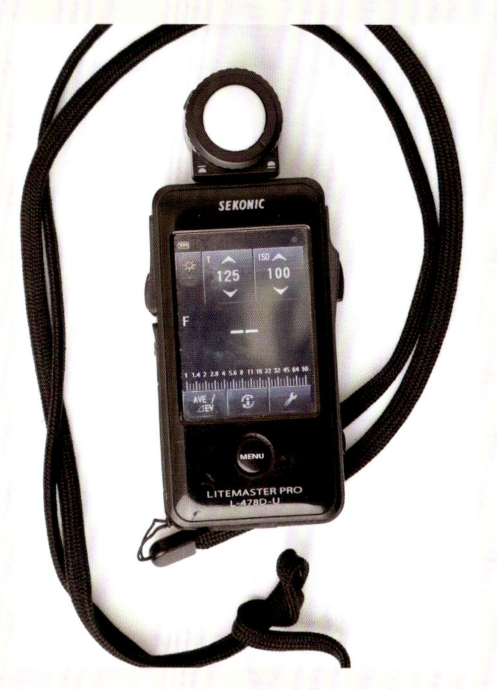


**FIGURE 2.13** This is my Sekonic meter set to natural light mode, indicated by the sunshine icon in the upper-left hand corner of the meter screen. Here I have the ISO set to 100 and the shutter speed set to 1/125 sec. When triggered, the meter will give me my aperture setting based on the available light.

## Film vs. Digital Sensors

While this is not a book on film photography, many family photographers (myself included) love the look of film and use it all the time in their work. And, when it comes to metering, there are fundamental differences between film and digital sensors that need to be addressed.

### Metering for Digital Cameras

Digital sensors are very sensitive to light, and you can easily blow out highlights and completely overexpose an image if a scene is not metering correctly. In fact, most digital photographers err on the side of underexposure for precisely this reason.

**FIGURE 2.14** shows a seven-stop exposure test taken with a Canon 5D Mark II. As you can see, the perfectly exposed image in the middle looks great. There is detail in both the highlights and shadows, and the overall photo is not too bright or too dark. But you may also notice that the images shot at one and two stops underexposure look pretty good as well. These images could easily be

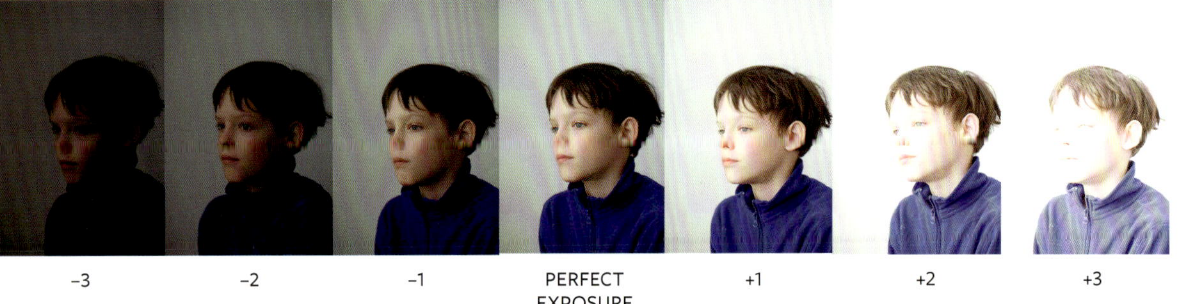


**FIGURE 2.14** A seven-stop exposure test taken on a Canon 5D Mark II

adjusted in post-production and be beautiful, usable photos. Even though they are technically underexposed, no information has been lost on either end, and there is enough detail in the highlights and the shadows to work with.

Now look at the images shot at one, two, and three stops overexposure. At one stop overexposed, the image is bright and the highlights look a little hot. While this is not an ideal exposure, there is still some information in both the highlights and the shadows, and this image could most likely be adjusted in post-production and be usable.

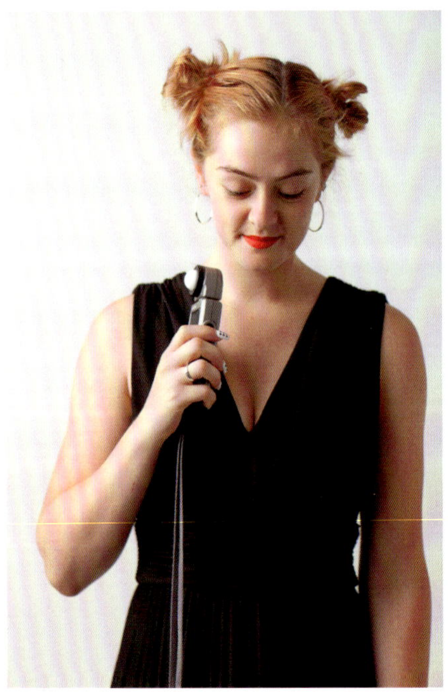

**FIGURE 2.15** To take a highlight reading, place your meter, bulb out, parallel to your subject's face, with the bulb facing the light.

By two stops over, however, we start to lose detail in the highlights on the face, meaning that there is no longer enough information in the highlights to make this a usable image. By three stops over, the highlights on the face are completely blown out and the image is unusable.

Digital sensors do not handle overexposure well. This is important to note in relation to metering. When working with a digital camera, make sure you are metering in a way that will protect your highlights, placing them at middle gray, Zone 5. To do this, meter for your highlights.

Notice in **FIGURE 2.15** how the meter is placed next to my subject's face as opposed to close to the light. This is important to note when metering for a portrait. Remember, the closer your subject is to your light source, the brighter the light will be, so if your meter is closer to your light than your subject is, you will not get an accurate reading for your subject.

### Metering for Color Film

When exposing with digital cameras, protecting the highlights is paramount. With film, especially color film, this is not a worry.

Film has incredible exposure latitude, especially on the overexposure side of things. You can overexpose most color film stocks up to five, even six stops over without losing detail or blowing your highlights, but underexpose a roll of film, and you'll end up with a big muddy mess (**FIGURE 2.16**).

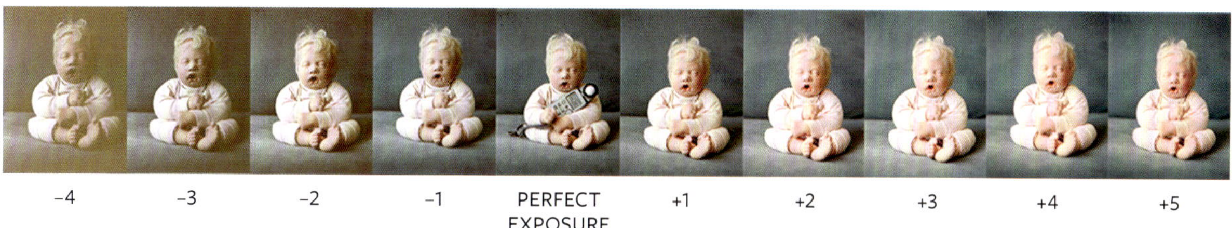


**FIGURE 2.16** This is a ten-stop exposure test shot on Fuji 400h color film. As you can see, there is still plenty of detail in the overexposed images, even when overexposed by five stops. The underexposed images, however, look dark and muddy.

This is the inherent difference between shooting digitally and shooting with film. When overexposing on a digital sensor, we lose information, especially in the highlights. When working with film, the opposite is true. Overexposing film a little actually adds information to the negative, creating what is known as a dense negative. Having a dense negative means that there is information in both the highlights and shadows.

**FIGURE 2.17A** and **2.17B** show the positive and negative of a perfectly exposed color film image. The dark parts of the negative show the highlights and the lighter parts of the negative show the shadows. As you can see, there is information in both the highlights and the shadows. Look at **FIGURES 2.17C** and **2.17D.** This image was captured at two stops overexposed. The positive image still looks great. The highlights are not blown and there is shadow detail. Now look at the negative. The entire image looks darker, telling us that more light hit the negative than in Figure 2.17B. This is an example of good density. By overexposing by two stops, I added information in the shadows without losing detail in the highlights. Finally, see **FIGURES 2.17E** and **2.17F.** This image was captured two stops underexposed. The positive looks dark and "muddy," and the overall negative is lighter, meaning less light hit the film. The shadows look thin, which means there is lost detail in those areas—which is why the positive scan of the images looks dull and dark.

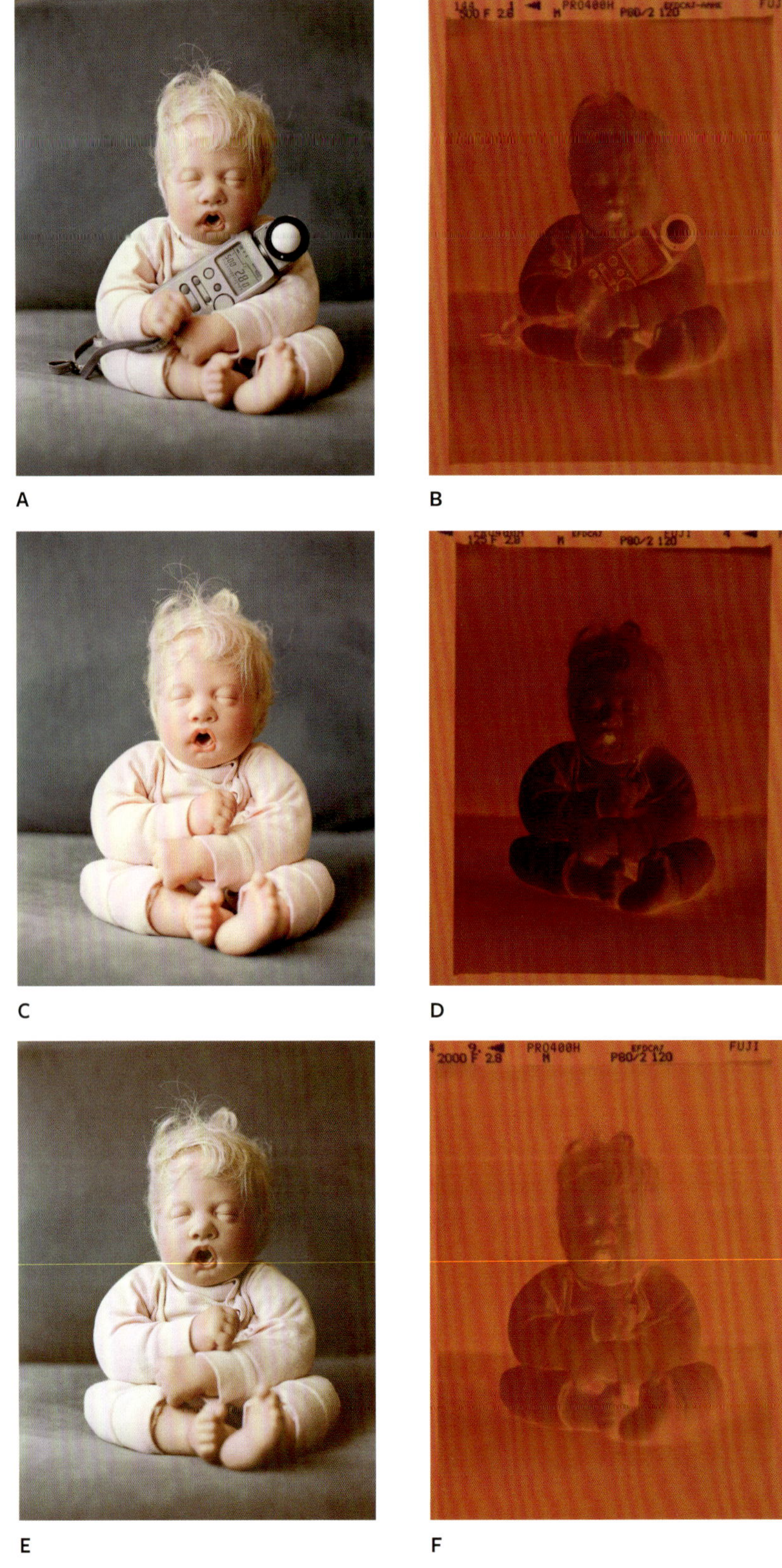


**FIGURE 2.17** Figures 2.17A and 2.17B show the positive and negative of a perfectly exposed color film image. In Figures 2.17C and 2.17D, the image was captured at two stops overexposed. Figures 2.17E and 2.17F was captured two stops underexposed.

When working with color film, creating a good, dense negative is always the goal. To achieve this goal, make sure your shadows, the darkest part of your image, have been properly exposed. To do this, meter for the shadows, which will place your shadows at middle gray. Your highlights will be two to three stops overexposed, which is perfectly fine for most film stocks, especially color film. You will not lose detail in your highlights the way you would on a digital sensor, and you will be creating proper density on your negative.

To take a shadow reading, enter your ISO and camera's sync speed into the meter, then place your meter next to your subject, bulb out, with the bulb facing into the shadows (**FIGURE 2.18**).

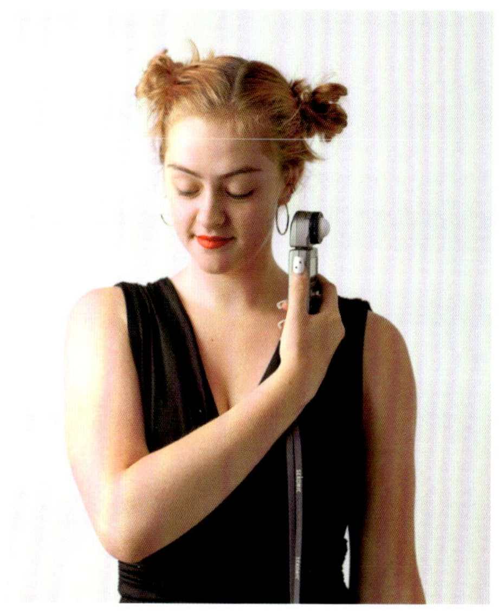

**FIGURE 2.18** Metering for the shadows

## Common Misconceptions

Photographers who are new to film often attempt to control the brightness of their photos through exposure. They think that to create a bright film image they must overexpose their film, and will go on to overexpose by four, five, or even six stops. This theory totally makes sense when you're used to working with a digital camera. Overexpose on a digital sensor and the image does indeed get brighter.

But that is not the case with film (refer to the ten-stop exposure test in **FIGURE 2.16**).

You'll notice that the image that was overexposed by five stops is no brighter than the image overexposed by one stop. With film, the brightness of your image has more to do with how your image is scanned or printed than it does with how much you have overexposed. While you will not blow your highlights by excessively overexposing your film, you will start to introduce color shifts and unwanted grain texture—so don't overdo it. Setting your ISO to the speed recommended by the manufacturer (printed on the box of film) and then metering for the shadows will overexpose your film by two to three stops, which is plenty. No need to add any extra exposure!

Remember, meter for the shadows with color film to ensure that there is enough light in the shadows to create good density—not to create a bright photo.

To make sure you are getting the look you want when using film, be sure to communicate your preferences to the lab you are working with. For example, when working with color film, I let my lab know that I meter for my shadows and would like my negatives scanned for the shadows as well. My style is bright, light, and airy, so I make sure to communicate those preferences!

When working with film, communication with your lab is key. Don't be afraid to tell them what you like!

### Metering for Black-and-White Film

Working with black-and-white film is much simpler than working with color film. Instead of being concerned with colors and tones, we can concentrate on highlights, shadows, and grain. It's a different kind of storytelling and a different way of seeing.

While each stock is unique, most black-and-white film has great exposure latitude. You can overexpose by two to three stops without blowing your highlights. You can even underexpose by a stop or two and, with a little work in post-production, get a usable image.

### An Exception to Every Rule: Metering for Slide Film

In 2018, Kodak Alaris re-introduced Ektachrome 100 to the film market. Ektachrome is color film. It is slide film, which means it is a color positive stock, not a color negative stock. Like most slide film, Ektachrome does not have the exposure latitude that we've come to expect out of our color film stocks. This is important to know in regard to metering.

Ektachrome handles more like a digital sensor than a color film stock. You can easily lose detail in your highlights and blow out an image if you overexpose this film. With Ektachrome, you do not want to meter for the shadows. For best results, treat it like a digital sensor and meter for your highlights or midtones.

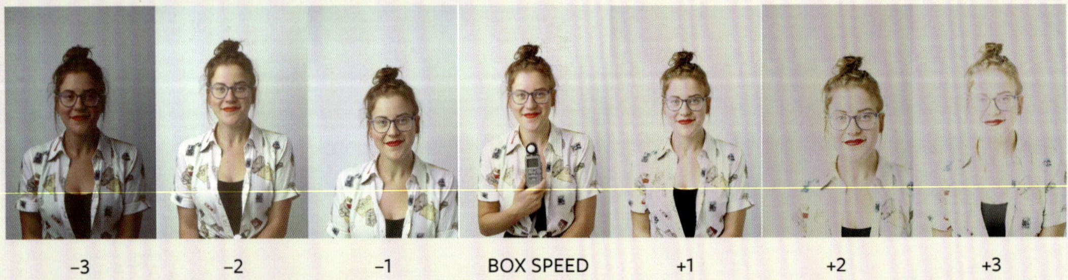

–3 | –2 | –1 | BOX SPEED | +1 | +2 | +3

**FIGURE 2.19** A seven-stop exposure test shot on Ektachrome 100. As you can see, at one stop over exposure the image is bright and the highlights are a little hot. By two stops over, details are lost in the highlights, and by three stops over, the image is completely blown out. This film stock does not like to be overexposed, so don't meter for your shadows. For best results, meter for your midtones and highlights when working with Ektachrome 100.

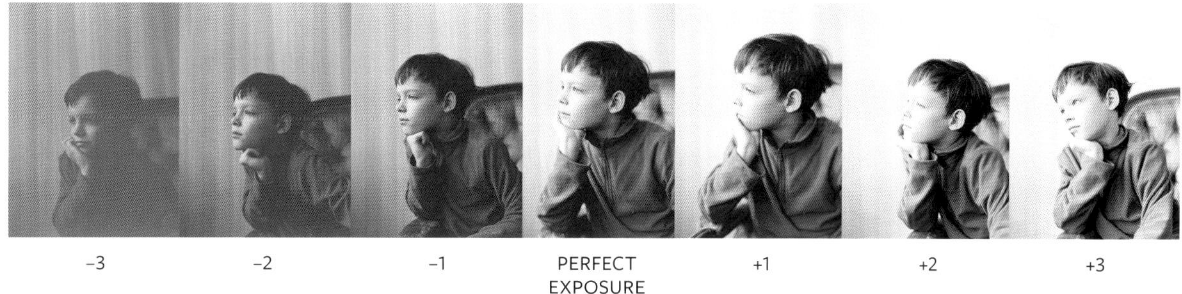


**FIGURE 2.20** A seven-stop exposure test shot on Kodak Tri-X 400

**FIGURE 2.20** shows a seven-stop exposure test captured on Kodak Tri-X 400. As you can see, the images shot at one, two, and three stops overexposure still have detail in the highlights. You may also notice that with black-and-white film, the images do get brighter as they are overexposed, similar to digital shooting. The images shot at one and two stops under are usable as well. Yes, we are losing some detail in the shadows, but they look contrasty and dramatic, not dull or muddy. We could push those exposures in processing (when pushing film, you leave the negative in the developer longer, adding contrast and grain) or import them into Photoshop and boost the blacks.

This is important to note from a metering standpoint. With color film, it's important to meter in a way that creates density in the darkest part of the image, so meter for the shadows. When metering for a digital camera, make sure to protect the highlights by metering for the highlights. With black-and-white film, however, there are no real rules. There are many different ways to use a stock, depending on the look you want to create.

If you want an image with lots of shadow detail, meter for your shadows (**FIGURE 2.21A**). Want more contrast with darker shadows? Meter for your highlights (**FIGURE 2.21B**). Just make sure to let your film lab know how you metered so that they can scan your negatives accordingly.

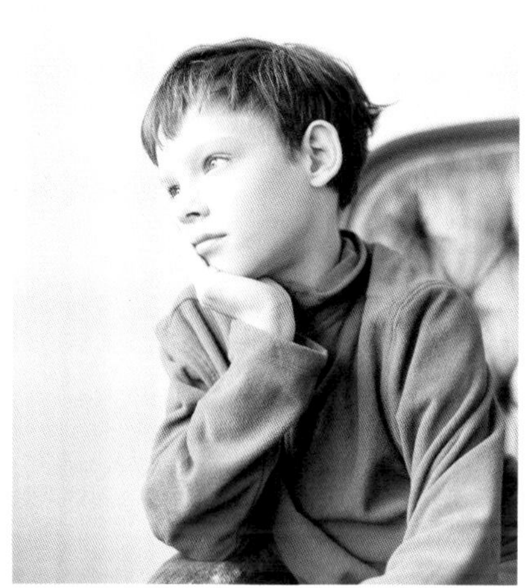

A

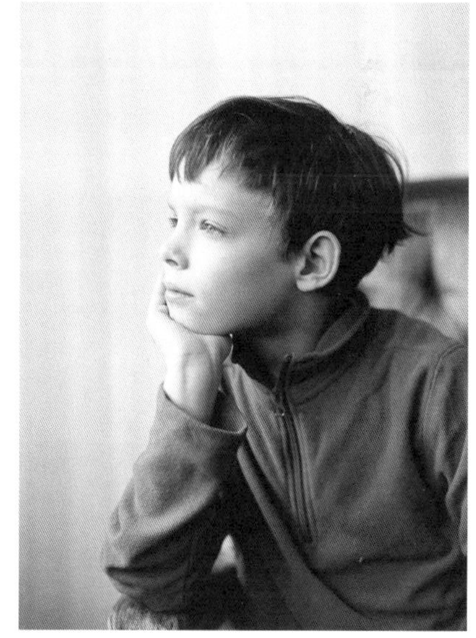

B

**FIGURE 2.21** Figure 2.21A was metered for the shadows, creating detail in the shadows and an overall bright image. Figure 2.21B was metered for the highlights, resulting in darker shadows.

## Metering Natural Light with a Handheld Light Meter

I use Sekonic meters and cannot recommend them enough. But, regardless of what brand and model you have, all light meters work the same way.

To take a reading, input two of the three components that make up the exposure triangle into your meter, place your meter in the light you wish to measure, and hit the trigger button. Once triggered, the meter will give you the missing third setting of the exposure triangle that you can set in your camera.

Where to place your meter when photographing people varies, depending on the medium you are using. When metering for digital cameras and slide film (E-6), meter for your highlights. When metering for black-and-white film, meter for where you want your detail to be. And when working with color film (C-41), meter for your shadows.

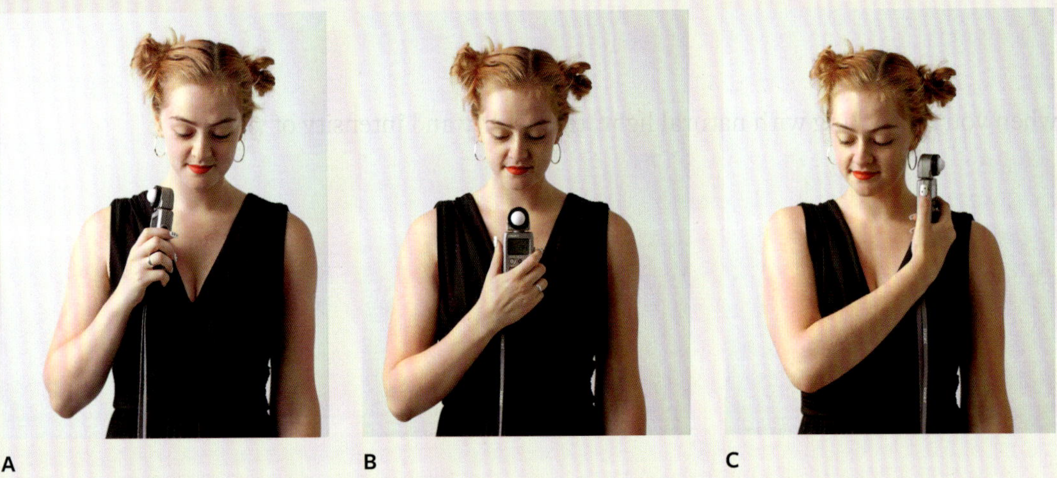

A B C

**FIGURE 2.22** Figure 2.22A is metered for the highlights. Figure 2.22B is metered for the midtones. Figure 2.22C is metered for the shadows.

## Identifying Your Ideal Light

Now that you understand how to meter and use your settings for proper exposure and visual interests, let's explore using light with intention.

Whether you realize it or not, you probably have a preferred lighting style. Most photographers do. Maybe you love the light and airy look, or maybe you are drawn to the drama of dark and moody images. Whatever your preferred style is, knowing how to identify it and create it consistently is how you begin to develop a signature style. And in the competitive world of family photography, having a signature style is key to setting yourself apart!

As mentioned in Chapter 1, the first step in developing your signature style is identifying your version of ideal light. Do you like hard light or soft light? What are your favorite lighting patterns? Do you prefer images with a lot or a little contrast between the shadows and highlights? Noticing these preferences gives insight into your personal lighting style and having that insight makes creating this style consistently much easier.

Light quality is defined by the shadows it produces. Hard light results in sharp, well-defined shadows and soft light results in gradual, less-defined shadows. Relatively small light sources produce hard light and relatively large light sources produce soft light—adding or removing diffusion and adjusting the proximity of your light source to your subject impacts the light's quality. Proximity also impacts the intensity of the light you are working with. The closer your light source is to your subject, the brighter the light will be. The farther away your light source is from your subject, the dimmer your light will be.

All of this is true whether you're working with natural light or artificial light, but, when you're working with natural light, the quality and intensity of your light is also impacted by the time of day and whether you are working outside or using window light inside.

## Natural Light Outside

When photographing families outside with natural light, your primary light source is the sun.

The sun is large, but its distance to the earth is very far, resulting in hard light. On overcast days, however, the clouds diffuse the light, making it softer. Pay attention to the weather forecast when planning to work with families outside. The weather will impact how comfortable your families are at their session, but it will also have a big impact on the quality of your available light.

The direction of your available light is another important factor to consider. Light direction and light intensity change throughout the day as the sun moves across the sky. In the Northern Hemisphere, morning light comes from the east, producing long shadows that shorten as you approach midday. At midday, your light will come from directly above, producing shorter, harder shadows. In the afternoon, light will come from the west, resulting in shadows that grow longer as you approach sunset.

There is a lot of information out there about how best to work with natural light at these different times of day but given the number of variables when working outside (weather, location, terrain), I prefer to keep it simple.

As I see it, when working outside you have four options on how to use your light. You can place your family in the shade, in direct sun, with the sun behind them, or photograph them in the hour just after sunrise or just before sunset, also known as the Golden Hour. These choices are the same regardless of the weather, location, or terrain you are working in. Knowing your preferred light quality and lighting patterns will help you decide how you are going to use the natural light to your advantage. For example, I prefer soft light. When working outside, my go-to lighting patterns are backlight and flat light. Knowing this helps me decide how to use the available light at my sessions to create images that are consistent and on brand.

The images in **FIGURE 2.23** were captured in the same location on different days and at different times of the year. **FIGURE 2.23A** was captured in the full sun of a hot summer afternoon. **FIGURE 2.23B** was captured on an overcast fall morning. I chose to backlight them both to produce images that are consistent with my style, despite the vastly different lighting conditions.

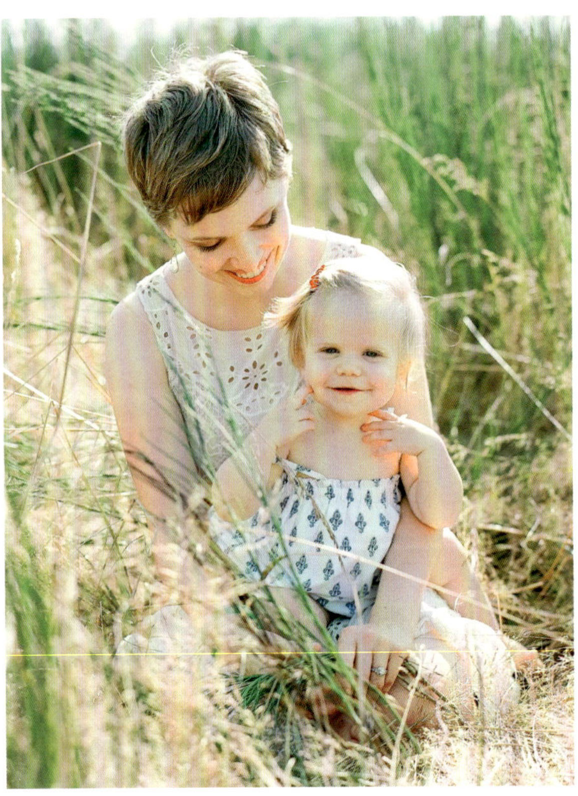

A

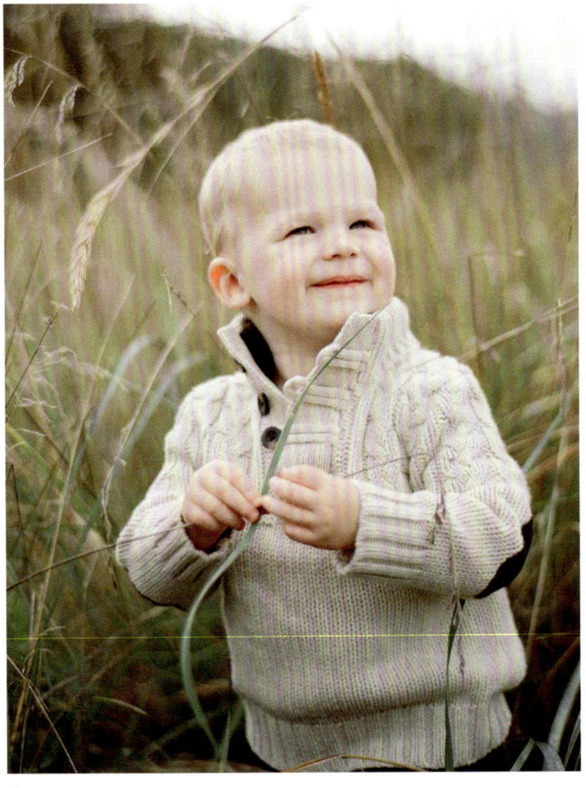

B

**FIGURE 2.23** Both images were captured in the same location and with the same lighting pattern (backlight). Figure 2.23A was captured in the full sun of a hot summer afternoon day. Figure 2.23B was captured on an overcast fall morning. Backlighting them both, even though the light I was working with was different in quality, direction, and intensity, is how I produced images consistent with my style, despite vastly different lighting conditions.

### Golden Hour

In the hour just after sunrise and just before sunset, the sun is low on the horizon and warmer in temperature, resulting in the golden glow that gives us the Golden Hour.

The light at Golden Hour is undeniably beautiful, making it a favorite time for scheduling photos for many photographers. Personally, I have found that scheduling sessions for the Golden Hour isn't always convenient. Most families (and family photographers for that matter) are not going to be ready for photos the first hour after sunrise, and catching the evening Golden Hour doesn't always work with schedules. I, for example, live and work in Seattle, Washington. At our latitude, the sun doesn't set until after 9:00pm in the summer, placing Golden Hour at a time of day that is just too late for most babies and toddlers to comfortably make it through a photo session.

Golden Hour can also fall around dinner time, which may present scheduling obstacles for you or the families you serve. If you do prefer to work in the Golden Hour, remember that the sun is low on the horizon at this time of day, creating intense light that can be challenging to work in. Paying attention to your lighting patterns and your metering is a must when working at this time of day!

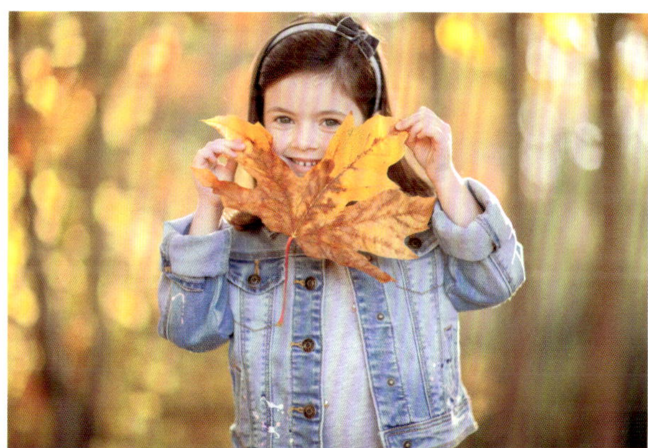

A

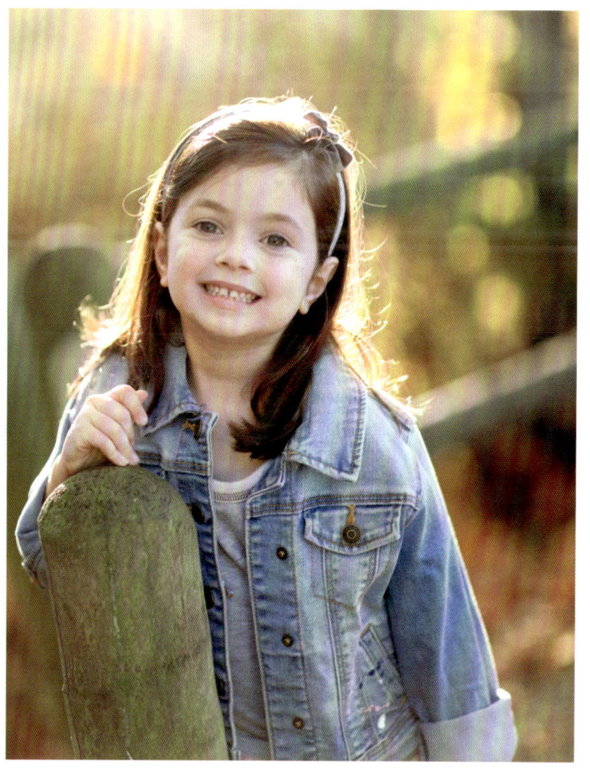

B

**FIGURE 2.24** Both of these images were captured at Golden Hour, just moments apart. In Figure 2.24A, I placed my subject in the shade to produce even, flat light on her face. In Figure 2.24B, my subject is backlit. I chose to place her in this position to create a beautiful glow around her.

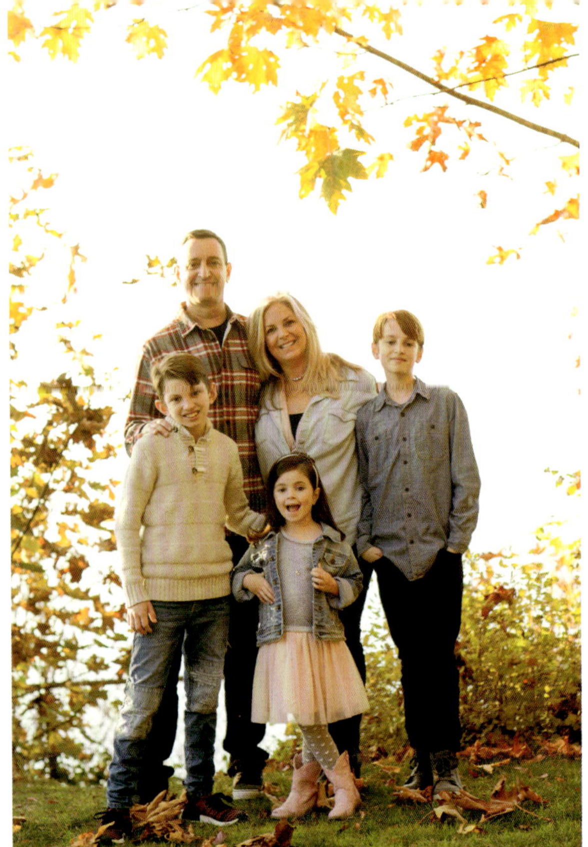

A

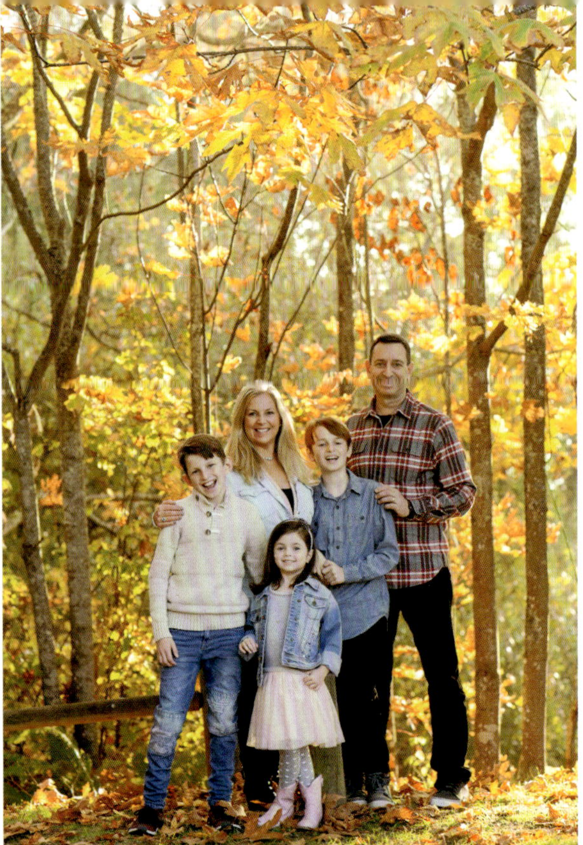

B

**FIGURE 2.25** These images show a family photographed in Golden Hour in the backlight position. Because we were working during Golden Hour, the sun was low on the horizon, producing very intense light. In Figure 2.25A, I placed the family in direct light, with a beautiful view behind them. But I did not want them in silhouette, so I metered for their faces, resulting in a completely blown-out background, losing the view we were trying to include. To solve the problem of the blown-out background, I moved the family in front of a darker backdrop—the trees in Figure 2.25B). We lost the view of the water but gained a view of the beautiful fall leaves and the "golden" light of Golden Hour. In this position, the family is in much better light for a portrait.

**FIGURES 2.25A** and **2.25B** were captured at the Golden Hour. The sun was low in the western sky at the time of our session. It was a very sunny day, not a cloud in the sky, so the light was low, bright, and intense. We were in a beautiful park with water and mountain views that the family wanted in their photos, but in order to keep everyone from being in silhouette I needed to meter for their faces. This resulted in a blown-out sky, effectively erasing the water and the mountains from the frame.

Luckily there was a patch of beautiful trees nearby. By placing the family among the trees in the backlight position, I was able to achieve proper exposure on their faces while also capturing the golden light of Golden Hour and the color of the fall foliage. In retrospect, a morning session may have been a better choice. We would have missed the Golden Hour, but the light would have been falling on the family in a way that would have allowed me to properly expose them and the beautiful view.

### Midday Light

As much as I love Golden Hour light, working at midday is much more convenient for me and my clients. I know a lot of photographers avoid working midday because the light is not ideal, but you can get beautiful images at this time of day by being intentional about your light quality and lighting patterns.

As I mentioned earlier, I prefer light that is soft in quality, and either flat light or backlight patterns when working outside. Placing my clients in the shade produces light that is soft in quality with a flat lighting pattern, even at midday. When I can't find shade, I backlight. Backlight is always flattering and always easy to find, regardless of the location or time of day.

## Natural Light Inside

While working outside has its merits, as someone who primarily photographs newborns, I do most of my sessions either in my studio or in client homes. When working with natural light in a client's home, windows are the primary light source, so knowing how to work with window light is very important.

Light changes throughout the day as the sun moves through the sky, which has a huge impact on window light. In the Northern Hemisphere, east-facing windows get direct light in the morning and shade in the afternoon, resulting in harder light in the morning and softer light in the evening. West-facing windows get the afternoon sun, resulting in shady, soft-light mornings and bright, hard-light evenings. South-facing windows get direct light all day, but the quality of the light they produce will change as the sun moves across the sky.

The quality of light from east, west, or south-facing windows also changes depending on the weather. Sunny days produce harder light than cloudy days. If you are working with a window with fluctuating exposure (east, west, or south-facing window), the quality of your light will change throughout the day and according to the weather.

The light produced from north-facing windows, however, is consistent. Because the sun arcs in the southern sky, north-facing windows never get direct light, which means you will have pretty much the same light throughout the day. North light is also not affected by the weather like other windows are. In addition to being consistent, north light is never direct, which means it is always soft in quality.

### "North Light" in the Southern Hemisphere

To achieve "north light" in the Southern Hemisphere, use south-facing windows.

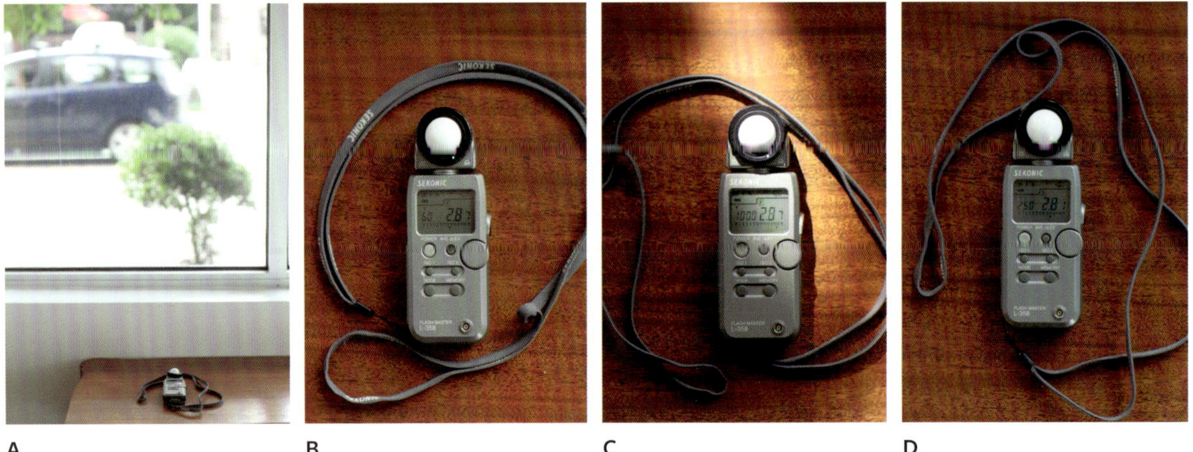

A B C D

**FIGURE 2.26** South light. To capture these images, I placed my meter on a table under a south-facing window (Figure 2.26A) and metered at 9:00 a.m., noon, and 5:00 p.m. Notice how the light moves and changes throughout the day. At 9:00 a.m. (Figure 2.26B), my reading was f/2.8, 1/60 sec., at ISO 400. At noon (Figure 2.26C), the reading changed to f/2.8, 1/1000 sec., at ISO 400. At 5:00 p.m. (Figure 2.26D), my reading was f/2.8, 1/250 sec., at ISO 400.

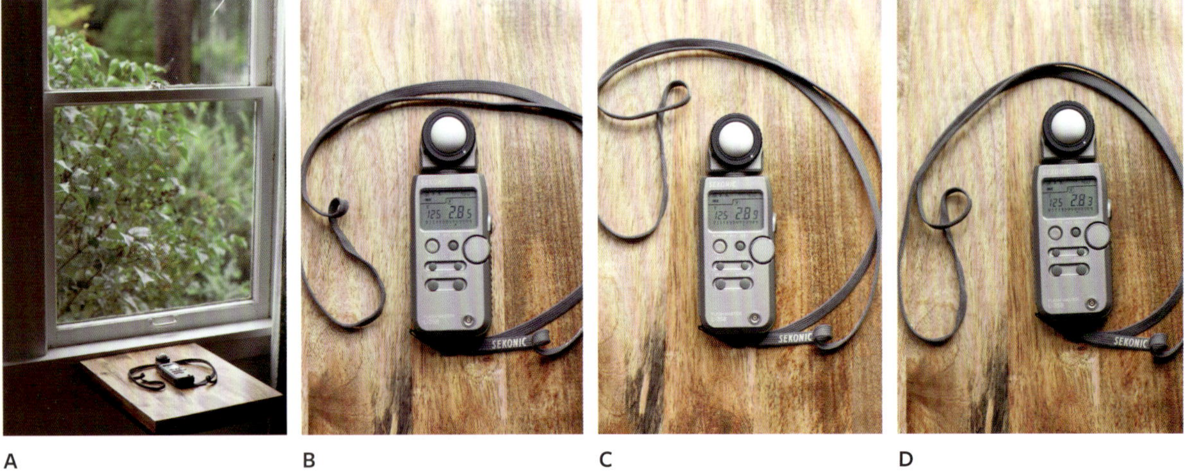


A B C D

**FIGURE 2.27** North light. I placed my meter on a table under a north-facing window (Figure 2.27A) and metered at 9:00 a.m. (Figure 2.27B), noon (Figure 2.27C), and 5:00 p.m. (Figure 2.27D). My readings were exactly the same all day long: f/2.8, 1/125 sec., at ISO 400.

North light is known for its consistency and softness. When used in portraiture, it results in glowing, luminous skin, and soft, subtle shadows, making it a favorite among many artists, myself included. But of course, not every home is going to have a perfect north-facing window to work with. And that is okay! You can create beautiful, natural-light images using any window, you just need to remember a few things.

First of all, what is your preferred light quality? East-facing windows will produce softer light in the afternoon than in the morning. West-facing windows

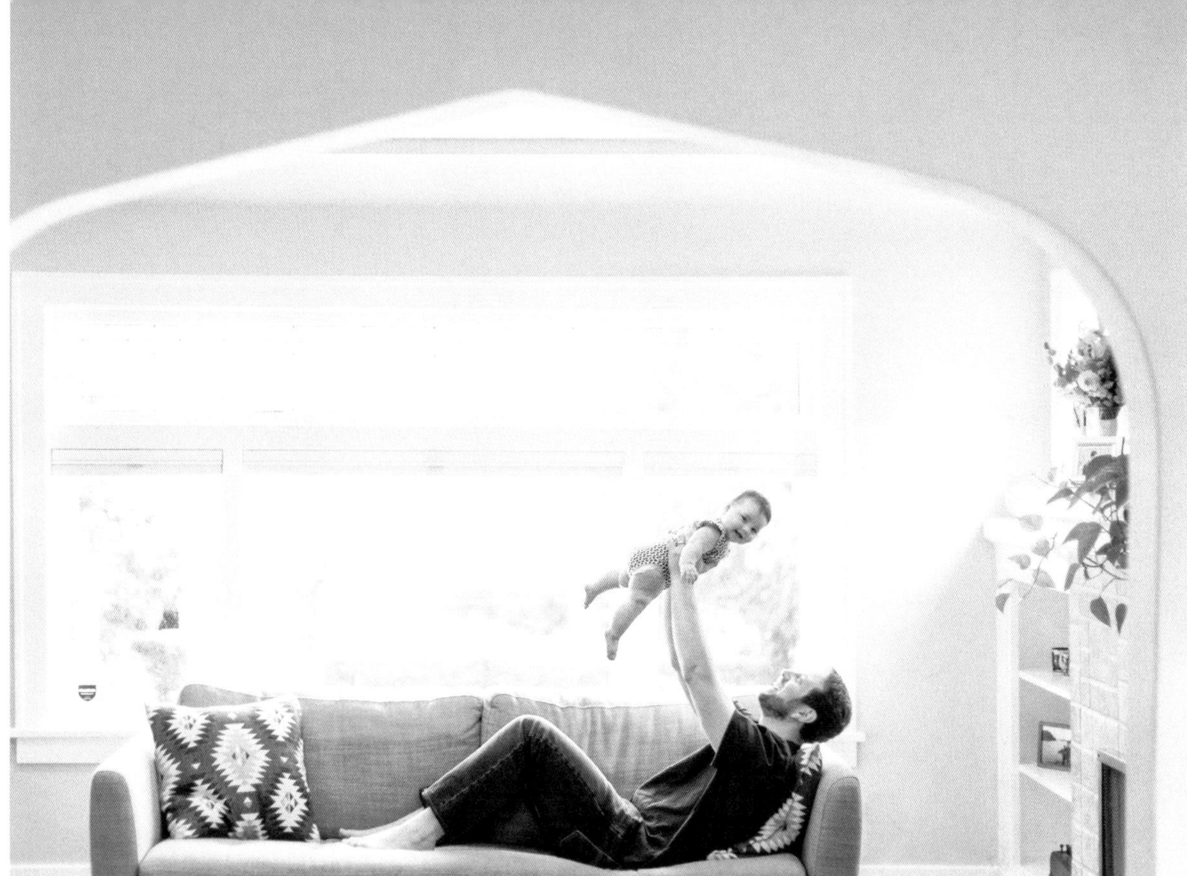

**FIGURE 2.28** East-facing window, midday

produce softer light in the morning than in the afternoon. North light will always be soft, and south light will fluctuate with the weather and the time of day.

Choosing windows to work with that produce your preferred light quality will help you create work you love and that is consistent with your style. I actually carry a little compass on my keychain to help me determine direction when on location. It's that important to me!

Remember that the size of your light source, level of diffusion, and proximity impact light quality as well. Going for soft light? Choose large windows, preferably with a level of diffusion, and position your subjects close. Want harder light? Look for smaller windows that have direct light and pull your subjects away from the windows when posing.

Next, what are your preferred lighting patterns? Move your clients around the window until you create your favorite pattern. My go-to lighting patterns when working inside are backlight, flat light and loop light. When working with windows, I'm always trying to create soft light and one of my go-to patterns. For example, **FIGURE 2.28** was captured at a midday session in a client's home. They had a large window in the living room that faced east. Because this was a midday session, the light coming in from that east-facing window was very bright, but not direct. The size of the window and my client's proximity to it resulted in light that was soft in quality. I chose to backlight my subjects to create this beautiful, playful image. I love the soft glow we got from the window light.

Remember to pay attention to your shadows and your catchlights when working with window light! The images in **FIGURE 2.29** were captured in a room with large north-facing windows. In **FIGURE 2.29A**, the baby was placed with her feet pointing toward the light source, creating a ghoul light pattern. Notice the catchlights in the bottom half of her eyes and the shadows that fall up her face. To fix this unflattering lighting pattern, I turned her around so that her head was pointing toward the light, creating a butterfly light pattern instead.

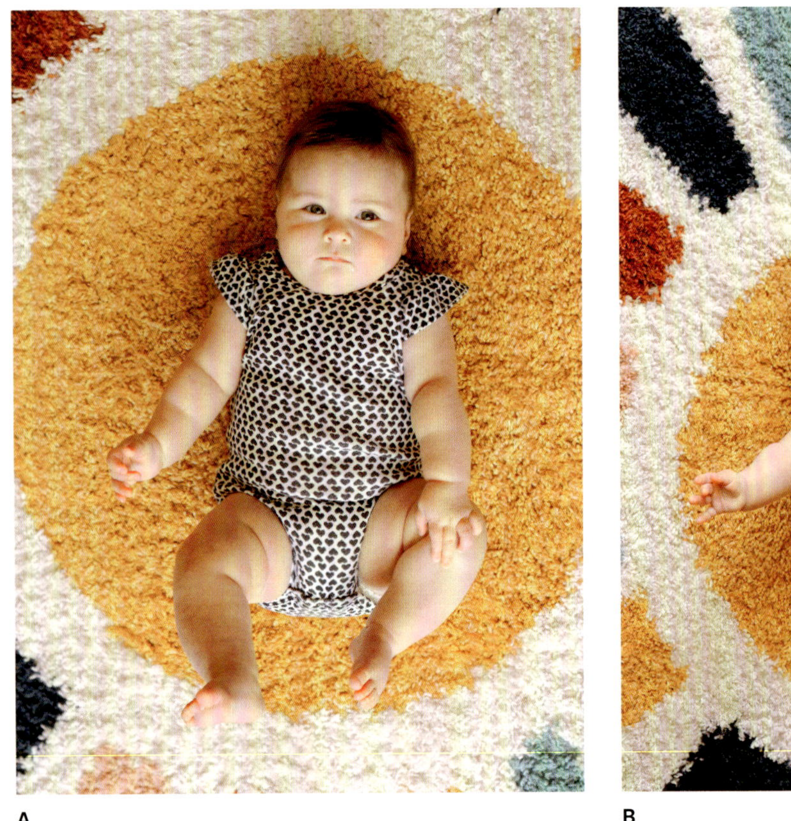

A

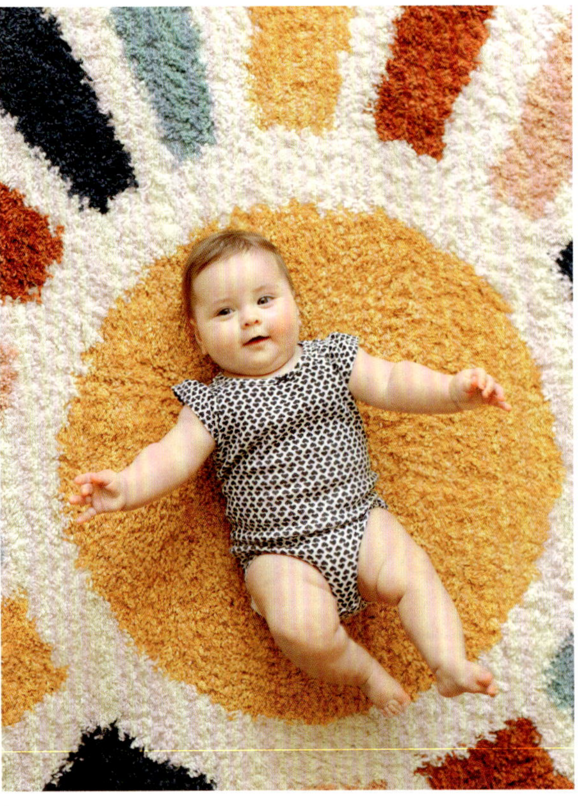

B

**FIGURE 2.29** Both images were captured using the soft light from a large north facing window. But in Figure 2.29A the baby was placed lying down with her feet pointing toward the window, resulting in a ghoul light pattern. In Figure 2.29B she is placed with her head pointing toward the window, creating a more flattening butterfly light pattern.

## Wrapping It All Up

Understanding how to work with natural light is one of the most important skills a photographer can have. It really is the foundation that everything else is built upon. Once you know how to read light, meter it properly, and use it with intention—indoors and out—you'll find yourself creating photos in your chosen style more consistently.

As you practice what you've learned in this chapter, take the time to notice what you're drawn to. Pay attention to the kind of light you prefer. In the next chapter, we'll take everything you've learned here and apply it to artificial light, so you can create your ideal light, anytime and anywhere, day or night!

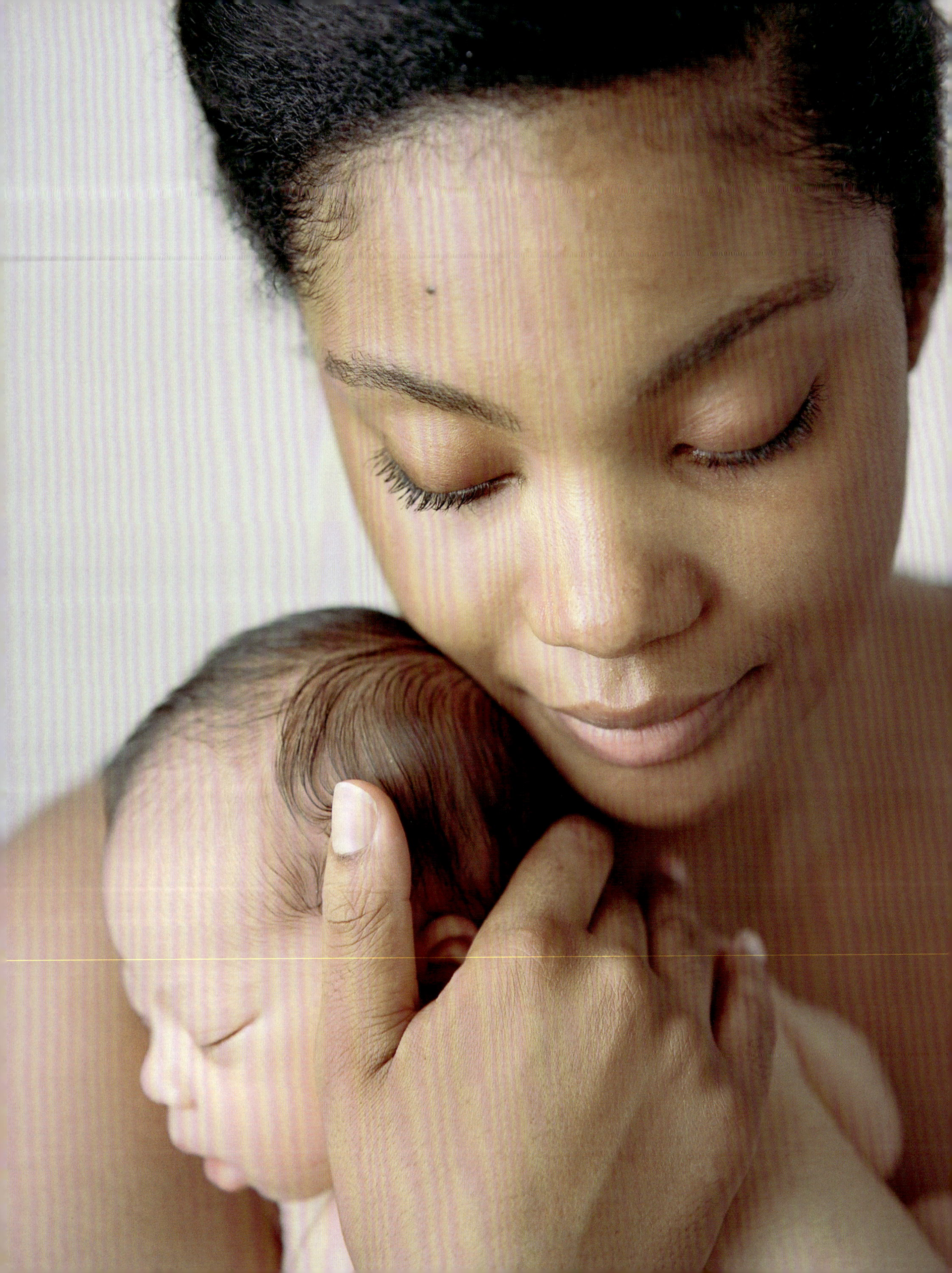

CHAPTER

# 3

# Working with Artificial Light

While natural light is beautiful, it's not always perfect. Sometimes it rains. Some days are dark. Some situations are just less than ideal. What do you do then? Make your own "natural light"!

I know a lot of family photographers stay away from using artificial light because it seems difficult and technical. They worry that setting up lights will mess with their "flow" and they don't want to navigate around a ton of equipment while also chasing toddlers and keeping babies happy. Luckily, you don't have to worry about any of that. The techniques I'm going to share require minimal gear and have a very small footprint. If you've always been intimidated by artificial light, don't worry. My approach is simple! If you know how to work with natural light (and you do!), then you know most of what you need to know to work with artificial light. Light is light, after all!

## Equipment

You do not need a ton of gear to create beautiful, natural-looking light with strobes and flash. Everything I do is done with one light, one light modifier, one stand, a trigger, and a light meter. Sometimes I don't even use all of that (as you will see in Chapter 4). So let me walk you through what you need, why you need it, and what to look for when purchasing equipment.

### Cameras

The first piece of equipment you need is a camera (obviously). All cameras are compatible with modern lighting equipment, including vintage film cameras. If you are working with a mirrorless camera, however, some settings, like exposure compensation, will need to be turned off when working with strobes and flash. Check your camera's manual for how to adjust this setting.

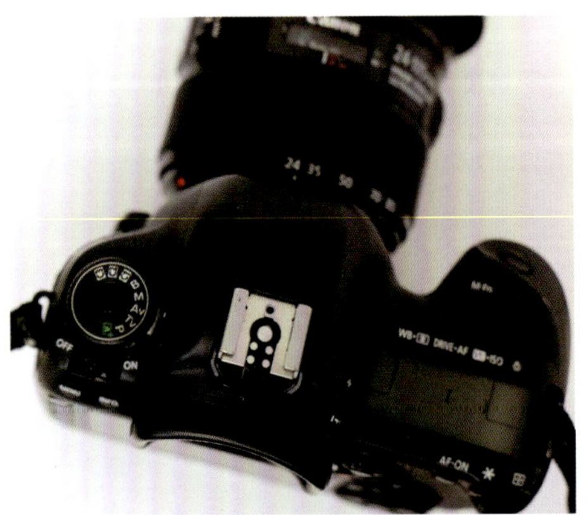

**FIGURE 3.1** Hot-shoe mount on a Canon 5D Mark IV

Regardless of the type of camera you are working with, understanding how your camera is designed to communicate with lighting equipment is a must. Different cameras do this in different ways.

### Hot Shoes

Most modern cameras come equipped with a hot-shoe mount (**FIGURE 3.1**). A *hot-shoe mount* is a metal bracket on the camera designed to attach to a flash or flash accessory, like a trigger. Hot-shoe mounts are electronically connected to the camera and designed to fire your flash or trigger whenever your shutter is released.

## Cold Shoes

A cold-shoe mount is a metal bracket designed to hold a flash or trigger. They look like hot-shoe mounts, but cold shoes are not connected electronically to the camera and will not fire a flash or trigger when you release the shutter. In order to fire a flash or trigger, you will need to connect it to the camera's sync port using a sync cord.

## Sync Cords

A sync cord is used to connect a flash or trigger to the sync port on your camera, enabling it to fire when the shutter is released. Sync cords come in a variety of shapes and sizes. Double check with your camera's manual to make sure you are getting the right chord for your camera.

## Sync Ports

A sync port is the spot on your camera where you attach your sync chord (**FIGURE 3.2**). Once plugged in, the cord will connect your camera to your strobe, flash, or flash accessory, triggering it every time your shutter is fired. Most sync ports are located on the camera, but they can also be located on the lens. Refer to your camera's manual to find the sync port on your camera.

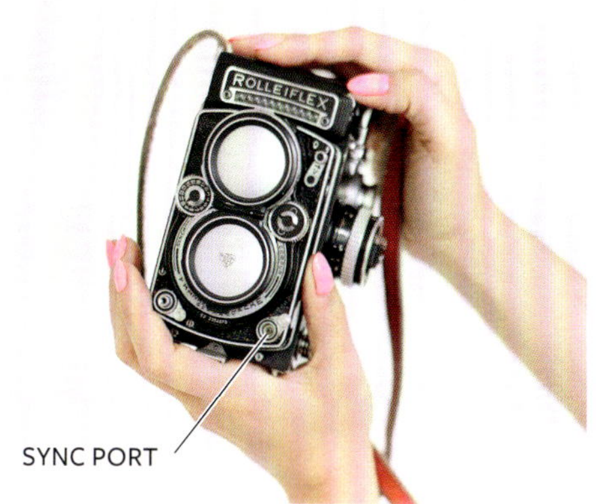


**FIGURE 3.2** Sync port on a Rollieflex 2.8 film camera

## Triggers and Receivers

Triggers and receivers enable your camera to communicate with your lights. The trigger connects to your camera via the hot shoe or by sync cord. It will send a signal to the receiver, which is located on or in your strobe or flash, every time you hit your shutter. Both a trigger and a receiver are required in order for your camera to communicate with your strobe or flash.

Modern systems, like the Westcott lights I use, have receivers built into their strobe and flash units. Most modern lighting systems have brand-specific triggers designed to work with their lights. Make sure your trigger is designed to work with your particular camera model. Luckily, many modern lighting companies, Westcott included, make universal triggers that are designed to work with all of the major camera brands (**FIGURE 3.3**).

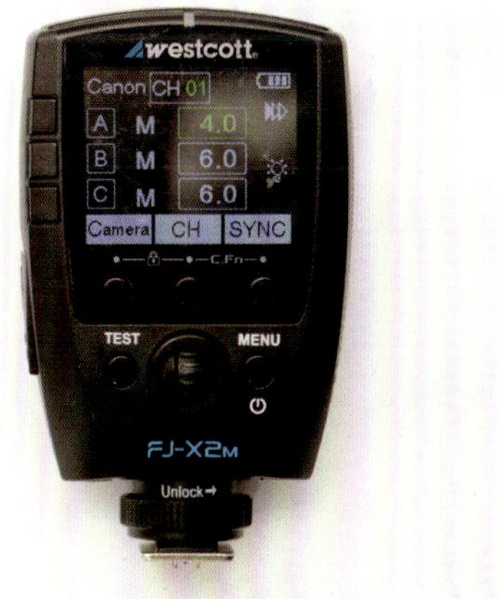


**FIGURE 3.3** The FJ-X2m Universal Trigger by Westcott. This trigger is set to work with my Canon cameras, but it can be formatted to work with all the major camera brands.

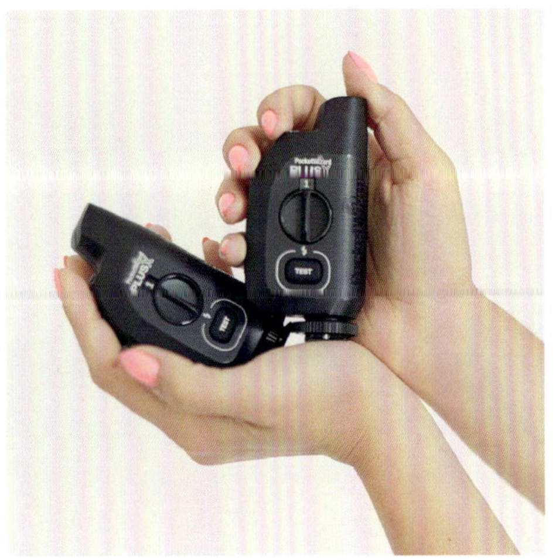

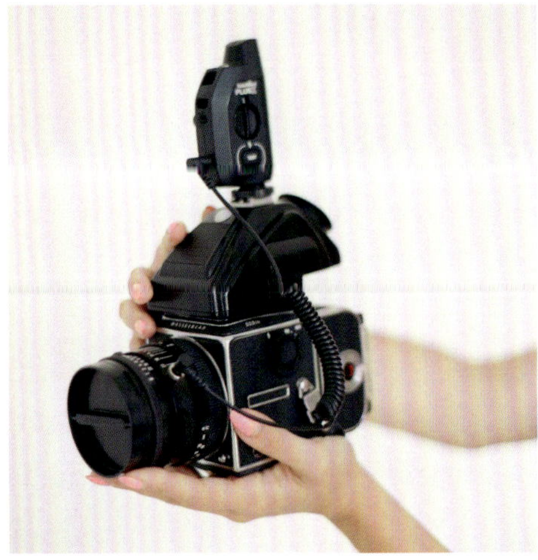

**FIGURE 3.4** PocketWizards. When using universal triggers, you need one to attach to your strobe (to act as a receiver), and one to put on your camera. PocketWizards work great on vintage film cameras.

Universal triggers and receivers, like PocketWizards, are designed to work with any camera or lighting brand. These triggers are great for connecting vintage cameras to modern lights. I keep a couple of sets of PocketWizards at my studio for this purpose. I use a sync cord to connect the PocketWizard receiver to my Westcott Light, and connect the PocketWizard trigger to my vintage camera, either on the hot-shoe mount or by sync cord. This allows me to use my film cameras with my modern lighting equipment (**FIGURE 3.4**).

Once your trigger is on your camera and your receiver is on your light, make sure they are set to the same channel and group to enable them to communicate with one another (**FIGURE 3.5**).

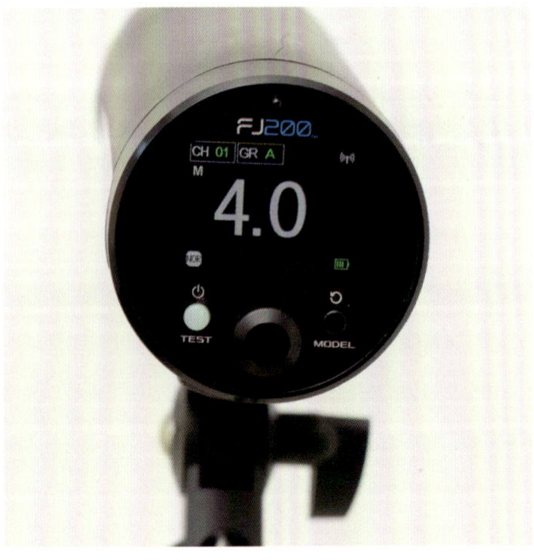


A

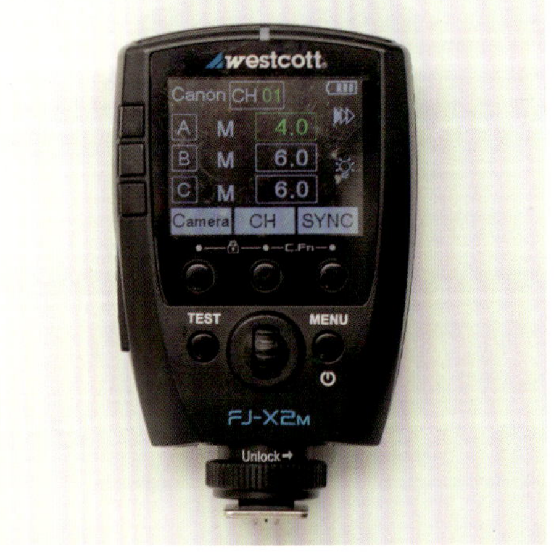


B

**FIGURE 3.5** The Westcott FJ200 strobe and Westcott FJ-X2m trigger are designed to work together, but in order to communicate, they must be set to the same channel and the same group. In Figure 3.5A, you can see that the strobe is set to Channel 1, Group A. In Figure 3.5B, you can see that the trigger is also set to Channel 1, Group A.

## Light Stands

When it comes to choosing a light stand, make sure the stand is strong enough to hold your light and your modifier. Also, think about how you'll be using your stand before making a purchase. Do you travel with your equipment? If so, look for a stand that folds up easily and packs up small. Do you work in a dedicated space, like a studio? If so, you may want to invest in something heavy and durable.

I have a small, portable light stand in my travel kit (Ulanzi TT43 Extendable Photography Light Stand), but in my studio I prefer heavier stands that I place on casters, like the Avenger Roller Stand, A5029 (**FIGURE 3.6**). The casters make moving my stands around the studio easy.

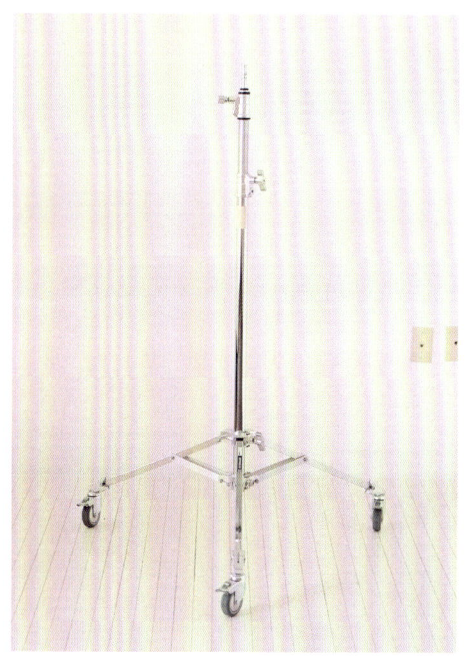

**FIGURE 3.6** The Avenger Roller Stand, A5029

## Handheld Light Meters

If you are a digital photographer, having a handheld light meter is optional. But trust me when I say, this little piece of equipment will save you so much time! And when you work with little kids, time is of the essence!

I'll go into detail on how to use your light meter when working with strobes and flash later in the chapter, but for now know that in order to use your meter with artificial light, you'll need an incident meter with the ability to read both natural light and flash. Whether you are buying online or in-store, this information will be listed in the description of the meter.

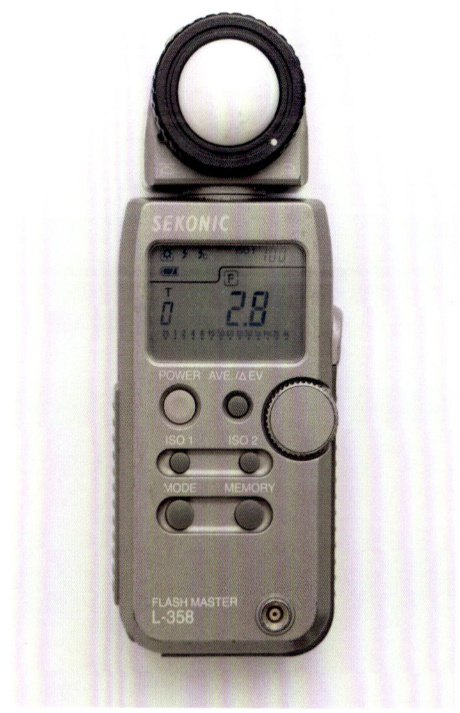


**FIGURE 3.7** Sekonic L-358 Light Meter. The meter pictured is set to read natural light, as is indicated by the highlighted sunshine icon.

## Modifiers

Modifiers are what you mount to your lighting unit to help you control and shape the light. When it comes to light modifiers, there are a lot to choose from! How do you know which one is the right one for you?

### Size

The size of your light source impacts the quality of your light. Relatively large light sources produce softer light than relatively small light sources. This is important to remember when choosing a modifier. A large modifier will create softer light than a small one will, just like a large window will produce softer light than a small window. If creating soft light is your goal, choose the largest modifier your space can hold!

### Color

Light modifiers come in different color options, as well. Some are black on the outside with white, silver, or gold on the inside. Some are all white. All-white modifiers and modifiers with white on the inside will produce soft, neutral light. Modifiers with silver on the inside produce a shiny, specular light with cool tones. Modifiers with gold on the inside produce a shiny, specular light with warm tones.

There is no right or wrong when it comes to choosing the color of your modifier. It's really just a matter of taste.

### Diffusion

Adding or removing diffusion is another way to control the quality of light you're working with. The more diffusion you add, the softer your light will be. Again, this is important to know when shopping for modifiers. Some modifiers come with diffusion panels built in (**FIGURE 3.8**), as well as an outer diffusion panel, and some do not.

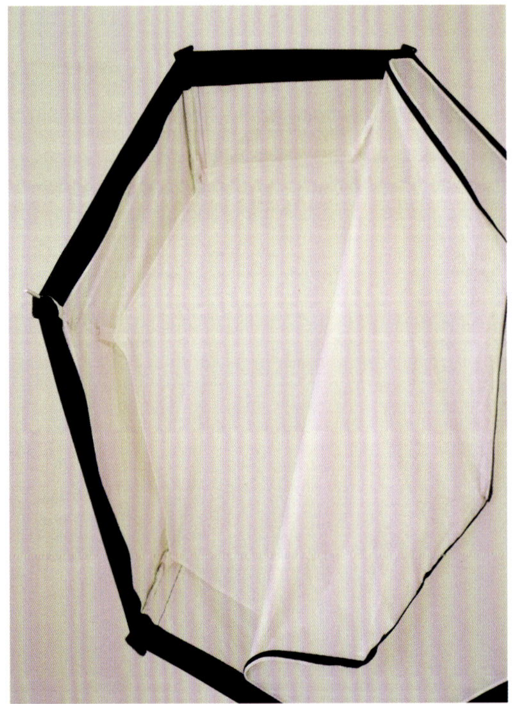

**FIGURE 3.8** This Photoflex OctoDome is an example of a modifier with an inner diffusion panel as well as an outer diffusion panel.

Other modifiers, like umbrellas, typically do not come with diffusion panels attached, but you can purchase diffusion panels to add separately. Adding a diffusion panel to an umbrella will help soften your light.

### Shoot-Through Vs. Reflective

How your light is positioned within the modifier will also contribute to how the light is diffused. Some modifiers are designed to "shoot through." With shoot-through modifiers, the strobe or flash faces forward and shoots through the diffusion panel or panels (**FIGURE 3.9**).

Other modifiers are designed to be reflective. With reflective modifiers, the strobe or flash faces toward the back of the modifier. When fired, the light hits the back of the modifier and bounces back through to the front (**FIGURE 3.10**).

With a reflective modifier, the bounce of light adds a level of diffusion. Adding an external diffusion panel to a reflective modifier will add a second layer of diffusion, further softening the light.

I use both shoot-through and reflective modifiers in my work, but I will often use my shoot-through umbrella as a bounce to add softness to my light.

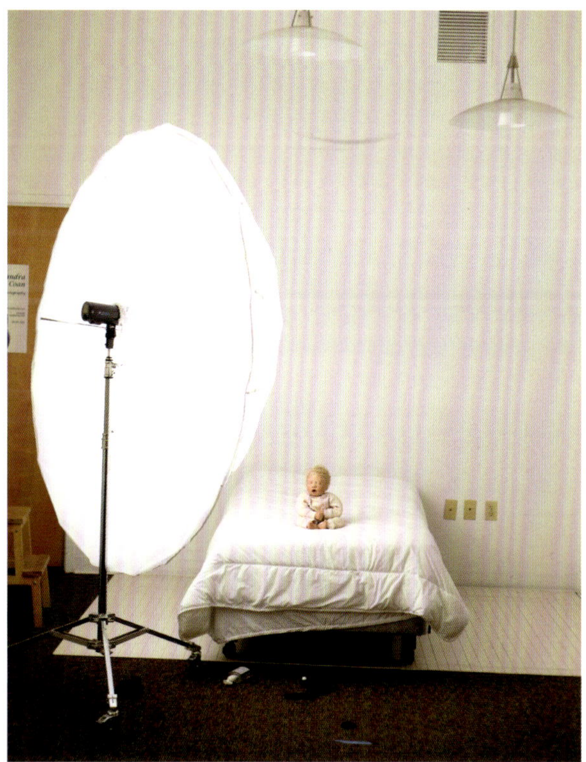

**FIGURE 3.9** The Westcott 7-foot Shoot-Through Umbrella

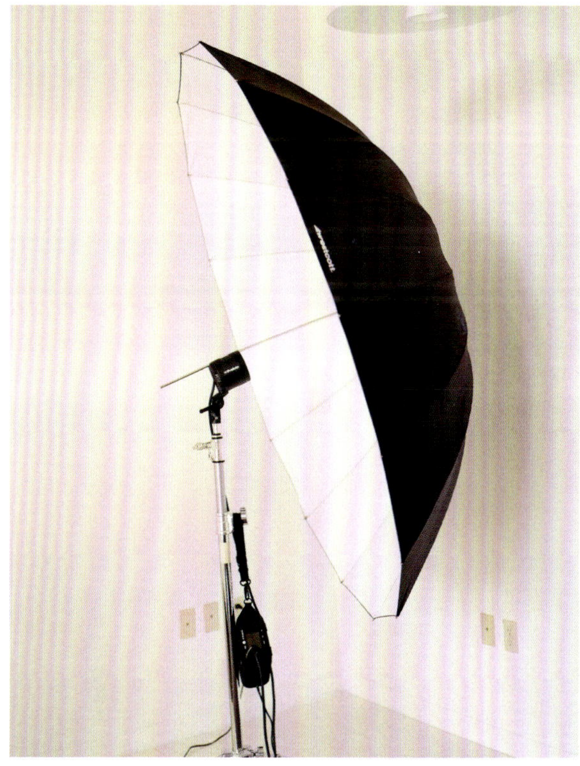

**FIGURE 3.10** The Westcott 7-foot Umbrella, a reflective style modifier. Notice how the light is facing the umbrella.

## "You're Using Your Light Modifier Wrong"

I commonly use my shoot-through umbrellas in the bounce position. As a result, I get a lot of people telling me that I'm using my modifier wrong. It's not wrong, but it is different.

When using a shoot-through in the traditional way, the light is positioned to shoot through the umbrella. Shooting through the umbrella creates one layer of diffusion and results in beautiful, soft light. When in the bounce position, the bounce results in one level of diffusion. I then add a diffusion panel on the front, creating a second level of diffusion. Two levels of diffusion add softness to my light, which I love. But, because I'm using a translucent umbrella to do this, light that hits the back of the modifier also escapes, bouncing around the space I'm working in. This results in an even spread of light on my backdrop and a bright, natural-light look.

This is my go-to set up for most of my sessions, but it doesn't work for every look. Using a shoot-through umbrella in the bounce position with an added diffusion panel (what I like to call The Sandra Coan Method), results in light that fills up the room, very little shadow detail on my subject.

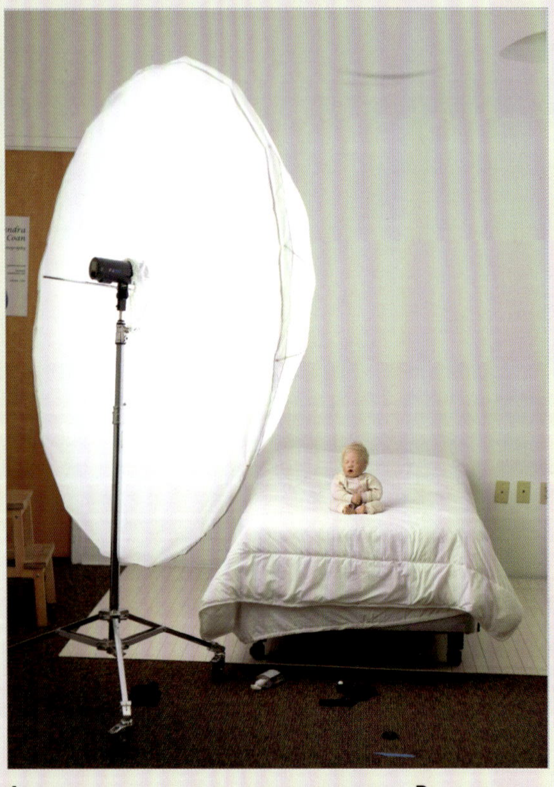

A

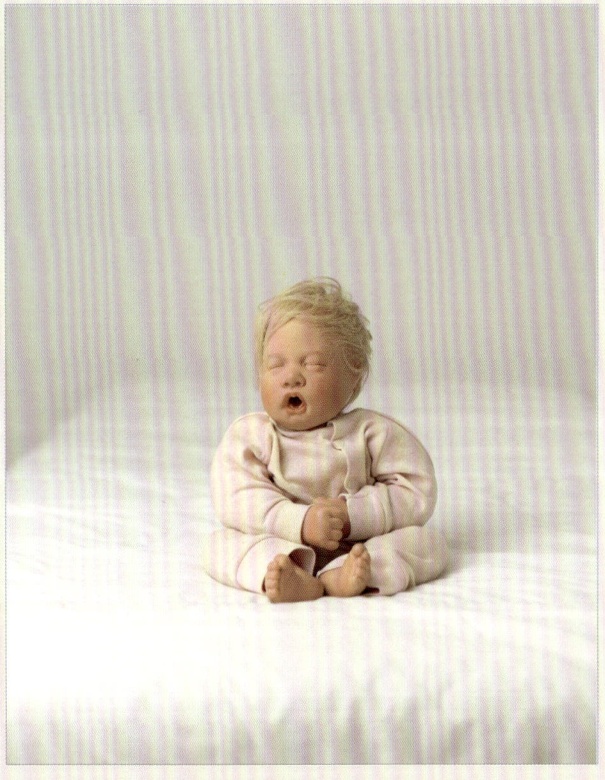

B

**FIGURE 3.11** Figure 3.11A shows a Westcott 7-foot Shoot-Through Umbrella set up in the traditional shoot-through position. Notice the bright patch of light on the bed, soft light on the posing doll, and the subtle shadow detail (Figure 3.11B).

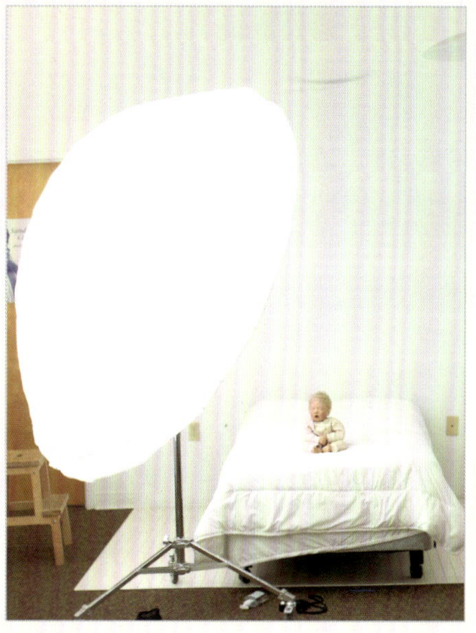

A

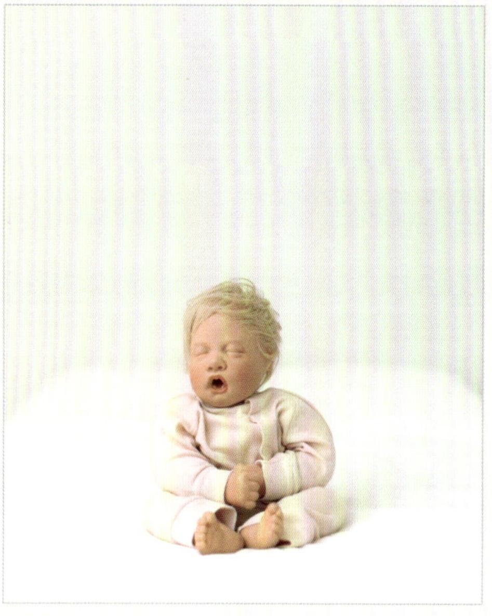

B

**FIGURE 3.12** Figure 3.12A shows the same white umbrella set up in the bounce position with an added diffusion panel on the front. Notice the bright, even light in the room, on the bed, and across the wall. The light is soft on the subject, with much less pronounced shadows than what we see when using the umbrella in the shoot- through position (Figure 3.12B). This is my go-to lighting setup, which I call The Sandra Coan Method.

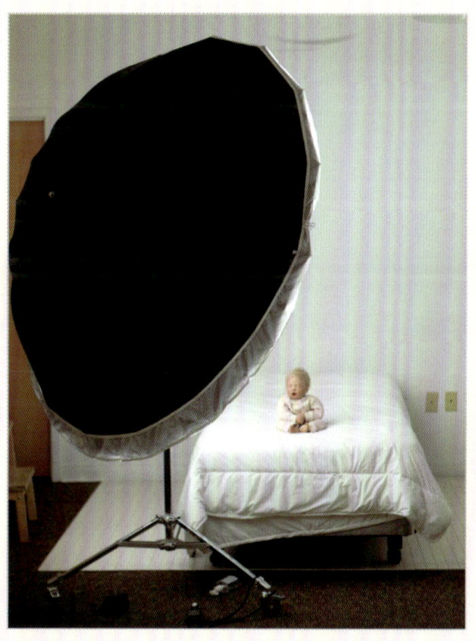

A

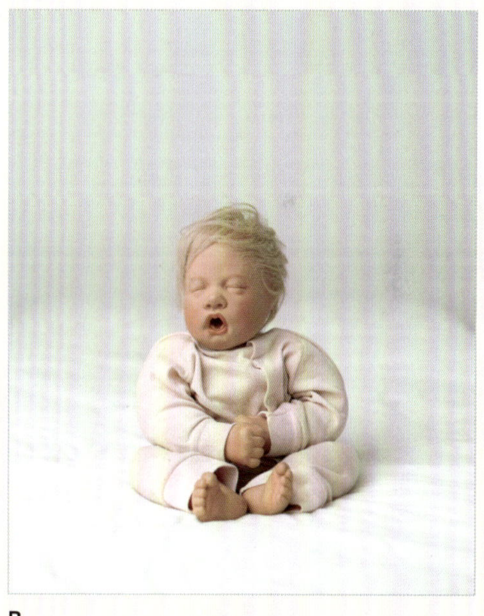

B

**FIGURE 3.13** Black umbrella in the bounce position (Figure 3.13A). This setup produces beautiful soft light due to the size and proximity of the umbrella, but because of the black backing, the light is controlled and focused, resulting in deeper shadows on the subject and less light spill on the backdrop (Figure 3.13B).

*continues on next page*

When I want more control and deeper shadows, I use a black umbrella with a white interior lining and an added diffusion panel on the front. With this setup, the black backing blocks the light from escaping, and bounces it all back onto the subject, resulting in soft, directional and more-focused light than I get when using a shoot through in the bounce position.

When I want deeper shadows and less light spill on my backdrop, I use an umbrella with a black backing. But when I want soft, even light that fills up a room, I use The Sandra Coan Method.

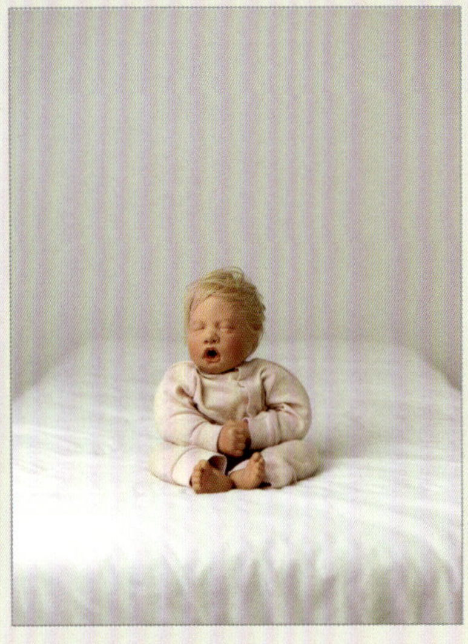

**A:** SHOOT THROUGH

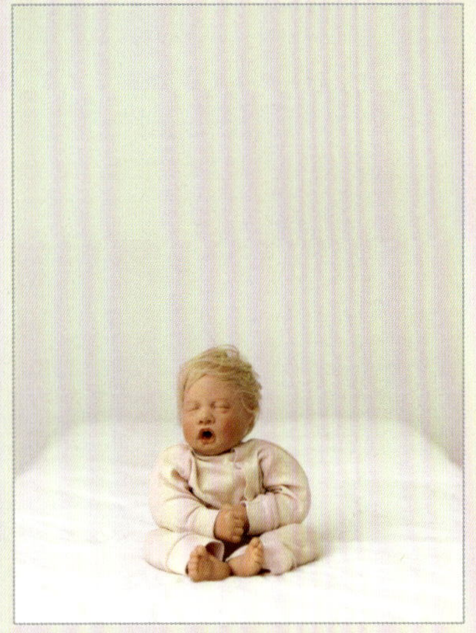

**B:** SANDRA COAN METHOD

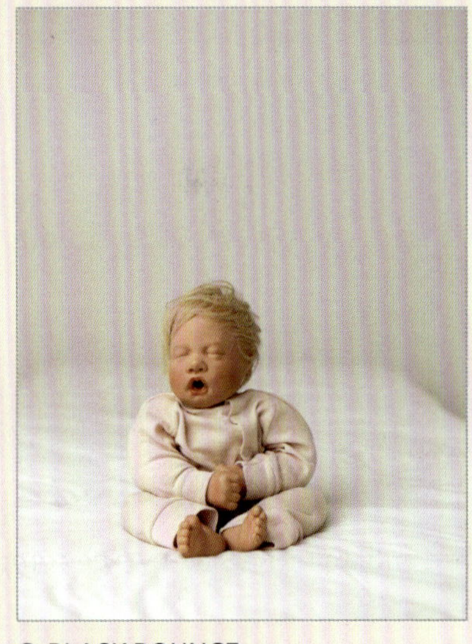

**C:** BLACK BOUNCE

**FIGURE 3.14** This side-by-side comparison highlights the visual impact of different umbrella lighting setups. Each image was created using a 7-foot umbrella fitted with a one-stop diffusion panel, positioned 3 feet from the subject. Figure 3.14A shows the traditional shoot-through umbrella, where light passes directly through the umbrella onto the subject. Figure 3.14B demonstrates The Sandra Coan Method, where the shoot-through umbrella is used in the bounce position. This creates a softer, more even wrap of light with minimal shadows. Figure 3.14C features a black bounce umbrella, which directs all the light forward and produces deeper shadows and more contrast.

## Does The Sandra Coan Method Only Work in My Studio?

Not at all—it can work anywhere! **FIGURES 3.15A** and **3.15B** were both captured in the same room, just moments apart, using a Westcott FJ200 strobe and a 45-inch umbrella with a diffusion panel in a loop light position. **FIGURE 3.15A** was created using The Sandra Coan Method—a 45-inch white umbrella in the bounce position. **FIGURE 3.15B** was captured with a 45-inch black umbrella and an added diffusion panel. Both setups used the same gear and location, but the lighting results are noticeably different. The Sandra Coan Method produces softer shadows, more balanced light across the subject and environment, and better tonal detail on surfaces like the bed and wall. This side-by-side comparison proves that this method can deliver beautiful, studio-quality results—even in a client's home.

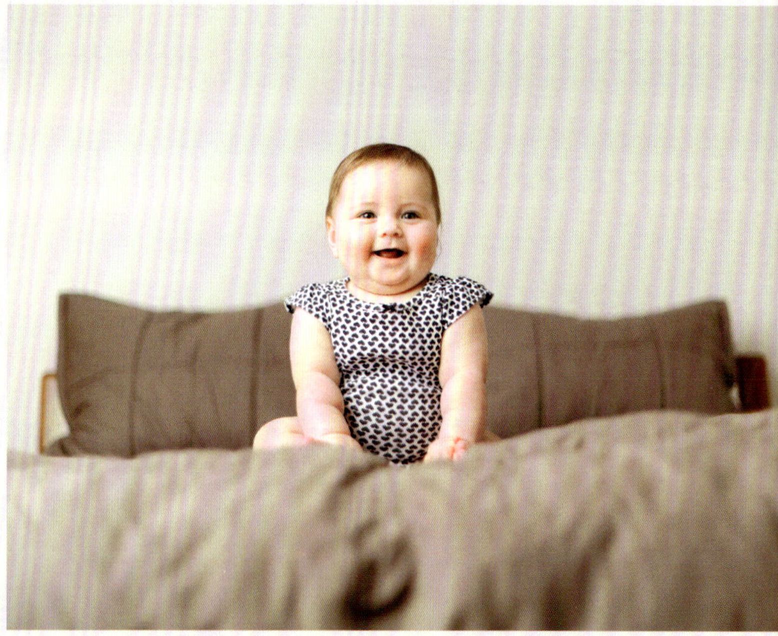

A

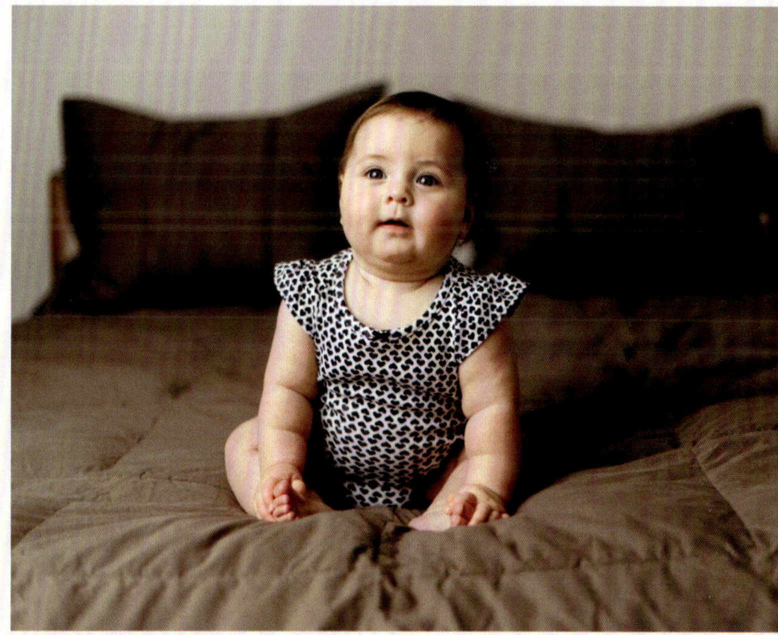

B

**FIGURE 3.15** Both images were captured in the same room, moments apart, using the Westcott FJ200 strobe and a 45-inch umbrella and diffusion panel in the loop light position.

### Shape

The shape of your light modifier is another thing to consider when purchasing equipment, as it will also impact the quality of your light and its spread.

Round and Octagon-shaped modifiers produce a wide spread of light while square and rectangle-shaped modifiers produce more focused light. These differences become less noticeable when using large modifiers. The shape of your modifier will also have an effect on the shape of your catchlights. Modifiers with curved edges, like umbrellas, produce round catchlights (**FIGURE 3.16A**); modifiers with straight edges, like softboxes, produce straight catchlights (**FIGURE 3.16B**).

This is important to note depending on the look you want to create. Small, round catchlights look like the catchlight we get outside from the sun, and large round catchlights follow the natural curve of the eye. Straight catchlights, large and small, look like the catchlights we get when working with windows.

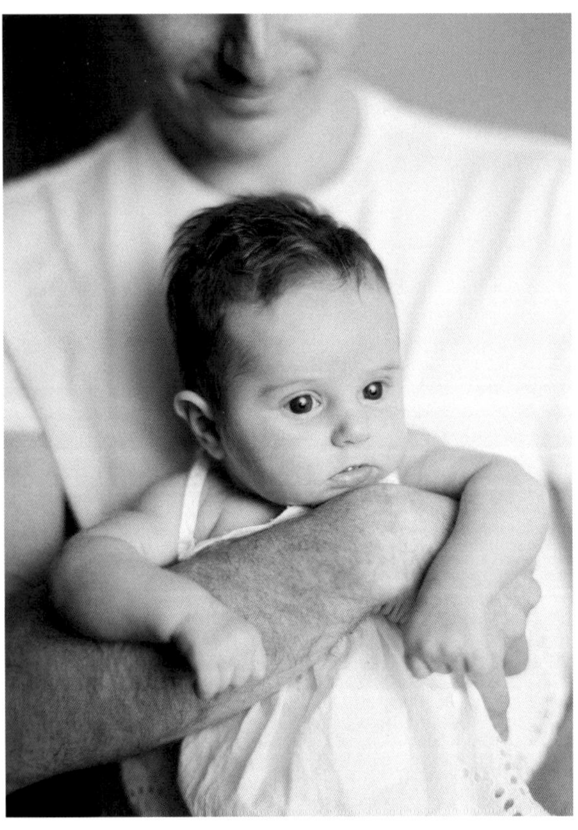

A

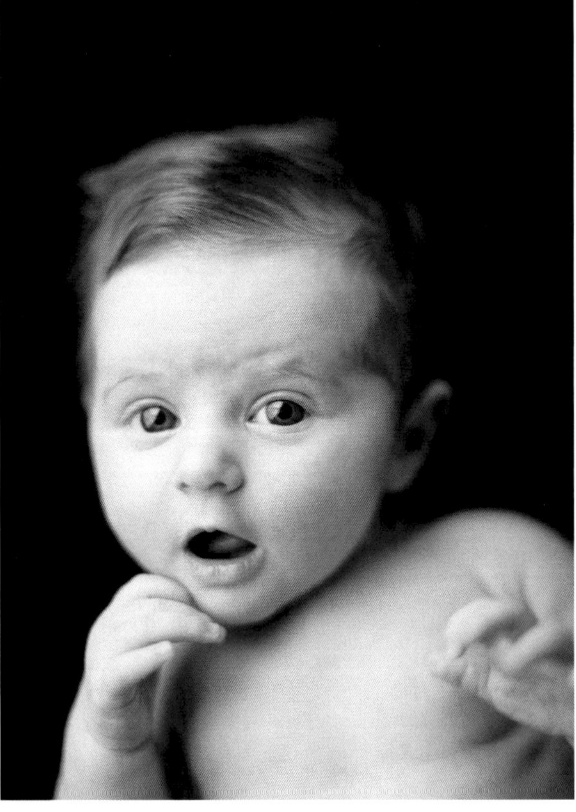

B

**FIGURE 3.16** Figure 3.16A was captured using a 24-inch Westcott shoot-through umbrella. Notice how the round catchlight mirrors the shape of the round umbrella. Figure 3.16B was captured using the 50 x 50 Westcott Apollo softbox. Notice how the catchlights take on the square shape of the softbox.

When I first started using strobes, my favorite softbox was the Westcott Apollo 50 x 50. Its large shape and level of diffusion created a beautiful, soft light, and its rectangular shape produced the window-like catchlights I wanted. Now I use large umbrellas, which produce a large catchlight that wraps around the eye, creating a similar look to the catchlights I get from a large window.

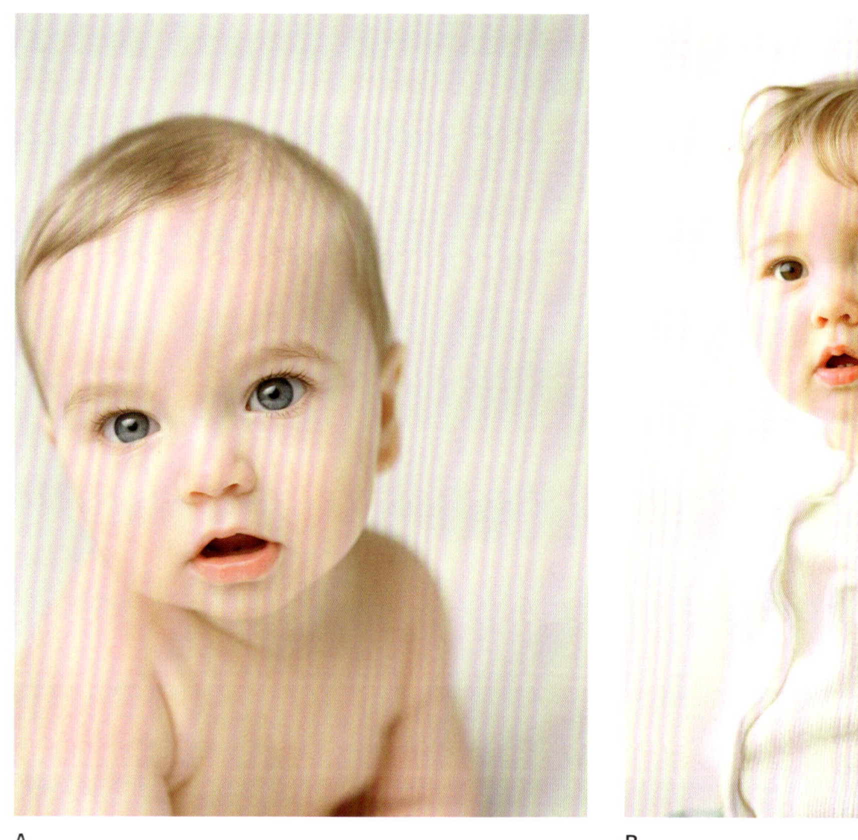

A

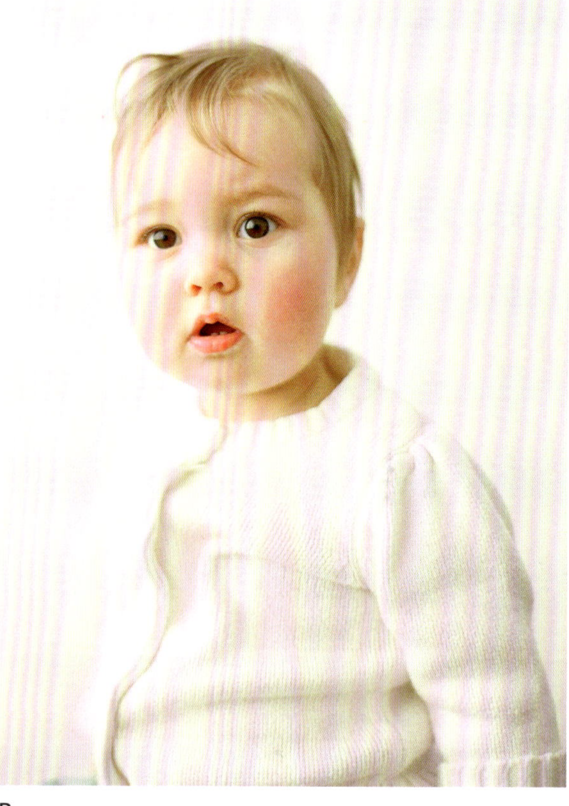

B

**FIGURE 3.17** Figure 3.17A was captured using the Westcott 7-foot Umbrella with a diffusion panel. Figure 3.17B was captured using light from a large window. Notice the similarities in the catchlights.

## Give It a Try!

Remember, when it comes to light and lighting, there is no right or wrong. There is only what you like and what works for you. So, I encourage you to experiment. Play. Think about your preferences and choose equipment that helps you achieve your desired light consistently.

## Strobes, Flash, and Continuous Lights

The last piece of equipment you'll need before you can start creating beautiful, natural-looking light is the light itself!

When it comes to lights, you have three categories to choose from: strobes, flashes, and continuous lights. You can create beautiful images with any of these light sources, but they each have a unique set of pros and cons.

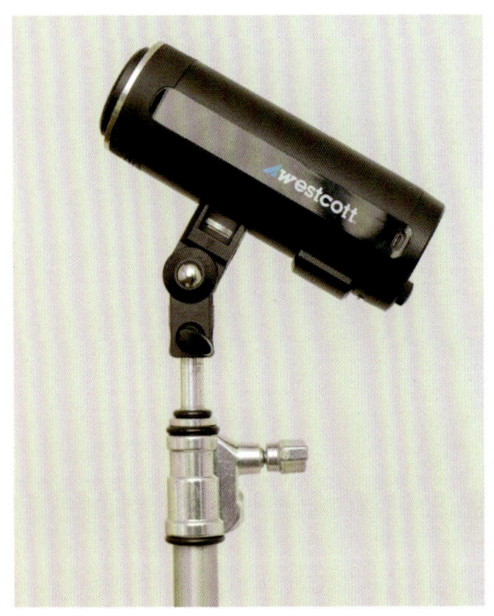


**FIGURE 3.18** The Westcott FJ200 strobe, my preferred strobe unit

### Strobe or Flash?

Strobes and flashes are very similar pieces of equipment in that they both fire a quick pulse of daylight-balanced light when triggered. The differences between the two are pretty subtle, but important, depending on your work and style.

### Strobes

Strobes are more powerful than flashes. They tend to be bigger (although they are getting smaller and lighter all the time!), have higher wattage, and have a broader range, meaning they can give off more light on the high end and less light on the low end than a flash can. Strobes also have two sets of lights in each unit: a model light and a strobe light.

The model light is one that can be left on at all times, making it easy to see your light and how it's falling on your subject. Model lights allow you to check your catchlights and shadow patterns before taking an image, and for me, provide some piece of mind. I like being able to see the light I'm working with! It's important to note however, that the model light is just there to assist. It is not the light that is used when taking the photo. The light that actually fires is the strobe light, which is the light that is used when taking the image.

Strobes can only be used off camera, and require the use of a light stand and a trigger. Strobes will also freeze movement in a photo the way a high shutter speed does when working with natural light.

### Flash

Flash units tend to be smaller than most strobes and can be attached to your camera's hot shoe, or used off camera and fired with a trigger.

Older flash units required batteries, and were known to have slow recycle time, requiring long pauses between shots. This is less of a problem with newer models. I have a Westcott FJ80 flash that is just as fast as my Westcott FJ200 strobe! And that is important when working with little kids!

A lot of older flashes do not have model lights, but most newer models do.

I always keep a flash in my to-go kit. They are super convenient to use when working in small spaces. Most come with a "foot" to place them on (**FIGURE 3.19**), so you can use them without a light stand!

If you plan on using an older flash off camera, you will need to attach a receiver to the camera using a sync cord (**FIGURE 3.20**). Most newer models have receivers built in.

Like strobes, the light from your flash will freeze motion.

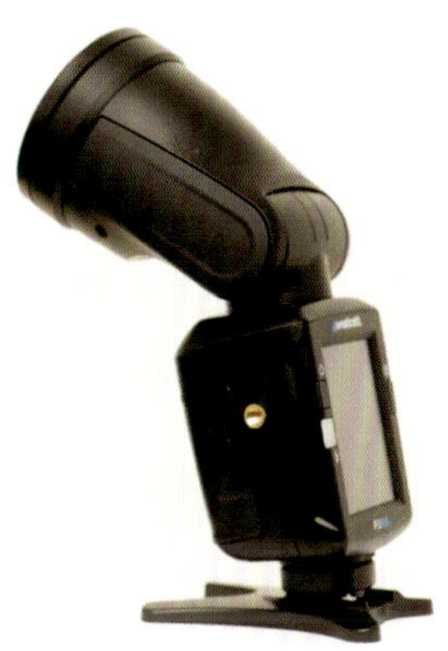

**FIGURE 3.19** The Westcott FJ80 flash standing on its flash "foot."

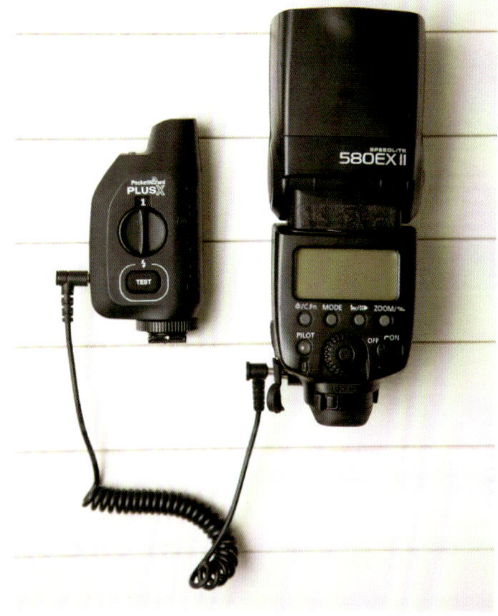


**FIGURE 3.20** The Canon 580EX II flash connected to a PocketWizard PlusX trigger by a sync cord.

## TTL or Manual?

Most strobes and flashes come with the option of a TTL setting. TTL stands for "through the lens" and functions like the "auto mode" setting on your camera. When in TTL, your strobe or flash will use reflective metering based on your camera's internal meter and adjust its own power setting. There are undeniable benefits to working in TTL mode. It's fast and convenient, especially for photographers who are new to artificial light. But, it's not always perfect. Because TTL uses reflective metering, the results may be affected by different clothing colors and skin tones. In my opinion, working in manual mode yields better, more consistent results.

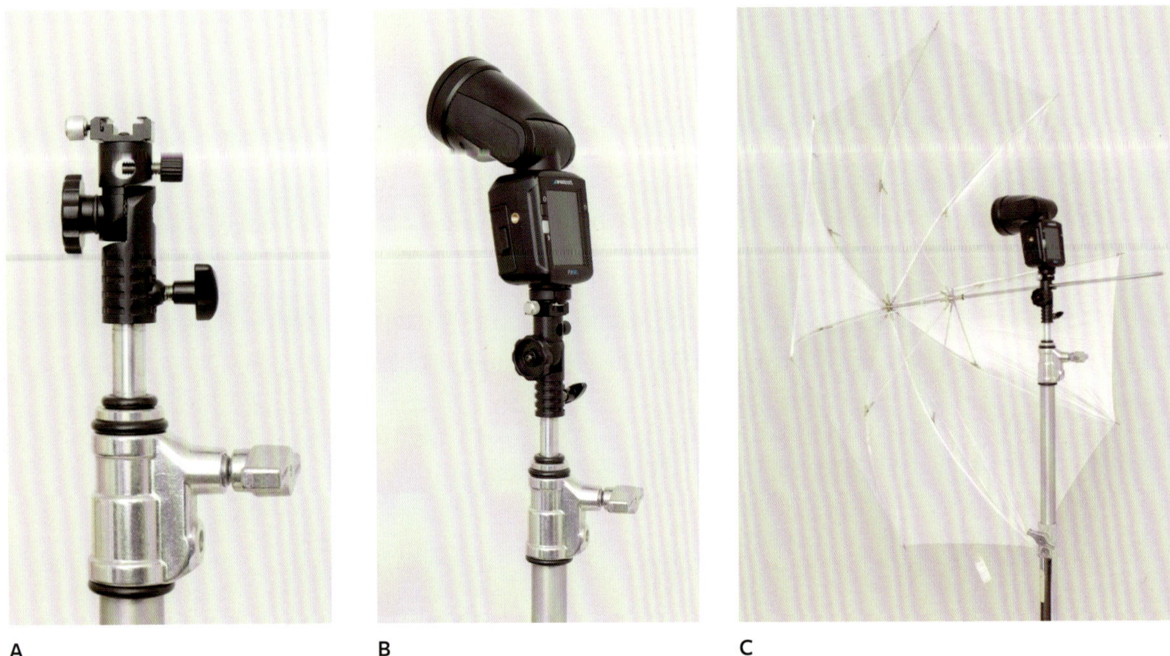


**FIGURE 3.21** Figure 3.21A shows the flash mount adapter on my light stand. Figure 3.21B shows my Westcott FJ80 flash on the adapter. Figure 3.21C shows the flash and adapter with an umbrella attached.

You can use a flash mount adapter to mount any flash unit on a stand so it can be used exactly like a strobe. A flash mount adapter is a small piece of equipment that attaches to the top of your light stand (**FIGURE 3.21A**). Most have a cold-shoe mount for securing your flash (**FIGURE 3.21B**). Most also have an opening for securing light modifiers, like umbrellas (**FIGURE 3.21C**).

### Continuous Lights

Continuous or constant lights are daylight-balanced lights that are left on while working. With continuous lights, the light you see is the light you get, making them a favorite for many photographers getting started with artificial lighting. You can easily see your catchlights and shadow patterns before taking your image. Using continuous lights feels very similar to working with window light. To use a continuous light, just mount it on a stand, add your favorite modifier, and turn it on! Remember what you've learned about light quality and lighting patterns, and meter like you would with window light. Easy peasy!

Despite the convenience of continuous lights, I have not always been a fan. Continuous light used to require bulky bulbs that would get *very* hot. I did not feel safe using them around small children. But technology is on our side, and these lights get better every year.

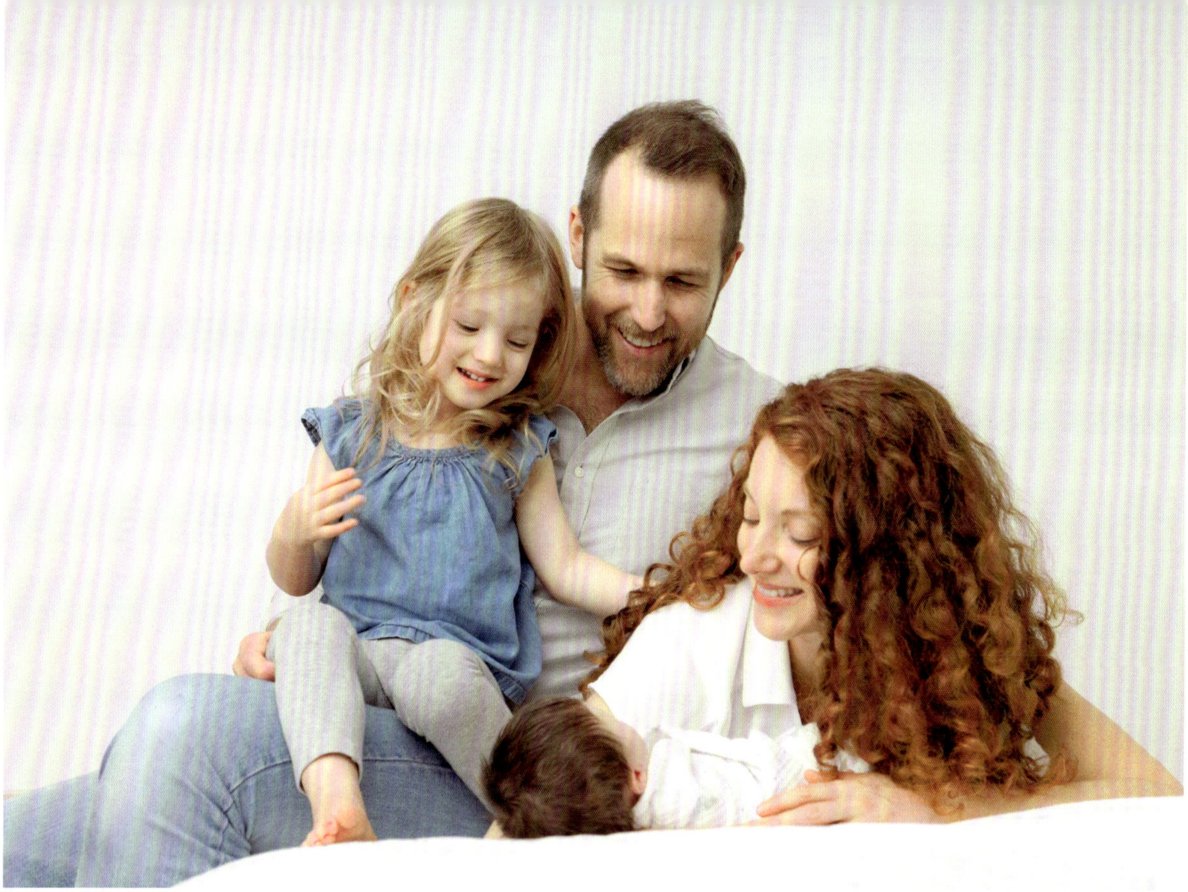

**FIGURE 3.22** Captured with the Westcott L120-B continuous light, f/4, 1/125 sec., ISO 400

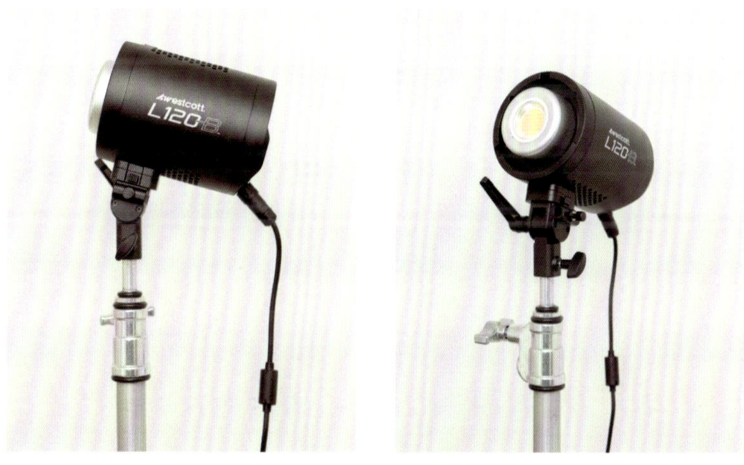

**FIGURE 3.23** The Westcott L120-B continuous light

I keep one Westcott L120-B continuous light at my studio and one in my travel kit (**FIGURE 3.23**). It's small, light, and bulbless, so I don't have to worry about it getting super hot and tipping over, which I love.

While the ease of continuous lights is undeniable, there are some disadvantages that you should be aware of.

When working with a strobe or flash, the light you are working with is delivered in a quick burst that lasts a fraction of a second. That means you can have the power on your light turned up very high without it feeling uncomfortable to your subject. Strobes and flash also have the ability to block out ambient light, allowing you more creative control over your images. Getting the same amount of light out of a continuous light isn't always possible. And continuous lights don't work for lighting techniques such as bouncing, which you'll learn in the next chapter.

Continuous lights also do not freeze motion the way strobes and flash do. I'll be sharing more on why that is later in this chapter, but for now, know that you will get motion blur with continuous lights (**FIGURE 3.24**) that you won't get with a flash or strobe.

**FIGURE 3.24** This image was captured at f/1.8, 1/125 sec., ISO 200 using the Westcott L120-B continuous light at full power. This little lady was moving fast, resulting in motion blur despite my shutter speed being set to 1/125 sec.

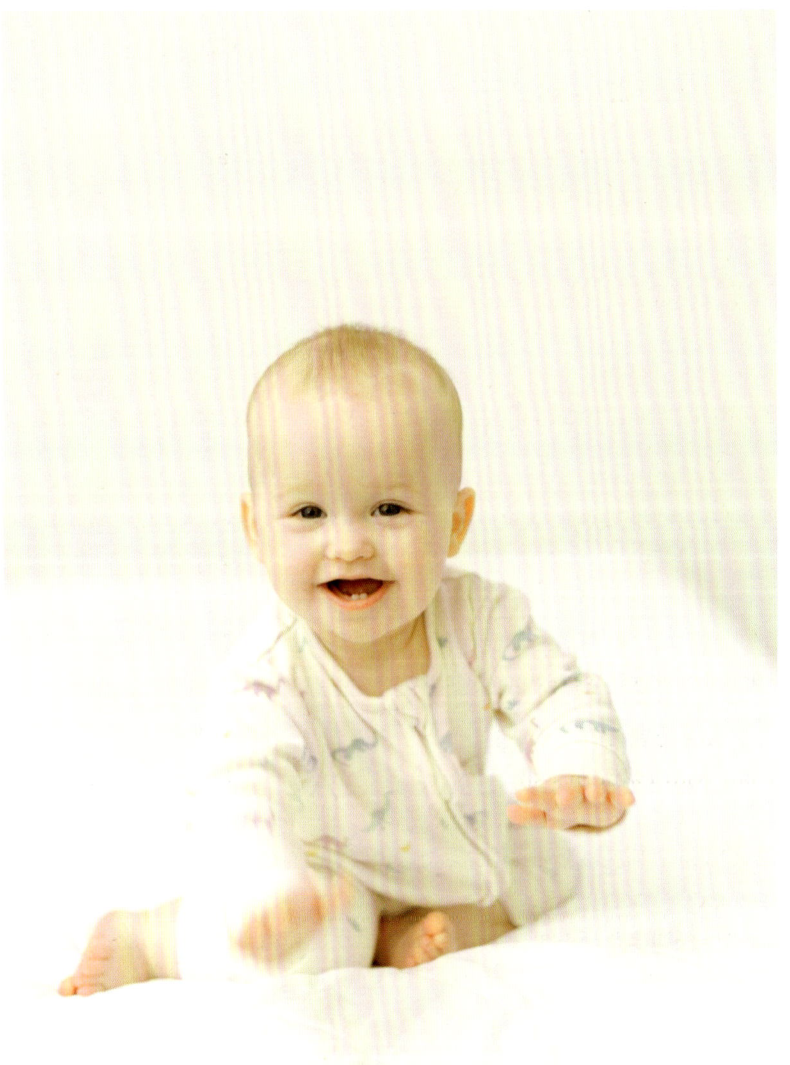

## What I Use in My Studio

- Cameras: Hasselblad H2, Contax 645, Rolleiflex 2.8, Canon R6 Mark II
- Lights: Westcott FJ200 strobe, Westcott L120- B continuous light
- Triggers and Receivers: Westcott FJ-X2m Universal trigger, PocketWizard Pro PlusX
- Stands: Avenger Roller Stand (AVA5029)
- Light Meter: Sekonic L-478D-U
- Modifiers: Westcott 7-foot Umbrella in white and black/white
- Extra Diffusion: Westcott 7-foot One Stop Diffusion Panel

All that said, continuous lights are a great tool, especially if you work in a dedicated space like a studio.

Now that you know what equipment you need and what it all does, let's talk about how to use it!

## Settings

Use ISO, aperture, and shutter speed settings to control exposure and create visually interesting pictures. This applies whether you are working with natural light, continuous light, strobes, or flash—with the exception of the shutter speed.

When working with natural light or continuous light, shutter speed is one of the ways your camera controls how much light it lets in, helping to balance exposure. You also use it to control motion. Low shutter speeds let in more light and more motion. High shutter speeds let in less light and freeze motion. That is not the case when working with strobes and flash.

Because the pulse of light that comes from a strobe or flash is so much faster than your camera's shutter, the amount of artificial light hitting your camera's sensor or film will not be affected by your shutter speed. When using strobes and flash, the pop of light takes over the traditional role of the shutter. The flash will freeze motion just like a high shutter speed does when working in natural light. **FIGURE 3.25** was captured with a Contax 645 film camera; the sync speed on the Contax 645 is 1/60 sec., but because I was using a strobe, the flash froze the motion, resulting in a blur-free photo.

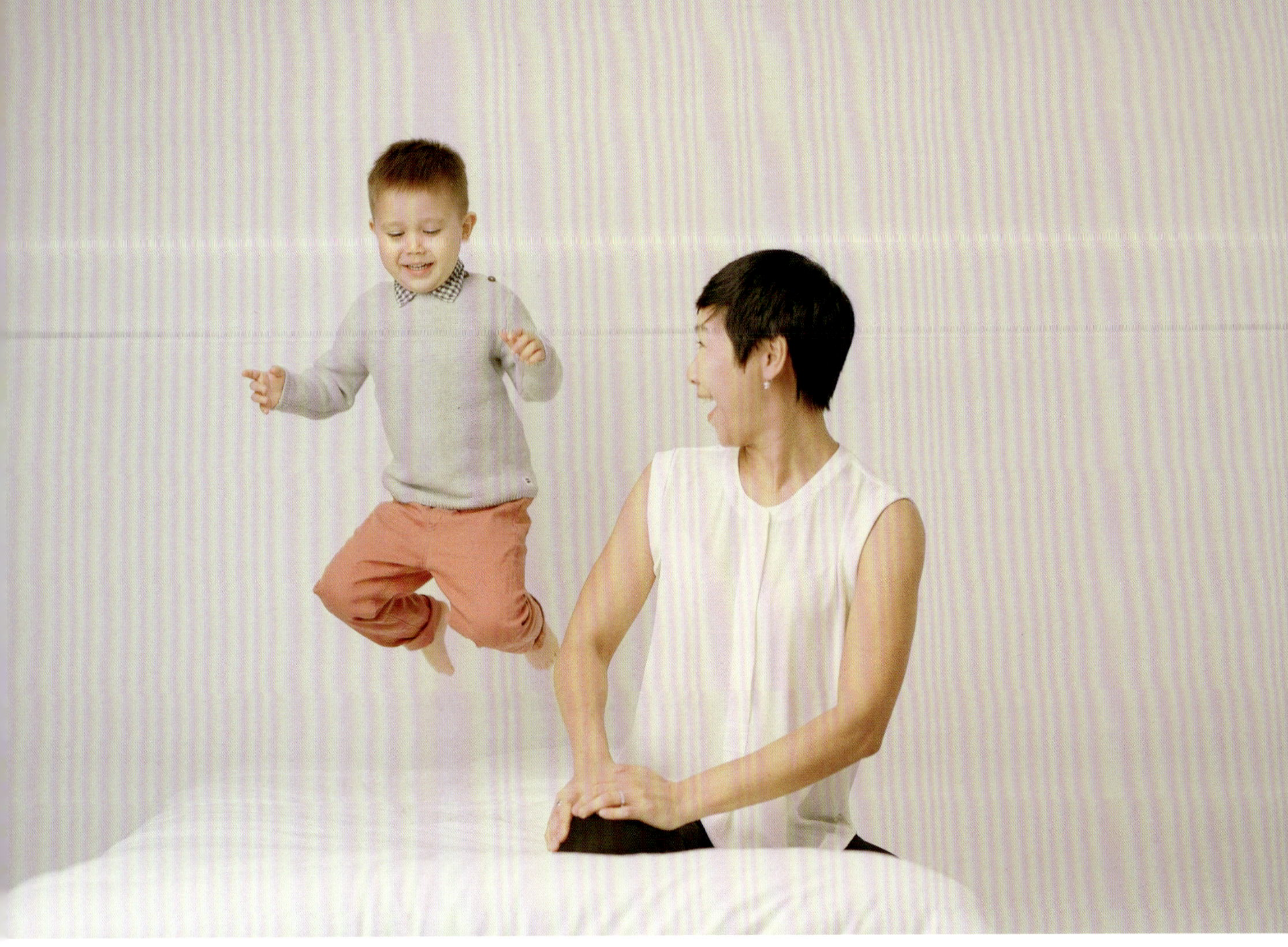

**FIGURE 3.25** This image was captured with a Contax 645 film camera with a sync speed of 1/60 sec., but because I was using a strobe, the flash froze the motion, resulting in a blur-free photo.

This is precisely why I prefer using strobes over a continuous light. A continuous light will give you extra light to work with on a dark day or in a low-light room, but it will not freeze motion the way a strobe or flash does.

When working with strobes and flash, your shutter speed will also not impact your exposure. Instead, proper exposure is achieved by balancing ISO, aperture, and the power of your light. **FIGURE 3.26** was captured with a strobe in a room with no windows and no other ambient light, at f/1.8, ISO 100, and at shutter speeds ranging from 1/30 sec. to 1/250 sec., a four-stop difference. Notice how the exposure stays the same even as the shutter speed changes.

### The Role of the Shutter When Using Strobe and Flash

When working with strobe or flash in a room with windows or other light sources, shutter speed is responsible for letting in or blocking out ambient light.

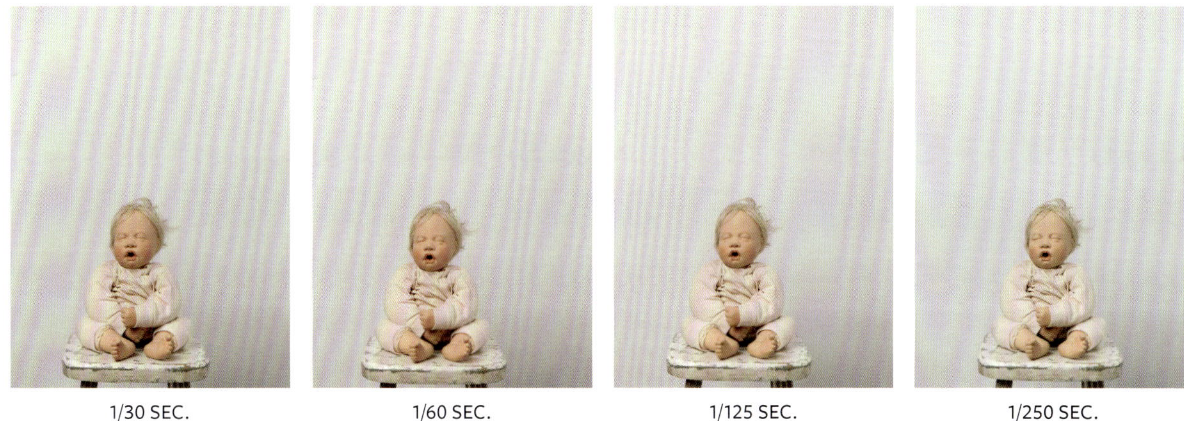


**FIGURE 3.26** These images were taken with a strobe in a room with no ambient light at f/1.8, ISO 100, and captured at shutter speeds ranging from 1/30 sec. to 1/250 sec., a four-stop difference.

This doesn't matter much if you're working in a dark studio with no windows or other light sources. But if you're working on location, in client homes, or—like me—in a bright, window-filled studio, understanding how shutter speed affects ambient light is essential.

When working with a strobe or flash, lower shutter speeds let in more ambient light and higher shutter speeds block it out. If you are working in a room with a window and you're using a strobe or flash, setting your shutter speed to a low number, like 1/30 sec. or 1/60 sec., will allow some of the window light into your image. Working at a higher shutter, speed like 1/125 sec. or 1/250 sec. will block out the ambient light.

Notice how the light on the walls in **FIGURE 3.26** looks quite similar to the images captured at shutter speeds of 1/125 sec. and 1/250 sec. in **FIGURE 3.27**, but looks noticeably different from the images captured at 1/60 sec. and 1/30 sec. This is because when working with a strobe or flash, your shutter speed controls how much ambient light is recorded in your image. In this setup, the ambient light was coming from a window. At 1/125 sec. and 1/250 sec. (**FIGURE 3.27**), the shutter was fast enough to effectively block out most, if not all, of the window light. So the only light you see in the images is from the strobe.

At 1/60 sec., the slower shutter allowed some of that ambient window light to register, which softens the shadows and adds a bit of fill—especially on the wall. At 1/30 sec., even more ambient light was captured, significantly affecting the overall exposure and giving a warmer, more blended look between the strobe and the window light.

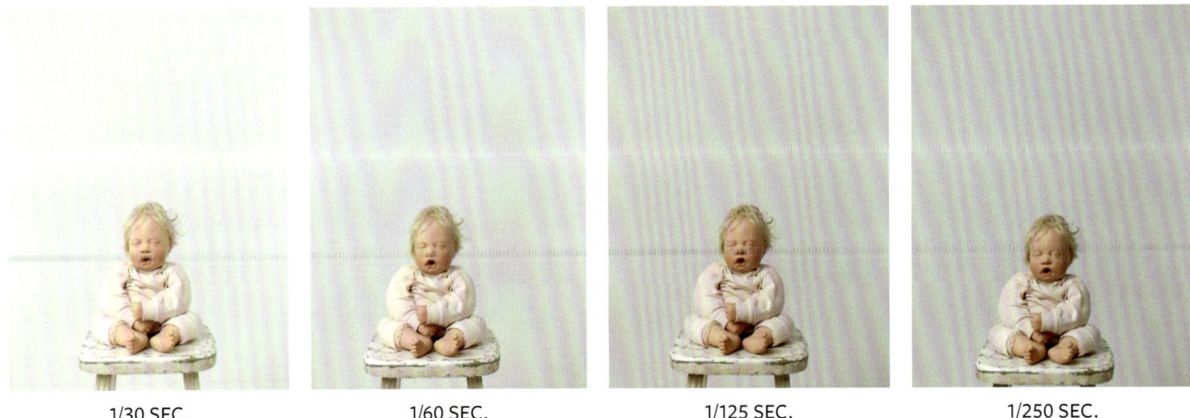


**FIGURES 3.27** These images were taken with a strobe in a room with large south-facing windows at ISO 100, f/1.8, and captured at shutter speeds ranging from 1/30 sec. to 1/250 sec., a four-stop difference. Notice how the brightness of the images changes as the shutter speeds get higher, blocking out the ambient light from the window.

If you want to eliminate ambient light and rely solely on your strobe, use a faster shutter speed. If you want to blend in ambient light for a more natural feel, slow down your shutter and adjust to taste.

### Shutter Drag and Ghosting

Intentionally setting a low shutter speed to create movement when working with both ambient light and strobe or flash is known as dragging your shutter. To drag your shutter, set your shutter speed to a slow setting, like 1/30 sec., 1/15 sec., or even lower, and either move your camera or let your subject move as you fire your flash. The flash will still freeze your subject, but the spill of ambient light through the shutter will also render an image, resulting in light streaks or a ghosting effect. The images in **FIGURE 3.28** were captured in a room with a mix of natural light and strobe at f/1.8, 1/60 sec., ISO 100. The window light combined with the low shutter speed created a ghosting effect as my little subject jumped on the bed.

To resolve the problem, I increased my shutter speed from 1/60 sec. to 1/250 sec., leaving the aperture and ISO the same. The faster shutter speed blocked out the natural light, allowing the pop of light from my strobe to freeze movement and resolve the ghosting issue (**FIGURE 3.29**)

Ghosting can be a cool effect when done intentionally to capture movement, but it can happen by accident when working in situations where the ambient light is brighter or at the same level as your strobe or flash. When accidental, however, ghosting looks like a mistake. To avoid ghosting, make sure that your

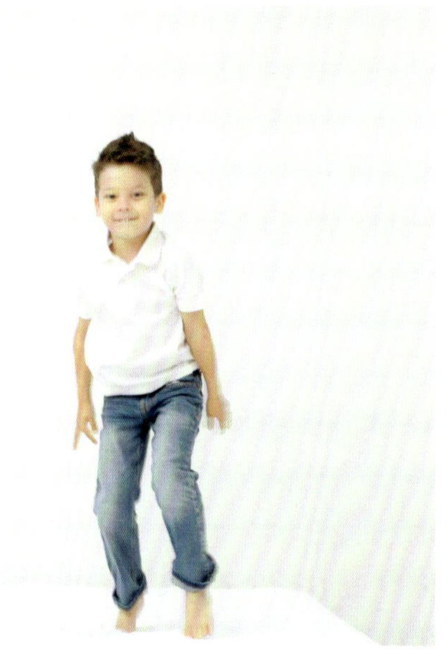
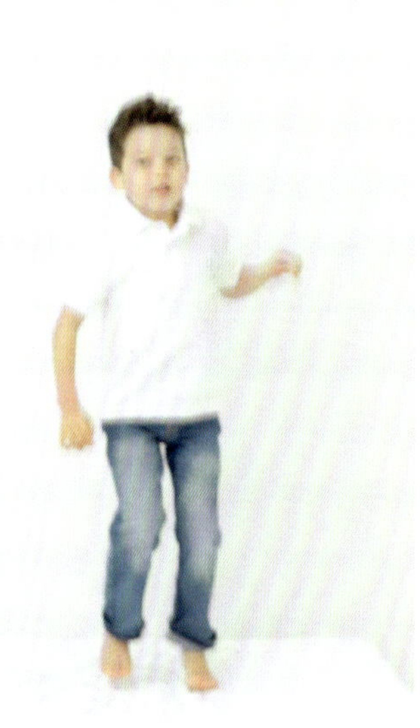

**FIGURE 3.28** Ghosting. These images were captured with a strobe in a room with bright window light (f/1.8, 1/60 sec., ISO 100). The low shutter speed of 1/60 sec. is letting a lot of the window light into the image, resulting in unintentional ghosting.

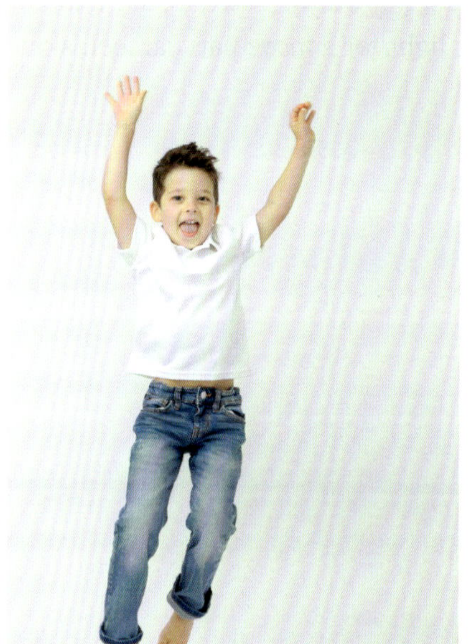
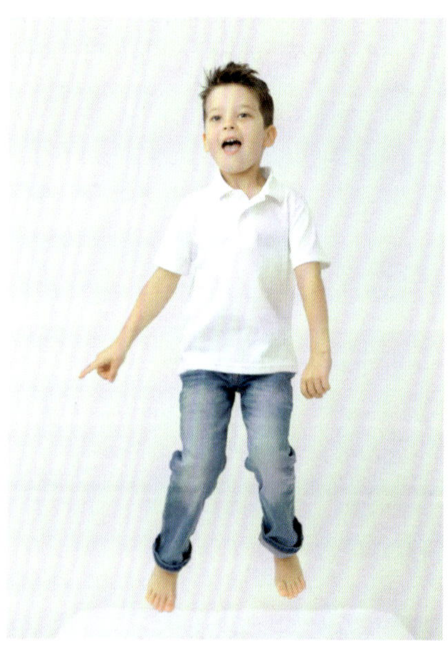

**FIGURE 3.29** These images were captured at f/1.8, 1/250 sec., ISO 100. Increasing the shutter speed to 1/250 sec. blocked out the ambient light and resolved the ghosting problem.

strobe light is the dominant light source in the room. Simply turning the power up on your strobe and adjusting your settings accordingly can solve a ghosting problem.

You can also control ghosting by increasing your shutter speed. Most cameras have a limit to how fast you can set the shutter speed when working with a strobe or flash, known as the sync speed. If you want to set your shutter speed above your camera's sync speed, you will need to program your strobe or flash to high speed sync.

## High Speed Sync

High speed sync (HSS) is a setting on your strobe or flash that allows you to use your lights at shutter speeds that exceed your camera's sync speed. Most modern lighting equipment will have a high speed sync option, but always double check before purchasing! This is especially useful if you are buying used gear, as older models may not have this capability.

### Sync Speed

The sync speed is the fastest shutter speed recommended for your camera when working with a strobe or flash of any kind. Older cameras, like most film cameras, tend to have lower sync speeds than digital cameras. My Pentax 67, for example, has a sync speed of 1/30th sec., whereas my Canon R6 Mark II has a sync speed of 1/250th sec.

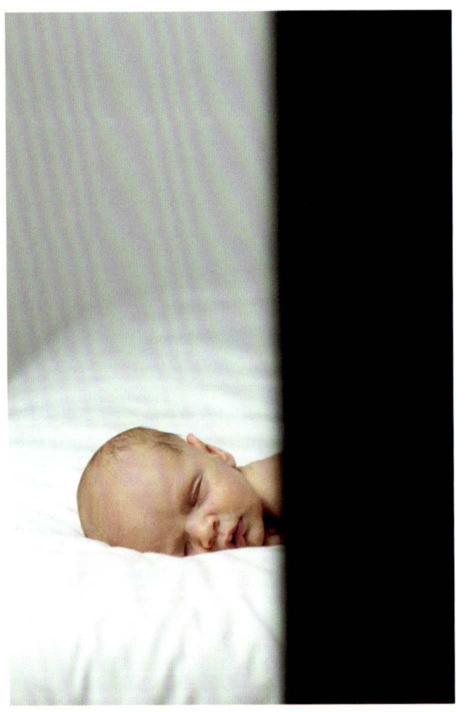

**FIGURE 3.30** This image was captured with a Canon 5D II at ISO 100, f/4, 1/500 sec. The sync speed on the Canon 5D II is 1/200 sec. Going over the sync speed resulted in a black bar (shutter shadow) through my image.

Staying within the parameters of your camera's sync speed is extremely important. Set your shutter speed higher than your camera's sync speed when working with a strobe or flash and your camera's shutter will not have enough time to get out of the way before your camera renders an image. This results in a shutter shadow, a black bar across your photo (**FIGURE 3.30**).

Sync speeds vary from camera to camera. And some cameras, like leaf shutter cameras, don't have sync speeds at all. So do your homework! You can find your camera's sync speed by looking in your camera's manual or online.

The takeaway is this:

- Know your camera's sync speed and do not exceed it, unless you have set your light to high speed sync.
- If your camera has a low sync speed, don't worry. Your flash will freeze motion for you.
- If you are working in a room with ambient light, such as a window, make sure that your flash or strobe is the dominant light source to avoid unintentional ghosting.

## Metering

When working with strobes and flash, I prefer to work in manual mode vs. TTL, which requires knowing how to properly meter. When it comes to metering with strobes and flash, using a handheld light meter is the gold standard.

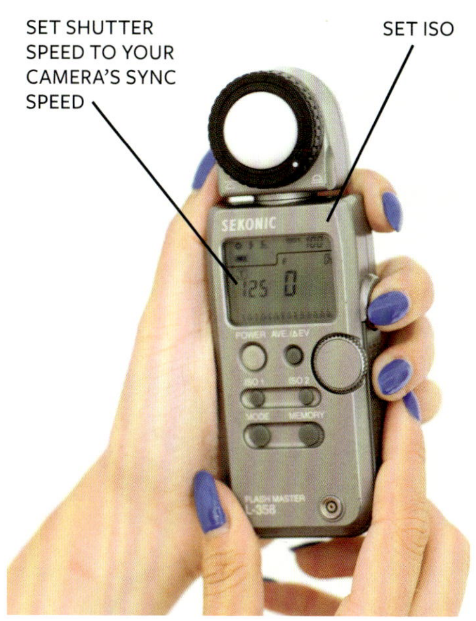


**FIGURE 3.31** Sekonic L-358 set to flash mode and ready to take an incident reading. Notice the ISO has been entered, and the shutter speed has been set to the camera's sync speed. Once triggered, the meter will pause and wait for the strobe to fire before giving an aperture setting.

### Setting Up Your Handheld Light Meter

To get perfect meter readings with strobes and flash, you need to make sure your handheld meter is set to flash mode. (Every meter is slightly different, so be sure to read your meter's manual to learn how to properly program this setting.) To get a reading, input two of the three components that make up the exposure triangle into the meter (**FIGURE 3.31**). When working with strobes and flash, it's important to not exceed your camera's sync speed, so enter your ISO and shutter speed into the meter. When triggered, the meter will give you an aperture reading.

To take a reading, simply press the button on the meter. When in flash mode, your meter will pause and wait for you to fire your light before giving an aperture setting. Taking a metering reading with a strobe or flash does require you to fire your light manually, so make sure your trigger and receiver are set to the same channel. Once everything is set, you can pop your flash by hitting the "test" button on the trigger (**FIGURE 3.32**).

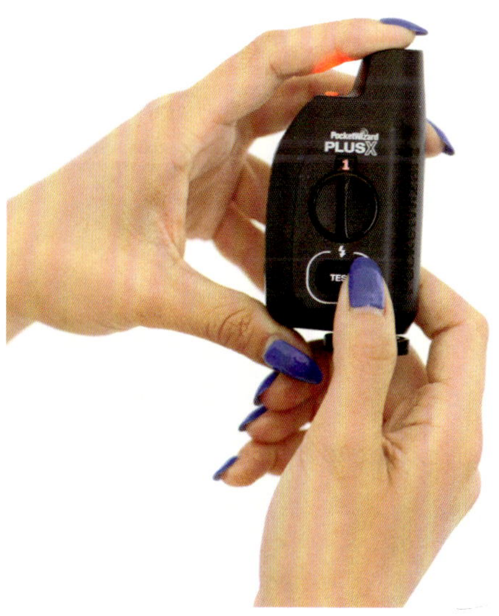


**FIGURE 3.32** To fire your light manually, simply press the "test" button on your trigger.

If you prefer a wide-open aperture, like f/1.8 or f/2, and the meter gives you a reading of something higher, like f/5.6 for example, then the power on your light is too high. Adjust the power on your light and re-meter until you've reached your desired aperture. If you are working with continuous lights, meter like you would if you were working with a window. Remember, knowing where to place your meter depends on the medium you are working with. Meter for your highlights when working with a digital camera or slide film. Meter for your shadows when working with color film. Meter for where you want your detail to be when working with black-and-white film.

## Know the Rules to Break the Rules

I'm old school and believe that it is important to know how to use a handheld light meter, especially when working with strobes and flash. I also work a lot with film, so a handheld light meter is a must since there is no digital display screen and built-in light meter. If you are a digital photographer, you can use the screen on the back of your camera as your guide. Simply set up your lights, input your ISO, camera's sync speed, and desired aperture, and take an image. If the light looks too bright on your screen, turn down the power on your light until it looks the way you want it to.

### A Two to Three-Stop Difference

Years ago, I noticed that when working with soft, diffused window light, I would have a two to three-stop difference between my highlights and my shadows (**FIGURE 3.33**).

This two to three-stop difference results in a soft, subtle shadow that gives dimension to photos without looking too contrasty or dark. Maintaining that two to three-stop difference between highlights and shadows when working with strobes gives me that "window-light" look.

I always meter both highlights and shadows when using lighting patterns that feature shadow detail (45-degree and 90-degree lighting) to make sure I'm within that two to three-stop range.

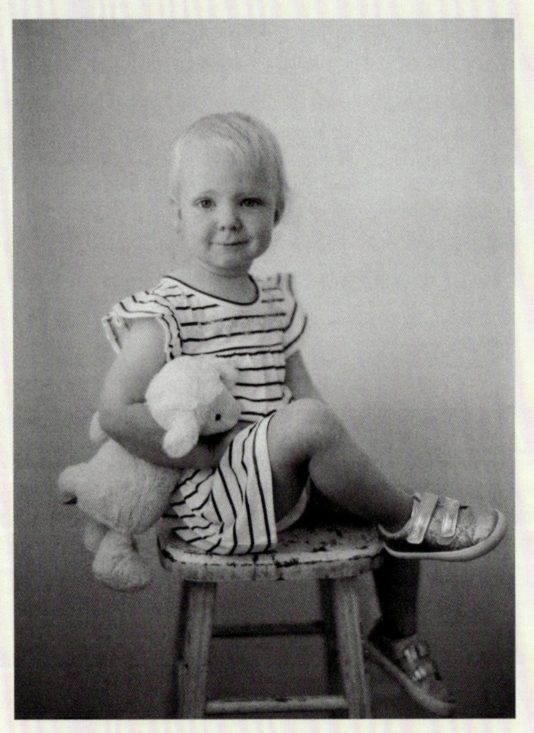

**FIGURE 3.33** This image was captured using diffused window light and Ilford Delta 3200 black-and-white film at f/2.8, 1/250 sec. There is a two-stop difference between the highlights and the shadows.

## Setting a Sekonic L-358 to Flash Mode

I still use my Sekonic L-358 handheld light meter that I bought way back in 2003. While this particular model has since been discontinued, it is possible to get them used for a very reasonable rate. They are fantastic meters. That said, I find all the Sekonic meters to be top-notch and would recommend any of their models.

To set the Sekonic L-358 to flash mode you'll want to start by holding down the Mode button. While holding down the mode button, use the side wheel to toggle from the sunshine icon (natural light) to the lightning bolt icon (flash). Once the lighting bolt icon is selected, you are in flash mode.

When in the flash mode, the meter will pause after you press the side button to take a reading. The meter will wait until you've fired your flash before giving you a recommended aperture setting.

While newer models of the Sekonic meters are a little different than my meter, the process for getting into flash mode is basically the same. Read your meter's manual, however, just to make sure you are in the proper mode.

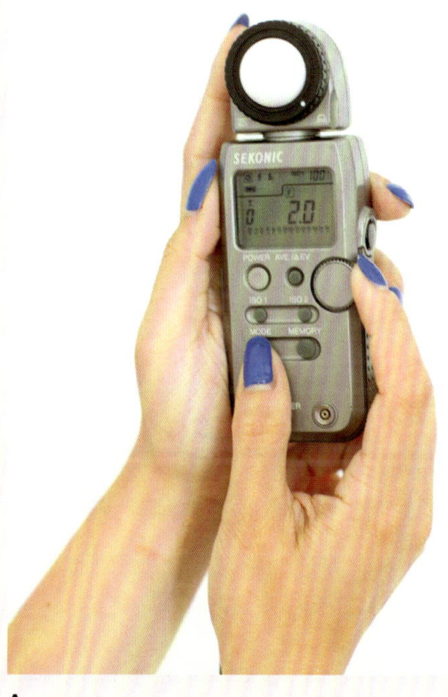


A

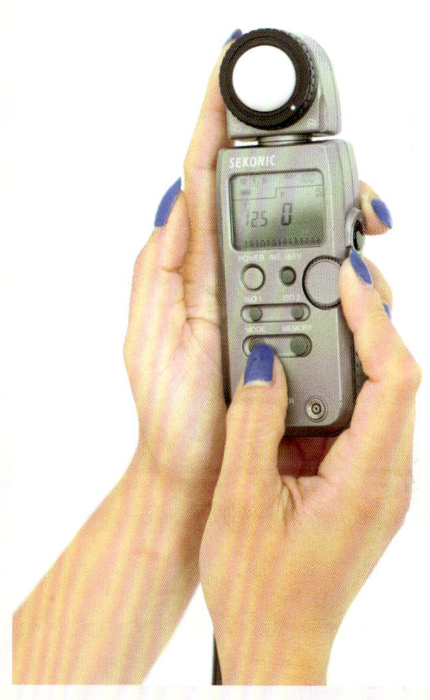


B

**FIGURE 3.34** To get into flash mode on the Sekonic L-358, hold down the Mode button and use the side wheel to toggle to the lightning bolt (flash) icon. Once the lightning bolt icon is selected, press the button on the side of the meter to take a reading. The meter will pause and wait for you to fire your strobe before giving an aperture setting.

## Putting It All Together

Ready to give it a try?!

1. Place your light on your light stand and add your modifier!

   In Chapter 1, you learned that the size of your light source impacts the quality of your light, and that adding or removing diffusion to a light source has an effect on its light quality, as well. Keep this in mind when choosing a modifier to purchase. If you prefer soft light, you'll want a relatively large modifier with diffusion. If you prefer harder light, then you will want to choose a relatively small modifier with less diffusion.

2. Set your light in the correct position to create your preferred lighting patterns.

   Remember that the size and shape of your modifier will have an impact on the size and shape your catchlights. Where you place your light and modifier will impact the location of the catchlights and the shadows you create.

   Review the lighting patterns from Chapter 1 and choose your favorite.

   Pay close attention to your catchlights to make sure your light is set up in a way that ensures a flattering effect. Catchlights should always be in the top half of the eye. Catchlights that appear in the bottom of the eye indicate light that is coming from below (ghoul light) and should be avoided.

   Remember, round modifiers produce round catchlights. Square and rectangular modifiers produce catchlights with straight edges. Large modifiers produce large catchlights and small modifiers produce small catchlights. The proximity of your light source will also impact the size of your catchlights. The closer your light source is, the larger the catchlights will be.

   If you like light and airy images, give The Sandra Coan Method a try! If you like images with more contrast, try a smaller modifier or a modifier with a black backing.

   I recommend renting modifiers from your local camera store if possible so you can experiment before committing to a purchase.

3. Meter and adjust the power on your light accordingly.

   When working with natural light, controlling light intensity can be a little tricky (you can't control the sun!). You can move your subject closer to or farther away from your light source, but that is about it. But when working with artificial light, you have the ability to adjust the power on your light, giving you complete control over its brightness! How great is that?!

All artificial light sources have a range in power that dictates the amount of light they will produce. Knowing where to set the power starts with knowing your preferred aperture. Do you like a deep or shallow depth of field? Choose your desired aperture, enter your ISO and camera's sync speed, and take a meter reading. If the meter gives you an aperture reading that doesn't match your desired aperture, simply adjust the power on your light and re-meter until it does.

4. Take some photos!

   Now the fun part begins! Grab your favorite posing doll. Bribe your children. Coerce your partner. Sit them in front of your lights and start taking photos. It may feel awkward at first, but the more you practice, the easier it will get! I promise!

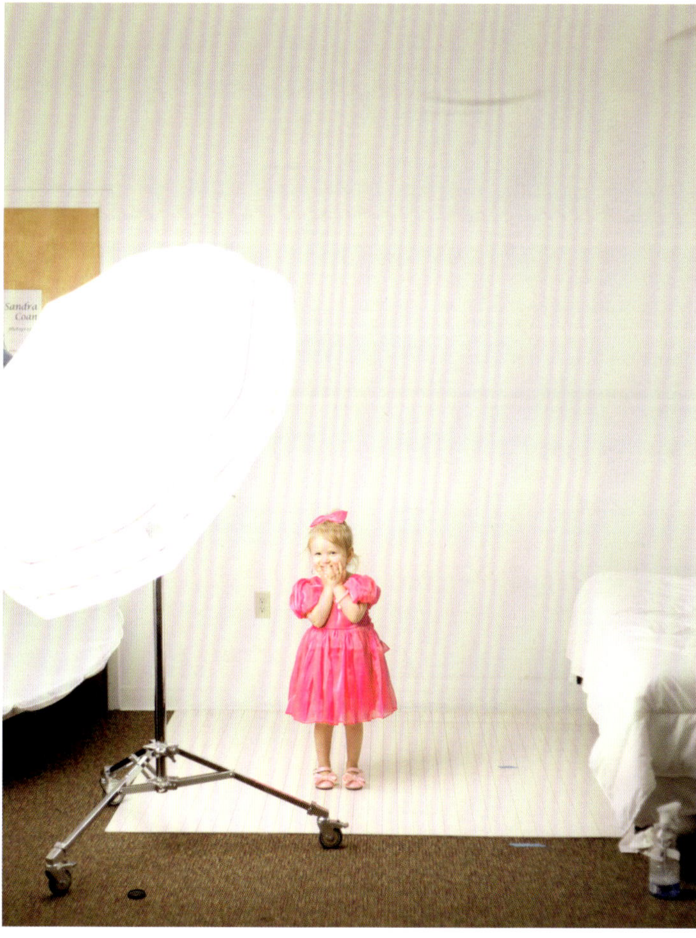

**FIGURE 3.35** This is my FJ200 strobe on my Avenger light stand with a Westcott 45-inch all white umbrella, with a diffusion panel placed 45 degrees to my subject to create a loop light pattern.

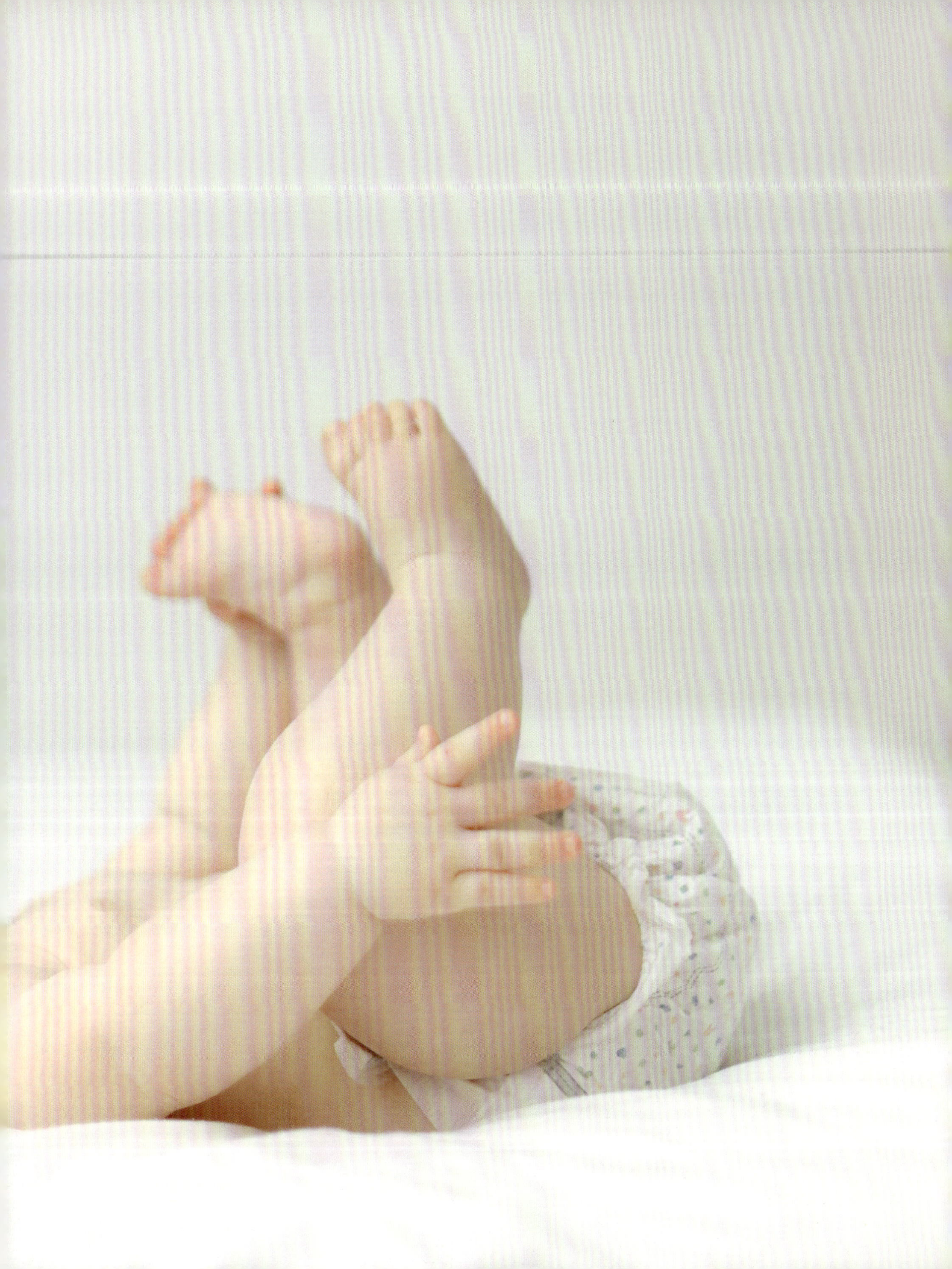

CHAPTER

# 4

# Lighting on Location

While it's true that the rules of light are the same whether you are working outside, inside, in a client's home, or in a studio, most of the resources available to photographers on the subject of artificial lighting showcase using strobes and flash in a studio setting. However, what works in a studio doesn't always work in a home!

In a studio, you have a blank slate to work with: Your space can be as cluttered or as uncluttered as you like. You can control the backgrounds and the ambient light. Your work environment is always the same. That is not the case when on location.

As an on-location photographer, you walk into a different work environment at every session. You have furniture to navigate, windows and overhead lighting to consider, and you need the skills to be able to walk in, assess your situation quickly, and make a plan for lighting your clients in the given environment.

When working on location, chances are you are also working in confined spaces, which affects what equipment you choose to use. When working in my studio, my go-to modifier is the Westcott 7-foot Umbrella. But that modifier is just too big to bring into most homes, so I have different, more appropriate equipment that I use when working on location that gives me the same soft, natural-looking lighting I love.

In this chapter, you will learn the common lighting problems photographers face when working in their clients' homes, and how to solve them by incorporating strobes and flash. I'll share the equipment I take with me when working on location and show you how to assess the environment you are working in so that you can decide whether to use natural light or artificial light to create an image. We'll consider light placement, how to use light modifiers when working in small spaces, and how to bounce light to create a natural-light look.

## Common Problems When on Location

Over the years I have heard more than one natural-light photographer say that they do not need to learn how to use artificial light because they are digital photographers and can simply increase their ISO when needed. And that is true! Digital cameras get better every year, and many can produce great-looking images, even at high ISOs. But increasing ISO for proper exposure only solves one problem. The truth is, there are many benefits to using artificial light beyond just increasing the light in a room.

## No Windows

For example, what if your client wants photos taken somewhere in their house that has no windows? You can increase ISO and try to work with overhead lighting or lamps, but most likely, the results will not be great. This is where artificial light comes to the rescue!

**FIGURE 4.1A** and **4.1B** were captured in a windowless hallway where the toddler I was photographing was happily playing. I wanted to capture the moment! So instead of moving him, I let him continue to play and brought my strobe to light the hallway (**FIGURE 4.1C**). It took me less than two minutes to set it up and it resulted in cute photos that his parents loved!

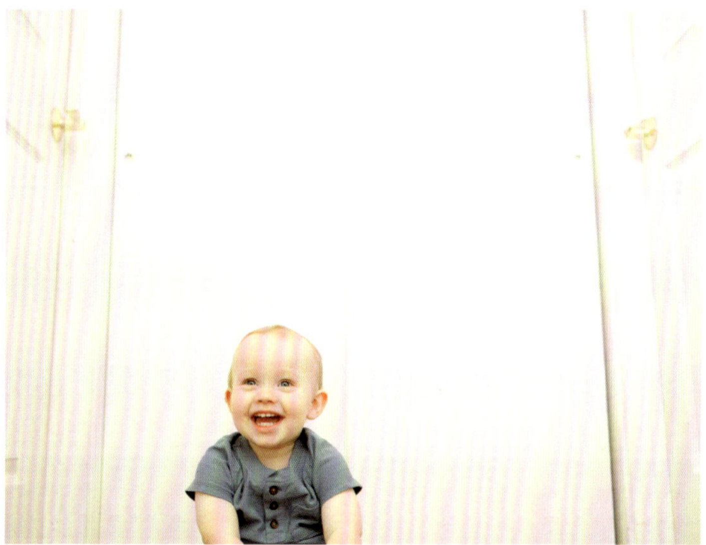

A

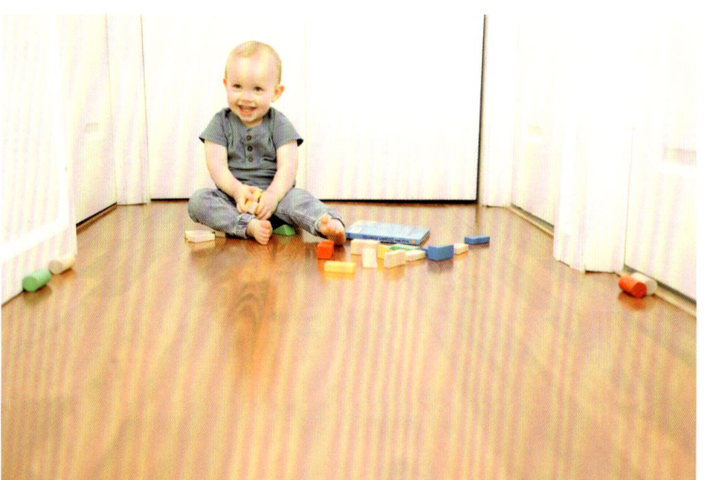

B

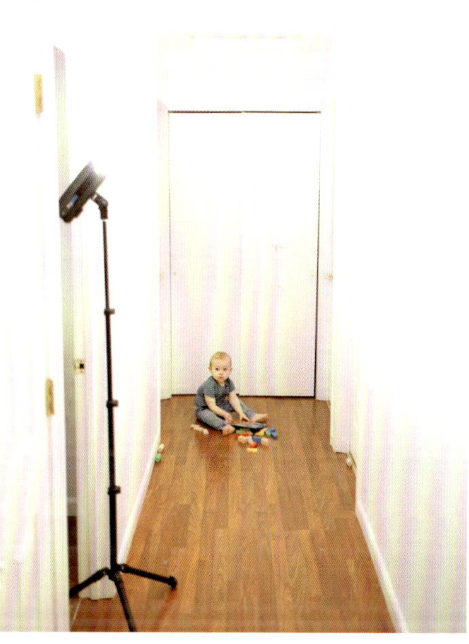

C

**FIGURE 4.1** These images show how artificial light can save the day when natural light just isn't available. To light this space, I used a strobe bounced off the ceiling to create soft, natural-looking light—all without interrupting the toddler's play. It took less than two minutes to set up, and the result was a series of joyful, well-lit images his parents loved.

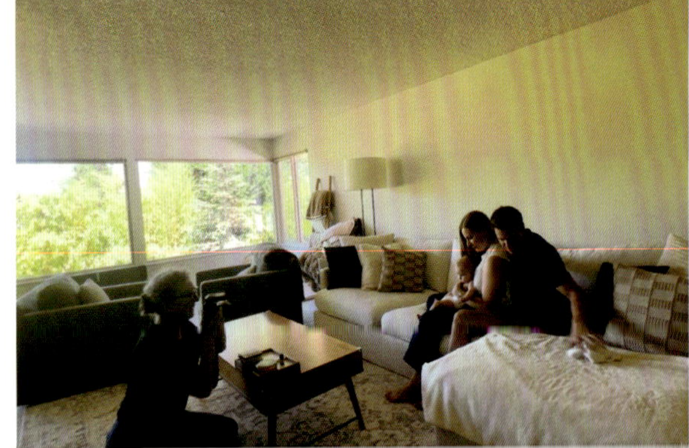

A

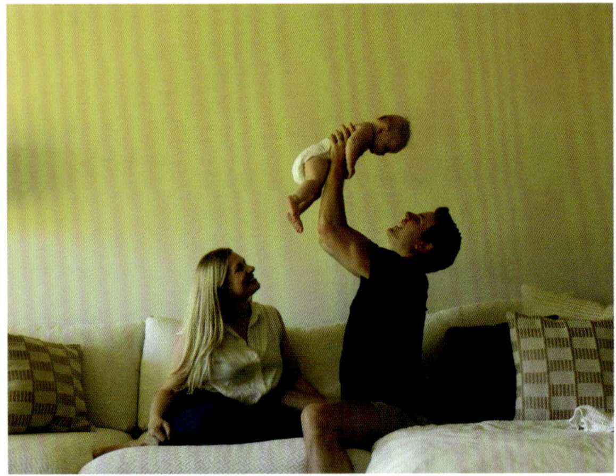

B

**FIGURE 4.2** As you can see in Figure 4.2A, this room had large, north-facing windows that provided plenty of beautiful light—but outside the windows, green trees reflected a strong green hue into the space.

## Light Temperature and Color Cast

Light temperature varies depending on time of day, location, and the weather. Objects outside of a window can also reflect light and bounce color back into a room. **FIGURE 4.2B**, for example, was photographed in a room with huge, north-facing windows. There was plenty of natural light to work with for proper exposure, but a bank of trees outside the windows was reflecting green light into the space, resulting in the unpleasant color cast.

To solve the problem, I set up my Westcott FJ200 strobe with a 45-inch white umbrella and diffusion panel and positioned it at a 45-degree angle to my subjects (**FIGURE 4.3A**). Strobes and flash are "daylight balanced," meaning they are set to 5500 Kelvin—a clean, neutral light. With this setup, the light from the strobe overpowered the ambient green cast in the room. With one simple change, I created beautiful images, straight out of camera.

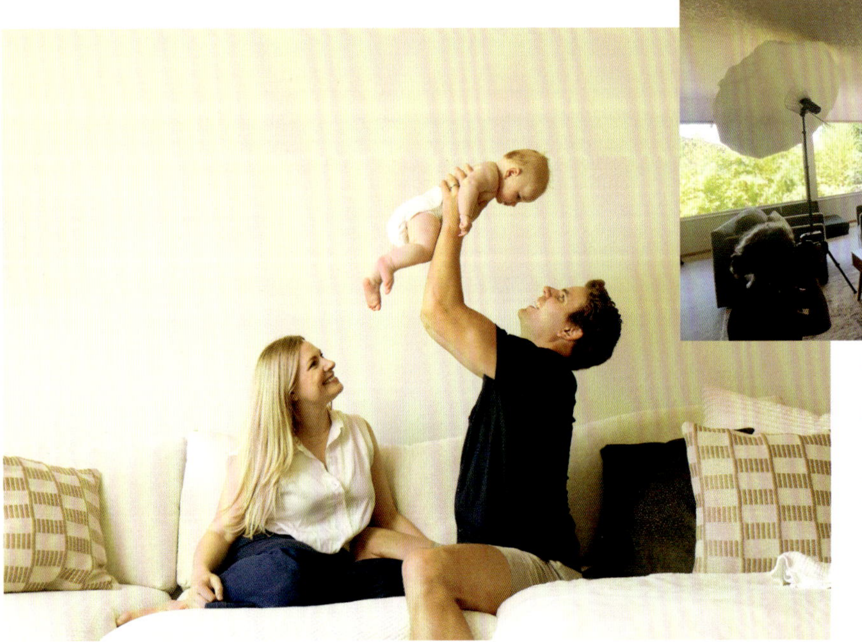

A

B

**FIGURE 4.3** Adding a strobe with a white umbrella neutralized the green color cast from outside reflections. The result is clean, natural light—straight out of camera!

As an added bonus, using strobes and flash to even out light temperature and remove color casts makes editing your photos much easier. When your light is clean and consistent, editing is a breeze!

## Unflattering Shadows

When working on location you can sometimes find yourself in a situation where you have enough natural light for a proper exposure, but the location of the light source results in unflattering shadows on your subject. Adding a light can solve this problem, as well.

**FIGURE 4.4** was captured in a basement nursery that had one window. The window was at the opposite end of the room from the crib we were using for photos, resulting in shadows that fell up the face (a ghoul light pattern).

To solve the problem, I set up my strobe on a stand and bounced the light off the wall closest to the crib (**FIGURE 4.5A**). The strobe eliminated the shadows, resulting in more flattering light and adorable pictures (**FIGURE 4.5B**).

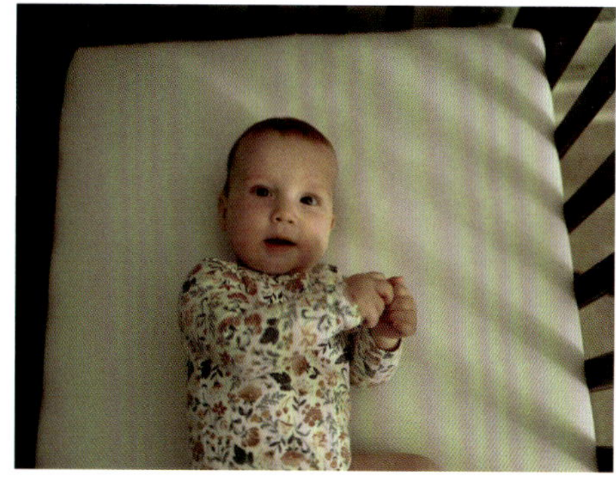

**FIGURE 4.4** This image was captured in a basement nursery that had one window, at the opposite end of the room from the crib we were using for photos, resulting in shadows that fell up the face, a classic ghoul light pattern. While the exposure is technically correct, the shadow pattern is unflattering.

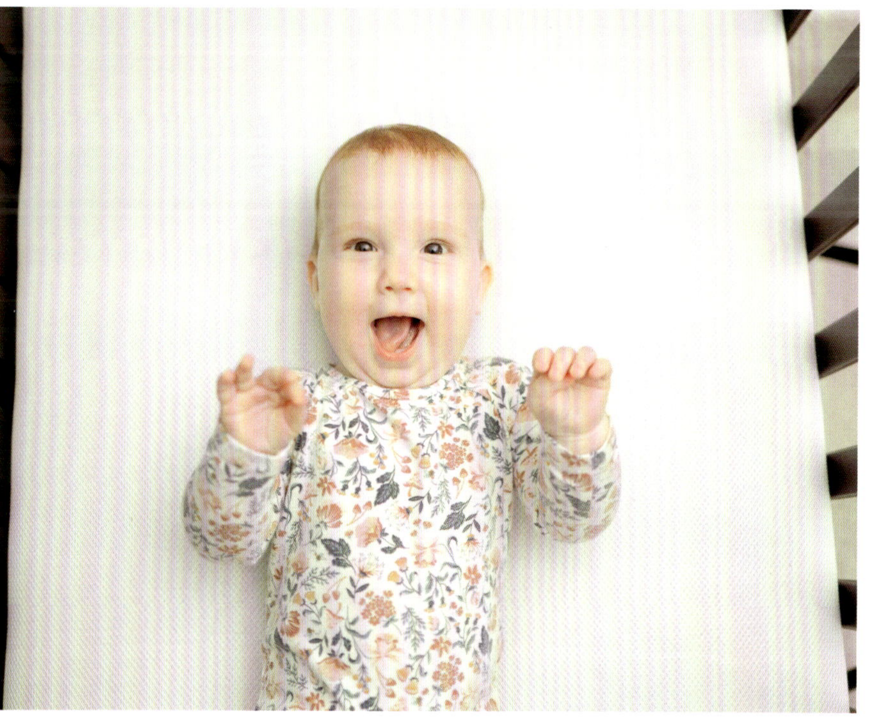

B

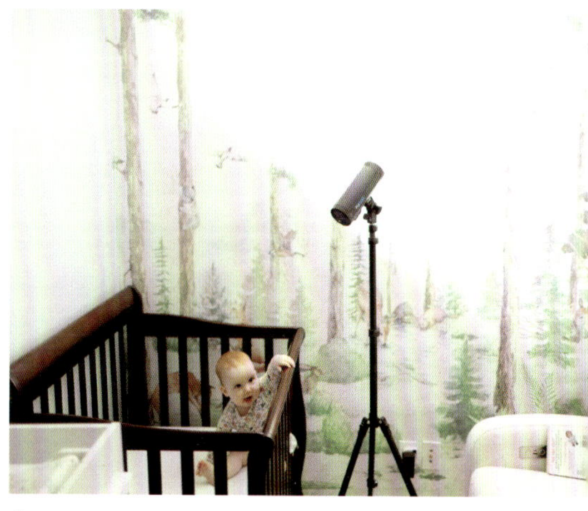

A

**FIGURE 4.5** I bounced the light from my strobe off the wall closest to the crib. This allowed me to redirect the light in the room, eliminating the unflattering shadows from the window light.

## What I Use on Location

You do not need a ton of gear to create natural looking light with strobes and flash. Everything I do is done with one light, whether I'm working in my studio or in a client's home. The difference is, when working on location, I need equipment that is easy to carry, easy to set up, and has a relatively small footprint, as most of the rooms I work in are smaller than my studio. I bring:

- A travel stand
- Westcott FJ200 strobe
- Westcott FJ80 flash
- Westcott universal trigger
- Westcott 45-inch convertible umbrella
- Westcott 60-inch convertible umbrella
- Westcott 53-inch diffusion panel

# Assessing Your Environment

Adding artificial light can solve many of the common challenges photographers face when working in client homes. But how do you know *when* to use it, and how do you decide *where* to place it to achieve the look you're after? This is one of the hardest parts of working on location.

Metering should always be your first step. It's a quick and easy way to determine whether you need additional light for proper exposure. But low light is just one of many issues that artificial light can help resolve.

When working in a client's home, I recommend asking yourself a few simple questions to guide your lighting decisions: Who? Where? What? And how?

### Who

Who are you going to be photographing at this session?

This information is helpful whether I'm working in my studio or in a client's home. After all, photographing a newborn alone is very different from photographing a newborn, three older siblings, two parents, and the family dog! And I like to be prepared. But this information is particularly important when working on location as it helps determine where to set up for photos in the home.

If I'm photographing a newborn alone, I can work in smaller spaces, no problem. But if I'm photographing a newborn with other family members in the photos, I will choose areas in the house that can accommodate them all comfortably.

## Where

After arriving at a client's home, greeting the family, and determining *who* will be photographed, I ask if I can look around the house to determine *where* to set up for photos.

Oftentimes families will want to highlight areas in their home that have sentimental meaning, like the nursery for example, and I always do my best to accommodate those requests. But I also look for places that I think will make creating flattering photos easy. When looking for places to set up, you are the photographer, which means you are probably better at determining what will and won't work than your clients are. Don't be afraid to suggest a space that your client may not think to point out (the dark basement, for example, may be the perfect spot when you know how to light it!). Don't be afraid to let your clients know if a space they suggest will not result in photos you can be proud of. Again, you see things differently than they do, and you're the expert!

If I'm photographing a large family, I'll choose to work in a larger space, like the living room. If I'm working with just a newborn or a newborn and their parents, then I have more flexibility and can work in smaller spaces. I always ask to use the primary bedroom for photos, regardless of the size of the family. I love using beds in my posing flow for newborns and babies (see Chapter 8) and the primary bed almost always has enough room for the entire family, big or small, and makes for cozy photos.

## What

Once I've determined where I'll be working, I'll decide what kind of light to use to create my images. Consider your style, preferred light quality, and lighting patterns when doing this. Is your style light and airy, or do you prefer more moody images? Do you prefer soft light or hard light? Do you like lighting patterns with a lot of contrast (like split light) or do you prefer patterns with less contrast (like flat light)? Knowing the answer to these questions will help you decide whether to use the available light in the room or to add your own light.

My style, for example, is light and airy. I love soft light with minimal contrast. My preferred lighting pattern is loop light when working indoors. I strive to create work that reflects these preferences whether in my studio or on location.

If the space I'm working in has no windows, I'll use artificial light to create my images. For this, I decide if I'm going to set up a stand, strobe, and modifier, or if I'll be using a bounced flash. If the room does have windows, I'll assess their size, determine what direction they face, look at the shadows they are

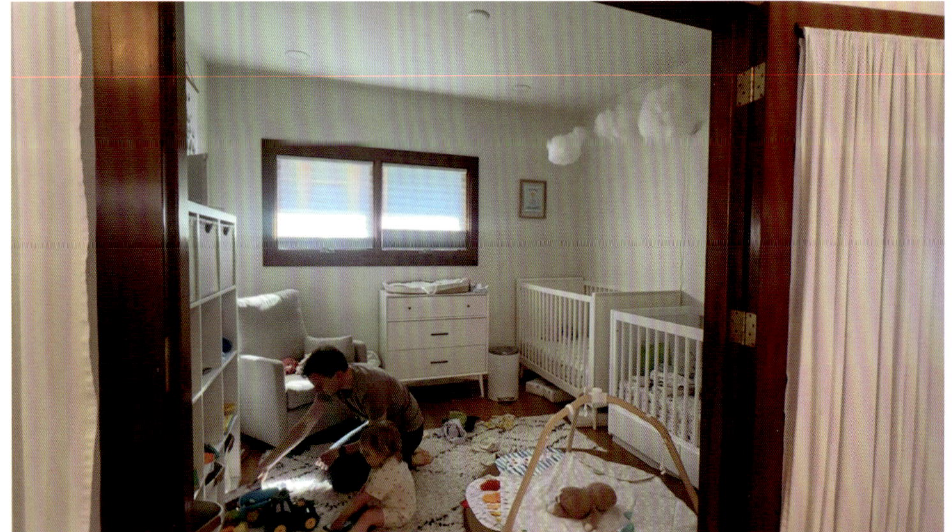

**FIGURE 4.6** I always take a quick photo of the space I'll be working in at the beginning of a session to help me assess the light in the room.

producing, and look for light temperature issues and unpleasant color casts. If I can achieve my desired look with just the windows, I'll use natural light. If not, I'll bring in a strobe or flash.

**Pro Tip:** Take a quick picture of the room to help assess your light. Cameras are better at noticing things like light temperature and color cast than the naked eye. **FIGURE 4.6** shows a pullback photo of a room in my client's home. The parents wanted photos of their toddler playing in her crib (which was the crib closest to the windows). Walking into this space, I noticed that the windows were relatively small. I also noted that they are west facing, and the light was blocked by the neighboring house. The test photo helped me see a greenish tint on the wall behind the crib closest to the window, as well as the shadow patterns the window light was creating (notice the dark corner behind the crib and the brighter patch of light on the wall).

## Window Size

I prefer soft light, so if the windows in the room are small, I'll most likely choose to create my own light. If the windows are large and have the potential to create the quality of light I prefer, I will move on to note the direction the window is facing as well as the time of day.

### Direction and Time of Day

In the Northern Hemisphere, north-facing windows always produce even light. But the light produced from an east, south, or west-facing window will change throughout the day as the sun moves through the sky, potentially changing

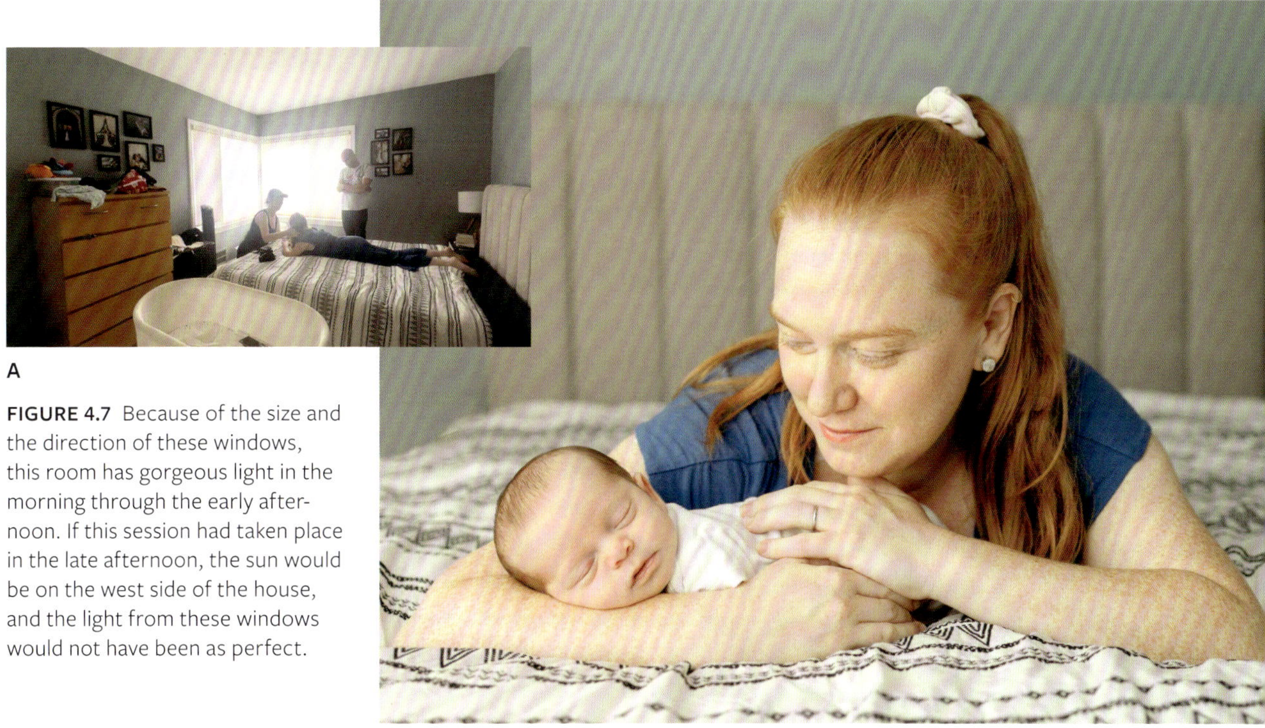

A

FIGURE 4.7 Because of the size and the direction of these windows, this room has gorgeous light in the morning through the early afternoon. If this session had taken place in the late afternoon, the sun would be on the west side of the house, and the light from these windows would not have been as perfect.

B

throughout your session. **FIGURE 4.7B** was captured in a small bedroom with relatively large corner windows that faced east and south (**FIGURE 4.7A**). It was a sunny day, and we were working at noon. The family had white blinds on the windows, which diffused the light, creating beautiful soft light, and the windows were in the perfect position relative to where I was posing the family on the bed to create the loop light pattern I love so much.

This was an ideal situation for using natural light, but if this session had taken place in the late afternoon, the sun would have been on the west side of the house, and the light from these windows would not have been as perfect. If this had been a late afternoon session, I most likely would have bounced a flash off the windows to create my light.

### Shadows

When assessing window light, it's important to take note of the shadows being cast. Noticing the shadows that are being created by a window will help you determine how to use the window light to create your desired look. If the shadows from a window create a pattern you love, then you may want to use the natural light; if you notice unflattering shadows, adding a strobe or flash can help correct the problem.

**FIGURE 4.8** is a great example of this. These images were captured with the natural light cast from a large south-facing window. There was plenty of natural light to achieve proper exposure at f/2.8, 1/125 sec., ISO 100, but the light coming in from the window was producing a slight ghoul light pattern on my client (**FIGURE 4.8A**). To solve the problem, I placed my strobe on a stand and bounced the light off the wall just above the windows (**FIGURE 4.8B**), redirecting the light to create a loop light pattern, instead (**FIGURE 4.8C**).

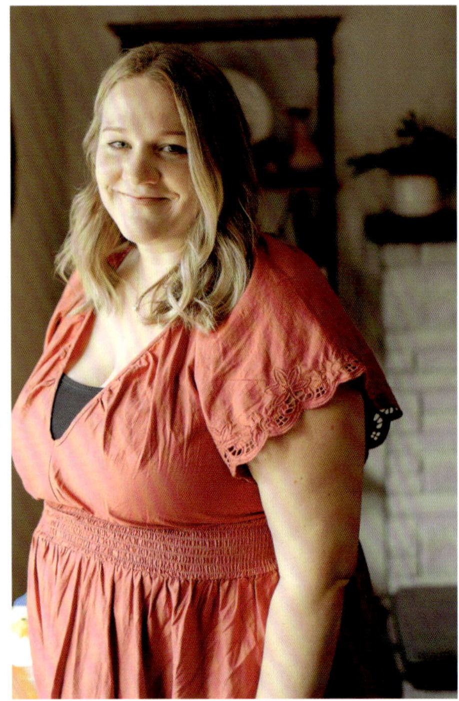

A

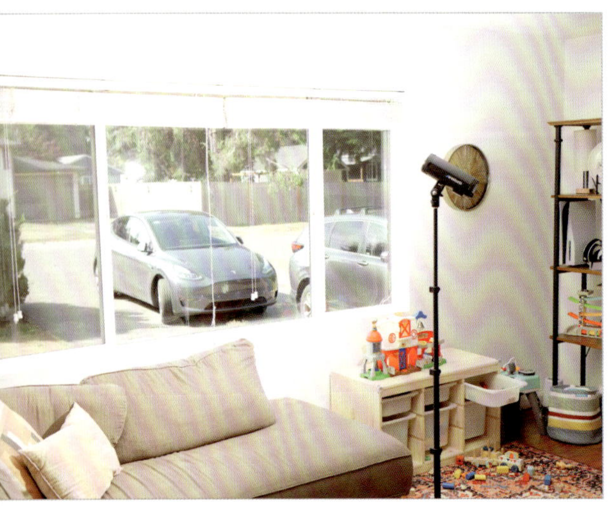

B

C

**FIGURE 4.8** The window light was creating an unpleasant ghoul light pattern on my client's face in Figure 4.8A. To solve the problem, I placed my strobe on a stand and bounced the light off of the wall just above the windows, redirecting the light to create a loop light pattern instead (Figure 4.8C).

## Why Large Windows Cause Ghoul Lighting

Ghoul lighting occurs when the majority of the light is hitting the client from below. It results in shadows that fall upward on the face—along the chin, nose, and cheeks—and catchlights in the lower half of the eyes. This is not considered a flattering lighting pattern for portraits.

Accidental ghoul lighting can occur when photographing newborns and babies who are positioned with their feet pointing toward the light source, but it can also happen when working in a room with large windows. In **FIGURE 4.9**, I positioned a client and her baby next to a large, north-facing window. The window's size and northern exposure provided beautiful, soft light, but because she is standing, her head and face are positioned in the top third of the window, while the remaining two thirds are below. This imbalance caused a slight ghoul light pattern on the mom and baby (**FIGURE 4.9B**). To correct the issue, I bounced light from my strobe off the top portion of the window (**FIGURE 4.9C**), redirecting the light so that the dominant light hit her from above. The result is a much more flattering lighting pattern, as you can see in **FIGURE 4.9D**.

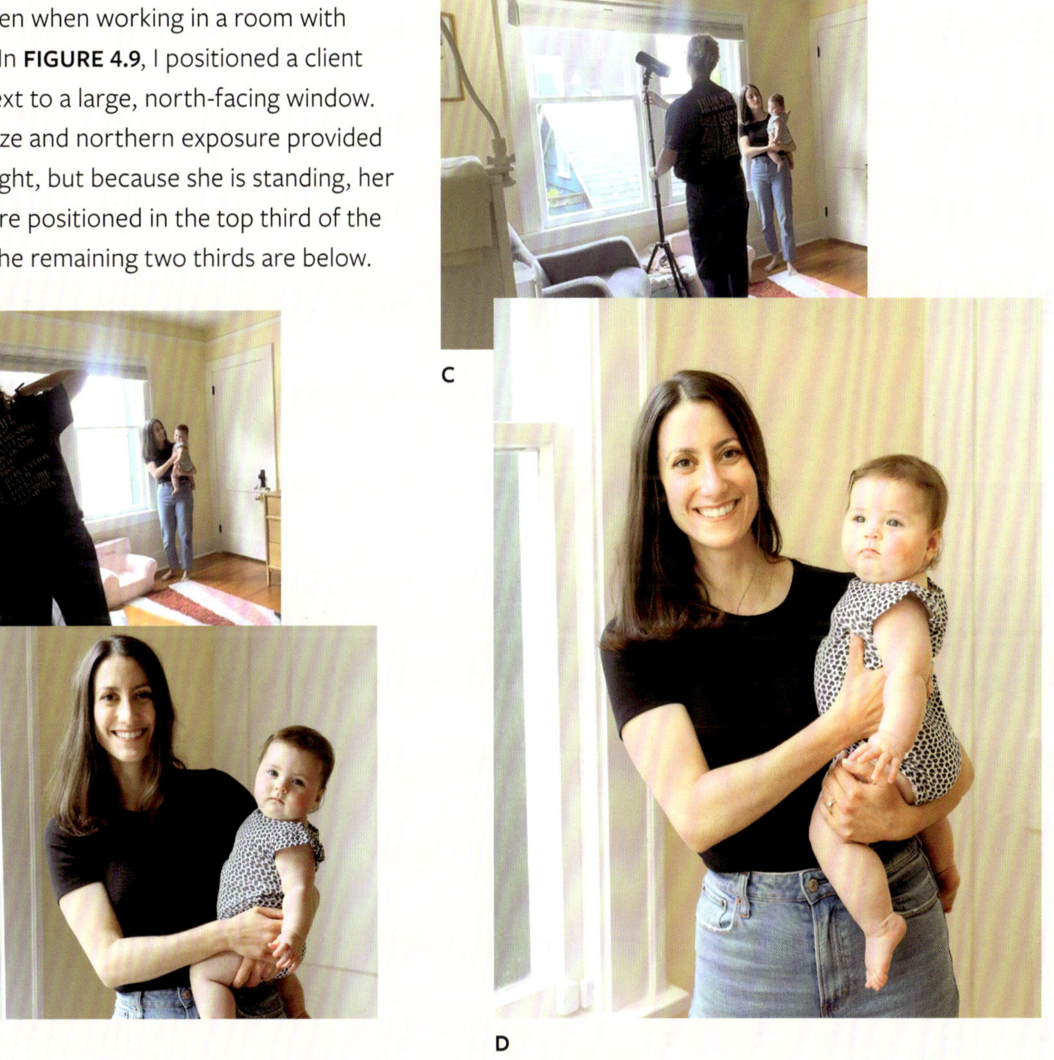

A

B

C

D

**FIGURE 4.9** The subject's head and face are positioned in the top third of the window, while the remaining two thirds of the window are below, resulting in a ghoul light pattern. Figure 4.9C shows how I set up my strobe to bounce light off the top half of the window. This increased the light coming from the top of the window frame, creating a more flattening light pattern on my client.

Shadows that are being cast by you or other people in the room can also present problems that are easily solved with the addition of a strobe or flash. **FIGURE 4.10** was captured in a room with huge, south-facing windows. The room was filled with beautiful natural light that I used for many of the images I created, but the windows were directly in front of the bed I was photographing the baby on. The layout of the room required that I had to stand between the window and the bed to get the photos I wanted of the baby, causing my body to cast a shadow.

To solve this problem, I set my strobe and 45-inch white umbrella with a diffusion panel at a 45-degree angle to the bed, redirecting the light and eliminating the shadow I was casting. The result was beautiful shadow-free photos of the baby.

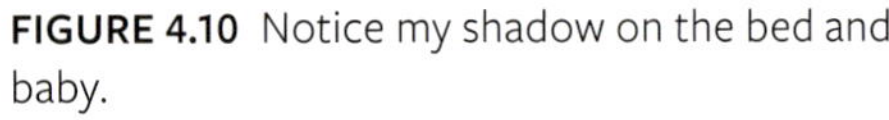

**FIGURE 4.10** Notice my shadow on the bed and baby.

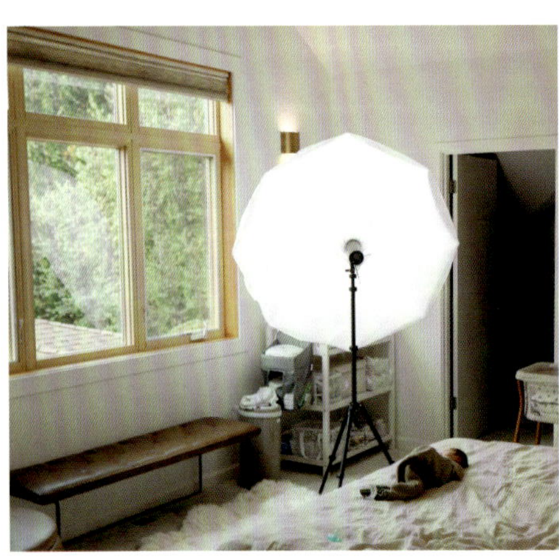

A

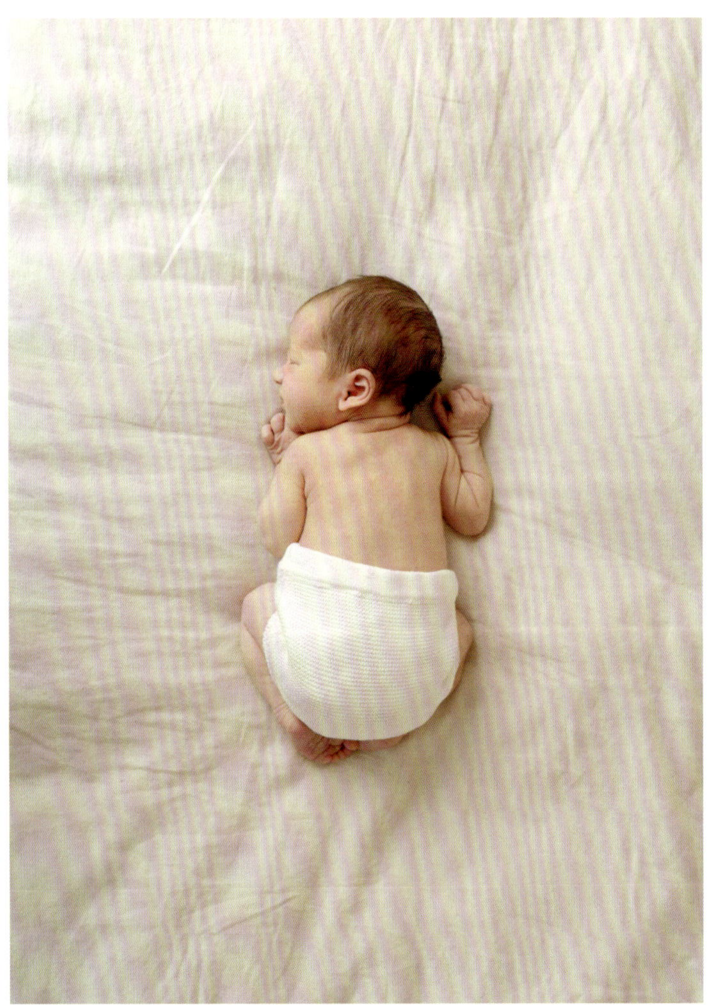

B

**FIGURE 4.11** The strobe and umbrella are set 45 degrees to the baby on the bed. Figure 4.11B shows the final image.

### Light Temperature and Color Cast

The last thing I look for when assessing the light in a room is light temperature and color cast. While these issues *can* be corrected in post-production, I personally don't enjoy spending time fixing problems in editing that could have been addressed at the session. And the final result is always better when you control your lighting in real time.

**FIGURE 4.12** is a great example. This image was taken in a basement nursery with just one window. The light coming through the window created a split light pattern on my clients that I did not like, and the green foliage outside caused a noticeable green color cast. Editing helped (**FIGURE 4.12B**), but it didn't fully eliminate the issues.

To solve both problems, I set up my strobe on a stand and bounced the light off the top corner of the window (**FIGURE 4.13A**). The light from the strobe neutralized the color cast and lightened the deep shadows on my client's face, solving two problems at once! As you can see (**FIGURES 4.13B** and **4.13C**), adding the strobe created a clean, soft light that was much more flattering—even straight out of camera.

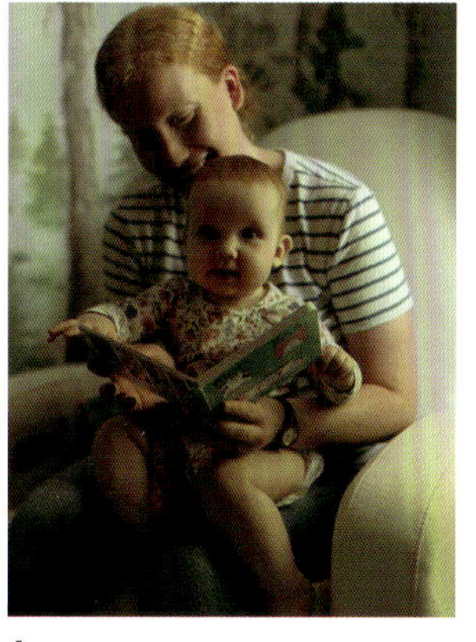

A

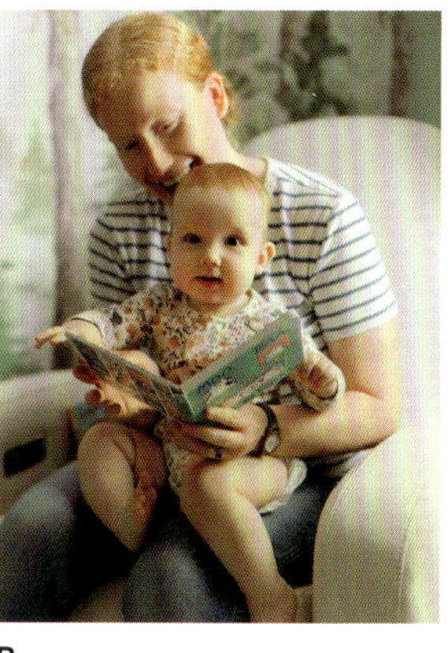

B

**FIGURE 4.12** Figure 4.12A shows the image straight out of camera, and the strong green color cast coming in from the windows. Figure 4.12B shows the edited version.

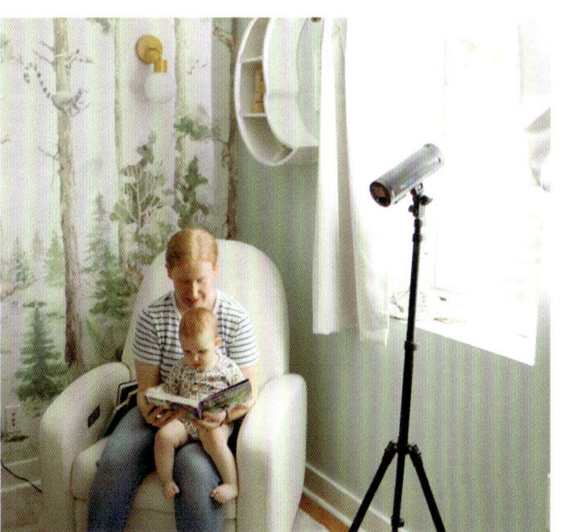

A

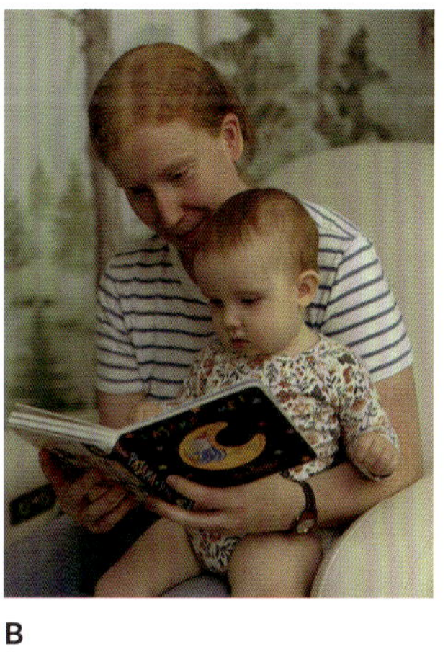

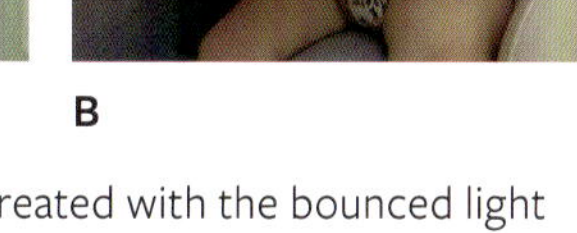

B

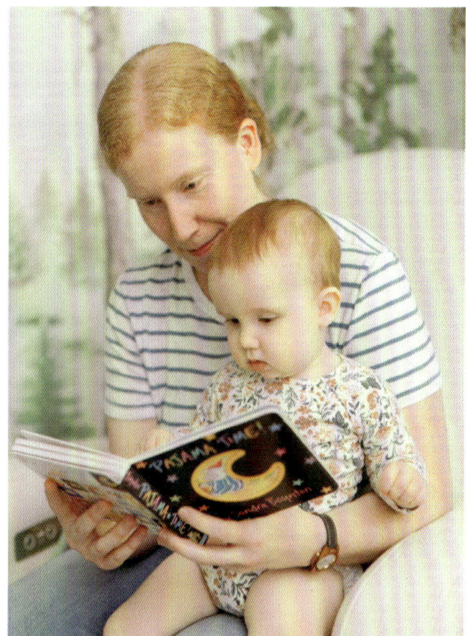

C

**FIGURE 4.13** Figure 4.13B shows the image created with the bounced light straight out of camera. Figure 4.13C shows the edited version.

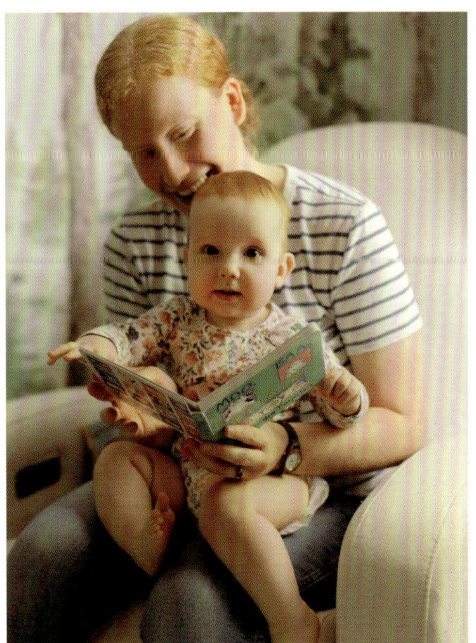

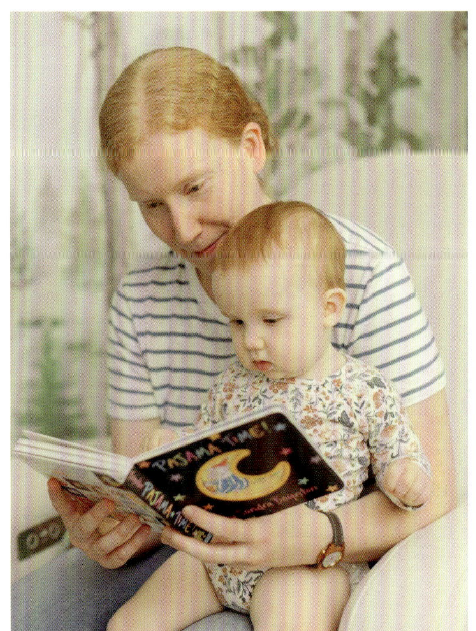


**FIGURE 4.14** These images show the difference between the edited versions of the natural light image and the image created with the strobe.

The side-by-side comparison of the edited versions of these images (**FIGURE 4.14**) shows just how impactful the additional light is. While editing improved the natural light image, the strobe photo required far less correction and yielded a more polished final result.

## How

Once you've assessed your space, it's time to determine *how* to light it. If you have plenty of natural light, the windows in the room are the proper size to result in your preferred light quality and lighting patterns, and there are no unpleasant shadows or wonky color casts, you can use the natural light! But if you have any of the problems I've outlined in this chapter, you'll want to bring in a strobe or a flash. Which light do you use? And how do you set it up and know where to place it?

### Where to Start

When using strobes and flash, my goal is always to create a natural-light look—light that is soft in quality and creates a pleasing lighting pattern. That goal is the same whether I'm working in my studio or in a client's home. But how I achieve it differs depending on the space I am working in.

Because the studio is a blank slate I can set up my light in the same place, creating the same lighting patterns at every session. And I do. In the studio, my light is almost always in the loop light position, and always to my left.

## Why Are the Unedited Pictures so Dark?

**FIGURES 4.12A** and **4.13B** were captured with my Canon R6 Mark II, a digital camera. Digital sensors are very sensitive to light, and photographers can easily overexpose their highlights to the point of no return. To protect against this, you should always meter for your highlights when working with a digital camera.

Metering for the highlights places the brightest part of your image at Zone 5. The rest of the image will shift into the darker zones, resulting in an image that looks darker overall. You can adjust the brightness of your image in post-production, lifting your highlights closer to Zones 7 and 8, without fear of losing information in your highlights.

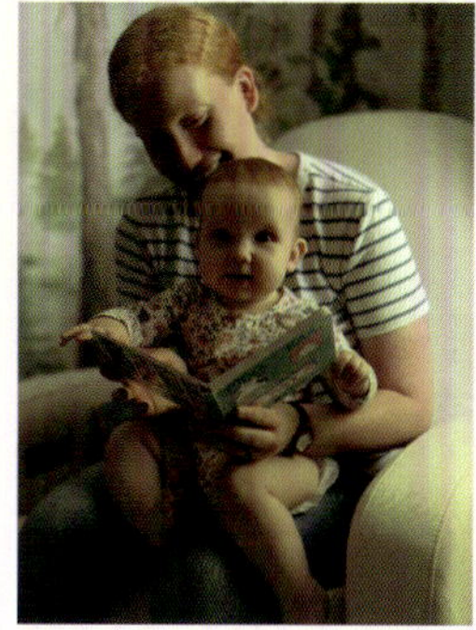

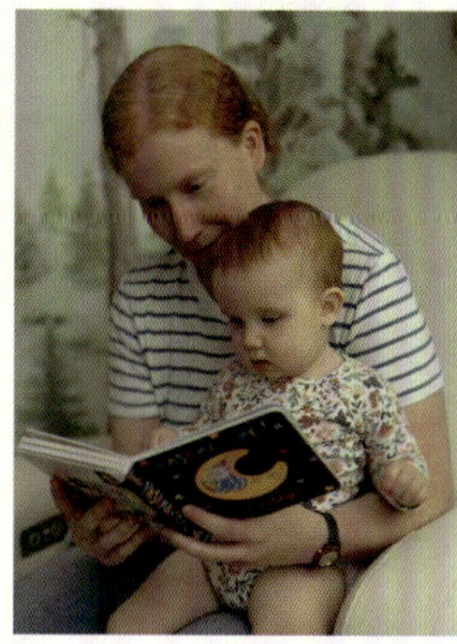

**FIGURES 4.14** These images look dark straight out of camera because I metered for the highlights on both.

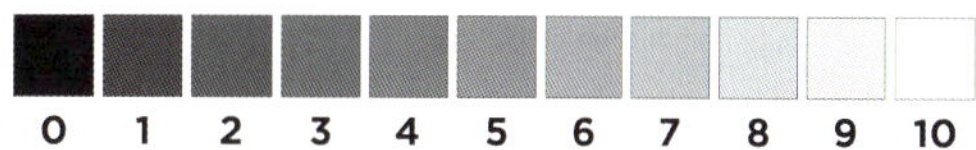


**FIGURE 4.15** The Zone System is made up of eleven zones that represent the gradation of tones between absolute black (Zone 0) and absolute white (Zone 10). Middle gray (Zone 5) is the perfect midpoint between total black and total white.

That is not the case when working on location. As an in-home photographer, my workspace is unique at every session, so my approach to lighting needs to be unique as well. But accepting that each in-home session is going to be "unique" doesn't mean that I go into them without a plan. I learned a long time ago that planning ahead makes my job as a family photographer much easier! So, even though every room I walk into in a client's home is different, I always start in the same place. If the room I'm working in has windows, I start by setting up my lights by the windows.

### Start by the Windows

Setting up my lights by the windows gives me a place to start. I also believe that starting by the windows helps me create light that looks natural in the space where I'm working.

As humans, what we see has an unconscious impact on how we feel. Ghoul lighting is a great example of this: It's commonly used in horror movies to make the viewer feel uneasy. It makes us feel this way because it is not a natural lighting pattern. Since the dawn of time, humans have seen the world lit by the sun. The sun is above us, and we are used to seeing light come from above. So, when we see light come from below, it signals to our brains that something isn't quite right

As photographers, I believe considering the unconscious impact lighting can have on our images and to our clients is important—wespecially when working in peoples' homes. When a person lives in a space, they are used to seeing it a certain way. If they have windows on the east side of their bedroom, for example, they are used to seeing light come from that direction, whether they consciously realize it or not. Setting up my lights on the window side of the room helps me light the space in a way that looks natural to my clients. And I believe it's one of the reasons why my clients are always impressed with how "natural" my lighting looks!

To illustrate this point, see **FIGURE 4.16**. My clients wanted photos of their daughter playing in her crib, but the windows in her room were relatively small, resulting in harder light than I like. There was a building just outside of the windows that was blocking some of the light and creating a blue/green color cast. And the room was dark. I knew I was going to need to add light to this space, and I wanted to create light that looked like an ideal version of the window light they were used to seeing.

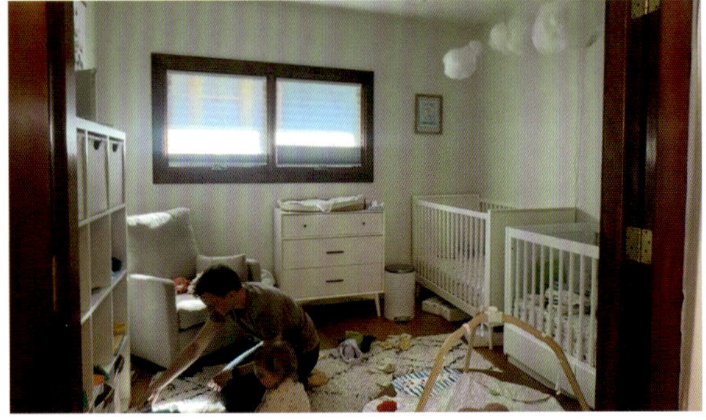

**FIGURE 4.16** There were many lighting problems in this room: It was dark; the windows were relatively small, resulting in harder light than I like; and there was a building just outside of the windows that was creating a color cast.

To achieve that goal, I set my flash on the dresser and pointed it toward the top of the windows, angled slightly toward the window on the left (**FIGURE 4.17**). By placing my flash at a slight angle and bouncing light off the far window, I created a slight loop light pattern that looked like the natural light my clients were used to seeing in this room—only better (**FIGURE 4.18**)!

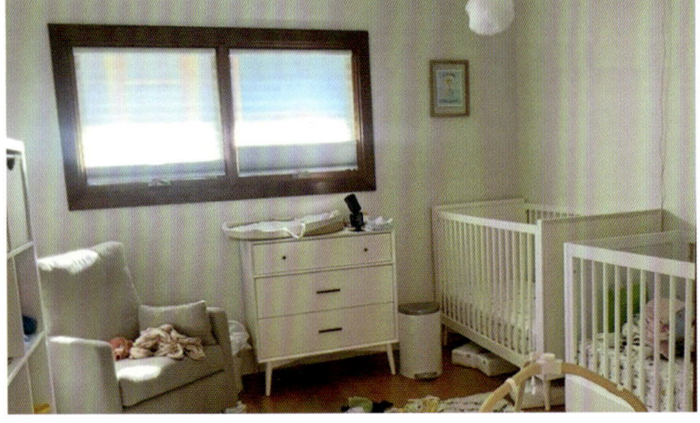

**FIGURE 4.17** To light this room, I set my flash on the dresser and pointed it toward the top of the windows, angled slightly toward the window on the left.

One of the biggest obstacles people face when using strobes and flash on location is learning where to set up their light! My advice is to start by the windows. Take a few images and assess. If the results are not quite what you want, move your light to a new spot and try again. It is okay to experiment!

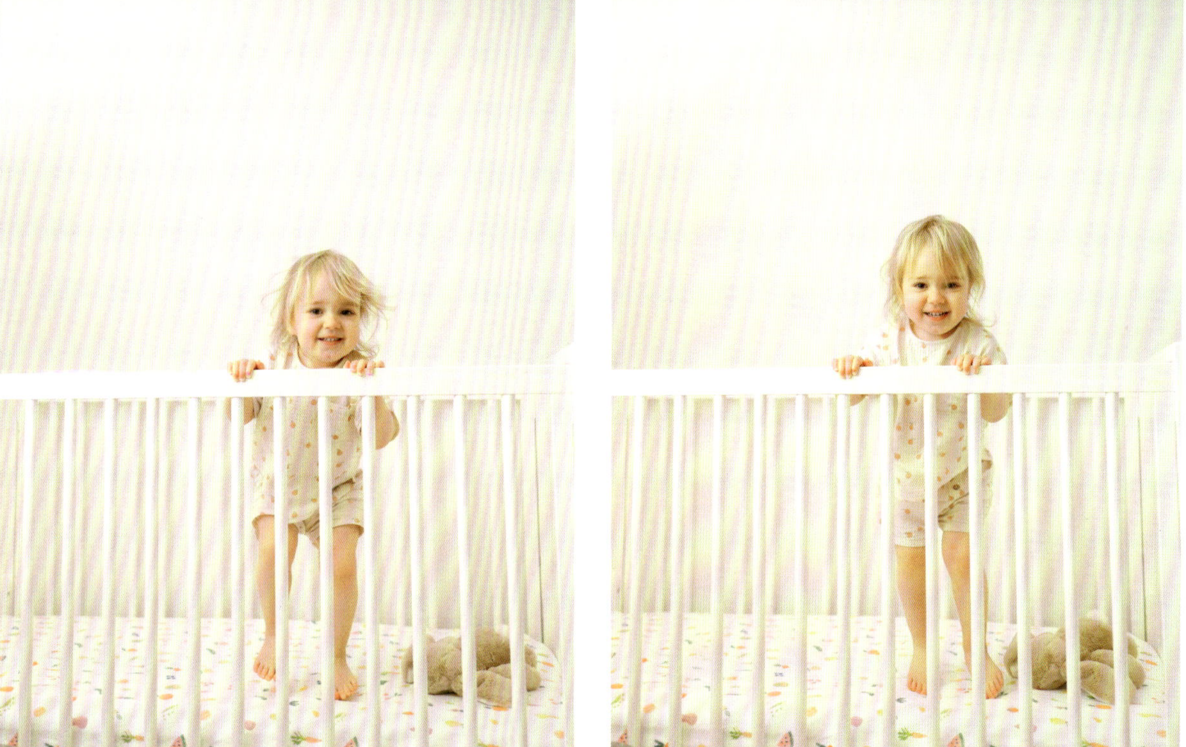

**FIGURE 4.18** These images were captured with just one light, my Westcott FJ80, bounced off the windows in the room.

### When Starting by the Windows Doesn't Work

When it comes to lighting on location, there are no hard rules. Every home—and every room—is different. Starting on the window side is a great baseline because it mimics the kind of light your clients are used to seeing. But if you don't love the results, move your light!

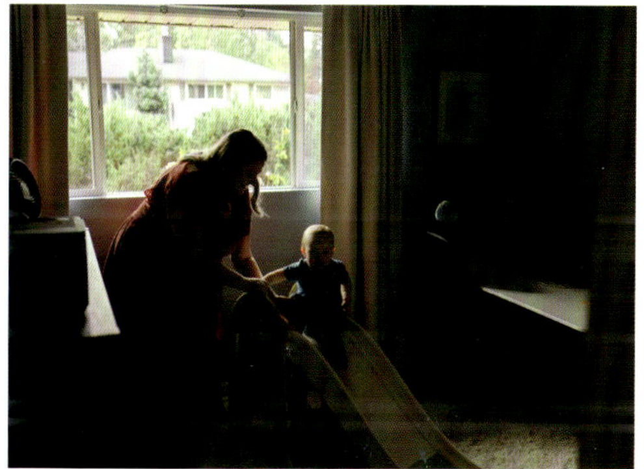

A

**FIGURE 4.19A** was captured in a small home office where my client had set up a slide for her son to play on while she worked. He loved the slide, and we both thought it would be fun to capture some photos of him playing on it.

The room had large, south-facing windows, but the direction of the light relative to the slide created strong backlighting, which cast deep shadows on the toddler's face (**FIGURE 4.19B**).

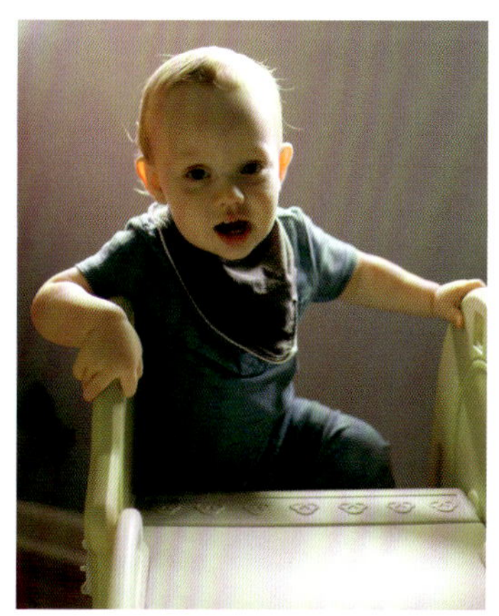

B

**FIGURE 4.19** Large, south-facing windows produced dark shadows.

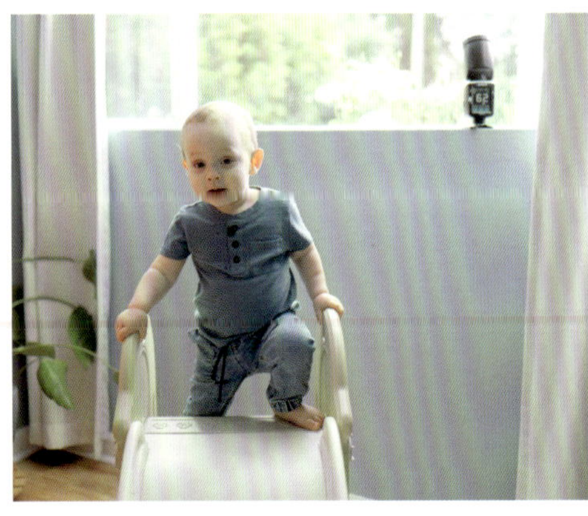

A

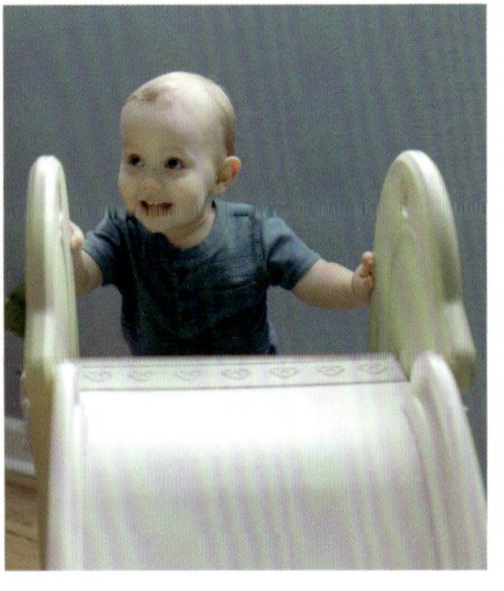

B

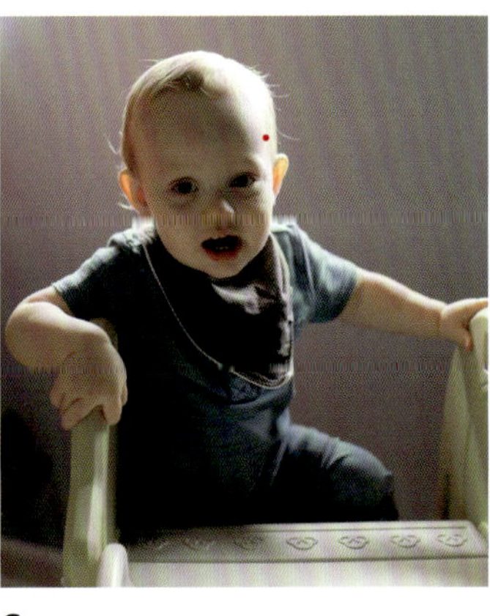

C

**FIGURE 4.20** Figure 4.20A shows how I placed my flash on the windowsill to bounce light into the room. The flash helped lift some of the shadows on my little client's face (Figure 4.20B), but not as much as I wanted—proof that sometimes even a good plan needs adjusting. Figure 4.20B shows the image taken with natural light and Figure 4.20C shows the image taken with the flash bounced off the window—better, but not perfect.

In this scenario, I placed my light on the window side of the room, but the room was tight that I didn't have space to set up a strobe on a stand. Instead, I placed my flash on the windowsill (**FIGURE 4.20A**), aimed it toward the upper corner of the window, and bounced light off the wall and around the room, hoping to fill in the deep shadows.

And it worked. *Sort of.*

The bounced flash helped—it brightened the space and filled in some of the facial shadows (**FIGURE 4.20B**)—but it didn't go quite as far as I needed. **FIGURES 4.20B** and **4.20C** offer a side-by-side comparison between the natural-light image and the one taken with the flash on the windowsill.

Since I still wanted more light on his face, I moved the flash off the windowsill and placed it on the desk across the room, pointing it toward the wall and up toward the ceiling (**FIGURE 4.21A**). This allowed the light to bounce off the top part of the wall and ceiling, then back onto my client—filling the shadows while keeping that pretty backlight glow (**FIGURE 4.21B**).

In **FIGURE 4.22**, you can see the full progression. **FIGURE 4.22A** is the original natural light image. **FIGURE 4.22B** shows the image with flash bounced off the window. **FIGURE 4.22C** shows the final version with flash bounced off the opposite wall.

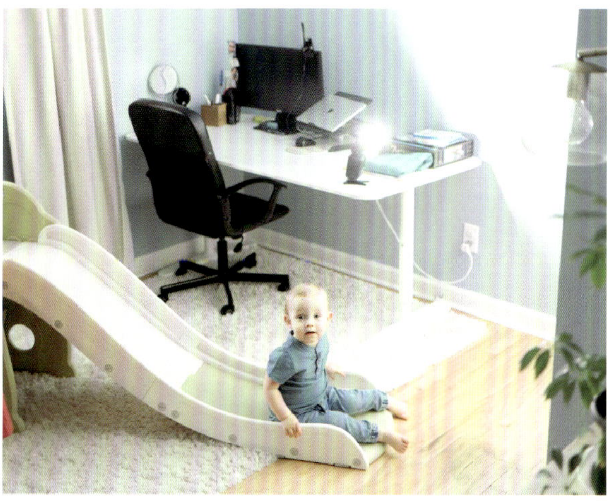

A

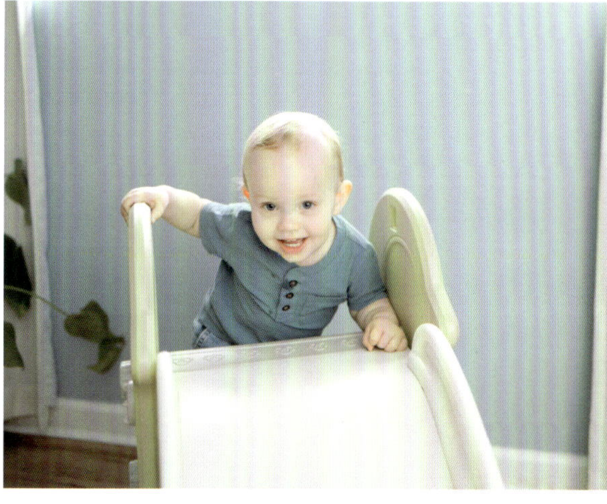

B

**FIGURE 4.21** I moved the flash off of the windowsill and placed it on the desk, facing the wall on the opposite side of the room. This allowed the light to bounce off the wall and back onto my client (Figure 4.21B), filling in the deep shadows while maintaining a slight glow from the backlight.

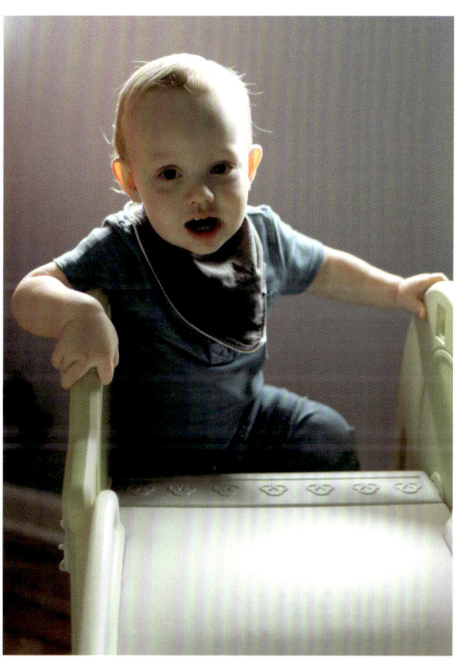

A

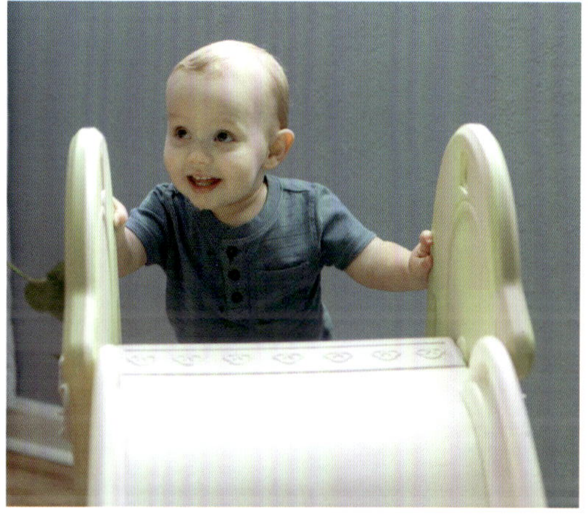

B

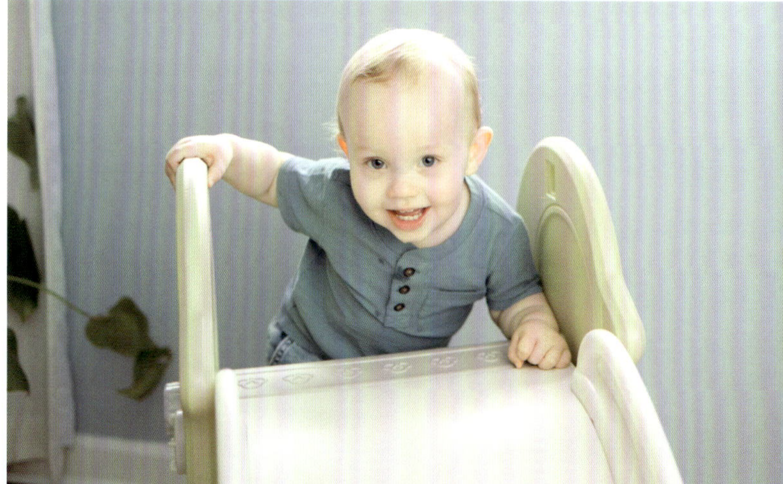

C

**FIGURE 4.22** Figure 4.22A is natural light only. Figure 4.22B includes bounced flash from the window. Figure 4.22C shows flash bounced off the far wall—offering the cleanest, most balanced light on my little client's face.

## A Word on Metering

I'm a big believer in using a handheld light meter, but I also know how crazy working with toddlers can be, and the reality is, you don't always have the luxury of pressing pause on the action when a child is in the middle of a fun activity. When I can, I always try to meter before bringing a child into the scene.

As you can see in **FIGURE 4.23**, I metered the light falling on the crib before having the parents place the child inside. This allowed me to get right to work once she was in position.

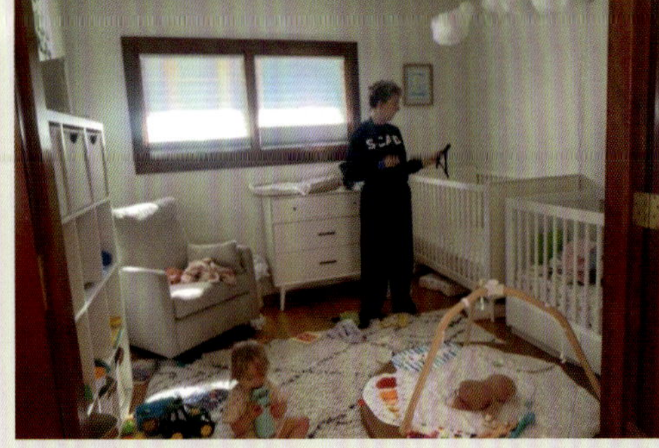

**FIGURE 4.23** I often meter my space before positioning my little clients so I can get right to work once the child is in position.

In the case of the boy on the slide (**FIGURE 4.22**) however, I did not have time to meter. He was moving fast, which meant I had to move fast too! For those photos I used the back of my digital camera as my guide. Not ideal, but sometimes a reality.

# Bouncing Light

Bouncing is my go-to lighting technique in client homes. It's fast, easy, and creates beautiful results. It also doesn't require a modifier—and when using a flash, it doesn't even require a light stand!

Best of all? It's incredibly convenient. You can bounce light off just about anything—TVs, sheets of paper, walls, ceilings, windows—literally any surface. But as always, the key is understanding how light behaves. Here are a few things to remember.

- **Size:** When you bounce light off a surface, that surface becomes your light source. A small bounce surface (like a small window) will create harder light. A large surface (like a wall or ceiling) will create softer light.
- **Distance:** The closer the bounce surface is to your subject, the stronger and softer the resulting light will be. If the wall or ceiling is far away, the light will be dimmer and harder in quality.
- **Color:** The color of your bounce surface will affect the color of your light. Neutral-colored surfaces (white, gray, beige, even light blue) will reflect clean, neutral light. But pigmented surfaces will reflect their color back onto your subject.

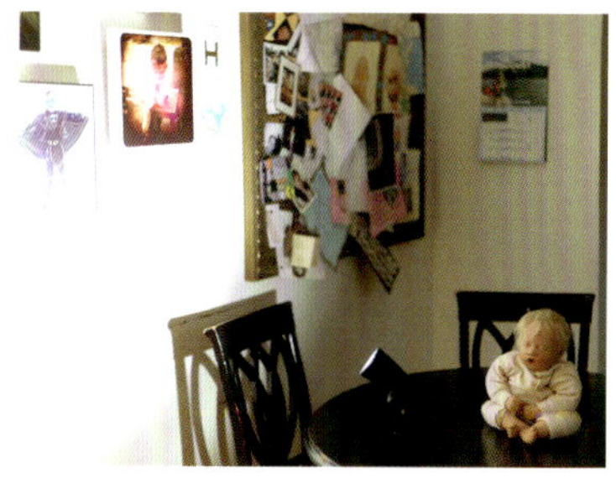
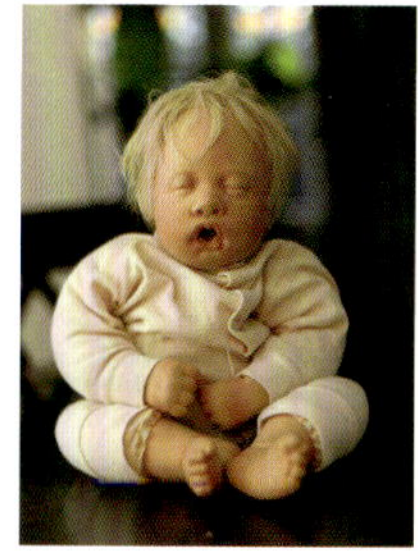

**FIGURE 4.24A** Flash bounced off a white wall. The light is soft and neutral—ideal for clean, natural-looking portraits.

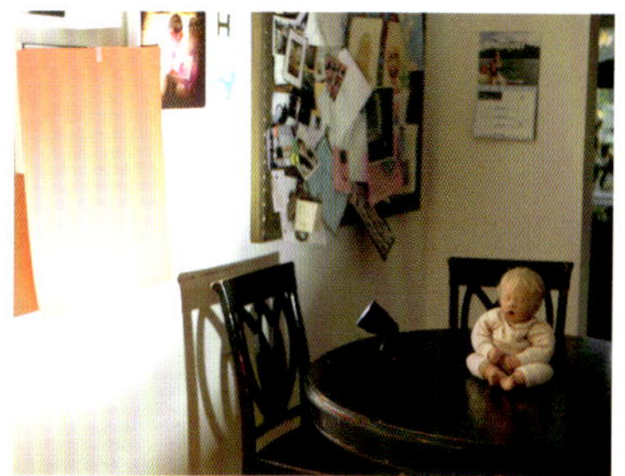
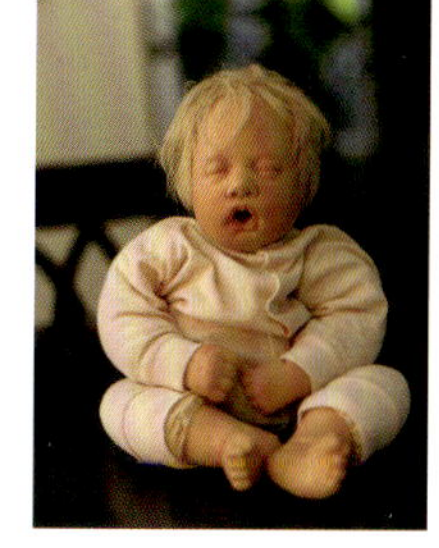

**FIGURE 4.24B** Flash bounced off red construction paper. Notice the red tint that appears on the subject.

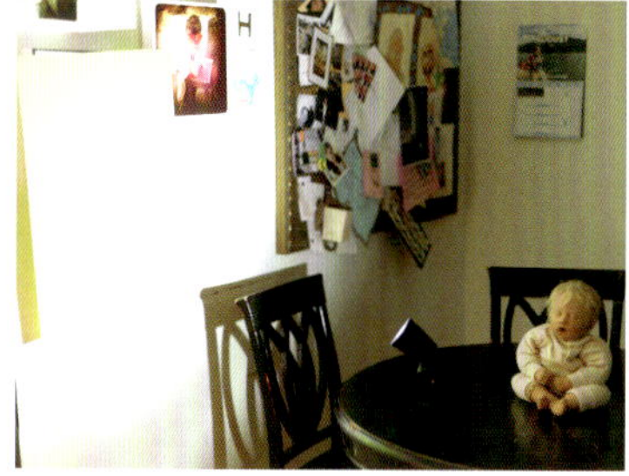
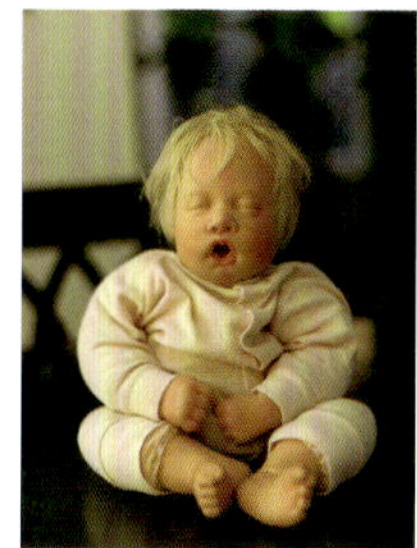

**FIGURE 4.24C** Flash bounced off light green construction paper. A subtle green cast is visible, especially in the highlights

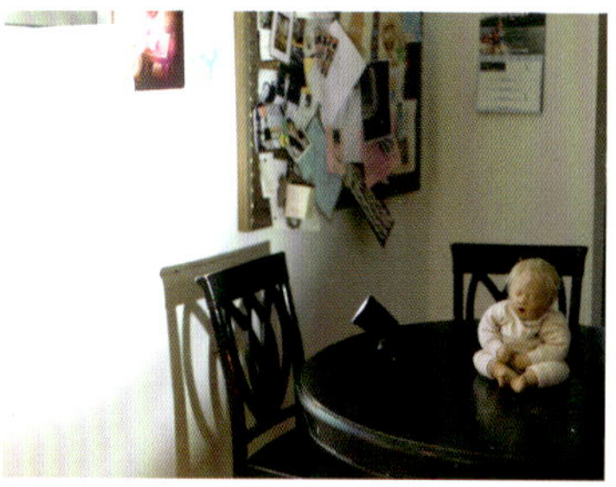
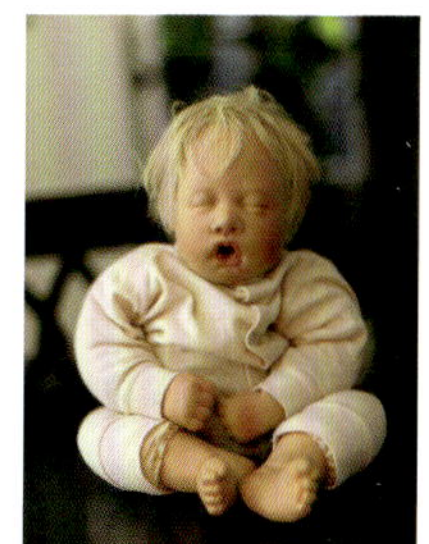

**FIGURE 4.24D** Flash bounced off light blue construction paper. The light takes on a cool tone but is more acceptable than any of the other colors.

Most ceilings are painted white, so bouncing light off them results in a clean, neutral tone. Windows also reflect neutral light well, even if there are trees or buildings outside. That's why ceilings and windows are my preferred bounce surfaces.

Bouncing off walls works great too—just make sure the wall isn't a bold or saturated color. Otherwise, you risk casting that color onto your subject. **FIGURE 4.24** shows this concept in action.

For these images, I posed my doll, Betty, on a table and placed a flash beside her. I first bounced the flash off a plain white wall, then taped different colors of construction paper to the wall and bounced off those. Notice how each surface affected the color of the light.

## How to Bounce Your Light

Bouncing light is a simple yet powerful technique to use when working on location. To bounce your strobe or flash, simply aim it at a nearby surface—preferably a white wall, ceiling, or window. The light will then hit that surface and reflect back, creating a soft, natural-light look.

Remember that the distance between your light and the bounce surface will impact the intensity and spread of light you create. **FIGURE 4.25** shows how pulling the light farther from the bounce surface results in a broader spread of light, but lower intensity, at the subject. This is due to the Inverse Square Law, which you learned about in Chapter 1. Each of the images shown here was taken at f/8, 1/125 sec., ISO 100. The only variable that changed was the distance of the light from the wall.

In **FIGURE 4.25A**, the light was positioned 1 foot from the wall. The result is a bright but narrow spread of light—notice how the beam is concentrated in a small area. In **FIGURE 4.25B**, I moved the light to 3 feet from the wall. At this distance, the light is slightly dimmer, but the spread is wider, illuminating a greater portion of the room. In **FIGURE 4.25C**, I pulled the light back to 6 feet from the wall. As you can see, the brightness decreases even more, but the coverage expands significantly, wrapping light around the space.

When possible, I like to position my light at least 3 feet from the surface I'm bouncing off. This allows the light to spread out more evenly, making it easier to light an entire room with just one source.

Once your light is in place, meter (or use the view on the back of your camera) to determine exposure, then adjust the power of your light as needed.

Remember: When you bounce your light, you're essentially turning the surface you're bouncing off into a light source. Bouncing off a large surface like a wall, ceiling, or large window will create light that fills the room. That's ideal if your style is light and airy, like mine. If your goal is to create darker, moodier images with more shadow detail, you'll want to avoid using this bounce technique and work with modifiers that offer more control.

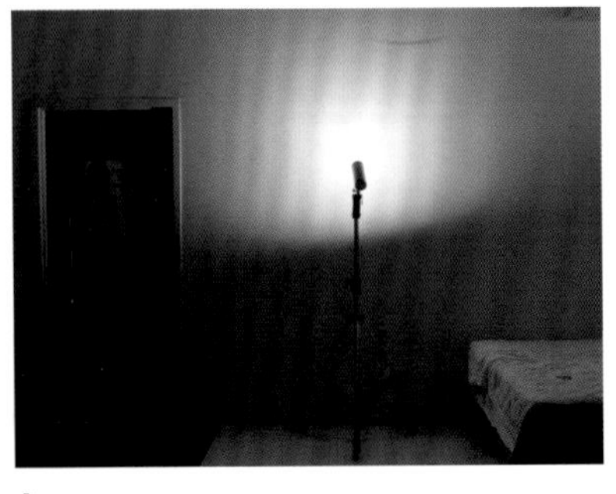

A

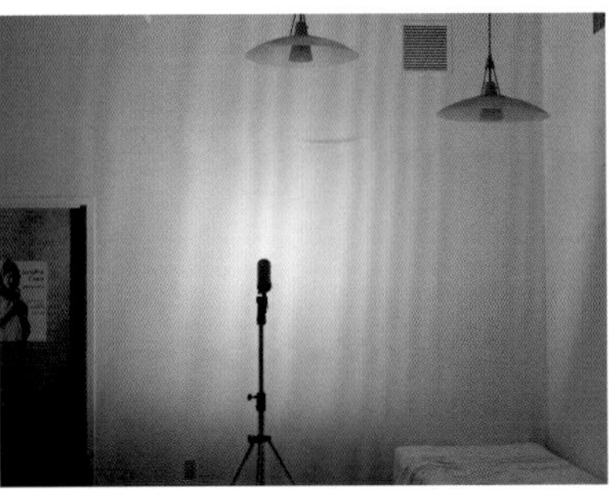

B

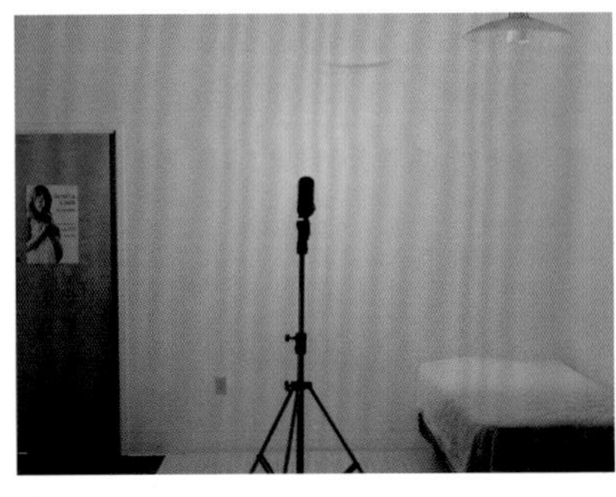

C

**FIGURE 4.25** These images demonstrate how the distance between your light and the bounce surface affects the spread and intensity of light. In Figure 4.25A the strobe is placed 1 foot from the wall. In Figure 4.25B, the strobe is 3 feet from the wall. In Figure 4.25C, the strobe is positioned 6 feet from the wall.

## What About On-Camera Flash?

Whenever I talk about bouncing light, I'm always asked about on-camera flash. Can you mount your flash on your camera and still bounce the light? Absolutely! Light is light, and the same rules apply! That said, I highly recommend taking your flash off-camera when working with families. When your flash is on-camera, your light moves every time you move, so maintaining consistency becomes tricky. Every time you change your position, you have to re-meter and re-adjust all of your settings. That can be hard to do during a fast-paced family session.

Your life will be much easier (and your work will be much better) if you take your flash off camera to bounce. I often use the flash "foot" that comes with my flash when taking my flash off camera (**FIGURE 4.26**) because it allows me to use my flash off camera without having to set up a stand.

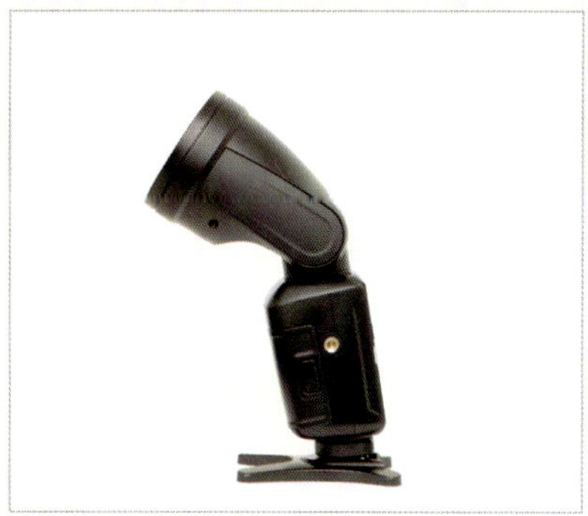

**FIGURE 4.26** A flash mount on its included "foot" allows for easy off-camera use without needing a full light stand. This setup is perfect for on-location sessions when space is tight, or you need to move quickly. It gives you the freedom to bounce light effectively while maintaining consistent placement and exposure.

**Pro Tip:** When lighting people, it's important to create flattering light patterns that fall down the face. Pointing your light up toward the top of the surface you are bouncing off will help ensure you are creating a flattering light pattern that mimics natural light.

### Using Light Modifiers

Even though I bounce my light the majority of the time when working in a client's home, my preferred lighting set up will always be a strobe and a large white modifier with a diffusion panel! Strobes have fast recycle times, model lights, and a great range in power. And using a modifier gives me the ability to shape, soften, and control my light in a way that is not possible when bouncing off a wall, ceiling, or window. So, if I have the space, I will set up a strobe and an umbrella every time.

Light modifiers come in all different shapes and sizes, but when working on location, I like to keep it simple, and work (almost) exclusively with umbrellas. Umbrellas are easy to travel with and easy to set up. My go-to for working on location are the Westcott 45-inch and 60-inch convertible umbrellas. These are great because they come with a white interior and a removable black outer

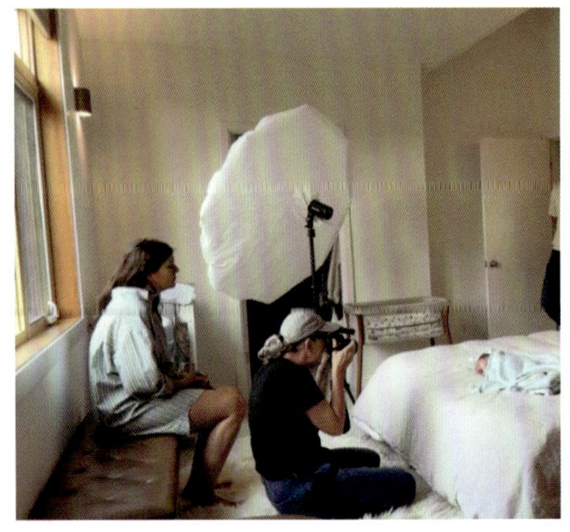

**FIGURE 4.27** Even though bouncing light is convenient, I love the control I get from using strobes on a stand with a modifier.

panel. I use the Westcott 53-inch diffusion panel on both umbrellas. **FIGURE 4.27** shows the Westcott 45-inch convertible umbrella with the black backing removed, and the 53-inch diffusion panel on the front.

### Black, White, or Bounce Light? What's the Difference?

Lighting techniques and modifiers have a huge impact on the final look of your images. The images in **FIGURE 4.28**, for example, were all captured just moments apart in the room shown in **FIGURE 4.29**, but with slightly different setups. **FIGURE 4.28A** was captured with natural light. **FIGURE 4.28B** was captured with a strobe, a 45-inch black umbrella, and a one-stop diffusion panel. **FIGURE 4.28C** was captured with

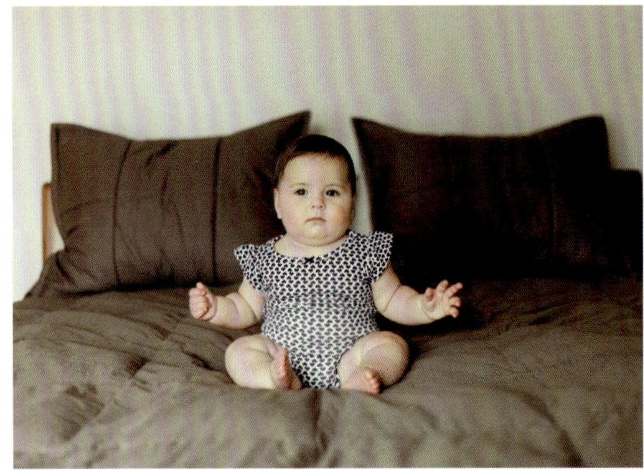

A

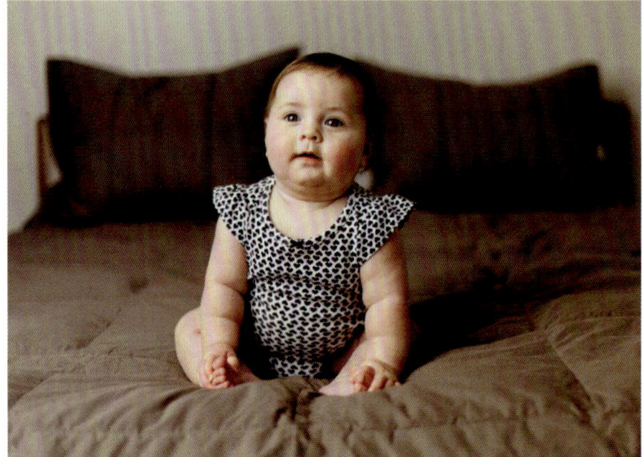

B

C

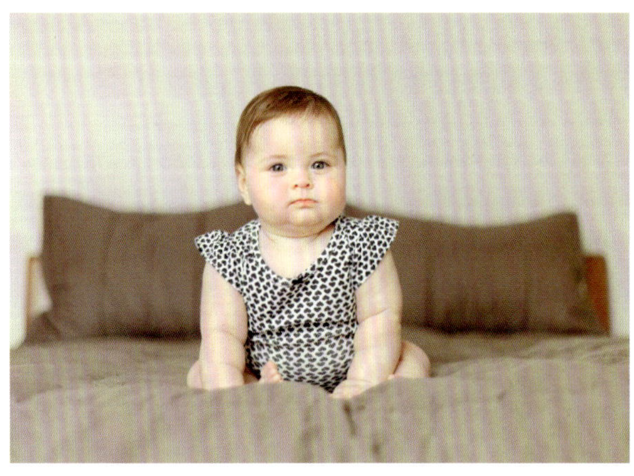

D

**FIGURE 4.28** The images above were captured with the following: **A)** natural light; **B)** 45-inch black umbrella and a one-stop diffusion panel placed 45 degrees to my subject; **C)** 45-inch all white umbrella and a one-stop diffusion panel placed 45 degrees to my subject; **D)** light from a strobe that was bounced off the window.

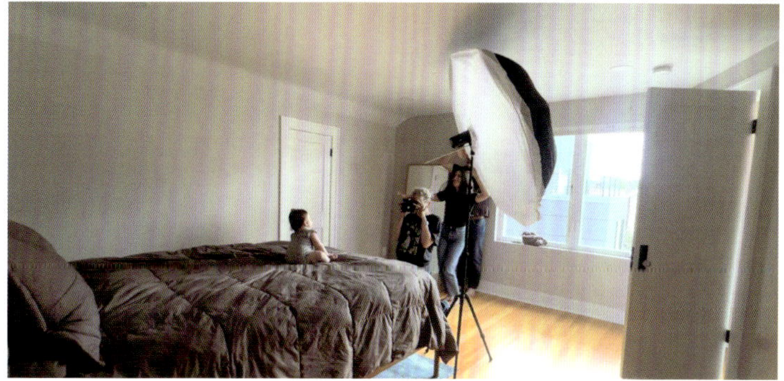

**FIGURE 4.29** In the natural-light image (Figure 4.28A), the window light was reflecting off the floor, causing a slight uplighting effect on the baby. The light was also uneven, and it introduced a greenish color cast—notice the darker shadows on the right side of the wall behind the baby. Figure 4.28D shows what happened when I bounced my strobe off the window. The entire room filled with clean, neutral light. It removed the color cast and evened out the shadows on the wall, resulting in soft, flat light on the baby—one of my favorite looks.

a 45-inch all white umbrella and a one-stop diffusion panel. This gave me a very similar look to bouncing light off the window (**FIGURE 4.28D**), but the umbrella gave me the ability to control the direction of my light more and allowed me to create a loop light pattern.

This series illustrates how subtle changes in your modifiers and lighting techniques can completely transform the look and feel of your photos. Try it yourself—use a posing doll or a willing family member, and photograph them with natural light, bounced light, and strobes with different umbrellas. Then compare the results. And pay close attention, you may discover the look that resonates most with your style!

**Pro Tip:** While bouncing light is quick and convenient, don't hesitate to set up a modifier and stand on location. It's just like working in the studio: place your light for the pattern you want, meter your exposure, adjust your power—and you're good to go. It's fast, easy, and totally worth the effort.

## Don't Be Afraid to Experiment

Using artificial light in a client's home can feel intimidating at first—but once you get comfortable with it, it becomes a superpower. Many photographers feel anxious about using flash or strobes in unfamiliar spaces because they're afraid of making a mistake. So let me say this clearly: you might make a mistake—and that's okay! If your initial lighting setup doesn't give you the look you were going for, change it. That's how we learn.

It's okay to be wrong at first. It's okay to try something and have it not work. It's okay to adjust your light—again and again—until you get it right. The truth is, changing your light's position takes very little time, and your clients will likely never notice you're making adjustments. More importantly, you'll learn so much by experimenting. That's how you grow. So don't be afraid to play with your setup—it's worth it!

## Dark and Moody?

A lot of the examples you are seeing in this section show work that is on the light and airy side, because that is the kind of light that I like and the kind of work I most often create. You can, however, easily use strobes and flash on location to create dark and moody images as well. To create dark and moody photos, consider what you know about light and light modifiers. Small light source produce harder the light, and modifiers will give you more control over your light then bouncing will. Modifiers with black backings will produce deeper shadows than all white modifiers will.

Now, put that all together! Dark and moody images tend to have more contrast and deeper shadows than light and airy photos, so you'll want to work with relatively small modifiers with black backings! **FIGURE 4.30A** is a natural light photo taken in a very bright room. To create a dark and moody look in this environment, I used a relatively small modifier (the small Westcott Rapid Box Switch Octa) on my strobe (**FIGURE 4.30B**). The small light source focused the light, keeping it from hitting and reflecting off the walls in the room. It also created light with more contrast, resulting in the dark and moody look I was going for (**FIGURES 4.30C** and **4.30D**).

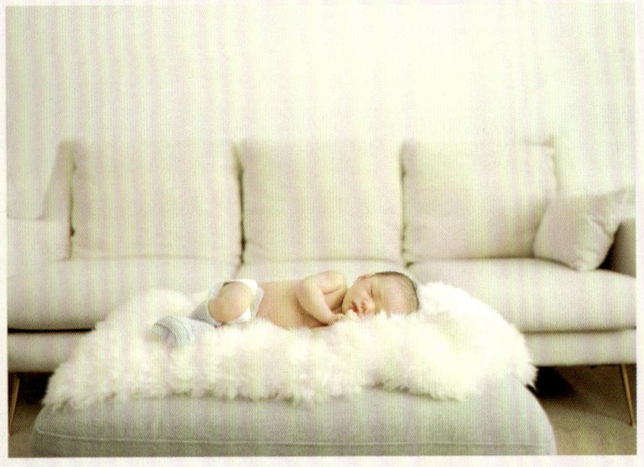

A

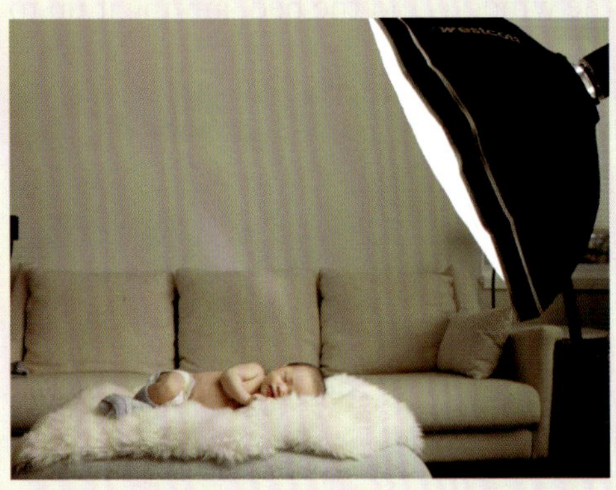

B

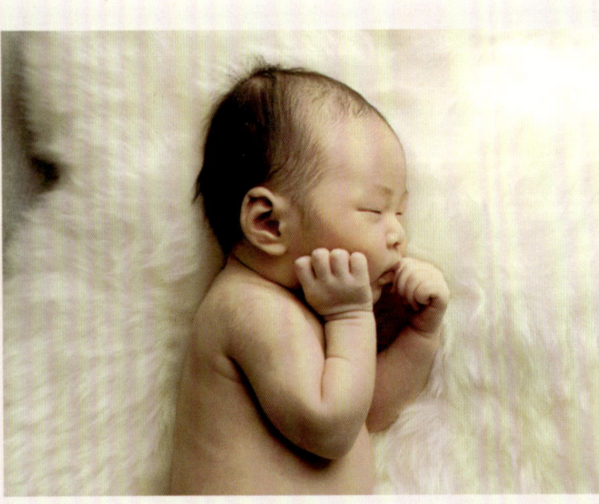

C

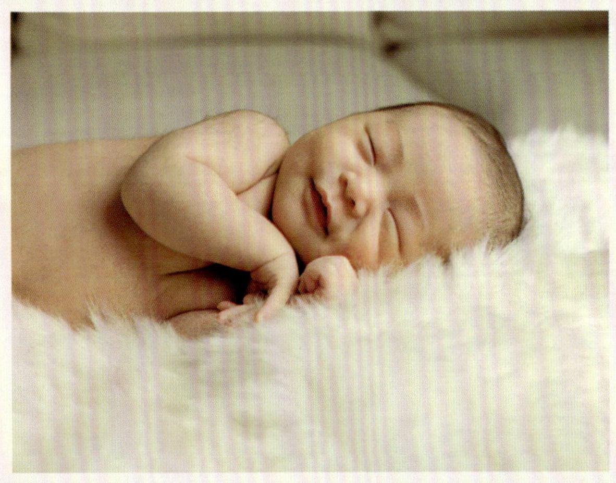

D

**FIGURE 4.30** Figure 4.30A shows how bright the natural light in the room was. To create more contrast and darker images, I used a relatively small modifier (Figure 4.30B) and was very happy with the results (Figures 4.30C and 4.30D).

## A Real-World Example

For this session (**FIGURES 4.31–4.34**), I was photographing a family of four in a small primary bedroom. The room had a large, north-facing window, but the light it produced was too dark for the look I wanted, and it created uneven split light.

There wasn't enough space for a full strobe setup with a stand and modifier, so instead I placed a flash on the dresser in the northwest corner of the room, facing upward to bounce light off the ceiling (**FIGURE 4.31A**). That created a beautiful, soft loop light pattern that filled the room evenly, and I immediately loved the results (**FIGURE 4.31B**).

The lighting looked great with this set up, but I decided to experiment further. Next, I placed the flash on the floor between the window and the bed, aiming it up to bounce off the window. My plan was to recreate the light coming from those windows and brighten up the room, but the space was too narrow, and the bounce didn't work—it produced harsh, uneven shadows and just wasn't pretty (**FIGURE 4.32**).

When I saw that position wasn't resulting in the light I wanted to create, I moved the flash again—this time to the

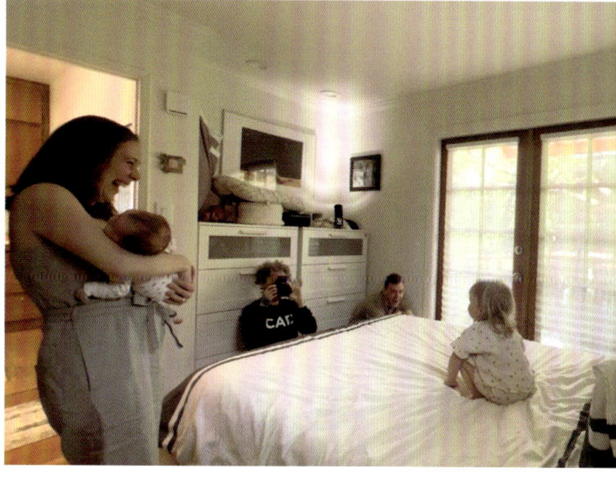

A

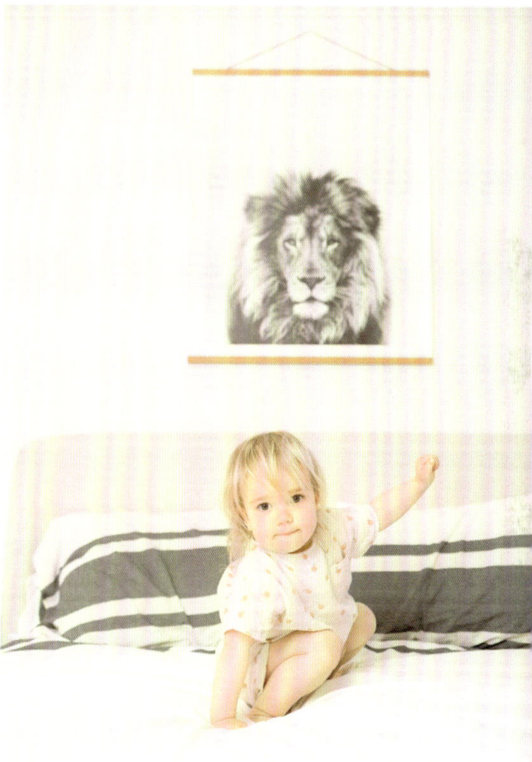

B

**FIGURE 4.31** Above: You can see the flash on the dresser behind me in Figure 4.31A. In Figure 4.31B, you can see the results of that lighting set up.

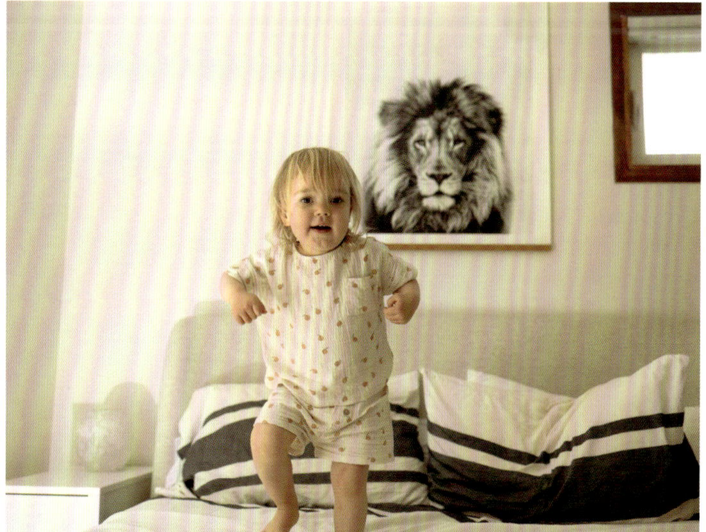

**FIGURE 4.32** Left: As you can see from this image, placing the flash on the floor and bouncing it off the windows didn't work.

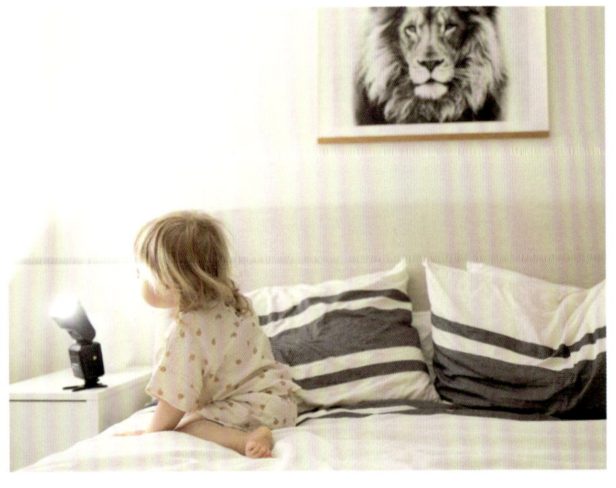

A

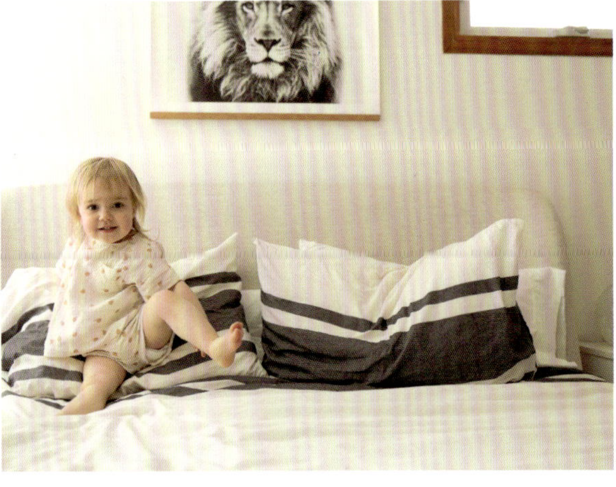

B

**FIGURE 4.33** This was my third attempt at light placement, and I didn't like it either.

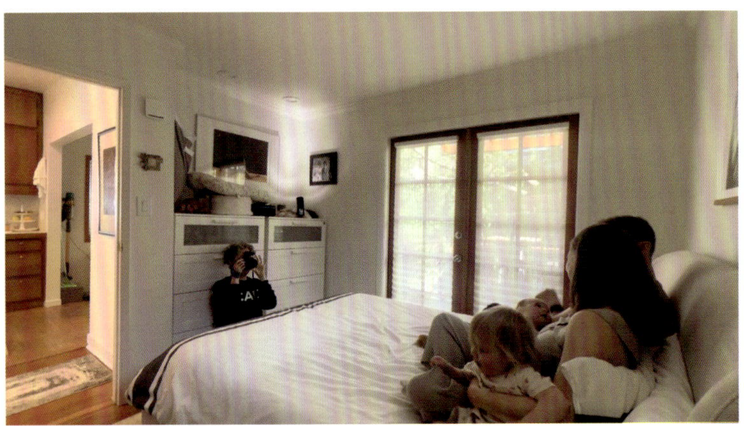

**FIGURE 4.34A** Figure 4.34A shows how I moved the flash back to its original spot on the dresser and finished the family photos on the bed (Figure 4.34B, next page).

nightstand, pointing it toward the top of the window, hoping to light the entire room (**FIGURE 4.33A**). Unfortunately, this setup didn't work either. The resulting light was similar to the natural light that the window was producing, and again, I didn't like the result (**FIGURE 4.33B**).

I finally gave up on the experiments and moved the flash back to the original spot on the dresser, bouncing it off the ceiling like I did at the beginning (**FIGURE 4.34A**). The soft, even light looked great, so I stuck with that setup and finished the session with a family photo (**FIGURE 4.34B**). Experimenting with light placement took just a few minutes, but it gave me confidence that I was photographing the family in the best possible way. And that's what matters.

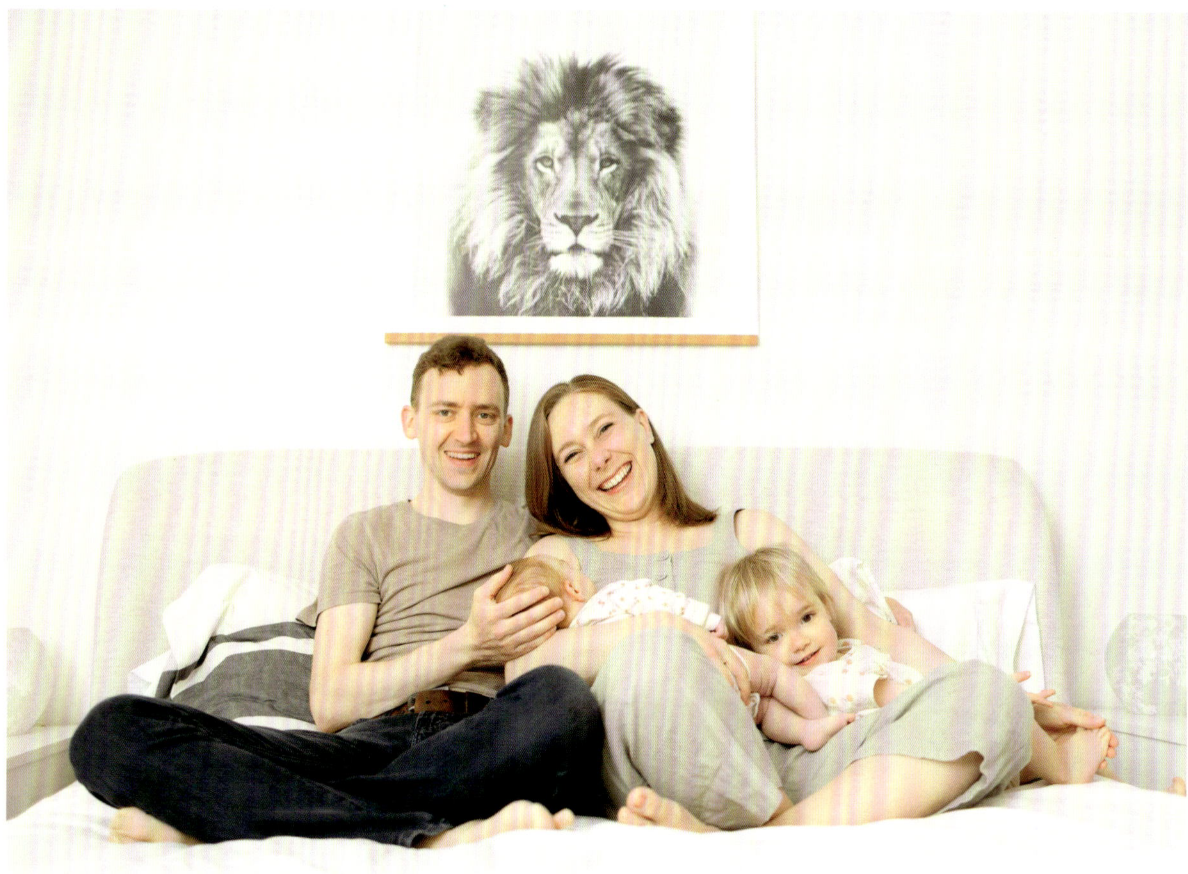

FIGURE 4.34B

## Next Steps

Next steps? Practice!

Start by lighting every room in your house using artificial light, even if you are only photographing a houseplant. Set up a strobe and modifier. Bounce your flash off the window, the ceiling, and the walls. Notice what works and what doesn't. Practice assessing the light of every room you walk into. Intentionally create your desired light quality and your favorite lighting patterns. When you start to feel confident, offer to photograph friends and family. And then, when you feel ready, start bringing your lights with you to client sessions.

It will feel awkward and clumsy at first, but the more you do it, the easier it gets! And *please*, share your results with me! You can tag me on Instagram (@sandracoan) or use #SCfamilyphotography when posting your images. I want to cheer you on!

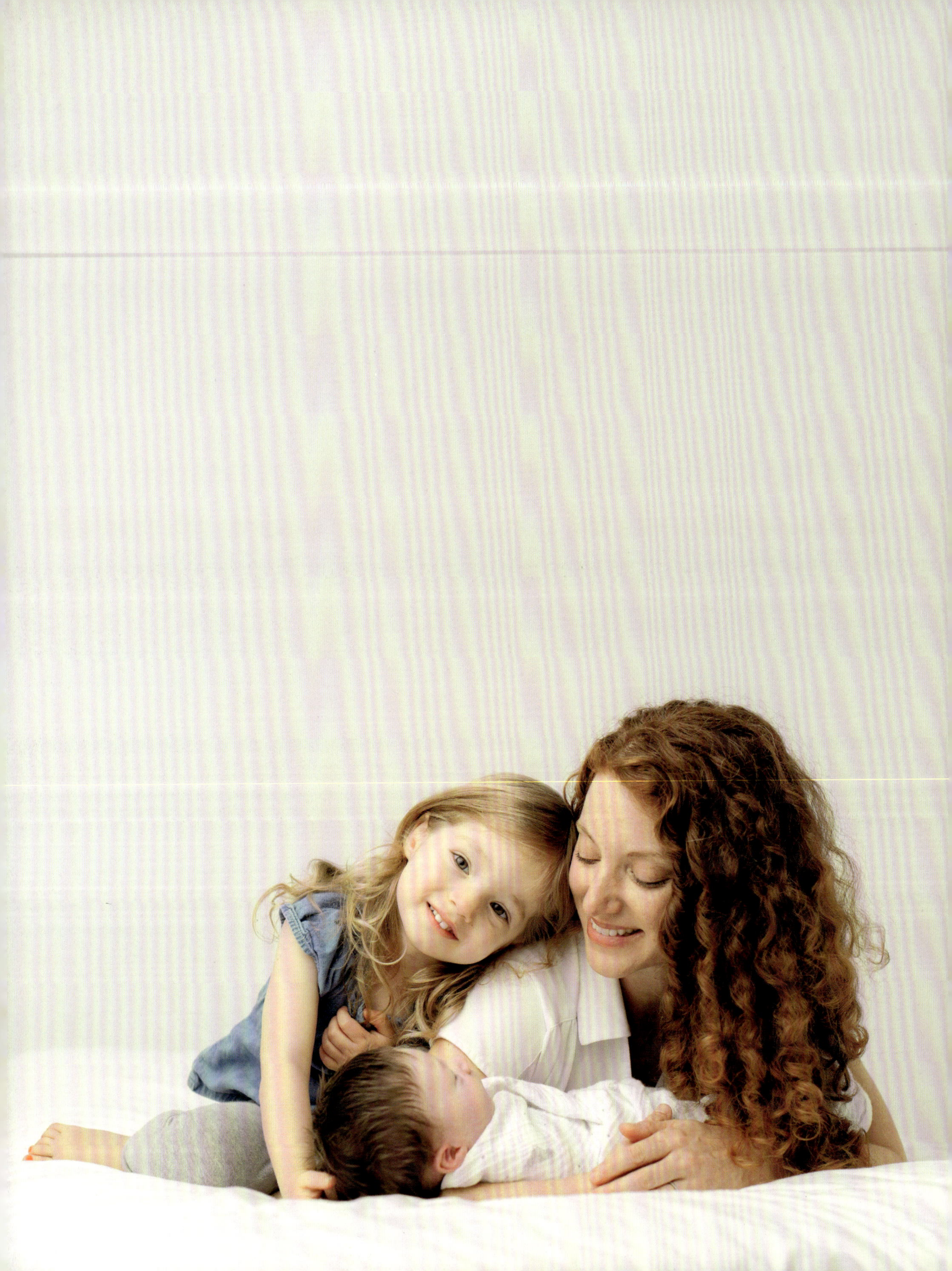

# Posing

Over the years, *posing* has become something of a dirty word among family photographers. Too many people associate posing with stiff, outdated portraits—the kind you'd find in a '90s mall studio. Think classic *Awkward Family Photo*. And nobody wants that.

But here's the truth: knowing how to pose your subjects is an essential skill for any family photographer, whether you're working in a studio, a client's home, or a local park. Yes, traditional studio photographers need to know how to pose. But so do "lifestyle" and "candid" photographers. Posing isn't the opposite of natural—it creates the space for authentic interactions to occur.

When you know how to pose people, you communicate confidence and authority. You show your clients that you know what you're doing—and that helps them relax. A relaxed session creates better photos, happier clients, and rave reviews. But just as importantly, it gives *you* peace of mind. When you have a posing plan, every session becomes more efficient. You know what you're going for, you know how to create it, and you can move quickly—an absolute must when working with kids and busy families. A solid posing flow gives you structure and direction, which creates ease—for you *and* your clients.

Posing also plays a key role in your brand. When paired with consistent lighting, it helps you create a polished portfolio and a signature style—which is good for your art, your reputation, and your bottom line.

## My Approach to Posing

To me, great portraiture tells us something about the person—or people—in front of the camera. It offers insight into a life, freezes a moment, and creates something lasting. Whether I'm photographing a newborn, a mother-to-be, or an entire family, that's always my goal.

I also believe every family photo has the potential to become an heirloom—something framed, displayed, and handed down for generations. So, I approach each session with timelessness in mind. I steer clear of trends and instead favor posing that feels natural—especially in my newborn work. While elaborate posing, intricate wraps, and prop-heavy setups are popular in newborn photography right now, they're not part of my style. I prefer a baby-led approach—posing newborns in ways that feel organic and comfortable to *them*. That's the style I'll be sharing with you throughout this book.

You will not find poses like "Froggie" or "Taco" in these pages. Those require advanced training and are typically created with Photoshop composites. My goal here is to teach you how to work simply and safely, creating beautiful, natural portraits in any environment.

Many photographers worry that using a consistent set of go-to poses will limit creativity, but I have found the opposite to be true. When you have a reliable posing flow, you're not stuck wondering what to do next. Instead, you're free to be present, connect with your subjects, and create truly meaningful work.

## What You'll Learn

In this section, you'll learn what posing really is—and what it isn't—specific to the genre of family photography. You'll explore how body language plays into your images and how to lead your clients into poses that feel relaxed and natural. I'll teach you how to craft both candid-feeling moments *and* classic, formal portraits. We'll talk about composition, visual interest, and how to use simple tools to create strong, emotive images.

I'll also walk you through the exact poses I use when working with maternity, newborn, and family clients. And finally, I'll show you how to create a posing system of your own—one that gives you confidence, clarity, and creative freedom.

## Patience and Practice

If you're new to posing, it might feel a little awkward at first. That's normal. Like anything else, it takes practice. So be patient with yourself. The more you do it, the more natural it will feel—and the more confident you'll become.

You've got this.

Let's get started.

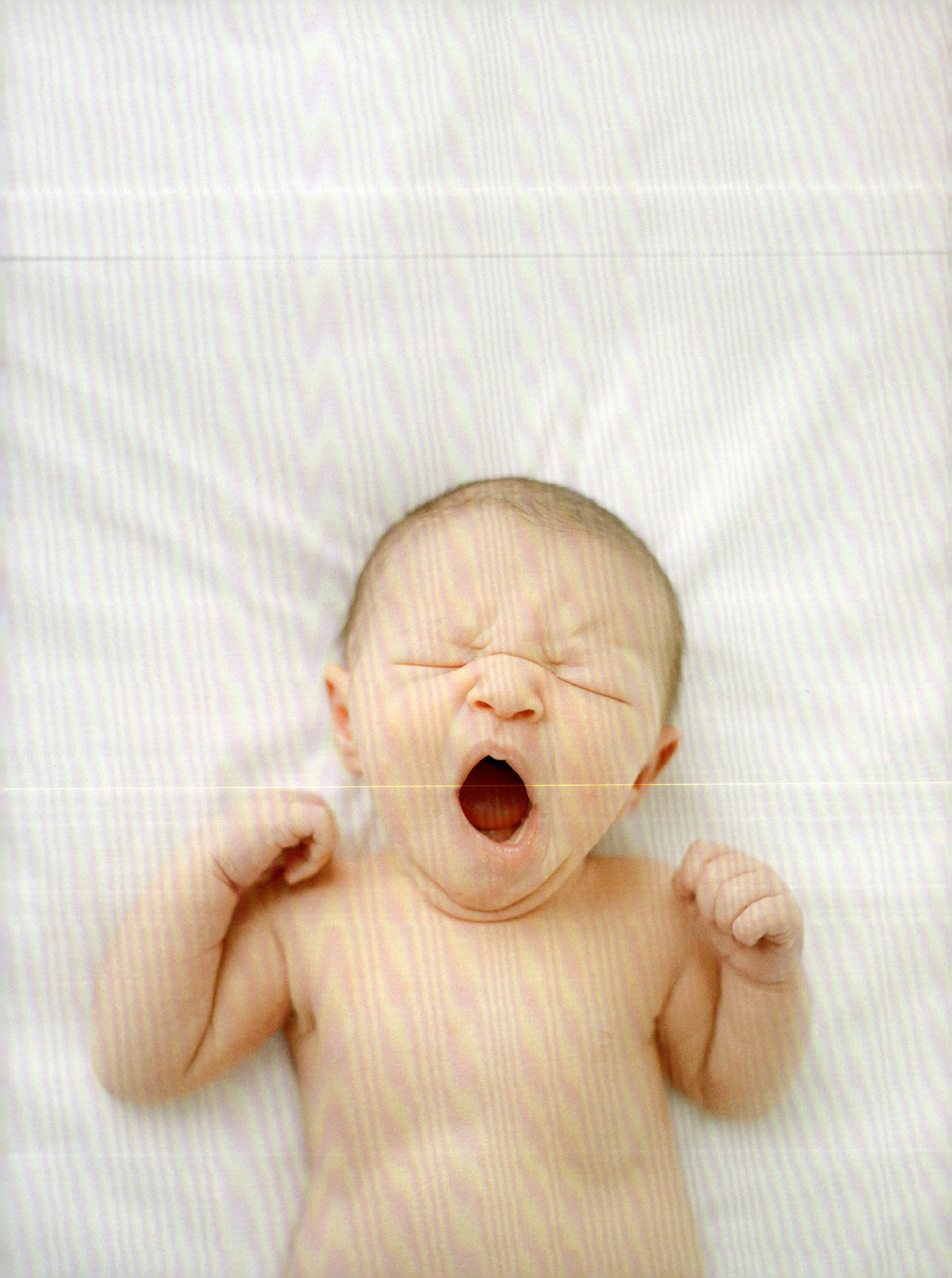

CHAPTER

# 5

# Posing Fundamentals

I started my photography career in the 1990s, when "photo-journalistic" family photography was all the rage! *Nobody* wanted "posed" pictures, including me. I wanted to create casual, candid photos that showed connection and "authenticity." I thought the way to do that was just to simply be a fly on the wall, observing and capturing the beautiful moments that would naturally happen when photographing families.

I'd show up to my sessions with my camera in hand, but no actual plan. I expected the families I was photographing to just know what to do. I'd tell them to "be themselves" and "act natural," but I didn't know how to help them do that. So, everyone felt stressed and self-conscious. The sessions were awkward, and the photos were not very good.

Fast forward to today. I still love candid photos, but now I know that part of my job as a photographer is to work with my clients to make those candid-looking moments happen. I'm the photographer, yes, but as the photographer, I'm also the director. As the director, it's my responsibility to create the vision for the session and to make sure that vision is realized. I'm responsible for choosing the location and deciding how to light the scene, and it's also up to me to direct the actors! Telling the people I'm working with where to stand, where to look, and how to position their bodies is an essential part of the job. Just like actors on a movie set, your clients will bring their personalities to the scene but your job as the director is to guide them and to bring out their best. Posing will help you do that.

## What Posing Is and Isn't, Specific to Family Photography

The first step to learning how to successfully pose families is having a clear understanding of the posing that's specific to our genre of photography. "Posing" is defined as "to move into and stay in a particular position in order to be photographed or painted." That makes me think of a mannequin that, once positioned, doesn't move. While that may work in some areas of photography, it's not a realistic expectation to have when photographing babies, kids, and families. A toddler for example, is not going to hold their arm or move their head just so and then hold it still while you take a photo. If only!

For family photographers, "posing" is less about positioning your clients in specific ways and more about helping them relax into positions that are flattering and create a sense of connection.

### Crafting Connection

The goals of an image differ depending on the genre of photography you are working in. Fashion photographers, for example, need to know how to direct the models they work with into poses that highlight the clothes they are wearing or the product they are promoting. In that line of work, perfection is the goal, and so fashion photographers need posing strategies that help achieve that.

In family photography, the job is to create images that showcase relationships, love, and joy. It's the small details—how a person holds their hands, where they look, and how they position their head and bodies—that have the biggest impact on the final look and feel of an image. For us, posing is more about creating connection than it is about achieving perfection.

### Body Language Matters

Because creating connection is so important to the work we do, paying close attention to your clients' body language is a must. As photographers, we have the unique challenge of conveying emotion without the use of words. We create still images after all, so the body language of our clients is 100% responsible for what is communicated in our photos. When that body language shows love and joy, we feel those emotions when we look at the image. And it's wonderful. But other emotions like stress and anxiety can also be captured and communicated, and we don't want people feeling those things when they look at their family photos.

I am not a scientist, nor do I claim to be an expert on the subtleties of body language. But I have been a portrait photographer since 1999, working specifically with babies, children, and families, and that experience has given me a lot of insight. I've become very good at detecting when a client feels nervous or stressed, and I've learned how to direct my clients into positions that make them look comfortable, connected, and engaged—even if they aren't feeling that way. In this section, I'll share that insight with you and highlight small adjustments you can make when photographing individuals, newborns, children, and families to create stronger, more polished images that look great and feel good.

## Hands

It's often said that the eyes are the gateway to the soul, but I personally believe that in portraiture, the true gateway is the hands. Hands can depict nurturing and caring, but they will also let you know if your client is nervous or feeling

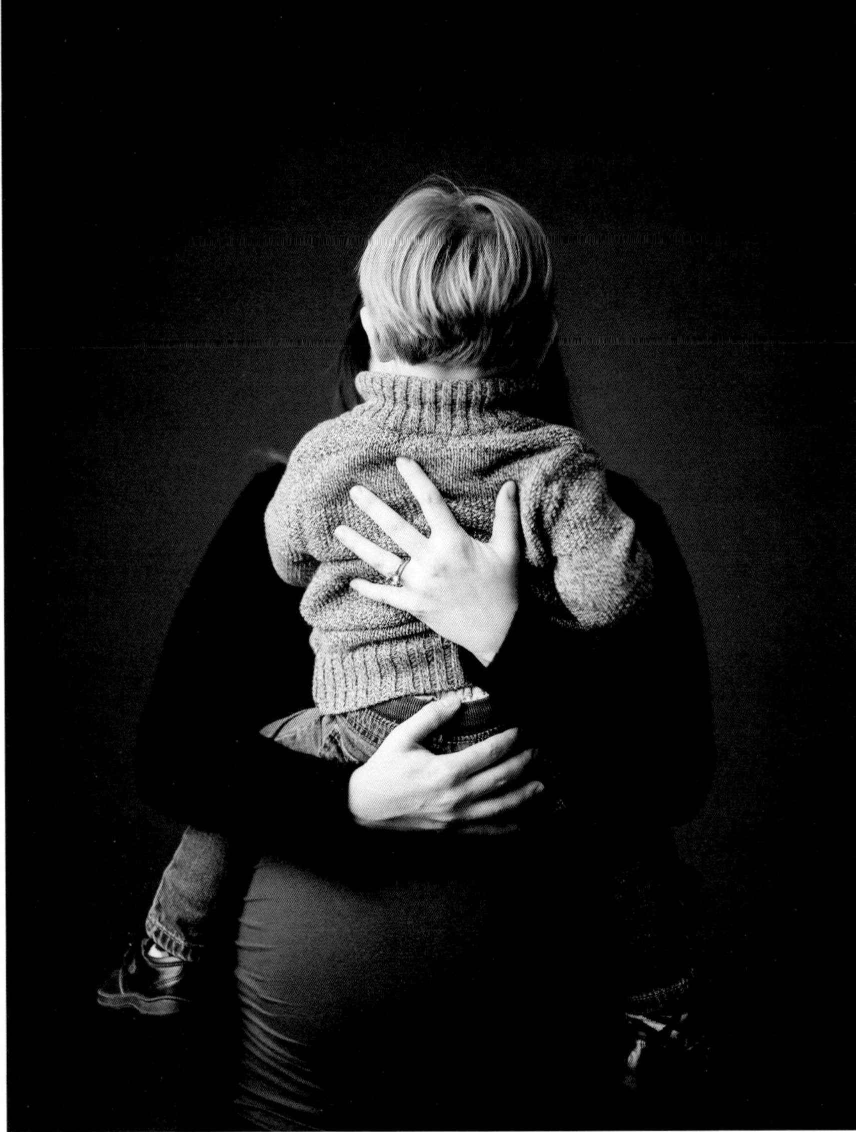

**FIGURE 5.1** An expecting mother holding her older child. Notice how the placement of her hands conveys a sense of support and comfort.

awkward. Paying attention to your clients' hands is a small detail that is incredibly impactful in the overall feel of your photos (**FIGURE 5.1**).

Figure 5.1 shows an expecting mother holding her older child. We can't see either one of their faces, but we don't have to in order to understand the story and feel the emotion of the moment. Her fingers are wide open, giving a sense of support and comfort. You can almost feel her pulling that child into her. You can tell they are connected. This is a nurturing, protective, and very loving image. And all of that is expressed through her hands alone.

Now look at **FIGURE 5.2**. This is also an image of a mother and child where all we can see of the mother are her hands. But in this image, the hands are communicating very different emotions—emotions that I'm sure parents everywhere can relate to.

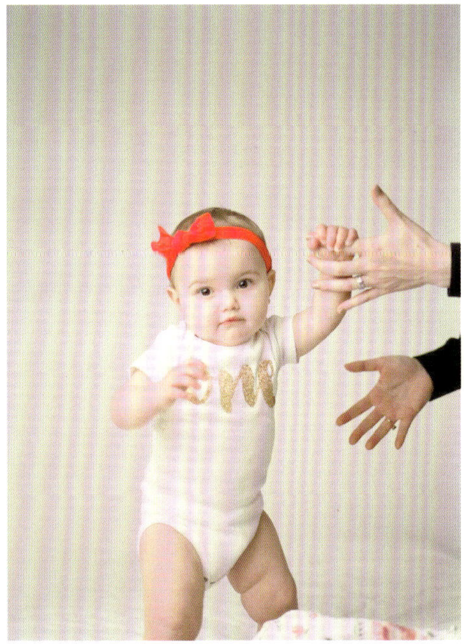

**FIGURE 5.2** A child being supported by her mother. Notice how the mother's hands in this image convey a sense of worry and alarm.

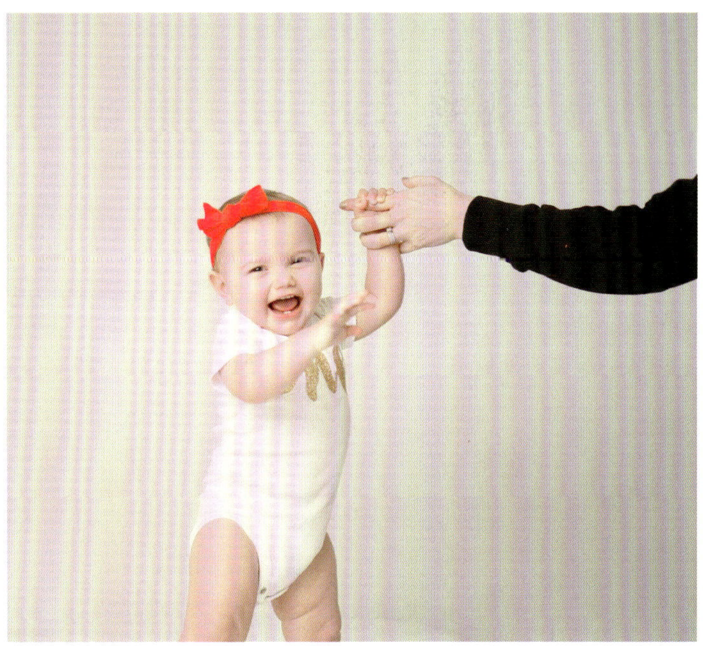

**FIGURE 5.3** The same mother, child, and setup as in Figure 5.2, but now the mother's hands are relaxed and assured.

These are "I'm gonna catch you" hands. They're protective, but they are also showing concern. These are nervous hands, and they make me as the viewer feel a little nervous as a result. When I look at this photo, I'm worried about that baby about to fall, and I feel a little on edge. **FIGURE 5.3** shows the same mother and baby in the same position, but in this image, the mother's hand is communicating calm and confidence.

You can tell that she has a watchful eye on her baby and is offering help, but this image conveys, "I've got this." The baby is perfectly supported. The mother's hand is strong and relaxed, so the viewer feels relaxed, as well.

This image is fun and cute. You can imagine that this baby is learning to take her first steps, and her mom is there to help her along. In Figure 5.2, it seems like the baby is about to fall and mom is ready to catch her. This small shift transforms the emotional tone of the image, conveying calm confidence.

Fear, concern, support, nurturing, encouragement—all of that is communicated through the hands in these images. Hands are important, and it's your job as the photographer and director to pay attention and help guide your client's hands into better positions when necessary.

## Barbie Hands

If your client is feeling nervous or awkward, you are going to see it in their hands first. Nerves translate into tension in the hands and result in what I call "Barbie hands" (**FIGURE 5.4**).

Barbie hands look very stiff. The fingers are close together and look fused, like a plastic doll. Barbie hands let you know that your client is nervous and hyper aware that they are being photographed. They want their hands to look perfect, and so they overpose. The problem is nobody holds their hands like this in real life. The result is an image that looks unnatural and makes the viewer feel tense.

This is something that I didn't know to look out for when I first started my business. I would sometimes notice that my images felt overly posed, but I wasn't sure why. When I finally realized Barbie hands were the problem, everything changed.

By simply directing clients to bend their fingers and spread them out a little, I was able to consistently create images that looked natural and much more relaxed. **FIGURE 5.5** highlights the difference: This image shows a very similar pose to Figure 5.4, but in this image, I directed my clients to relax their hands—a small adjustment with a big impact!

Whereas Figure 5.4 looks posed, Figure 5.5 looks like a candid moment—like the couple was just naturally standing like this and I happened to capture it.

Here are a few more examples. **FIGURE 5.6** shows two mothers and their babies in the same pose. In **FIGURE 5.6A**, the mother's hands are in the Barbie hands

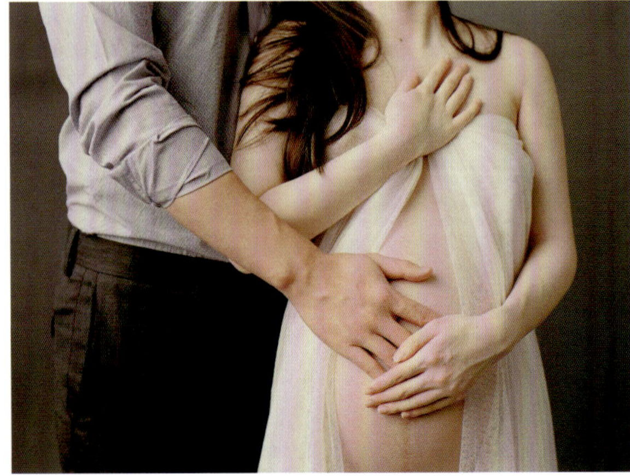

**FIGURE 5.4** This is an example of "Barbie hands." Barbie hands are a sign that your client is feeling nervous and will result in an image that looks overly posed.

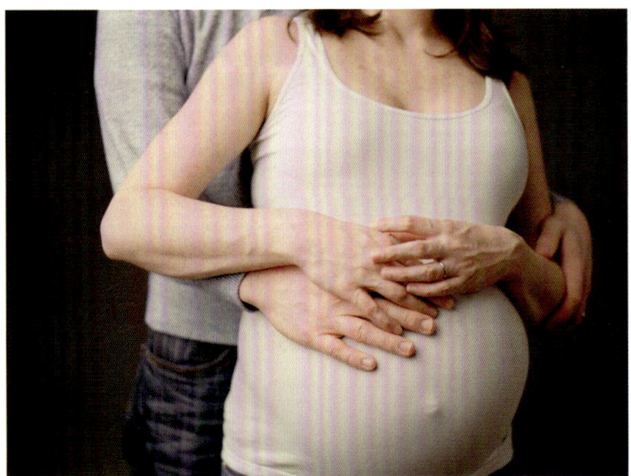

**FIGURE 5.5** While similar to the pose in Figure 5.4, in this image, I directed my clients to relax their hands, resulting in a candid look.

position; in **FIGURE 5.6B**, the mother's hands are relaxed, and the image looks more natural.

In **FIGURE 5.7**, we have two babies, both photographed in their father's hands. Note the difference between the Barbie hand and the relaxed hand.

Be on the lookout for Barbie hands when posing your clients, and if you notice them, ask your client to separate their fingers and bend them a tiny bit. That little adjustment will have a huge impact on the look and feel of your photos!

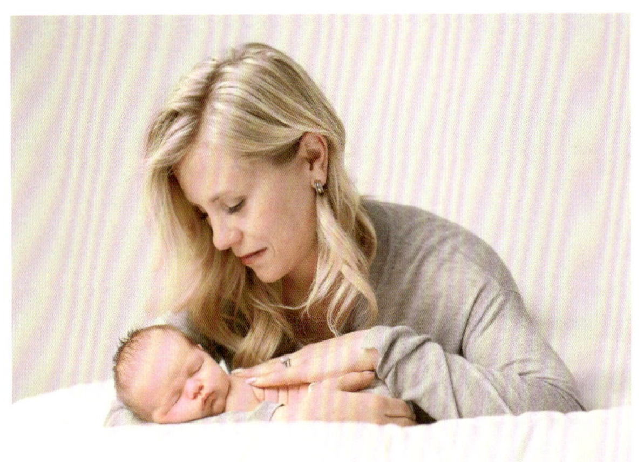

A

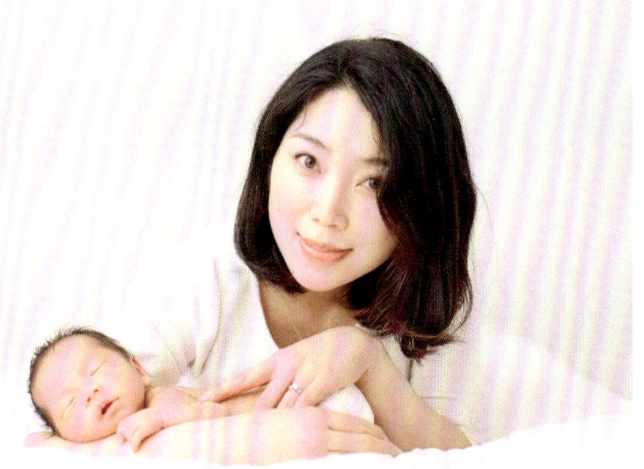

B

**FIGURE 5.6** Note the difference between the stiff "Barbie hand" and the more natural-looking pose with a relaxed hand.

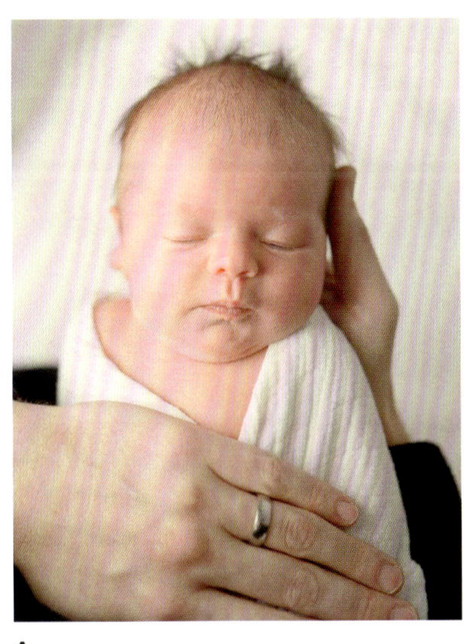

A

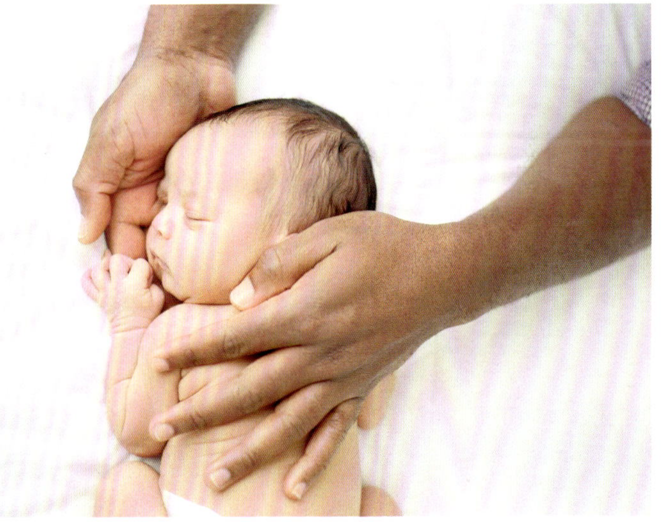

B

**FIGURE 5.7** Two babies photographed in their father's hands. In Figure 5.7A, the father is in the Barbie hands position, and the image looks stiff and overly posed. In Figure 5.7B, the father's hands are relaxed, and his fingers are separated and slightly bent, giving the overall image a calm, nurturing feel.

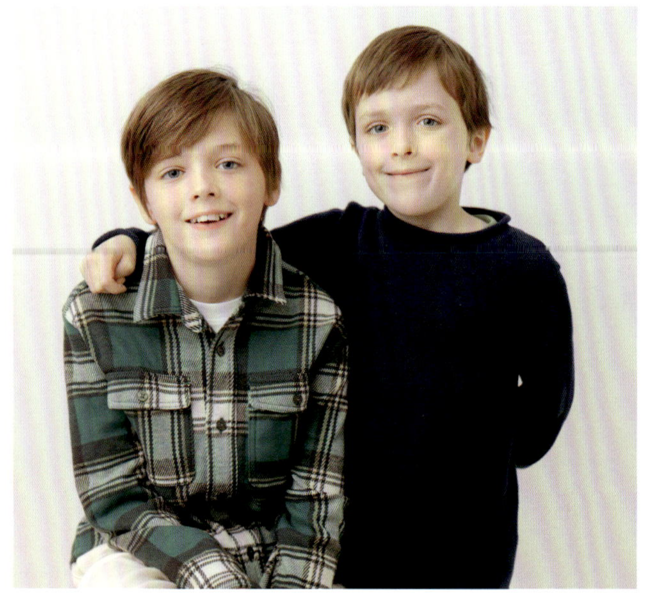

A

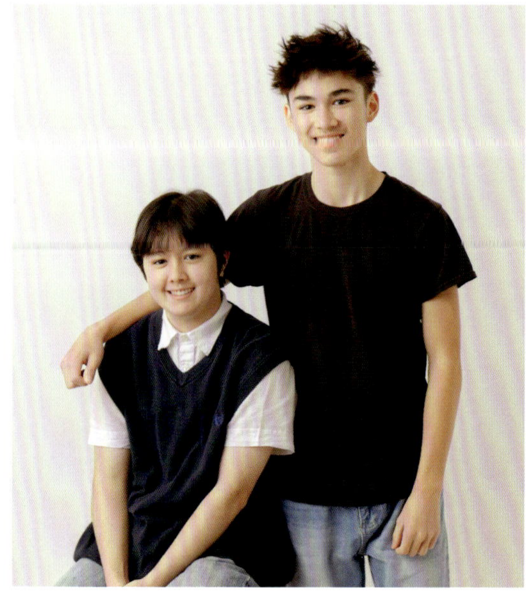

B

**FIGURE 5.8** The Claw!

## The Claw

Another common hand position that people go to when feeling nervous or uncomfortable is what I call "the Claw." This is one I see most often when photographing pre-teens and teens, especially when they are asked to put their arm around a sibling. They will ball up their hand into a fist position rather than relaxing their fingers (**FIGURE 5.8**).

The Claw is less common than Barbie hands, but when I see it, I know that my client is feeling awkward and needs a little direction to look more at ease in their photo. When the Claw appears, I instruct my client to open their fist and allow their fingers to spread out a little. I'll do the movement myself as I explain it so that they can see the difference.

## The Crotch Hold

Often, when parents scoop up their child to hold them, they'll place their hands between the child's legs for support (**FIGURE 5.9**). This hand position doesn't convey tension or nervousness—it's simply a secure and practical way to hold a baby. However, it's not the most flattering position for photos, so when I notice it, I gently guide my clients into a different position.

Remember, as a family photographer, you are potentially creating heirloom images every time you pick up your camera. So, pay attention to the details!

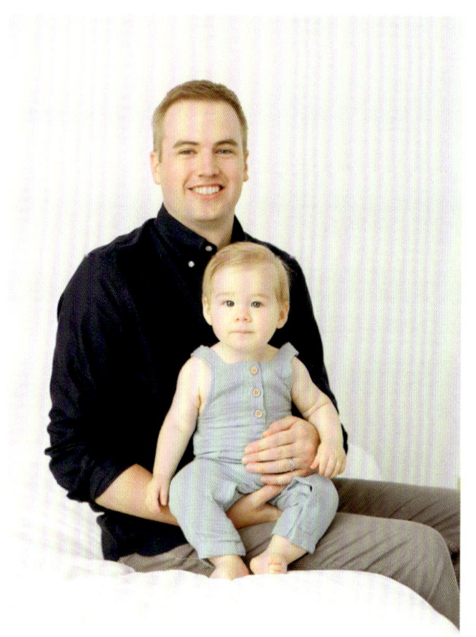

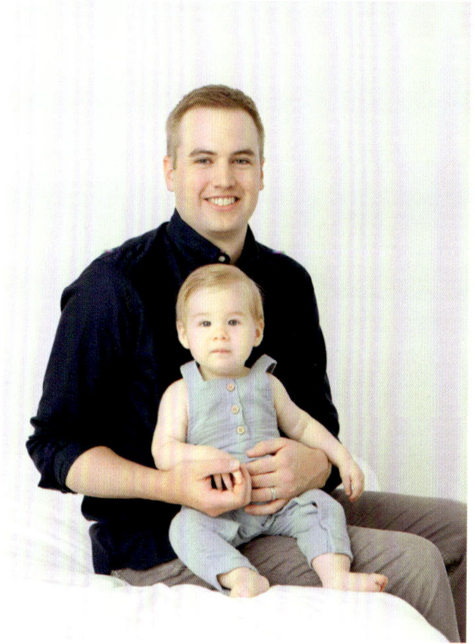

**FIGURE 5.9** The Crotch Hold. When I notice it, I instruct my clients to place the child on their lap and secure them with a hand on their belly.

## Eyes

While hands can communicate emotion, the eyes are the focal point of a portrait. They draw the viewer in, creating an immediate sense of connection and conveying a multitude of emotions. Through the eyes, we gain insight into who a person is and how they are feeling. The slight crinkle at the corners during a smile, for example, signals genuine happiness. Wide eyes express surprise and sometimes fear. A steady gaze can communicate confidence, curiosity, or even aggression.

Paying attention to your clients' eyes, especially young children, will help you understand their emotional state (**FIGURE 5.10**). Giving them direction on where to focus their gaze will help you control the look and feel of your portraits.

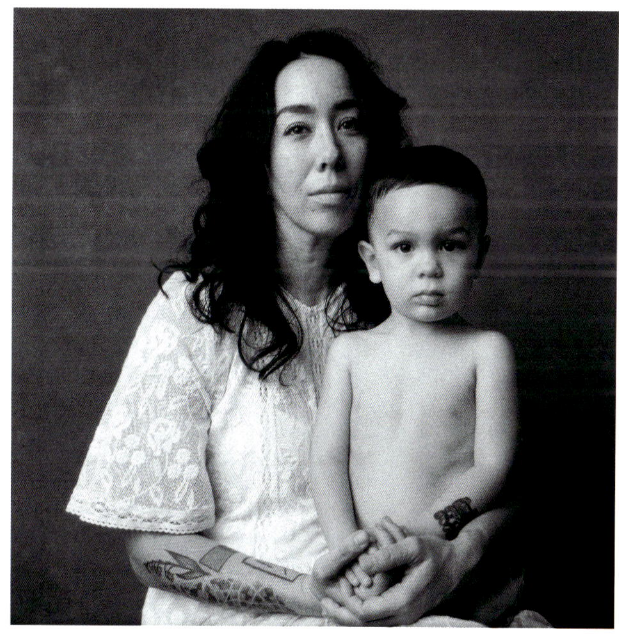

**FIGURE 5.10** Eye contact is a powerful and effective way to pull the viewer into a photo, creating a sense of connection with the subject.

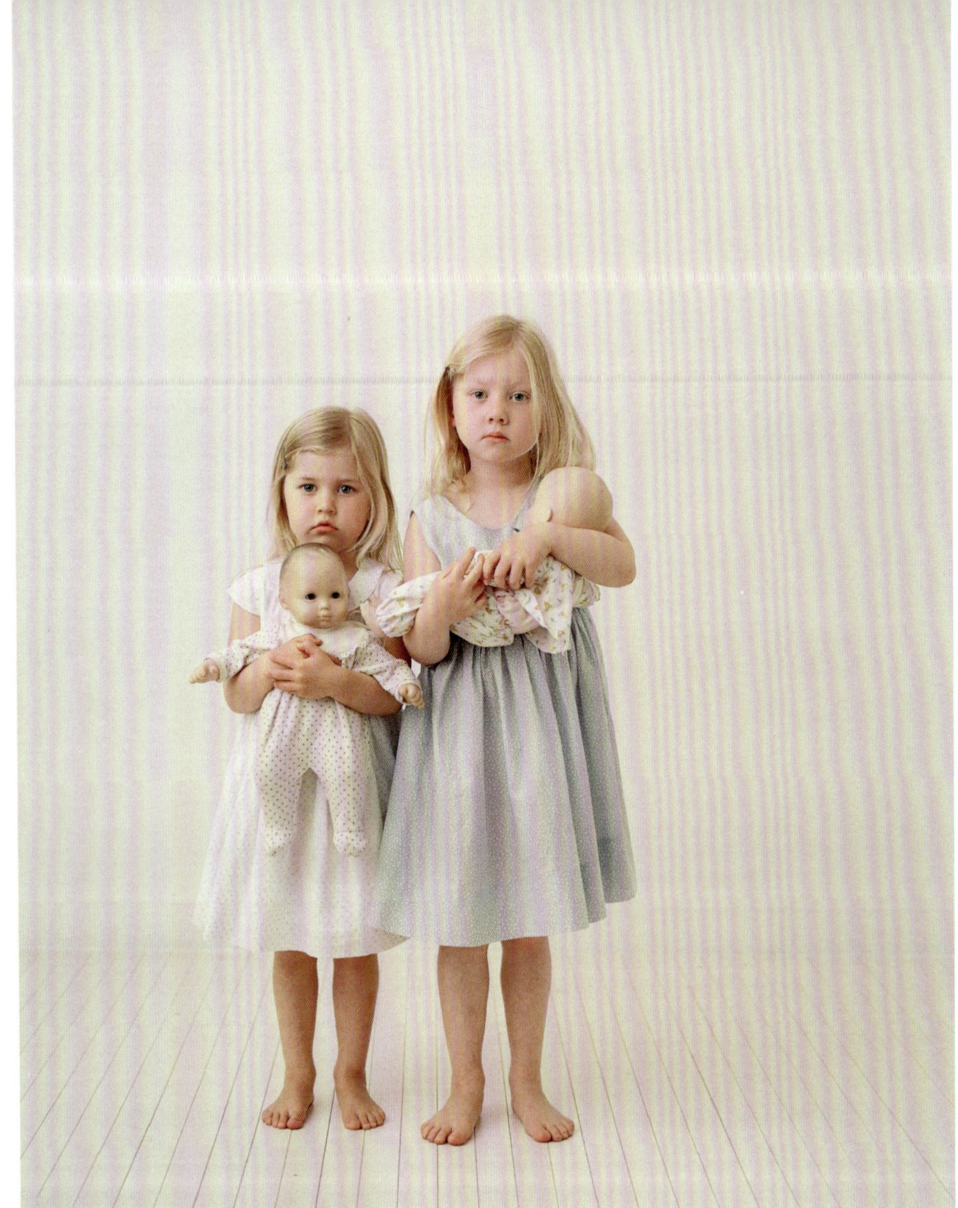

**FIGURE 5.11** Photographing children at eye level invites us into their world. It places the viewer and child on an equal plane, and I believe that allows us a glimpse into who they are as people, not just as children.

Eyes really matter in portraiture, so carefully consider how you position your camera relative to your clients' eyes. Positioning yourself at eye level to your client allows you to meet their natural gaze and gives the viewer a sense that they are interacting with the subject. This is true regardless of the age of your client, but I believe it takes on extra importance when photographing newborns, babies, and children (**FIGURE 5.11**).

I was a kindergarten teacher before becoming a photographer, and one thing I learned from teaching is that getting down to a child's level when interacting with them helps that child feel more comfortable. In addition, it will help your small clients feel more at ease. This adjustment in perspective will transform the impact of your portraits, both artistically and technically.

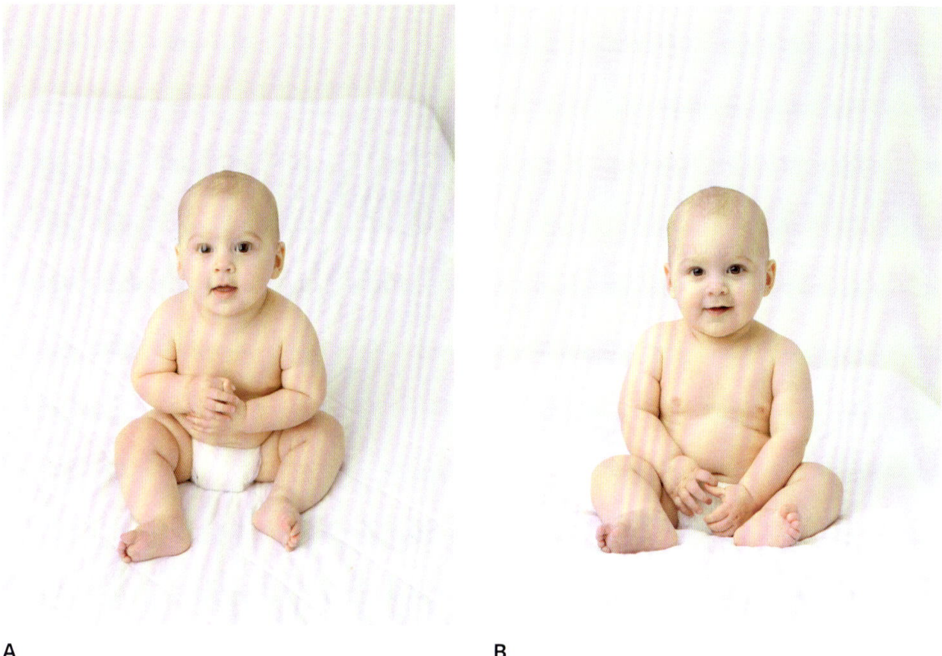

A B

**FIGURE 5.12** Figure 5.12A shows a baby photographed from a standing position—a common viewpoint for adults. Figure 5.12B was captured at eye level with the baby. This perspective is much more engaging and looks more professional.

Photographing children at eye level elevates the emotional appeal and looks more polished and professional, but it also improves the quality of the work by eliminating "perspective distortion" and other technical mistakes (**FIGURE 5.12**).

## Perspective Distortion

Perspective distortion is a visual effect caused by the differences in how the camera and the human brain see depth and scale. For example, when we look at a baby sleeping on a bed, our eyes (and brain) will adjust to see the baby as proportional, whether we're standing near their head or their feet. A camera, on the other hand, doesn't make these adjustments. Instead, objects closer to the lens appear larger, while objects farther away appear smaller, creating an exaggerated sense of scale in the photo.

In **FIGURE 5.13A**, I positioned myself near the baby's feet. Notice how the baby's bottom, being closer to the camera, appears larger, while their head and eyes, which are farther away, seem small. This creates an exaggerated proportion where the bottom half of the baby dominates the image. Compare this to **FIGURE 5.13B**, where I adjusted my position to align with the baby's eyes. At this angle, the baby appears balanced and proportional.

**FIGURE 5.13** Perspective distortion creates an exaggerated proportion. Adjust your position to align with the baby's eyes. At this angle, the baby appears balanced and proportional.

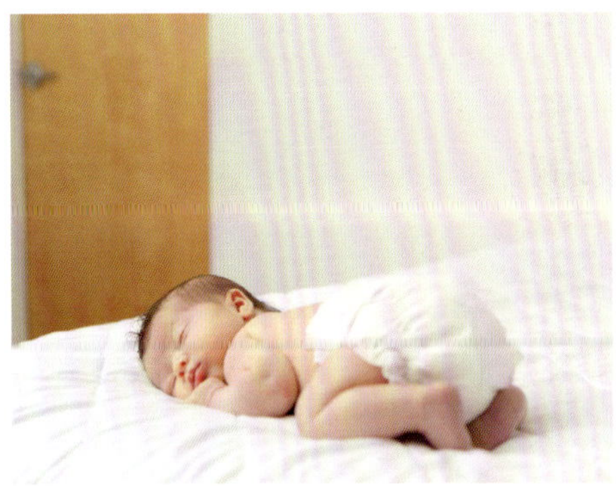

A

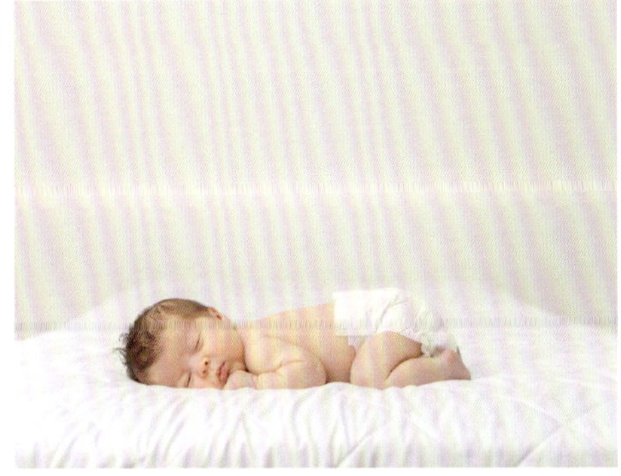

B

Photographing your subject at eye level is a quick and easy way to avoid perspective distortion, regardless of the age of your client, but it is something to keep top of mind when photographing newborns and babies, in particular. Babies and newborns are so small that the position of the photographer can easily change what is emphasized in the photo. Positioning yourself eye level will ensure that you are capturing their natural proportions. (It will also help you avoid the common mistake of "shooting up the nose.")

## Shooting up the Nose

"Shooting up the nose" is another mistake to avoid when photographing newborns and babies in particular. It occurs when your camera angle is too low relative to the face of the baby you are photographing. In addition to causing perspective distortion, this angle will emphasize the nostrils, making the baby's nose the focal point of your image (**FIGURE 5.14**).

The best way to avoid "shooting up the nose" is to always position yourself eye level with a newborn.

**FIGURE 5.14** "Shooting up the nose" occurs when your camera angle is too low relative to the face of the baby you are photographing. Avoid this by positioning yourself in line with the eyes of the baby you are photographing.

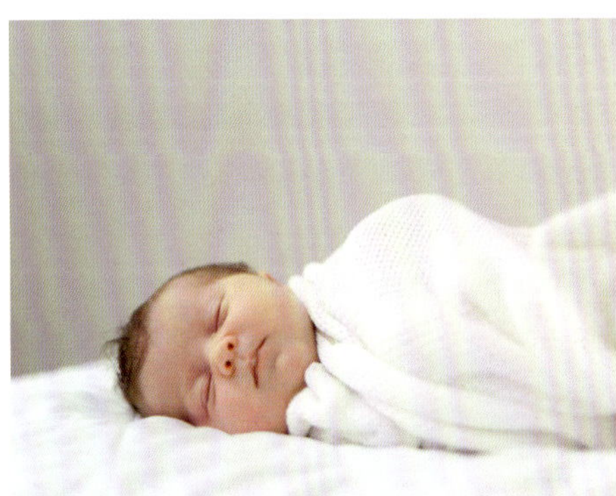

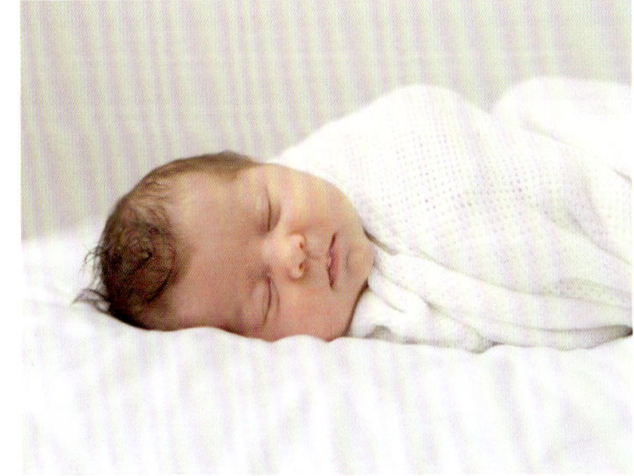

## Play with Perspective

I'm a big believer in photographing children at eye level, but I am not afraid to try different perspectives, as well, and I encourage you to do the same.

Shooting from below, for example, can be a great way to photograph children under the right circumstance, as it adds an element of storytelling to a photo, especially if you're capturing a child in the context of play or exploration.

Shooting from below when capturing children at play gives your photo the feeling that the children are larger than life, mirroring the feelings children often have when tapped into their imagination. I also love to capture children from below when photographing them jumping or being thrown in the air by their parents. Again, the low angle changes the perspective, and makes the child appear higher in the air than they actually are, adding to the playful energy of the image.

So don't be afraid to play around with perspective. A small change in your point of view can have a big impact on your final image.

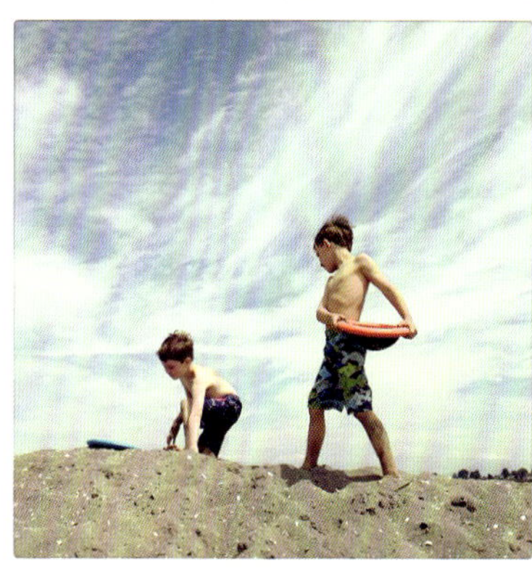

**FIGURE 5.15** Shooting from below when capturing children at play.

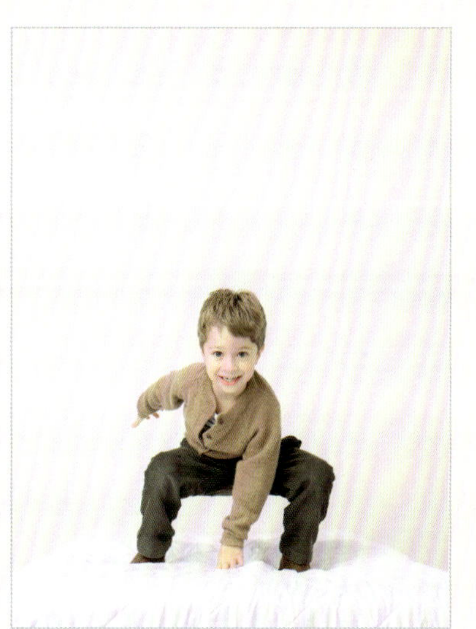

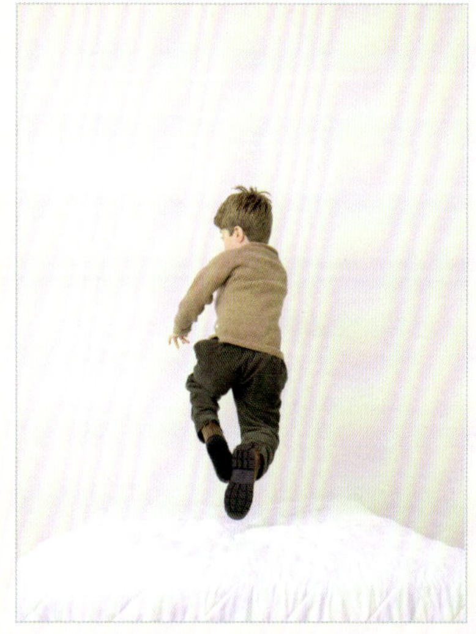

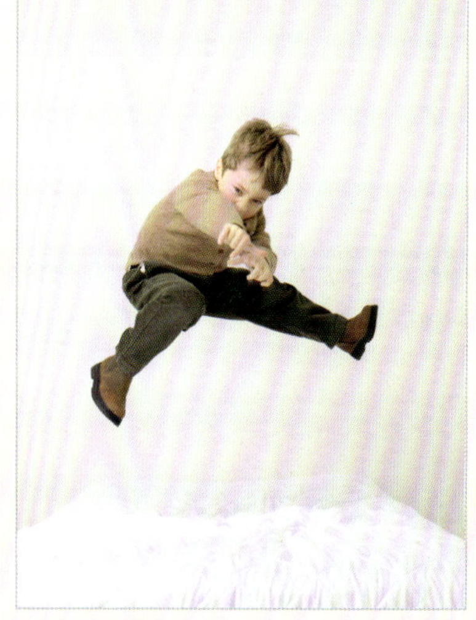

**FIGURE 5.16** I love to capture children from below when photographing them jumping or being thrown in the air by their parents. The low angle makes the child appear higher in the air than they actually are, adding to the playful energy of the image.

## Creating Candids

At the beginning of this chapter, I shared my preference for candid-looking photos. My clients often comment on how much they love the natural feel of my images. The truth is most of the "candid" photos I share in my portfolio are actually posed.

I create "candid" images by giving people direction on where to look, and I create formal portraits the same way. Directing your clients where to look during a photo session is a quick and easy way to create a robust set of images by getting the most out of each pose.

### Eye Contact

The difference between a formal portrait and a candid-looking photo is eye contact. Eye contact in photography denotes a formal portrait approach, especially if everyone in the image is looking into the camera. If people are not looking into your lens, your photos will look candid. See the difference in **FIGURE 5.17.**

Directing my clients on where to look allows me to maximize my poses, getting multiple looks from one pose in a matter of moments. For example, in **FIGURE 5.18A**, I directed both parents to look down at their new baby to create

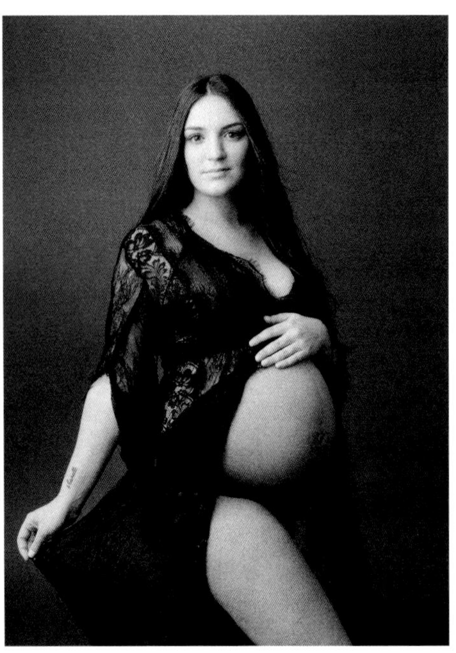

A

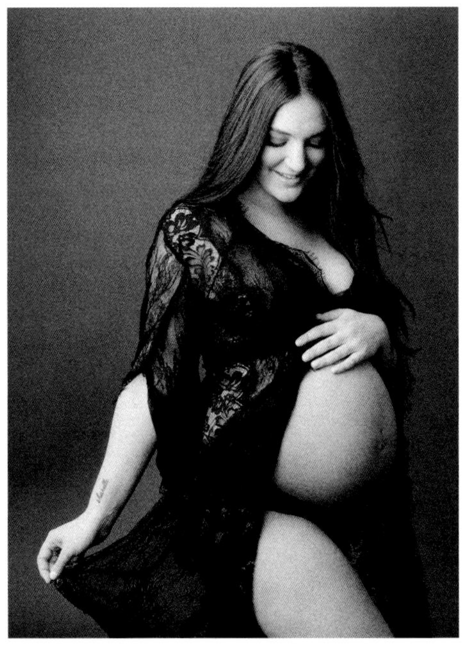

B

**FIGURE 5.17** These two images have an identical pose, but in Figure 5.17A, my client is looking into the camera, creating a formal looking portrait. In Figure 5.27B, I asked her to look down toward her belly and laugh, resulting in an image that feels like a candid moment.

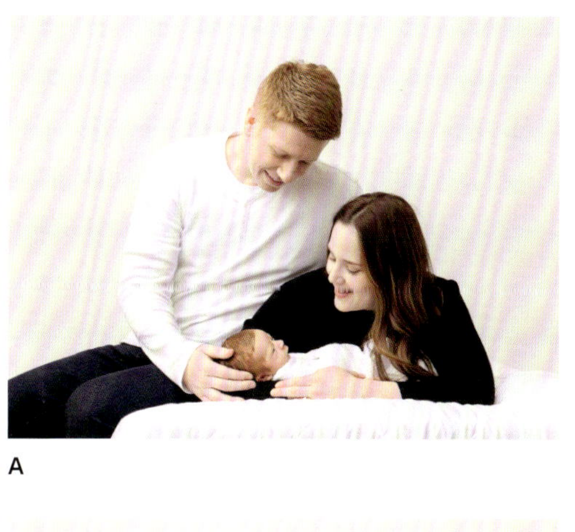

A

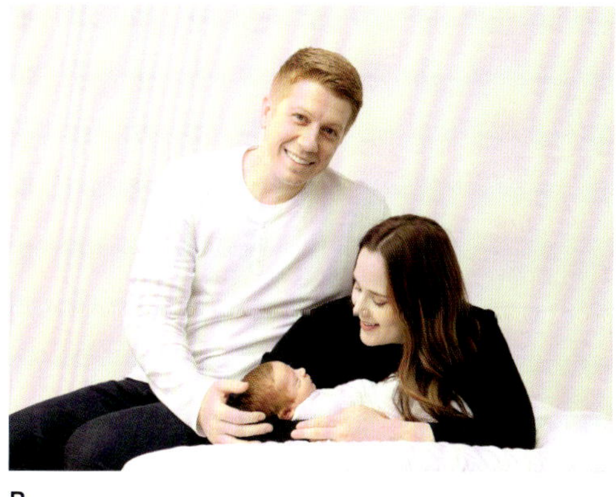

B

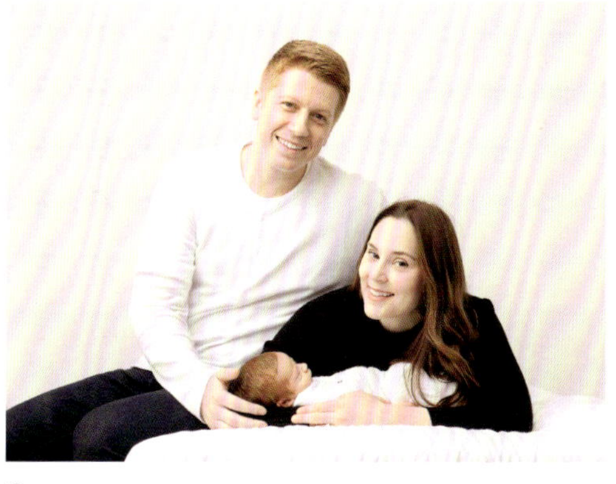

C

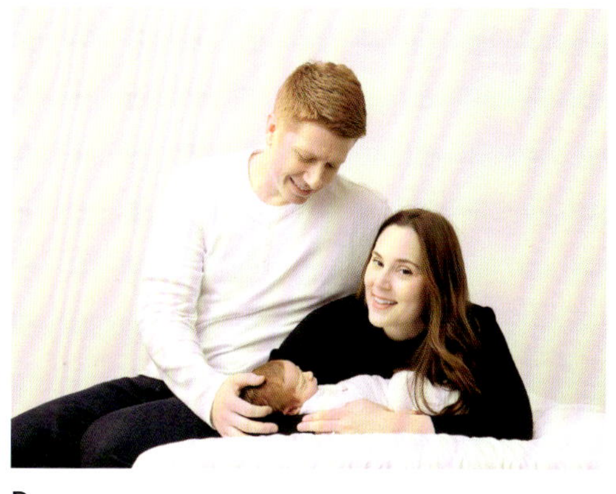

D

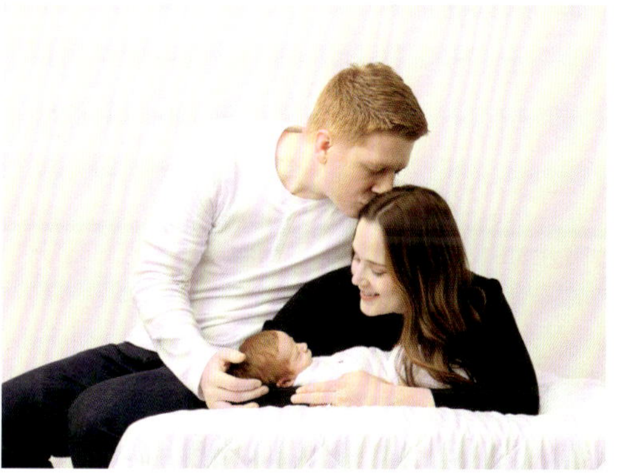

E

**FIGURE 5.18** Giving my clients direction on where to look allows me to get multiple looks from one pose in a matter of moments.

a candid-looking photo. From there, I asked the mom to continue looking at the baby and directed the dad to look at me (**FIGURE 5.18B**). Then I asked both parents to look at me (**FIGURE 5.18C**), which resulted in a formal-looking portrait. After I captured that image, I had the dad look at the baby and asked that the mom continue to look at me (**FIGURE 5.18D**). For the last image, I asked them both to look back down at the baby, only this time I directed the dad to kiss the top of his wife's head (**FIGURE 5.18E**). Five looks from one pose!

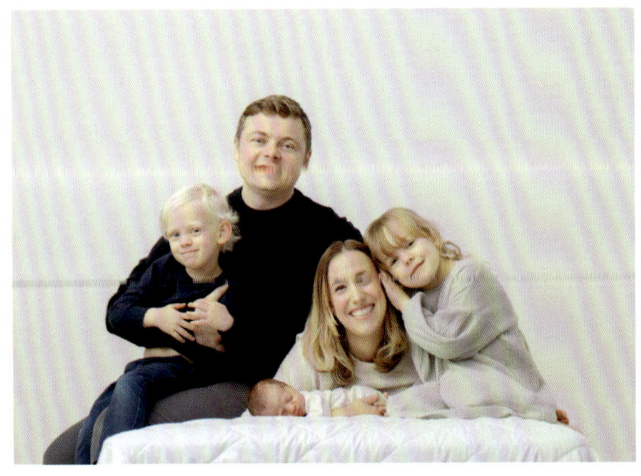

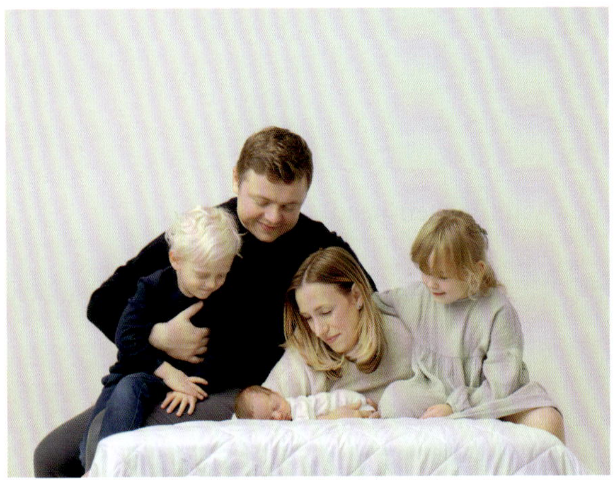

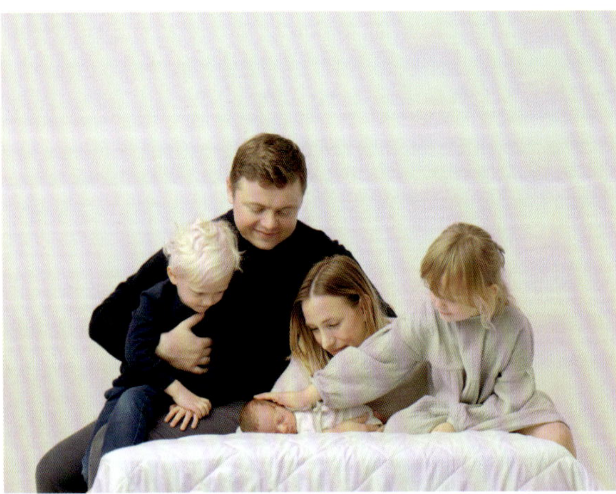

**FIGURE 5.19** I asked everyone to look at me, then at the baby. While the family was looking at the baby, the older sister reached out and gently stroked the baby's head, allowing me to capture a sweet candid moment.

Another benefit of giving this kind of direction is that it opens up space for truly candid moments to occur, especially when working with little kids. **FIGURE 5.19** shows three images taken within a few seconds of each other. asked everyone to look at me to create a formal family portrait, then I asked everyone to look at the baby. While the family was looking at the baby, the older sister reached out and gently stroked the baby's head, allowing me to capture a sweet candid moment that resulted from a controlled and directed situation.

This sort of spontaneity happens with adults, too. In **FIGURE 5.20** I posed this couple with their twins, directing them to look at the camera, then down at the baby their partner was holding. The mom leaned into her husband to look down at the baby on his lap, and as she did, he leaned in and kissed her shoulder. A sweet spontaneous moment born out of directed space.

I believe these spontaneous moments happen because being directed helps my clients relax. If I were to sit a family down and just tell them to act natural (like I used to at the beginning of my career), they wouldn't know what to do. Most likely, they'd sit down and smile at the camera, resulting in images that look like snapshots.

Being posed and directed takes the pressure off your subjects. It lets them know that you are in charge and you are going to make them look their best. That results in trust. When people trust you, they are more likely to be themselves in front of your camera.

**Pro Tip:** Remember, as a family photographer, you are also the director, so don't be afraid to give your clients direction! Be specific on where you want your clients to look. If you want to

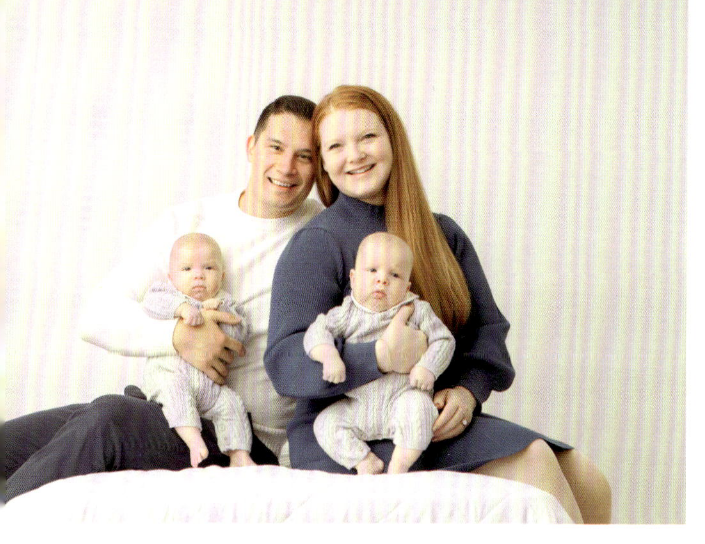
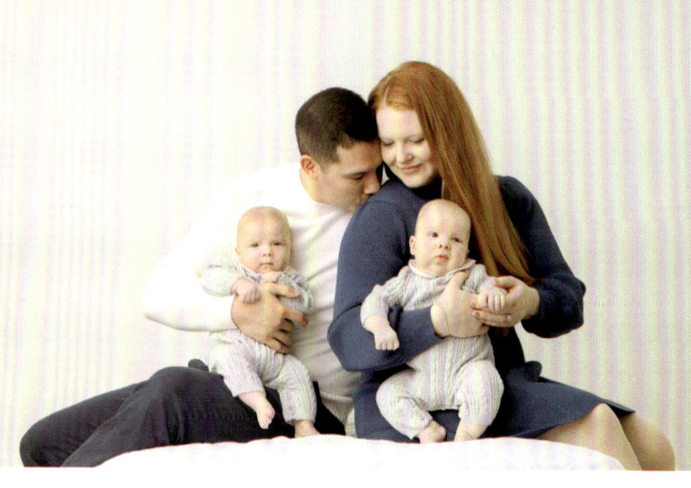

**FIGURE 5.20** Directing clients opens up the space for truly candid moments to occur.

create a formal portrait, ask your clients to look at you. If you want to create a candid moment, direct them to look at something else. One challenge that can arise when directing clients on where to look is that they will tilt their head too far, emphasizing their forehead or the top of their head rather than their face (**FIGURE 5.21**) To avoid this, direct them to look at a specific point that will result in a flattening angle. I give my clients detailed directions, often telling them to look at their wrist, or hand, or at the top of their child's head instead of simply saying "look down at your baby" or "look at your belly." Giving specific direction like this helps you create candid looking images that are controlled and flattering.

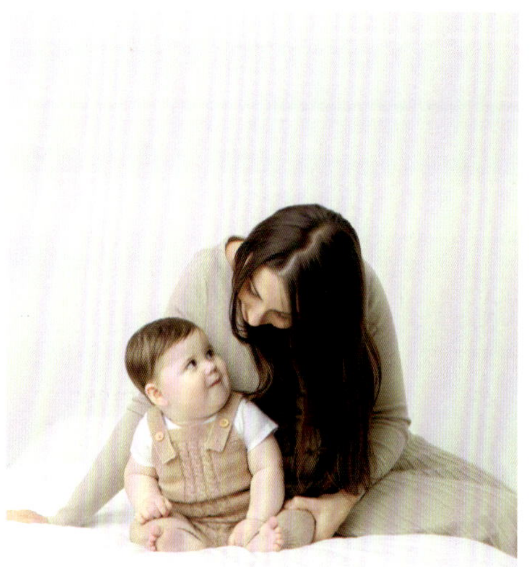
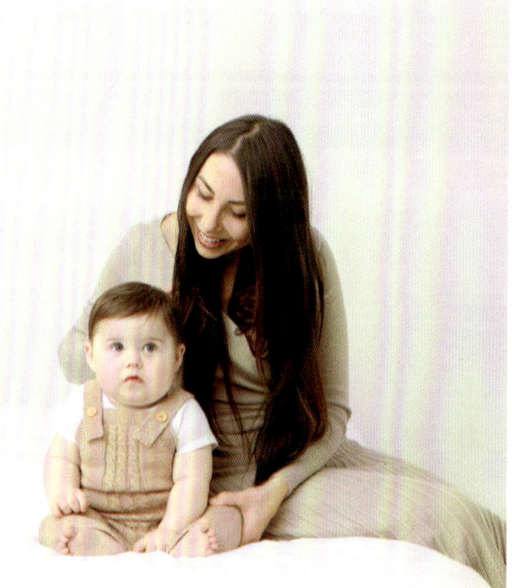

**FIGURE 5.21** I asked my client to look down at her son and she did what most parents do: She bent all the way forward so she could look into his eyes. This created an angle that emphasized the top of her head, not her face.

## Chins and Jawlines

The final detail to consider when directing your clients into a candid pose is their chin and jawline.

While I love encouraging my clients to look down rather than directly into my camera, I can't tell you how many times someone has joked or worried about ending up with a double chin. And honestly, I get it! Everyone wants to look their best. Asking someone to look down can unintentionally create an unflattering angle, and your clients are often aware of this. Taking the extra step to ensure they look their best isn't just thoughtful—it's good customer service.

While photographing your clients at eye level is an effective way to create connection in your portraits, shifting your perspective slightly above their eye line can help prevent the appearance of a double chin when they look down. When you position yourself just above their eyes, you capture the tip of their chin, avoiding any skin below it. This subtle adjustment makes a significant difference, resulting in flattering, polished portraits that your clients will love (**FIGURE 5.22**).

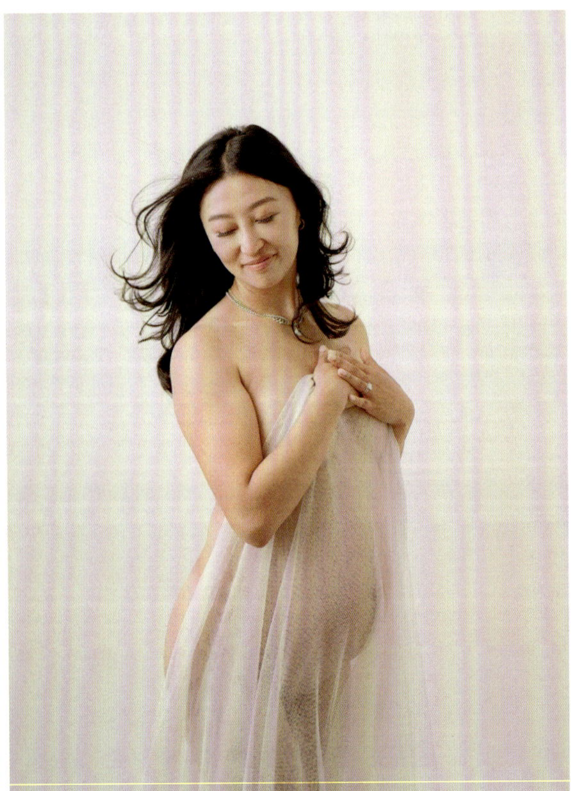

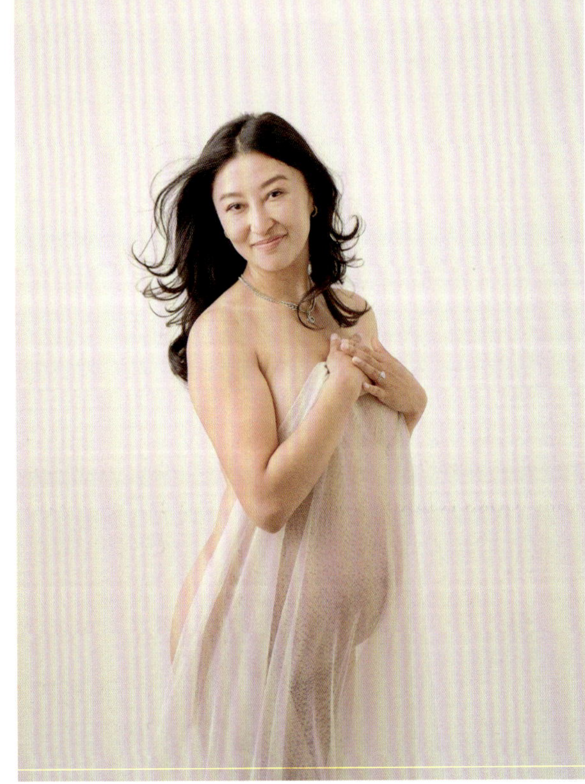

**FIGURE 5.22** The left image was captured at eye level to my client. In the right image, I positioned myself ever so slightly above her eyes as she looked down to ensure a flattering angle on her chin and jawline.

## Focus is Key!

In portraiture, your clients' eyes are always the focal point. This is true whether your subject is making eye contact in the image or not. If the photo is of a person, the viewer will naturally be drawn to the eyes. Therefore, maintaining a sharp focus on the eyes is a must!

If the eyes are out of focus, the entire image will feel off. So, pay extra attention when focusing! Especially when working with a wide-open aperture.

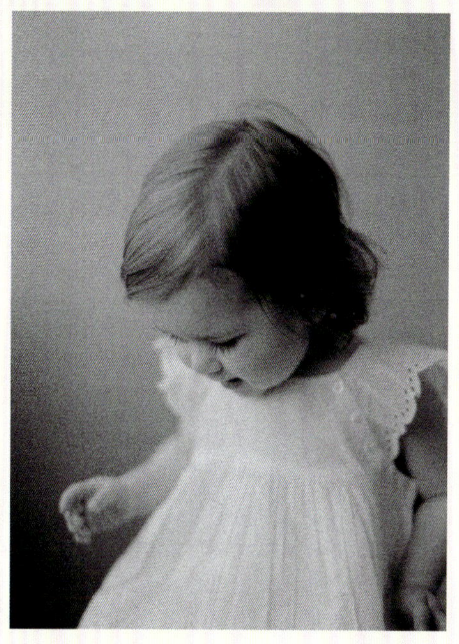

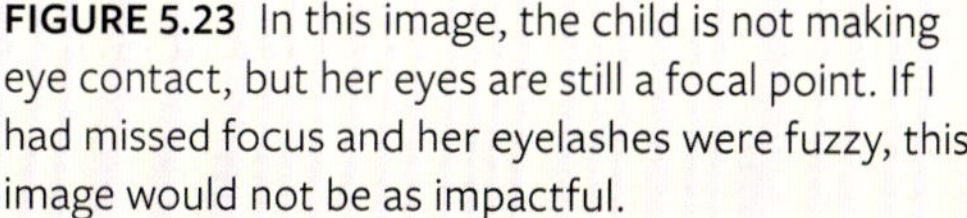

**FIGURE 5.23** In this image, the child is not making eye contact, but her eyes are still a focal point. If I had missed focus and her eyelashes were fuzzy, this image would not be as impactful.

# Heads and Faces

Like eye contact, how a person holds their head can have a significant impact on the look and feel of a portrait. For example, the images in **FIGURES 5.24** were all taken within seconds of each other. The lighting, composition, eye contact, and camera position is the same across the photos. The only variable is the position of my client's head. Notice how this subtle change alters the overall impression of each image.

In **FIGURE 5.24A**, she's holding her head in neutral position, resulting in an image that looks relaxed and approachable. For **FIGURE 5.24B**, I asked her to raise her head slightly, conveying power and confidence. For **FIGURE 5.24C**, she tilted her head down, creating a more playful look. Three distinct looks that evoke three unique feelings, all achieved with minor adjustments to head position.

I direct my clients on how to hold their head to intentionally create a mood in an image. By having your client look into the camera, you create a formal portrait, but by having your client look at the camera and lift their chin slightly, you can create a formal portrait in which they look strong and confident (a look I love to see on my maternity clients in particular!) (**FIGURE 5.25**).

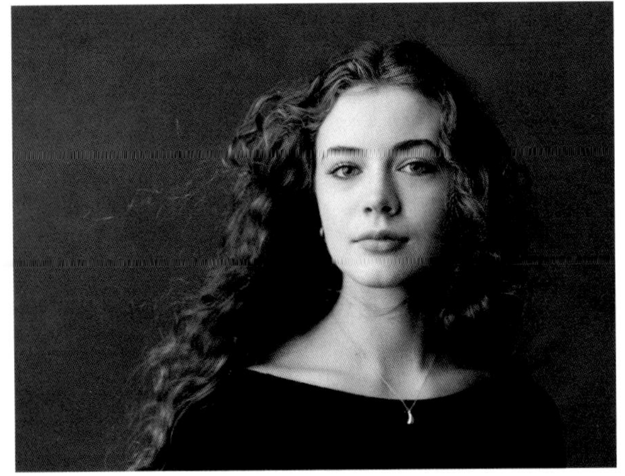

A

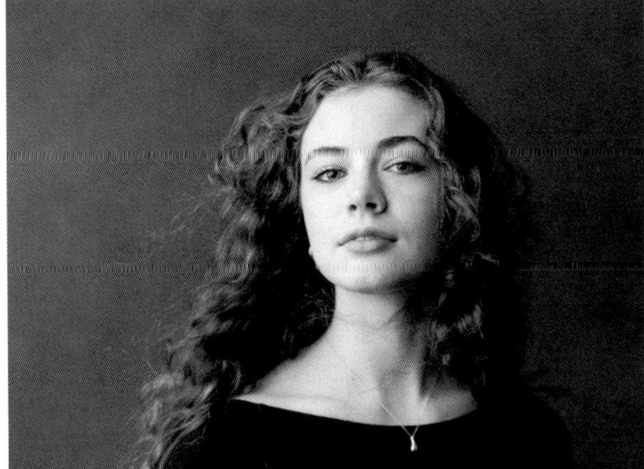

B

**FIGURES 5.24** (Above and right) The only thing that changed across these images was the tilt of her head. That small chance has a big impact on the look and feel of the photo.

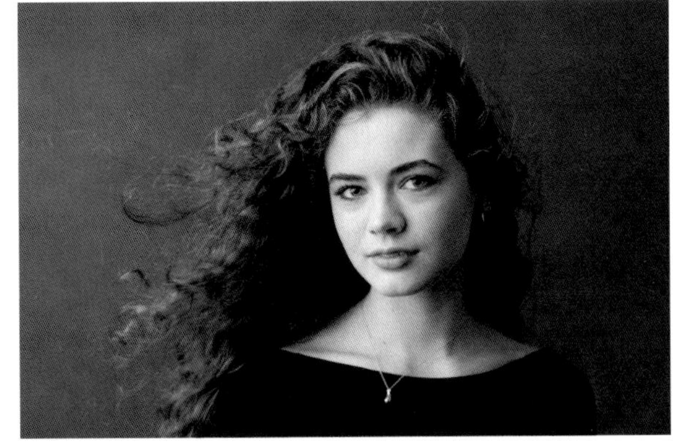

C

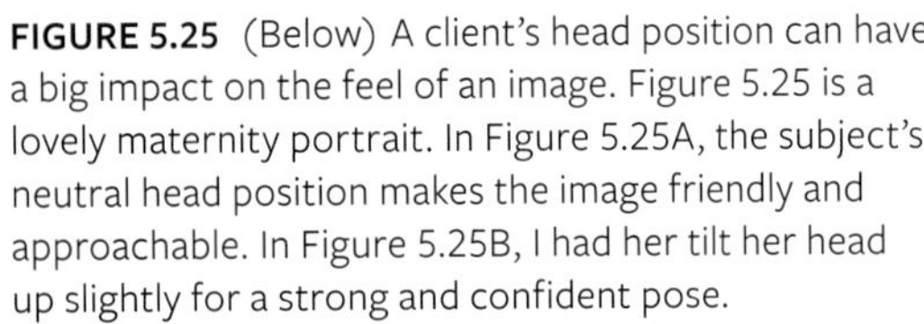

**FIGURE 5.25** (Below) A client's head position can have a big impact on the feel of an image. Figure 5.25 is a lovely maternity portrait. In Figure 5.25A, the subject's neutral head position makes the image friendly and approachable. In Figure 5.25B, I had her tilt her head up slightly for a strong and confident pose.

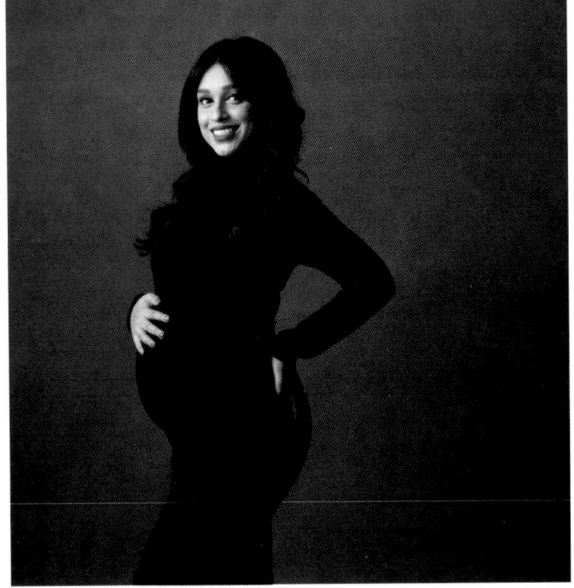

A

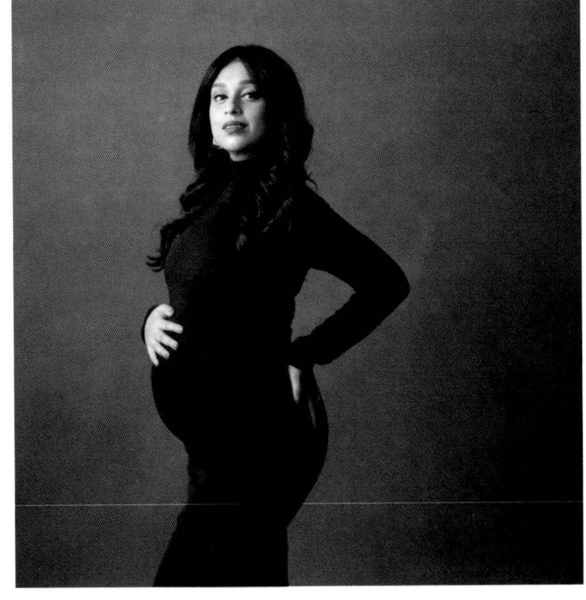

B

## Head Position for Children

Directing adults and older children into specific head positions is somewhat easy, as they can follow directions. A baby, toddler, or young child on the other hand, cannot. Instead of giving directions when working with babies, toddlers, and young children, I pay attention to what they are naturally doing, then work on adjusting my behavior to draw a specific look from them.

For example, babies, toddlers, and young children will often tilt their heads to the side when they are feeling shy or playful. When I see a head tilt in a child that indicates they are feeling shy rather than playful, I will work on helping them feel safe and confident. Having them hold a parent's hand or sit next to a sibling often helps (**FIGURE 5.26**).

This little girl was feeling shy, as indicated by the way she's tilting her head and not making eye contact with me. She wasn't scared, but she also wasn't 100% sure she wanted to be standing there by herself. To help her relax, I invited her mother over and asked them to hold hands. The close presence of her mother shifted her confidence, and we were able to get **FIGURE 5.26B**.

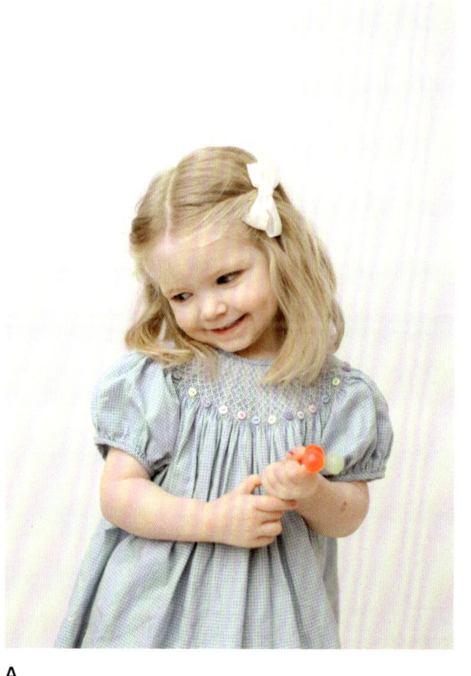

A

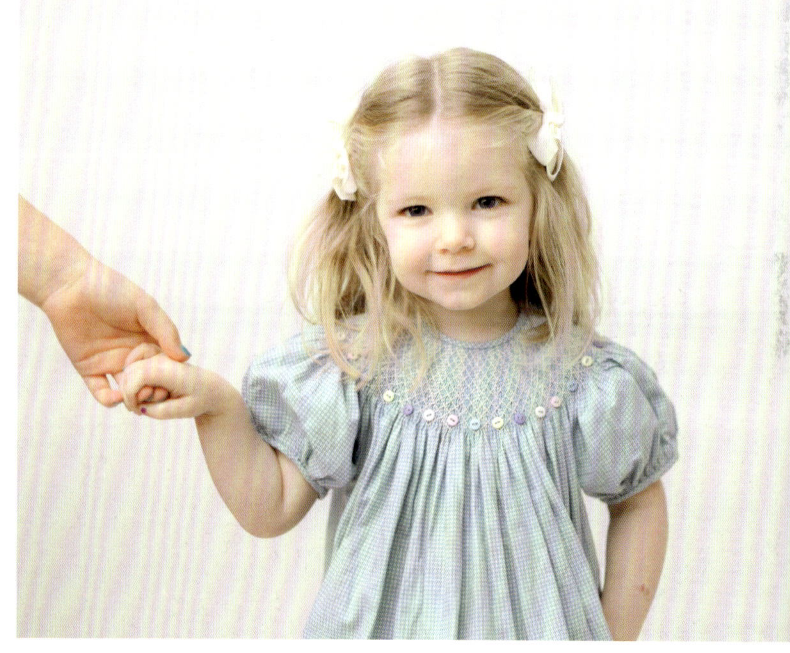

B

**FIGURE 5.26** This is an adorable image, but the head tilt and lack of eye contact let me know that this little girl was feeling shy. Holding her mother's hand shifted her confidence. Her head is now straight, but relaxed, and she is comfortably making eye contact.

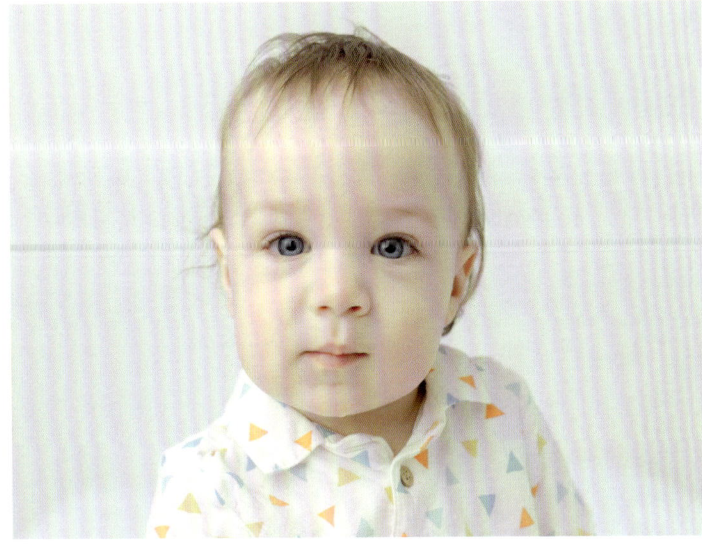

A

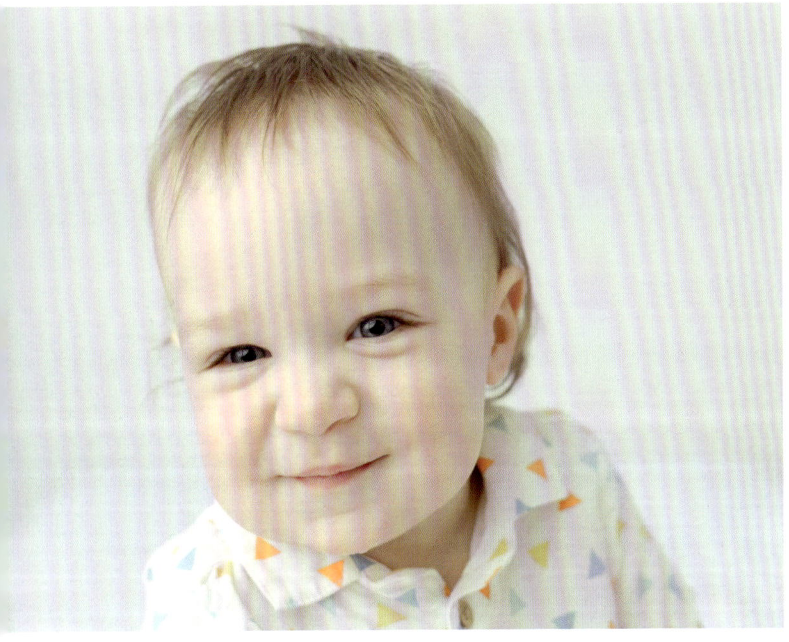

B

**FIGURE 5.27** This little boy was unsure at the very beginning of his photo session, but after a while, he relaxed. Here we can see the playful head tilt.

When a toddler or small child feels curious, unsure, or on guard, they will hold their head straight and look you in the eye. Little kids often do this at the very beginning of their session. I love this look, and will always grab a few photos, but when I see a child doing it, I take care to give them space. This look tells me that they don't trust me yet, and this will end in tears if I get too close. So, I keep my distance. I let them stare me down as I slowly take pictures, talking and/or singing to them the entire time. After a few minutes they learn that I'm someone they can trust and will relax into a more playful mood.

**FIGURE 5.27A** is a perfect example of "the stare down." You can tell he is trying to figure me out. He's not feeling shy, but he's also not feeling entirely secure. He's cautiously curious. His head is straight, and he is staring directly into the camera. After a few minutes, however, he realized that I'm friendly, and he relaxed. In **FIGURE 5.27B** we see a genuine smile and a playful head tilt.

Paying attention to the body language of the children you are working with will help you tap into how they are feeling and inform you on how to proceed. If a child looks shy, grab a few photos to show that side of their personality, then work to make them feel more comfortable. If the child is curious, satisfy that curiosity by allowing them to stare, giving them the time they need to feel more comfortable. Meeting them where they are at is the secret to success!

## Perfect Posture

I am not a fan of perfect posture in family photography. To me, perfect posture results in images that look stiff and overly posed. Perfect posture tells me that the person I am photographing is feeling nervous or awkward, and I don't want that to come through in their images.

I want my work to have a relaxed, natural look, so when I notice someone overdoing it with their posture, I'll direct them into softening their stance. If they are standing, I'll ask them to shift their weight into a hip or onto one leg to create movement in the body. If they have a child in front of them or on their lap, I'll ask them to lean slightly toward the child. If they are sitting, I'll simply ask them to take a deep breath and release it, sinking into a slight slouch.

When giving this kind of direction, I always create the movement with my own body so they can see what I'm asking of them. Small details like how a person is sitting or standing can have a huge impact on the look and feel of your images, so don't be afraid to give your clients feedback and direction, especially when you know it will result in better-looking photos.

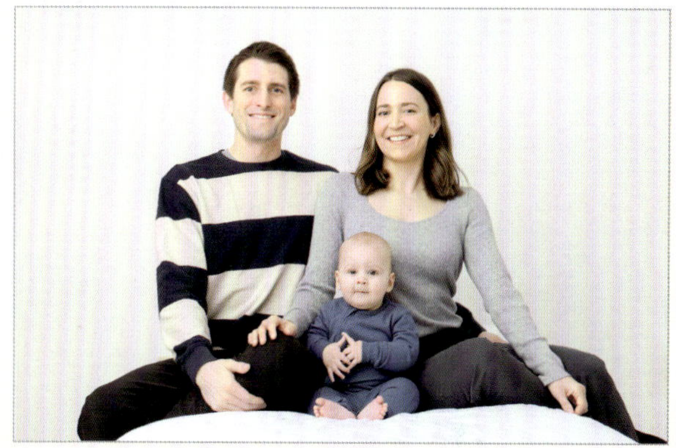

**A**

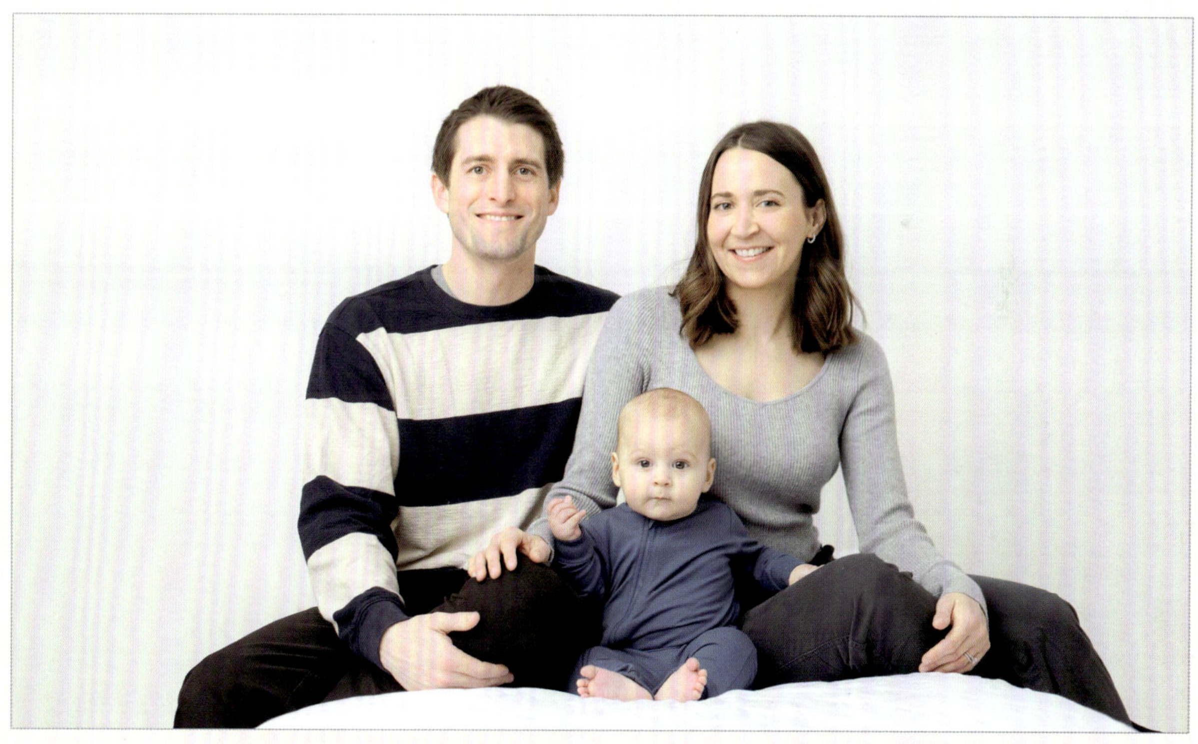

**B**

**FIGURE 5.28** In the first image, the couple's posture is a little too perfect. I asked them to lean slightly toward their baby, resulting in an image that feels more natural and relaxed.

## Head Tilts in Adults

Head tilts are not just for children! A head tilt on an adult will soften the image, creating a portrait that feels approachable. Two adults tilting their heads toward each other conveys a feeling of connection and intimacy. Most of the time, you will need to direct the adults you are working with into these positions.

Adults often hold themselves perfectly upright when having their photos taken, even when holding a newborn or sitting with their children. This comes from years of conditioning about how one should look in a picture. The better the posture, the better the portrait. Right?

Well, maybe not. I find that perfect posture in family photography results in images that look overly posed, similar to the Barbie hands problem. I often direct the adults I work with to tilt their head slightly when setting up a pose (**FIGURE 5.29**).

A simple head tilt toward a child or a partner creates a feeling of connection. And when a person tilts their head, they will naturally tilt their body in the same direction, reinforcing that feeling of closeness. You can see this in action in **FIGURE 5.30**. Notice how the slight head tilt and subtle lean change the feeling of these photos from something formal to something that looks (and feels) organic.

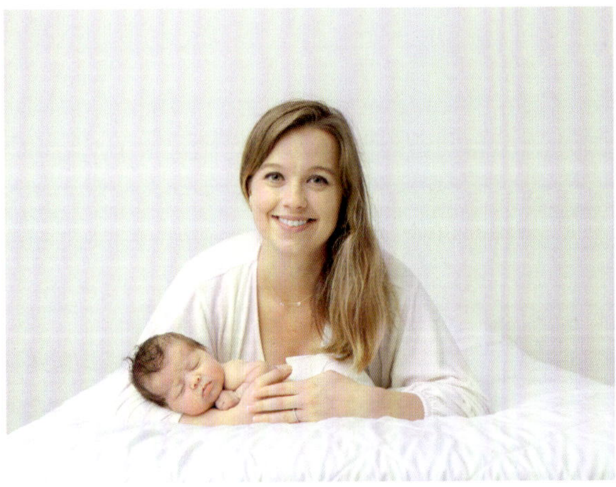

**FIGURE 5.29** The head tilt on the mom contributes to the soft, approachable feel of this formal portrait.

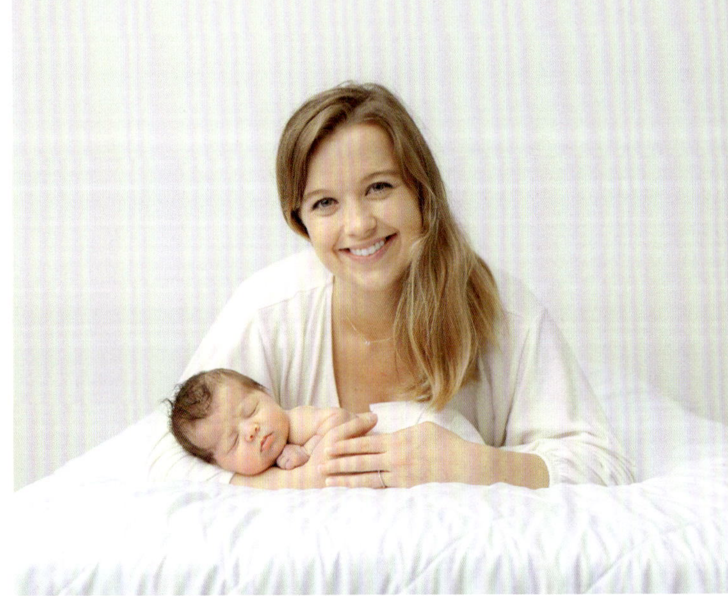

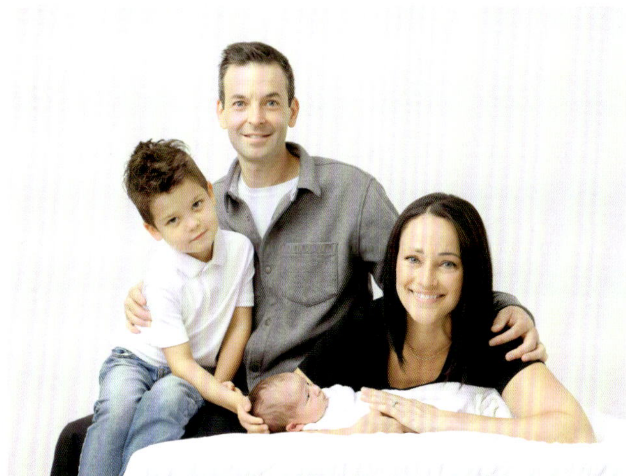

A

**FIGURES 5.30** Figure 5.30A is a formal-looking image. In Figure 5.30B, I asked the dad to tilt his head toward his son, changing the feeling of the photo. It's still a formal portrait, but the dad's head tilt makes the image feel more relaxed and intimate.

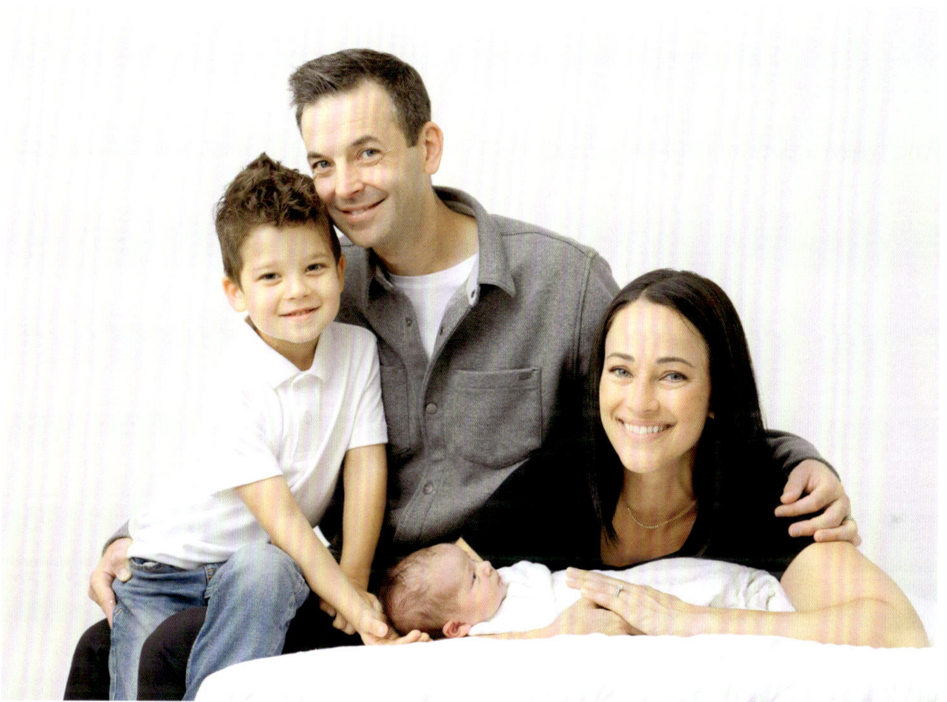

B

## The Takeaway

Remember, as the photographer, you're not just capturing moments; you are creating them. Posing is more than just arranging people for a photograph—it's about creating space for connection. When you use posing as a tool, you elevate your work and strengthen the emotional impact of your photographs. By embracing your role as both a photographer and a director, you can create images that are authentic, timeless, and full of life.

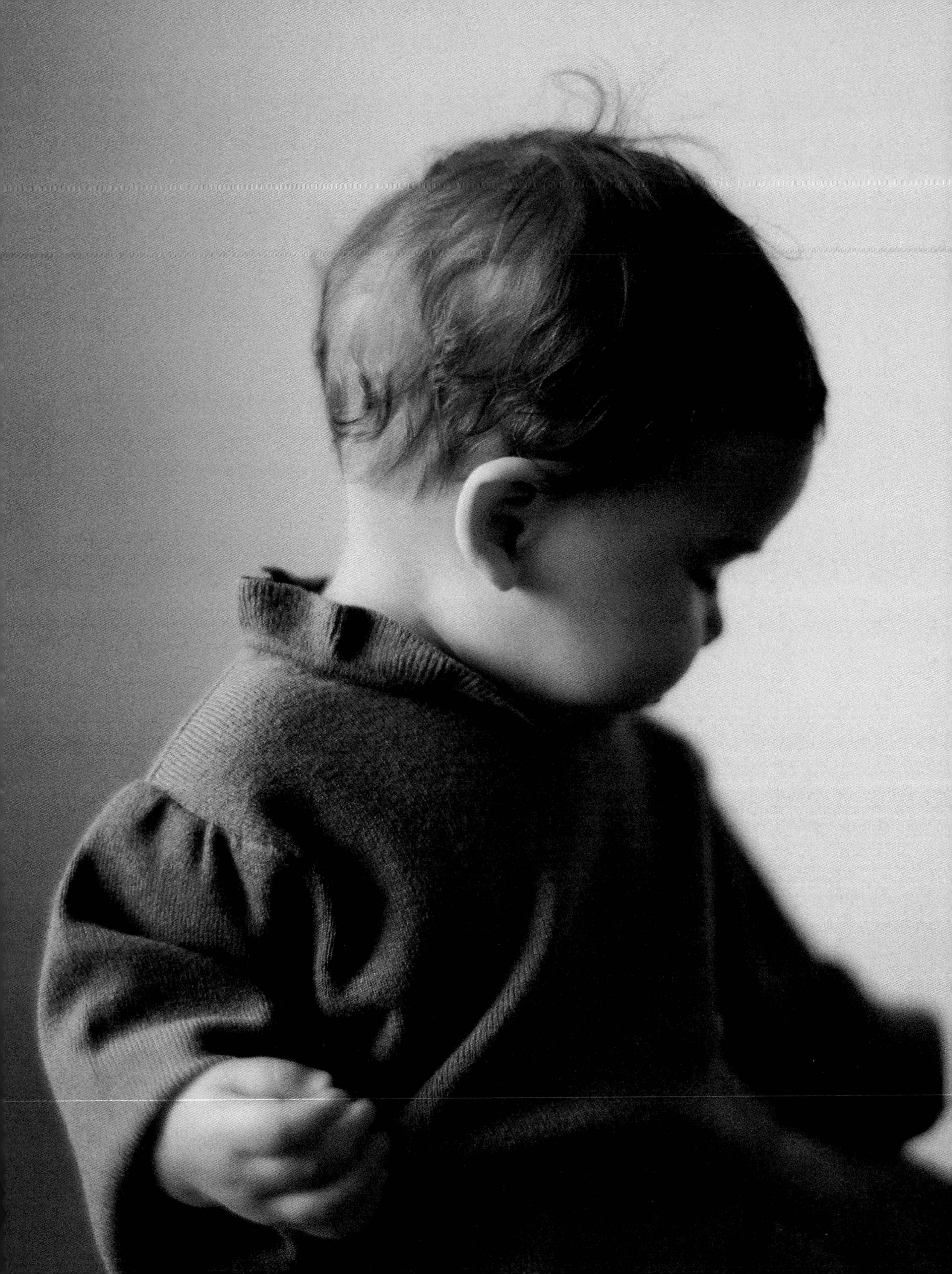

CHAPTER

# 6

# Composition

At the beginning of my career, I didn't fully grasp how much composition influenced the final look of my images. I was much more concerned with creating photos that showed love and connection than I was with incorporating "the rule of thirds" or "leading lines." I also worked primarily in a studio, and as a studio photographer, I didn't have competing elements to worry about. I was working with people in front of a white wall or gray seamless backdrop, so creating interesting and artful compositions just wasn't top of mind. As a result, my images were pretty boring.

Over time, I came to realize that making a compelling image of one or two people standing against a blank wall is one of the greatest challenges of studio photography. When in a studio, everything else is stripped away. All you have to work with are the people in front of you. How you choose to pose them helps you create a sense of connection, but how you choose to compose the image of that pose is what will elevate your art.

While the studio strips away distractions, outdoor and on-location photography challenge you to incorporate the environment around you creatively. Using the rules of composition can help guide the viewer's eye and emphasize the people in your photographs, setting them apart from the busyness around them.

In this chapter I'll share my favorite composition techniques and show you how to use them in your family photography. I still primarily work in a studio, so the majority of the examples I share are studio images. However, these rules of composition are the same regardless of where you work.

## Creating Triangles

The word "composition" always made me think of using the environment you are in to create an artistic image. But when photographing families, composition isn't just about the surroundings. It's also about how you position the people you are photographing within the frame. By creating interesting shapes, you can craft engaging portraits that are both visually appealing and emotionally compelling. And the best shape of all is the triangle!

In art, triangle shapes are used to create a sense of strength and harmony. Their simple structure naturally appeals to our human brains, guiding our eyes from one subject to the next. And their wide base creates a sense of stability, translating into strong, grounded images. If you photograph people, learning to see and create triangles in your portrait work is a must. But be warned, once you start creating them, you'll see them everywhere! I, personally, have become obsessed.

## Posing One Person

Because a person's head and shoulders naturally form a triangle, creating this shape can be done pretty easily when photographing one person. Filling the frame to show only your subject's head and shoulders is one way to achieve this look, as you can see in **FIGURE 6.1**.

Pulling back to capture your client's head, shoulders, and arms will also create triangles. When taking this approach, I like to direct my clients to bring their hands together in front of them. This creates two triangles in the frame, one formed by their head and shoulders, and another formed by their arms (**FIGURE 6.2**).

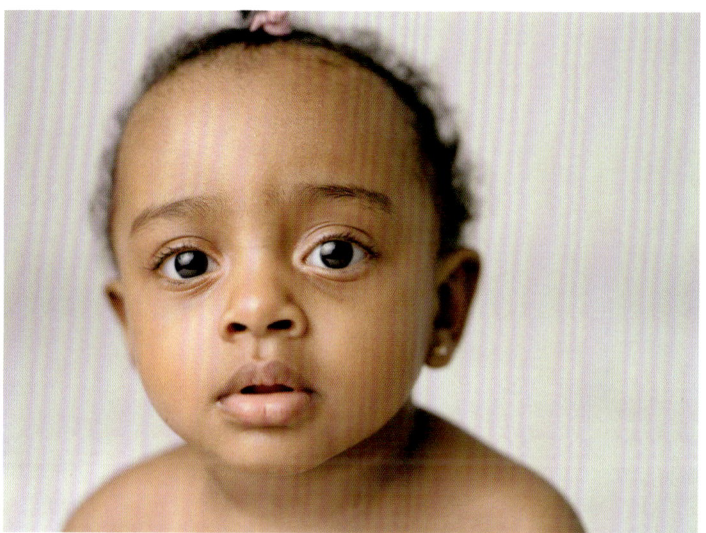

**FIGURE 6.1** Because a person's head and shoulders naturally form a triangle, creating this shape can be done easily when photographing one person.

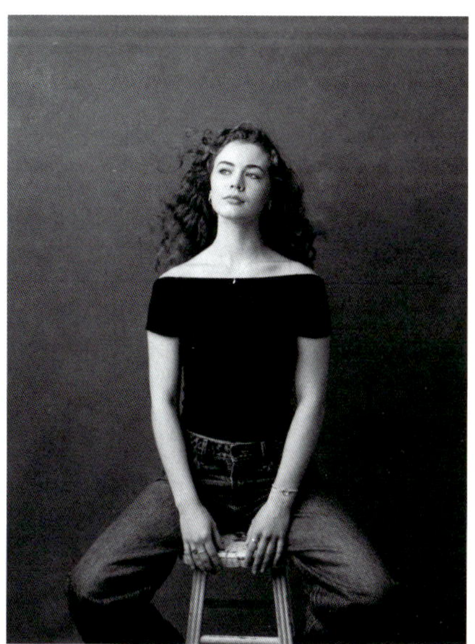

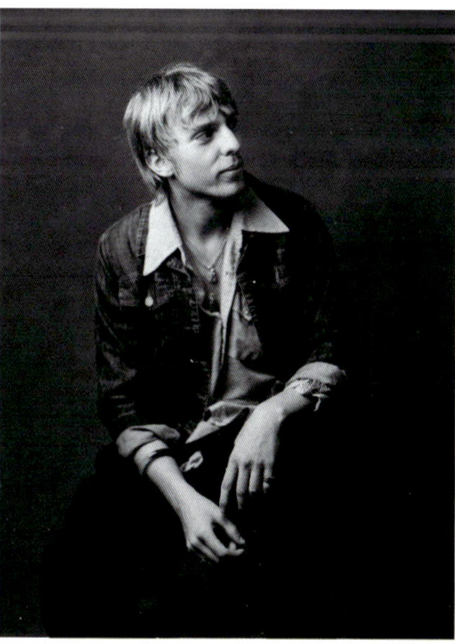

**FIGURE 6.2** Directing your subject to bring their hands together forms two triangles—one at the head and shoulders and another with the arms—for added visual interest.

When working with older babies (five to twelve months old), placing them on their belly with their arms under them for support will create a triangle (and make for adorable portraits) (**FIGURE 6.3**).

If they are old enough to sit on their own, having them sit facing the camera with both arms in front or to the side will also create a triangle. Babies naturally sit this way, so capturing a pleasing triangle shape is easy to do when photographing kids this age (**FIGURE 6.4**).

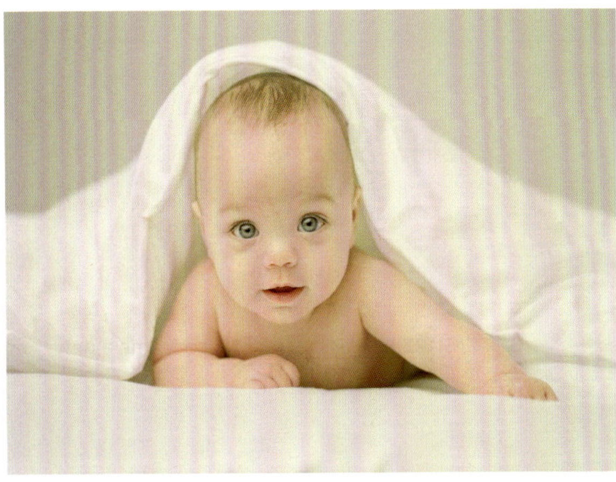

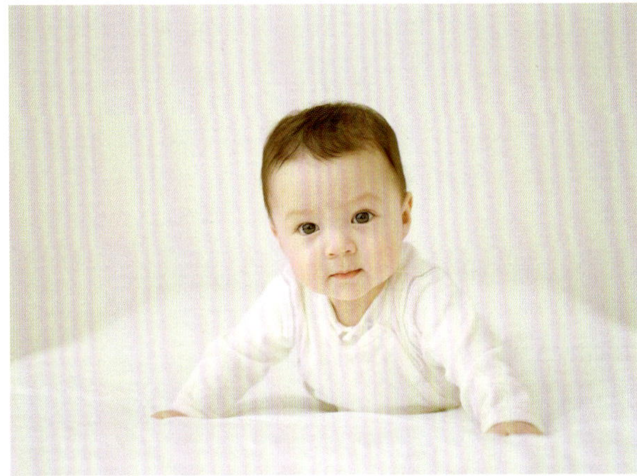

**FIGURE 6.3** Placing an older baby on their belly naturally creates a triangle shape, and makes for an adorable, visually pleasing portrait.

**FIGURE 6.4** Older babies sitting with their arms forward or to the side naturally create a triangle shape.

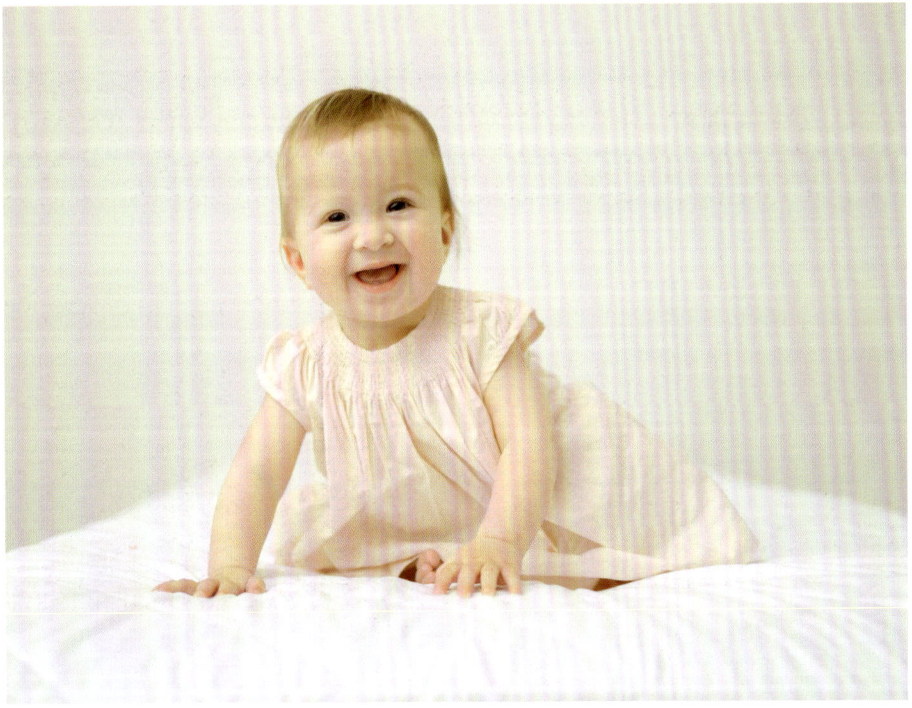

Positioning yourself eye level to your subject will help accentuate the triangle shape in all of these looks and create a sense of connection in the viewer.

When photographing newborns, I use blankets to make triangles (**FIGURE 6.5**). This builds visual interest into the photo while also framing the baby's face.

Having your client place one arm across their body is an effective way to create a triangular shape when photographing individuals. Small children will often do this naturally, so be ready to capture the moment when it occurs (**FIGURE 6.6A**). For adults, you can intentionally direct them into this position to achieve the same pleasing effect. For example, I frequently ask my maternity clients to drape an arm across their belly—this arm placement forms a flattering triangle that also highlights the pregnant form. A win-win (**FIGURE 6.6B**)!

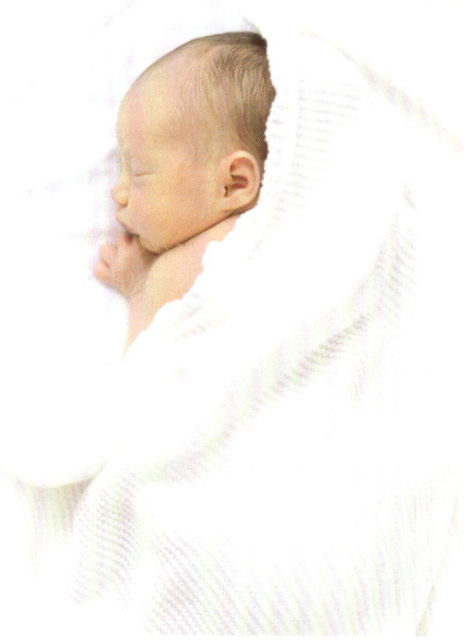

**FIGURE 6.5** Using blankets to frame a newborn creates soft triangles that guide the viewer's eye.

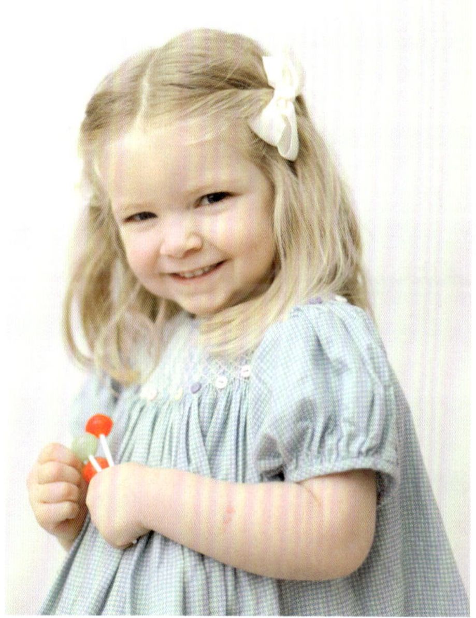

A

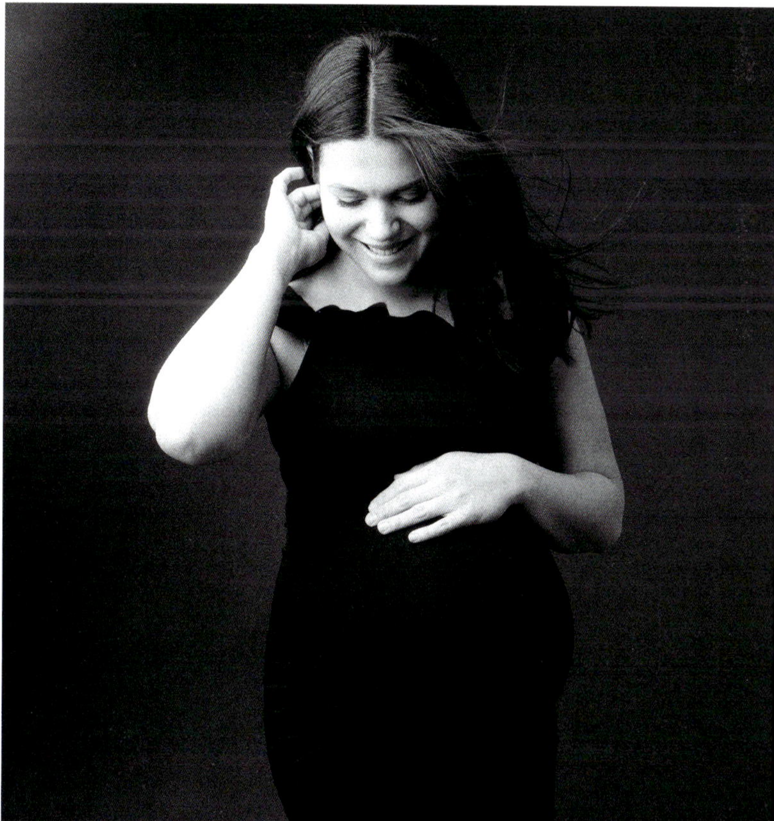

B

**FIGURE 6.6** Children will often naturally form triangle shapes by crossing an arm across their body. You can get the same look when posing adults by instructing them where to place their arms.

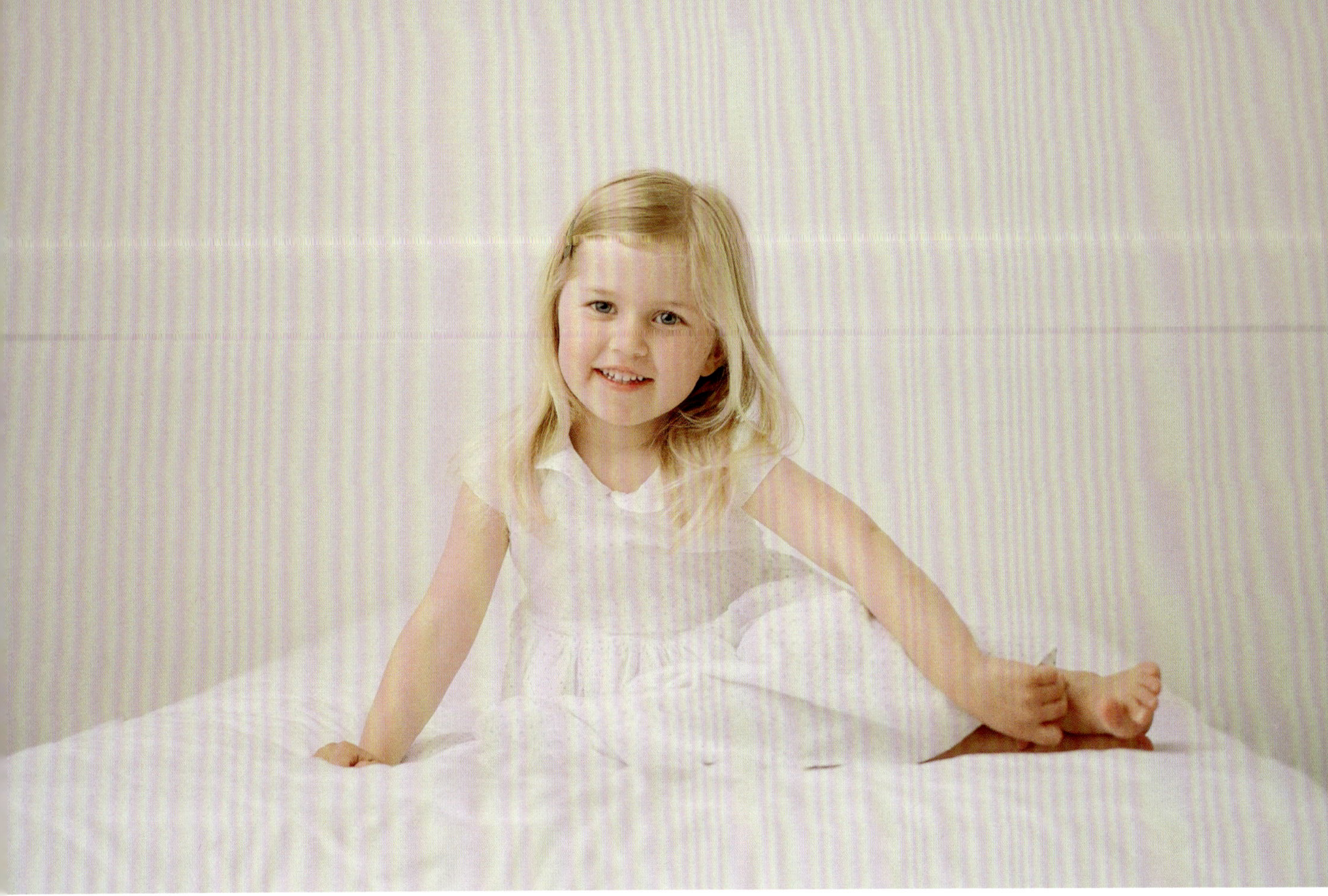

**FIGURE 6.7** The "mermaid pose" creates a beautiful triangle shape that's especially flattering for young children.

When working with school-aged children, I create triangles by directing them to sit with both legs to one side. I call this the "mermaid pose" (**FIGURE 6.7**). This pose results in a lovely triangle shape and is much more flattering than the traditional "crisscross applesauce" position that children learn at school, especially when the child you are working with is wearing a dress. I demonstrate the mermaid pose by doing it myself as I'm explaining it, but most little kids know exactly what I mean when I ask them to sit like a mermaid!

## Posing Two People

When using triangles while posing groups of two or more, the shape adds another layer of meaning as it creates a sense of cohesion and togetherness. This shape is very easy to create when photographing two people, especially when one of those people is a baby.

I love to photograph the newborns I work with on a bed. The bed's elevated height makes it easy for me to position myself eye level to the baby, and beds provide a comfortable, relaxed area for family members to sit for group photos. I have a twin bed in my studio, and when on location, I always ask to use the primary bedroom for photos.

When photographing a newborn with one parent or a sibling, I start with the baby on a bed, either on their belly or swaddled and on their back. I then ask their parent or older sibling to lie on their stomach, perpendicular to the end of the bed and facing the baby. Then I gently lift the baby's head to place it in the crook of their arm. Directing the parent or older sibling to look at you, look at the baby, and even bend down to kiss the baby is a great way to create multiple looks from this one pose, each one featuring a pleasing triangle shape.

If the older sibling I'm working with is too young to safely hold their newborn brother or sister, placing them on the bed, slightly behind the baby and instructing them to place a hand on the baby's head or bottom (or both) is another way to set up a safe and sweet sibling pose, while also creating a triangle shape (**FIGURE 6.8**)

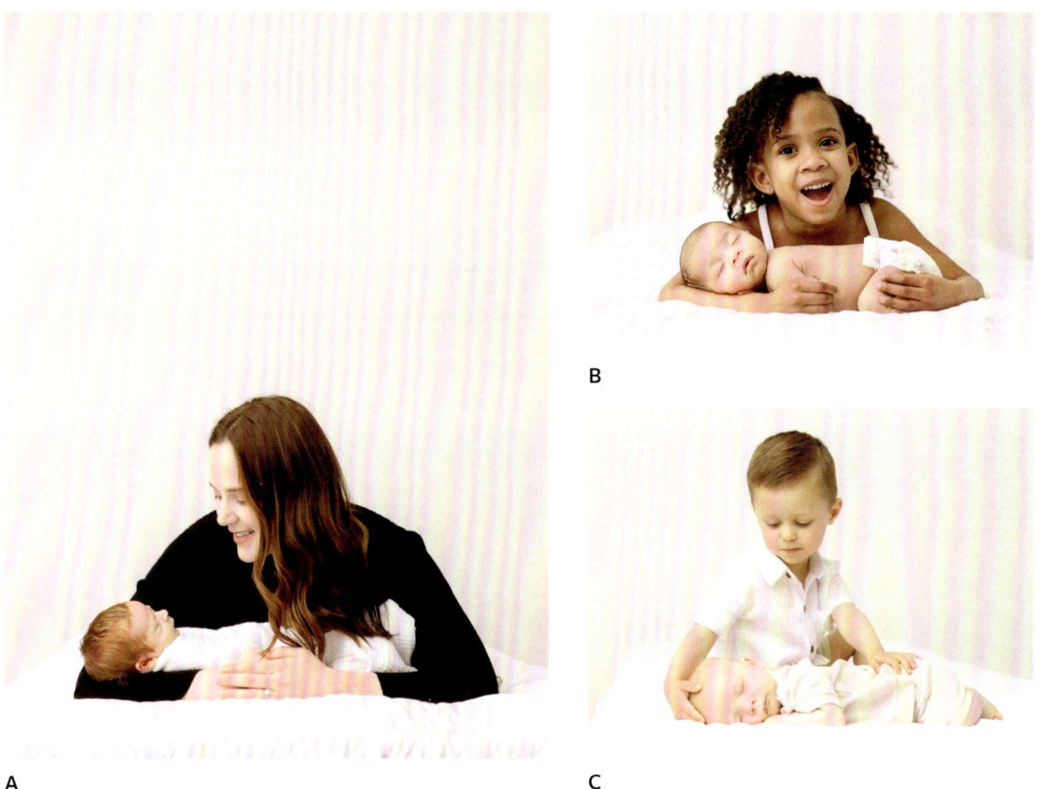


**FIGURE 6.8** Creating triangles when posing a newborn with a parent or sibling helps build a strong sense of connection, as well as visual interest.

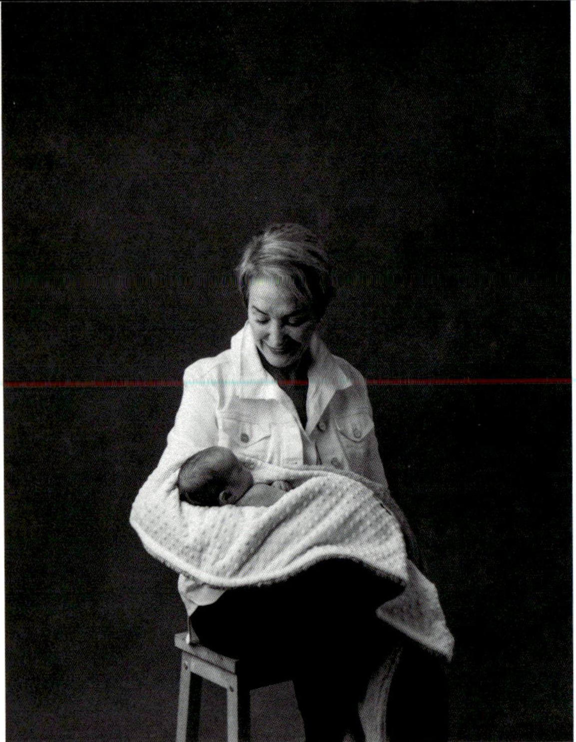
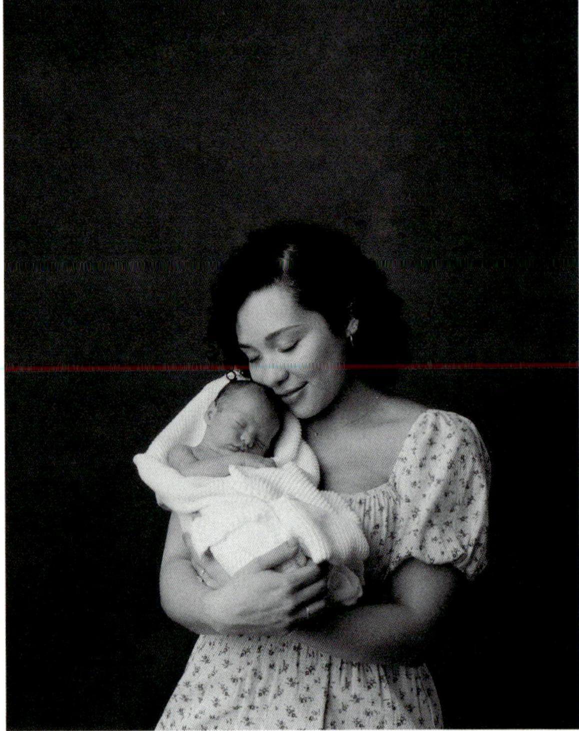

**FIGURE 6.9** Cradling a baby in the arms forms a natural triangle, while also creating a beautiful portrait.

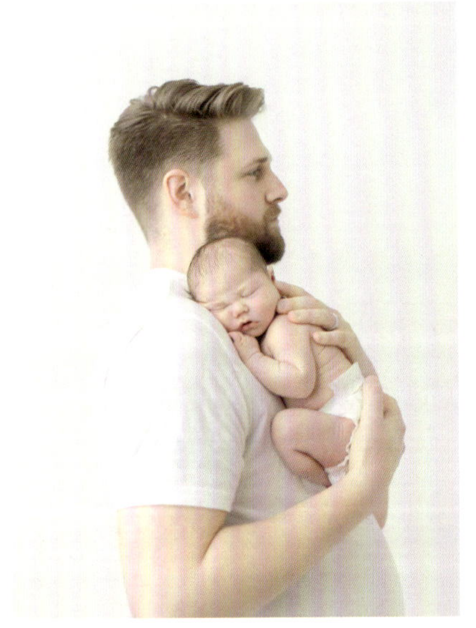

**FIGURE 6.10** This is one of my favorite newborn poses. It's sweet and supportive and features a natural triangle shape!

You can create beautiful triangles by having your client hold their baby in a cradle or a high cradle. Like when photographing individuals, the natural shape of their head and shoulders will create a triangle that is then emphasized by the bend in their arm as they hold the baby (**FIGURE 6.9**).

Positioning a parent profile to the camera and placing their baby on their chest with the baby's head resting on their shoulder will also create a triangle shape (**FIGURE 6.10**). This is one of my favorite poses for new fathers. Position yourself eye level to the baby and focus on the baby's face to capture the image.

When working with older children and adults, directing them to tilt their head and body toward each other will create a triangle shape. This works in both sitting and standing poses and is a quick and easy way to create the triangle shape. For **FIGURE 6.11**, I directed the husband to stand next to his wife with his back to me, drape one arm across his wife's belly, and look down at the top of her head. I then asked her to hold on to his arm with one hand, cradle her baby bump with the other, and tilt her head toward her husband, resting it on his shoulder. This is a lovely pose in and of itself, but the tilt of the head creates a relaxed sense of intimacy while also adding to the pleasing triangle shape.

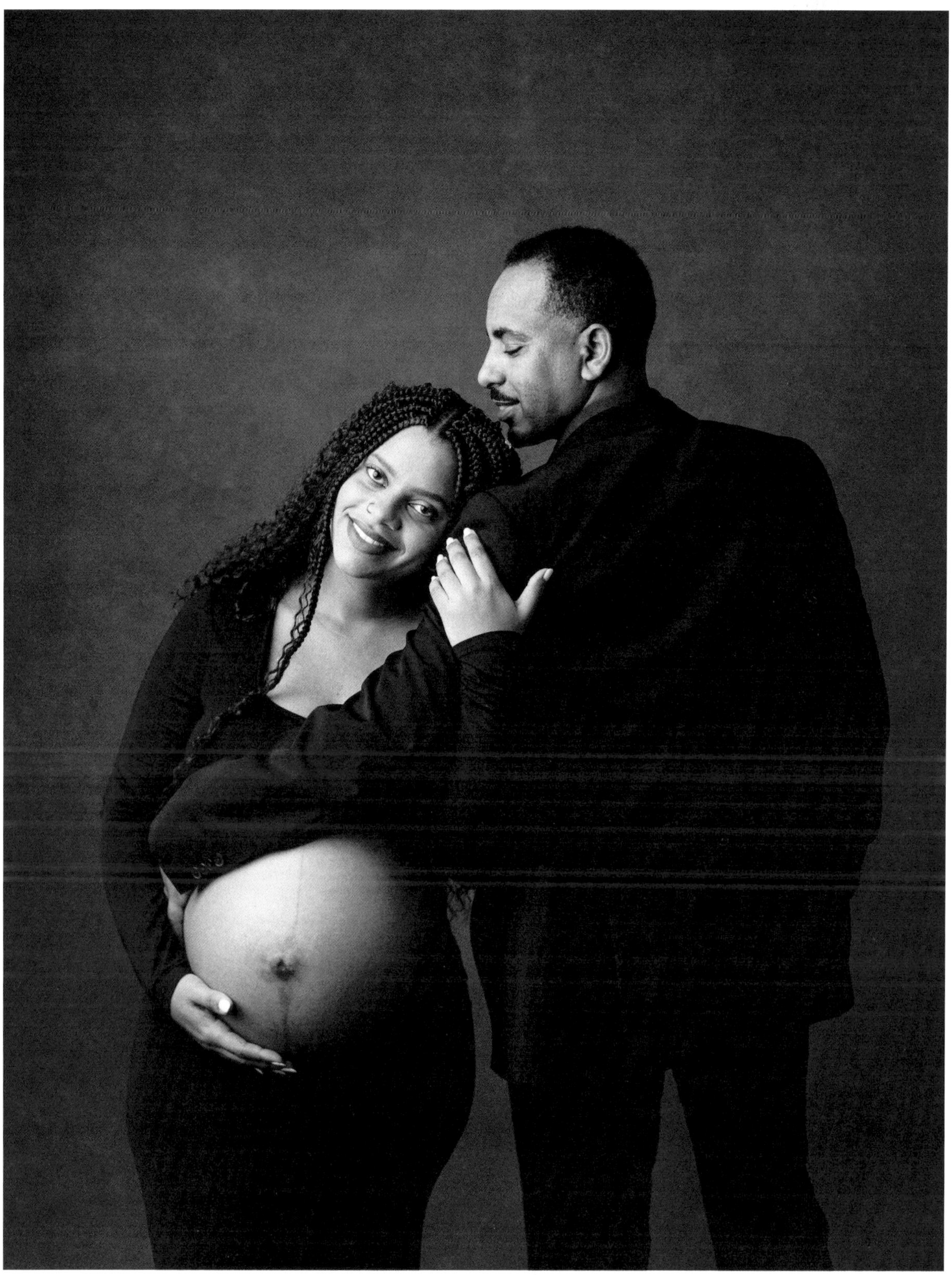

**FIGURE 6.11** Triangles help create a sense of connection when used in portraiture.

## Pro Tip: Giving Clear Direction is Essential When Working with Children

Years of working with children have taught me the importance of giving clear, specific direction when posing clients.

At the beginning of my career, I used to ask children I worked with to hug each other, for example, to create a nice shape and sense of connection in a photograph. I quickly learned however, that asking a child to hug their sibling is a recipe for disaster. Hugs can very easily turn overly enthusiastic when working with school-aged children (**FIGURE 6.12A**). Most of the time it's unintentional, but you don't want anyone getting hurt at your sessions. Learn from my mistakes!

When photographing children together, I give very clear directions on what I want them to do. Instead of saying, "Hug your brother or sister," for example, I'll say something like "I want you to stand next to your (brother or sister) and I want you to both look at me. (Older sibling), gently place the arm that is next to your (brother or sister) on their back. Use your other hand to hold their hand and lean your heads toward each other" (**FIGURE 6.12B**).

I mirror what I'm asking them to do as much as I can. And I always have a lot of stickers and lollipops on hand for rewards.

This may seem like a lot to explain but trust me! The extra time it takes to set up a pose in this way is worth it.

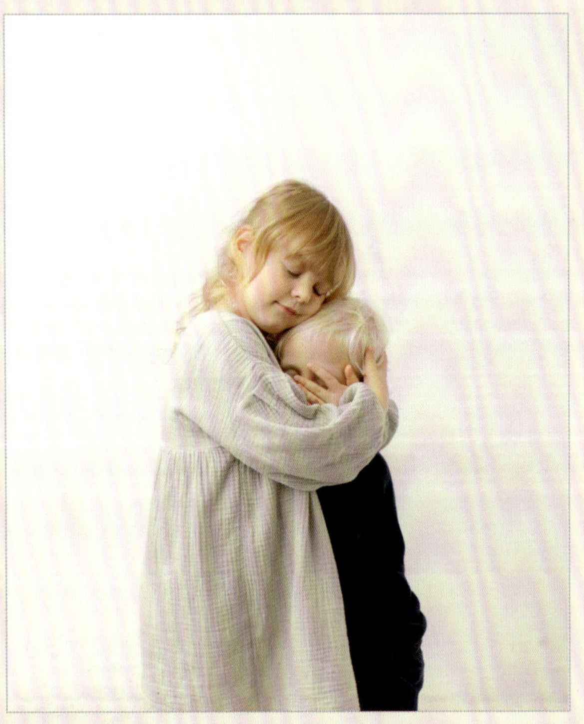

A

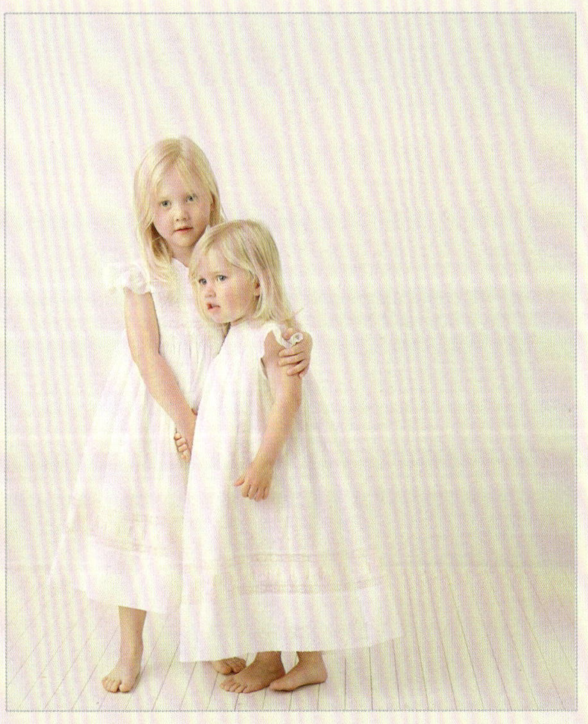

B

**FIGURE 6.12** Be specific with your instructions to avoid over-enthusiastic "hugs" that can quickly get rough! Clear direction helps children pose comfortably while also forming a perfect triangle.

## Posing Three or More

The key to posing groups of three or more is to avoid creating straight lines. And while that sounds easy, it can be challenging, especially when photographing larger groups.

When photographing families with children of varying heights, I find it helpful to start with one person, then build the shape as I add people into the frame, creating triangles as I go. **FIGURE 6.13** shows how I do this when working with children. At this session, my goal was to get an image of three children together—two older girls and their baby brother.

To set up the photo, I posed the youngest of the two girls on the bed in the mermaid pose (**FIGURE 6.13A**). Then I asked her older sister to sit next to her (**FIGURE 6.13B**). Next, I placed the baby on the older sister's lap (**FIGURE 6.13C**). I noticed however, that his head was directly under hers, forming a straight line rather than a triangle, so I helped her shift the baby slightly to one side, and asked the two girls to tilt their heads toward each other. The result is a lovely portrait of the three, and a pleasing triangle shape (**FIGURE 6.13D**).

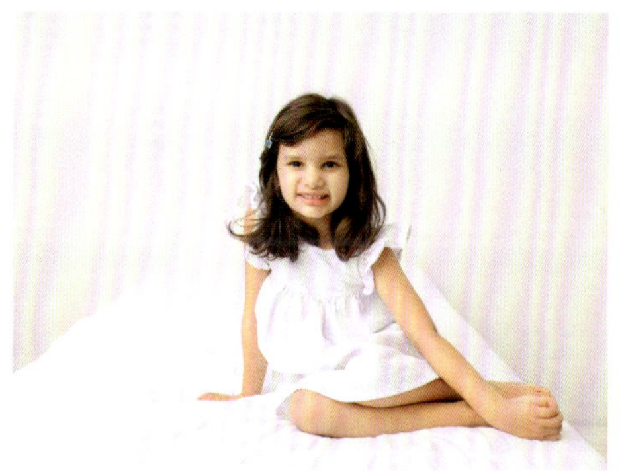

A

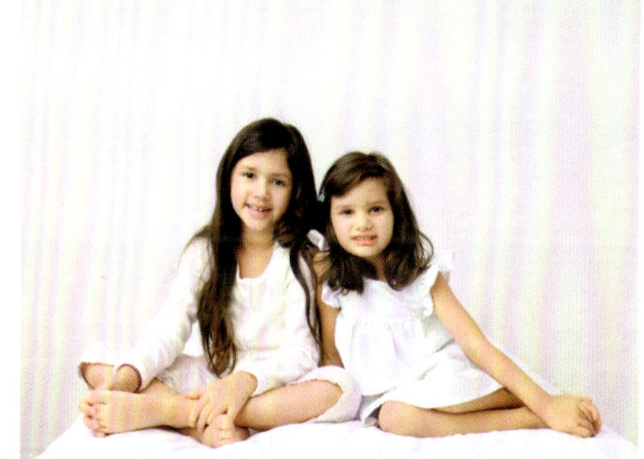

B

**FIGURE 6.13** Building a group pose one person at a time helps avoid straight lines and create pleasing shapes.

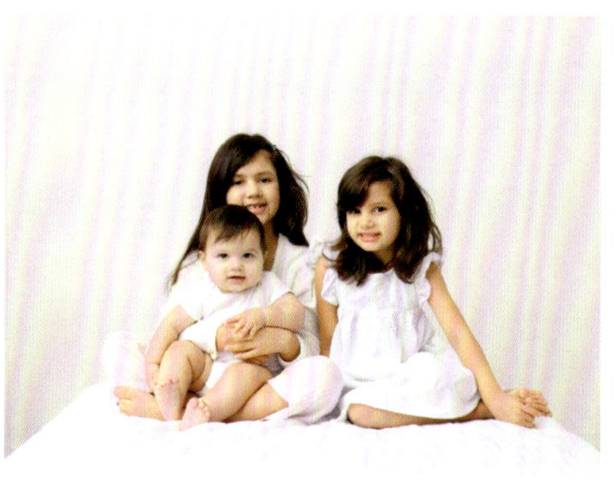

C

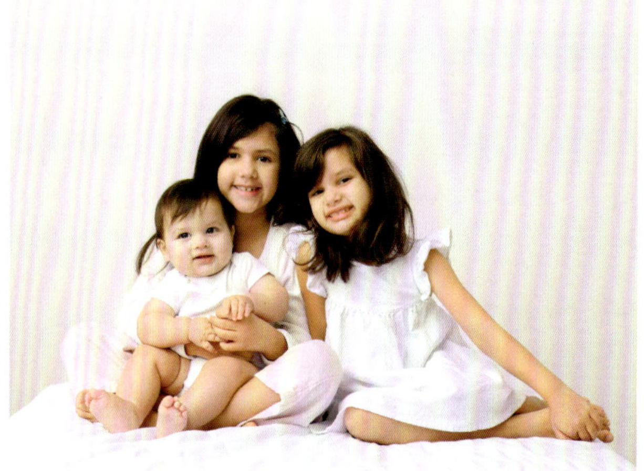

D

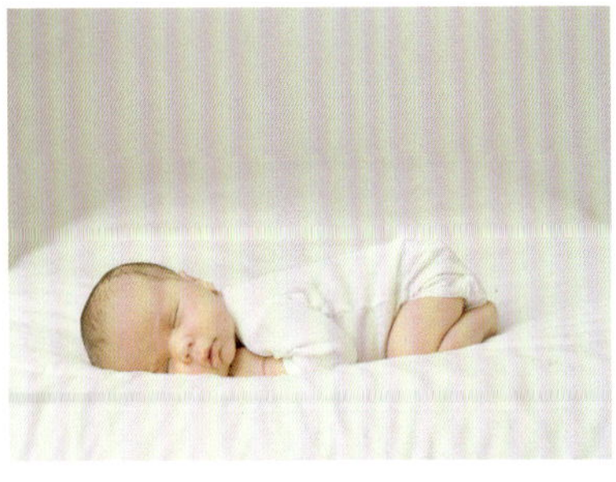

A

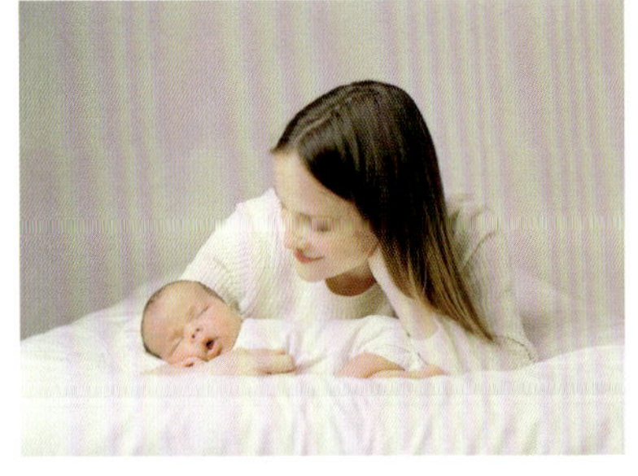

B

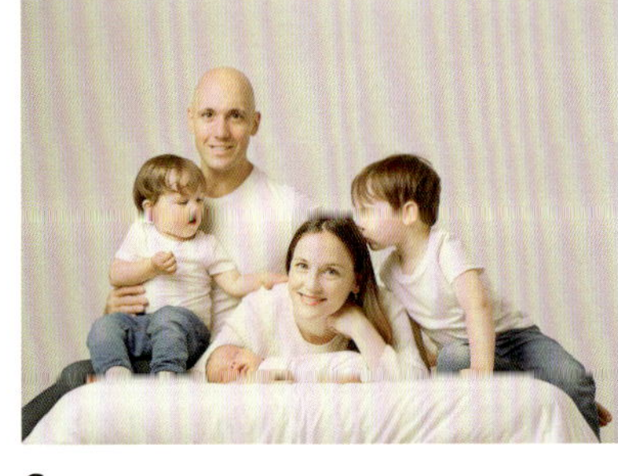

C

**FIGURE 6.14** Building a family portrait step-by-step.

I build all of my family portraits using the same approach: I start with one anchor person and then add other family members in one at a time, carefully avoiding straight lines and intentionally creating triangles as I go. **FIGURE 6.14** shows this in action. I began with the newborn (**FIGURE 6.14A**), then added the mother (**FIGURE 6.14B**), and then incorporated the father and two older children to complete the full family portrait (**FIGURE 6.14C**).

When photographing groups of adults (or groups with adult-sized children) who are roughly the same height, you can use stools of varying heights to stagger your group.

Creating triangles with your posing takes practice, but the more you do it, the easier it will become. Look for this shape when photographing individuals and remind yourself to build it when working with groups. It will absolutely change the quality of your photos for the better!

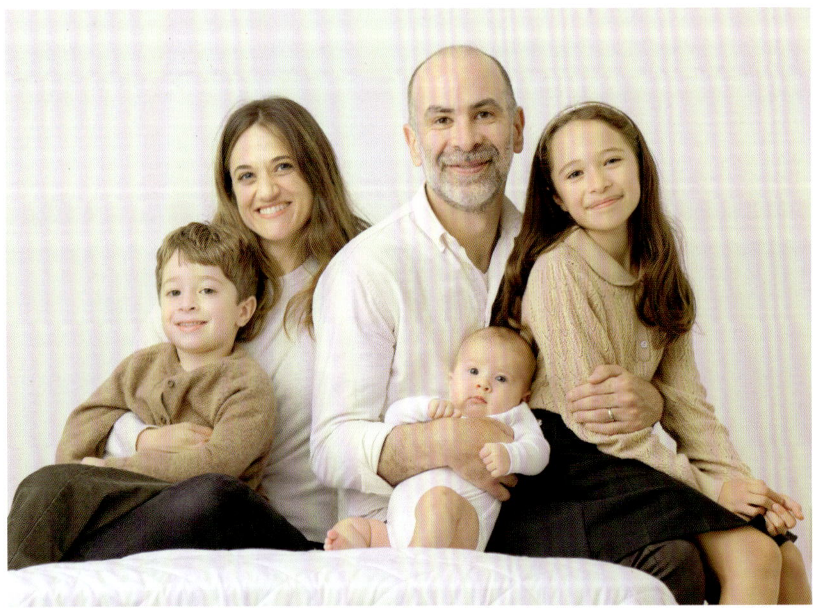

**FIGURE 6.15** Family of five, posed to create triangles.

## Rule of Thirds

While triangles form the foundation of strong, compelling photos, other compositional techniques—like the rule of thirds—can add balance, variety, and visual interest to your work.

The rule of thirds is a classic for a reason. It consistently enhances images, whether you're working in a studio or on location. It's also incredibly easy to apply, even in the midst of a fast-paced family session.

To use the rule of thirds, imagine your frame divided into nine equal parts by two horizontal and two vertical lines. The idea is to position the key elements of your photo along these lines or at their intersections. Doing so draws the viewer's eye to the subject and creates a composition that feels natural, balanced, and engaging.

In portraiture, one simple way to apply the rule of thirds is by placing the subject's eyes off-center, roughly along one of the upper horizontal lines. This is a technique I use frequently in the studio with clients of all ages (**FIGURE 6.16**).

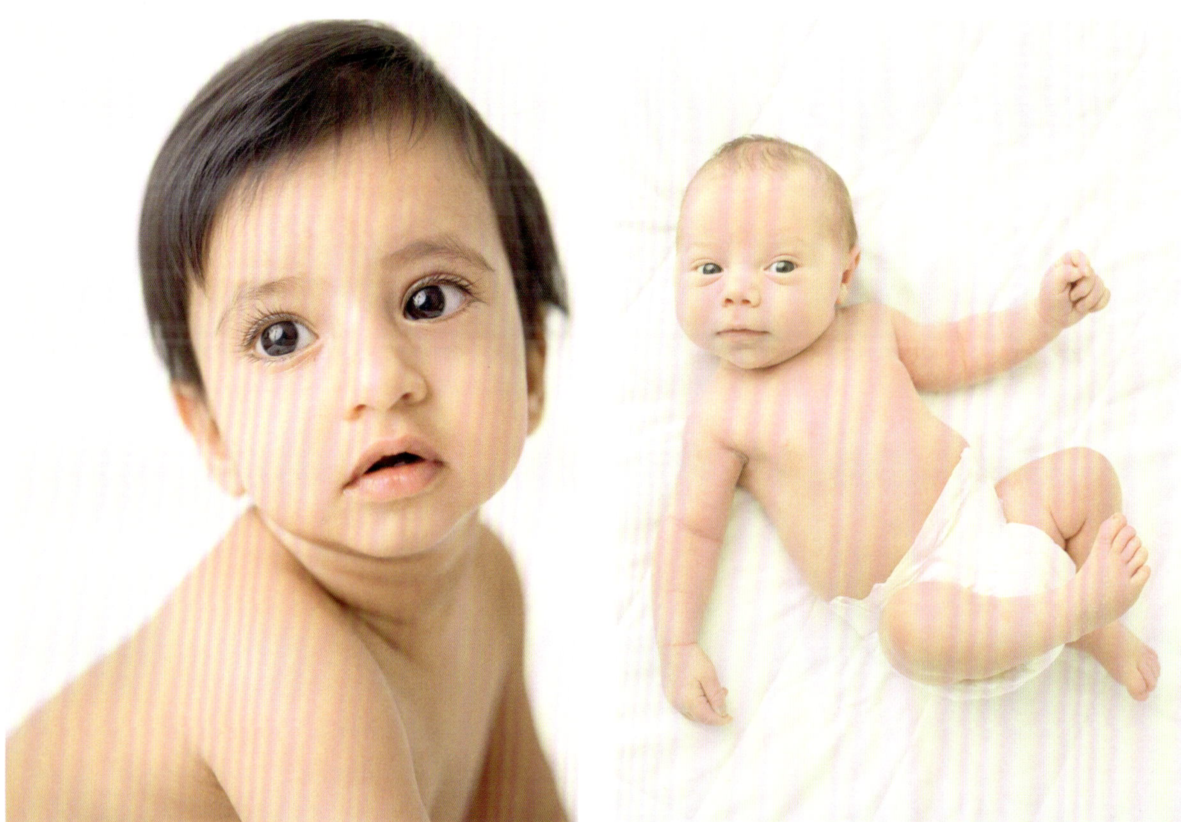

**FIGURE 6.16** Rule of thirds.

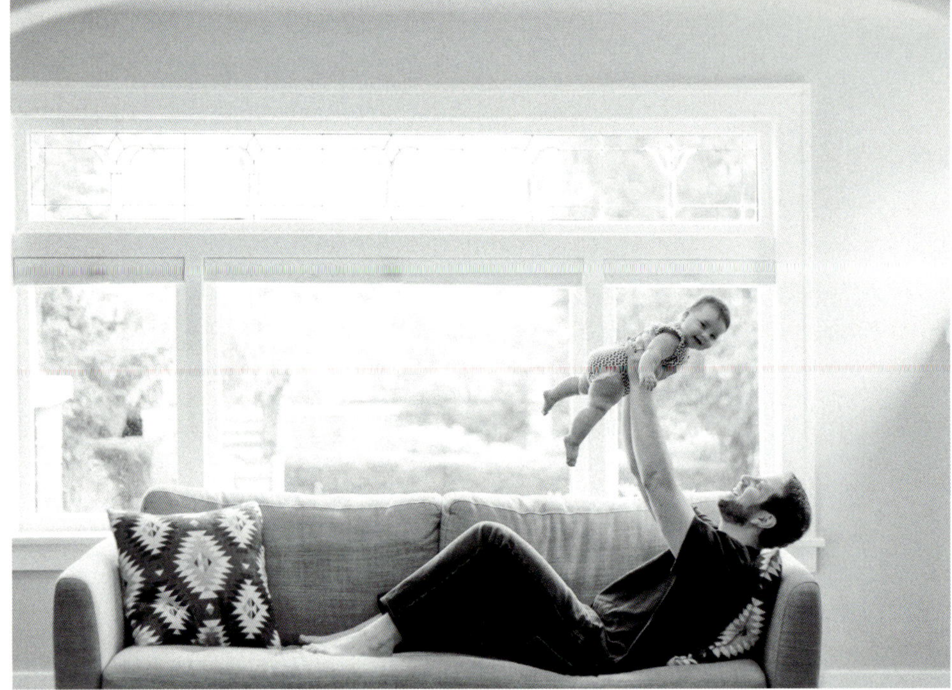

**FIGURE 6.17** Pulling back and placing your subject in one third of the frame to incorporate the surrounding environment adds storytelling elements to your rule-of-thirds composition.

Placing the subject's eyes off-center, roughly along one of the upper horizontal lines in your photo grid, is a quick and easy way to compose using the rule of thirds. You can also incorporate the surrounding environment—whether in the studio or on location—by pulling back and placing your subject in one third of the frame. This technique not only highlights your subject but also tells a richer story by including more of the setting (**FIGURE 6.17**).

Many modern cameras offer a feature that displays a grid in the viewfinder. If your camera has this option, turning it on can be incredibly helpful for composing with the rule of thirds—and for training your eye to see strong compositions naturally.

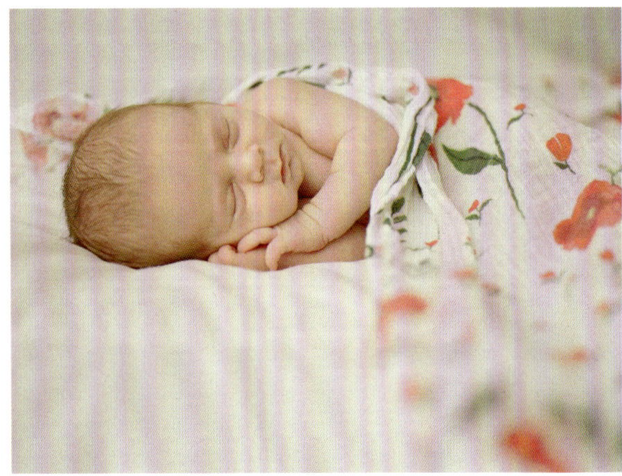

**FIGURE 6.18** In this image, I positioned the baby in the top third of the frame to create a soft, balanced, and visually engaging composition.

You can also build this skill by simply practicing placing your subject off-center. Take time to experiment with positioning your subject in different areas of the frame (**FIGURE 6.18**). This exercise will not only strengthen your eye for composition, it will also make it second nature to spot interesting framing options during your family sessions.

While the rule of thirds is lovely, sometimes breaking it by centering your subject can produce powerful and striking images, especially when paired with negative space.

## Negative Space

Negative space is the empty area in a photograph that surrounds your subject. This space draws attention to that subject and gives a little bit of drama. I love using it when working with clients in my studio, paired with a center composition (**FIGURE 6.19**). To create an image using negative space, simply place your subject(s) within the frame, leaving plenty of empty space around them. You can choose to place your subject anywhere within the empty space.

Negative space is one of my favorite composition techniques. You will see it in a lot of my work.

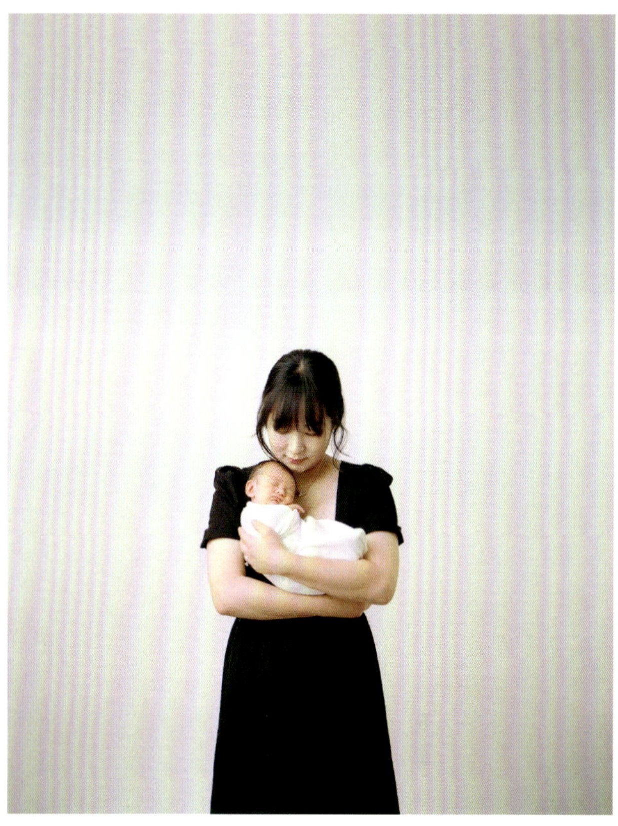

**FIGURE 6.19** Negative space combined with a center composition draws attention to the subject and adds a sense of drama.

## Fill the Frame

Filling the frame is basically the opposite of negative space. When filling the frame, you want to zoom in so that your subject(s) takes up all or most of the image.

Filling the frame removes the environment from your photo, allowing the viewer to focus solely on the people in the image. It also creates a sense of intimacy between the subject and the viewer, like being invited into a special private moment (**FIGURE 6.20**).

I like switching between negative space and filling the frame as a way to get multiple looks from one pose. **FIGURE 6.21**, for example, is the same mother and baby that we saw in Figure 6.20, but in this image, I zoomed in to create a tight portrait of the two of them. Same pose, but very different look and feel.

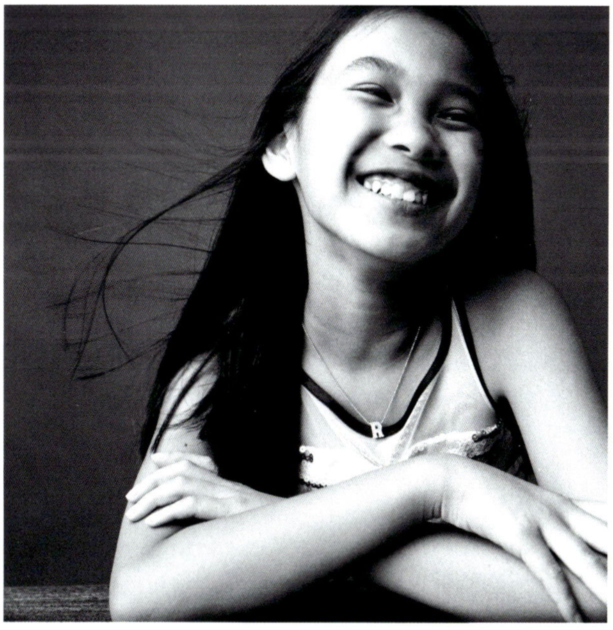

**FIGURE 6.20** Filling the frame with your subject removes distractions and allows the viewer to focus fully on them.

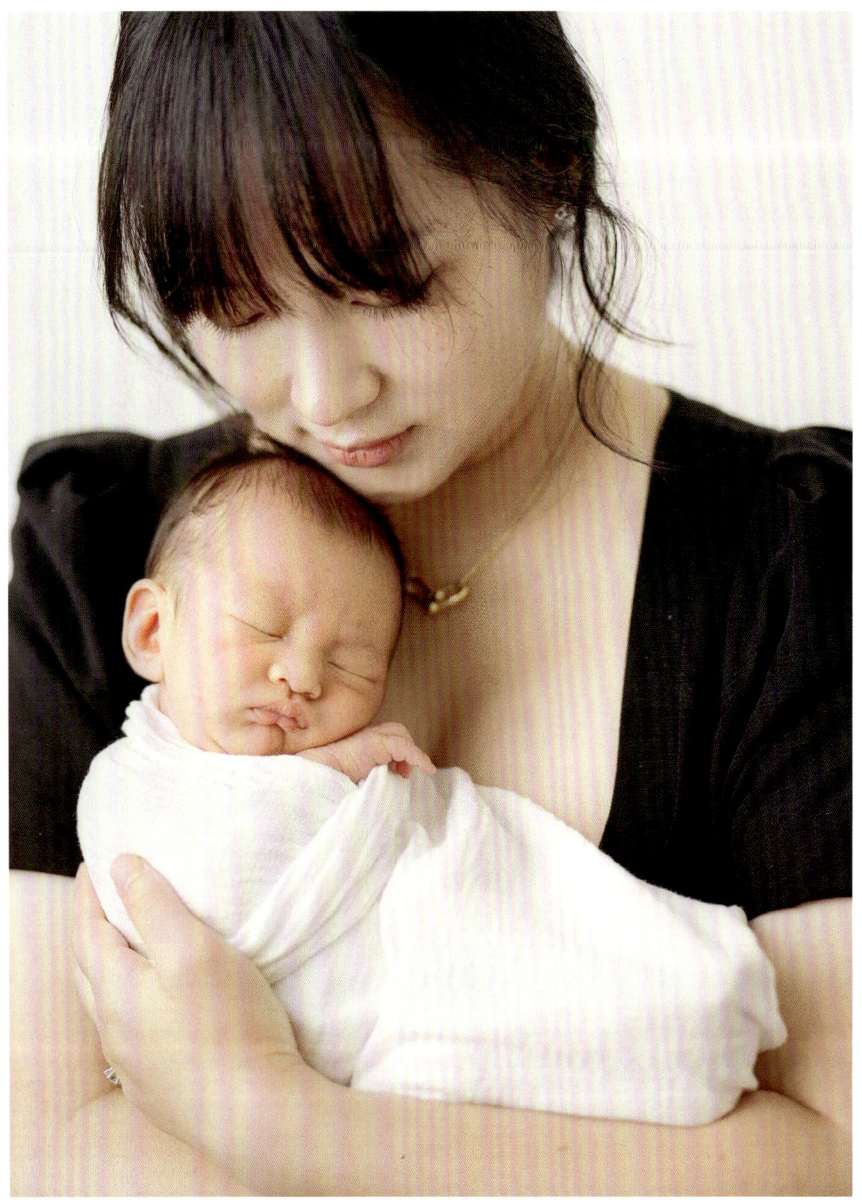

**FIGURE 6.21** Switching from negative space to filling the frame is a simple way to create variety from a single pose.

## Leading Lines

**FIGURE 6.22** is a photograph I took of my sons many years ago while visiting the tulip fields in the blooming season. It's also a great example of leading lines.

Leading lines in a photograph draw the viewer's attention to the subject. They can be natural or man-made, curved or straight, obvious or subtle. If they draw the viewer's eye to your subject, they're leading lines, and can be used to add visual interest to a photo.

Look for lines when photographing families and use them to your advantage by either placing your subject(s) where the lines converge, or by using the lines to point directly to the people you are photographing. Pay attention, because once you'll start looking for them you will notice lines everywhere! For example, I work in a very simple studio. My work is extremely minimalistic, and yet, I use leading lines in my photos all the time. The twin bed I use when posing newborns, children, and families creates two perfect lines that I use to draw attention to the people I photograph (**FIGURE 6.23**).

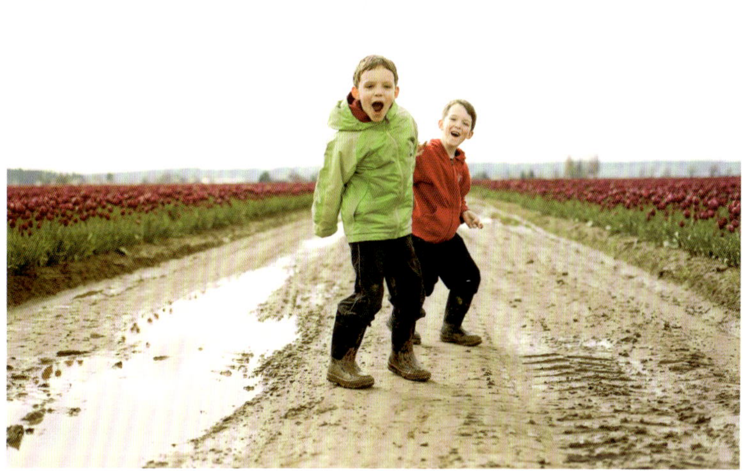

**FIGURE 6.22** Leading lines, like the tulip rows in this photo, naturally draw the viewer's eye toward the subjects.

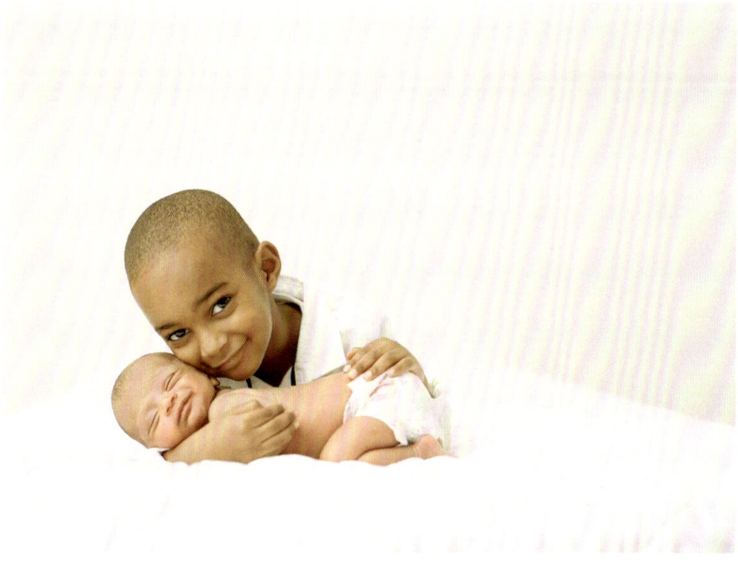

**FIGURE 6.23** Even minimalistic settings, like a studio bed, offer opportunities to use leading lines to guide focus.

## Putting It All Together

Spend some time playing around with all these techniques. I often use more than one compositional rule at a time in my work, as you can see in **FIGURE 6.24**, and I encourage you to do the same.

Always start by posing your clients with the intention of capturing or creating triangles as you go. Then step back and decide how to frame the image.

Working with the rules of composition will allow you to create visually appealing photos that will also connect with your audience on a deeper level. Don't forget to capture the same pose using different composition techniques. This is a quick and easy way to add variety to your galleries.

As you practice, these techniques will become second nature, allowing you to focus on what matters most—connecting to the families you photograph! So, start small, experiment, and let composition transform your photographs, one intentional frame at a time.

**FIGURE 6.24** (Opposite page) Don't be afraid to use more than one compositional element at a time. This is a photo of one of my sons playing on the beach one foggy morning. As you can see, I used the rule of thirds, negative space, and leading lines in this image. And the natural shape of his head and arms makes a pleasing triangle shape!

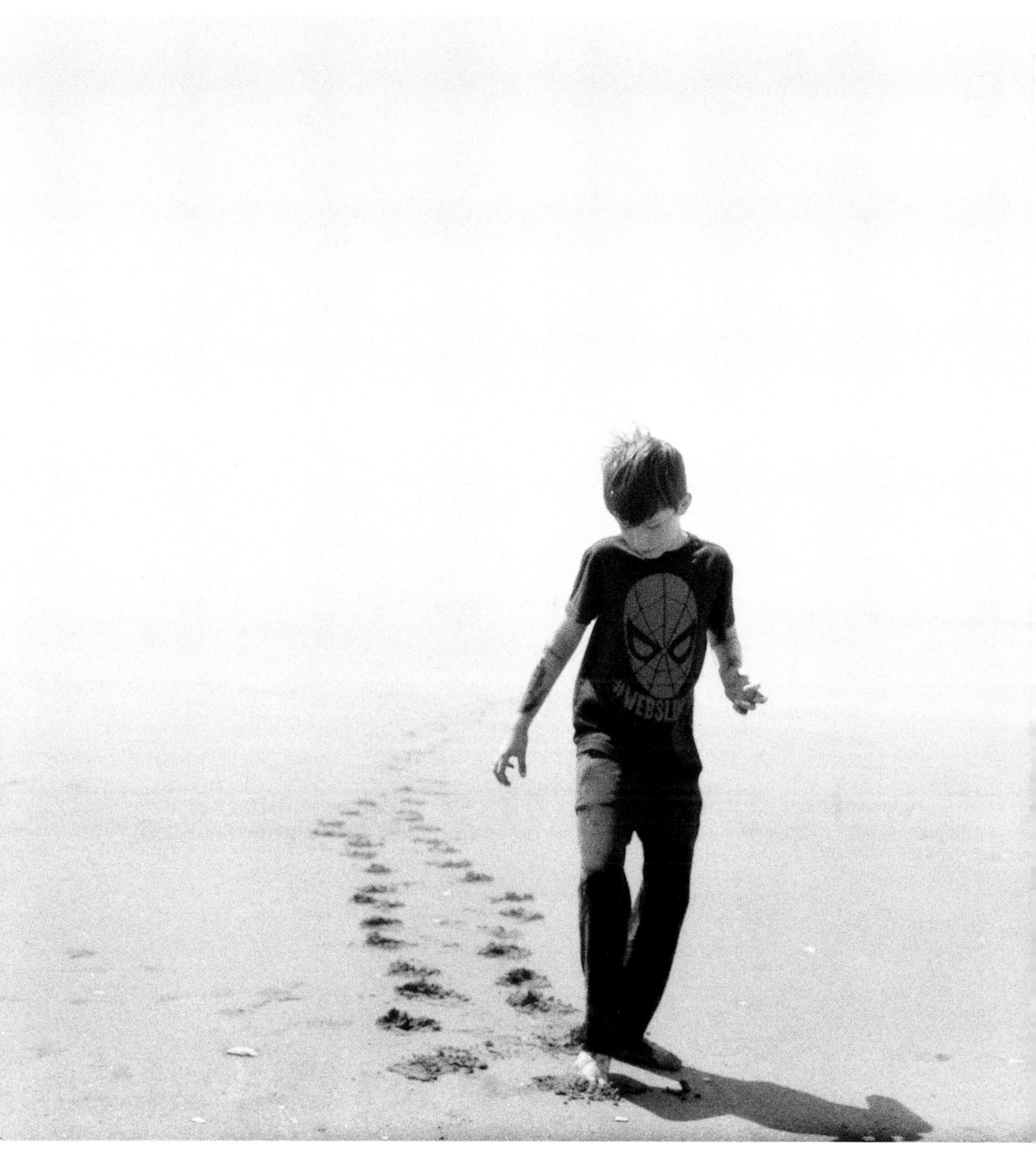

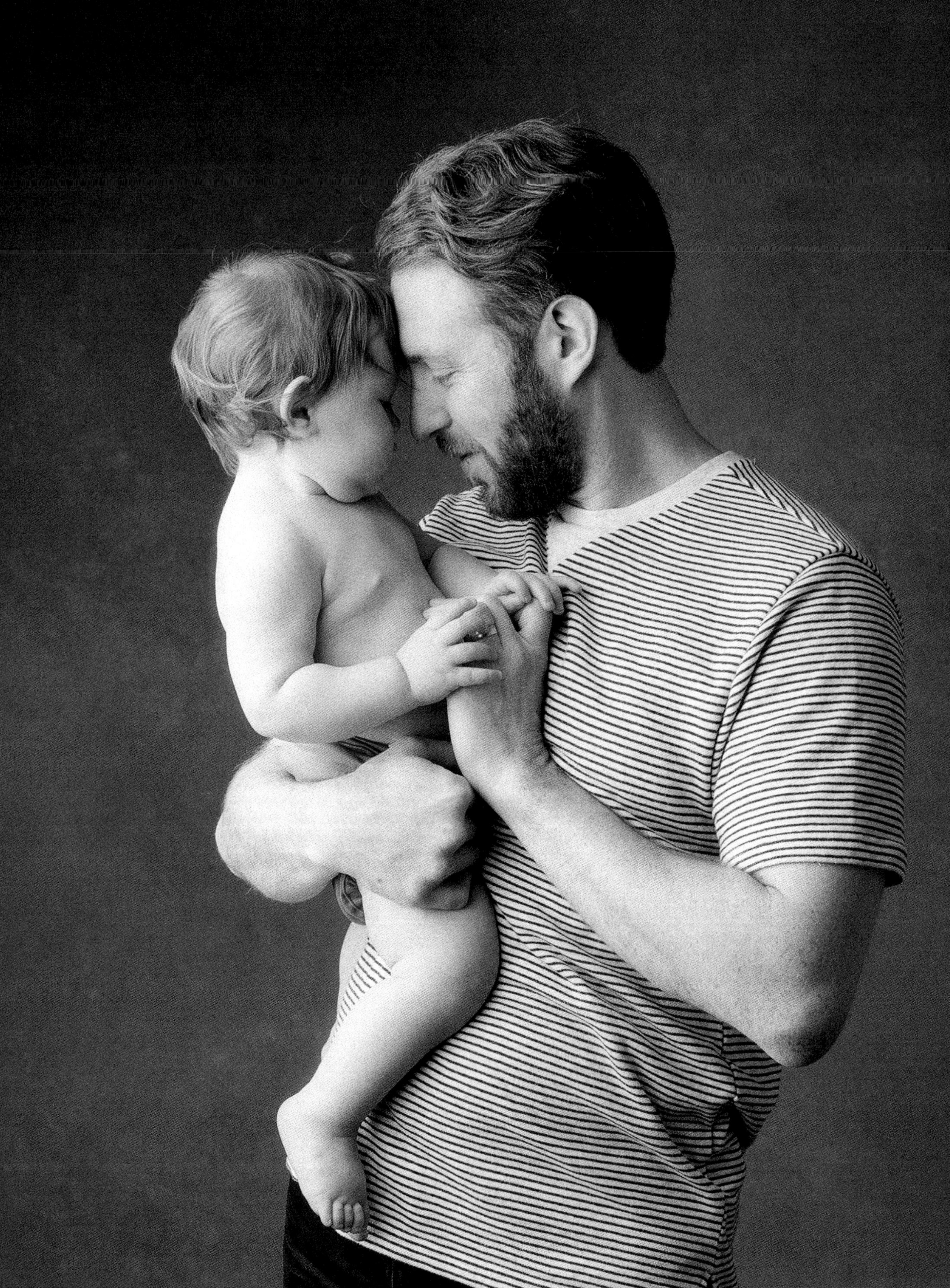

CHAPTER

# 7

# Posing Flow

Remember, as a photographer, you are also a director. And as the director, it's your responsibility to have a clear vision for the scene you're creating. Setting expectations for your work and creating a plan to meet those expectations are essential steps in bringing your vision to life. Establishing a posing flow that includes a set of go-to poses used in the same order at every session will help you achieve this goal.

A consistent posing routine removes the stress of trying to create flattering poses on the fly. It gives you a structured plan to follow, so you never have to worry about what to do next. And that ensures that you can create a well-rounded, robust gallery for your clients while also maintaining order during busy family photo sessions. Your photoshoots will run smoothly and efficiently, and your clients will be thrilled with the results.

In this chapter, I'll share why creating consistent, predictable routines for your posing is so beneficial to your work as a family photographer. I'll share the posing flows I use in my work, and I'll teach you how to create a system for yourself. For the sake of explanation, I use the terms "mother" and "father" in my descriptions, but these flows work beautifully with all kinds of families.

## Consistent, Predictable Routines

Consistent, predictable routines (CPRs for short) are something I learned about in graduate school while earning my teacher accreditation. The concept is simple but powerful: CPRs are routines we create for ourselves to intentionally form habits.

The human brain is always searching for ways to simplify and automate tasks. This is why we often develop unintentional habits without realizing it—driving home from work the same way every day, for example. Once a habit is established, we can perform it on autopilot without much thought. Again, looking at driving as an example, how many times have you arrived at your destination without even remembering the drive? It's a pretty amazing ability. Our brains are designed to work this way. So why not use it to our advantage?

Consistent, predictable routines provide structure for us to follow, thereby reducing stress and anxiety. They help us with time management, giving us a clear framework to follow and allowing us to anticipate what action to take next. This helps with prioritizing important tasks. Over time, these CPRs turn into healthy habits, which frees up our conscious mind to focus on other things.

In classrooms, consistent predictable routines help children complete mundane tasks without distraction so they can focus on learning. When applied to your photography business (and to posing specifically), CPRs have a profound impact on efficiency, the quality of your work, and your client experience. This is something I had to learn the hard way.

### Creating Order out of Chaos

Despite my background as a kindergarten teacher, I didn't use CPRs in my photo sessions at the beginning of my career. Like many photographers, I believed that relying on the same poses in the same order at every session would stifle my creativity. Instead, I would show up to my photo shoots without a clear plan, hoping the family I was photographing would inspire me and the magic of the moment would just happen.

Sadly, that was rarely the case. Instead of feeling inspired and creative, I felt stressed. Without a plan, I had no idea how to start or what to do next, which made every session feel chaotic. I was working without direction, desperately trying to capture every interaction, every laugh, every little moment, while simultaneously worrying that I was missing something important. I didn't know how or when to end the session either, and so I would just shoot and shoot and shoot. It was exhausting for me and my clients. My sessions were a disorganized mess, a far cry from the professional experience I wanted to create for my clients.

At one session in particular, the children I was working with were extra rambunctious, the parents were visibly frustrated, and I was completely overwhelmed. I had no plan, no control, and no idea how to pull things back together. The session felt like a disaster. The pictures weren't great. And sadly, this was not the first time this had happened to me. Something had to change.

Driving home that day I couldn't stop thinking about how different my photography sessions felt compared to my days in the classroom. Back then, I'd managed an entire room full of five-year-olds, and it never felt chaotic. My classroom was fun, calm and productive: a lovely place to learn and work.

The difference? The classroom had consistent, predictable routines. The kids knew what to expect and so did I, which made everything run smoothly. I decided to incorporate the same idea into my photography business. If consistent, predictable routines could create order out of the chaos of a kindergarten classroom, surely they could do the same for my photoshoots.

And they did.

Establishing CPRs for my posing flow changed everything. Instead of walking into a photoshoot hoping for inspiration to strike, I started with a plan. That plan gave me confidence. I knew exactly what I was going to do, how I was going to do it, and when I was done. That structure allowed me to focus on my clients rather than scrambling to come up with poses on the fly. I could slow down, connect with the families I was working with, and think about how to make them look and feel their best.

Once I implemented CPRs, my stress levels plummeted, and my creativity went through the roof. With the foundation of the predictable flow, I was free to focus on other things, like compositions, connection, and all the small details that take a photo from good to great. And that boosted my confidence—an unexpected but welcome outcome.

## Enhancing the Client Experience

Another unexpected outcome of implementing CPRs was the positive impact they had on my clients' experiences. They helped me create a calm, organized environment for the people I serve. In that light, I look like the professional I am, and the people I'm working with trust me.

Because I have a well-formulated plan, I'm able to start every session by explaining exactly what we'll be doing and in what order, so my clients know what to expect. For example, at newborn sessions, I let the parents know that we'll begin with photos of the baby alone, then move on to photos of the baby with their mother, then photos with both parents, and end with photos of the baby and their dad. Sharing the plan in this way reassures the parents that I've got everything under control. They can relax and just enjoy the experience. It also gives them the chance to share any special requests they might have, which helps me make sure I'm capturing images they will treasure for years.

If a family has older children, I share the same level of detail with them. I let them know I'm going to photograph the baby alone, take their photo with the baby, and take some photos of the entire family. I also make it crystal clear that there are rewards at the end, once we're done. Children thrive on predictability and letting them know what they can expect from our time together helps them feel more comfortable, cooperative, and like they are an important part of the day—which of course, they are.

Because I'm working from a plan, my photoshoots run smoothly and efficiently. My clients often comment on how seamlessly my sessions flow, and I've lost count of the number of glowing reviews I've received where people specifically mention my ability to work quickly and calmly, even with babies and toddlers in the mix. That's the beauty of CPRs. They don't just help me as the photographer—they directly enhance the client experience as well. When clients leave the session feeling like it was easy, fun, and stress-free, they're more likely to come back for future sessions, leave positive reviews, and refer me to their friends!

Consistent, predictable routines truly are a game changer, and best of all, they are fairly easy to create.

## How to Create Your Own CPRs

To set up your CPRs, start by making a list of the types of sessions you do. For me, that includes newborn, family, and maternity sessions.

### Start with Your "Must Haves"

Outline the images you want to capture at each session. This step is about identifying the must-have photos that will form the foundation of your gallery. Don't worry about what poses you will use, yet. That will come later. For now, it's important to just have a firm idea of the kinds of photos you want to create for each type of session you do.

For example, at a newborn session, I always aim to capture:

- The baby alone
- The baby with each parent
- The baby with siblings (when applicable)
- The baby with the entire family

For a family session, I want to make sure I get:

- The child(ren) alone
- The children together, if there is more than one child
- The child(ren) with each parent
- The entire family

For maternity sessions, my foundational images include:

- Profile images to the left and to the right
- Straight-to-camera photos
- Cropped images of just the belly
- Photos with the partner or other children, if present

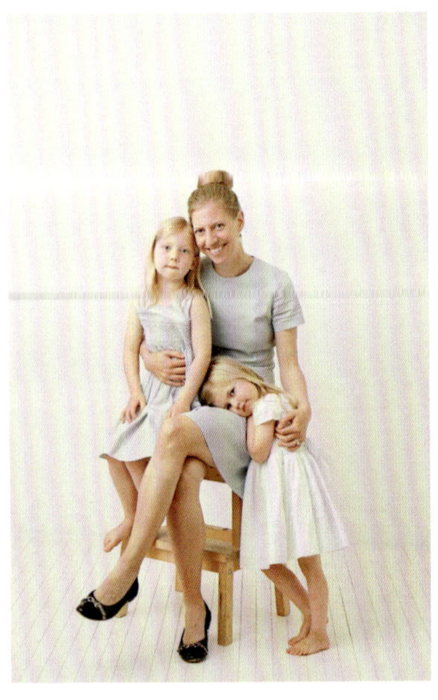

A

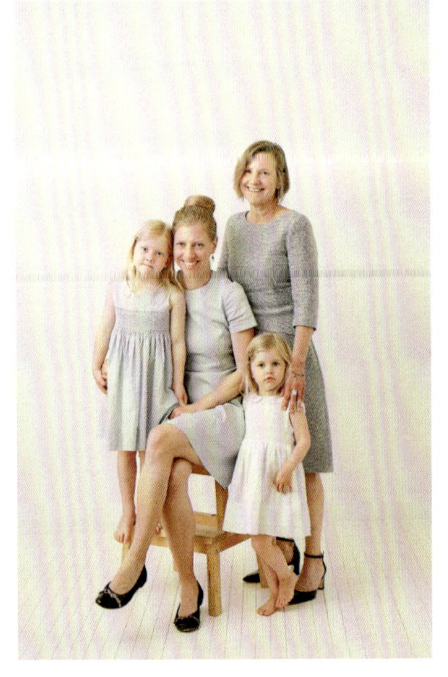

B

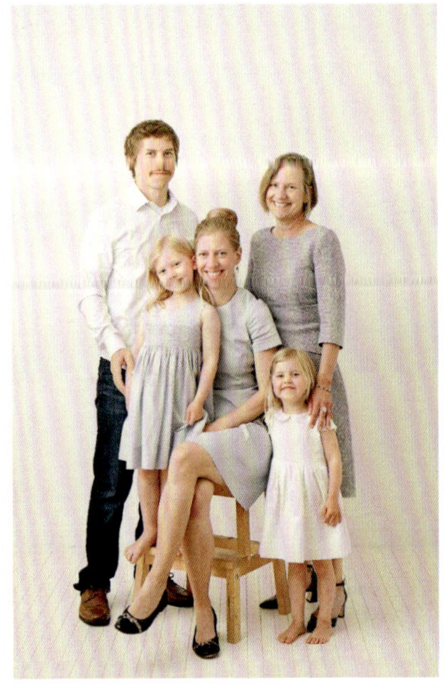

C

**FIGURE 7.1** Start with an "anchor": For these images, I started by posing the mother. I added her children (Figure 7.1A), then grandmother (Figure 7.1B), and finally the father (Figure 7.1C) to create a full family portrait.

### Establish an Order

Once your shot list is established, decide on the order in which you'll take your photos. Take the time to think through the entire session when doing this. Knowing what you know about your clients, where is the best place to start? How would you like the session to end? What flow makes the most sense for efficiency?

### Start with an "Anchor"

When photographing families or groups of people, I recommend starting with one person as your anchor. Pose that person first, then bring others into the frame until you have all, or most, of your must-have images.

In **FIGURE 7.1**, I started with the mom as my anchor. Once she was seated and posed, I brought her children to her for a photo (**FIGURE 7.1A**). Then I added her mother into the frame to get an image of the mother, daughters, and grandmother (**FIGURE 7.1B**). From there, I included her husband and captured the full family photo she requested (**FIGURE 7.1C**). Starting with an anchor and building from there is quick and efficient, and it gives you the time to construct your groupings, building triangles as you go. As you learned in Chapter 6, constructing triangles and being aware of composition in your poses helps add visual interest to your photos.

### Posing Flow: Newborns and Family

When working with newborns, my goal is to keep the baby I'm working with relaxed, calm, and happy, and so I start my newborns sessions with photos of the baby alone. Starting with the newborn gives me the time I need to soothe the baby and ease them into a comfortable pose.

Once the baby has been photographed (**FIGURE 7.2A**), I move on to capture photos with their mother (**FIGURE 7.2B**). From there, I'll bring the father in and get some family portraits (**FIGURE 7.2C**). I end with photos of father and baby (**FIGURE 7.2D**)

This flow allows me to get the majority of my must-have photos without having to disturb the baby. In fact, once the baby is posed, I don't pick the baby up until the very end of the session, when I hand them to their father for some standing poses.

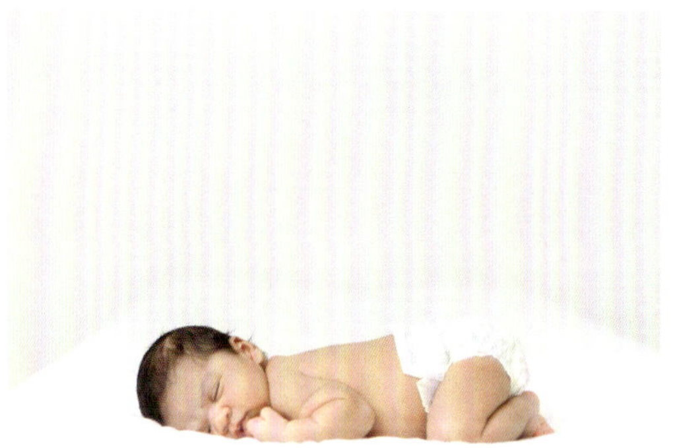

A

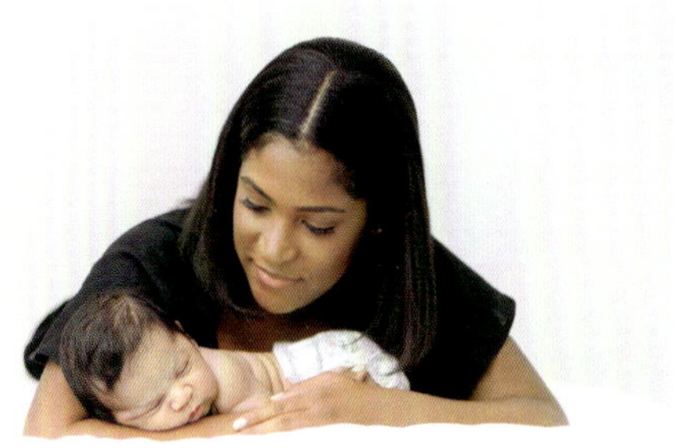

B

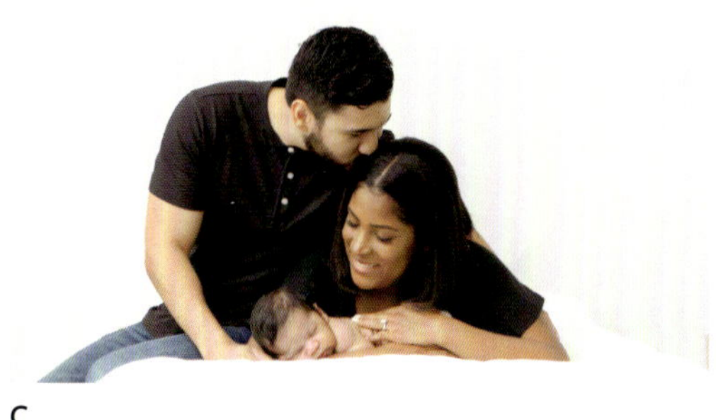

C

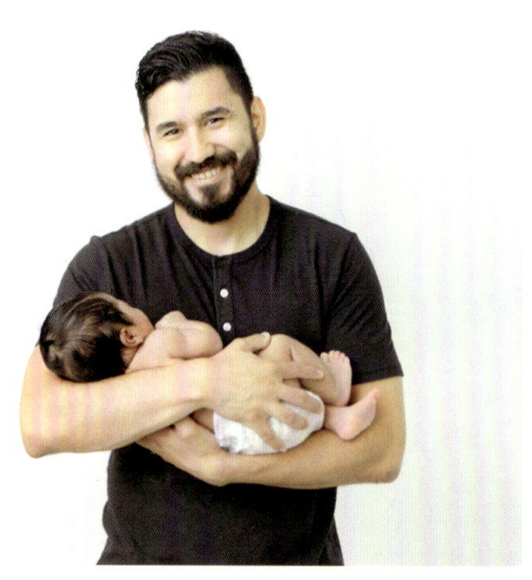

D

**FIGURE 7.2** My newborn flow: Start with baby alone (**A**), add the mother (**B**), add both parents for family photos (**C**), and end with baby and father (**D**). This routine works great when in the studio and when working with newborns and families on location.

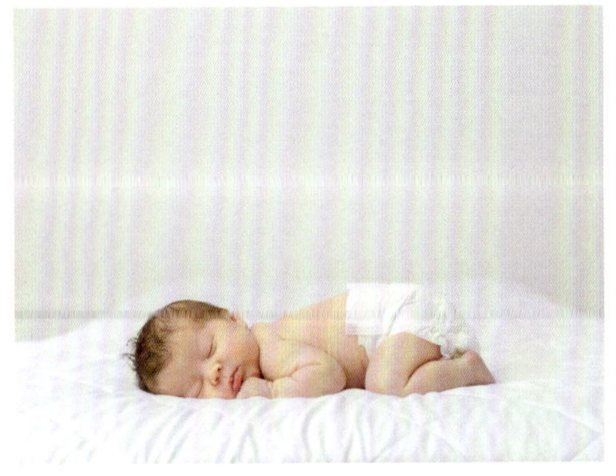

A

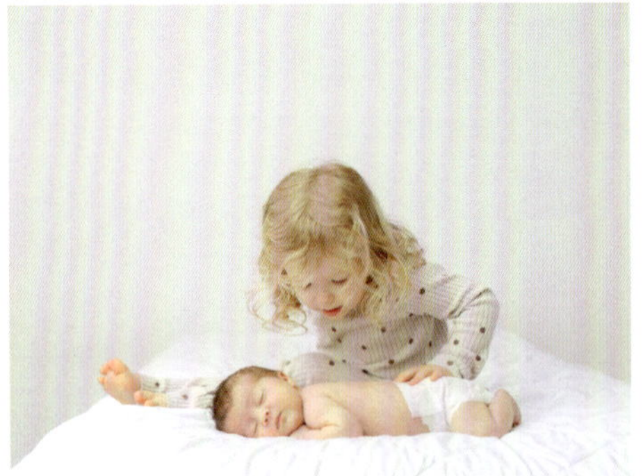

B

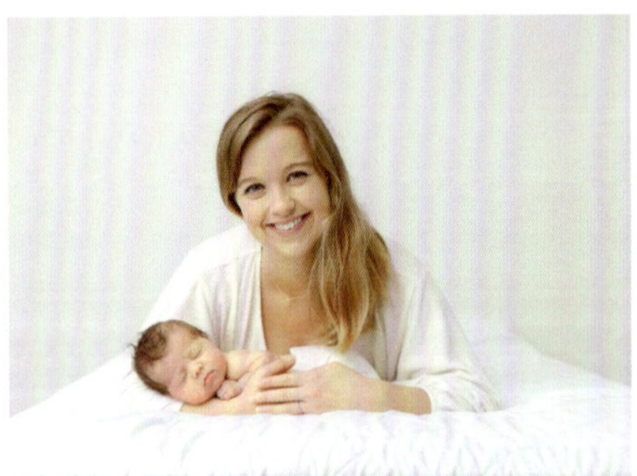

C

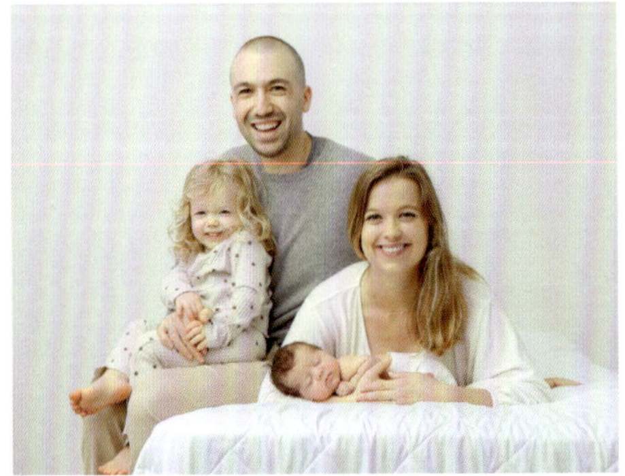

D

**Pro Tip:** Moving a sleeping baby too much may wake them up. To keep your little client content, comfortable, and happy throughout the session, build a posing flow that minimizes handling and allows the baby to rest comfortably as you work.

### Posing Flow: Newborns and Family with Older Kids

If the family I'm photographing has older children, I can easily adjust my newborn flow to include images of the baby with their sibling(s) just after photos of the baby alone, but before images with the newborn and their mother. The framework, however, stays the same. The newborn is the anchor, and I bring everyone else to them until the very end when I pick them up and place them in their father's arms. **FIGURE 7.3** shows this flow in action.

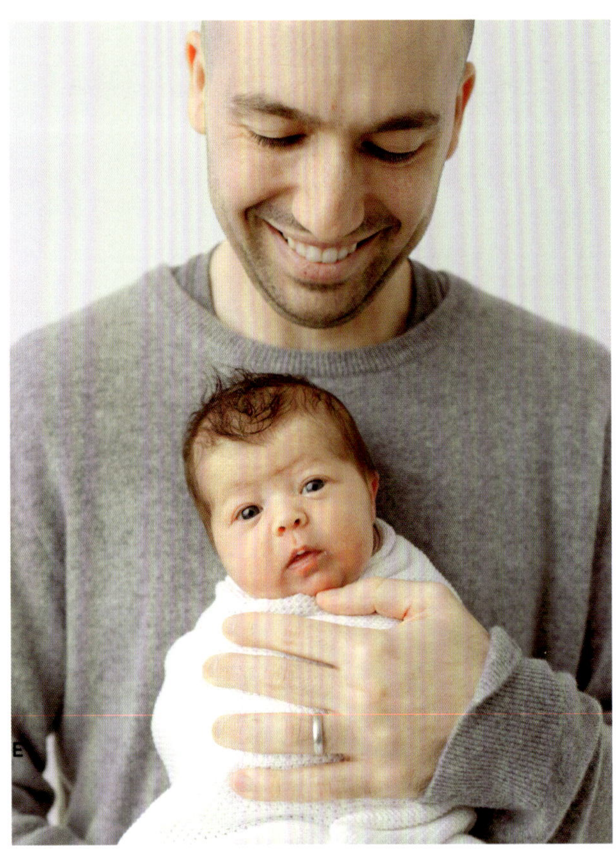

E

**FIGURE 7.3** Newborn posing flow with older siblings: After photographing the baby alone (**A**), I bring in the sibling(s) for photos of the children together (**B**) before moving on to parent and family photos (**C**, **D**, and **E**). The newborn remains the anchor throughout.

### Posing Flow: Older Children and Family

My CPR for working with older children and their family is exactly the same. I start with individual photos of the child, using the child as my anchor (**FIGURE 7.4A**). After capturing images of the child alone, I'll photograph them with their mother (**FIGURE 7.4B**), then with both parents for a nice family photo (**FIGURE 7.4C**) end with the child and their father (**FIGURE 7.4D**).

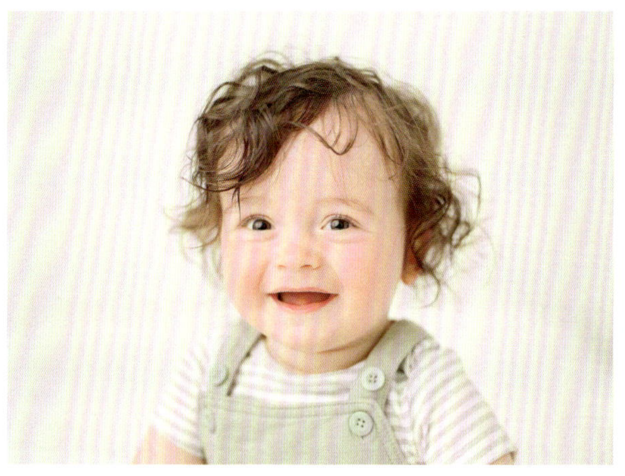

A

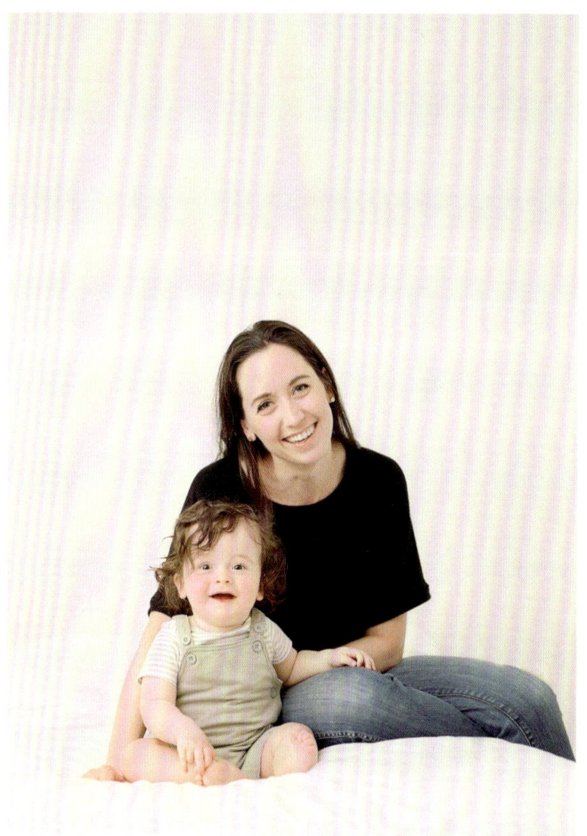

B

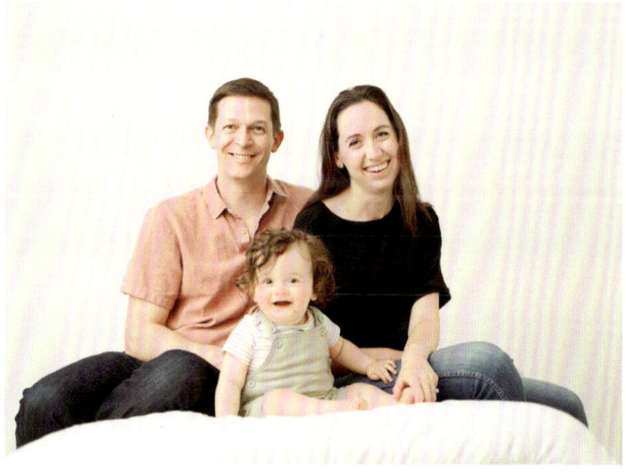

C

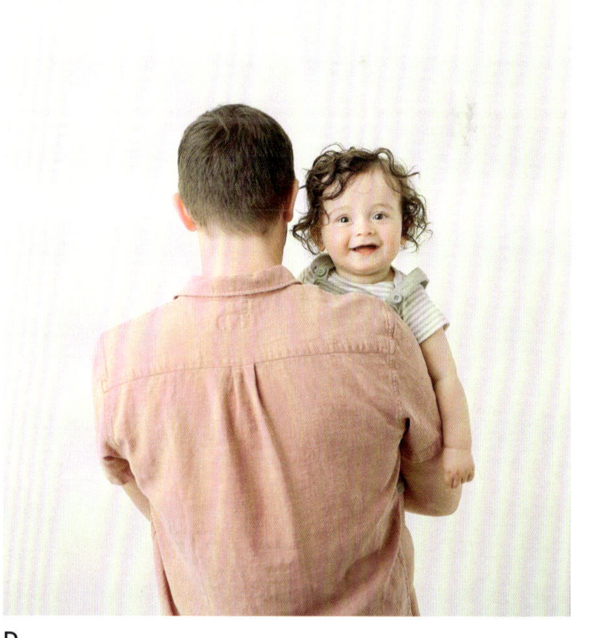

D

**FIGURE 7.4** My posing flow with older children is the same as when working with newborns. I start with individual portraits of the child, then bring in the mother, add both parents for a full family photo, and finish with the child and father.

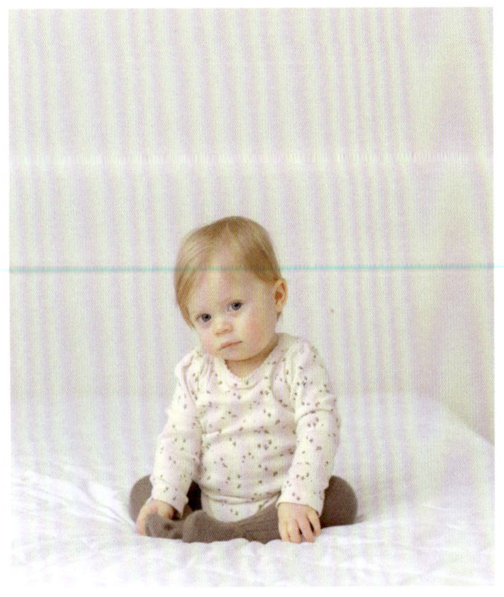

A

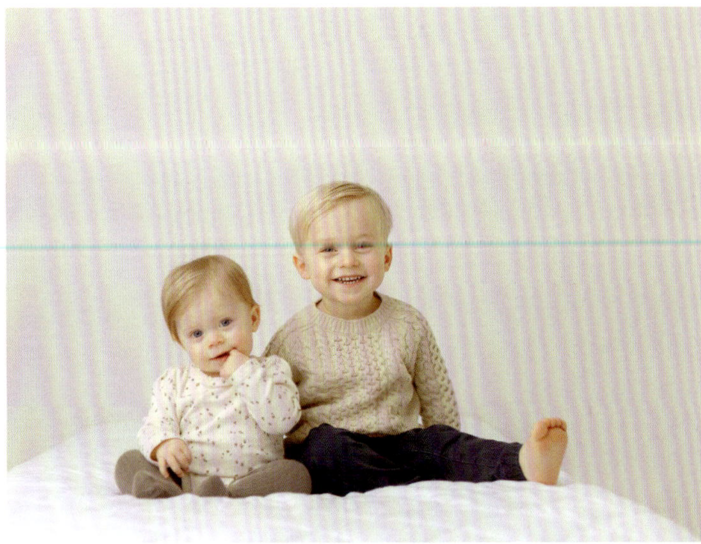

B

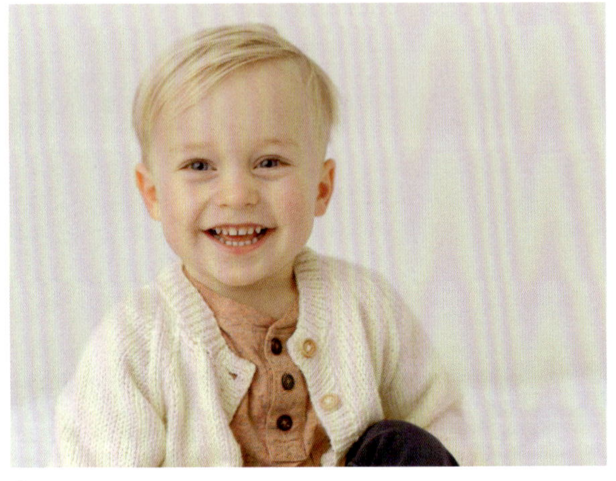

C

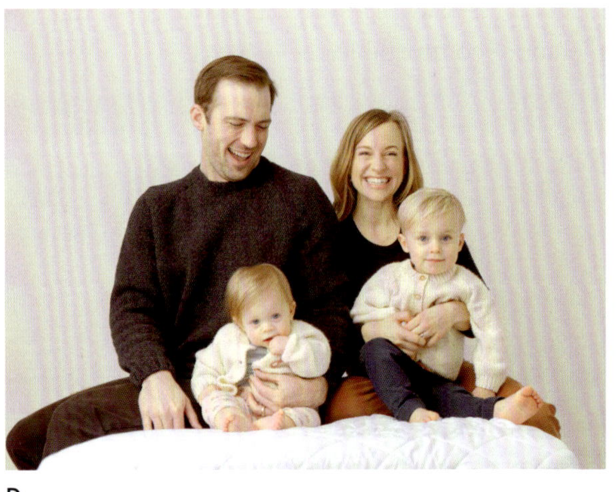

D

**FIGURES 7.5** When working with multiple children, I start with the youngest, then capture sibling photos, individual portraits of the older child, and end with family images. This flexible flow keeps everyone happy and engaged.

If there is more than one child, I'll start with the youngest one first, then get photos of the children together, and then the older child before moving on to photos of the family together (**FIGURE 7.5**).

**Pro Tip:** When working with multiple children, I like to start with the youngest. Older kids usually have more patience and can handle waiting their turn. That said, if the youngest isn't quite ready, it's easy to adjust the flow and rearrange the order as needed.

## Flexibility within CPRS

Even though CPRs might seem rigid at first glance, they actually offer a great deal of flexibility—which is essential. Every session is unique, after all, and being able to adapt to different family dynamics is a must.

For example, if a family brings grandparents to the session, my CPR makes it easy to incorporate them seamlessly. I start with the child(ren), then bring in the mother, followed by the father, and then the grandparents. From there, I'll ask the parents to step aside for a moment so I can capture a few images of the grandparents with the child(ren) alone. Then wrap up the session the way I always do—with some final images of father and child(ren).

If I'm working with a shy toddler, I can start with images of the toddler and their mother to help the child feel more secure. From there, I continue with my flow. After capturing images of the toddler and their mother, I'll bring in the father for family photos. Then I take some images of the toddler with just their father, and finally, end the session with images of the toddler alone—once they feel more comfortable.

Sometimes I'll even omit a must-have photo or rearrange the flow at the family's request.

In **FIGURE 7.6**, for example, the family had a set of nine-month-old twins and a four-year-old. Their priority was to get good photos of the twins together, their older son, and all three boys, but they were a little nervous about the potential of the twins getting tired and being unhappy. For their flow, I started with the youngest—in this case the twins—and photographed them together. After their photos were complete, their older brother joined them for photos of the boys together. Then I photographed the older child alone, and then the whole family. Once we finished our must-have photos, I checked in on the twins, who were still happy, so we quickly grabbed some individual images of each of them before calling it a day!

That's the beauty of an established CPR: it provides a dependable structure while leaving room for creativity and adaptation.

Over time, your consistent, predictable routine will become second nature, giving you the flexibility to drop into the sequence wherever it makes the most sense for the situation. Once the sequence is memorized, you can start at any point, because you'll know exactly what to do next! When your flow is muscle memory, you can easily make accommodations with little stress or worry, knowing how to pick up where you left off.

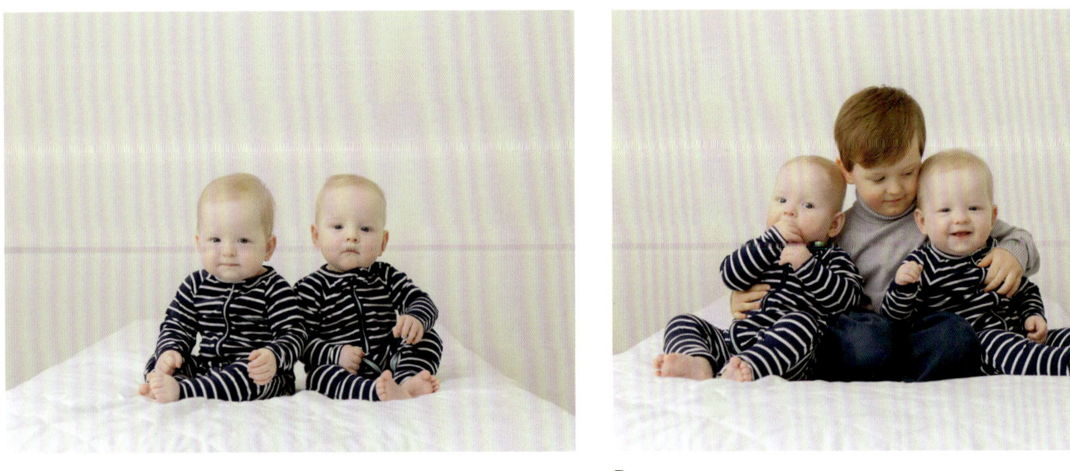

A

B

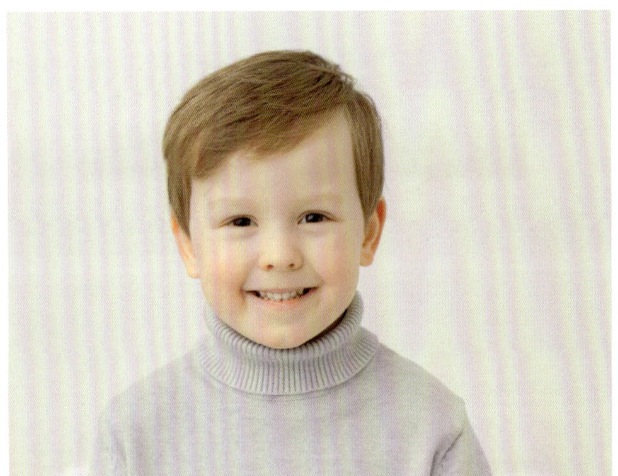

C

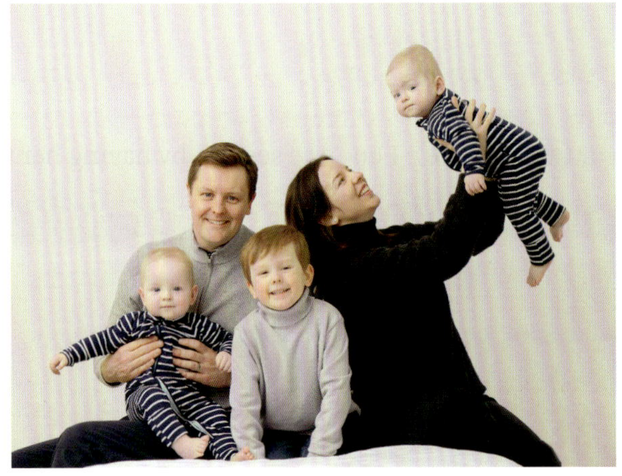

D

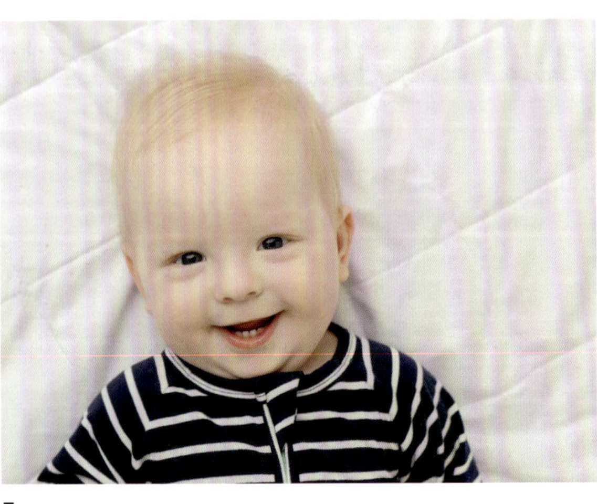

E

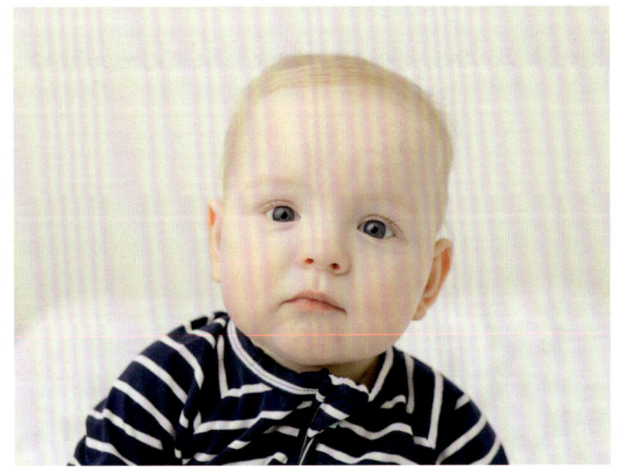

F

**FIGURE 7.6** Adapting the flow for young twins and siblings: I prioritized must-have images early—twins together, big brother with the twins, solo portraits of the older brother—then moved to family photos, adjusting based on the needs of the family. Remember, flexibility is key when working with children.

## Photographing Individuals

While CPRs are incredibly effective for family and newborn sessions, they're just as impactful when working with individuals. I have a maternity CPR, for example, that I use every time I work with a maternity client.

A lot of my maternity clients come to their sessions alone. This is a time to celebrate their pregnancy and honor the incredible transformation their body undergoes while creating a baby. I believe this is a sacred time, and my goal is to create images that reflect all the magic of the moment.

Because there is just one person at these sessions, there is no need to designate an "anchor" like I do in my family photo shoots. I still follow a consistent routine so that my sessions have a clear flow that is easy for me to remember and implement. For my maternity session, I always start by posing my client in profile, turned to my right (**FIGURE 7.7A**). From there, I have her face the camera (**FIGURE 7.7B**). I end the session by having her turn to my left (**FIGURE 7.7C**). If she has an outfit change, I go through the flow starting in a drape, then again in any outfits that she brought with her.

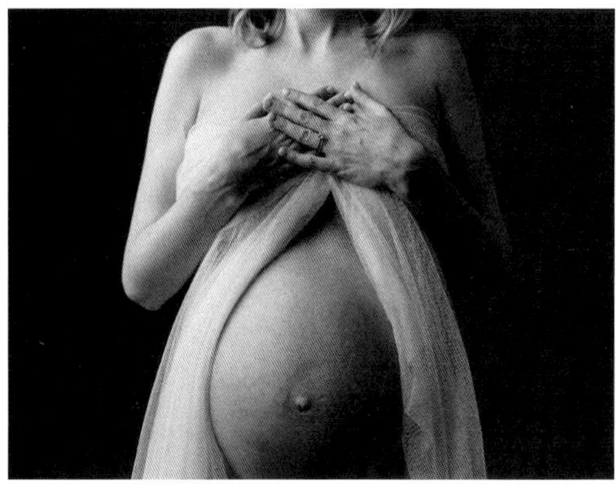

B

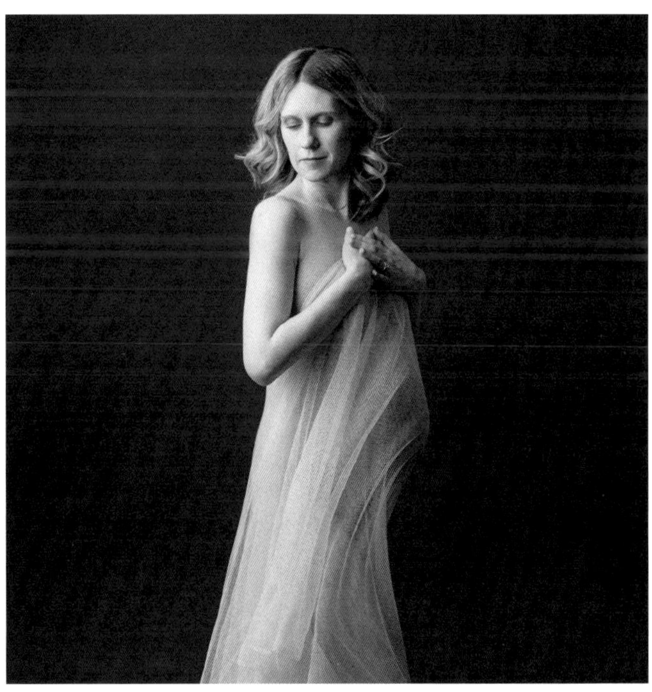

A

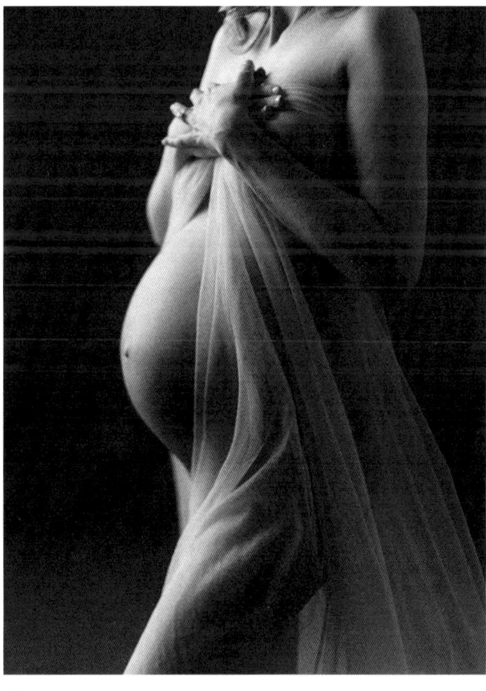

C

**FIGURE 7.7** My maternity posing flow for individuals: Start with a right-facing profile, move to a straight-to-camera pose, and finish with a left-facing profile. A simple, beautiful sequence to celebrate this special time.

If she has her partner or her other children at the session, I'll go through the session flow as usual, then end with photos of her and her partner and/or her children (**FIGURE 7.8**).

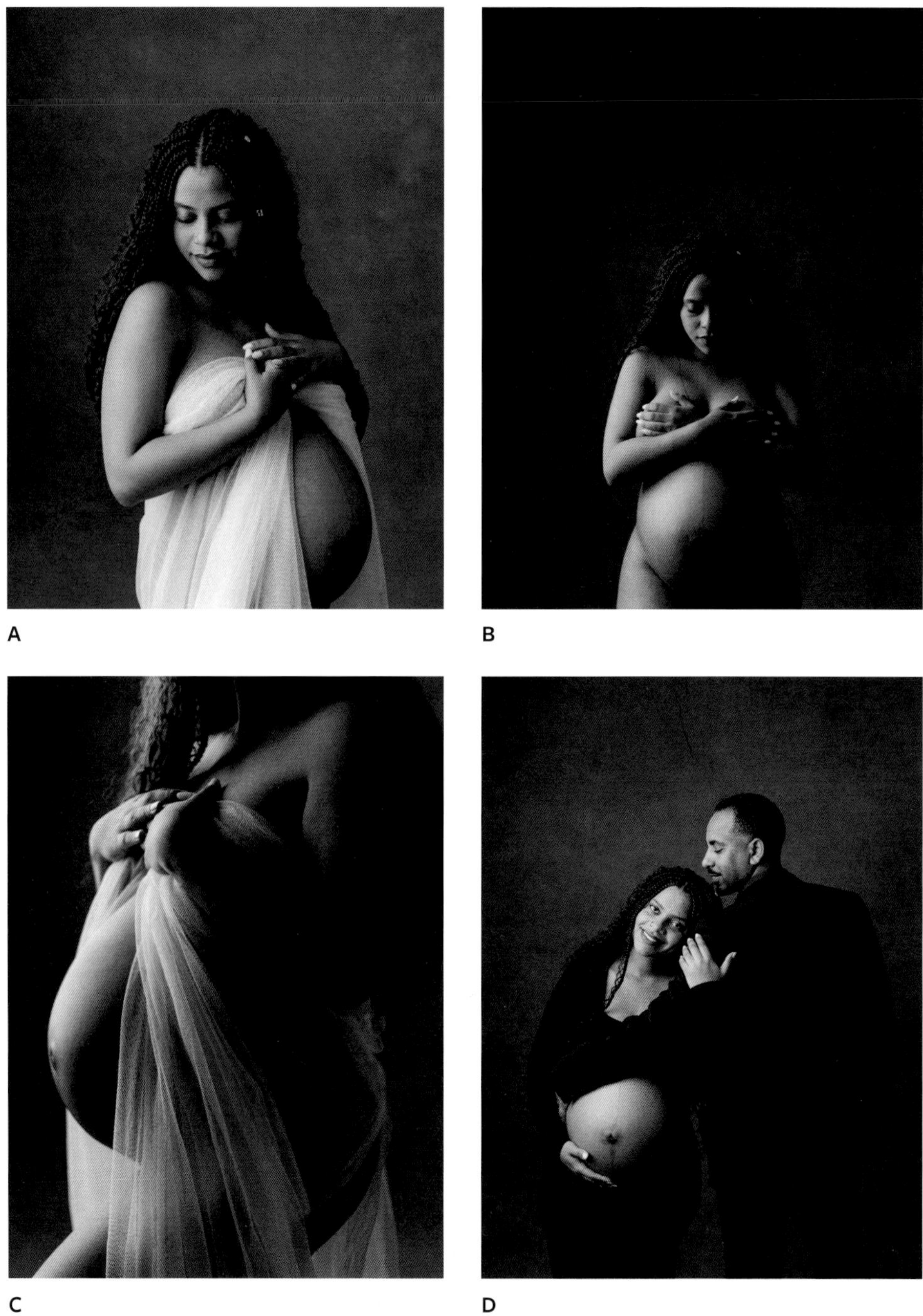

**FIGURE 7.8** Adding partners and children to maternity sessions. After completing the solo maternity flow, I bring in partners or children at the end to create portraits that celebrate the entire family-to-be.

Remember, when drafting your CPR, don't worry about the specific poses you will use. That will come. At this phase, think about the flow of your sessions: how you want them to start, what to do next, and how you want them to end. Establishing a clear sequence like this keeps your sessions organized and eliminates guesswork. When you know where to start, what to do next, and when you're done, your sessions will flow with ease.

## Keep It Simple

Your consistent, predictable routines don't have to be long or complicated to be effective. A short shot list is easier to remember, and easier to implement within the time frame of a typical family session. You'll notice that my CPRs only have four to five must-have shots. I create full galleries from those short lists by using specific poses for each line item, then maximize each pose by using different lighting patterns, adjusting my angles, experimenting with different compositions, and giving clear directions to my clients—guiding them on where to look and what to do—to create a mix of formal and candid-looking images.

Think of your CPRs as the foundation for your sessions. Take the time to think about it and write it out. Once your CPR has been established, you're ready to focus on creating the poses you'll use for each image.

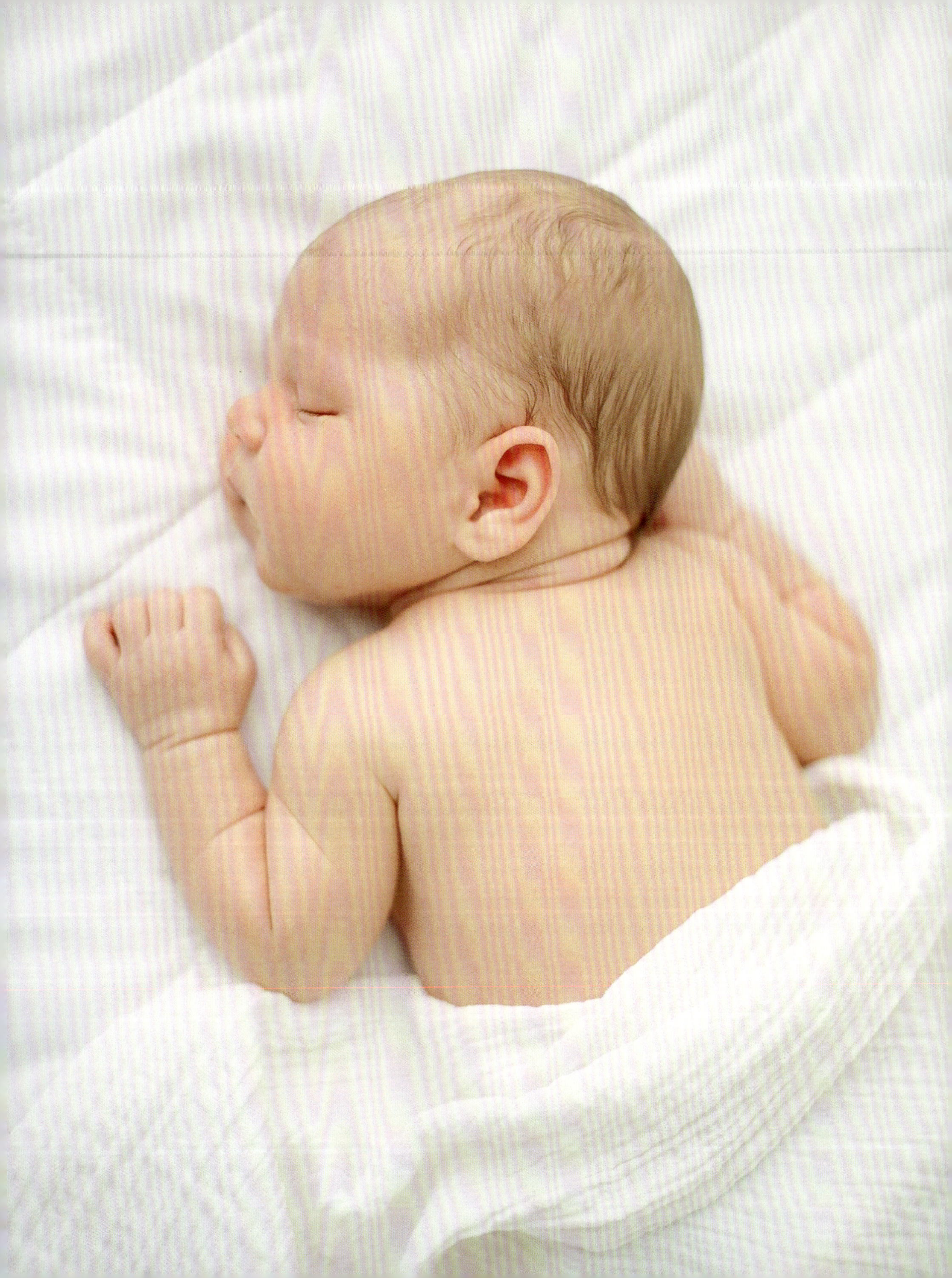

CHAPTER

# 8

# Posing Newborns, Babies, and Small Children

As you learned in Chapter 7, I'm a big believer in having a consistent, predictable routine (CPR) for session flow. I approach every session the same way—starting with the child alone as my "anchor," and then building the rest of the poses around them. This method keeps sessions running smoothly and ensures I capture all my must-have images. But my CPR approach doesn't stop at session flow, it also applies to how I work with each pose, allowing me to make the most of each one for a variety of looks quickly and efficiently.

In this chapter, you'll learn the poses I use when working with children of all ages. I'll share how to set them up and how to get multiple looks from each one, all while keeping the kids you are photographing happy, comfortable, and engaged. Many of the examples in this chapter were captured in my studio, but these poses—and my posing system—work beautifully in clients' homes, as well. My hope is that the poses I share will serve as inspiration for you. Try them, tweak them to fit your style, and make them your own.

## My Approach to Posing Children

As a portrait photographer, it is my job to capture the people I'm photographing as they are in this current moment. That job is the same whether I'm working with a person who is 80 years old or 8 days old. I use posing as a way to bring out their best and tell their story. But not all poses will work for all ages. There are developmental milestones that must be considered when posing babies and small children. Understanding these milestones is an essential part of your job as a family photographer.

I see my style as classic portraiture, with a relaxed natural feel. I want my images to look organic, even when posed. And I photograph the children I work with as I would photograph my own children—respecting their abilities and their limits. I work hard to create poses that are developmentally appropriate and allow the children I'm photographing to feel relaxed, comfortable, and safe.

Because I believe in photographing children this way, I practice a baby-led approach to newborn posing. In this style, newborns are placed on their bellies, sides, or backs. I intentionally avoid highly stylized poses that require specialized training or Photoshop composites and only place newborns in positions that are natural and safe. That doesn't mean I don't position the babies I work with; the baby-led approach still involves posing, and great care is taken to create images that are flattering, safe, and comfortable for my tiny clients.

I take a similar approach when working with older babies, toddlers, and children. All the poses I use are in line with what can be expected from the child based on their age and are easy and comfortable for little ones to hold.

## Maximizing Each Pose

At the beginning of my career, I made the mistake of thinking that the longer my sessions were (the more time I spent with my clients), the better and more robust my galleries would be. The truth is babies, toddlers, and small children don't have the patience that adults do. They get tired fast, and when they're done, they're done. No amount of extra time is going to result in better photos if you are working with a child who has hit a wall. If you're going to be a successful family photographer, efficiency is key!

My sessions move quickly. Most last an hour or less, even my newborn sessions (and yes, I allow time for feedings and diaper changes). I'm able to work at that pace because I have a consistent, predictable routine in place for my session flow. I also have a consistent, predictable routine that helps me maximize each of my poses. This routine enables me to get multiple looks quickly without having to repose the child. I approach every pose the same way:

1. Start with a full-body photo. Capture both vertical and horizontal images.
2. Move in for a close-up of the face. Again, capture vertically and horizontally.
3. Capture details, like tiny fingers, toes, and eyelashes—these are the images that parents love.

This simple yet effective system allows me to get a variety of looks from a single pose without unnecessary repositioning, keeping the session efficient and stress-free for both the child, their parents, and me. This is a pattern I use when photographing children of all ages, and one you will see repeated throughout all my posing instruction.

## Newborns

Babies are considered newborn from birth to one month old. I'll photograph a baby at any point in their development, but I encourage my clients to come in for their newborn session within the first ten days, if possible.

Babies tend to be very sleepy in the first couple of weeks after they are born. The earlier you can get in, the more likely it is that they will sleep through their session. While it's not necessary for the baby to be asleep for their session, it does make posing much easier. Also, common problems like baby acne and cradle cap (both normal skin conditions in newborns) don't usually present until week two or three, so working with newer newborns will help cut down the time you'll need to spend in post-production cleaning up skin.

Newborns do not have muscle control. They cannot roll over on their own, and they are not strong enough to support their own heads. Care must be taken when handling and posing a newborn to ensure that they are properly supported, especially their head and neck.

This is one of the main reasons why I practice baby-led posing. With this approach, babies are only put in positions that are safe and natural, which means their head and neck are always supported. Another reason I love the baby-led approach is that it does not require any special equipment or props. All you need is a bed!

I have a twin bed in my studio that I use for posing. When working on location, I always ask to use the primary bedroom so that I can have access to the family bed.

## Pose: Baby on Belly

Newborns are very responsive to slight pressure. It helps them to calm down and feel relaxed and is one of the reasons why new parents are taught to swaddle their babies. Positioning a sleeping baby on their belly is one way to provide this comforting pressure for a newborn without swaddling.

Because newborns find this position so soothing, I start my sessions by positioning the baby on their stomach with their face turned toward the camera. From there I will move around the baby to "maximize the pose," getting different angles, crops, and compositions. (Please note, it is not safe let a newborn sleep on the stomach unsupervised for naps or overnight. This position is for fully supervised photo sessions only.)

To set this pose up, place the baby on their belly with hands up by their chin and their feet tucked up under them. Take time to soothe the baby as you're placing them in this position. If the baby takes a pacifier, offering them one may help them relax. I also place one hand on the baby's head and one hand on their

## The Newborn Sleep Smile

Nothing melts a parent's heart like seeing their baby smile for the first time.

Newborn smiles usually happen when the baby is sleeping. And years of experience has taught me that if you can capture one in a photograph, your clients will love you forever!

No one knows for sure why newborns smile in their sleep, but we do know that it usually happens when the baby is in a state of sleep known as REM (Rapid Eye Movement). In adults and older children, REM is the stage of sleep in which we dream. In newborns, however, researchers believe that REM sleep is when they are working on their reflexes and muscle development. You can tell when a baby is in this stage of sleep by looking for these signs.

- Changes in breathing pattern. They will have short moments of sped up breathing while in this state.
- Rapid-eye movement. You will notice their eyes moving. Sometimes they will open or roll their eyes, even though they are asleep.
- Their hands and feet may twitch

The baby in **FIGURE 8.1** is in REM sleep. They started breathing quickly, twitching slightly, and rolling their eyes. When I notice a newborn doing these things while sleeping, I will position my focus on their face and wait for the sleep smile to happen. It may take a few minutes, but the smile always comes (**FIGURE 8.1C**)!

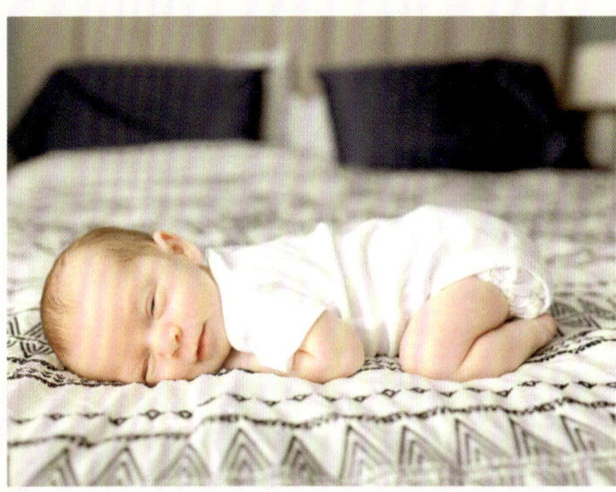

**A**

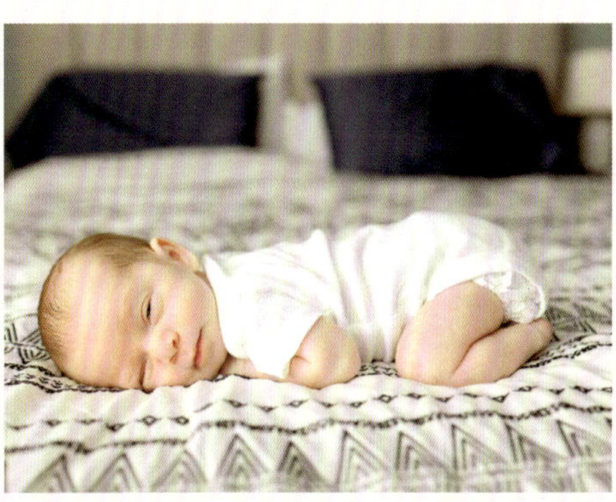

**B**

**C**

**FIGURE 8.1** To capture sleep smiles when working with newborns, watch for rapid breathing, eye movement, and twitching. These signs indicate a likely sleep smile is coming—just like the one captured here.

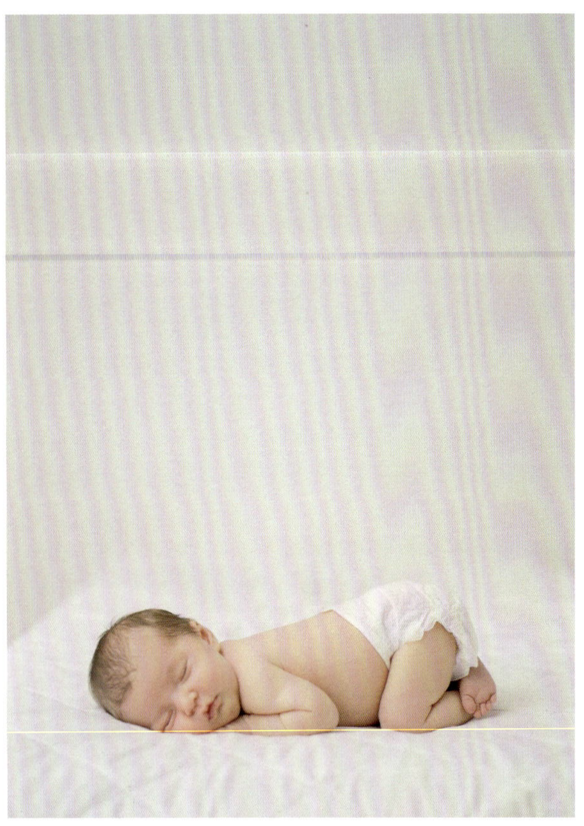

FIGURE 8.2 Baby on Belly. This pose provides soothing pressure and is a great starting point for newborn sessions.

back, providing light pressure until the baby settles in. Once the baby is relaxed, position yourself eye level to the baby and capture an image of their full body (**FIGURE 8.2**).

From there, zoom in to get close-up photos of the baby's head and shoulders (**FIGURE 8.3**) and any details you would like to capture. You can drape a baby blanket over the baby for added texture. And remember to take both vertical and horizontal images to add variety.

Once you have captured the baby on their belly from the side, stand over them to capture their entire body (**FIGURE 8.4A**), their head and shoulders (**FIGURE 8.4B**), and their feet (**FIGURE 8.4C**).

***Safety First!* Always wear your camera strap around your neck when standing over a baby.**

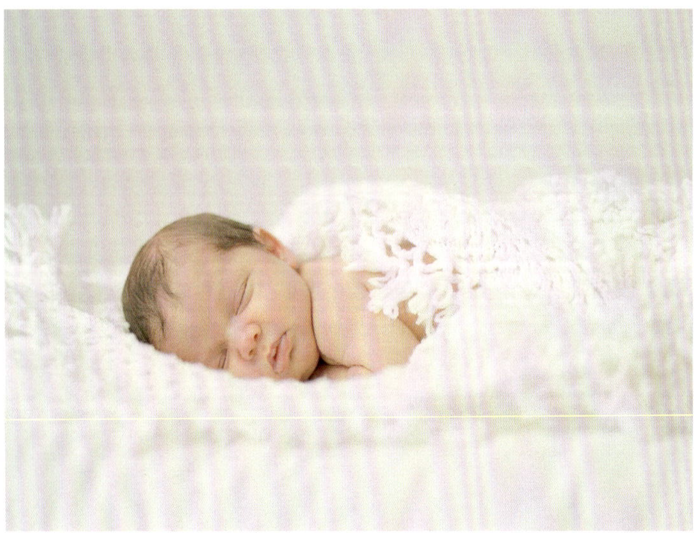

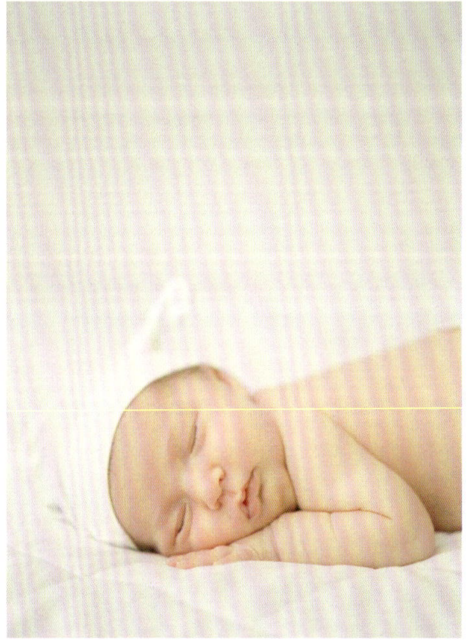

FIGURE 8.3 Close up photos of the baby's head and shoulders. Remember to take both vertical and horizontal images!

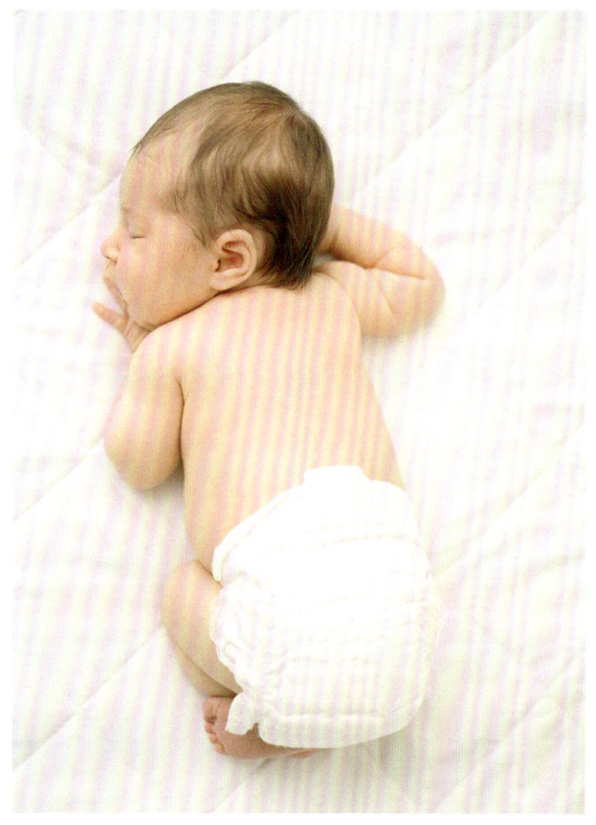

A

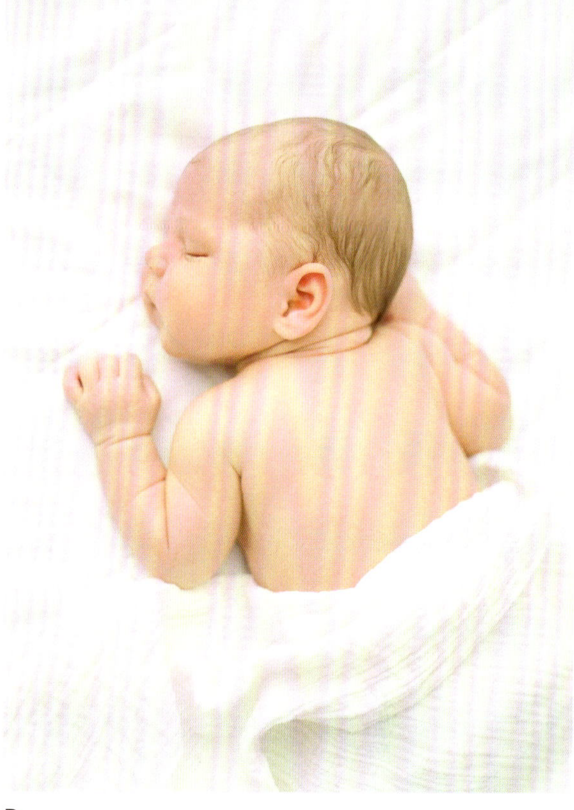

B

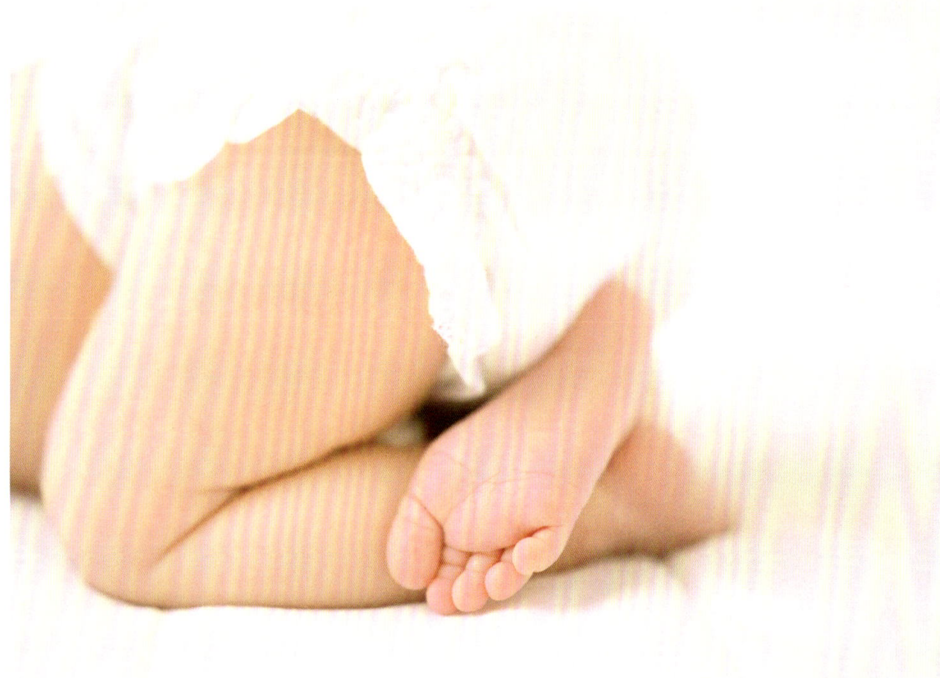

C

**FIGURE 8.4** Stand over the baby to get images of the baby's entire body, head and shoulders, and feet.

# Must the Baby be Sleeping for These Poses to Work?

Not at all. In fact, some of my favorite photos are of wide-eyed newborns staring into my lens!

All of the poses shared in this chapter can be done with a baby who is wide awake, but the baby must be well fed and happy for the session to run smoothly. I ask my clients to change and feed their baby before leaving for the studio. I also ask that the baby arrive in an outfit they would like them photographed in, or an outfit that is easy to remove.

Most babies will fall asleep on the car ride over. If they are ready to go when they arrive, I gently take them out of their car seat while they are sleeping and position them on their belly on the bed to begin the session. If the baby is awake, I'll check to see if the baby is hungry before placing them on their belly. You can tell if a baby wants to eat by softly rubbing their cheek. Newborns have a strong "rooting" reflex, and will turn their head, mouths open and ready, toward the touch when they need to be fed. If they are hungry, I ask the parents to feed them before we proceed. If they're not hungry, we go right into the pose.

When working in a client's home, I'll ask that the baby be fed and in the outfit they will be photographed in when I arrive so I can go right into the same routine I use when posing in my studio. Most of the time, a well-fed baby will be happy and relaxed, even when awake, but some babies will continue to root when placed on their stomach, even when not hungry. When that happens, I simply skip the "Baby on Belly" and "Baby on Side" poses and go straight into working with the "Baby on Back" pose.

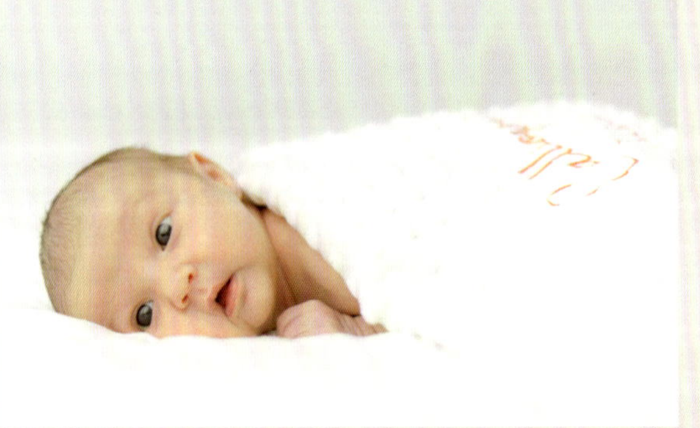

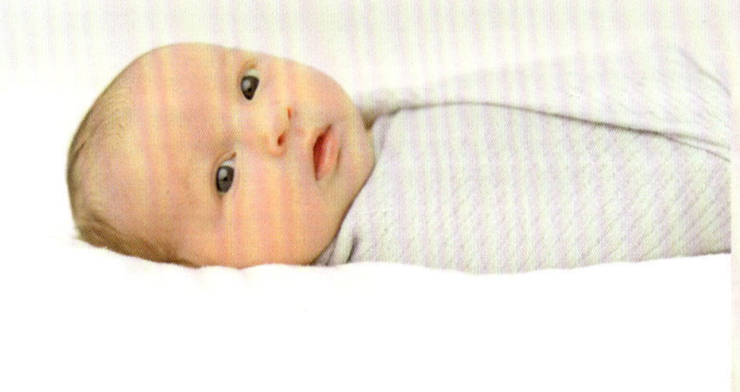

**FIGURE 8.5** Wide-awake babies in the belly and back positions. These poses work beautifully when the baby is alert and content.

## Pose: Baby on Side

After photographing the baby on their belly, gently roll them onto their side for a second pose. Take your time with this. Newborns have a strong reflex, known as the Moro reflex, that causes them to startle, throwing out their arms and legs in a wide, sudden movement. This reflex often happens when the baby is positioned on their side or on their back without being swaddled.

The Moro Reflex is a normal, healthy thing for a newborn to do, but it can result in waking them from sleep. If you are going to position the newborn you are working with into a new pose, go slowly and apply light pressure to their hips and shoulders as you roll them. See **FIGURE 8.6** for an example of what this looks like. Allowing them to rest in the new position with light pressure for a few minutes helps them settle into the pose.

Once the baby is positioned and relaxed, move around the baby to capture a variety of angles, crops, and compositions, just like with the Baby on Belly pose. Start by positioning yourself over the baby, looking down to capture their entire body (**FIGURE 8.7A**). While positioned above the baby, take an image of the baby's head and shoulder (**FIGURE 8.7B**) and of their legs and feet (**FIGURE 8.7C**). Remember to look for triangles (or create them by using blankets) and play around with filling the frame and negative space for varied composition.

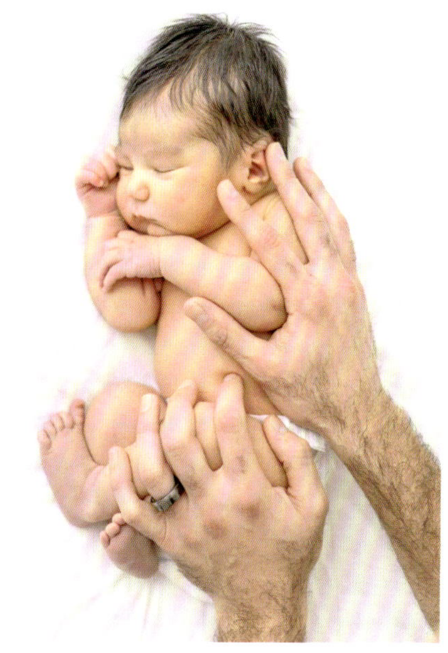

**FIGURE 8.6** Newborns respond to light pressure. It helps them relax and will help to avoid triggering the Moro reflex.

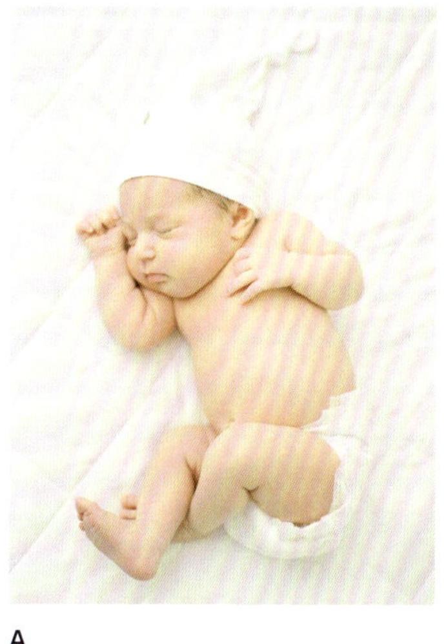

A

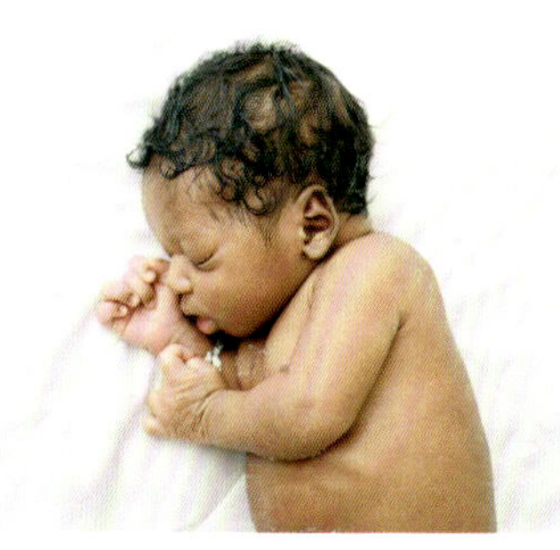

B

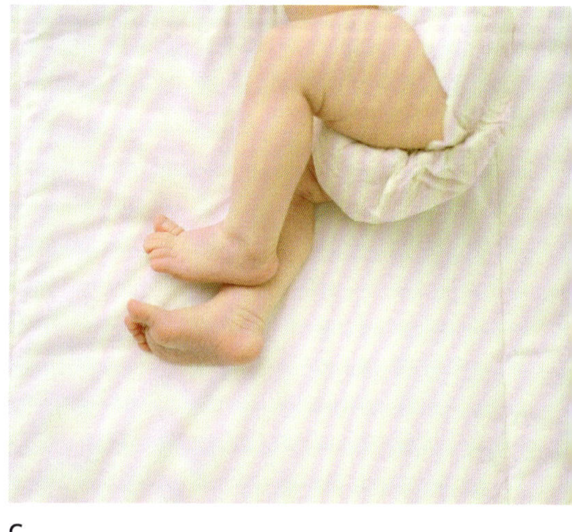

C

**FIGURE 8.7** Overhead images of the baby: full body, head and shoulders, and feet.

Once you've taken all your baby-on-side photos from above, position yourself eye level to the baby and take an image of the baby's full body (**FIGURE 8.8A**). Then zoom in to capture their feet and legs (**FIGURE 8.8B**) and head and shoulders (**FIGURE 8.8C**).

Remember to add variety to your gallery by taking both vertical and horizontal images, adding a blanket for texture, and using different compositional rules, like the rule of thirds and filling the frame.

**Pro Tip:** Newborns often move their arms while on their side, creating opportunities for fun and unique images! I can't tell you how many times I've taken a photo of a baby after they've moved themselves into a new position, only for the parents to laugh and tell me they have an ultrasound image of the baby in that exact same position! In my opinion, this is one of the best parts of baby-led posing—it lets the baby show us a little glimpse of their personality!

**FIGURE 8.8** Eye-level full-body image and photo of the baby's feet. Newborns often move their arms while on their side, creating opportunities for fun and unique images, like in Figure 8.8C! If the baby you're photographing stretches or shifts, be sure to capture it.

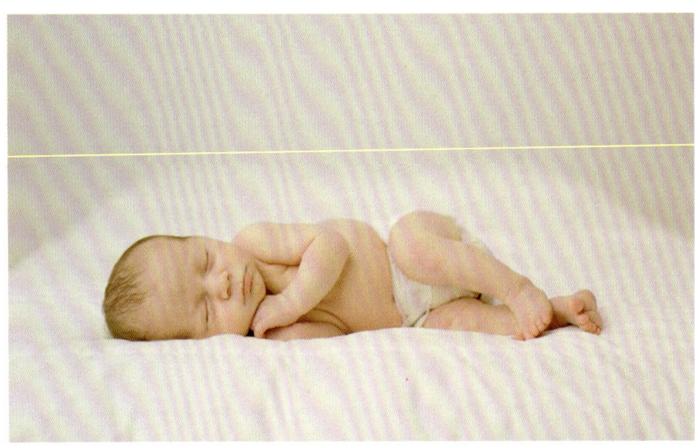

A

B

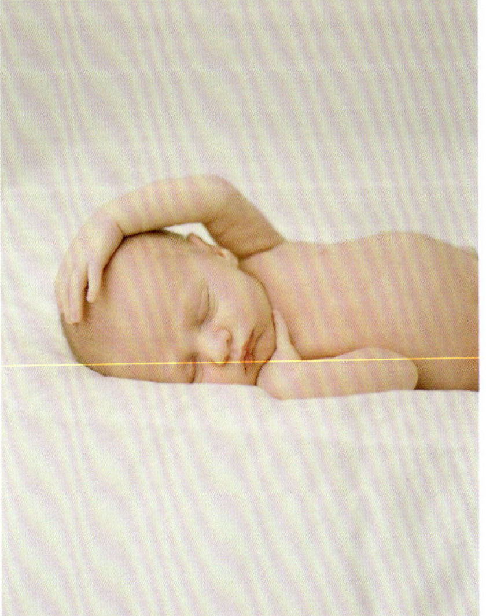

C

### Pose: Baby On Back

Placing the baby on their back is the last pose I use when photographing a newborn alone. Like all of our newborn poses, this is a natural (and comfortable) position for newborns, but unless the baby is in a deep sleep or very relaxed, being positioned on their back will cause them to startle. If you notice this, swaddle the baby to help them relax.

## The Simple Swaddle

In keeping with my goal of creating timeless images for my newborn clients, I shy away from swaddling trends and opt for a simple technique that keeps the babies I work with snug and happy (and photographs well). I call it the simple swaddle.

Step One: Fold your swaddle blanket into a triangle shape. Place the baby in the middle of the blanket, head pointing away from the point of the triangle (**FIGURE 8.9A**).

Step Two: Place the baby's right arm along the side of their body. Grab the right side of the swaddle blanket and pull it firmly across the baby's chest, keeping the right arm under the fabric. Tuck the blanket that was pulled across the baby's chest under their body (**FIGURE 8.9B**).

Step Three: Place the baby's left arm along the side of their body. Pull the left side of the blanket down over the baby's left shoulder toward their chest (**FIGURE 8.10A**). Secure the blanket with one hand on the baby's chest and fold the remaining left side of the blanket (**FIGURE 8.10B**). Pull it across the baby's body and tuck the remaining fabric under them and tie a knot or twist the blanket that is down by their feet (**FIGURE 8.10C**).

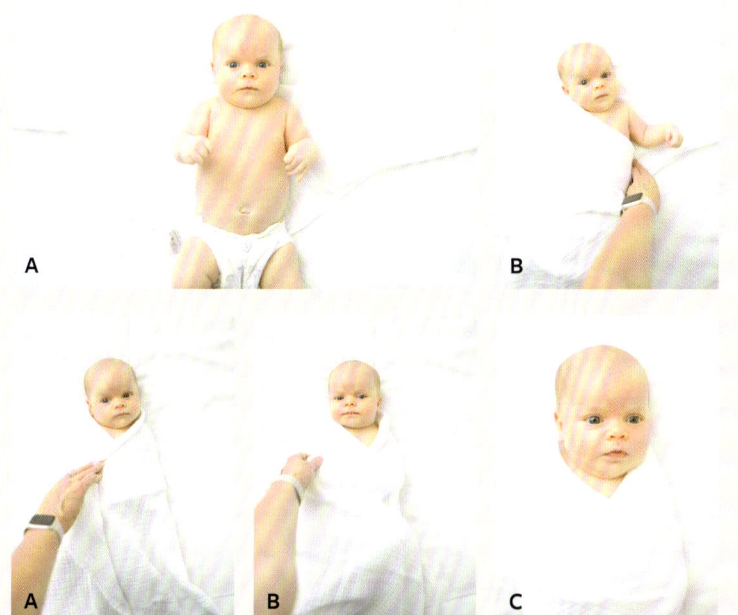


**FIGURE 8.9** Position the baby in the middle of the triangle. Tuck the right arm under the fabric and wrap the swaddle across the baby's chest.

**FIGURE 8.10** Pull the left side of the blanket down over the baby's left shoulder toward their chest. Secure the blanket, fold the remaining left side of the blanket, then pull it across the baby's body.

Once the baby is resting comfortably on their back, get to work moving through the routine (full body, as in **FIGURE 8.11A**; zoom in to get images of their face, as in **FIGURE 8.11B**); then get the legs and feet (**FIGURE 8.11C**) and any other details!

**Don't forget to wear your camera strap when standing over a baby! I know I've said this before, but I can't stress its importance enough. Baby safety should always be your number one priority.**

**Pro Tip:** Rolling the baby onto their back will potentially wake them from sleeping, which means the baby may yawn and stretch. Be ready to capture those movements when working with a baby in this position as they make for adorable photos!

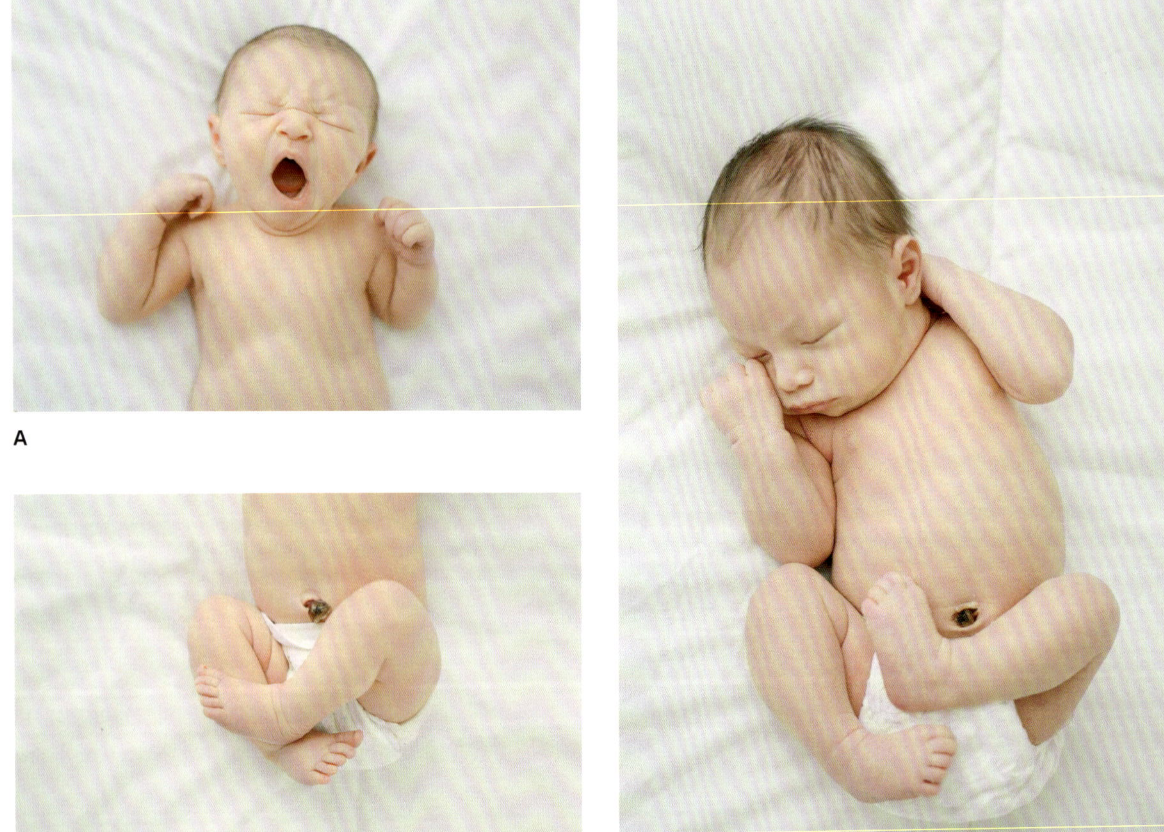

A

C

B

**FIGURE 8.11** Make the most of your poses with headshots and full-body shots. To capture the look in Figure 8.11C, shoot the legs and feet from above. While this look can be done while the baby is swaddled, I prefer it with an unswaddled baby, as you can capture the baby's umbilical cord if it's still attached!

While the baby is posed on their back, you can also position yourself eye level to the baby and capture them from the side (**FIGURE 8.12**). I'm obsessed with baby profiles, so images from the side like this are always some of my favorites!

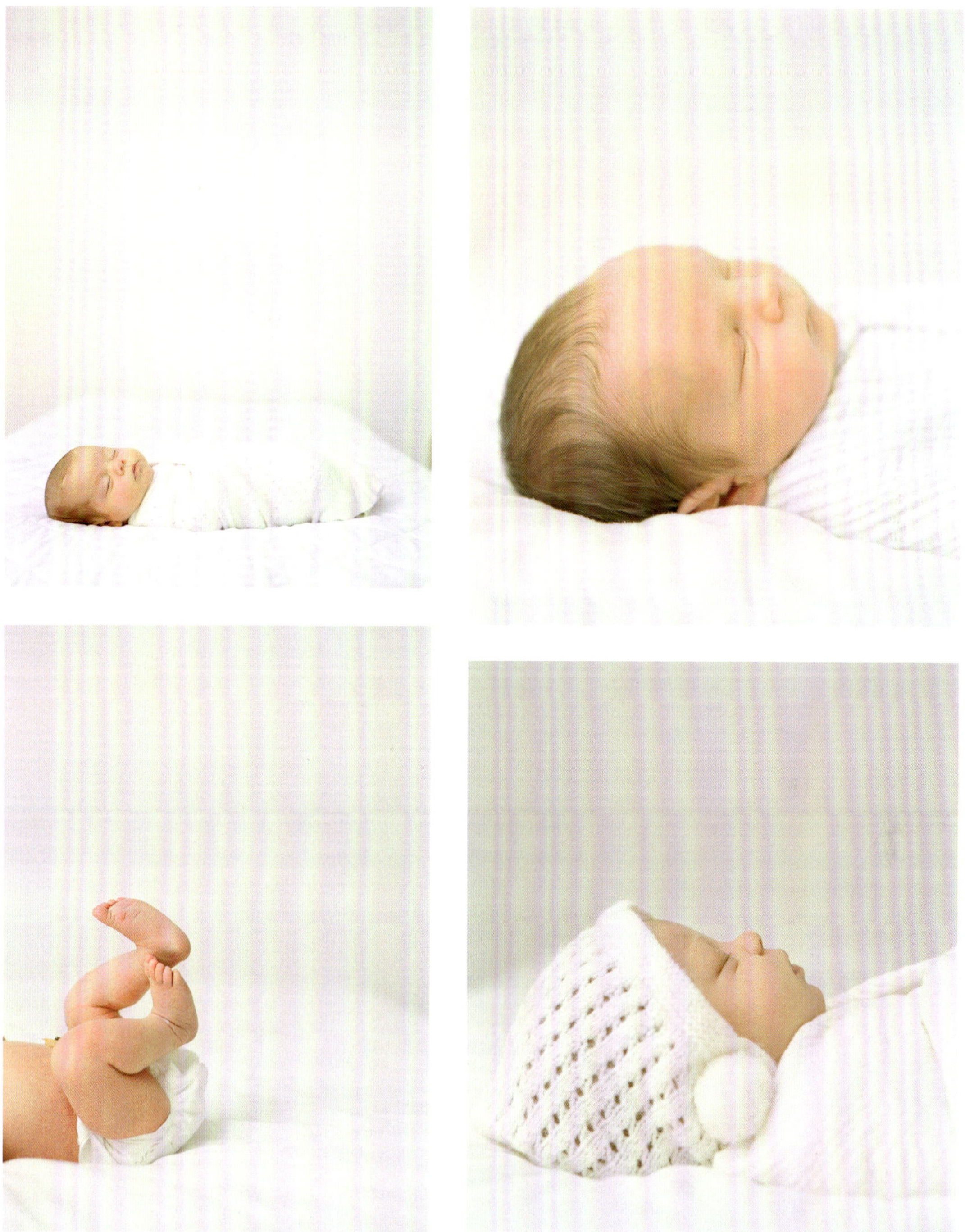

**FIGURE 8.12** Side-angle views of the baby on their back: full body, face, feet, and profile.

## Don't Feel Pressured to Move the Baby Through All Three Poses

While my goal at every newborn session is to get as many beautiful images of the baby alone as possible, not every baby can handle being placed in multiple poses. Babies are very sensitive to touch, and too much handling can overstimulate them (this is especially true with babies who were born prematurely). If you notice that the baby you are working with reacts by startling, waking, or crying every time they are moved, they are probably overstimulated. Get them soothed and comfortable, then focus on just one pose rather than attempting all three. The baby in **FIGURE 8.13**, for example, was very sensitive to touch and movement, so I kept him on his belly for all his photos.

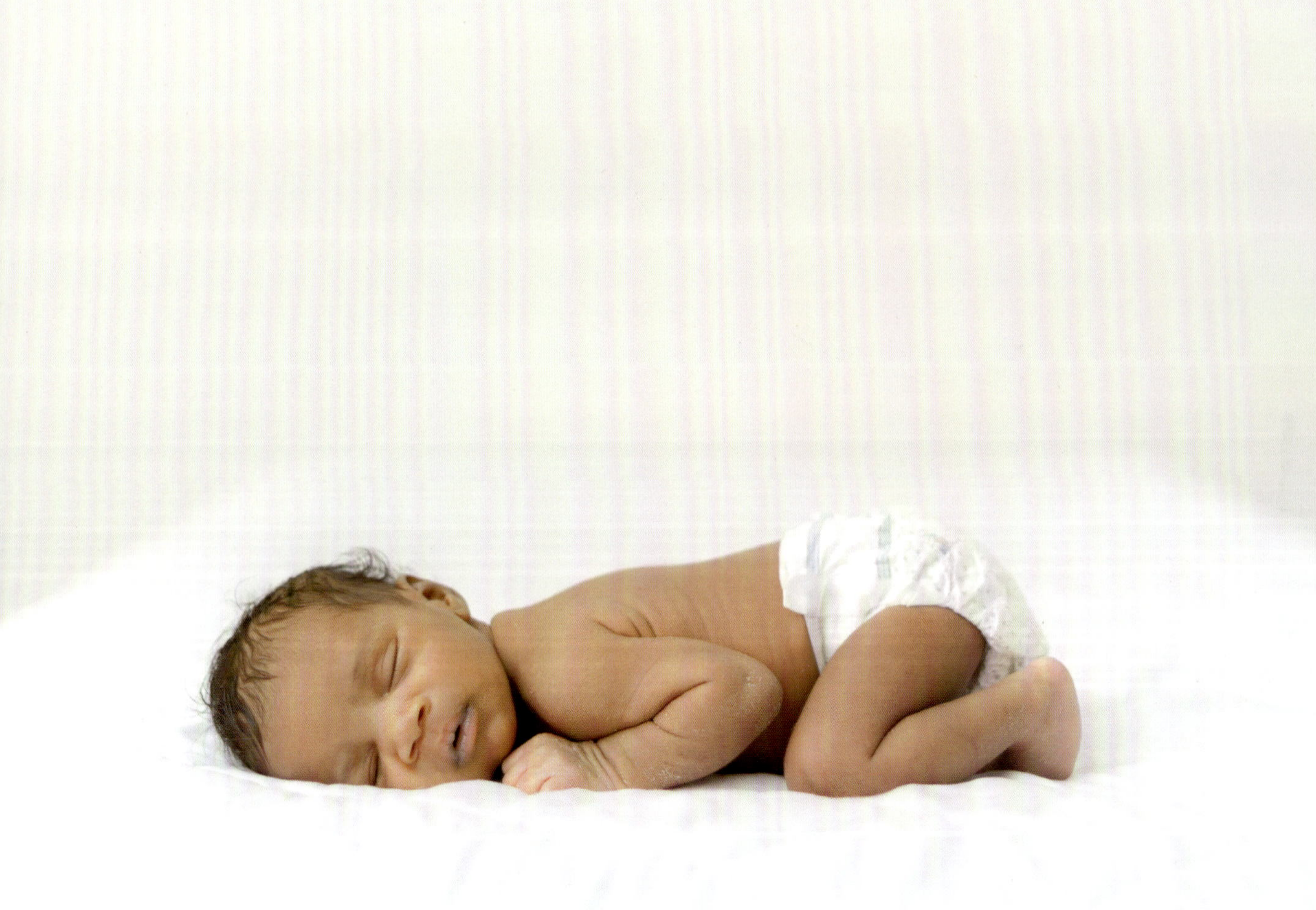

**FIGURE 8.13** A sensitive newborn photographed entirely on his belly, using angles and variations to create a full gallery.

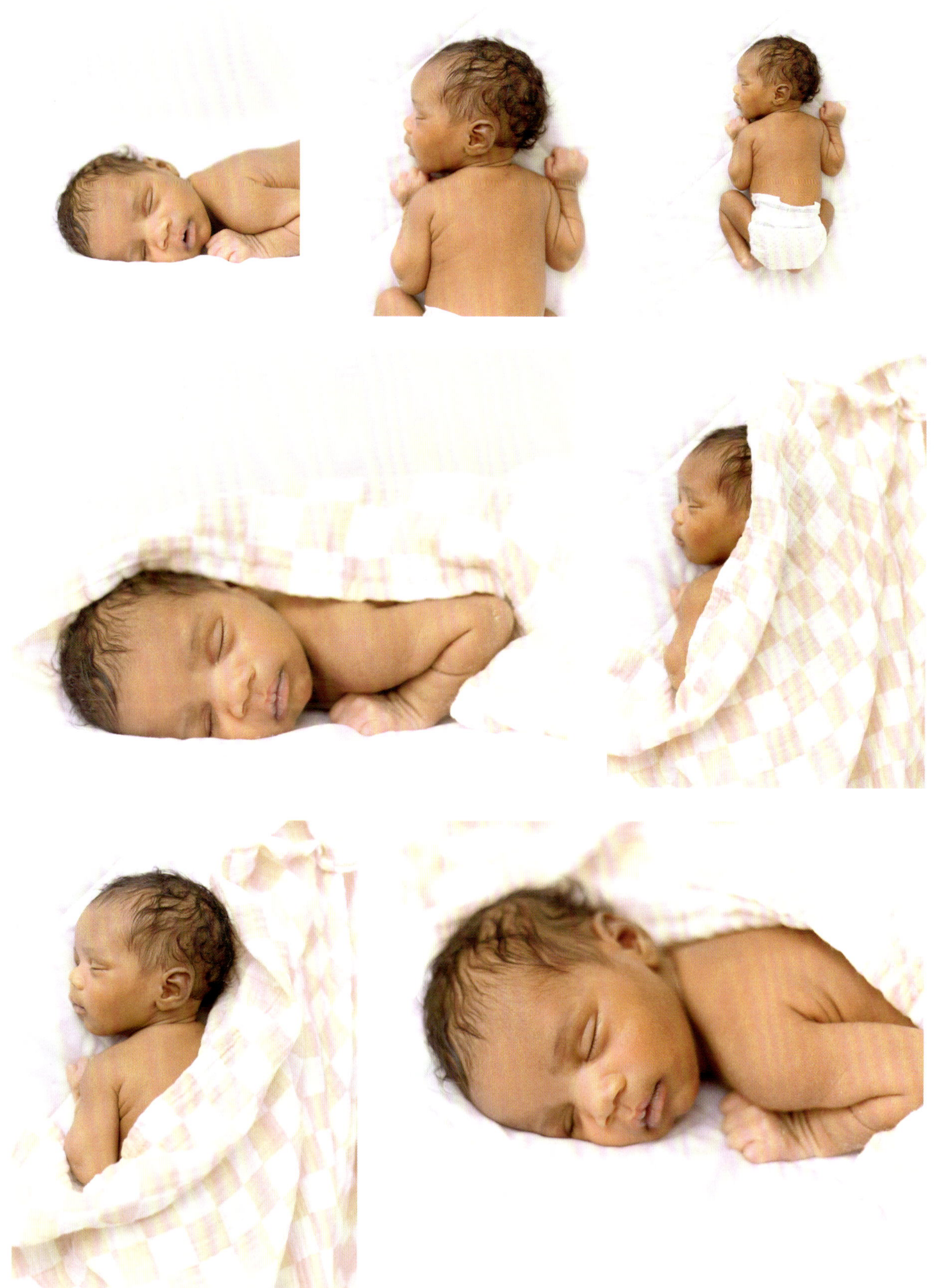

## Three Months

The newborn phase is wonderful, but it can be hard and overwhelming for new parents. As a result, a lot of families miss the "newborn" window for photos. And that is okay! I remind my clients that every stage of a baby's first year is special and worth capturing. But, if they missed newborn photos and are disappointed, I encourage them to book a three-month photo session.

By three months of age, a baby still cannot roll over, but they can support their head and often do when placed on their belly. They also have more control over their arms and legs and can intentionally put their hand in their mouth or grasp and hold onto objects.

At this age, babies are becoming social. They turn their heads to follow noises and objects, smile at people (especially people they know), and even babble and coo. For all of these reasons, this is one of my favorite ages to photograph.

My poses for a three-month-old baby are very similar to my newborn poses. I place them on their belly, on their side, and on their back, and I maximize each pose by getting full body images, close-up portraits, and details (in a mix of vertical and horizontal images). With three-month-olds, however, I make some slight variations to my poses to account for where they are developmentally.

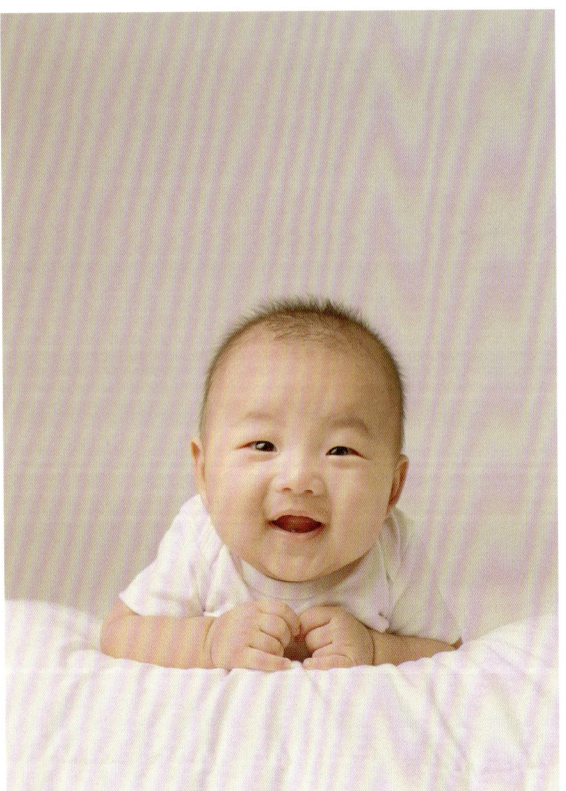

**FIGURE 8.14** A three-month-old engaging with the camera.

### Pose: Baby on Belly

While I work to help the newborns I photograph fall asleep for their session, I prefer my three-month-old babies to be awake. I love the bright eyes and sweet smiles that accompany this age and want to make sure I capture them in photos for the family. Like at the newborn session, I start these sessions with the baby on their belly, but because they are usually awake, I position them so that they are facing me, rather than in profile.

At this age, most babies will push up on their arms when placed on their bellies, lifting their head to engage with me and the camera (**FIGURE 8.14**). But if they're not quite strong enough to do that yet, I will place a pillow under their arms for support and position their arms up under their chin to help them in lifting their head.

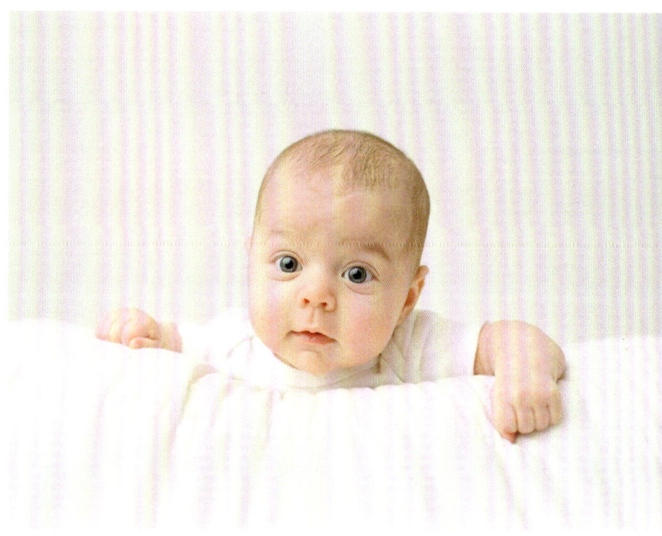

FIGURE 8.15 I ask parents to stand to the side so the baby will make direct eye contact with me.

To capture this look, position yourself eye level to the baby and engage them in conversation. I talk and sing to thc babics I work with and am usually gifted with eye contact and smiles as a result. Remember, this is a social age, so take advantage of that fact!

**Pro Tip:** If a parent is standing behind you, the baby will look at their parent rather than you. I explain this to my clients and ask them to stand to the side when I'm engaging their baby. This helps me get great eye contact in my three-month-old portraits (**FIGURE 8.15**).

Once you've placed the baby you're working with in this pose, move fast. This position requires a lot of work on the part of the baby, and they will tire quickly! Babies can go from all smiles to tears in seconds (**FIGURE 8.16**), so I try to respect their limits and only spend a minute or two in this pose.

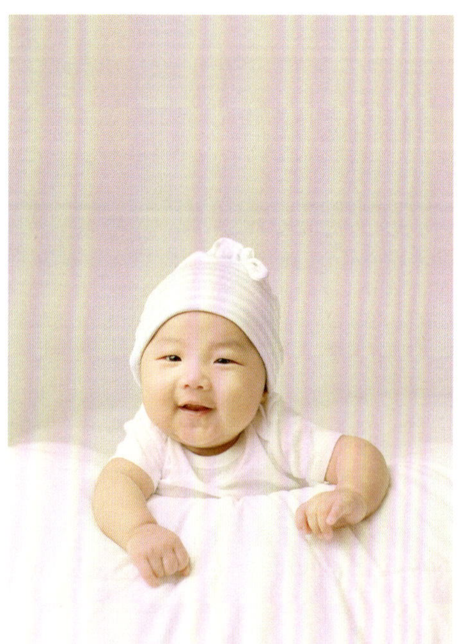

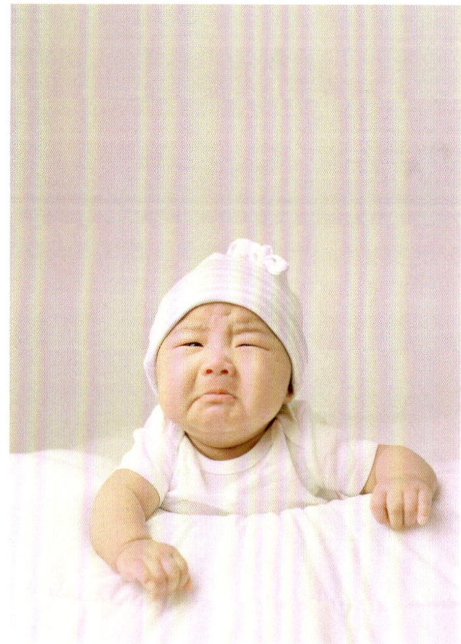

FIGURE 8.16 These images were taken less than a minute apart. In the first image, the baby was all smiles. Moments later, he was tired and let us know!

### Never Wake a Sleeping Baby!

If the baby is asleep when the session begins, let them sleep. Trust me. Waking a sleeping baby is a recipe for disaster. If they are sleeping, place them on their belly just like you would at a newborn session and work all the angles to maximize the pose!

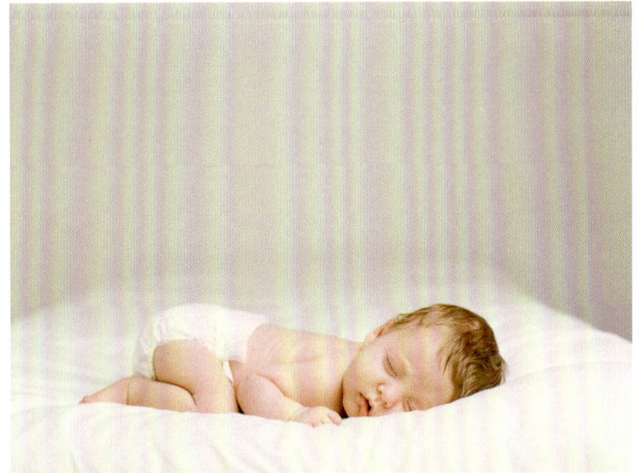

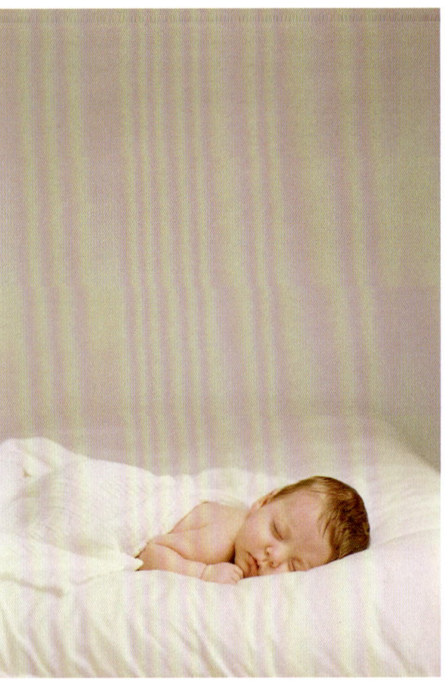

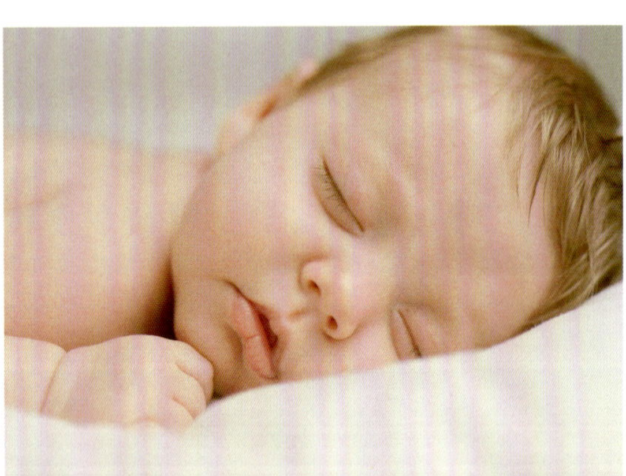

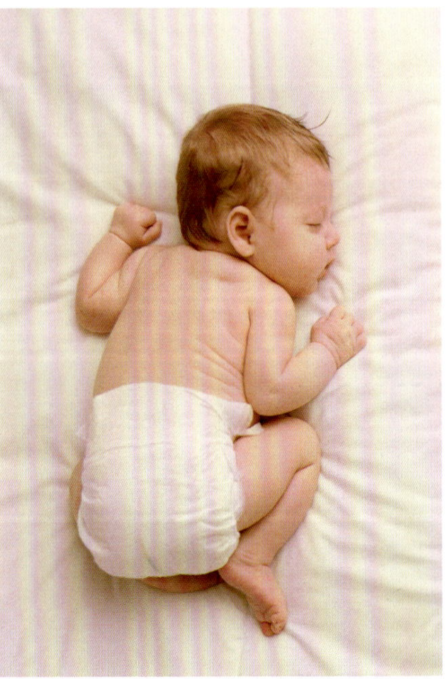

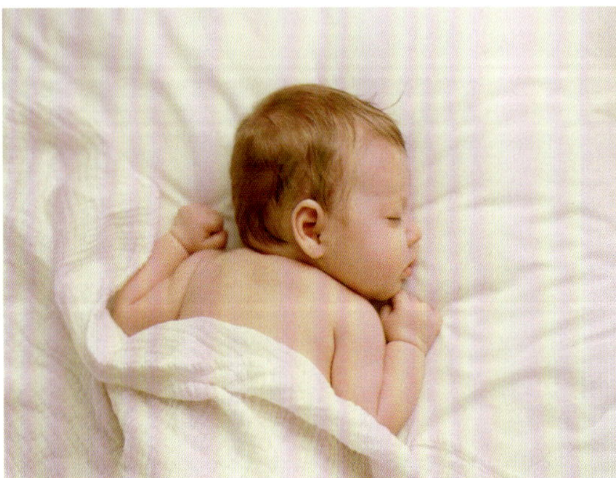

**FIGURE 8.17** If the three-month-old you are working with is sleeping during their session, pose them as you would a newborn and move through the same session flow.

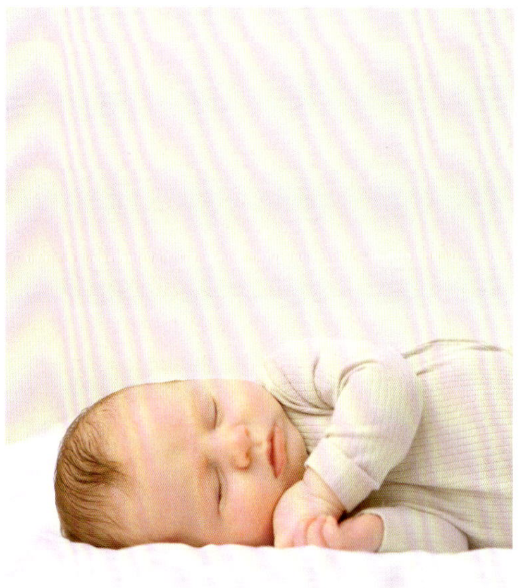
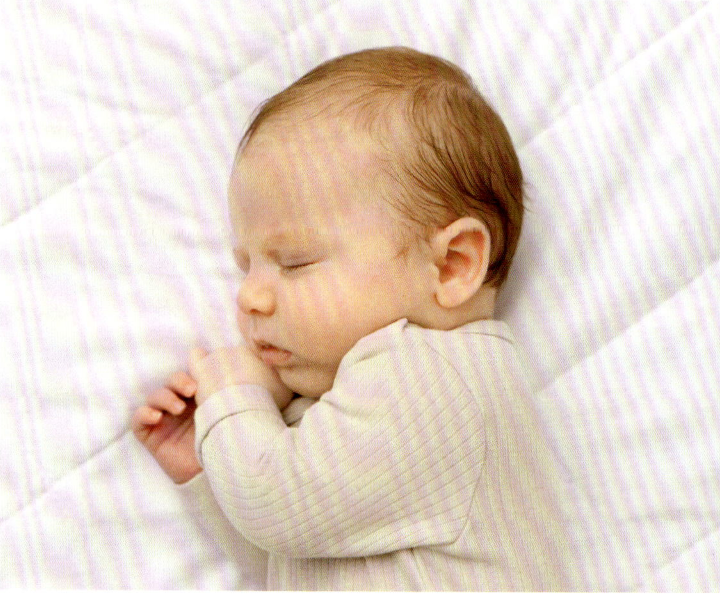

**FIGURE 8.18** The Baby on Side pose with a three-month-old—only used when the baby is asleep and settled.

## Pose: Baby on Side

If the three-month-old I'm working with is sleeping, after capturing the Baby on Belly photos, I'll gently roll them onto their side into the Baby on Side pose, capturing all the angles and variations that I do when photographing a newborn (**FIGURE 8.18**). If the baby is awake, I skip the Baby on Side poses and go straight to placing the baby on their back.

Remember, babies are very social at this age. If they are awake, they want to look at you and interact. That's hard for them to do when they are on their side, and they will most likely just get frustrated. I save this pose for the sleeping babies only.

## Pose: Baby on Back

The last pose I use for my three-month-old session is the Baby on Back pose. At this age, babies have some control over their arms and legs. They can grasp and hold objects for a short amount of time, for example, but they still lack the strength and coordination to move their arms and legs extensively. This is an important fact to know when posing them on their backs.

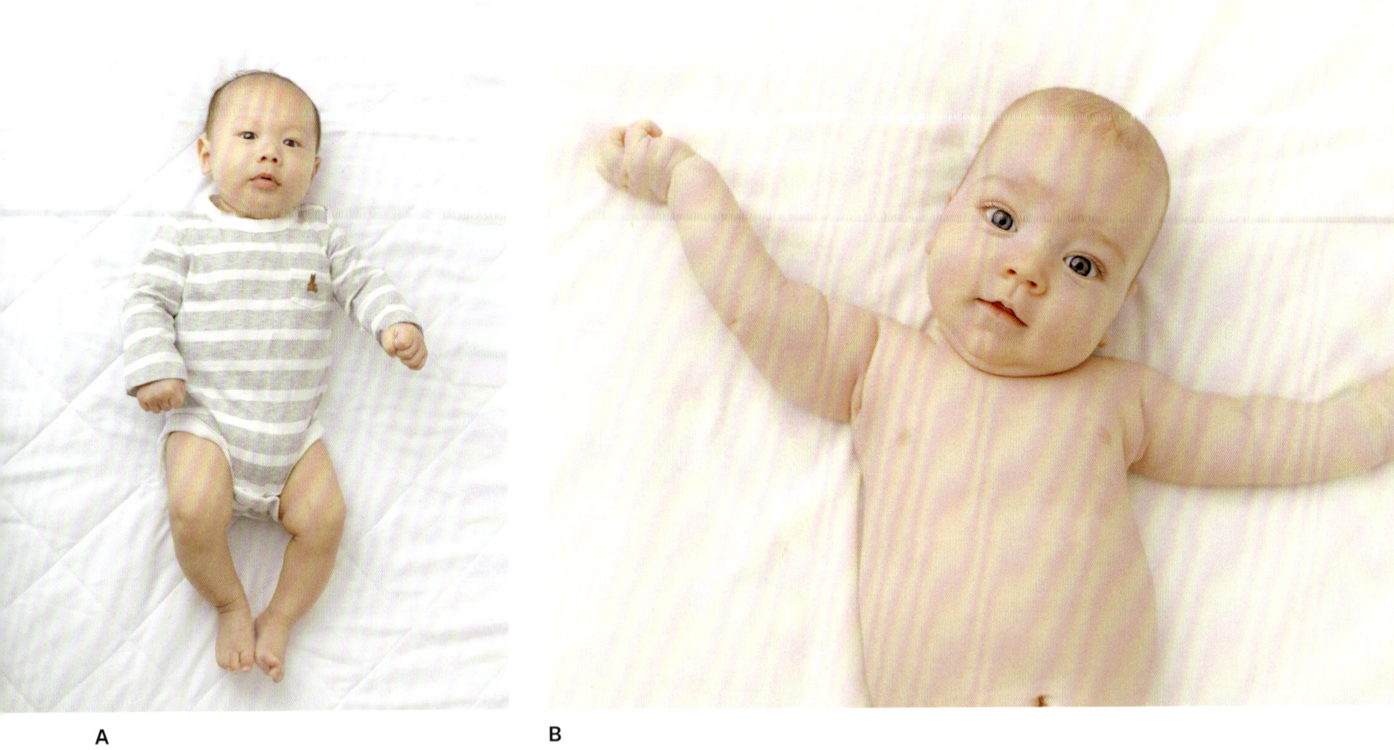

A B

**FIGURE 8.19** The first image shows the typical body position of an awake three-month-old baby on their back. The second image shows how I prefer to photograph this age when they are on their back.

As newborns, when placed on their backs, babies will curl up, similar to how they were positioned in the womb. By six months of age, they will lift their legs and reach for their toes. But at three months of age, they do neither. When placed on their back, a three-month-old will look up at you, and smile and coo. They may place a hand into their mouth or stretch to the side. But for the most part, they will lie with their legs and arms stretched straight beside them (**FIGURE 8.19A**). For this reason, I tend to skip the full body images from above and focus on getting tight headshots, instead (**FIGURE 8.19B**).

**Pro Tip:** A lot of babies still enjoy being swaddled at this age. And they look super cute when they are (**FIGURE 8.20**)!

Next, I'll position myself eye level to the baby and get some photos from the side. Remember, when awake, these babies will turn their heads to look at you or their parents (**FIGURE 8.21**), so take advantage of their interest and engage! If you talk to them, they'll "talk" back with smiles and coos! Some of the best conversations I have are with three-month-old babies!

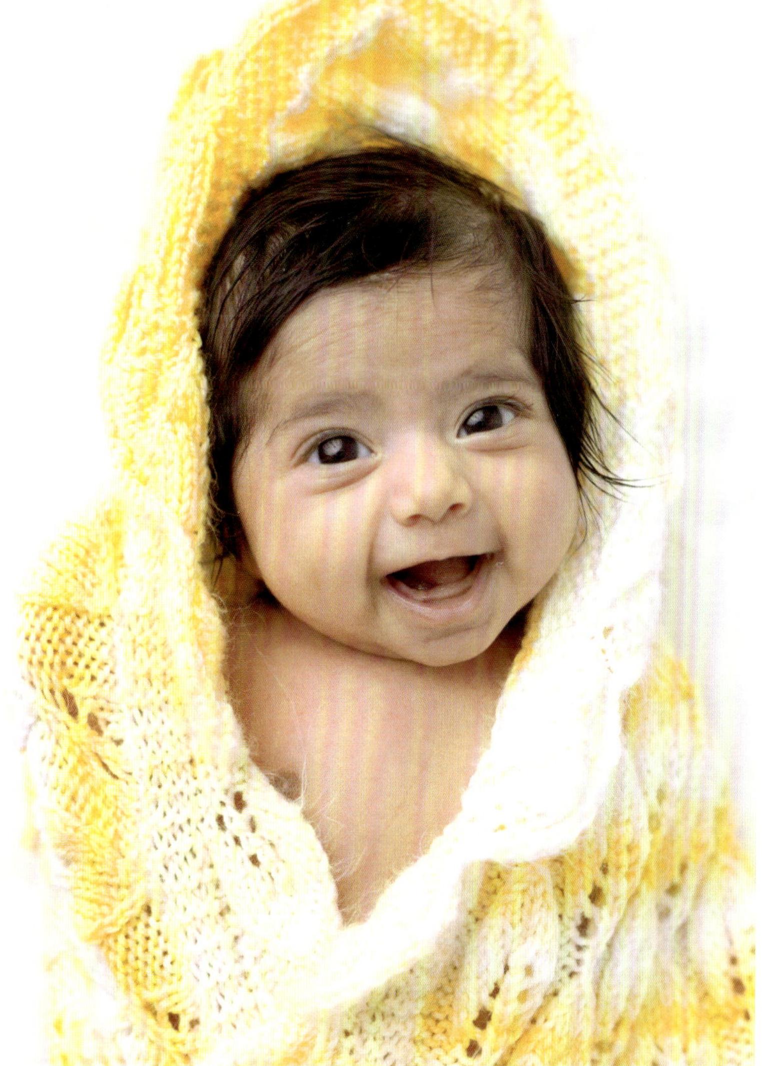

**FIGURE 8.20** A smiley three-month-old, swaddled and adorable!

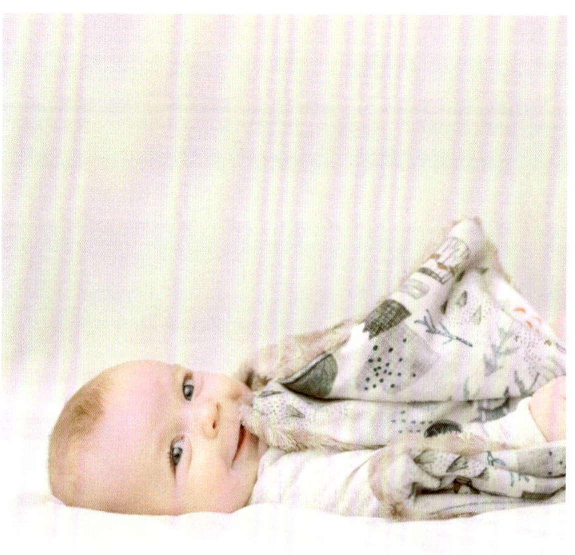

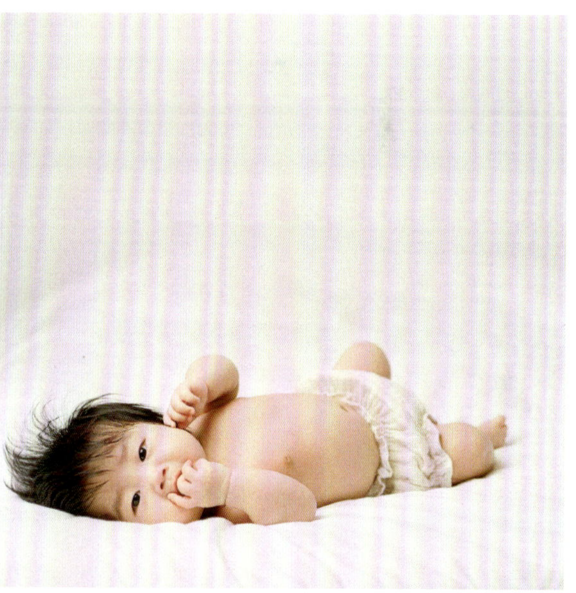

**FIGURES 8.21** When awake, three-month-old babies will turn their heads to engage with you. Take advantage of their interest!

# Sitters

Most babies can sit on their own, unsupported, anywhere between 5 and 9 months of age. At this stage, they can also roll over on their own and push themselves up into a crawling position. Some may even crawl.

When it comes to photo sessions for babies this age, I encourage my clients to schedule when their babies can sit on their own but are not yet crawling. We call these "sitter" sessions.

Sitter sessions are a blast. Babies this age are very social. They smile, babble, and coo. Because of their increased strength and muscle control, they are also capable of new movements and positions.

These sessions are fun but fast-paced! Sitters bring a lot of energy to a session, but they also get tired really fast. I rarely shoot for longer than 30 minutes when working with a sitter.

## Pose: Baby Sitting

Sitter sessions are all about showing off the baby's new skill—sitting! I start every session with them in this position. To set this up, simply ask the parent to sit the baby on the bed, facing you. Position yourself eye level to the baby and then work on maximizing the pose by getting pull-backs of the baby's entire body, as well as tight portraits and details (**FIGURE 8.22**).

Babies this age are curious and will be very interested in you as a new person. Talk to the baby you are photographing. Play games, like peek-a-boo. Clap and cheer them on for everything they do. Six-month-olds love a good time!

**Pro Tip:** Even though most babies are not officially crawling at their sitter sessions, they do move! They will roll, lunge forward or to the side, and get up on all fours and rock, sometimes falling to one side or forward (**FIGURE 8.23**). If you are going to be working with a baby of this age on a raised surface, like a bed, make sure you have an adult within arm's reach to spot the baby. I always have one of the parents positioned next to the bed for this reason (**FIGURE 8.24**).

### Stranger Danger

"Stranger Danger," the fear of unknown people, is a normal developmental stage in babies anywhere between 6 to 9 months. Babies this age will look at you, and even smile and engage, but they may not want you to get too close or to touch them. Respect their boundaries.

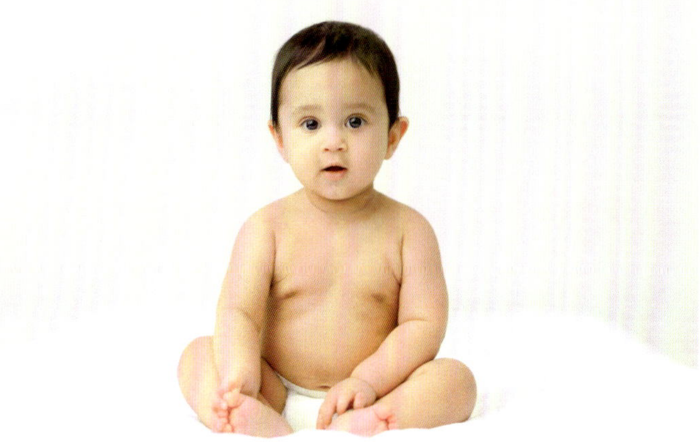

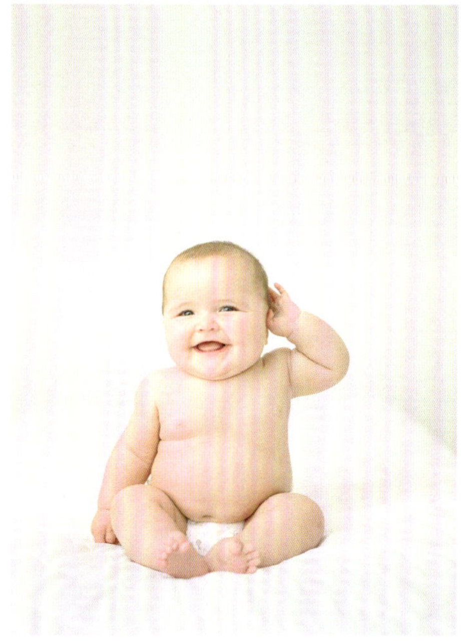

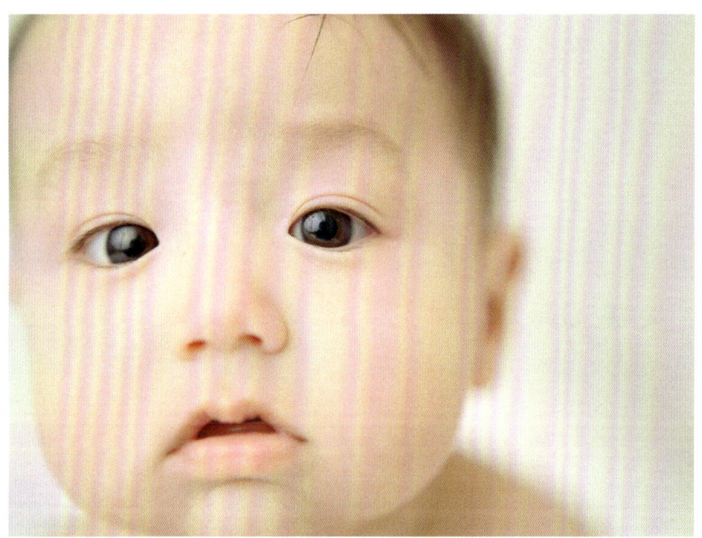

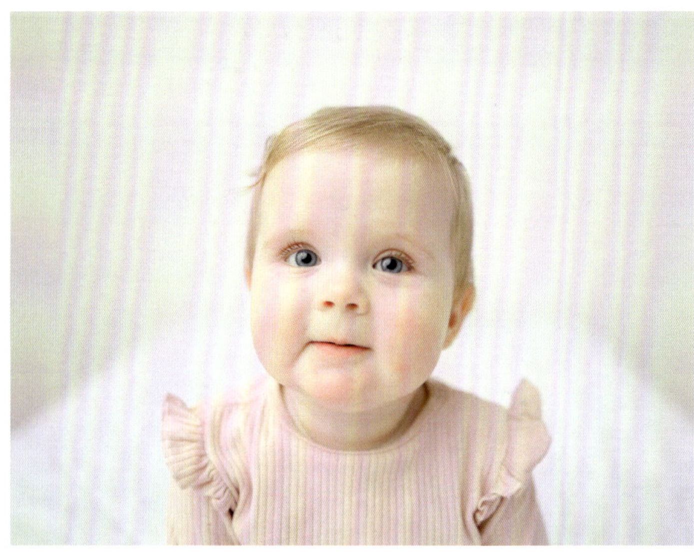

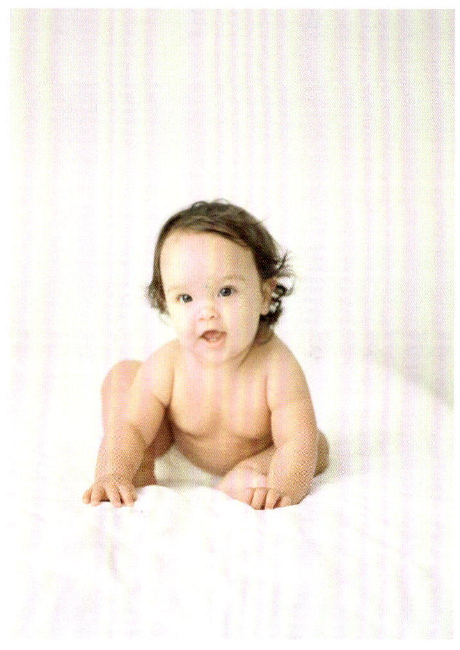

**FIGURE 8.22** Sitters doing what they do best—sitting and looking at the camera!

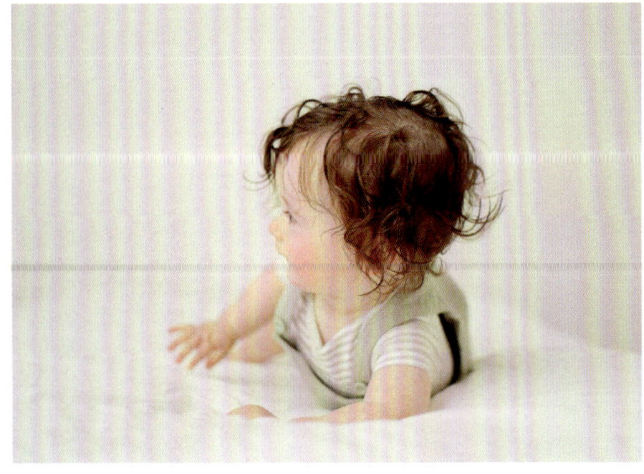

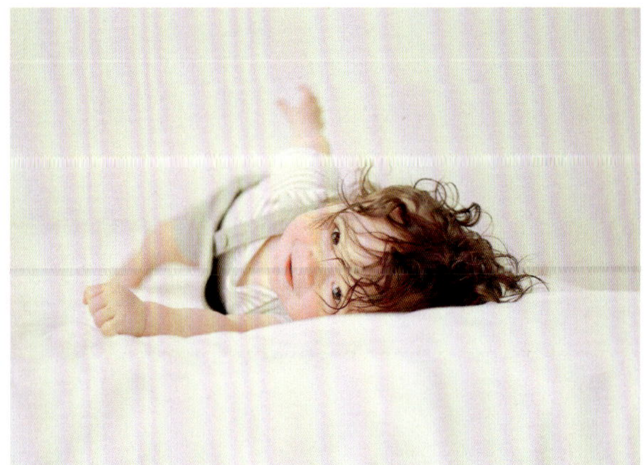

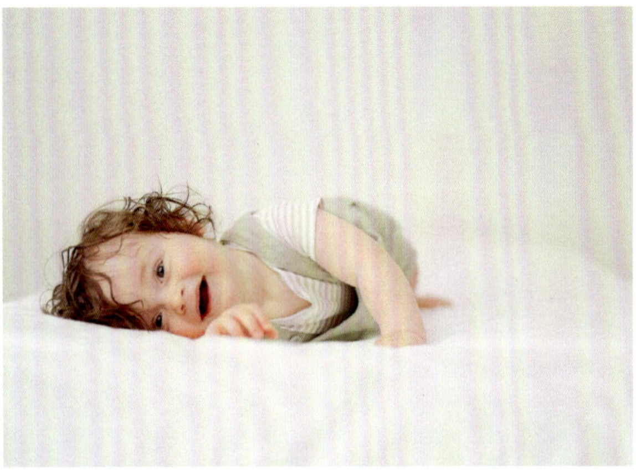

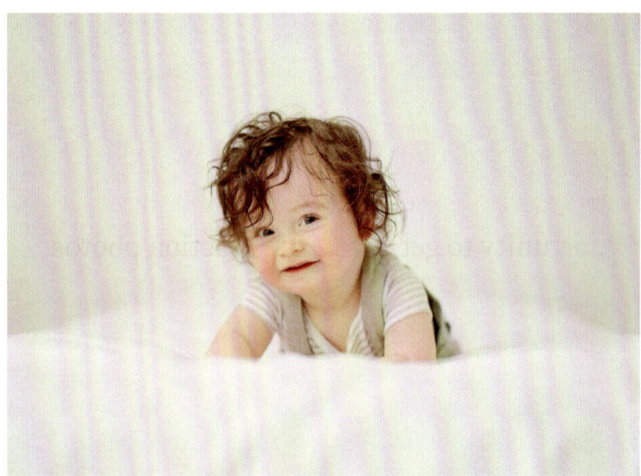

**FIGURE 8.23** Babies this age can move quickly, so be prepared!

**FIGURE 8.24** Safety first! Always have an adult at arm's length when you have a baby on a raised surface, like a bed.

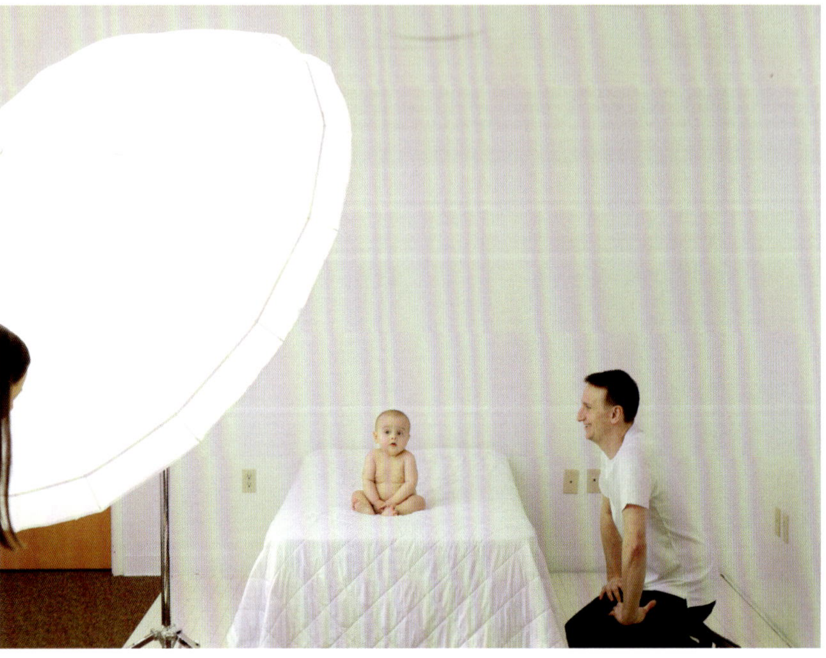

If you notice a baby lean back as you approach, or if they reach for a parent when you talk to them, back off a little and keep your distance. Ask a parent to move the baby from one pose to the next and only touch the baby if they engage you first.

Babies will reach for you (or your camera) when they are ready. I wait for the babies I'm working with to show me they're comfortable before I scoot in to get a close headshot, for example. If they don't invite me in, I'll keep a reasonable distance for the entire session.

Even when a baby this age is totally comfortable, they will keep a close eye on their parents. They often turn to make sure their parents are near, even when playing and having a good time with me. It helps them feel safe and gives me the opportunity to get some cute reaction photos and profile shots (**FIGURE 8.25**).

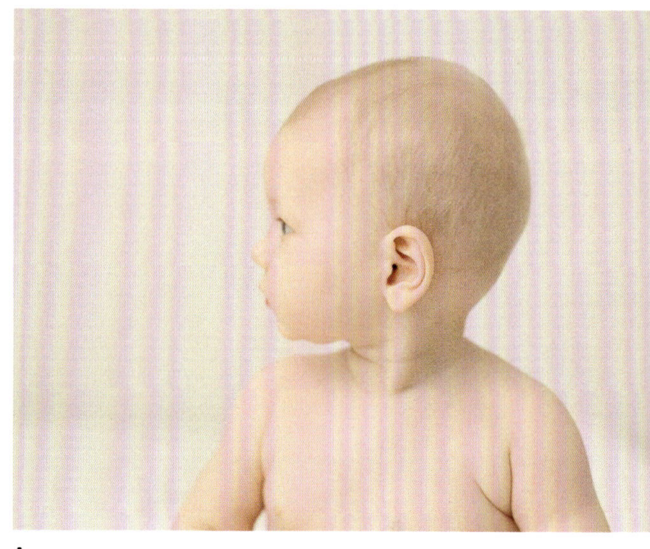

A

B

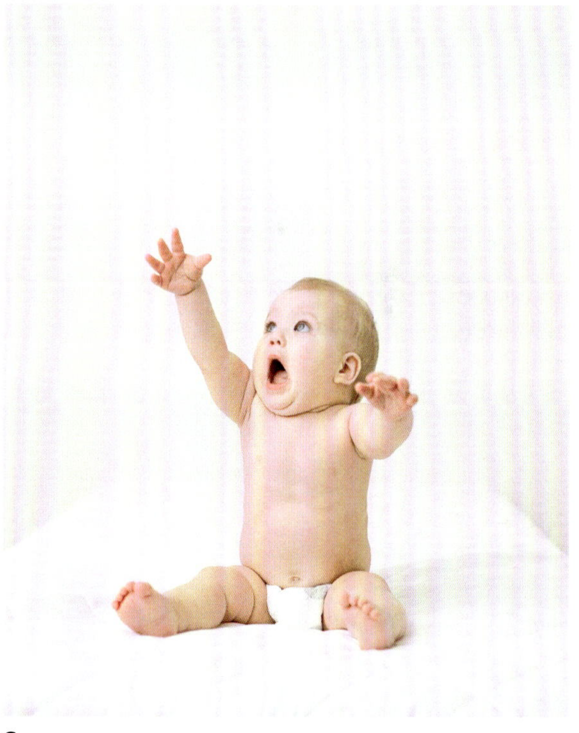

C

**FIGURE 8.25** Sitters will often turn to look at their parents, even when having fun at a session. Figure 8.25C was taken as one parent played peek-a-book with the baby from behind my strobe and umbrella. Such a hilarious capture!

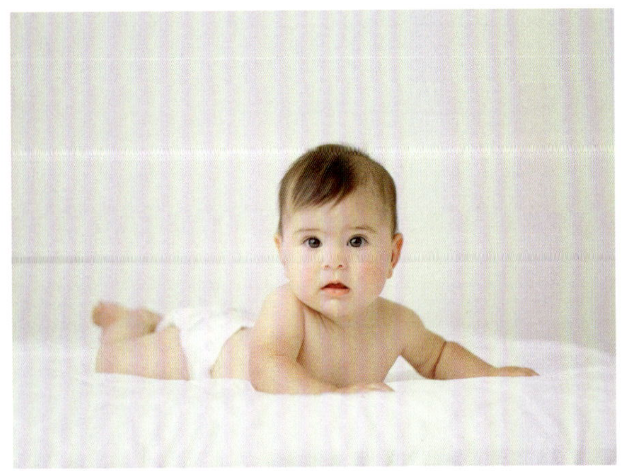

A

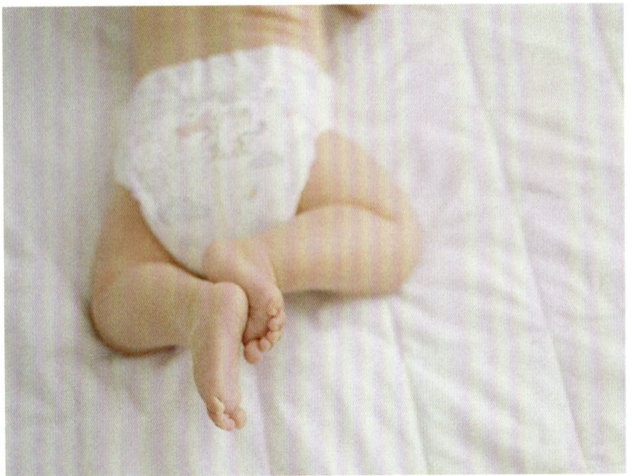

B

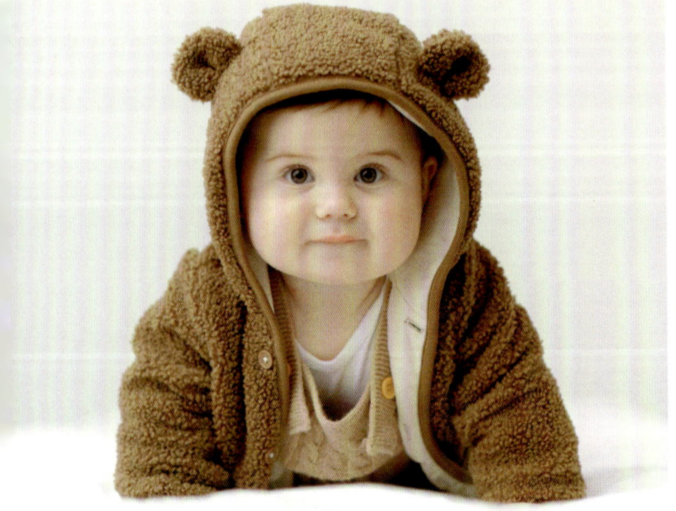

C

## Pose: Baby on Belly

After completing the sitting poses, ask one of the parents to place the baby on their belly. Position yourself at eye level and get to work! Some babies will happily stay in the position, allowing you to get all the angles—the pullback shots (**FIGURES 8.26A** and **8.26C**), the close-ups, and details (**FIGURE 8.26B**).

Some babies want to practice crawling when placed on their belly. They'll push themselves up onto all fours and rock back and forth. I love watching babies do this! It's amazing to me that they just figure out how to move, without being taught! And it makes for some fun organic poses (**FIGURE 8.27**).

## Pose: Baby on Back

The last pose I work through with a sitter by themselves is the Baby on Back pose. When placed on their back, babies this age will lift their legs and feet into the air and reach for their toes with their hands. This is a classic 6-to-9-month position that I make a point to always capture (**FIGURE 8.28**).

To set this pose up, have the parent place the baby on their back, profile to you, and position yourself eye level to the baby. Make sure there's space between the baby and the end of the bed, as the baby may roll. And always have an adult within arm's reach, for safety. Get images of the baby's entire body from different angles, vertical and horizontal images, details, and close-up portraits (**FIGURE 8.28E**).

**FIGURE 8.26** Classic Baby on Belly pose for a sitter. Pullback shots (**A**, **C**) and a details shot (**B**).

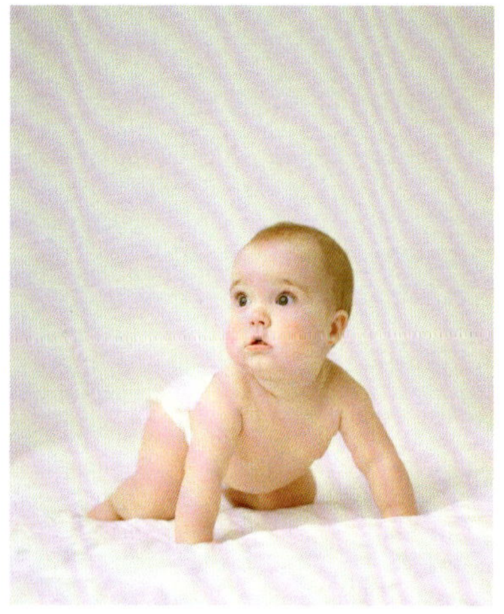
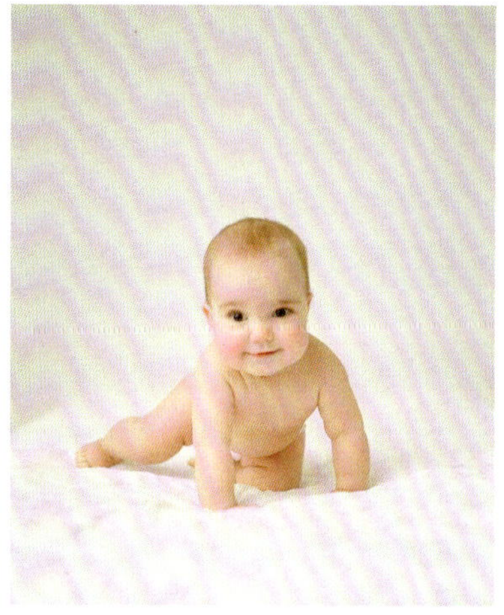
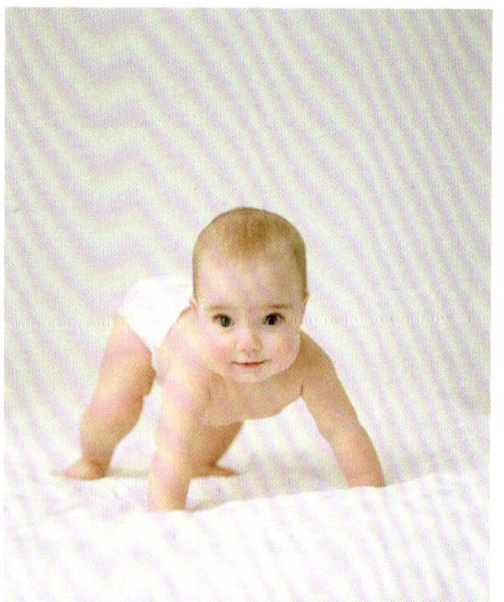

**FIGURE 8.27** A sitter practicing crawling during a session.

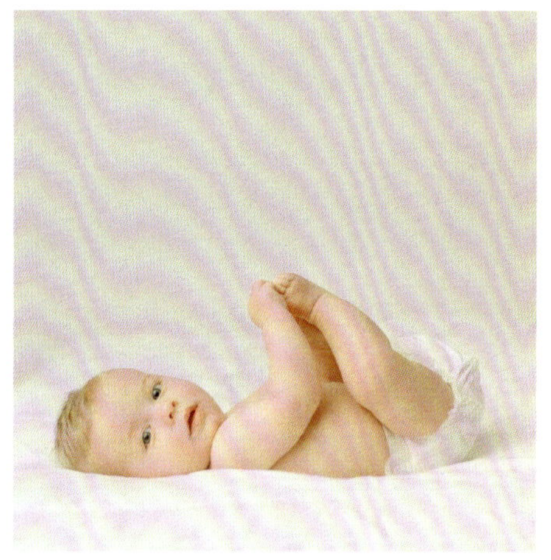

A

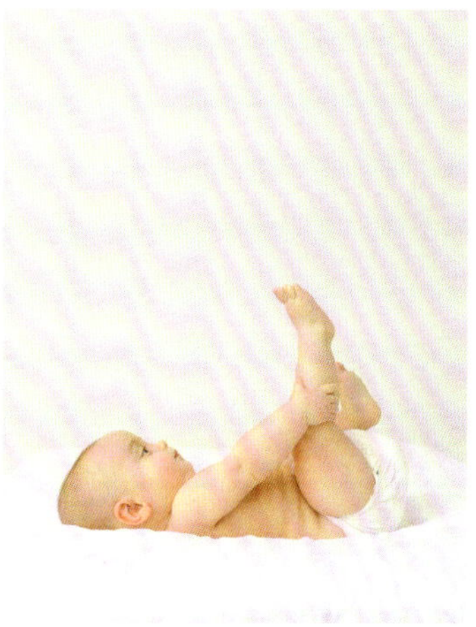

B

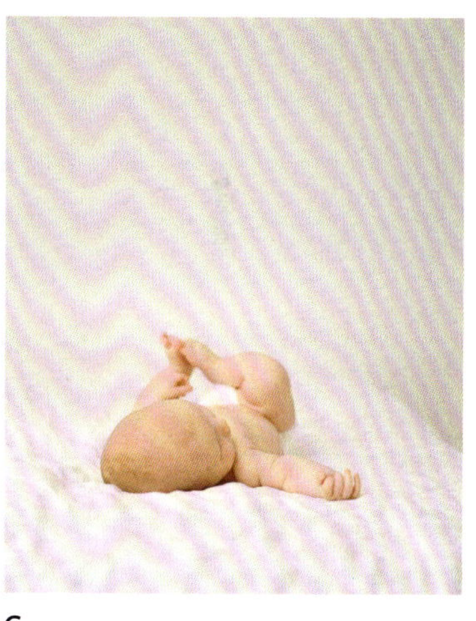

C

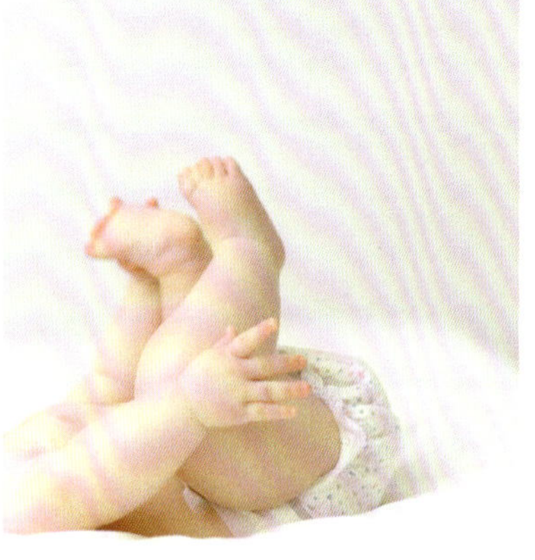

D

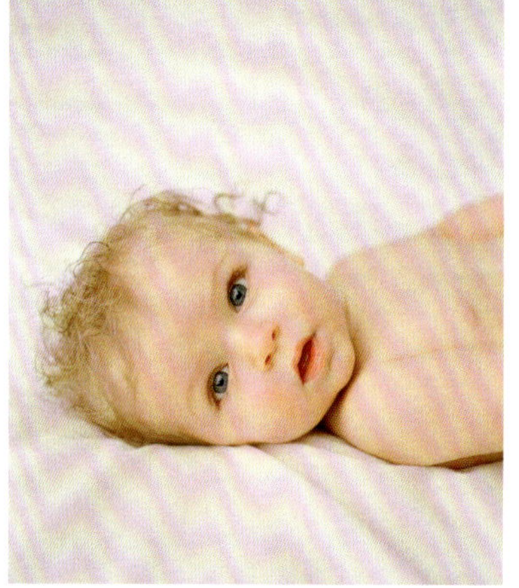

E

**FIGURE 8.28** When placed on their back, babies this age will lift their legs and feet into the air and reach for their toes with their hands. Sitters are very social and will look into the camera and engage.

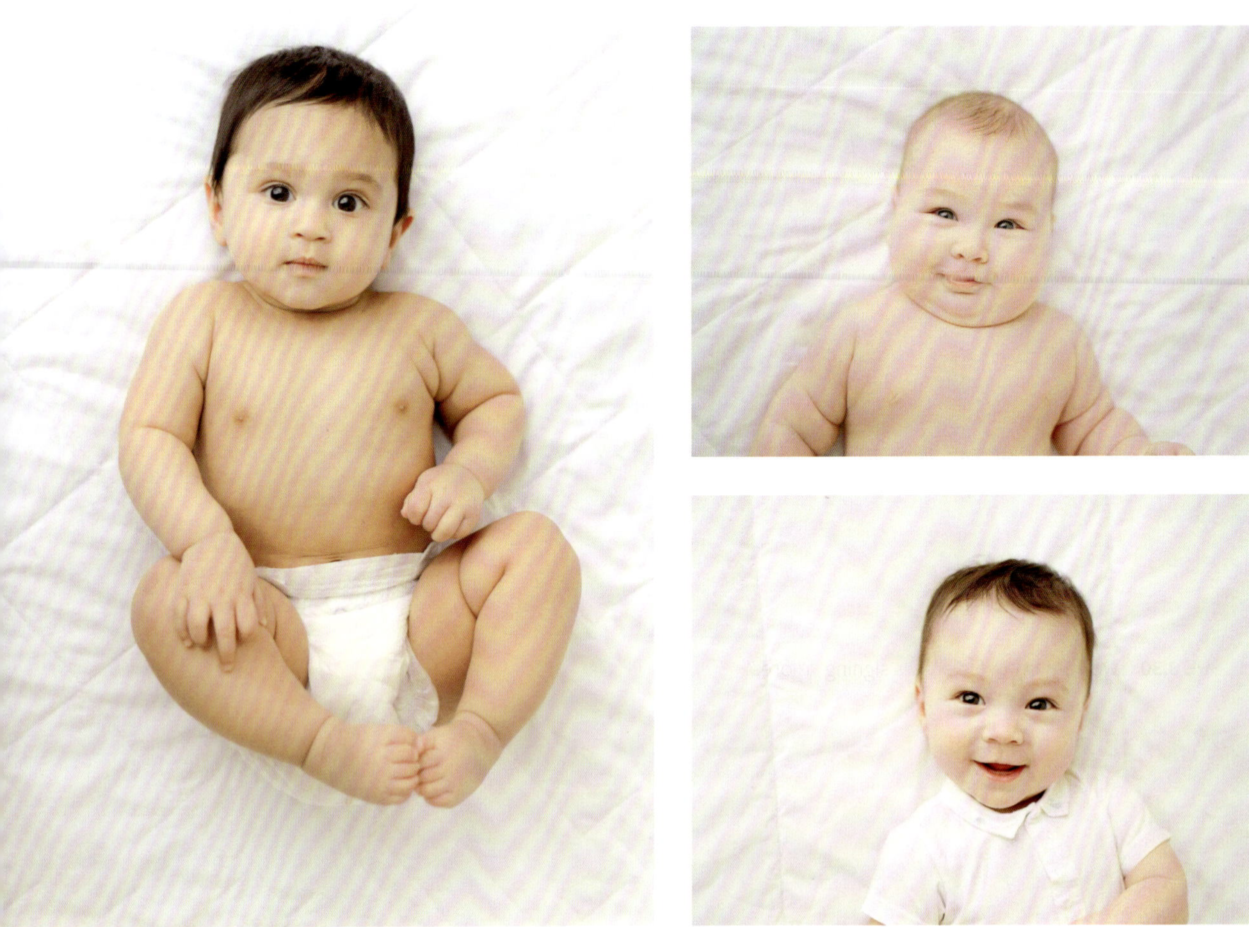

**FIGURE 8.29** Always place your camera strap around your neck when standing over a baby!

Once I have photographed the baby on their back from the side, I will quickly stand over them for some images from above (their entire body and tight portraits) (**FIGURE 8.29**). Be sure to engage with the babies you are working with! And always wear your camera strap when standing over a baby.

## One Year

By 12 months of age, most babies have a pretty impressive skill set. Most are crawling, and many can stand, cruise (walk while holding onto something or someone for assistance), and walk on their own. They also understand simple words, and will wave, clap, dance, and play games. Some may use sign language (if they have been taught)!

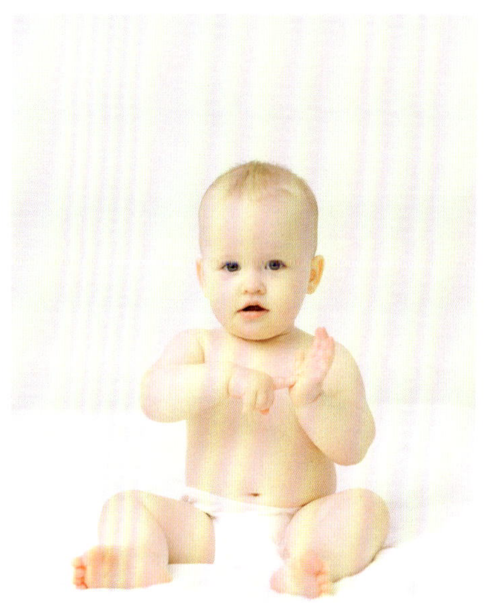

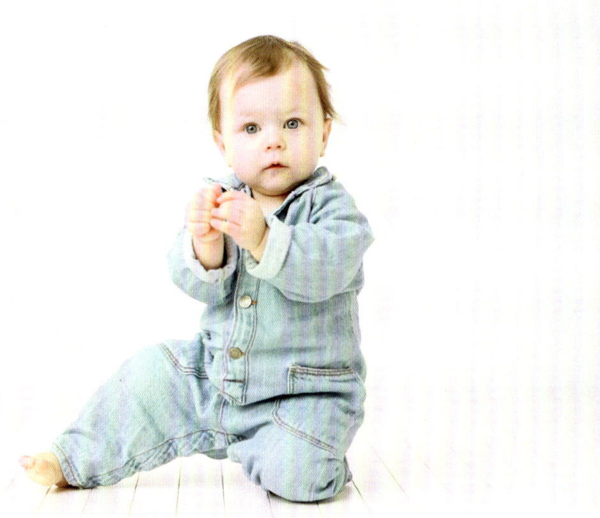

**FIGURE 8.30** Twelve-month-old babies signing "more."

I highly recommend familiarizing yourself with common words used in baby sign language. Doing a quick internet search will help you learn. My small clients often use signs with me, and I'm thrilled to be able to communicate with them in this way. The images in **FIGURE 8.30**, for example, both show babies signing "more."

## Pose: Sitting

I start my one-year-old sessions with a sitting pose. Ask the parent to place the baby in a sitting position facing you and position yourself eye level to the baby. Most one-year-old babies are a little cautious at the beginning of their session. The stranger danger they developed at around 6 months of age is still very strong, so they may need a few moments to warm up. When in this cautious state, they will sit still and stare directly at you and your camera. They want to check you out to make sure they can trust you. Keep your distance and speak to them in a soothing way, and make sure a parent is close by. Once they warm up to you, they will begin to smile and move. And once they start to move, you'll have to work extra fast to keep up with them, so use the moment of stillness at the beginning of the session as an opportunity to capture portraits of the baby sitting still and looking directly into your camera. Pull back to get full-body photos, then zoom in to capture tight headshots and details.

The first two images in **FIGURE 8.31** show a one-year-old at the beginning of the session with that tentative stare so common at this age. **FIGURE 8.31C** shows the same child later in the session after she becomes more comfortable.

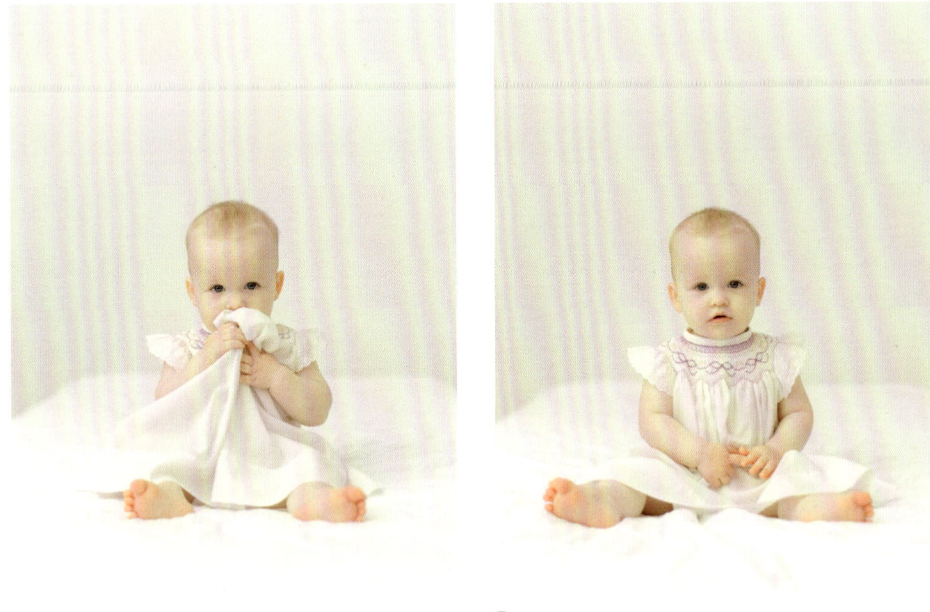

A

B

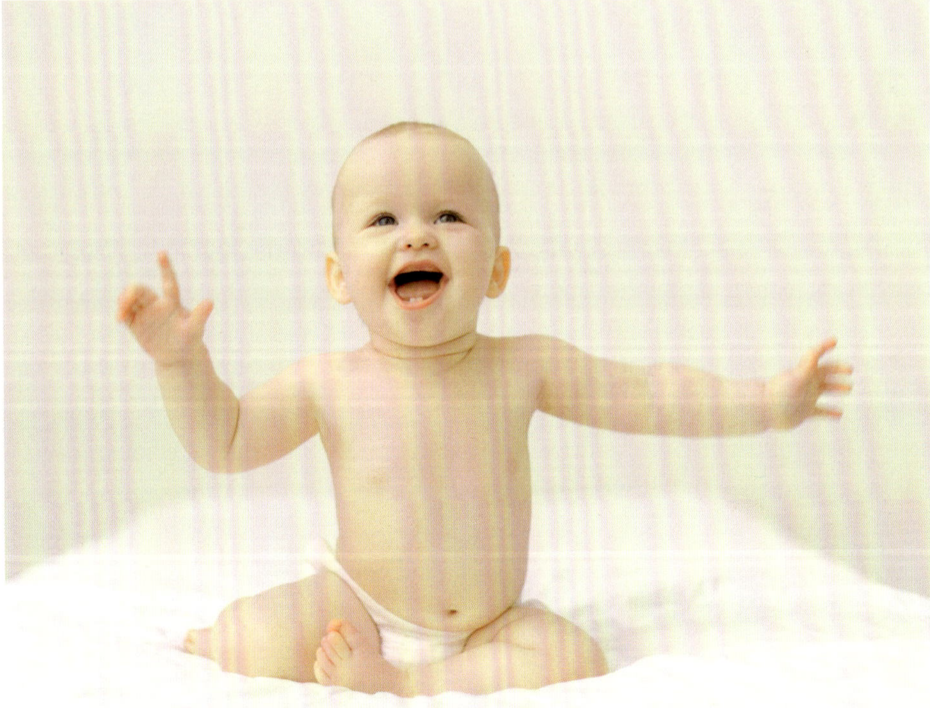

C

**FIGURE 8.31** Twelve-month-old babies will often be a little shy at the beginning of their session but will warm up quickly.

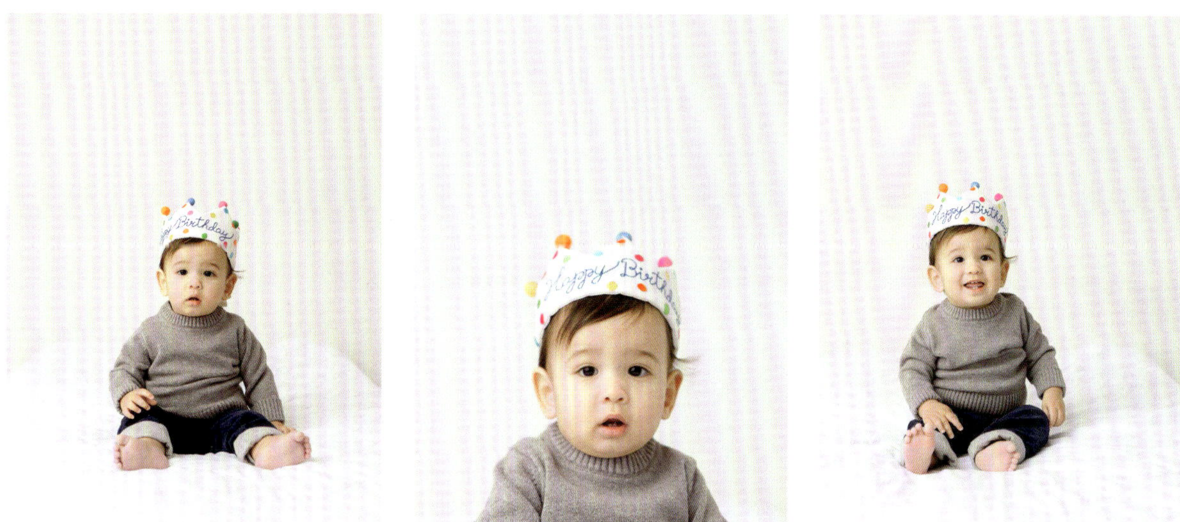

**FIGURE 8.32** Take photos with birthday accessories at the very beginning of your session, while the baby is still and cautious.

**Pro Tip:** If your clients have birthday accessories, like a hat, that they want the baby photographed in, take those photos at the very beginning of your session, while the baby is still and cautious (**FIGURE 8.32**). Once they get comfortable, it will be hard to keep that hat on their head!

## Pose: Baby on Belly

After the sitting pose, I move the baby onto their belly. Some babies will push themselves up on their arms or on all fours and stay still while you photograph them, but most will use the opportunity to move. And move they will!

Because babies this age are so mobile, a lot of these poses will blend together. You may start the session with the baby sitting, for example, but then they'll decide they want to crawl and move themselves into a belly position. Or you may place them on their belly, but they'll decide they'd rather sit up or roll over. Stay flexible and move fast, because if they do decide to move, it's usually quite quickly.

To set up the poses in the images in **FIGURE 8.33**, ask the parent to place the baby on their belly at the opposite end of the bed from where you are positioned. If the baby chooses to crawl, you will have to reset several times, as babies move fast! This one-year-old was placed on their belly, and the images were captured only moments apart, as he was moving fast. As you can see, at one point he chose to sit up and make sure his parents were close by before continuing to crawl toward me and my camera.

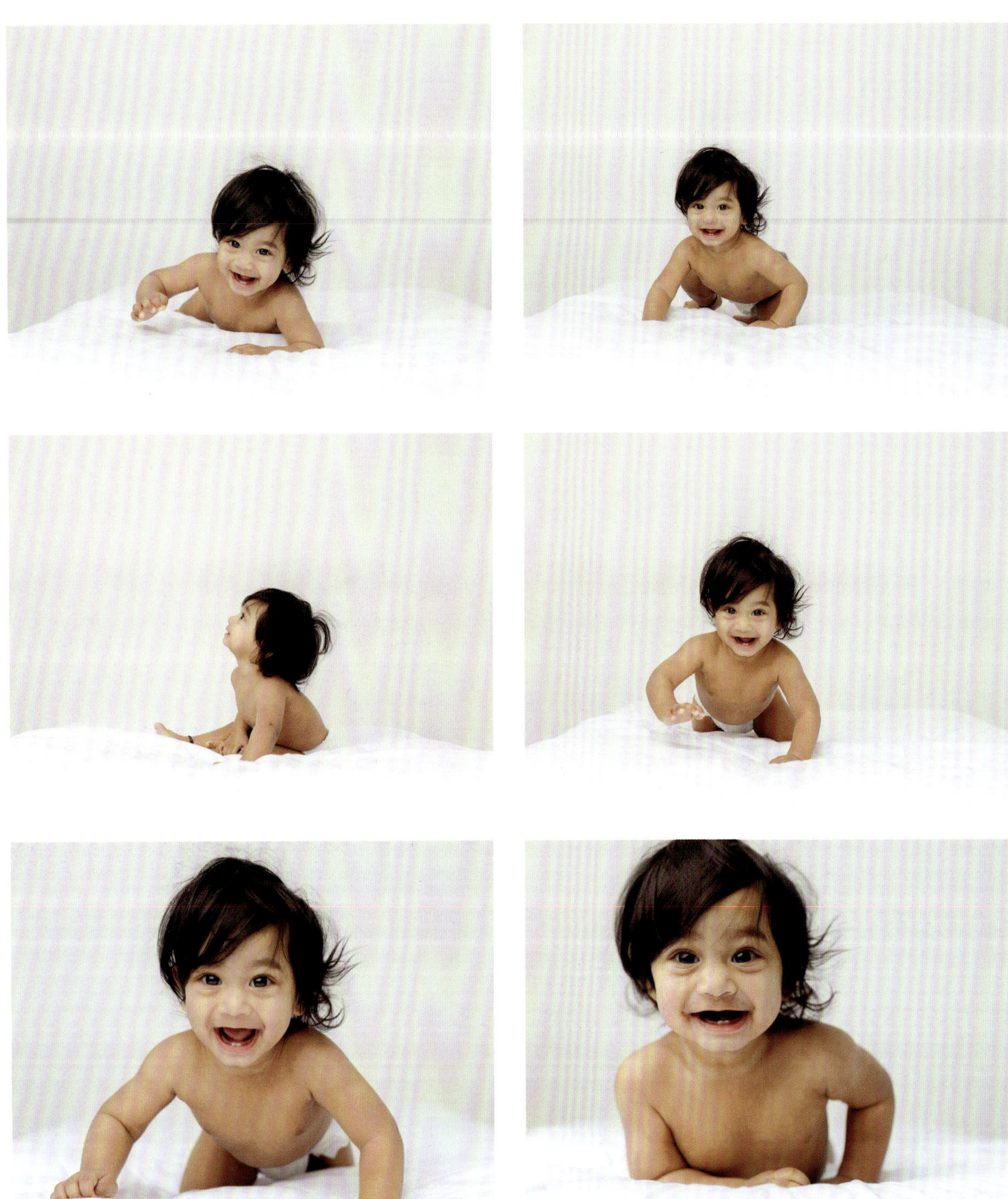

**FIGURE 8.33** One-year-old in motion!

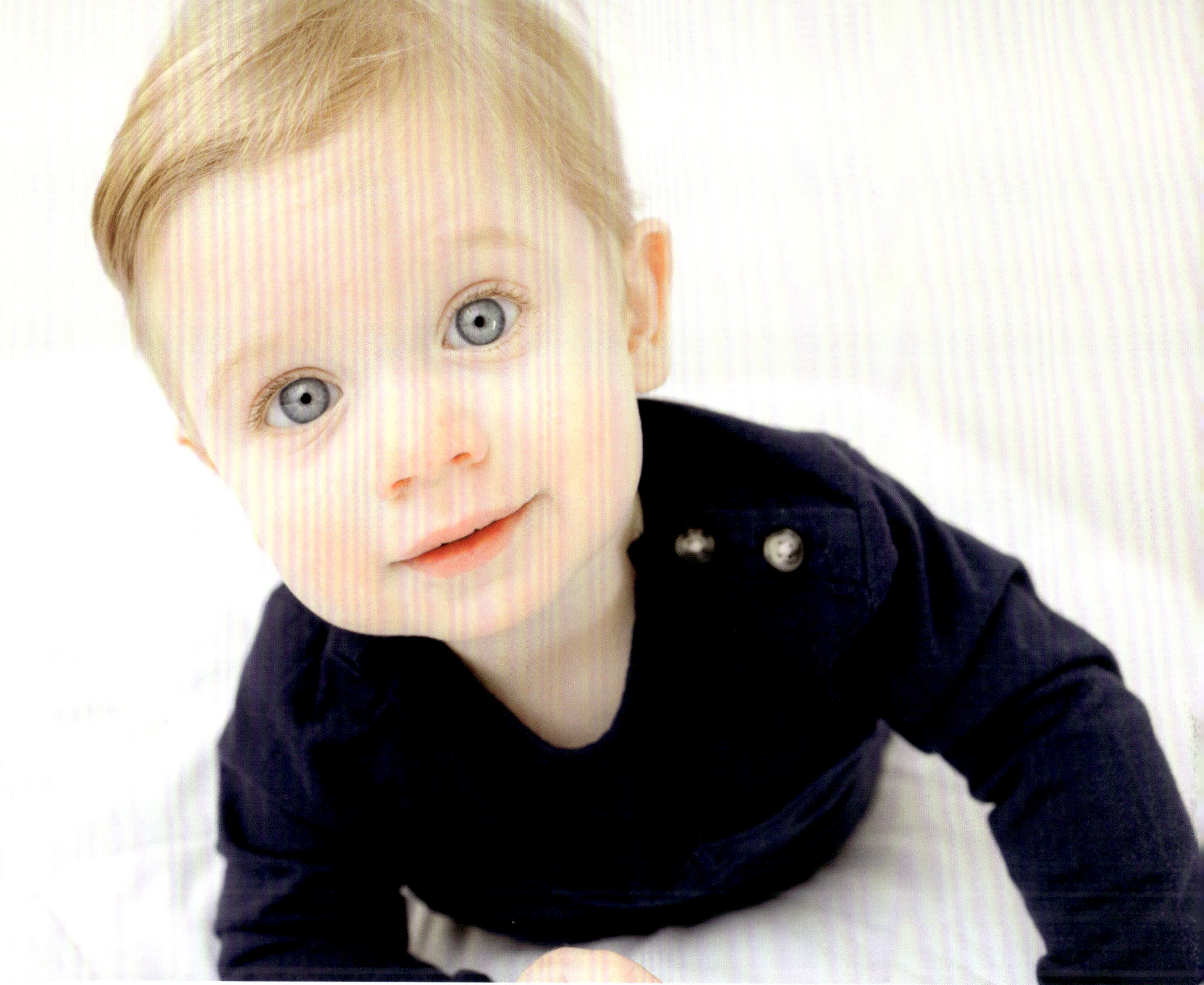

**FIGURE 8.34** A curious one-year-old in the Baby on Belly pose.

If you are photographing a child in this pose on a raised surface, like a bed, have an adult positioned within arm's reach to spot the child. Remember to get pull-backs of the baby's entire body as well as tight headshots whenever possible.

**Pro Tip:** I prefer placing the baby on a bed for Baby on Belly poses rather than on the floor because it provides a defined space. When a baby is placed on the floor in this position, they can go anywhere, and you'll end up chasing them around the room. When they're on a bed, however, their movement is limited, which will make your job much easier!

## How to Slow a Baby Down

Once a baby has developed a new skill, like moving, they want to use it! Crawling babies love to explore their environment, which can make photographing them a challenge. To slow down a moving baby, provide interesting distractions that give them something to focus on. For example, I use stickers.

Placing stickers on the floor or on the bed in front of the baby you are photographing is a great distraction (**FIGURE 8.35A**) as they are small, easy to place, and easy to remove in post-production (**FIGURE 8.35B**). I will often place stickers in the path of a crawling baby when I need to slow them down, and it works every time!

**Pro Tip:** Your stickers don't have to be fancy to work. I use round label stickers. They come in bright colors that catch the baby's attention and are relatively inexpensive.

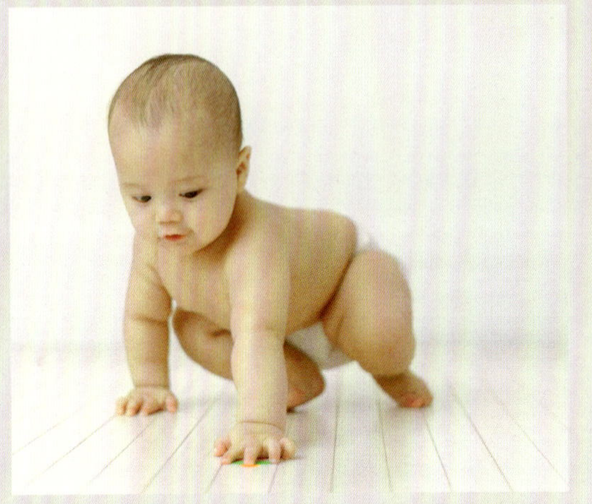

A

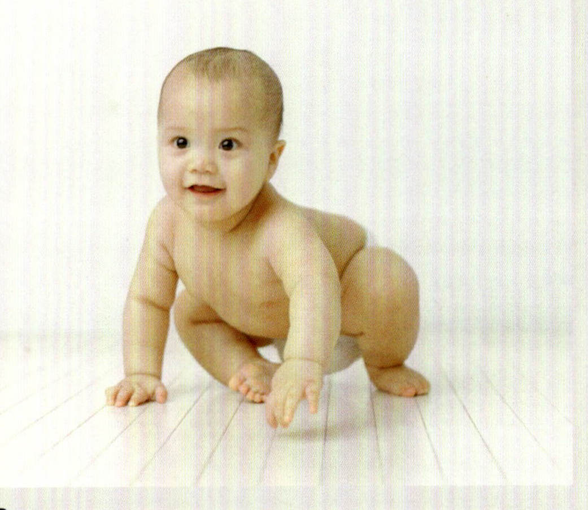

B

**FIGURE 8.35** This crawling baby is reaching for the stickers I've placed on the floor to get his attention (underneath his hand). In the second image, you can see that the stickers were removed in post-production.

### Pose: Standing

Because every baby develops at their own pace, the standing pose will look different for every child you photograph (**FIGURE 8.36**). Some babies need the support of a parent, either holding on to their hands, or supporting them securely around the waist. Some babies can support themselves by holding on to a solid object, and some can stand completely on their own. The good news is all scenarios result in adorable pictures of this important milestone. Once the child is positioned, work quickly (especially if they are standing unsupported).

This pose is all about capturing the child standing, so you'll want most of your images to be of the baby's entire body. Capture these vertically and horizontally to add variety and play around with different compositions for visual interest. If the baby is doing well in the standing position, zoom in to get some tight headshots, as well.

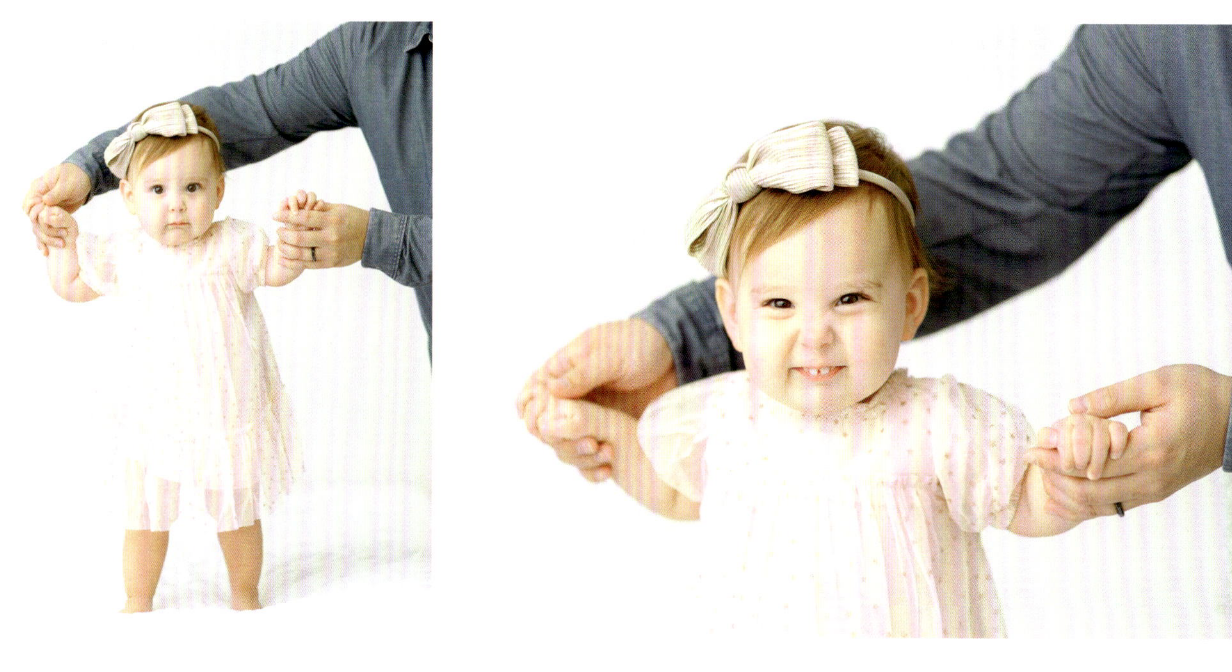

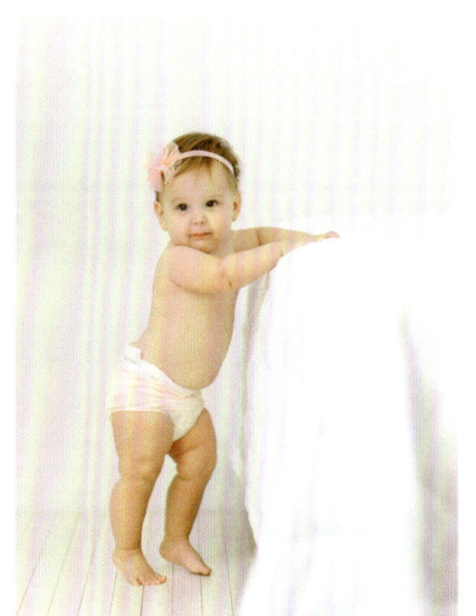

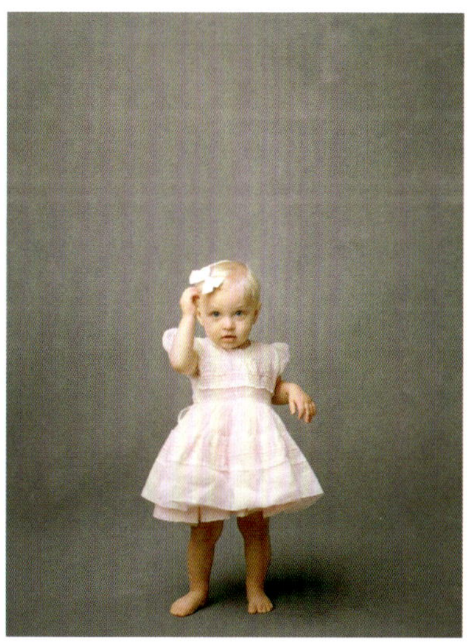

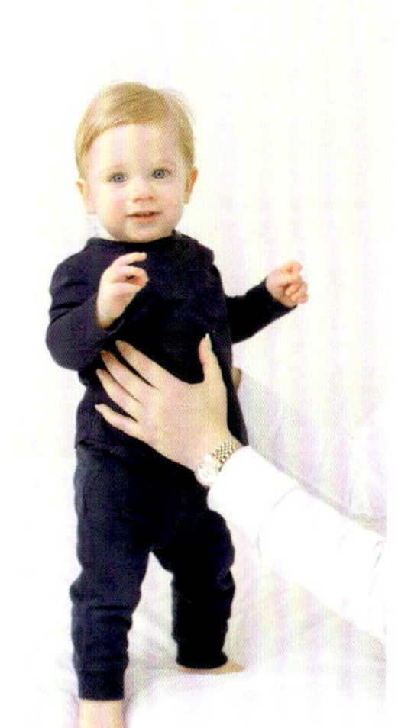

**FIGURE 8.36** Standing babies with varying levels of support—from held by a parent to fully independent.

# Toddlers

Children between the ages of one and three years old are considered toddlers. By this stage, they have mastered an array of new skills: they can stand, walk, run, and climb. They understand language and are learning to express themselves. They comprehend commands and requests, and they most definitely have opinions.

Toddlers are delightful little people—when they get to do what they want. They are naturally curious and adventurous, but they do not appreciate being bossed around (and really, who can blame them?). Trying to force a toddler to do something they don't want to do will almost certainly result in a tantrum—and tantrums are best avoided whenever possible!

## Ask Constructive Questions

One of the ways I maintain control when working with toddlers is by being intentional with the questions I ask. I only ask questions when I know the answer will lead to the outcome I want.

For example, if I need a toddler to sit for a photo, I won't ask, "*Would you like to sit down so I can take your picture?*" That question leaves room for a *no*, and in reality, *no* is not an option. Instead, I'll reframe the question to offer controlled choices: "*Would you like to sit on the stool or on the bed?*" This way, the child feels a sense of autonomy by making a decision, while still doing what's needed for the session to move forward.

## Toddler "Poses"

When it comes to "posing" toddlers, keep it simple. There are really only two basic options: they can sit, or they can stand. And whenever possible, I let them decide how.

Most two- and three-year-olds don't yet have the coordination to sit "criss-cross" or in the mermaid pose, so I never force those positions. If they're sitting on the bed, I simply let them sit however they feel most comfortable. This keeps them happy and relaxed, which makes for more natural photos.

Once they're settled, I adjust my framing—zooming out to capture full-body photos and zooming in for tight headshots. By letting toddlers move in ways that feel natural to them, I can focus on capturing genuine expressions and personality-filled portraits (**FIGURE 8.37**).

If they choose to sit on a stool instead of a bed, I position them sitting in profile to me, with a parent standing in front of them for support and safety. I prefer this positioning because it helps eliminate perspective distortion (see Chapter 5) and creates visually interesting shapes in the composition (**FIGURE 8.38**).

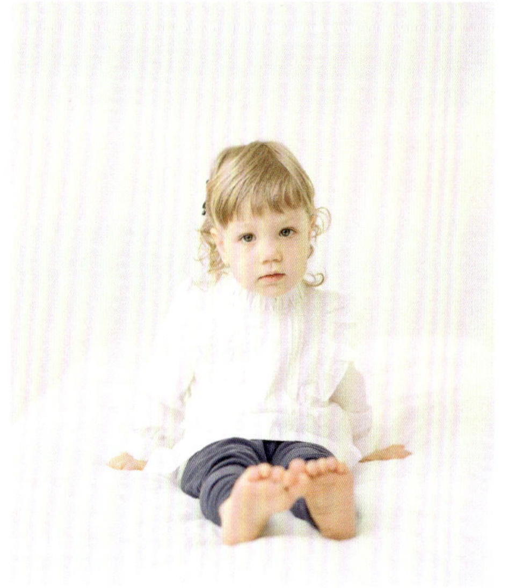

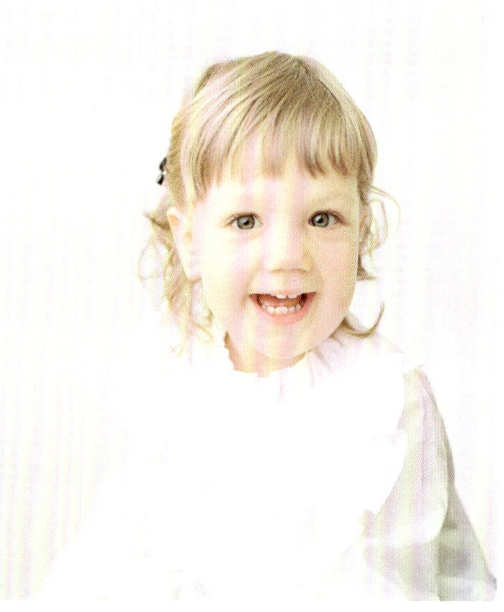

**FIGURE 8.37** I let toddlers sit however they feel most comfortable.

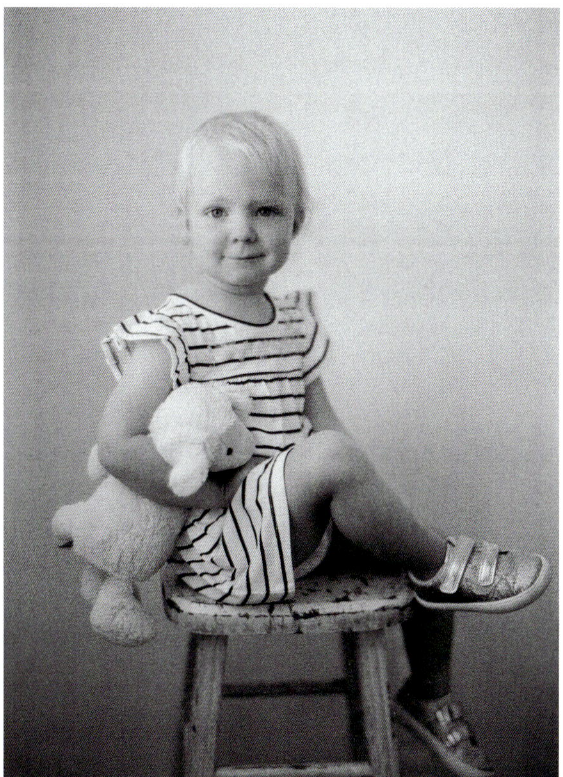

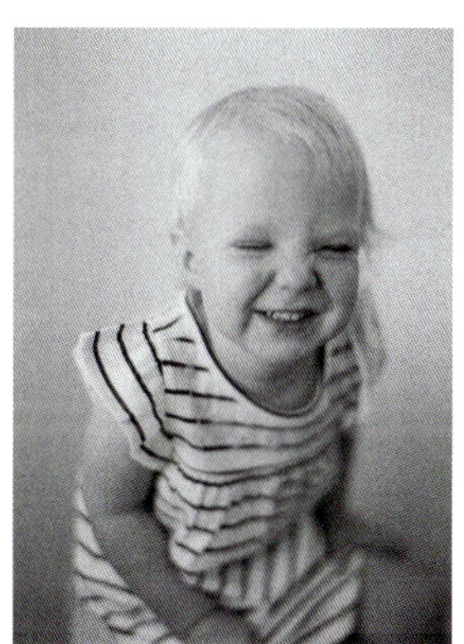

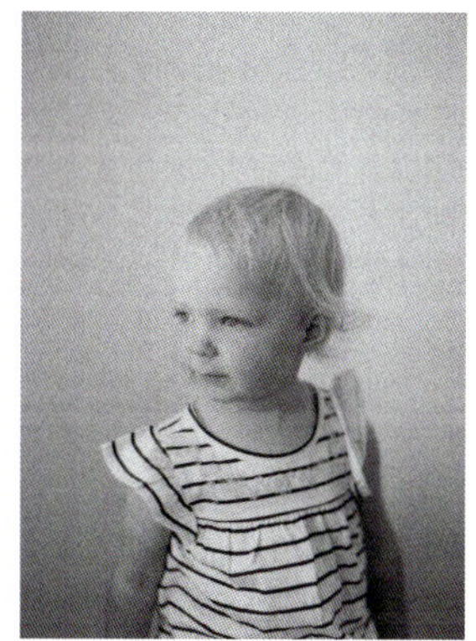

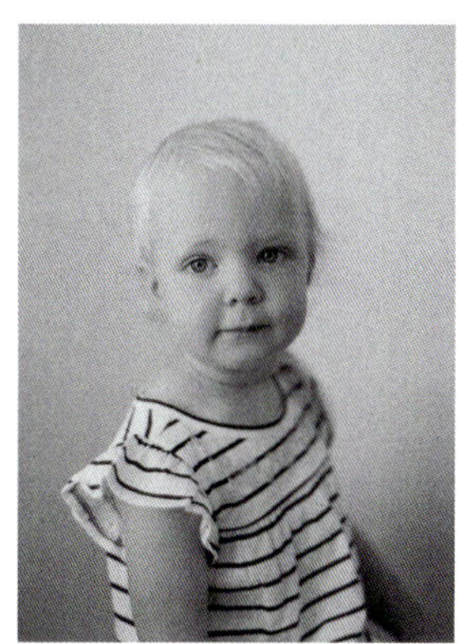

**FIGURE 8.38** This toddler posed sitting on a stool while I captured a mix of full-body photos and tight headshots.

### Keep Things Fun!

When working with toddlers, keep things fun! Sing, clap, play music—whatever it takes to create a playful, engaging environment for the little person in front of your camera. A happy toddler is a cooperative toddler, and the more fun they're having, the better the photos will be.

### Bribe When Necessary

I always keep stickers and lollipops on hand as incentives. If I'm working with a reluctant child, I'll grab a handful of lollipops and ask them to pick their favorite color. Then, I'll place a sticker on the ground where I want them to stand—or on the bed or stool where I want them to sit—and ask them to sit or stand on it. I'll let them know that when they do, they get to hold their lollipop. Sometimes, I'll end up giving toddlers an entire bouquet of lollipops just to keep them engaged (**FIGURE 8.39**). The best part? Lollipops not only hold their interest but also look adorable in photos—a win/win!

**Pro Tip:** Always ask a parent's permission before offering a lollipop or any kind of treat. Some children have allergies, and some families have specific rules about what their kids can eat. If a parent says no to sweets, stickers work just as well!

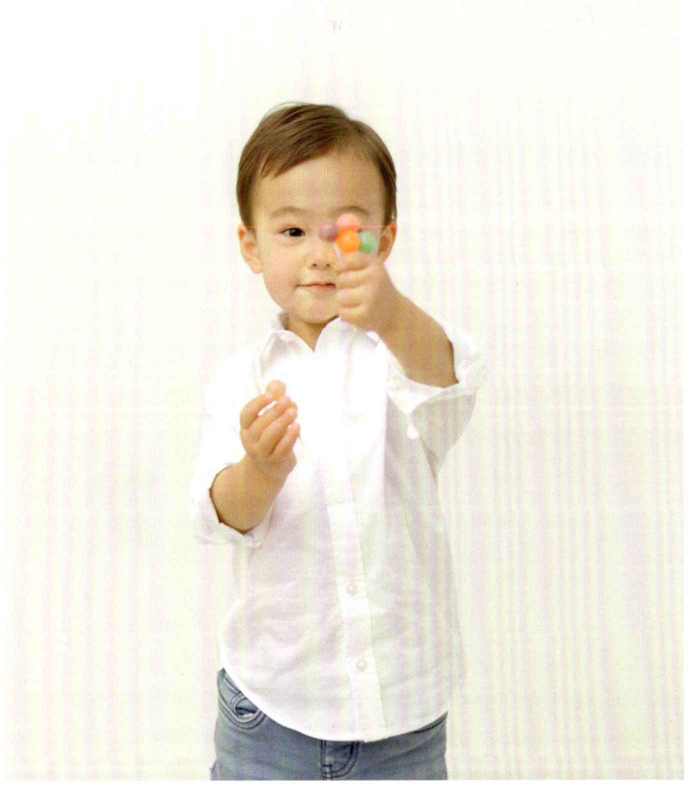

**FIGURE 8.39** Toddler holding a lollipop bouquet—a sweet, effective incentive that photographs well.

## School-Age and Beyond

Once a child turns five, they are considered "school-age" until they reach their teenage years. While there are many milestones between ages 5 and 12, I approach these sessions much like I do when photographing toddlers. The main difference is that older children can follow directions more easily, allowing for more structured posing. I typically use a mix of sitting, standing, and lying-down poses, adjusting my approach to keep the session fun and natural.

### Pose: Sitting

Because older children take direction better than toddlers, you can be more intentional with posing. Look for ways to create triangles in your composition and give clear, simple instructions.

If the child is sitting on a bed or the ground, for example, guide them into a position that feels comfortable for them while also maintaining a flattering shape. I often use the mermaid pose (see **FIGURE 8.40**). To set up this pose, ask the child to sit with both legs facing the same direction, and to bring one arm down for support. I ask them to imagine that their legs are fused together, like a mermaid's tail, and demonstrate the move myself while explaining it. This is my favorite pose for older kids who are sitting on a bed or on the ground. It's flattering (especially if the child is wearing a dress or skirt) and it results in a pleasing triangle shape. That said, sitting crisscross or on their knees also works well for children this age. If the child is sitting on a stool, ask them to sit in profile to you, and have them turn their head toward the camera for the photos (**FIGURE 8.41**). Remember to add variety to your seated poses by directing the child where to look. Shoot vertically and horizontally and get both full-body shots and headshots.

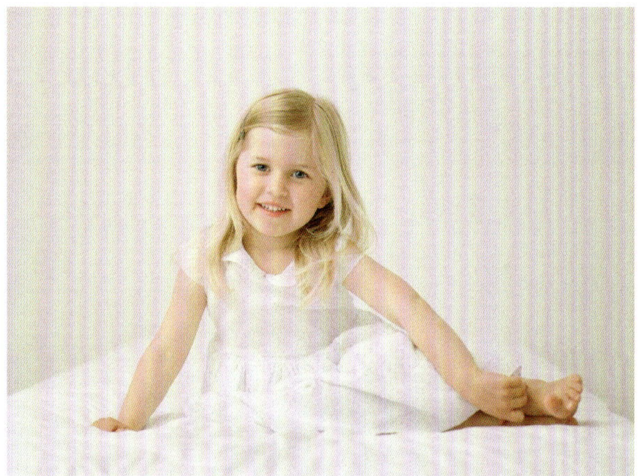

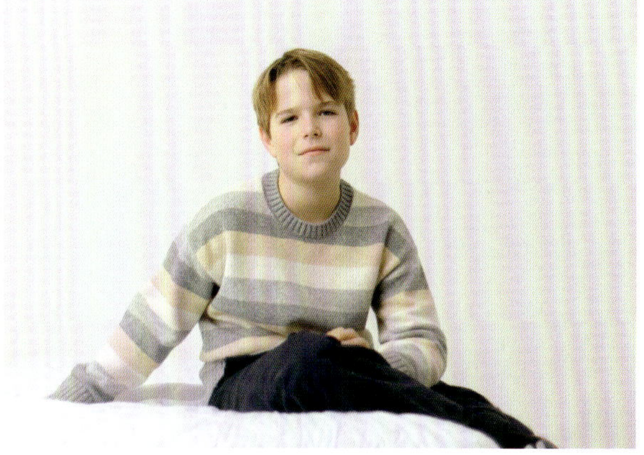

**FIGURE 8.40** Two examples of the mermaid pose.

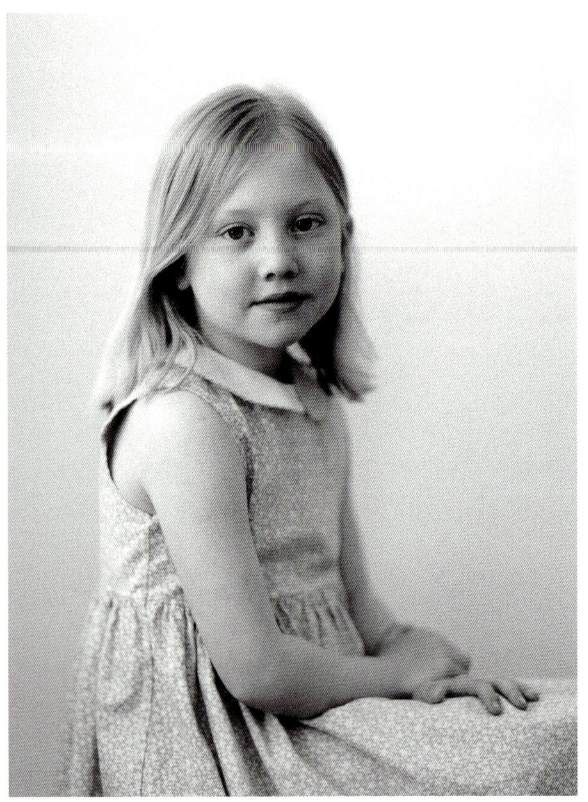

**FIGURE 8.41** Sitting on a stool. Ask the child to sit in profile to you and turn their head toward the camera for the photos.

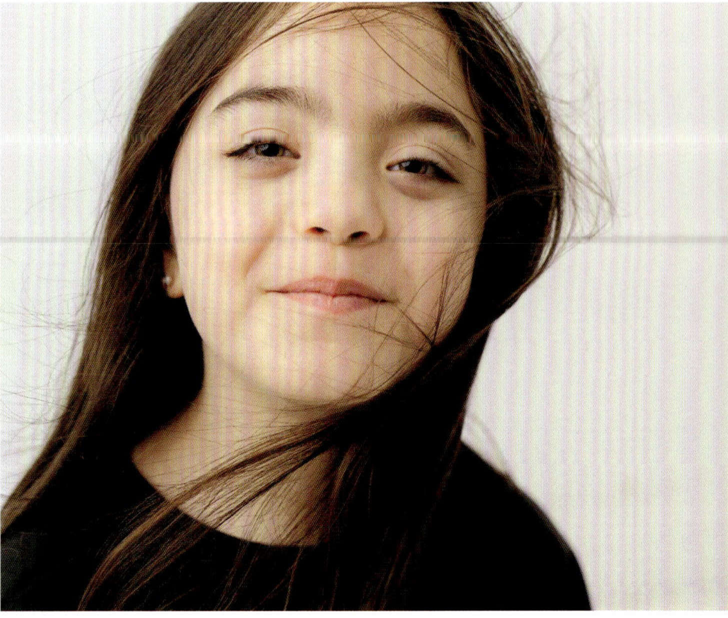

**FIGURE 8.42** Adding a fan to a sitting pose adds fun and flair—kids love it, and it shows!

**Pro Tip:** Nothing brings out a child's inner rock-star quite like a fan. If the child you are photographing has long hair, use a fan to create a sense of fun and movement (**FIGURE 8.42**). This is something I like to add to my sitting poses.

## Pose: Standing

Standing poses can look awkward, especially when working with older children. The key to pulling these poses off is, again, giving clear direction. If a child looks stiff or nervous, give them something to do—have them place a hand in one pocket, shift their weight onto one leg, or ask them to hold their own hands or place them onto their arm (**FIGURE 8.43**).

I often have school-age kids stand on my bed instead of the floor and encourage them to jump. Jumping on a bed is fun and brings out genuine smiles. It also results in dynamic, joyful photos (**FIGURE 8.44**).

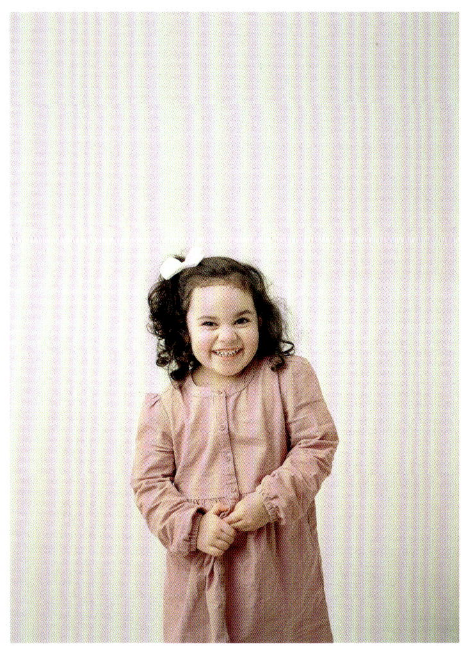

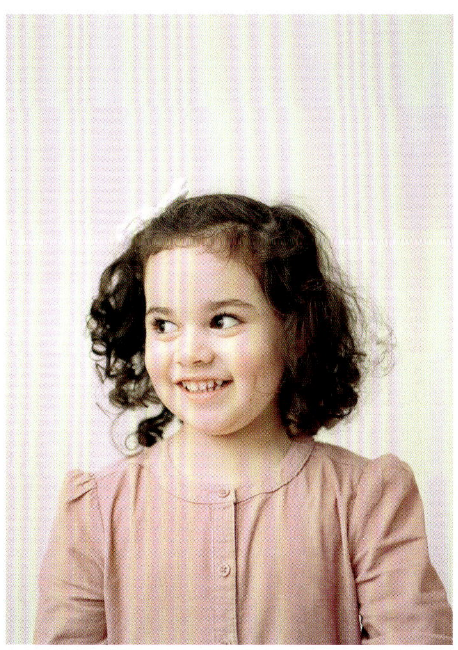

**FIGURE 8.43** An adorable school-age child in a standing pose.

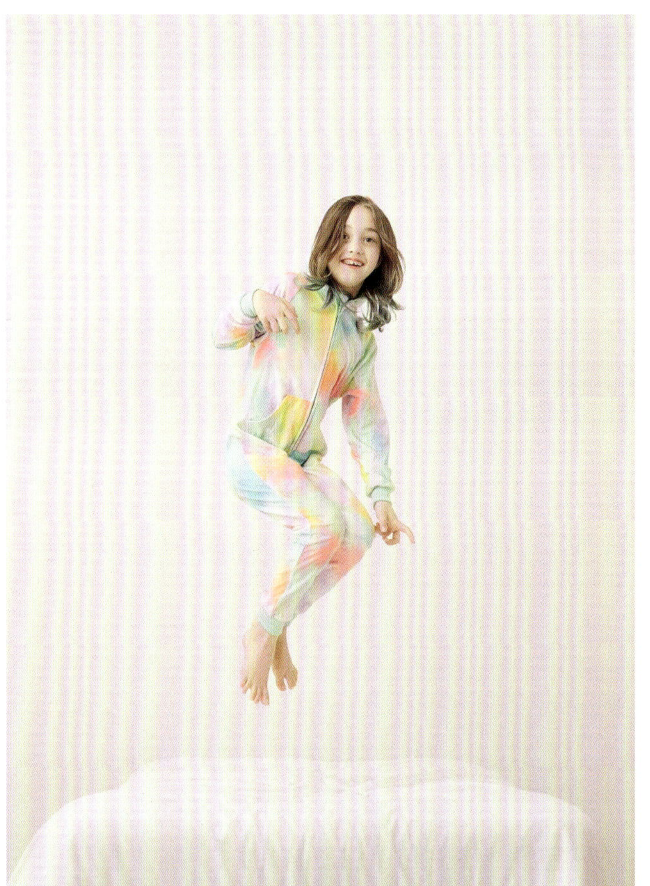

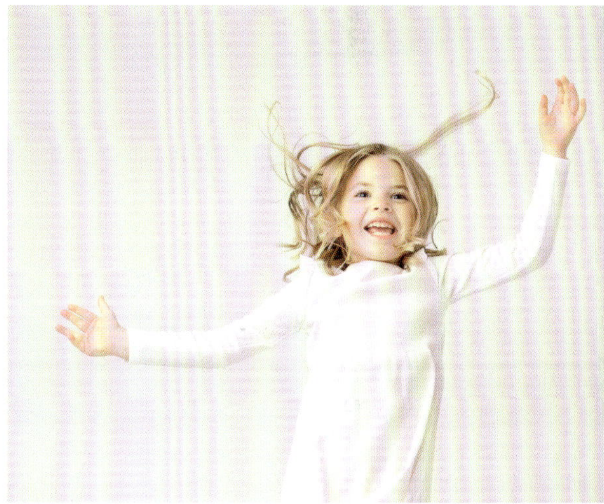

**FIGURE 8.44** Jumping on the bed results in fun photos!

## Managing Silliness

One of the things I love about working with school-aged children is they are a lot of fun. They'll joke, strike crazy poses, and really go for it when given the chance. All of that makes for great photos. But that fun energy can also quickly snowball into chaos if not properly managed. When working with silly kids, I maintain control by giving them very clear rules to follow.

If they're jumping on the bed for example, I will let them know that they are allowed to jump on the bed as long as they freeze when I tell them to and keep the jumping *on* the bed. No jumping on and off! When in standing poses, I give them something specific to stand on (a sticker on the floor of the studio or a particular spot when working on location). I let them know that if they stay on that spot, they can be as silly as they'd like—but if they move, we'll have to stop. This approach allows the child to have fun and express themselves but keeps things from getting out of control. It also results in photos that showcase the child's personality, which clients love!

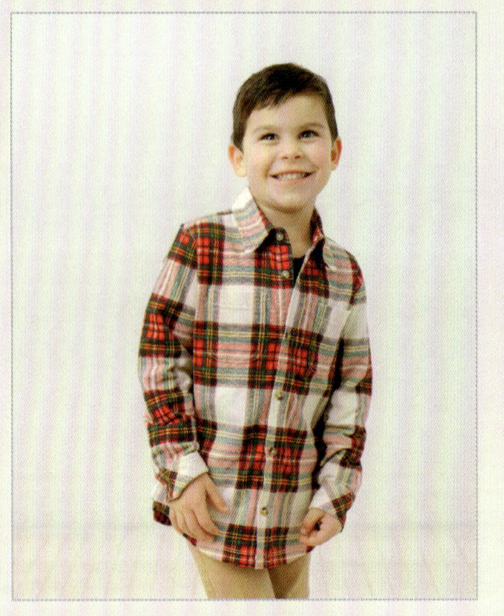

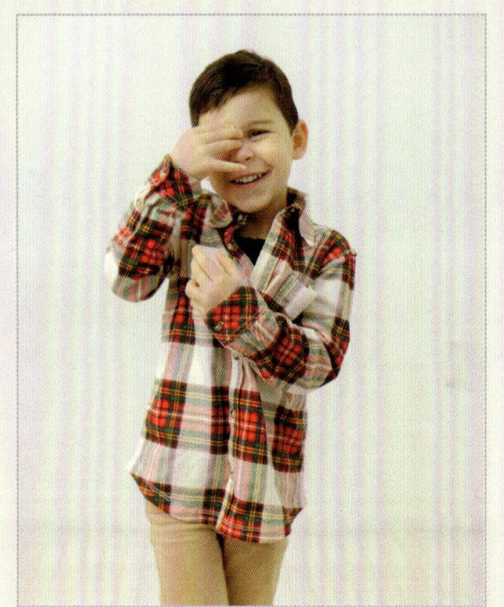

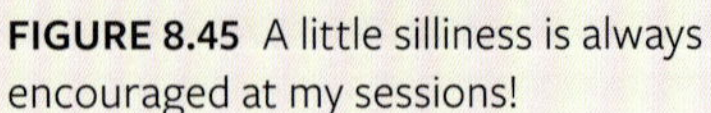

**FIGURE 8.45** A little silliness is always encouraged at my sessions!

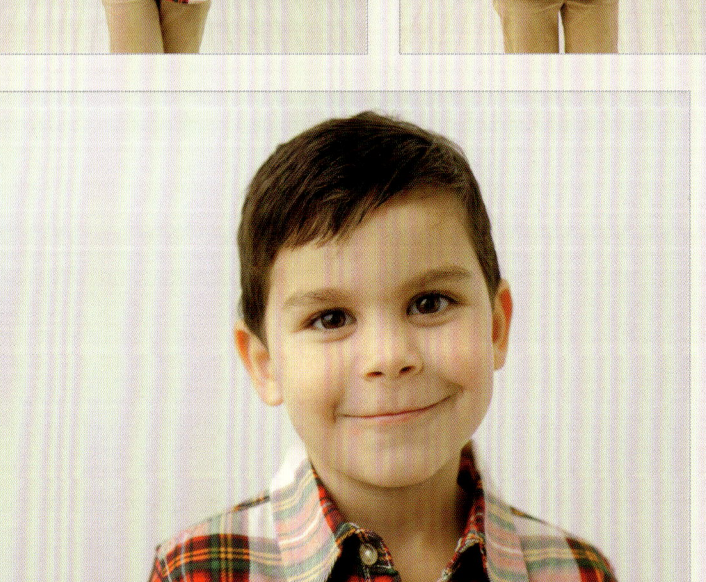

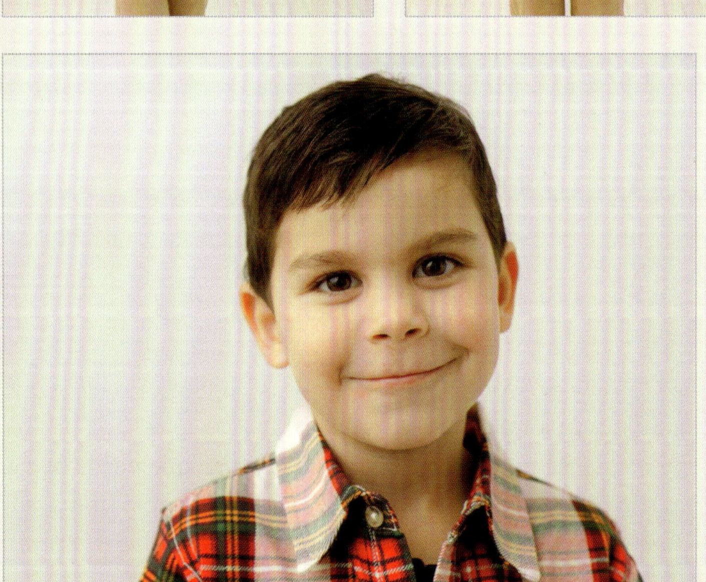

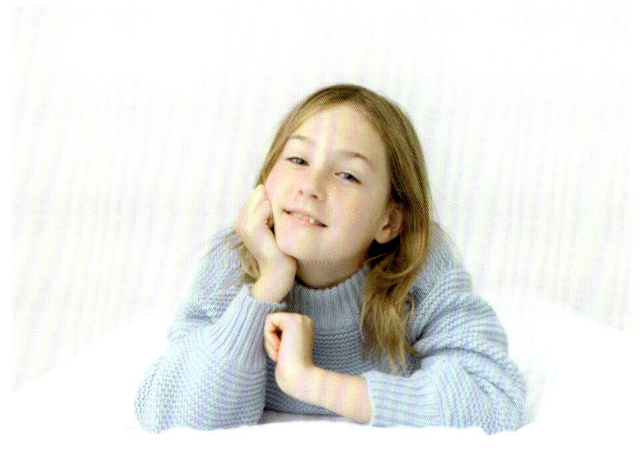

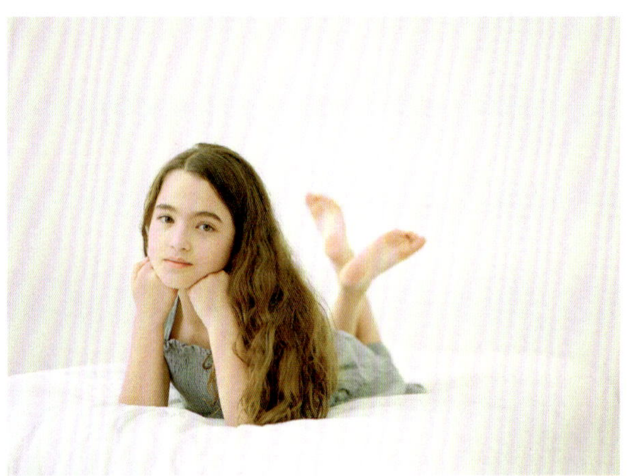

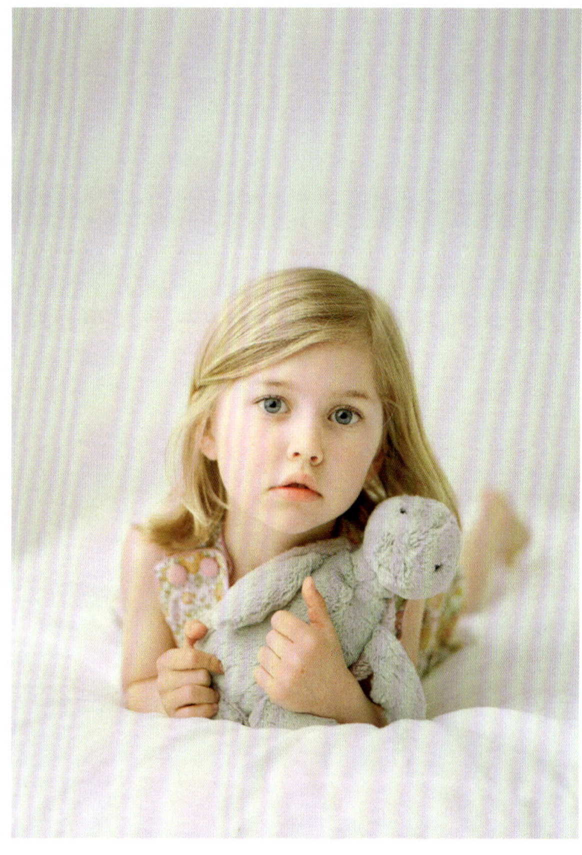

**FIGURE 8.46** Instruct the child to position themselves up on their elbows or with their head in their hands.

### Pose: Lying Down

The lying-down pose is also very cute for school-age children. For this pose, ask them to lie down on a bed or on the ground, facing you. Instruct them to position themselves up on their elbows, or with their head in their hands (**FIGURE 8.46**).

## Next Steps

Posing newborns, babies, and small children requires skill, practice, and a little bit of patience. My hope is that the techniques, insights, and poses in this chapter will serve as a guide. Use them as inspiration, but don't be afraid to adjust and refine them to fit your style and the unique needs of each child you photograph. In the next chapter, we'll build on these concepts as we explore posing families.

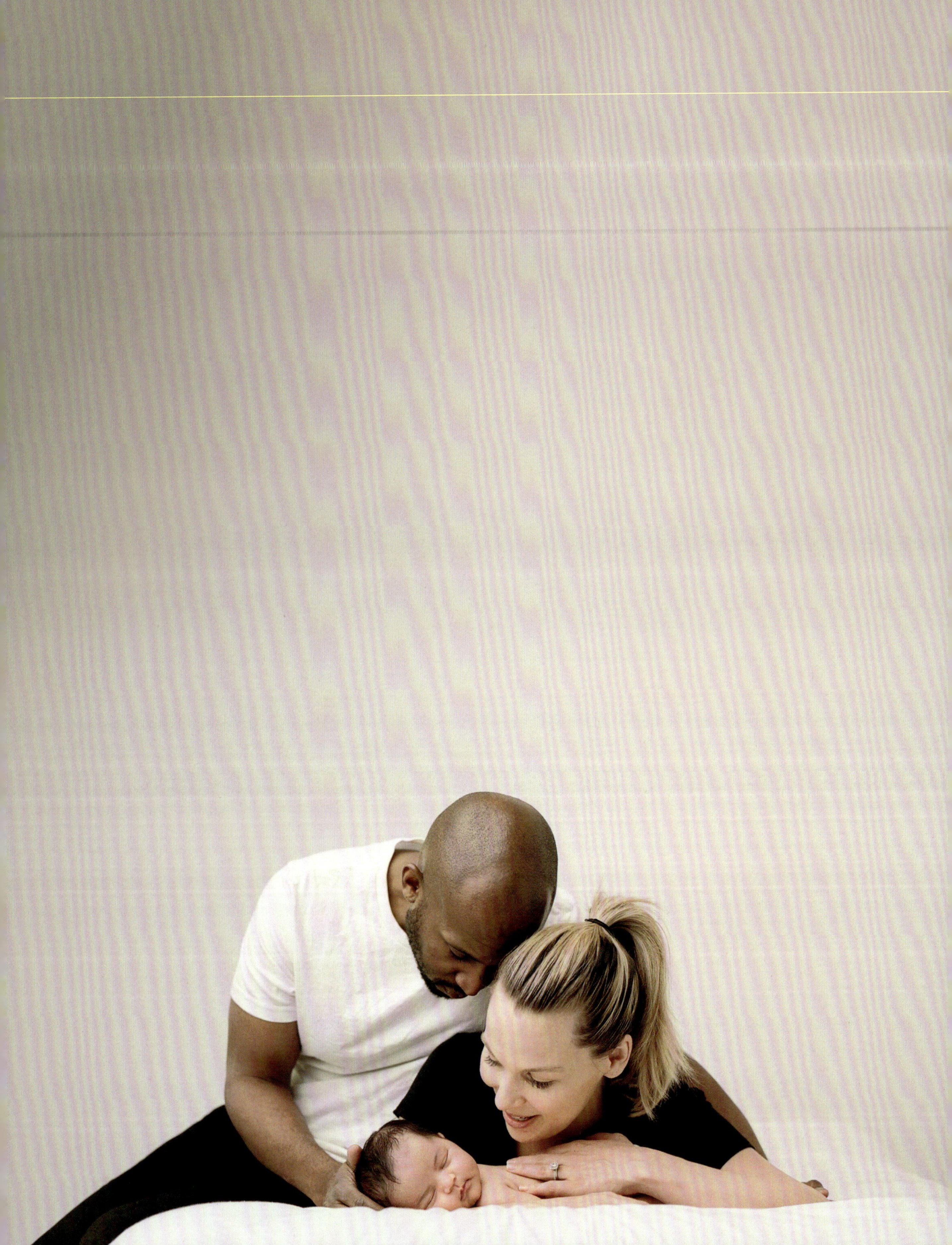

If they choose to sit on a stool instead of a bed, I position them sitting in profile to me, with a parent standing in front of them for support and safety. I prefer this positioning because it helps eliminate perspective distortion (see Chapter 5) and creates visually interesting shapes in the composition (**FIGURE 8.38**).

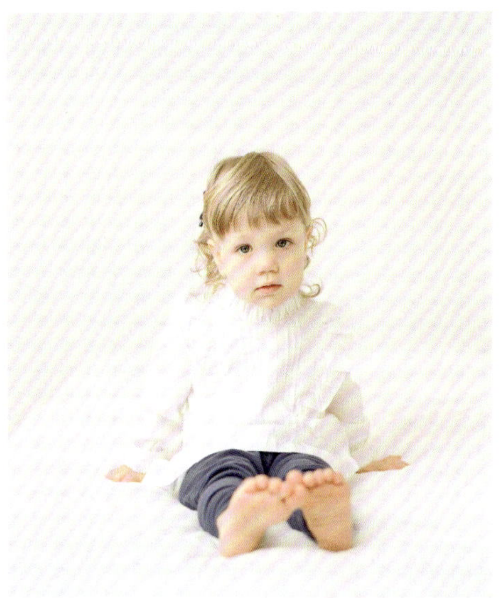

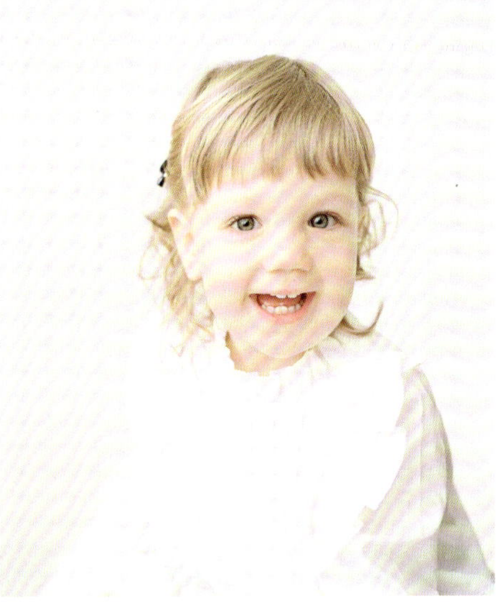

**FIGURE 8.37** I let toddlers sit however they feel most comfortable.

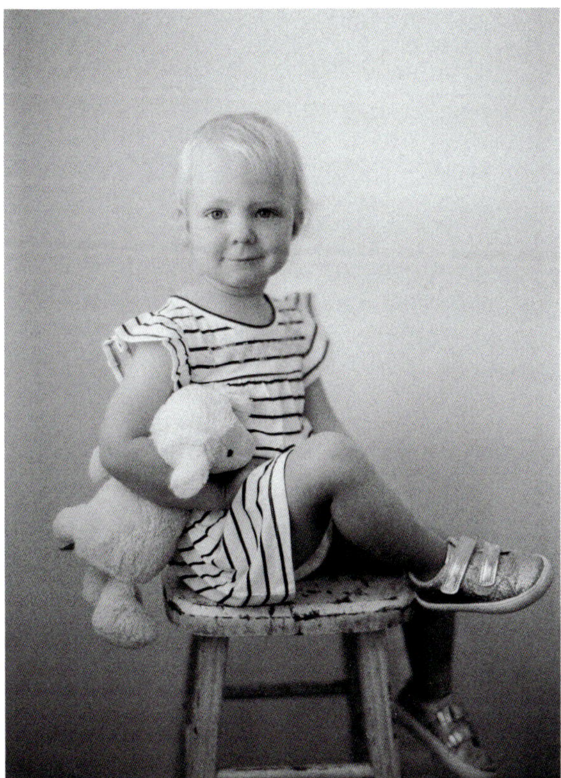

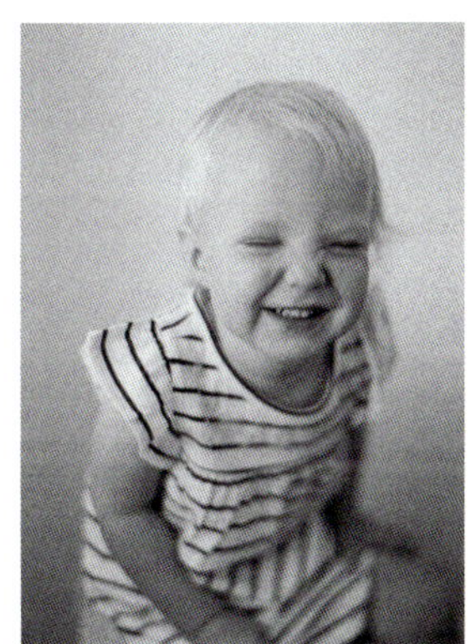

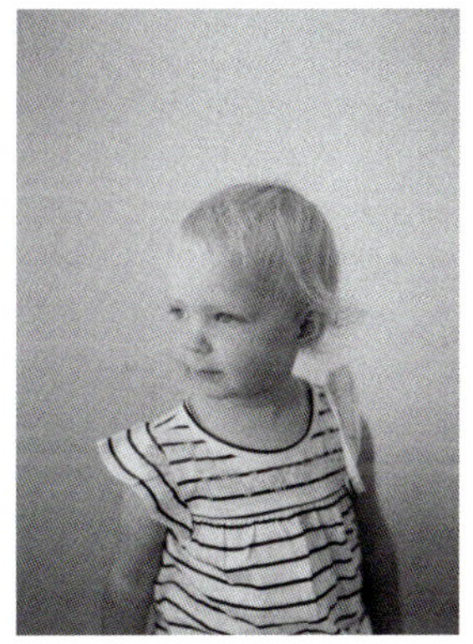

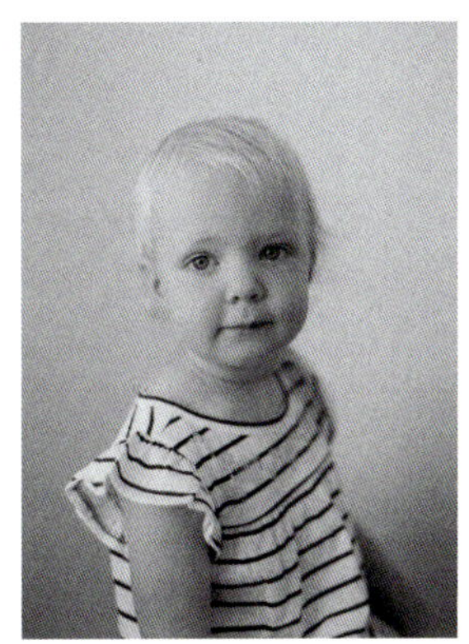

**FIGURE 8.38** This toddler posed sitting on a stool while I captured a mix of full-body photos and tight headshots.

### Keep Things Fun!

When working with toddlers, keep things fun! Sing, clap, play music—whatever it takes to create a playful, engaging environment for the little person in front of your camera. A happy toddler is a cooperative toddler, and the more fun they're having, the better the photos will be.

### Bribe When Necessary

I always keep stickers and lollipops on hand as incentives. If I'm working with a reluctant child, I'll grab a handful of lollipops and ask them to pick their favorite color. Then, I'll place a sticker on the ground where I want them to stand—or on the bed or stool where I want them to sit—and ask them to sit or stand on it. I'll let them know that when they do, they get to hold their lollipop. Sometimes, I'll end up giving toddlers an entire bouquet of lollipops just to keep them engaged (**FIGURE 8.39**). The best part? Lollipops not only hold their interest but also look adorable in photos—a win/win!

**Pro Tip:** Always ask a parent's permission before offering a lollipop or any kind of treat. Some children have allergies, and some families have specific rules about what their kids can eat. If a parent says no to sweets, stickers work just as well!

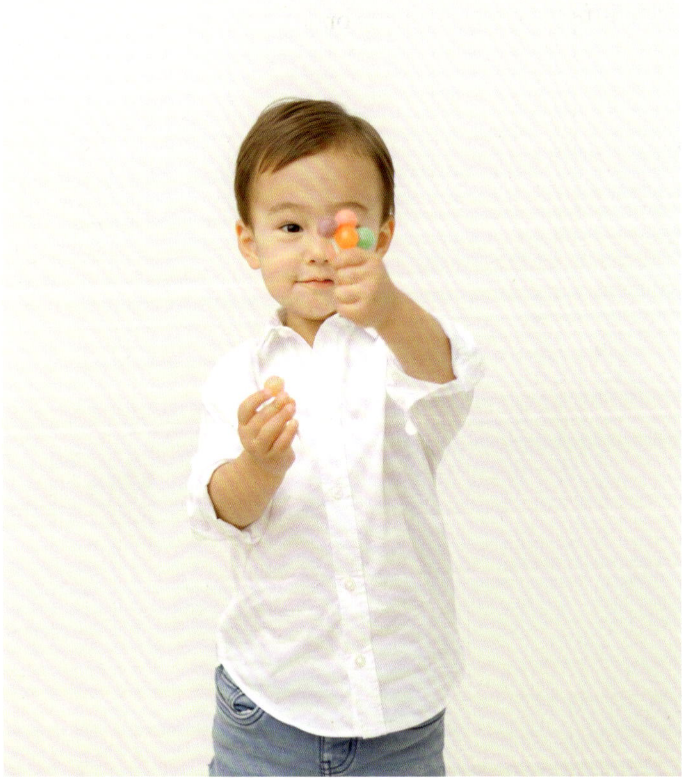

**FIGURE 8.39** Toddler holding a lollipop bouquet—a sweet, effective incentive that photographs well.

## School-Age and Beyond

Once a child turns five, they are considered "school-age" until they reach their teenage years. While there are many milestones between ages 5 and 12, I approach these sessions much like I do when photographing toddlers. The main difference is that older children can follow directions more easily, allowing for more structured posing. I typically use a mix of sitting, standing, and lying-down poses, adjusting my approach to keep the session fun and natural.

### Pose: Sitting

Because older children take direction better than toddlers, you can be more intentional with posing. Look for ways to create triangles in your composition and give clear, simple instructions.

If the child is sitting on a bed or the ground, for example, guide them into a position that feels comfortable for them while also maintaining a flattering shape. I often use the mermaid pose (see **FIGURE 8.40**). To set up this pose, ask the child to sit with both legs facing the same direction, and to bring one arm down for support. I ask them to imagine that their legs are fused together, like a mermaid's tail, and demonstrate the move myself while explaining it. This is my favorite pose for older kids who are sitting on a bed or on the ground. It's flattering (especially if the child is wearing a dress or skirt) and it results in a pleasing triangle shape. That said, sitting crisscross or on their knees also works well for children this age. If the child is sitting on a stool, ask them to sit in profile to you, and have them turn their head toward the camera for the photos (**FIGURE 8.41**). Remember to add variety to your seated poses by directing the child where to look. Shoot vertically and horizontally and get both full-body shots and headshots.

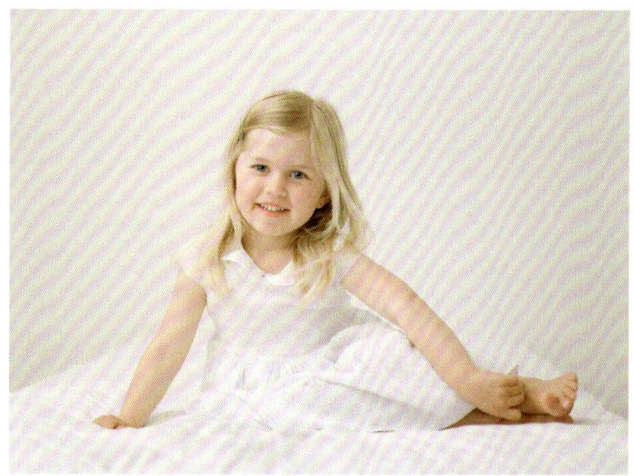

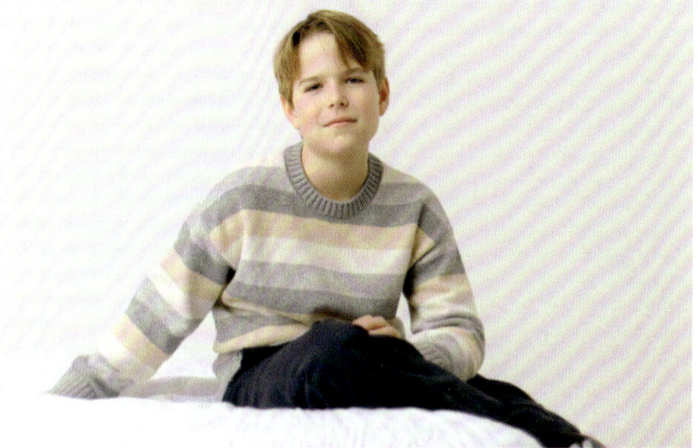

**FIGURE 8.40** Two examples of the mermaid pose.

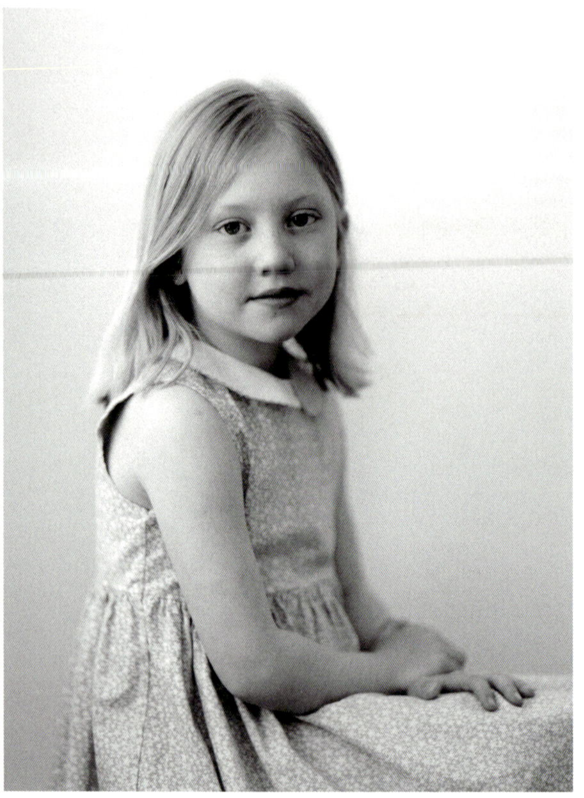

**FIGURE 8.41** Sitting on a stool. Ask the child to sit in profile to you and turn their head toward the camera for the photos.

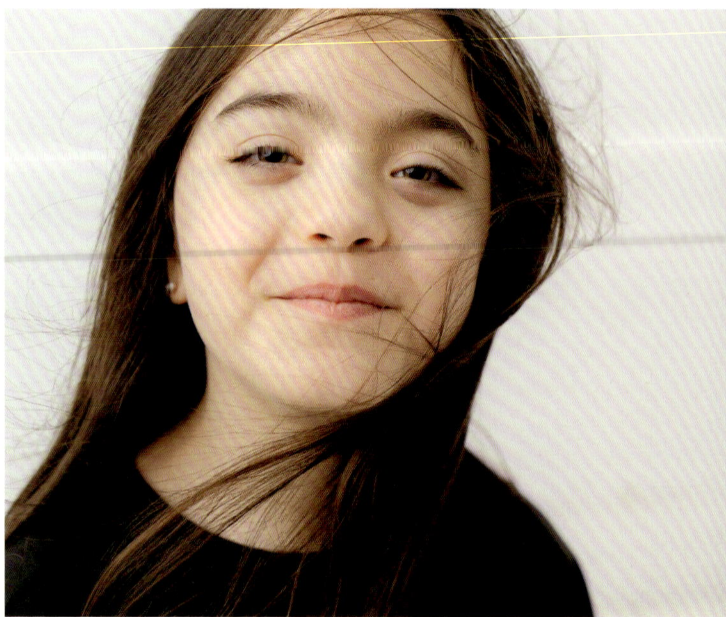

**FIGURE 8.42** Adding a fan to a sitting pose adds fun and flair—kids love it, and it shows!

**Pro Tip:** Nothing brings out a child's inner rock-star quite like a fan. If the child you are photographing has long hair, use a fan to create a sense of fun and movement (**FIGURE 8.42**). This is something I like to add to my sitting poses.

## Pose: Standing

Standing poses can look awkward, especially when working with older children. The key to pulling these poses off is, again, giving clear direction. If a child looks stiff or nervous, give them something to do—have them place a hand in one pocket, shift their weight onto one leg, or ask them to hold their own hands or place them onto their arm (**FIGURE 8.43**).

I often have school-age kids stand on my bed instead of the floor and encourage them to jump. Jumping on a bed is fun and brings out genuine smiles. It also results in dynamic, joyful photos (**FIGURE 8.44**).

CHAPTER

# 9

# Posing Siblings and Families

Before we dive into the specifics of posing families, let's take a moment to review what you've learned so far.

We've already covered the fundamentals of posing, and how small but impactful adjustments can elevate an image. You've explored how composition works in family portraiture, and how to create a consistent, predictable posing routine that helps with your session flow and instills confidence in both you and your clients.

In Chapter 7, I introduced my go-to posing system—a structured sequence that helps me keep sessions running smoothly and efficiently: It begins with photos of the child(ren) alone, then sibling portraits (when applicable), followed by images of the child(ren) with one parent, then full family portraits. It ends with photos of the child(ren) with the other parent. This consistent, predictable routine allows me to build most of the session around the child(ren), which is especially helpful when working with newborns or babies. By keeping the baby comfortable for the majority of the session, I can work quickly and produce a wide variety of beautiful, natural images without ever having to disturb the baby until the very end of the session.

In Chapter 8, we focused on how to pose children on their own—from newborns to school-age kids—and how to get the most out of each pose by adjusting angles, crops, and compositions for variety. In this chapter, we'll expand that foundation to include posing children together, with their parents, and in full family groupings. As I share my specific poses, I'll walk you through the posing system I use in the same order I follow during my sessions so you can see exactly how it flows in practice. I'll also show you how to adapt each pose to accommodate children at different developmental stages.

We have a lot to cover—let's get started!

## Working with Siblings

Every parent dreams of a beautiful photo of their children together. But as every photographer knows, capturing that perfect sibling image can be a challenge—especially when the children are at different ages or developmental stages. Having a set of go-to sibling poses that you know like the back of your hand is essential. When your posing is second nature, you don't have to think about logistics—you can focus entirely on connecting with the children in front of your camera. And that connection is what makes great photos.

## Newborns and Babies with Older Children

The sibling bond is special and deserves to be captured, but it's also important to prioritize safety, especially when newborns or babies are involved. Many children, especially toddlers, have no understanding of just how fragile a newborn or baby is, so it's your responsibility to use poses that look great and prioritize the physical safety of all the children involved.

### Sibling Pose: The Safe Hold

When it comes to posing newborns and babies with their siblings, the Safe Hold is one of my favorite poses. This pose is beautiful, comfortable for both children, and allows the older child to feel that they are holding the baby while keeping the baby safe and secure.

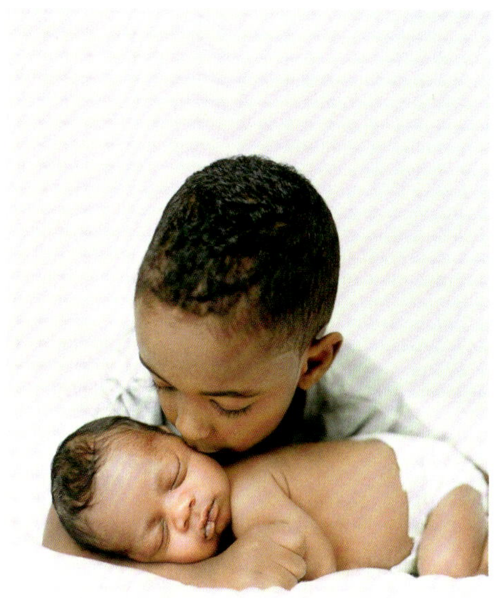

To set up this pose with a newborn, place the baby on their belly, then ask the older child to lie on their stomach and get up on their elbows, perpendicular to the end of the bed and facing the baby. Gently lift the baby's head and place it in the crook of their sibling's arm. Have the older child place their other hand gently on the baby's back. Position yourself eye level to the baby and have the older child look at you.

This pose works best with a sleeping baby, but it can be done with a baby who is awake, as long as the baby is content! This pose works with babies up to three months of age.

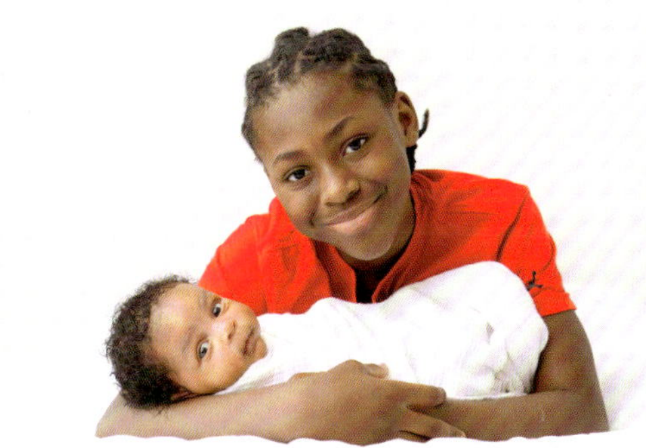

**FIGURE 9.1** The Safe Hold with the baby on their belly and swaddled on their back.

If working with an older baby, or if the newborn you are working with is awake, place them in a simple swaddle on their back instead of in the belly-down position, then follow the steps outlined above. Swaddling the baby will keep them from lifting their hands and blocking the face of their older brother or sister.

Once you have the pose set up, ask the older child to look at you, look at the baby, and even give the baby a gentle kiss on the cheek or on the head. All the adorable variations on this pose will quickly become your client's favorite images from the session.

### Sibling Pose: The Pretend Hold

Not all children are comfortable with or capable of "holding" their baby brother or sister, even in the Safe Hold. When that is the case, the Pretend Hold is the perfect pose. To achieve this, position the baby just as you would when setting up the Safe Hold. Ask the older child to lie on their stomach and get up on their elbows, perpendicular to the end of the bed and facing the baby. For this pose, do not place the baby in their arms. Instead, let them choose if they'd like to be up on their elbows, looking over the baby, or place one arm on the bed next to the baby's head. Position yourself eye level to the baby to capture the image.

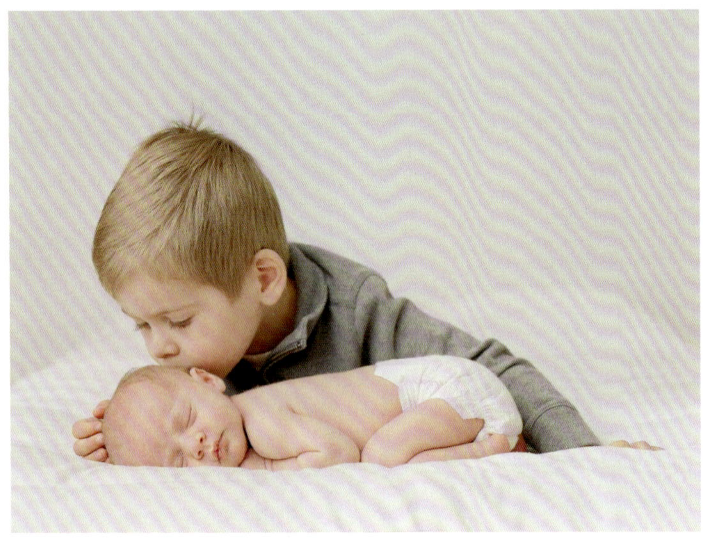

A

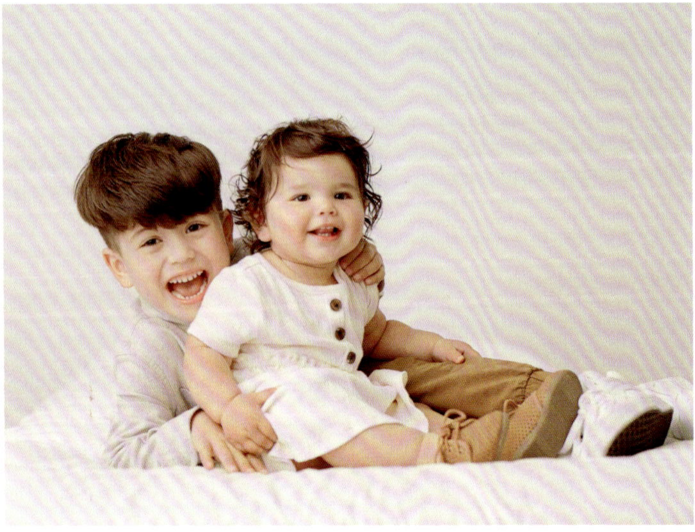

B

**FIGURE 9.2** The Pretend Hold. This pose is great for photographing newborns and older babies with their siblings.

This pose is great for photographing newborns and older babies with their siblings. I use it when photographing newborns and a sibling (**FIGURE 9.2A**) up through sitters with a sibling (**FIGURE 9.2B**). Remember to maximize this pose by directing the older child where to look and what to do, and by capturing the pose vertically and horizontally.

### Sibling Pose: Sit and Point

When the child you are working with is too young to "hold" their baby or follow complex instructions like the ones given for the Safe Hold and Pretend Hold, the Sit and Point pose is a great alternative. To achieve this look, place the baby parallel to the end of the bed, either on their belly or swaddled on their back. Have the older child sit next to the baby and then ask them to point at the baby.

I like to turn this into a game when working with toddlers. Once I have both the baby and the toddler in position, I will ask the toddler a question like, "Do you have hair? Show me your hair. Does the baby have hair? Show me the baby's hair." Once the toddler is engaging and pointing to the baby's hair (or feet, or nose, or whatever we're talking about in our little game), I'll quickly capture some images (**FIGURE 9.3**).

This pose works best with babies up to 3 months old and their siblings. If the baby you are working with is awake, place them in a swaddle on their back rather than in the belly-down position.

**Pro Tip:** Sometimes younger children will use their baby sibling as a pillow when placed in the Safe Hold or Pretend Hold position which can be uncomfortable for the baby (**FIGURE 9.4A**). If that happens, repositioning the children into the Sit and Point pose is a great alternative (**FIGURE 9.4B**).

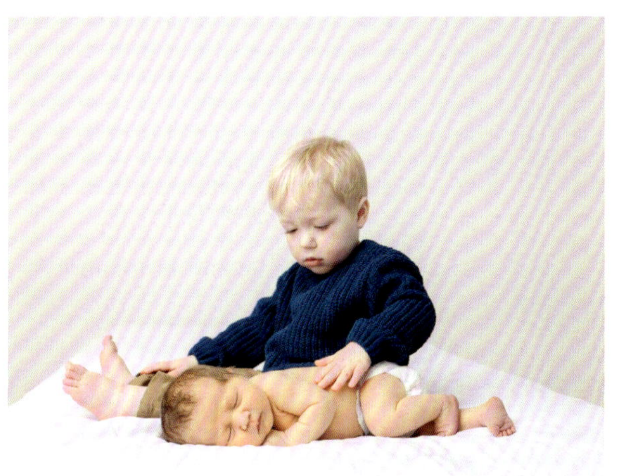

A

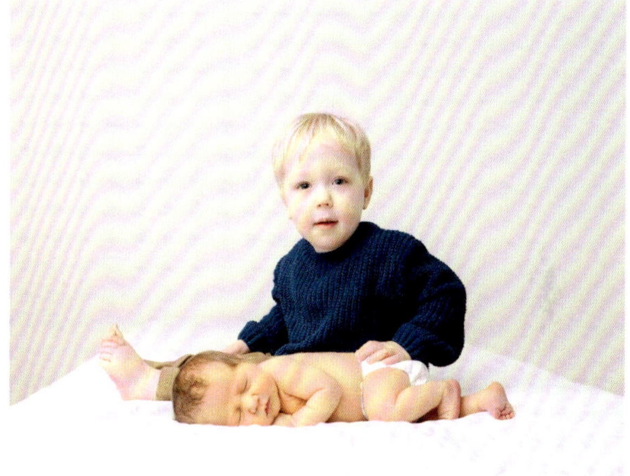

B

**FIGURE 9.3** The Sit and Point pose with a newborn and their two-year-old brother.

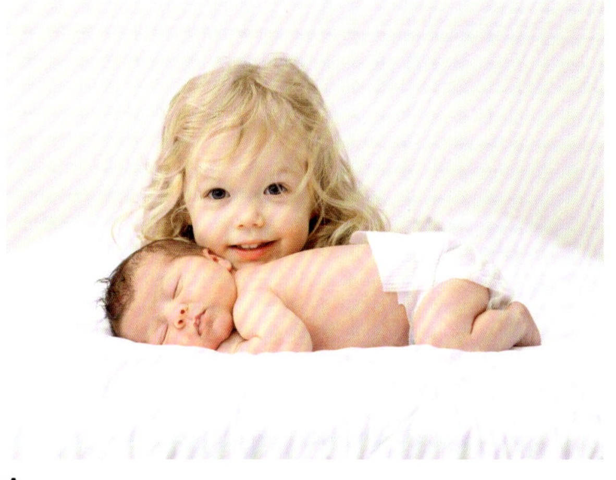

A

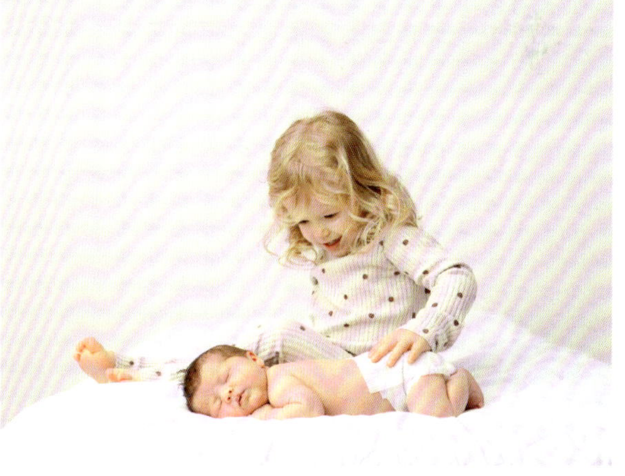

B

**FIGURE 9.4** I initially posed this adorable three-year-old with her newborn sister in the Safe Hold, but the baby quickly became a pillow (Figure 9.4A). To keep the baby comfortable, I repositioned them into the Sit and Point pose (Figure 9.4B).

### Sibling Pose: Kiss on the Head

This is a great pose for children who are not comfortable being on the bed with their sibling, especially when that sibling is a newborn to three-month-old baby. To set this up, ask the older child to stand on the edge of the bed closest to the baby's head. Once positioned, ask them to lean over and kiss the baby on the head (**FIGURE 9.5**).

Having a step stool on hand will help small children get close enough to achieve this look. I also keep small stickers nearby and will sometimes place one on the baby's head as an incentive. A toddler is more likely to "kiss the sticker" if they get to keep it afterwards!

**FIGURE 9.5** An older sibling gently kisses a newborn on the head—an ideal pose for older siblings who may not feel comfortable lying or sitting with the baby on a bed.

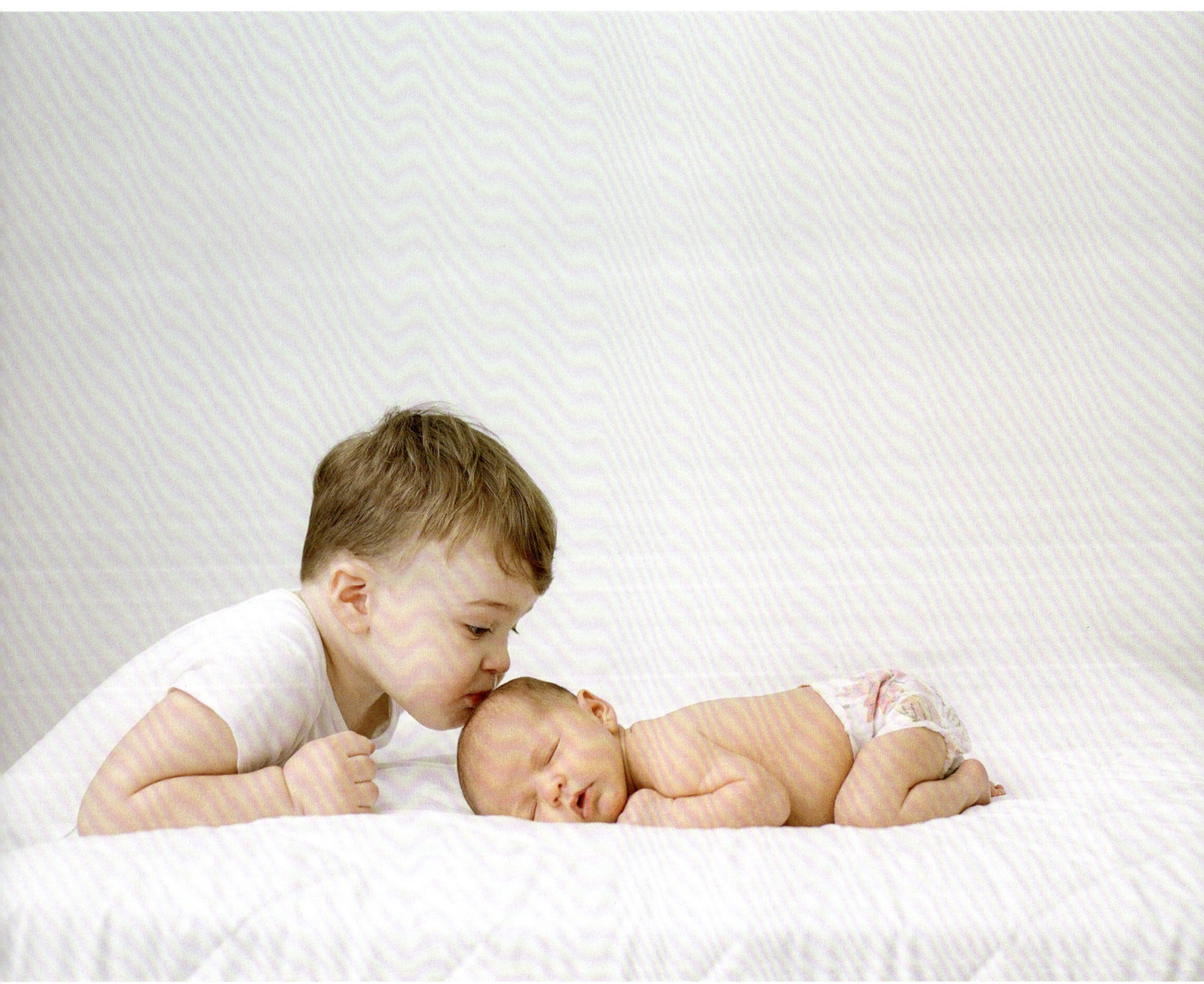

## You Can Do This Pose with Other Family Members!

While the kiss on the head is one of my go-to poses when working with newborn and three-month-old babies and their older siblings, it's a pose that I use for adults as well—especially fathers (**FIGURE 9.6**). Ask the adult to kneel by the side of the bed closest to the baby's head. Have them gently slide one hand under the baby's head and rest the other on the baby's back. Direct them to look down at the baby and give the baby a kiss on the head. Be sure to take some photos of just the baby in their parent's hands to really make the most of this pose (**FIGURE 9.6C**).

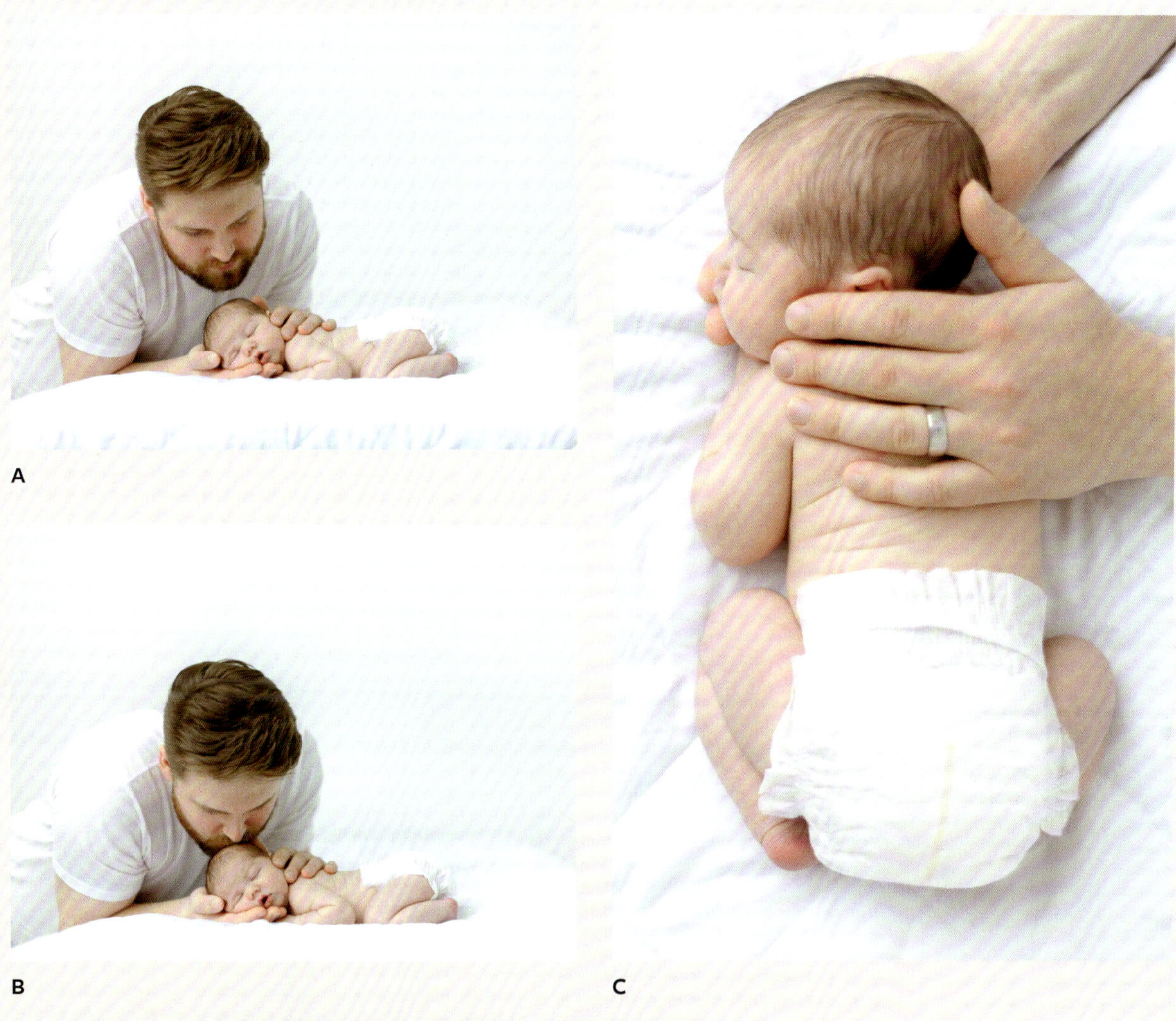

A

B

C

**FIGURE 9.6** The kiss-on-the-head pose works beautifully with parents too!

## Posing More Than One Child with a Newborn or Baby

When working with a family who has more than one other child, I position the oldest child in the Safe Hold pose (**FIGURE 9.7**), then add in the other sibling, creating triangles as I go. Once the children are in place, I position myself eye level to the baby and create multiple looks by directing the older children where to look. For more formal photos, ask them to look at you and for "candid" images, ask them to look at each other or down at the baby.

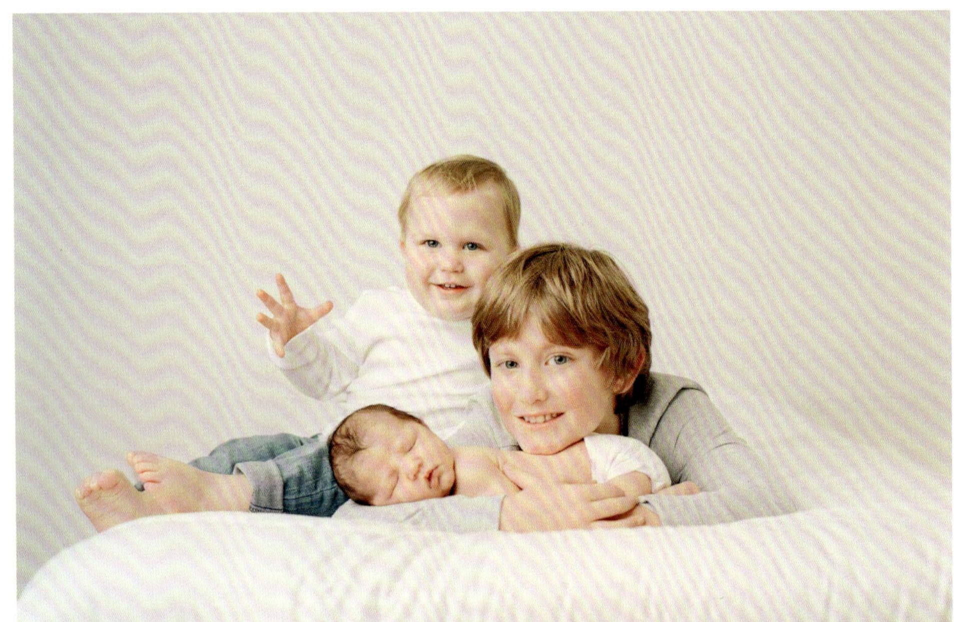

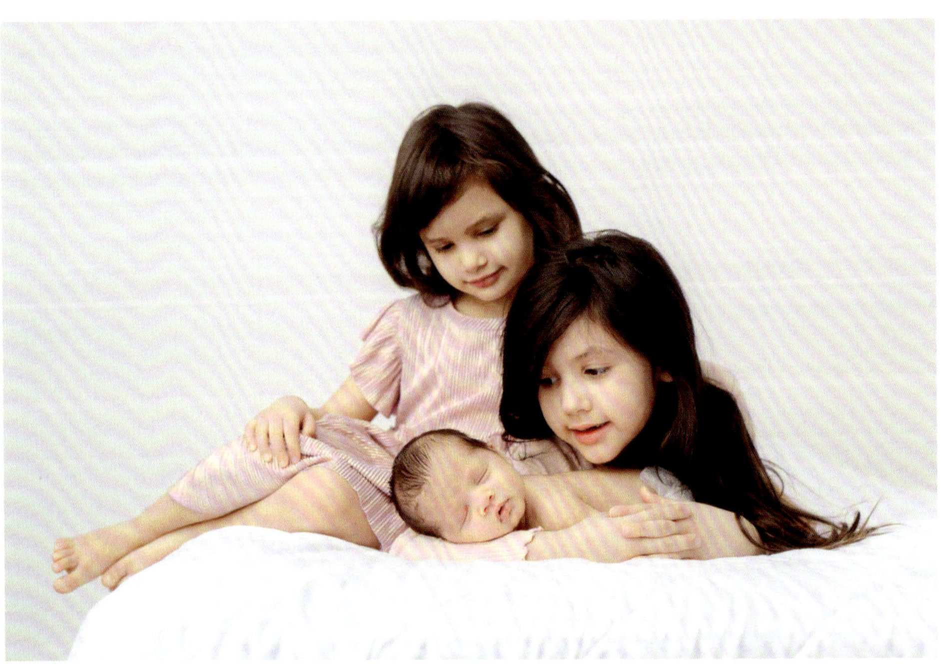

**FIGURE 9.7** Poses featuring multiple children with an infant.

## What if an Older Child Doesn't Want to Participate?

Not all children are excited about being in photos with the new baby in their lives. If a child *really* does not want to be in a photo with their new baby brother or sister, I will respect their boundaries. What I've found, however, is when I don't force the issue, they usually come around. **FIGURE 9.8** shows great examples of this. At this session, my client really wanted photos of her toddler with the new baby. Her toddler, however, was *not* interested.

Instead of pushing him, we continued photographing the baby alone and then moved on to capturing images with the newborn and his parents. Eventually, the toddler became curious about what we were doing. He moved from across the room to next to the bed, then eventually asked to get on the bed, but he still kept his distance from the baby (**FIGURE 9.8B**). Once he was on the bed, I asked him questions about himself and about the baby, things like, "Can you show me where your ear is? Can you show me where the baby's ear is?" Eventually he began to engage and we got the photo we needed.

Most toddlers take some time to warm up, even if they're being photographed in their own home. Having fun activities for them to engage with is a great way to get them loosened up and ready for pictures. Giving them time to observe you working also helps. Be sure to keep stickers and lollipops on hand so that when a child does decide to participate, they are rewarded.

If a child still does not want to participate, even after you've tried all above suggestions, move on to taking photos of the baby with mother and with family poses, then try again later in the session. In my experience, most children come around eventually. But if they don't, don't force it. Insisting that a toddler does something they don't want to do is a recipe for a meltdown. And nobody wants that!

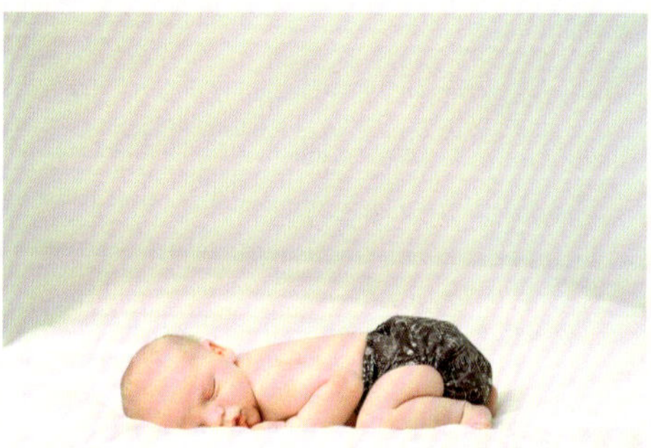

A

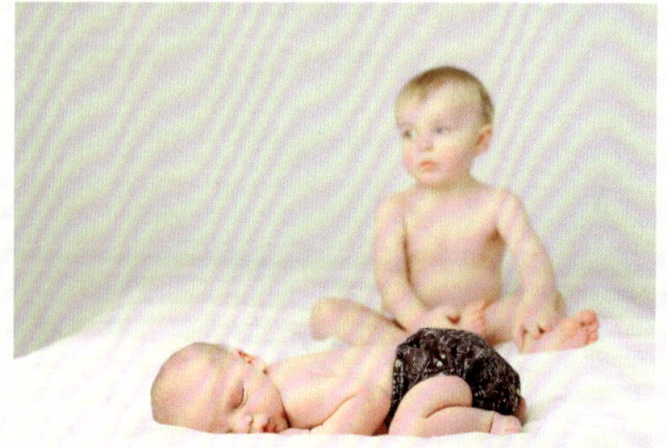

B

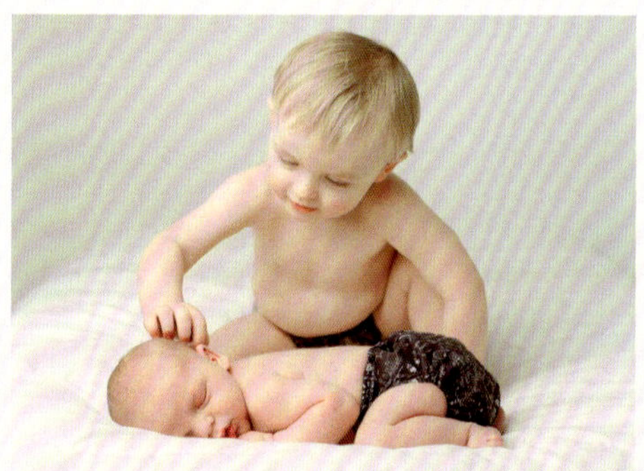

C

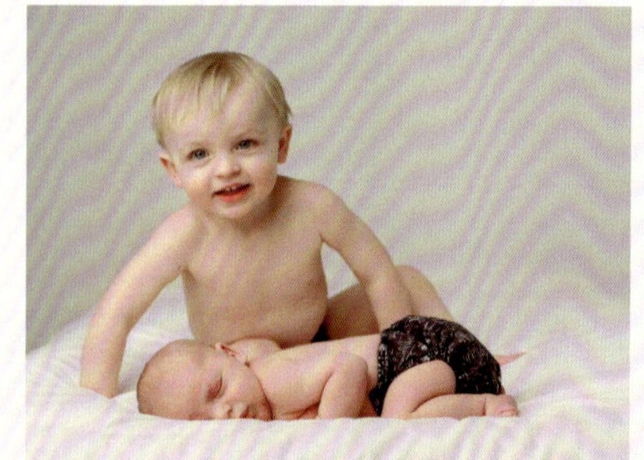

D

**FIGURES 9.8** Toddlers aren't always eager to jump into photos with a new sibling—and that's okay. Sometimes, giving a child time and space is the best strategy.

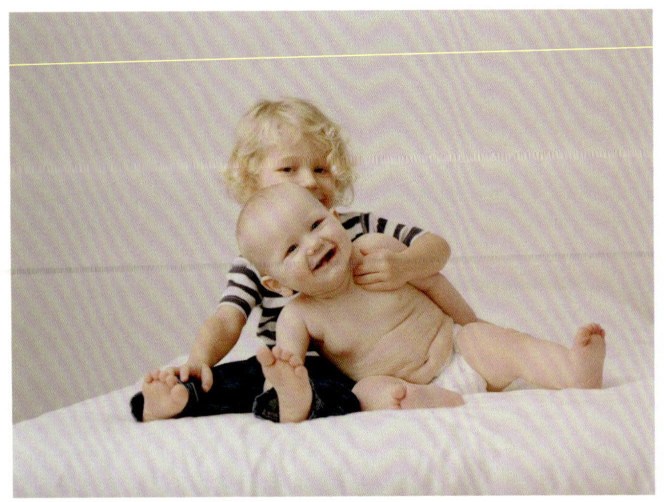

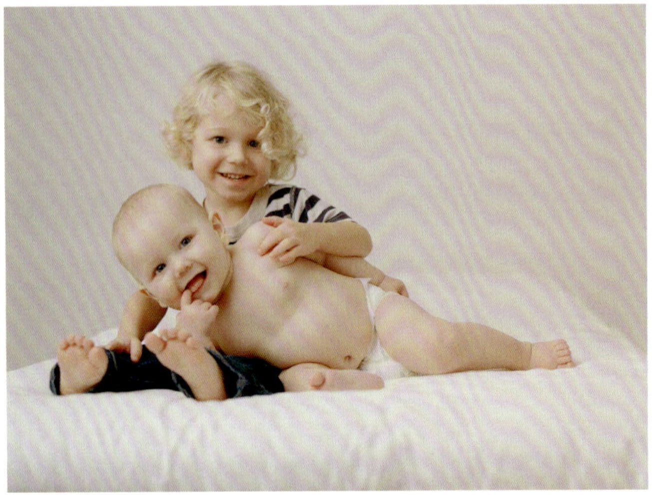

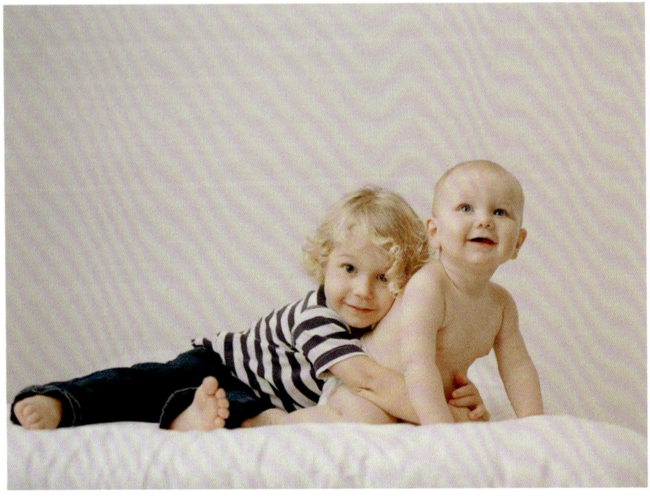

## Older Children

Posing older children with newborns and babies requires skill and practice, but in a lot of ways, it's the easiest of the sibling poses to achieve because newborns and small babies don't move! The trick to pulling these poses off is working with the developmental stages of the children. **FIGURE 9.9** shows images from a session with a one-year-old baby and their three-year-old sibling. These children were at very different developmental stages: The one-year-old was a very proficient crawler and had no interest in sitting still. The three-year-old was good at following directions but was too young to sit in the mermaid pose, or even crisscross. To get images of the two of them together, I sat them on the bed, side by side, and asked the three-year-old to hold onto their younger sibling. I had a parent on each side of the bed for safety and worked quickly. There was a lot of silliness, but we ended up with an image we all loved.

### Sibling Pose: Sitting

If the youngest child can sit on their own, I'll position them in a sitting pose and bring their older sibling in to sit next to them. If the older child is capable of sitting mermaid style, I'll ask them to sit that way. If not, I'll allow them to sit however is most comfortable (**FIGURE 9.10**).

**FIGURE 9.9** Posing older children can be surprisingly challenging. For success, keep it simple and work quickly!

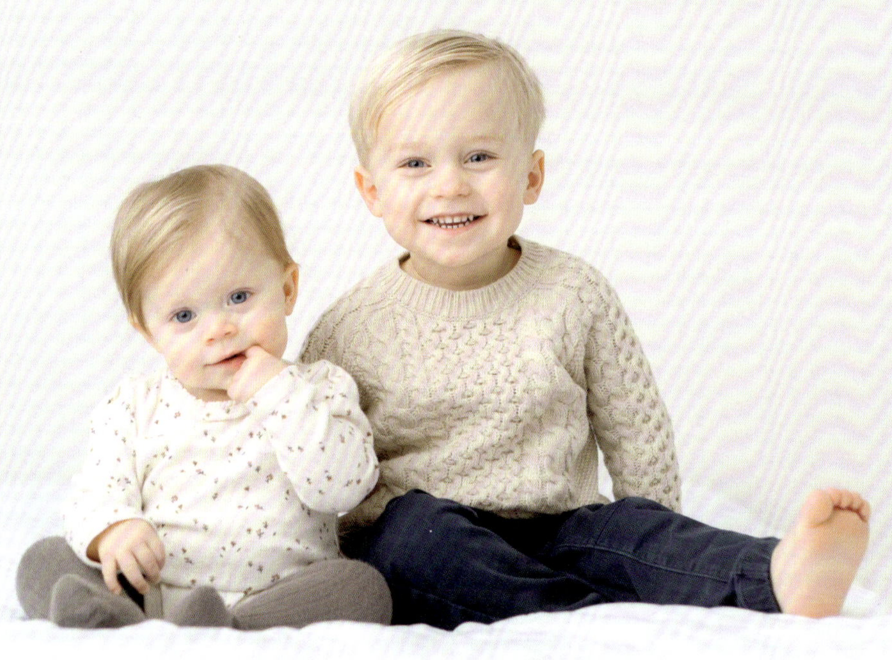

**FIGURE 9.10** This baby was old enough to sit on her own, and the brother was old enough to follow directions, but not quite old enough to sit in the mermaid pose, so I had him sit in a position that felt comfortable and captured this sweet photo.

To help set up a sitting pose, have one parent position the children so that their legs or hips are touching. This creates a sense of closeness in the image and a pleasing triangle shape. Position yourself eye level to the children, then talk or sing—whatever it takes to get them looking at the camera. This pose can be done on the floor or on a bed. If working with the children on a bed, remember to have at least one adult within arm's reach at the side of the bed for safety.

If both children are old enough to sit on their own and follow directions, I'll position them intentionally to create triangles. When working with two children, have one sit on their knees or crisscross, and have the other sit like a mermaid (or have both sit in the mermaid pose with their legs in opposite directions (**FIGURE 9.11**) and direct them to lean in toward each other to create the triangle shape.

I prefer to pose children on a bed or on the ground rather than stools because I find it easier to create the shapes I want when they are on a bed.

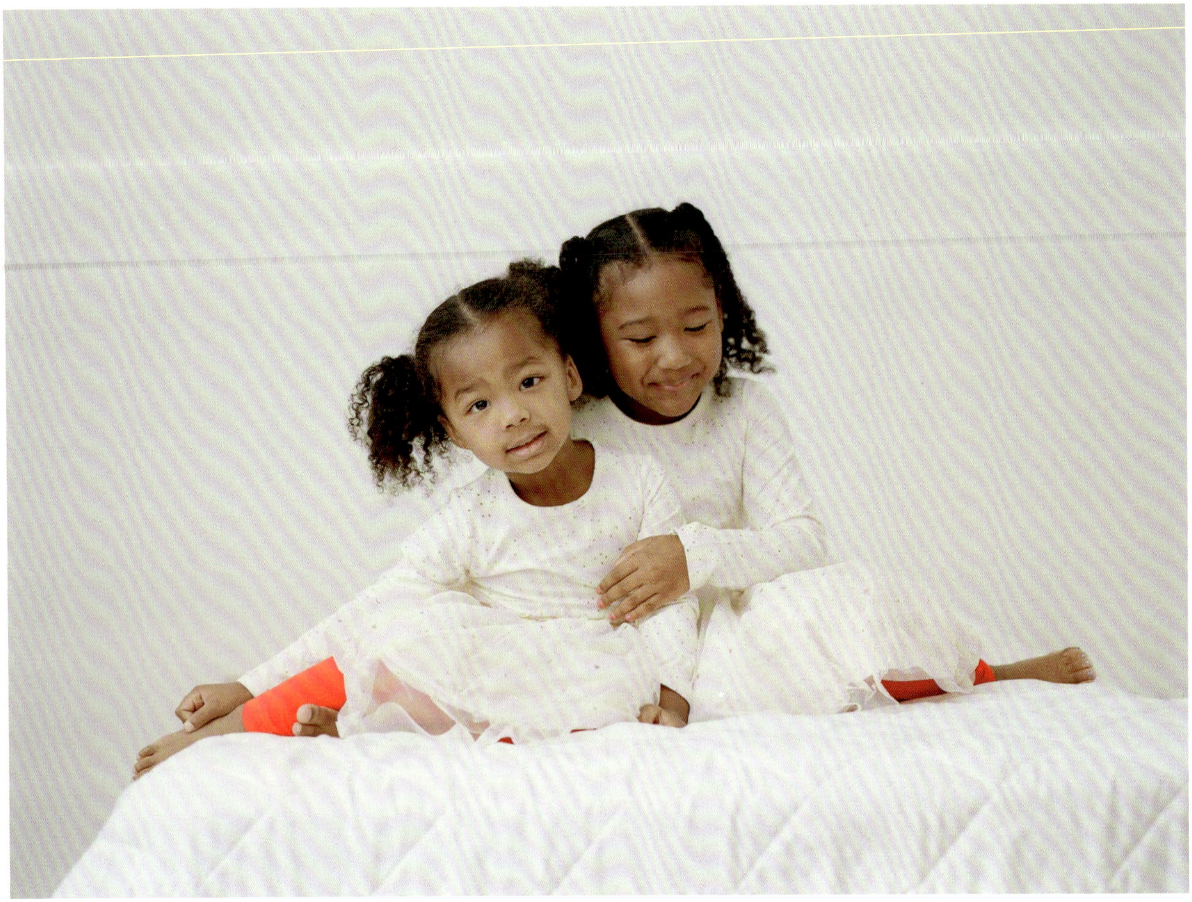

A

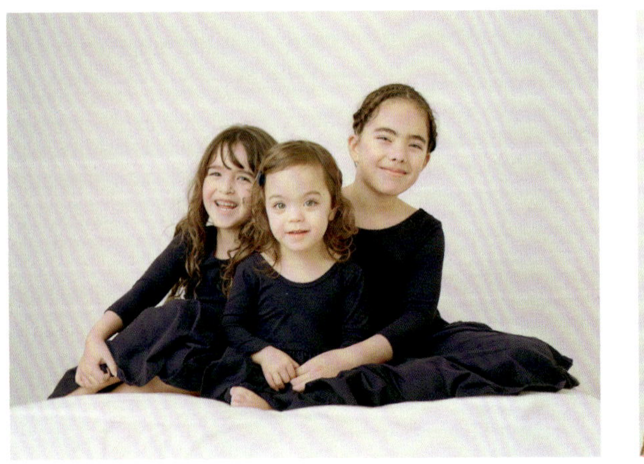

B

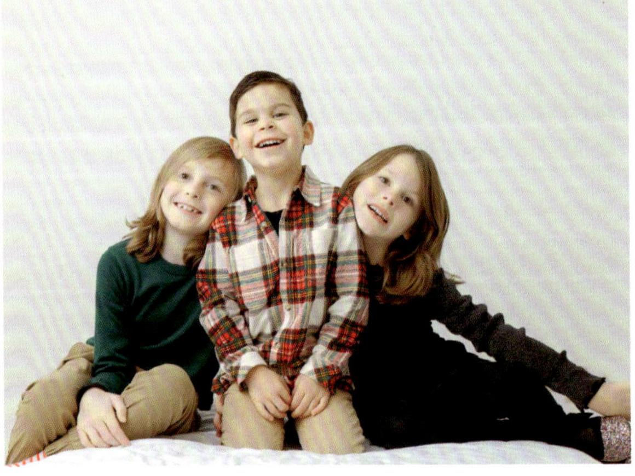

C

**FIGURE 9.11** Two school-age children in a seated pose, both sitting like a mermaid (**A**). If there are three children, I'll position the child in the middle (usually the youngest) on their knees or sitting crisscross, and the others to each side in the mermaid pose.

### Sibling Pose: Standing

Standing poses only work when all children can confidently stand on their own. Look for ways to stagger their heights to create triangles. I like to have the children I'm working with hold hands, or I'll instruct the older child to gently place an arm around their sibling. Position yourself at eye level to the children to create a sense of connection. All these poses can be used in a studio, in your client's home, or even on location (**FIGURE 9.12**).

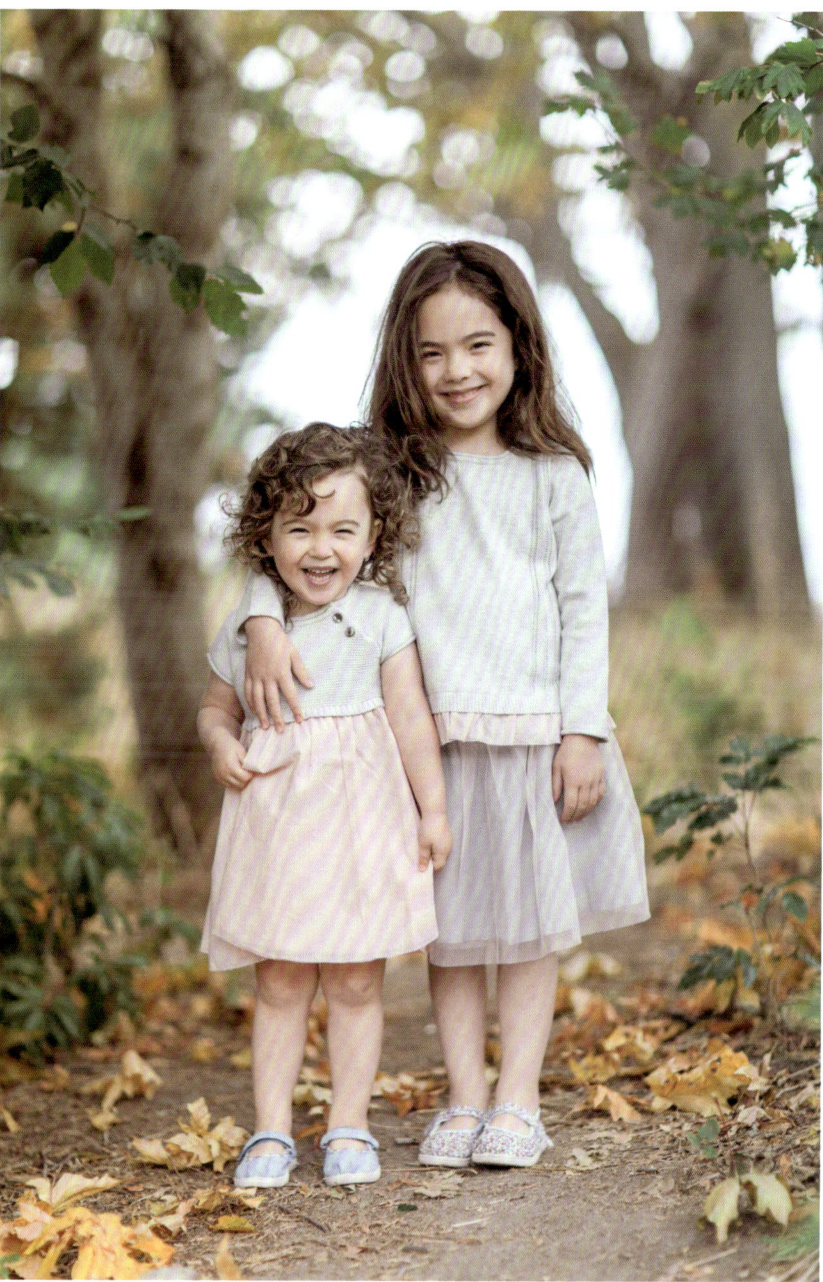

**FIGURE 9.12** A simple standing pose.

# Adding the Parents

Once I've finished capturing photos of the child or children alone, and after I've finished the children together (when applicable), I move on to capturing portraits of the child or children with their parents.

## Child(ren) with One Parent

I generally add one parent to the mix, usually the mother, and take photos before adding the second parent for family shots.

### One Parent Pose: Lying Down

When working with newborns and babies, my favorite pose involves having the parent lie down on the bed with the child. This position allows me to capture some beautiful photos of parent and child without having to move or disturb the baby in any way. It's an extremely flattering pose for the adult, and it keeps the baby out of a feeding position, which helps them stay asleep or calm and relaxed.

To set up this pose, leave the baby where they were for their individual photos, either on their belly or swaddled on their back (when working with newborns and babies) or in a seated position (when working with sitters and one-year-olds).

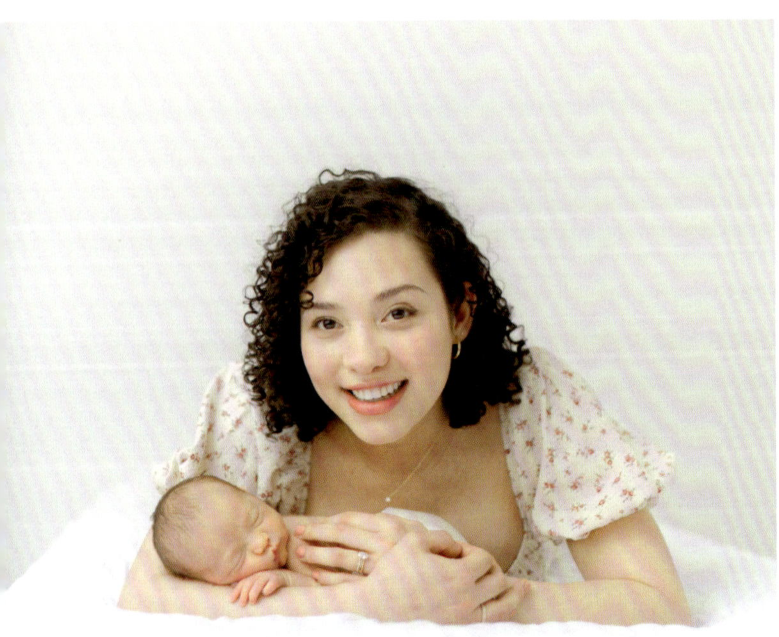

**FIGURE 9.13** Mother and child in the lying-down pose.

When working with a newborn or three-month-old baby, ask the parent to lie on their stomach, up on their elbows, perpendicular to the end of the bed, facing the baby. Gently lift the baby's head and place it in the crook of their parent's arm. Have the parent place their other hand gently on the baby's back. If photographing a woman in this pose, ask her to bend her knees and cross her ankles. This adds a feminine touch to the pose when captured from a ¾ angle. Position yourself eye level to the baby and have the parent look at you (**FIGURE 9.13**).

One thing I love about this pose is its versatility. You can get multiple looks by directing your clients where to look and by changing your point of view and composition (**FIGURE 9.14**). Direct your client to look down at the baby, then ask them to give it a little kiss. Take some photos head on and some from a ¾ angle. Capture frames using negative space, and by filling up the frame, and capture each variation horizontally and vertically.

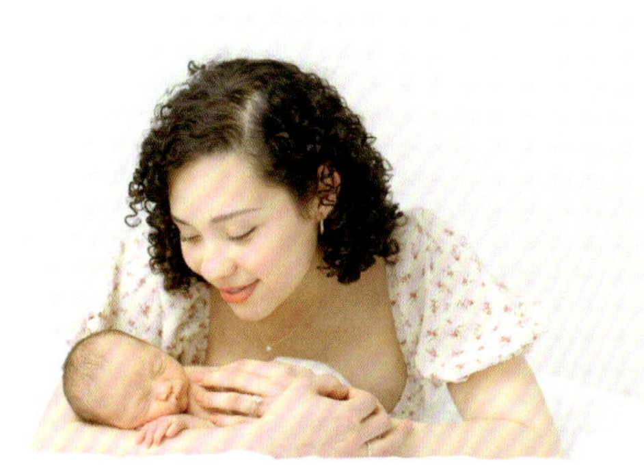

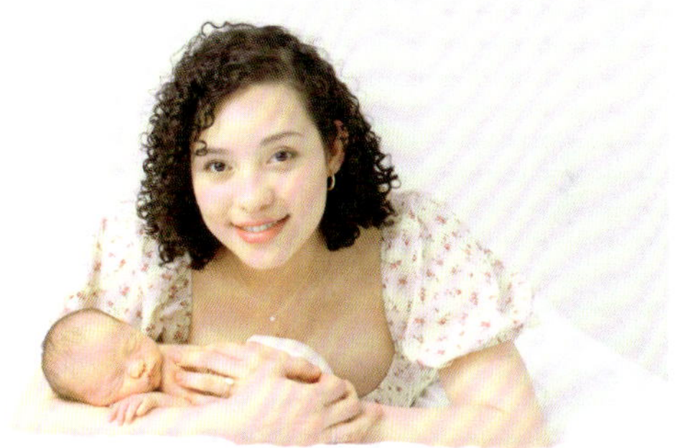

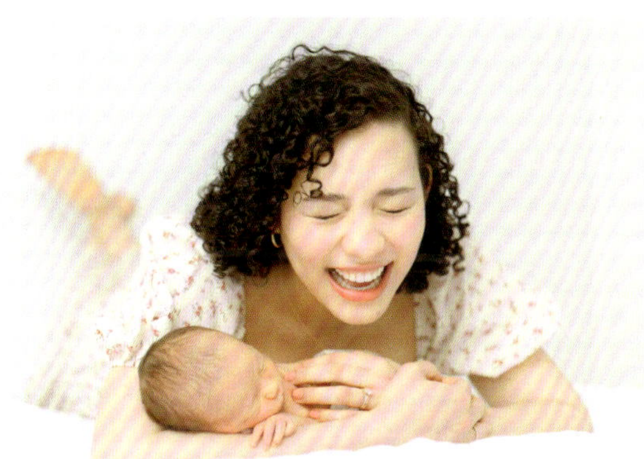

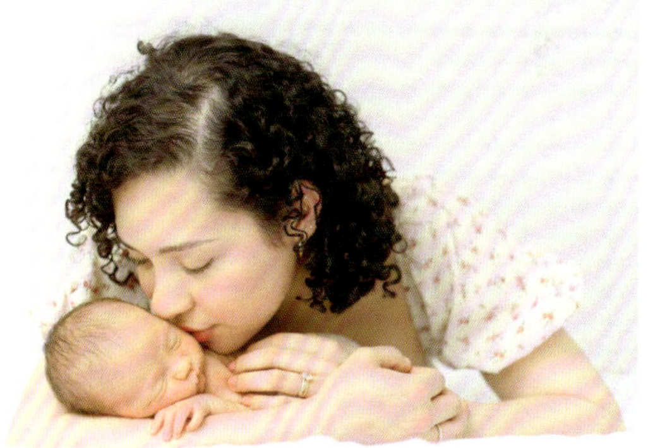

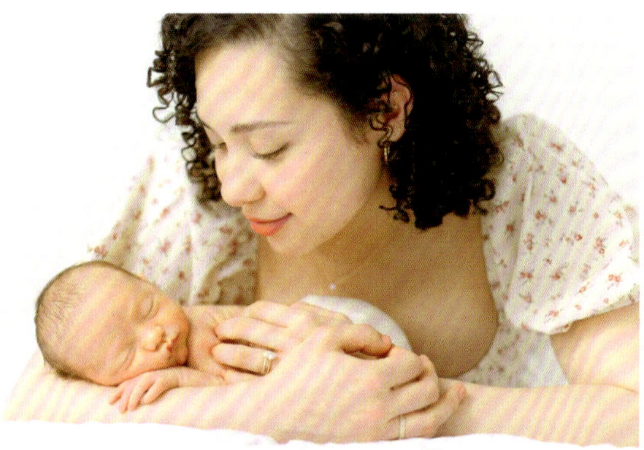

**FIGURE 9.14** A mother and her newborn in the lying-down pose. I was able to get multiple looks from this one pose by directing my client on where to look and by changing my perspective, crops, and composition.

Before placing a new mother in this pose, always ask if she is comfortable being on her belly. She may not be, especially if she recently gave birth and/or had a C-Section delivery. If she is not comfortable lying down, you can place the father (or the parent who did not give birth) in this position instead (**FIGURE 9.15**).

This pose works beautifully with newborns but it's also great to use with older babies, especially once they've started to smile! If you place a two- to three-month-old baby in this position, for example, they will almost always greet their parents with a huge smile (**FIGURE 9.16**).

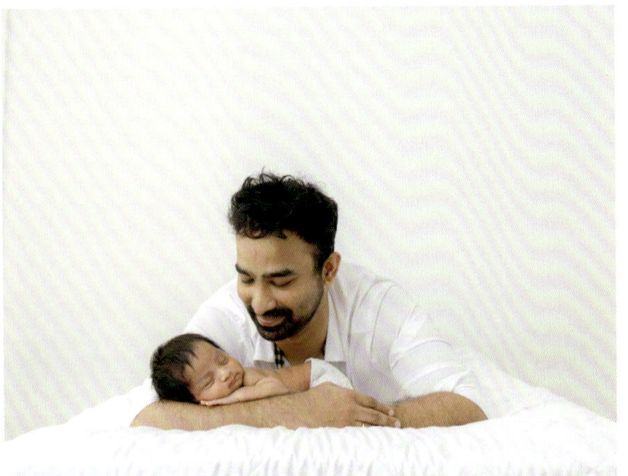

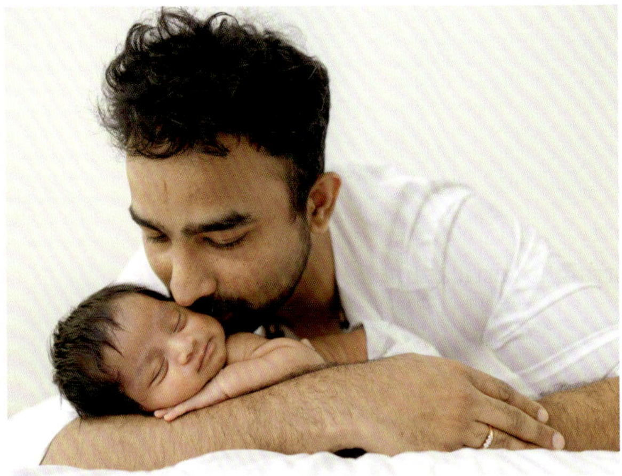

**FIGURE 9.15** A father in the lying-down pose.

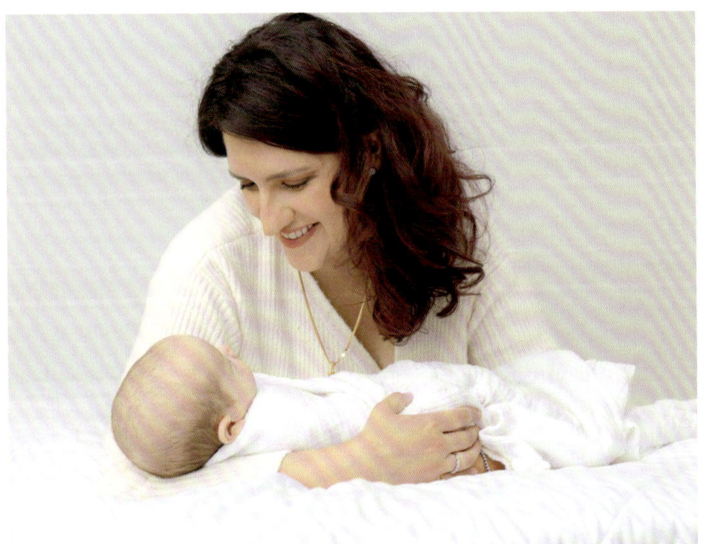

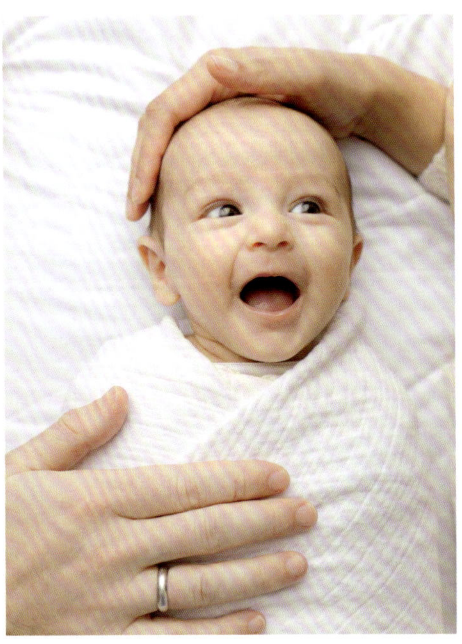

**FIGURE 9.16** By shifting my perspective to looking over the mother's shoulder, I was able to get some adorable pictures of the baby smiling at their mother.

When working with a sitter or one-year-old, simply ask the parent to lie on their stomach and get up on their elbows, perpendicular to the end of the bed, facing the seated child (**FIGURE 9.17**).

### One Parent Pose: Sitting

When photographing older babies, toddlers, and school-age children, I prefer to have the parent sit with their child instead of having them lying down.

Often older babies—typically between 6 and 12 months—prefer standing. If the baby wants to stand, ask the parent to sit slightly to one side of the child so that their heads are not stacked in a straight line. The parent can offer support by gently holding the baby's hands or by securing them around the waist (**FIGURE 9.18**).

If the child prefers to sit, they can be placed either beside the parent or on the parent's lap. When seated on a parent's lap, have the parent lean slightly to one side. Again, this creates visual interest by preventing them from aligning in a straight vertical line.

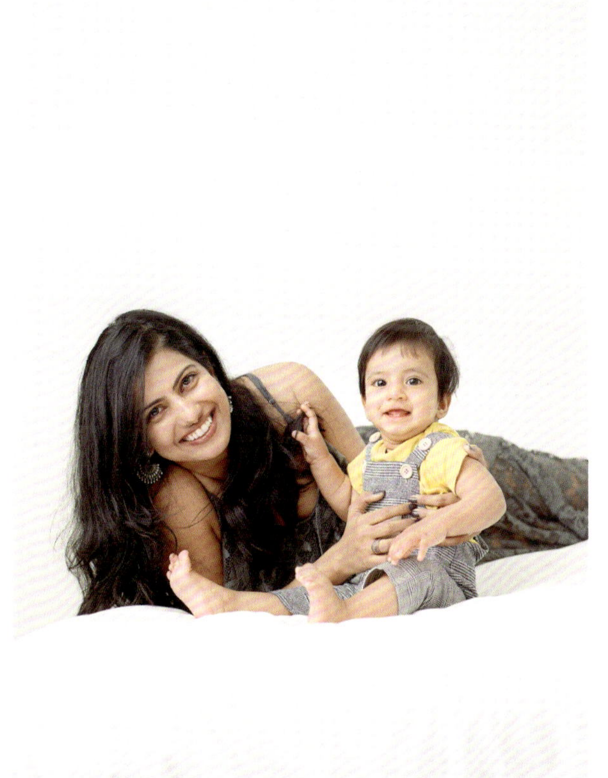

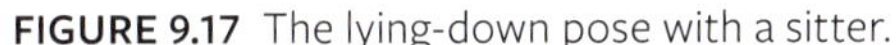

**FIGURE 9.17** The lying-down pose with a sitter.

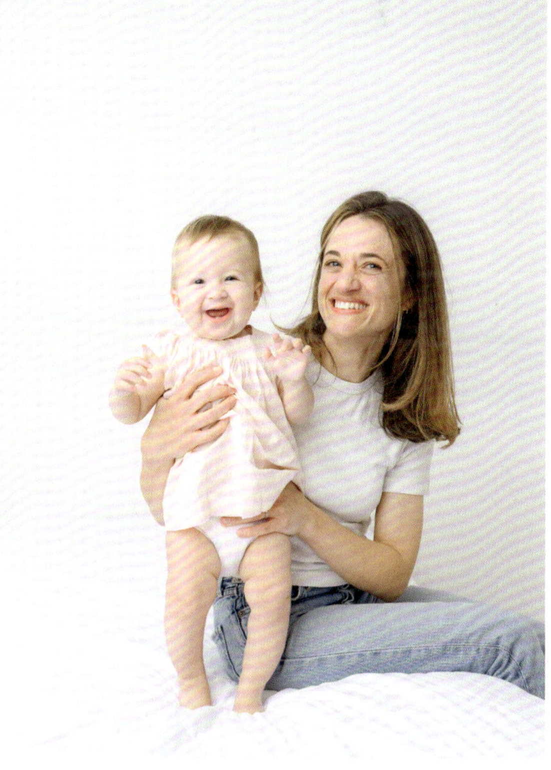

**FIGURE 9.18** A one-parent sitting pose with an older baby.

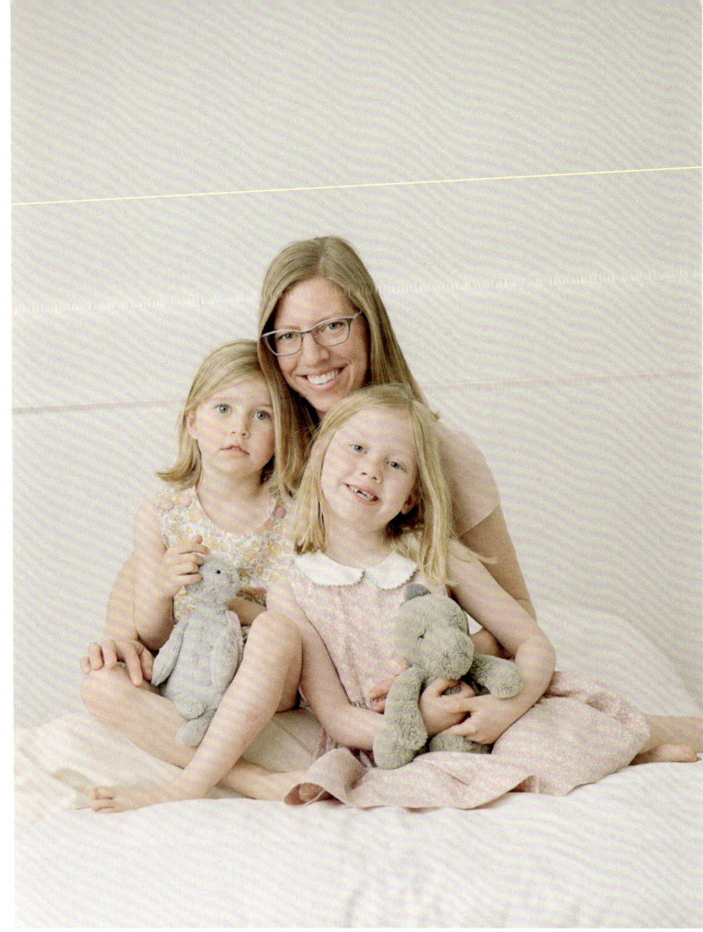

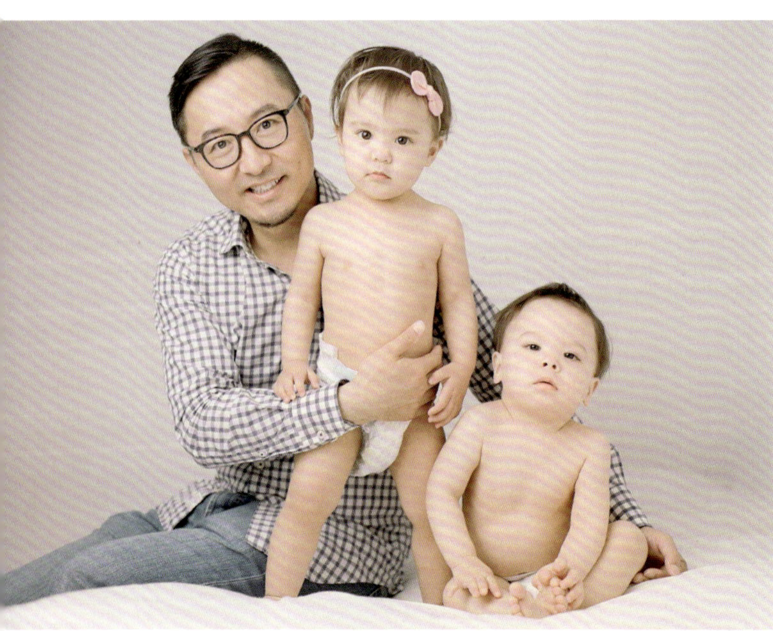

**FIGURE 9.19** When photographing multiple children with a parent, staggering their positions to create a natural triangular composition while keeping everyone relaxed and comfortable.

When working with multiple children, have one child sit on the bed next to the parent and one sit or stand in front, slightly to one side of the parent. This helps stagger their heights, and create triangles, while also making sure everyone is comfortable (**FIGURE 9.19**).

## Family

After capturing images of the child or children with one parent, transitioning into family photos is simple. Just invite the parent who isn't currently in the frame to join the others for a few family portraits.

### Family Pose: Lying Down

To create a family portrait using the lying-down pose, have the parent who is not already on the bed with the baby or child sit next to their partner. Ask this parent to place one arm over their partner and the other hand gently on the baby's head or their partner's elbow.

If there's an older child, have them sit on the seated parent's lap, slightly to one side. If there's more than one child, place the youngest on the seated parent's lap and position the oldest on the other side of the parent who is lying down with the baby (**FIGURE 9.20**). Position yourself at eye level with the baby and have everyone look at you to create a connected and balanced portrait. This pose can be done with newborns and older babies, up to six months old.

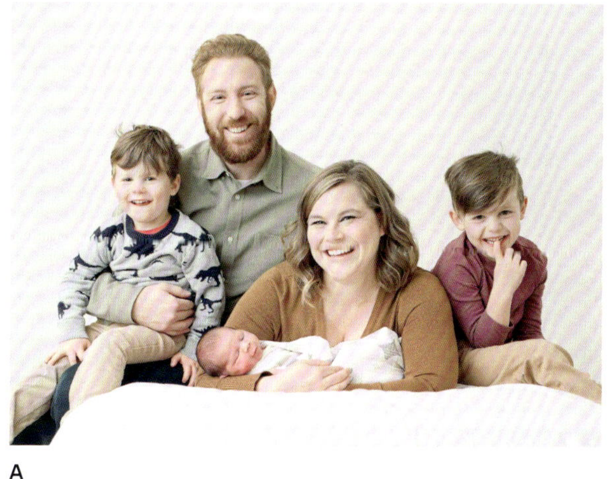

A

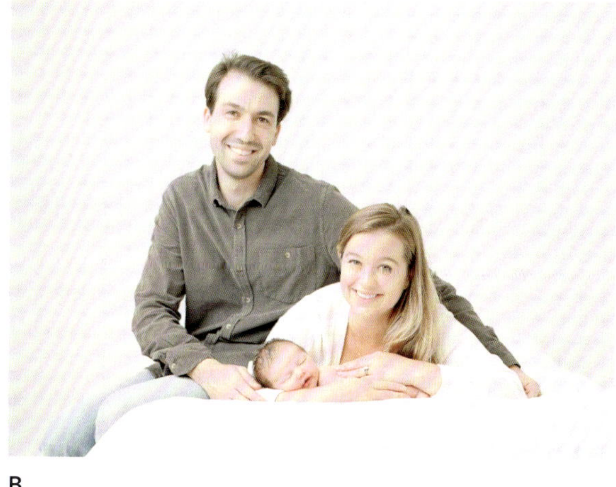

B

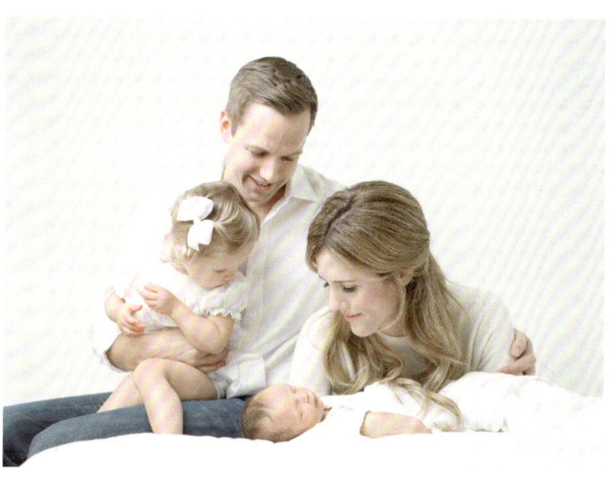

C

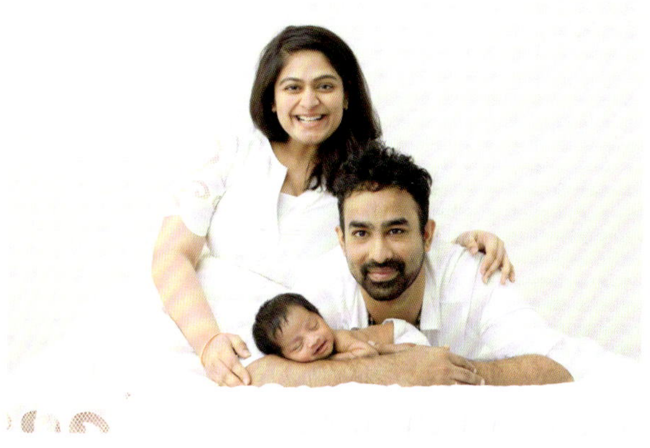

D

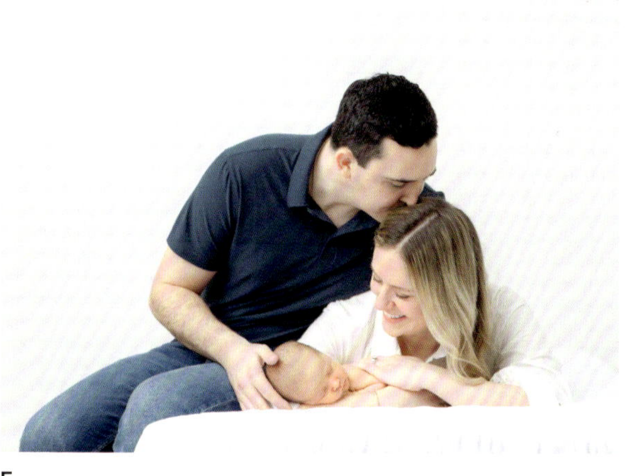

E

**FIGURE 9.20** Figure 9.20A shows a family of five, but the lying-down pose works well with families of all sizes! If working with a mother who is not comfortable lying down, you can have her partner lie down with the baby and seat her next to them (**D**). Remember to get multiple looks from this one pose by directing your clients where to look and what to do.

**Pro Tip:** If you are working with older children, instruct the parents to continue looking at the camera with a smile while you interact with the older child or children. Parents will often want to look at their other children to try to help get them to smile, but oftentimes, that just results in awkward-looking photos of the parents. Give the parents clear direction, then play with the kids to get the expressions you want.

### Family Pose: Side Kiss While Lying Down with Baby

This pose is very similar to the side-kiss pose from the earlier section on posing siblings. For this version, ask the parent who is on the bed with the baby to stay where they are, and instruct their partner to kneel on the floor next to the bed. Position yourself eye level to the baby and have the parent who is kneeling on the side of the bed snuggle or kiss the baby on the top of the head (**FIGURE 9.21**). Have both parents look at the baby and then look at each other, creating a candid-looking image that your clients will love! And of course, be ready to capture any truly candid moments that may occur as you work.

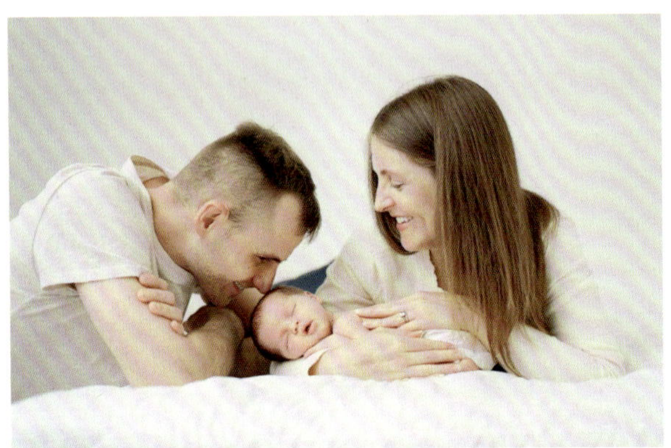

A

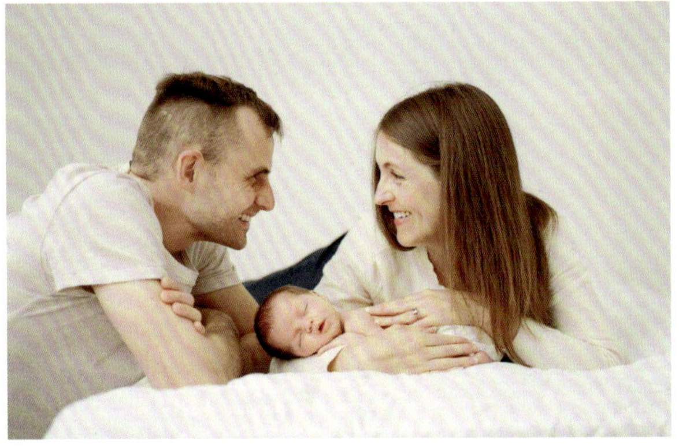

B

**FIGURE 9.21** The Side Kiss. Figures 9.21A and 9.21B. Figure 9.21C was a spontaneous moment that happened in this directed pose.

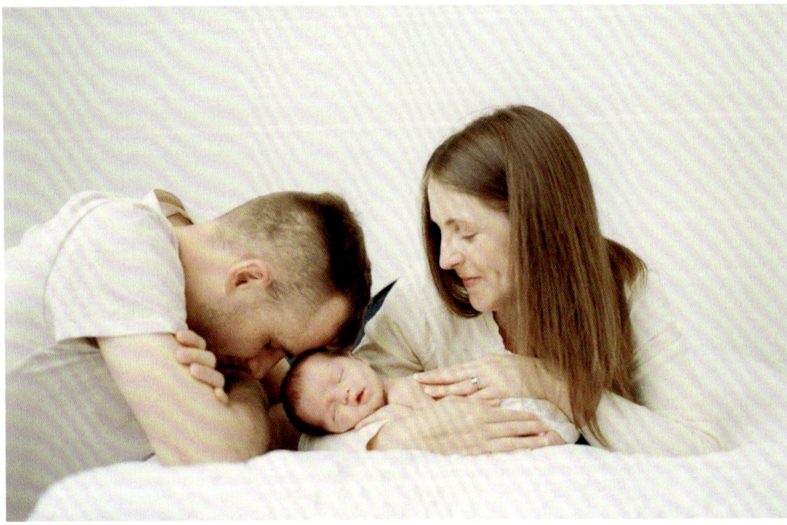

C

### Family Pose: Sitting

If you are working with older babies or children who are sitting, the same rules apply! **FIGURE 9.22** shows this flow at a sitter session.

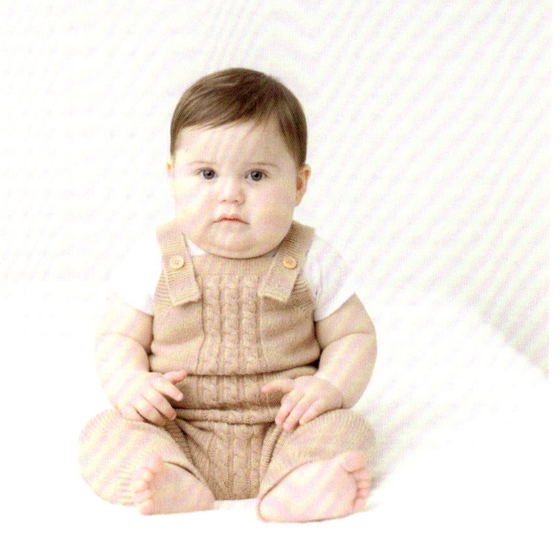

A

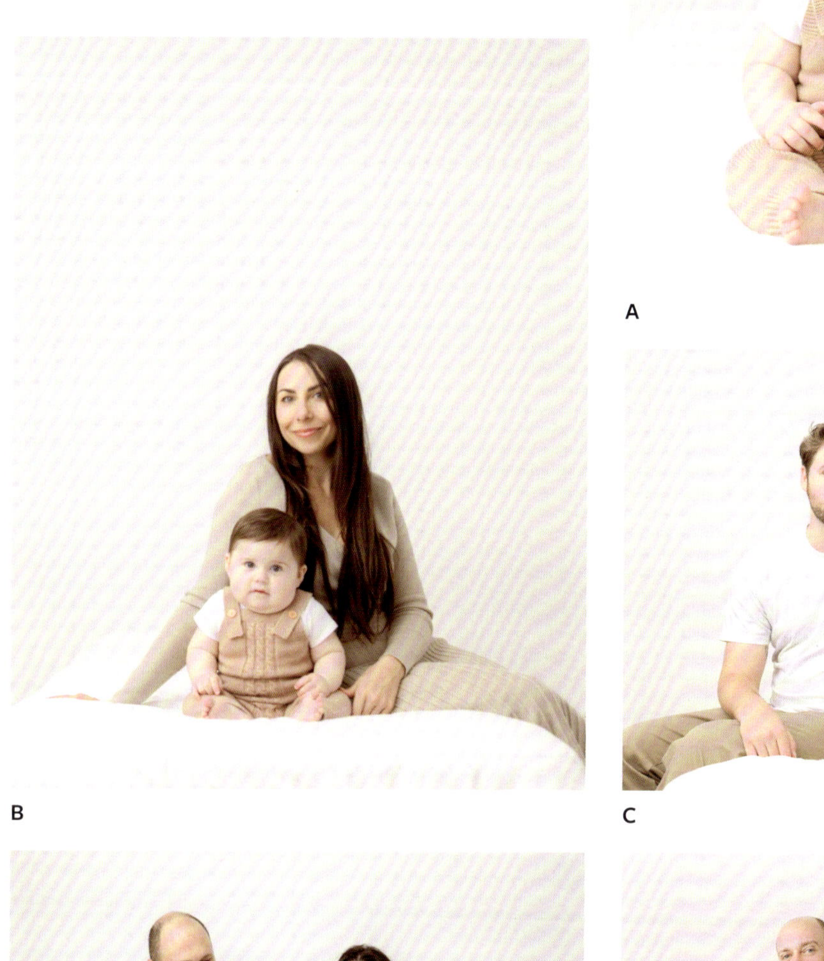

B

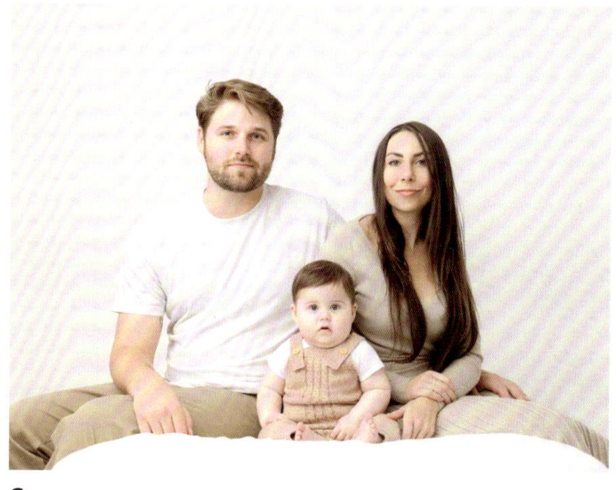

C

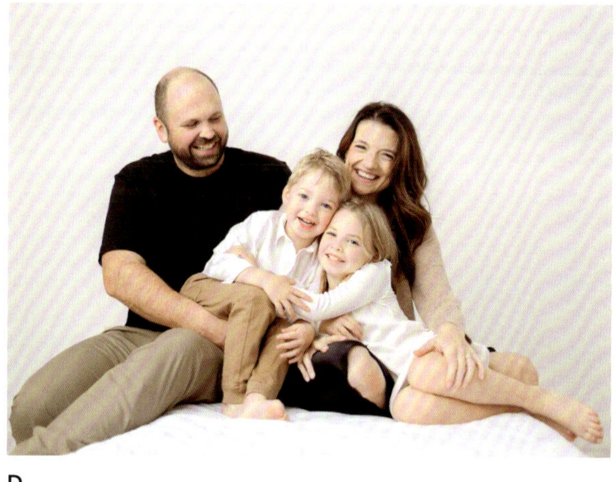

D

E

**FIGURE 9.22** Baby alone (**A**), baby with mother (**B**), then baby with both parents (**C**). Figure 9.22D shows this pose with a family of four. The children were both school-age and could follow directions, so I asked the little boy to sit on his father's lap. I asked the girl to sit mermaid style next to her mother. The hug between the siblings was entirely spontaneous! Figure 9.22E shows this pose with a family of six.

### Family Pose: Airplane

I'm pretty sure that every parent has played "airplane" with their child at some point. It's fun for the child and makes for cute photos. A true win/win! Position one parent on the edge of the bed, in profile to you, and have the other parent sit in the mermaid position next to them. Ask the parent who is sitting in profile to lift the child into the airplane position and ask both parents to look at the child (**FIGURE 9.23**).

This pose works well with a single parent, as well. Have the parent position themselves parallel to you and lift their child into the air (**FIGURE 9.24A**). You can add variety to this pose by asking the parent to turn their back to you so that you can see the child's face (**FIGURE 9.24B**). This pose is only appropriate for children who have developed good muscle tone, so six months and up. Also be aware that this pose can be a workout for the parent, depending on the size of the baby, so you will have to work quickly!

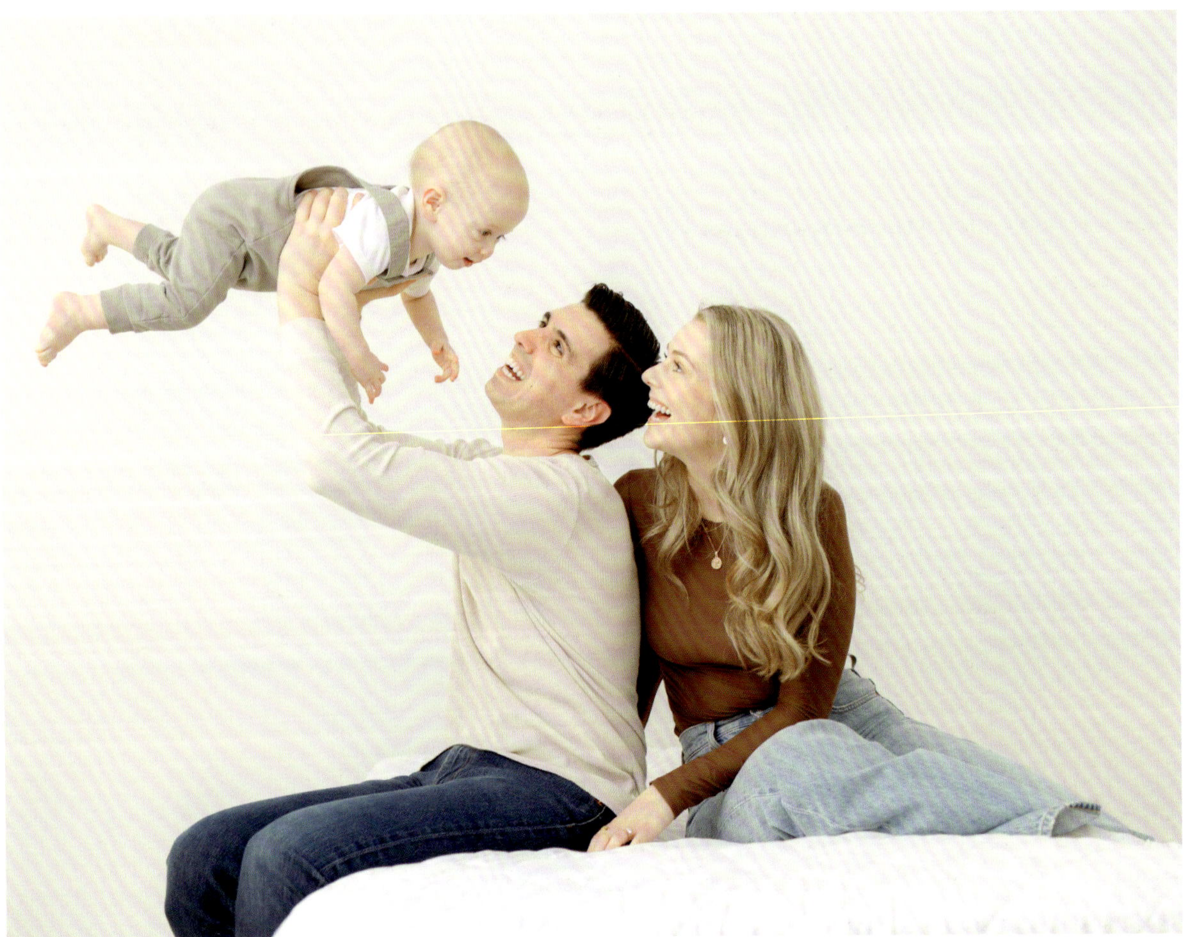

**FIGURE 9.23** Airplane pose with the entire family.

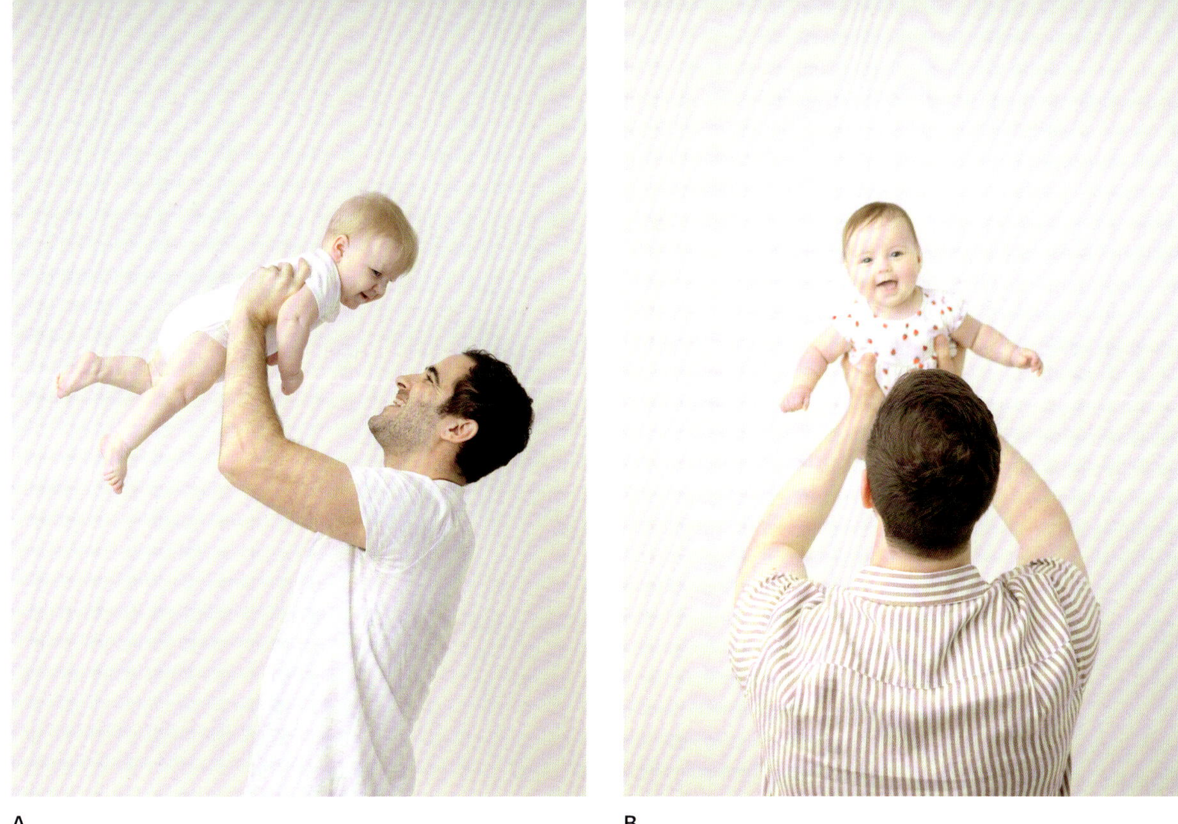

A B

**FIGURE 9.24** The airplane pose is a fun way to add variety to your sitting poses when working with older babies and toddlers.

## Child(ren) with the Other Parent

After capturing photos of the family together, I move on to portraits of the child or children with their remaining parent. When working with a newborn or young baby, once I've posed the child, I try not move them for the majority of the session. All the other poses I create involve positioning family members around them. Even with my sitters, one-year-olds, and toddlers, I bring the parents to them for photos rather than moving the child multiple times throughout the session.

This strategy allows me to build out a gallery of multiple looks without having to disturb the children I'm working with. As a result, the child is happy and comfortable for most of the session, allowing me to work quickly and efficiently, all while creating plenty of beautiful photos for my clients. I save moving the baby until the very end of the session when I transition into standing poses. These poses are usually created with the father, but they work beautifully with either parent.

**Pro Tip:** If the baby you are working with is sleeping, it's very likely that they will wake up when being moved into some of the standing poses—and that's okay! Babies can be awake or asleep for any of these poses.

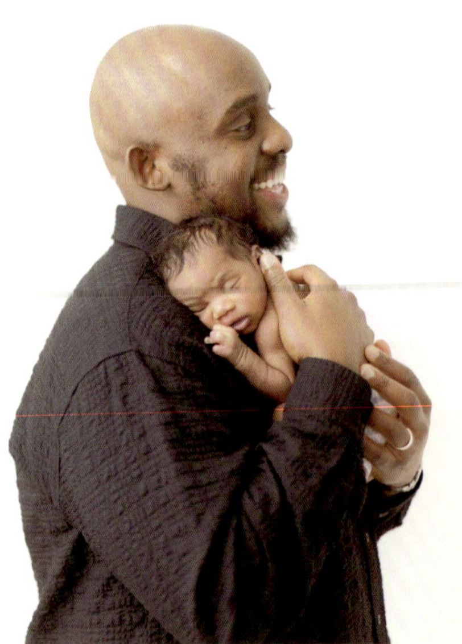
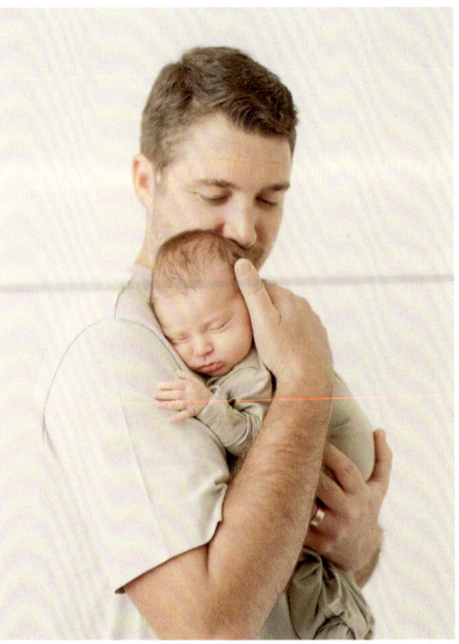
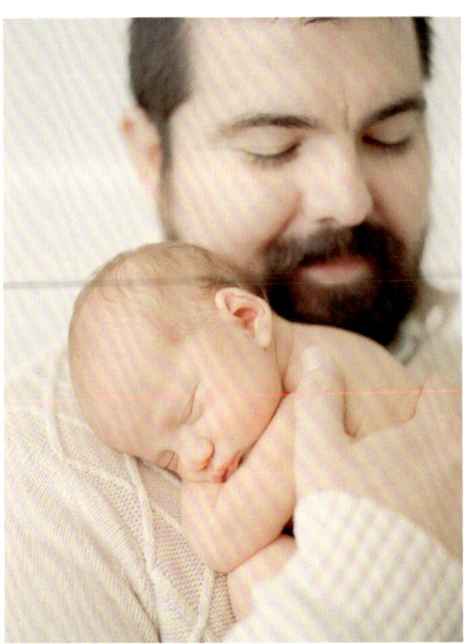

**FIGURE 9.25** Profile poses with baby on shoulder. Make the most of this pose by guiding your client where to look and experimenting with different compositions.

### One Parent Pose: Standing with Baby on Shoulder

This is one of my favorite poses for newborns and babies up to three months of age. Ask the parent you are photographing to stand in profile to the camera. Gently pick the baby up off the bed and place them in their parent's arms, high on the chest so that their head is resting on their parent's shoulder, face toward the camera. Have the parent look straight ahead. Position yourself eye level to the baby, focusing on their face (**FIGURE 9.25**).

### One Parent Pose: Standing with Baby on Chest

After capturing some images of the baby on the parent's shoulder, ask the parent to turn and face the camera directly. Slide the baby down from the position on the shoulder until their head rests in the middle of the parent's chest. When working with newborns and sleeping babies, face the child toward the parent's chest as in **FIGURE 9.26A**. When working with older babies or babies who are awake, face the child out so that they can look into the camera (**FIGURES 9.26B**, **C**, and **D**).

**Pro Tip:** Before positioning the baby, check to see if the person holding them is wearing anything—like buttons, zippers, or textured fabrics—that could scratch or irritate the baby's skin. If you spot something that might be uncomfortable, gently slide your hand under the baby's cheek and chest as they're being positioned to protect their skin and ensure a smooth transition into the pose.

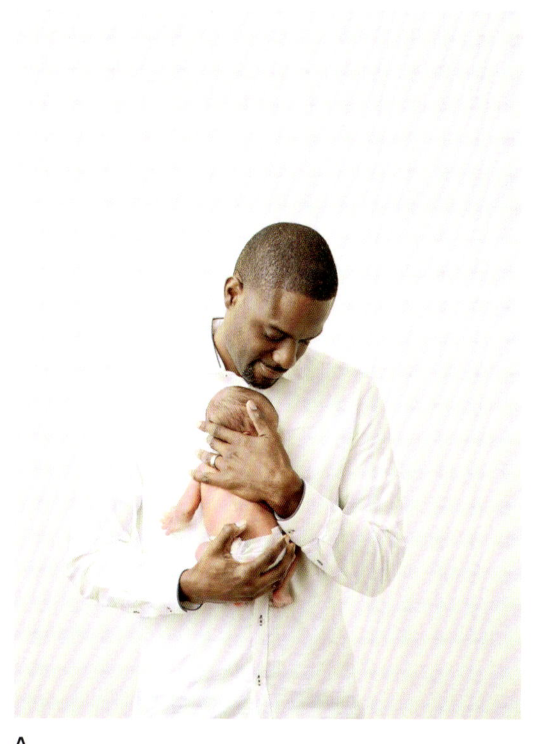
A

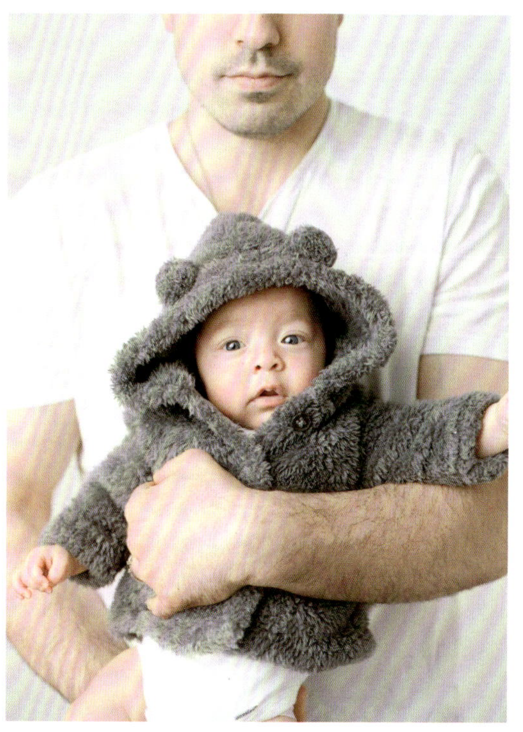
B

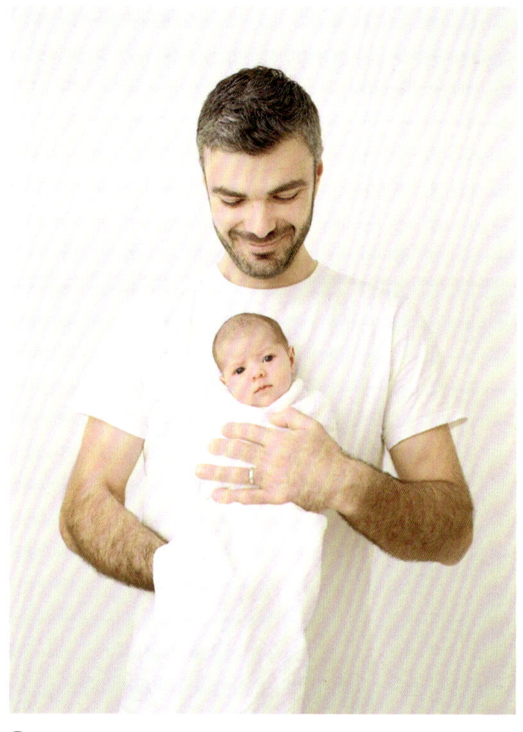
C

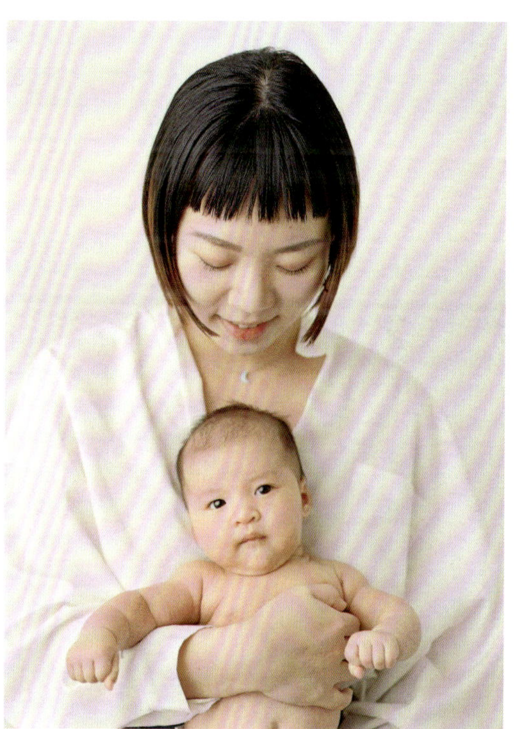
D

**FIGURE 9.26** Baby on chest

### One Parent Pose: Cradle Hold

Another simple but beautiful standing pose when working with newborns and young babies is the cradle hold (**FIGURE 9.27**). To set this up, have the parent face the camera and cradle the baby. I do this with both men and women but find it's a particularly nice pose for mothers who are not comfortable in the lying-down poses soon after birth. It's a natural and nurturing way to hold a baby and results in lovely images.

Because the cradle hold is often used when feeding, it may elicit the rooting reflex in a newborn, especially when in their mother's arms. You'll have better luck with this pose if the baby you are working with is sleeping or already well fed. When using this pose, be sure to point the top of the baby's head toward your light source to avoid accidentally uplighting the baby.

**Pro Tip:** Sometimes sleeping babies will wake up when lifted off the bed and into their parent's arms, and they may cry. If the baby does start to fuss, ask the parent to turn so that the top of the baby's head is pointing toward the camera, as in **FIGURES 9.27C** and **9.27D**). This will allow you to get some quick photos before pausing to comfort the baby.

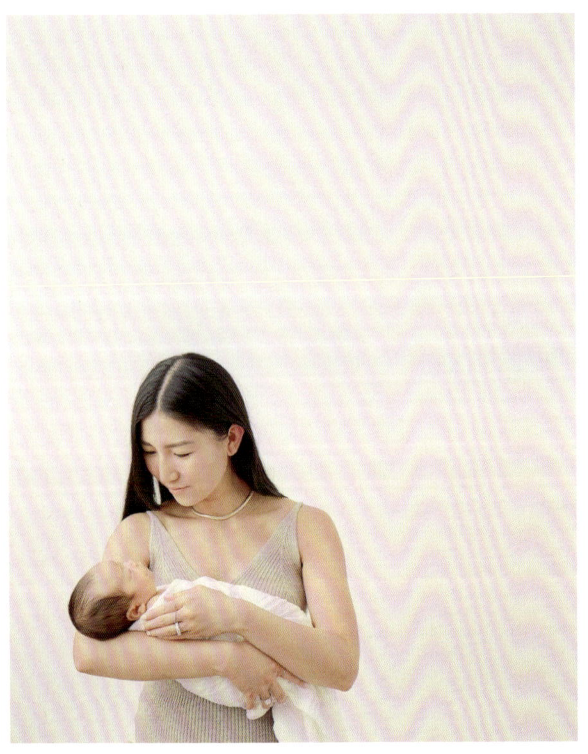

A

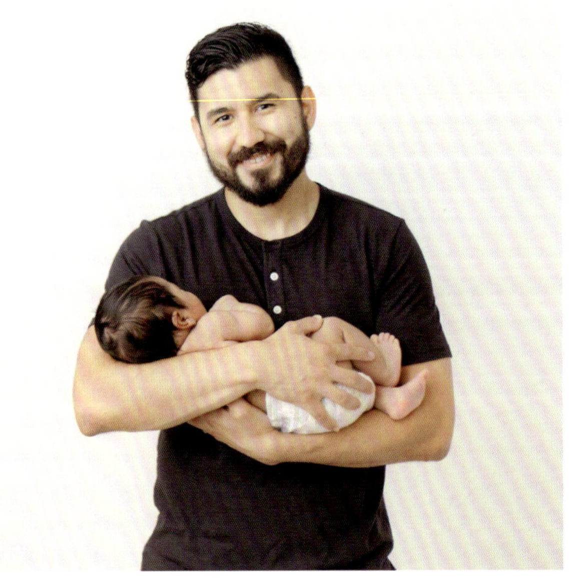

B

**FIGURE 9.27** The cradle hold. This pose also works beautifully when your subject is sitting, as in Figure 9.27E. It can also be easily done with twins (Figure 9.27F).

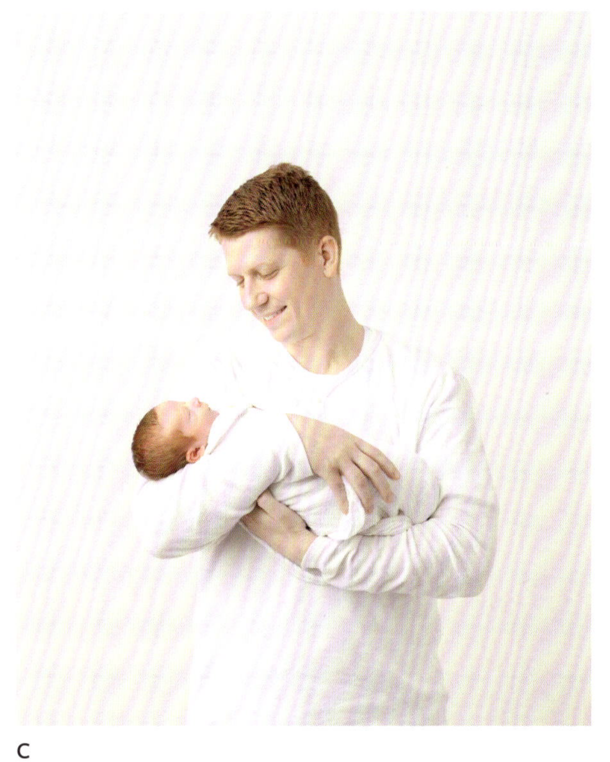

C

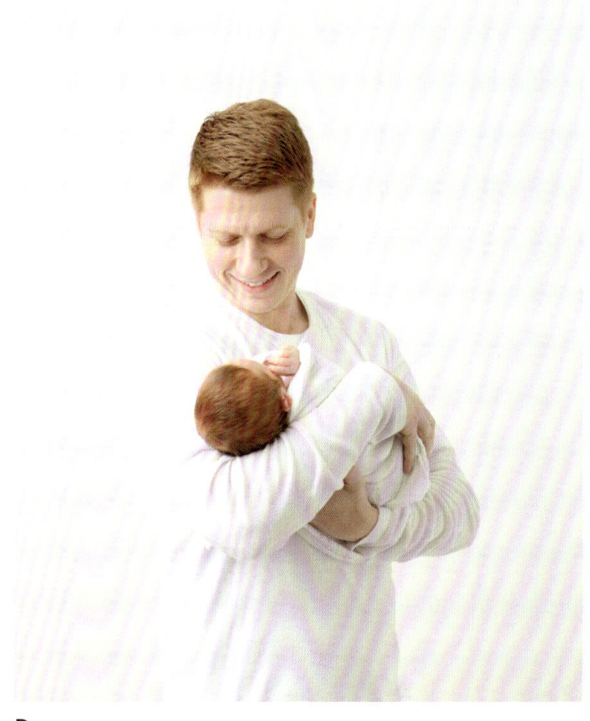

D

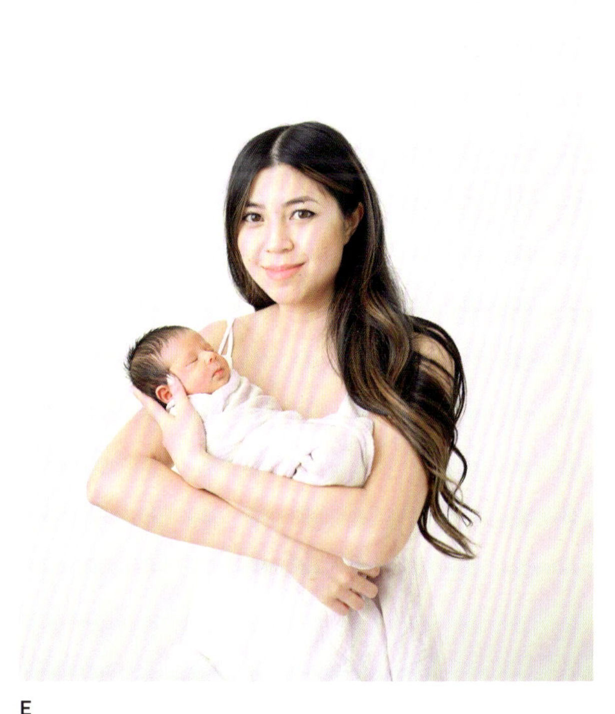

E

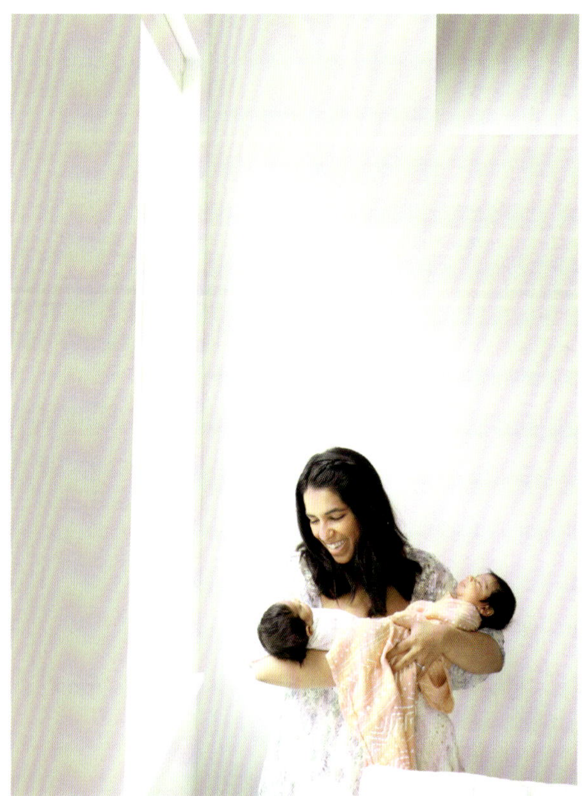

F

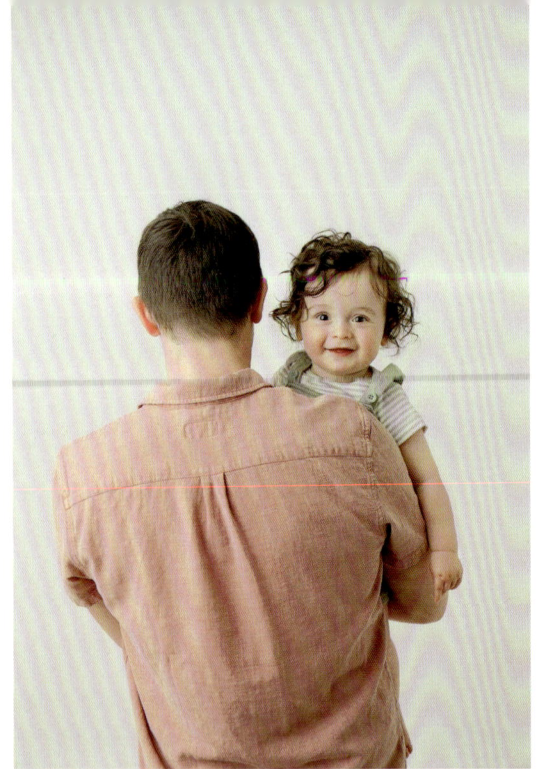

A

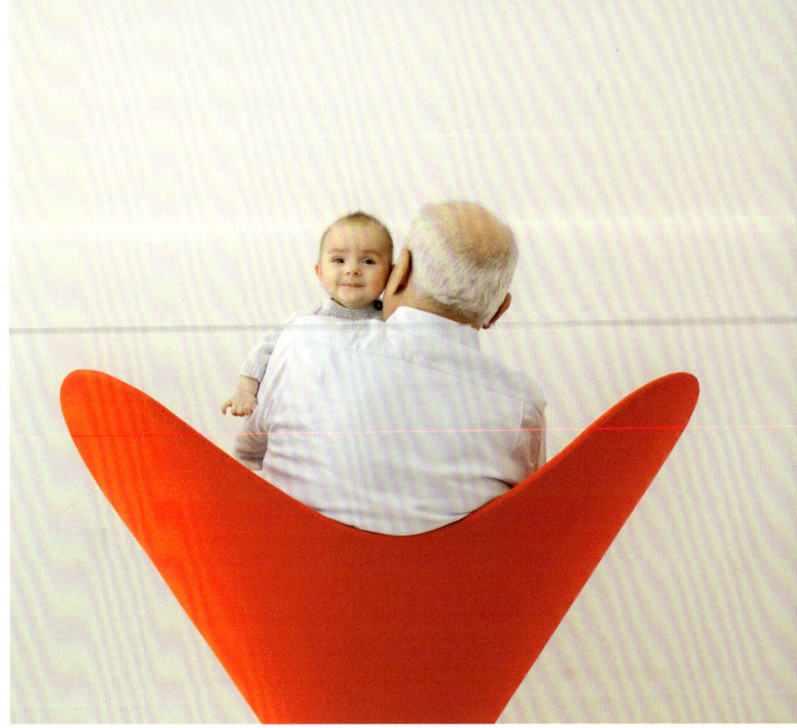

B

**FIGURE 9.28** Peek-a-boo!

### One Parent Pose: Peek-A-Boo

If the child you are working with is old enough to hold up their head, try the peek-a-boo pose! Simply ask the parent (or, in the case of **FIGURE 9.28B**, the grandparent) to position themselves so that their back is facing the camera. Have them hold the child so that the child is peeking up over their shoulder at you. This cute pose works well whether your client is standing or sitting.

### One Parent Pose: Squat and Stand

The Squat and Stand pose can be used with six-month-old babies through school-age children. For this pose, have the parent stand behind the standing child and squat down so that you can get both of their faces in the frame. If the child needs some help standing, have the parent support them by holding their hands or holding them around the waist. Pull back to get both parent and child in the frame (**FIGURE 9.29A**) and zoom in to get the child's face and the parent's hands (**FIGURE 9.29B**).

### Family and Baby: Standing

Most of the time, once I've finished with the parent and baby standing poses, the session will be done. But, if the baby is still happy or asleep, I will sometimes invite the other parent and other child(ren) (when applicable) back into the frame for a few standing family photos.

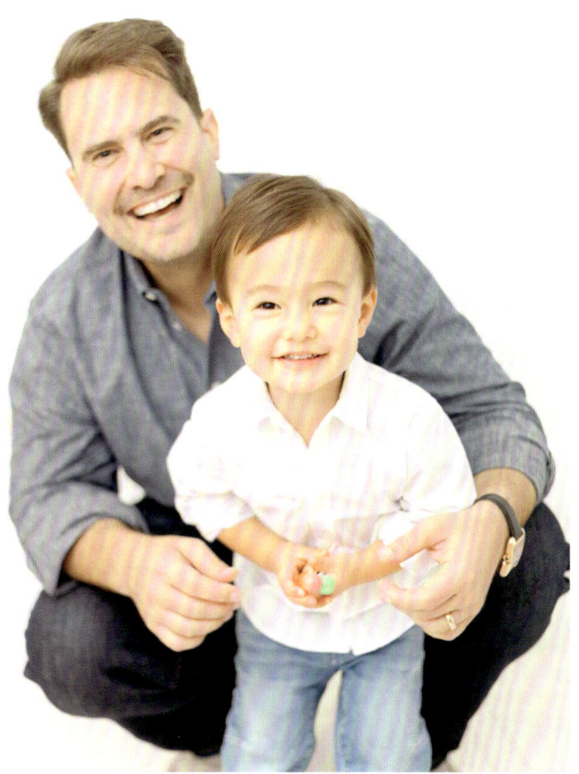

A

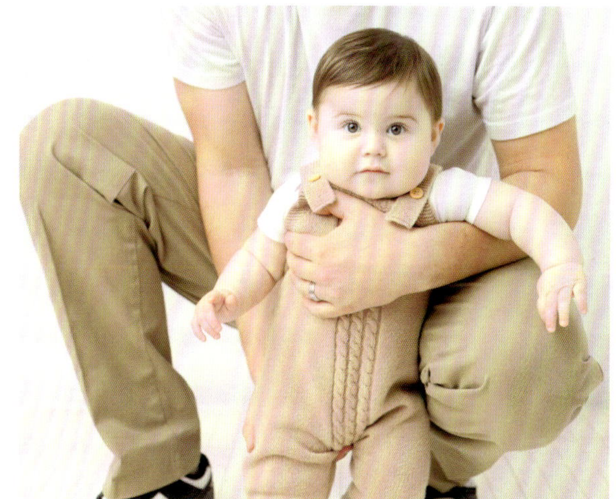

B

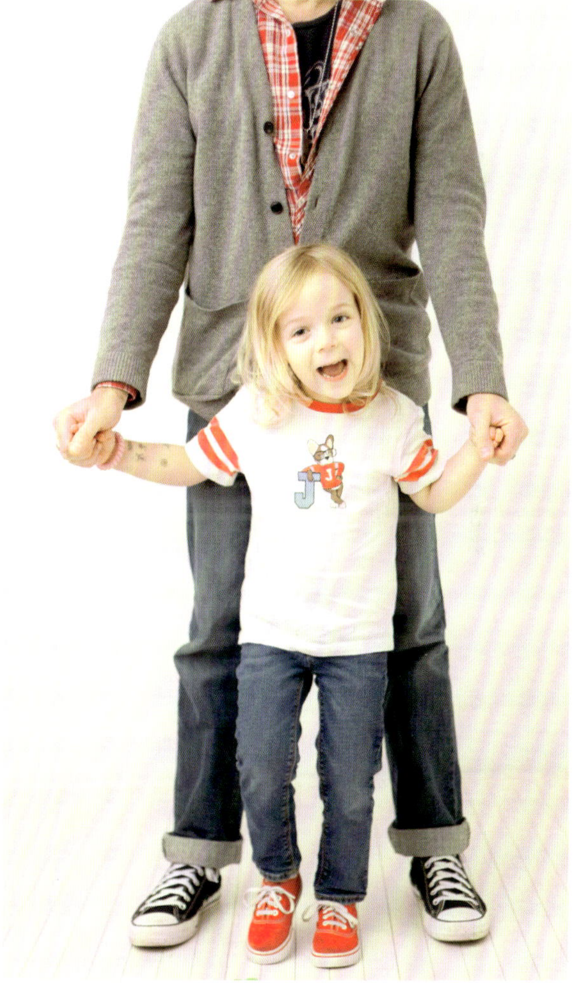

C

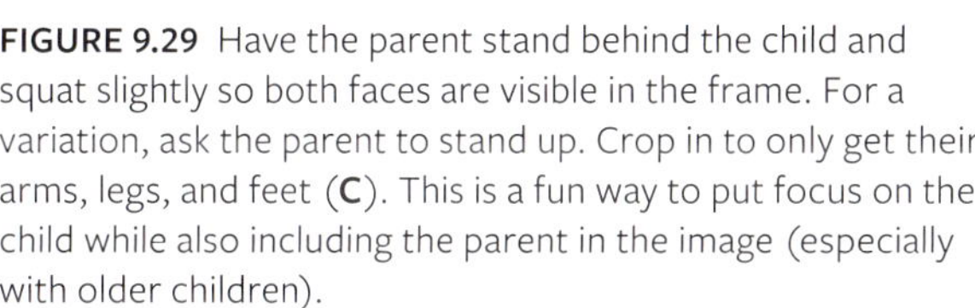

**FIGURE 9.29** Have the parent stand behind the child and squat slightly so both faces are visible in the frame. For a variation, ask the parent to stand up. Crop in to only get their arms, legs, and feet (**C**). This is a fun way to put focus on the child while also including the parent in the image (especially with older children).

## Pose: Baby Sandwich

The baby sandwich is a classic pose that can be done with newborns up through school-age children (**FIGURE 9.30**, next page). When working with a newborn or baby, start with the baby on the parent's chest or shoulder. With older children, have one parent hold the child in a comfortable position and ask the parent who is not holding the baby to stand next to their partner. Have the two adults turn toward each other, keeping the child in the middle, and direct the parent who is not holding the child to wrap their arms around their child and partner to create a "baby sandwich."

### Pose: Back Snuggle

This is another super sweet family pose that can be added in at the end of the session, when one parent is holding the child (**FIGURE 9.31**). To set this pose up, ask the parent who is holding the child to stay put, and invite their partner to stand slightly behind them and wrap their arms around their partner.

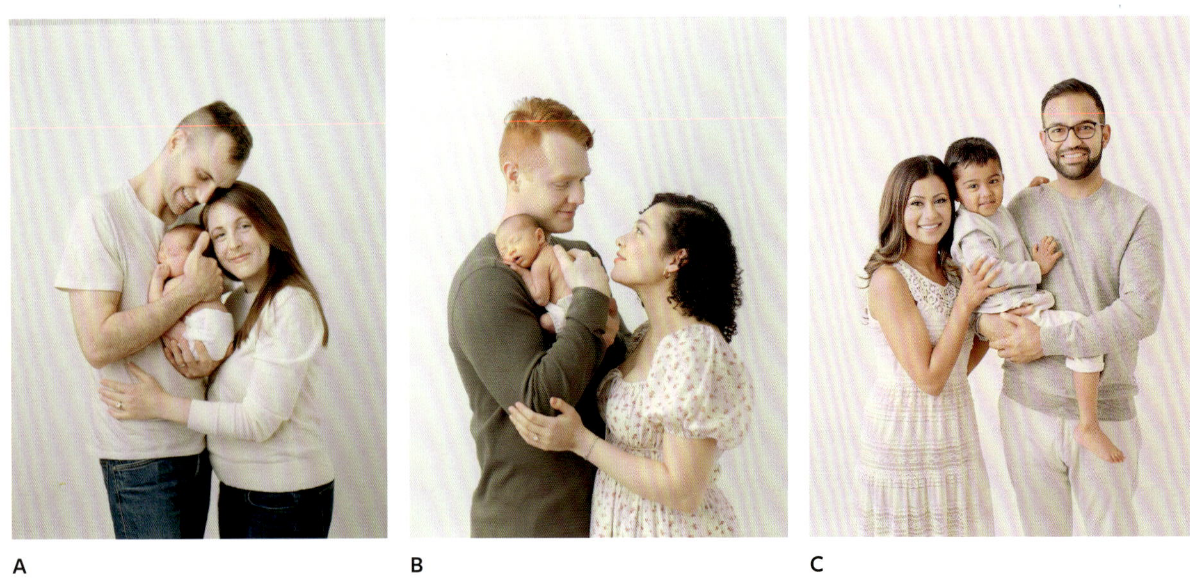

A B C

**FIGURE 9.30** Figures 9.30A and 9.30B show a baby sandwich with a newborn; Figure 9.30C shows the pose with a four-year-old.

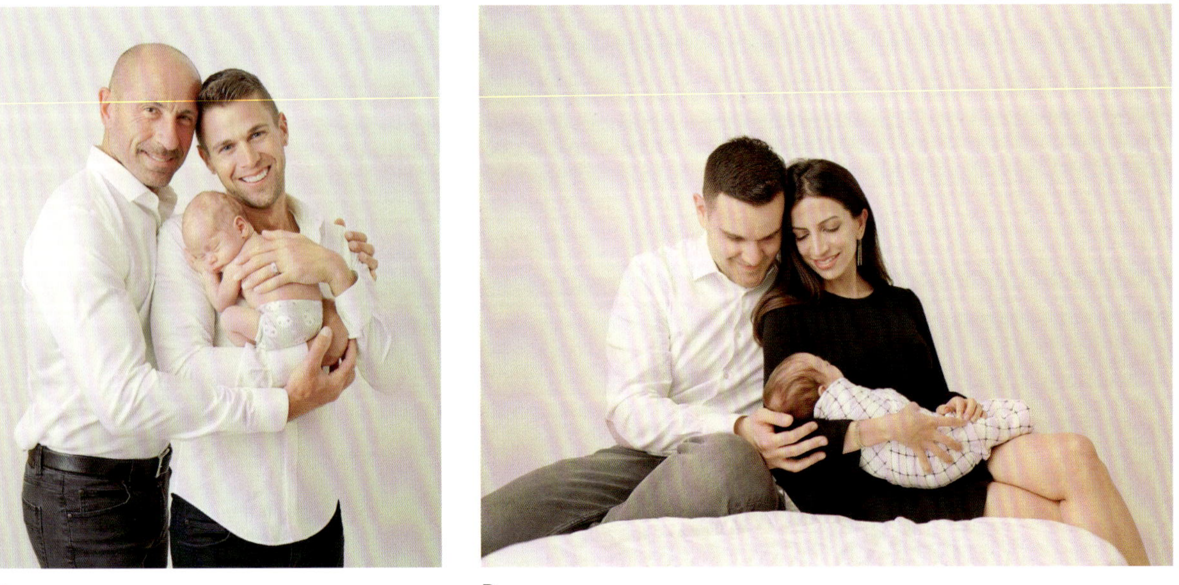

A B

**FIGURE 9.31** The back snuggle. This pose can be done with babies up to one year in age. It also works well as a seated pose, as shown in Figure 9.31B.

### Pose: Side Snuggle

The side snuggle is very similar to the back-snuggle pose and works beautifully with babies up to one year of age. For this pose, direct the parent who is not holding the baby to (you guessed it) to stand to the side of their partner and snuggle up. Have both parents look into the camera and look down at the baby to add variety (**FIGURE 9.32**).

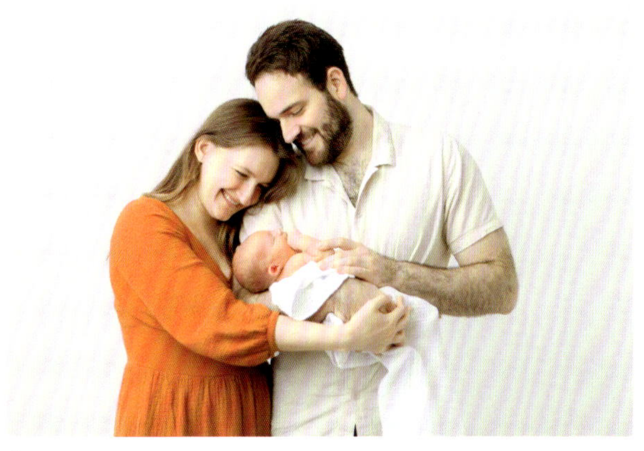

A

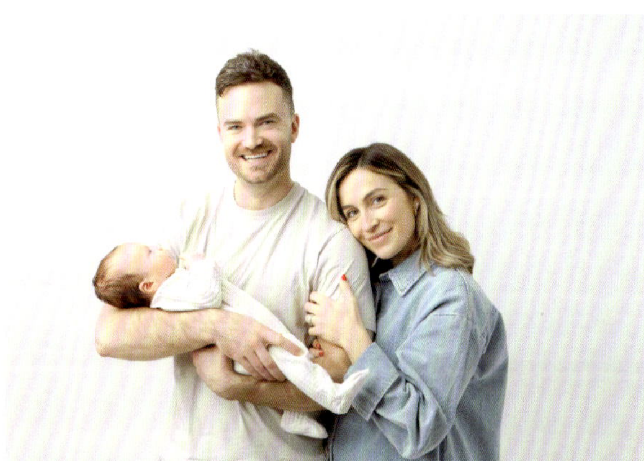

B

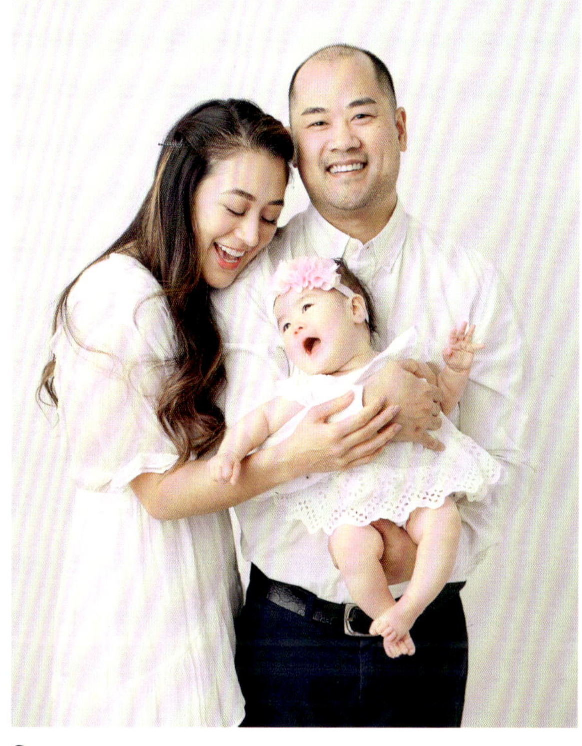

C

**FIGURE 9.32** Side snuggle with a newborn (**A**), three-month-old (**B**), and sitter (**C**).

## Make These Poses Your Own

When it comes to posing, remember that every family is unique. Some are small, others are large, and many are somewhere in between. The key to successful family posing is to embrace these differences. Use the poses shared in this chapter as inspiration and make them your own (**FIGURE 9.33**, next pages). Nearly every pose can be adapted to accommodate larger families, older children, and multiple generations. Trust your creativity and consider the dynamics of the family you're working with when posing them. With a little practice, posing families will become second nature.

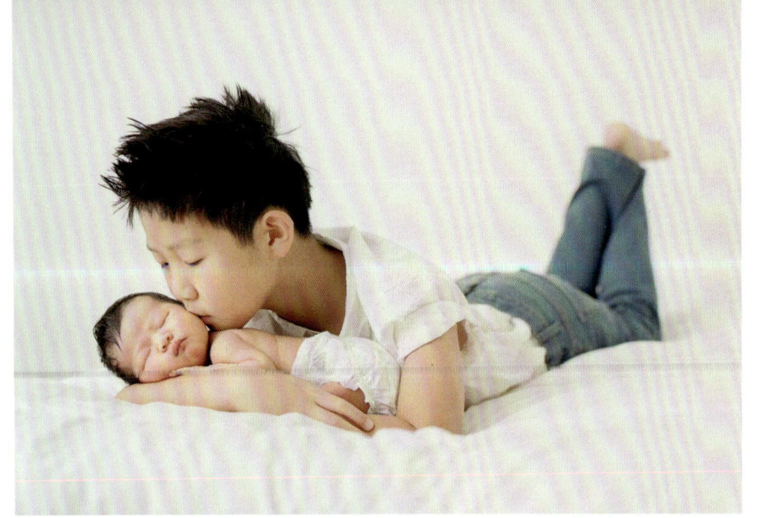

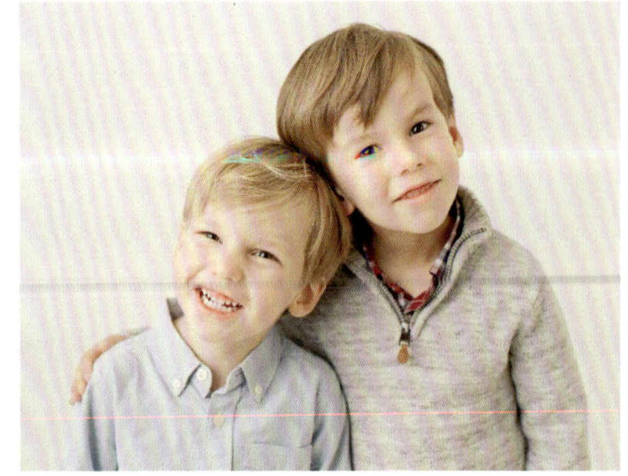

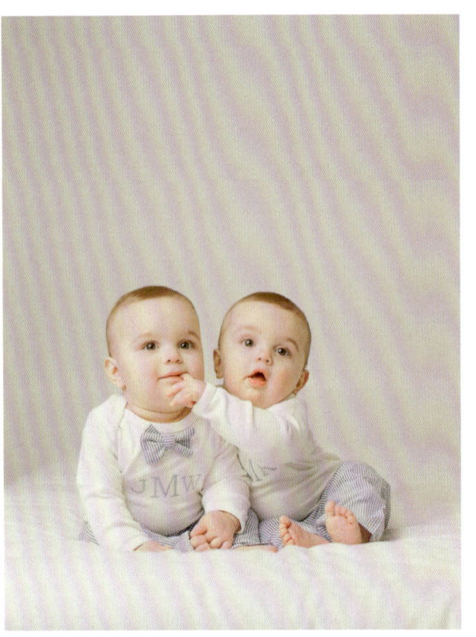

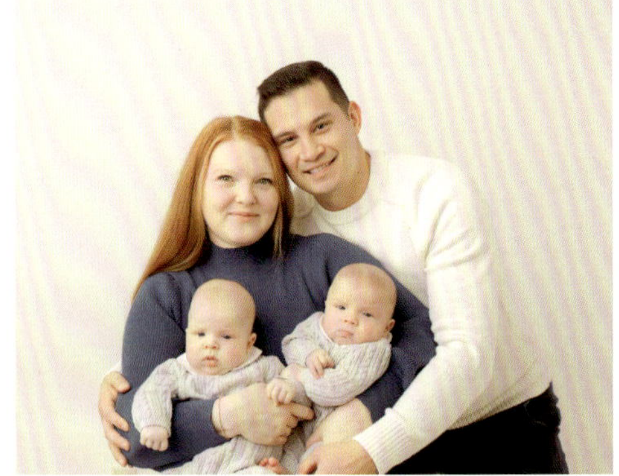

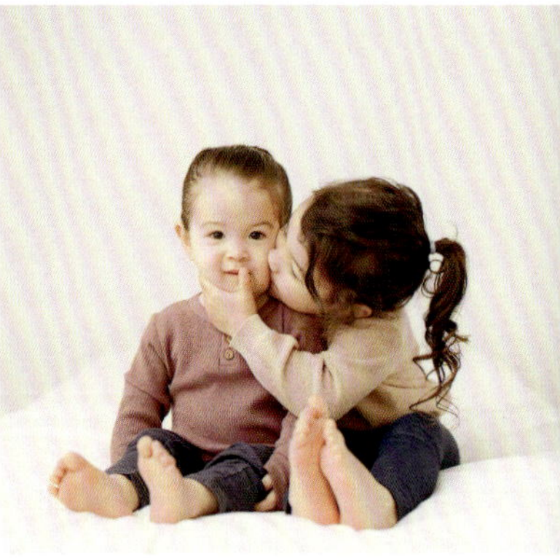

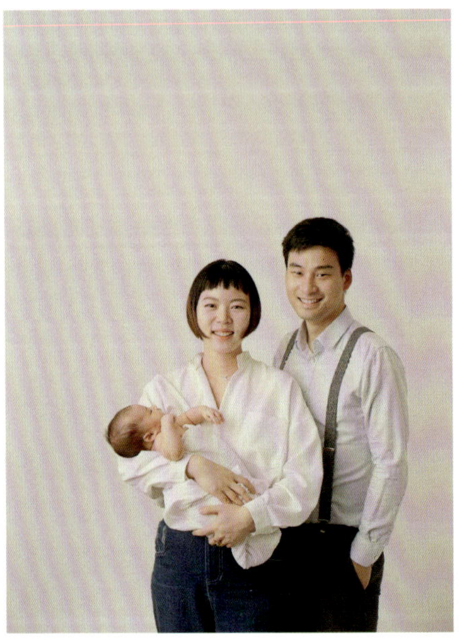

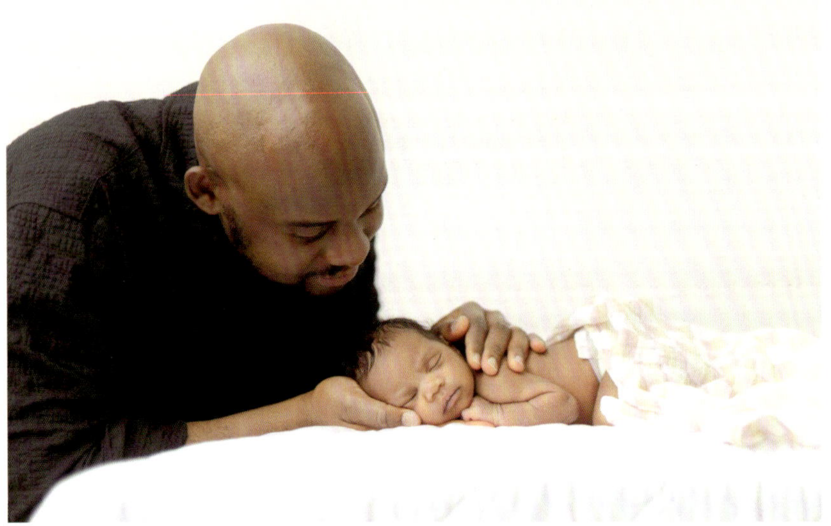

**FIGURE 9.33** All these images show different variations on the family poses shared in this chapter.

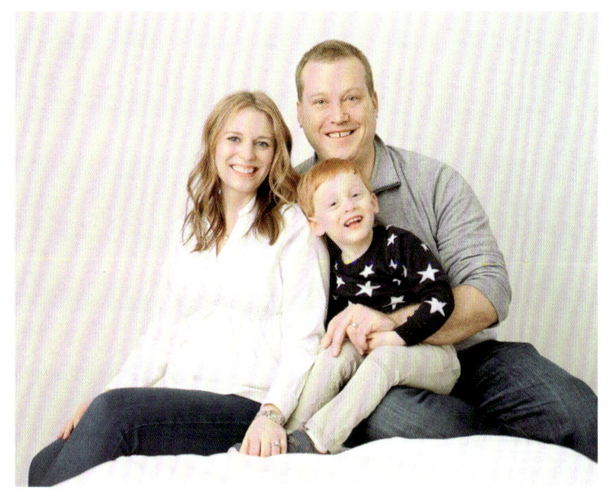

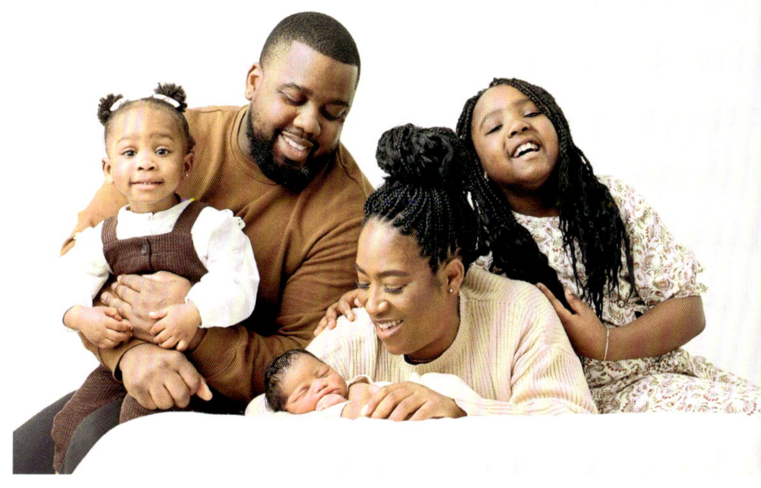

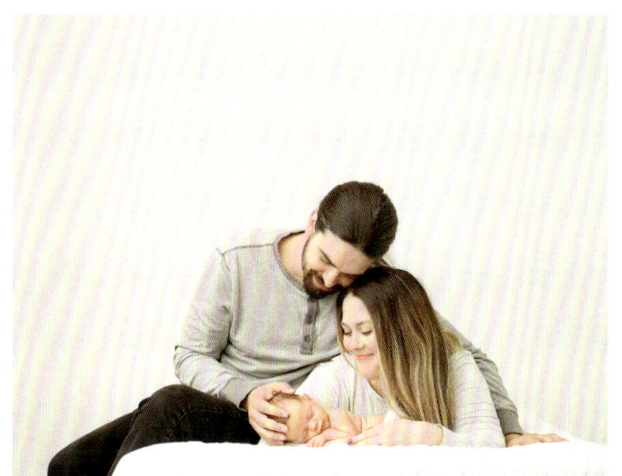

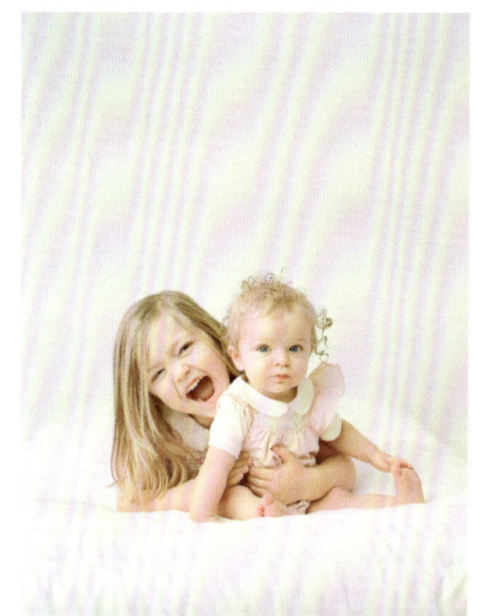

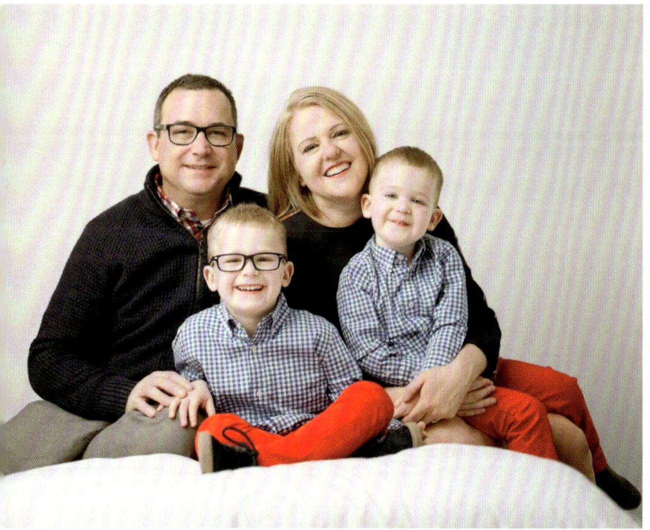

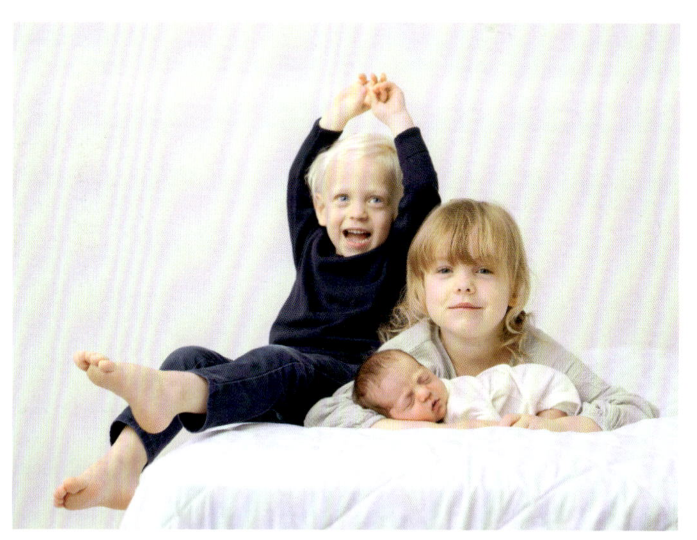

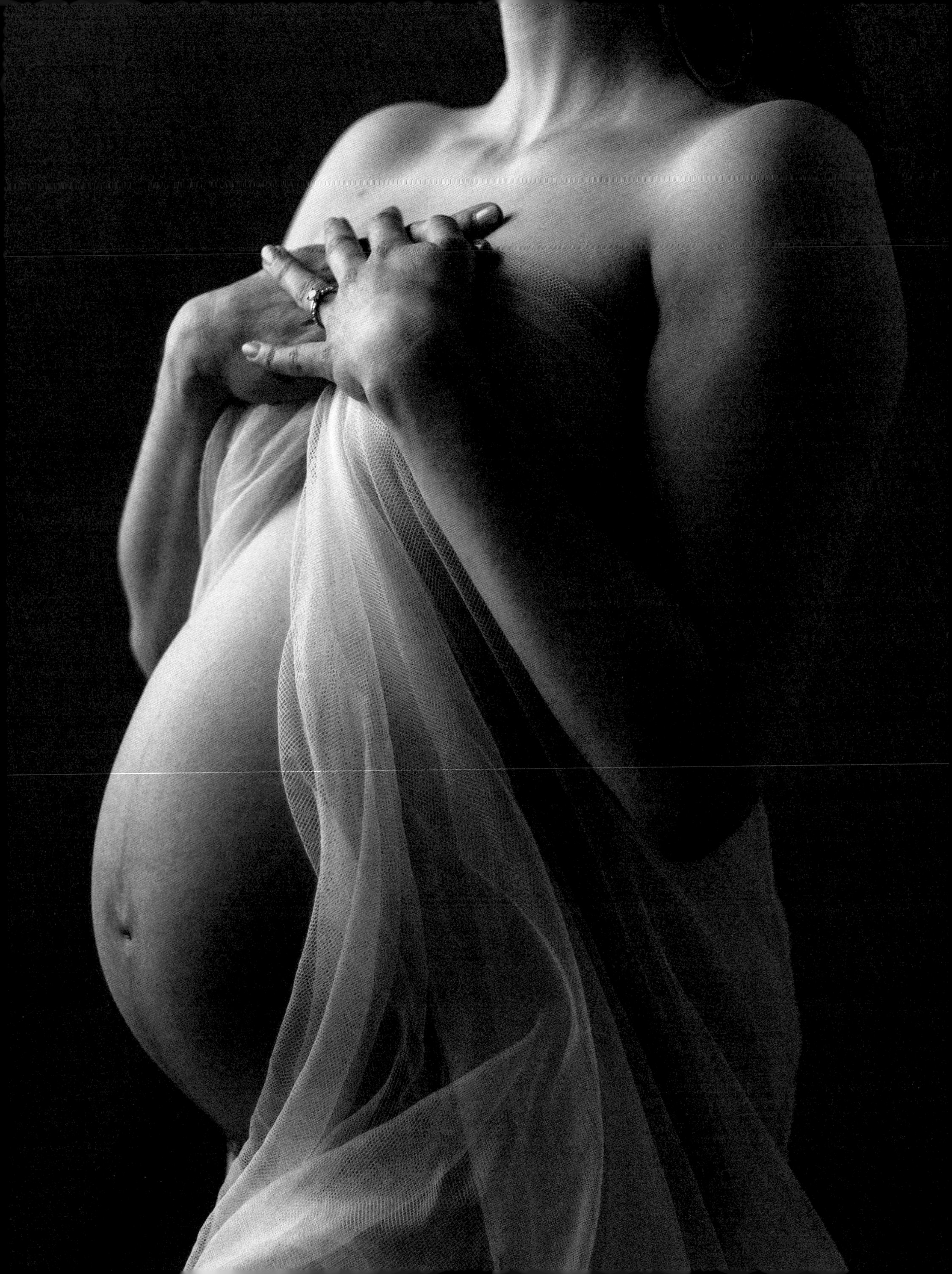

CHAPTER

# 10

# Maternity Posing

Maternity photography is my first love. It's how I launched my business back in 1999, and after all these years, it still inspires me. At the beginning of my career, I loved working with pregnant women because pregnant women are beautiful. But the importance of this work didn't really hit me until I had my own children in 2006. Before then, I thought maternity photography was all about capturing the pregnant form. Pregnancy lasts a very short time, and only a handful of those months is a woman visibly pregnant. The transformation deserves to be captured.

Being pregnant taught me that the transformation we capture as maternity photographers is about so much more than documenting the changes in a woman's body. A pregnant woman is in a state of metamorphosis. Yes, she's creating a child, but she's also turning into a mother. And while the archetype of a mother is someone sweet, nice, and nurturing, mothers are also fierce, wildly protective, and strong as hell.

Pregnancy is not for the faint of heart. It can be hard and scary and uncomfortable, as well as miraculous and beautiful. And *all* of that deserves to be captured.

## When to Schedule

Maternity sessions are best when scheduled between 28 and 36 weeks of gestational age. By 28 weeks, most women are showing and have a big enough bump to showcase their pregnancy in a portrait. They also tend to be more comfortable and can hold poses longer than a woman who is farther along. Some women, however, want to wait until their bump is really showing and will schedule closer to their due date. For these women, I advise scheduling before their 36th week.

Babies are considered term by 37 weeks, and while most deliveries take place around week 40 or 41, it is not uncommon to go into labor early. If a woman goes into labor at 36 or 37 weeks, her doctor will not try to stop it, and she will deliver. And you don't want your clients to miss the opportunity to capture this special time. When working with women who are carrying multiples, I encourage them to come in between 24 and 32 weeks, depending on their comfort. Women with multiples tend to deliver early, and again, you don't want anyone missing out on their portraits!

# How to Prepare

To prepare for the session, advise your clients to stay away from wearing anything that will leave a mark or indentation on their skin. When pregnant, women retain a lot of extra water. Things like elastic waistbands, socks, and elastic hair bands worn on your wrist will leave a mark that will take a long time to disappear. I advise my clients to wear a light-fitting dress and sandals the day of their session, and, if they feel comfortable, no panties or bra. I want their skin to be as smooth as it can be for their photos.

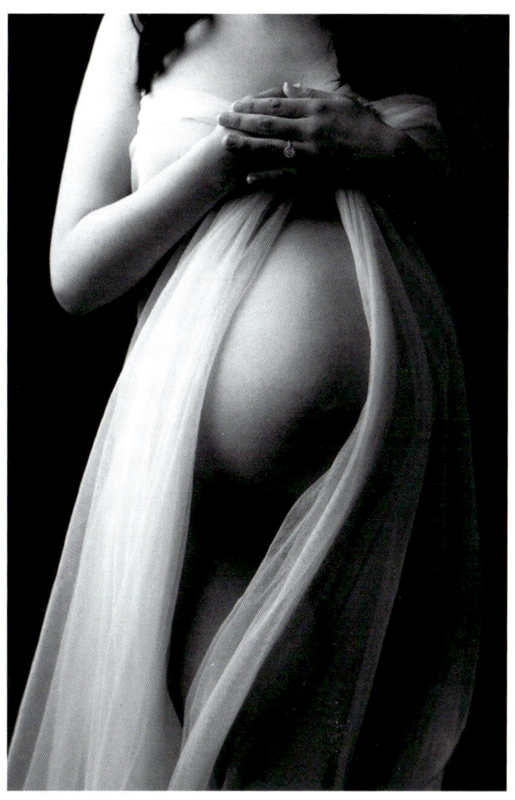

**FIGURE 10.1** Notice how the play of light and shadow on the skin helps accentuate the shape to the belly.

## Nude, Draped, or in Clothing?

I prefer photographing my maternity clients draped or nude, rather than in an outfit. As we'll discuss later in this chapter, clothing absorbs light and can take away from the shape of the body. When nude or in a drape, light reflects off the skin, making it much easier to see curves (**FIGURE 10.1**).

I provide draping for my clients, and my clients often do the entire session either in the drape or in nothing at all. My favorite drape is literally drapes—sheer curtains I get from Ikea! They are inexpensive and washable (win/win), but any sheer fabric will do.

If your client does want to bring an outfit or two to the session, let them know the tighter the better! Loose fitting maternity clothes and dresses hide the shape of the body whereas tighter clothing clings to curves and photographs better (**FIGURE 10.2**).

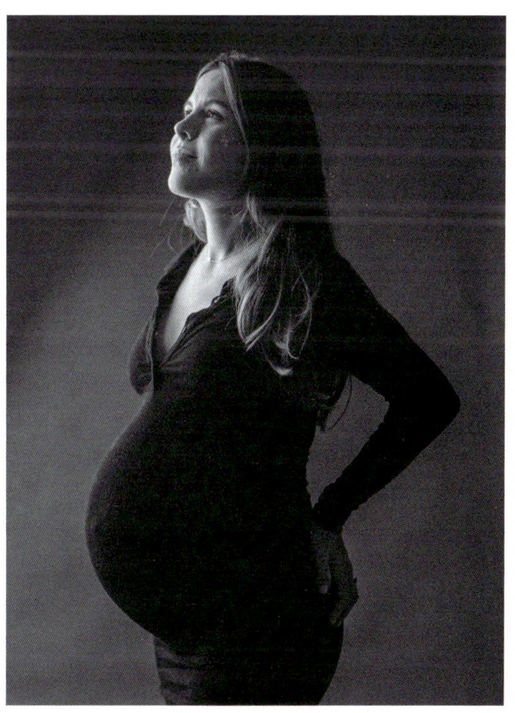

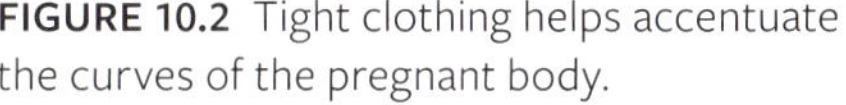

**FIGURE 10.2** Tight clothing helps accentuate the curves of the pregnant body.

## How to Drape

I love incorporating draping into my maternity sessions. It provides coverage while still allowing light to fall beautifully across the client's skin, creating depth, highlights, and shadows. I use my drape two ways: open in front (**FIGURE 10.3A**), or open in back (**FIGURE 10.3B**).

Before draping your client, ask them to remove their bra and underwear. This allows for a smoother, more natural look in the final images and saves time in post-production by eliminating the need to edit out visible undergarments. You can layer and fold the draping fabric to provide more or less coverage based on your artistic vision and your client's comfort level.

### Open in Front

Opening your drape in the front will showcase the belly and create a soft, flattering frame around your client's body. It offers more coverage than a full nude (covering the backside and legs) while still highlighting the pregnancy in a timeless manner.

To create this look, wrap the fabric across your client's back and bring it forward just under the arms. I often tell my clients to imagine wrapping themselves in a towel after a shower. Bring each side of the drape to the front and loosely cross it over the breasts. Ask your client to hold it in place using their palms rather than gripping it with their fists—this looks more relaxed and elegant.

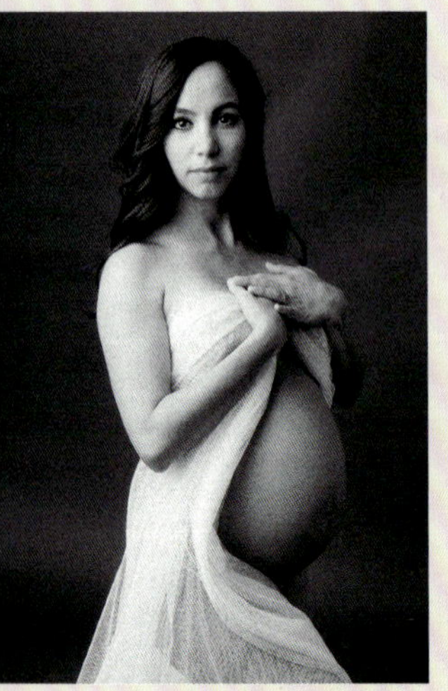

A

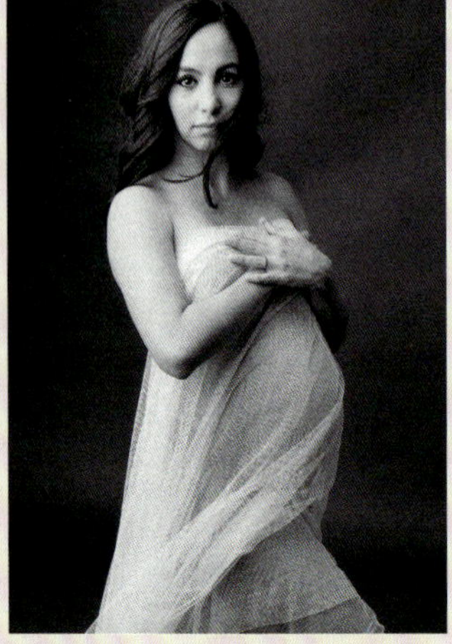

B

**FIGURE 10.3** My go-to draping styles: Open in front (**A**) and open in back (**B**).

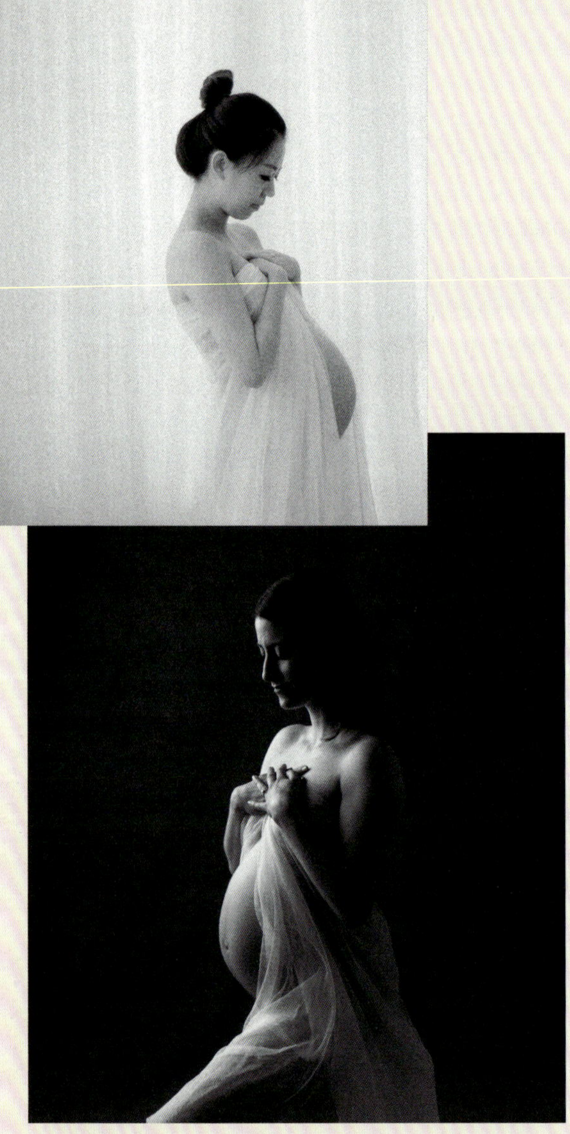

**FIGURE 10.4** Open-in-front draping

Once the fabric is secured, open it to expose the belly. Take a moment to adjust as needed, creating folds for coverage and shape. Direct your client to bend the knee closest to you and wrap some of the drape around that leg for added visual interest and modesty.

## Open in Back

For the open-in-back look, reverse the drape so that most of the fabric wraps around the front of the body, covering the belly while leaving the back exposed. (I tell my clients to imagine putting on a hospital gown.) You can cross or twist the fabric at the back and tuck the ends in securely. Although the back won't be in the frame, securing it may help your client feel more comfortable. Alternatively, you can let the fabric fall naturally to the side, adding softness and movement to the image. Adjust the front as needed for coverage and shape, based on your client's comfort level and your desired look. Folding the fabric will make it appear more opaque while a single layer creates a sheer, ethereal look.

**Pro Tip:** Using a fan while photographing a draped client adds subtle texture and shape to the fabric. I used a fan in **FIGURE 10.5A** to create movement and folds in my draping. This helps the fabric follow the curves of the body, emphasizing shape while providing coverage. It also gives the image a touch of magic—and who doesn't love a little extra magic in their photographs?

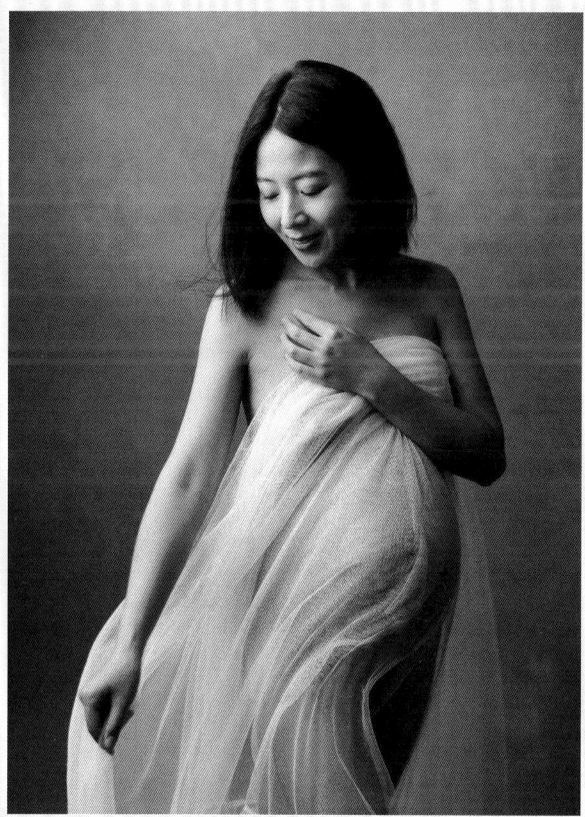

A

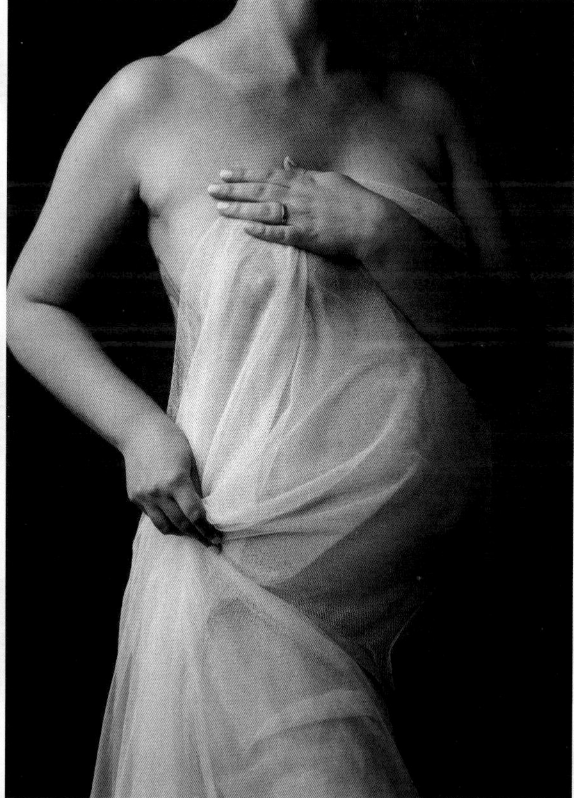

B

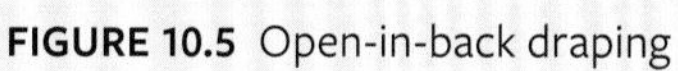

**FIGURE 10.5** Open-in-back draping

## Safety

I am not a medical professional, but I've worked with pregnant women long enough to know that anything can happen when you're expecting. I've had women go into labor at their session, and I've had women miss their session because they went into labor and delivered early. Scheduling your clients in the 28- to 36-week window helps avoid some of these situations, but preterm labor is also a risk and is a very serious condition—something I know first-hand.

I went into labor with my twins at 22 weeks. Luckily, we caught it early and were able to stop it. But that situation landed me on hospital bed rest until I delivered at 36 weeks. I know just how scary preterm labor can be, and I take it very seriously.

Some poses, especially poses that require a pregnant woman to arch her back, look pretty, but can sometimes cause sciatic pain (nerve pain that runs from the back down the leg), or trigger contractions. Sciatica is not dangerous (just very painful), but contractions can be.

Most of the time, contractions are a normal part of pregnancy. A lot of women experience what are called Braxton Hicks contractions—mild, irregular contractions that are thought to prepare the body for labor. These are often harmless, but my experience with preterm labor taught me that *all* contractions have the potential of leading to labor. So, I make sure the poses I place my clients in can be comfortably held without putting stress on the body.

I use mostly standing poses for this reason and encourage my clients to tell me if any pose causes discomfort. Contractions are not always painful—they can present as a sudden feeling of dizziness, a "hot flash," or just feeling "off." If my clients feel any of those symptoms, we stop. Photos are not worth putting a mother's or baby's health at risk.

Keep water on hand for your clients, as dehydration can cause contractions as well. Also, remind your clients not to lock their knees—this is a common reaction when feeling nervous, but it can cause fainting during pregnancy.

## Body Position

As you learned in Chapters 8 and 9, when photographing babies and children, posing is all about working within the child's developmental stages to make the most of a moment. We don't worry so much about posing "rules," because babies and young children can't follow them.

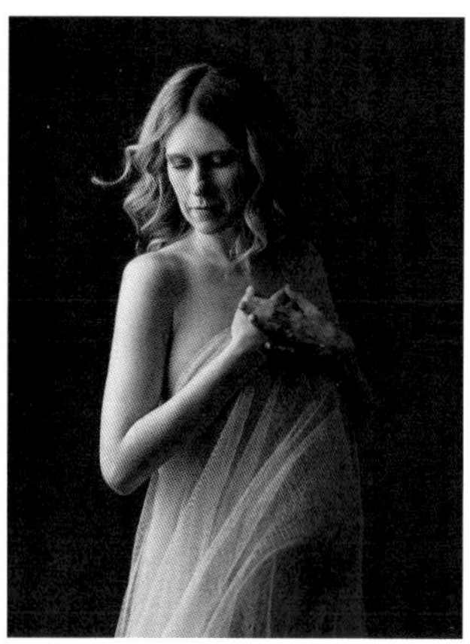
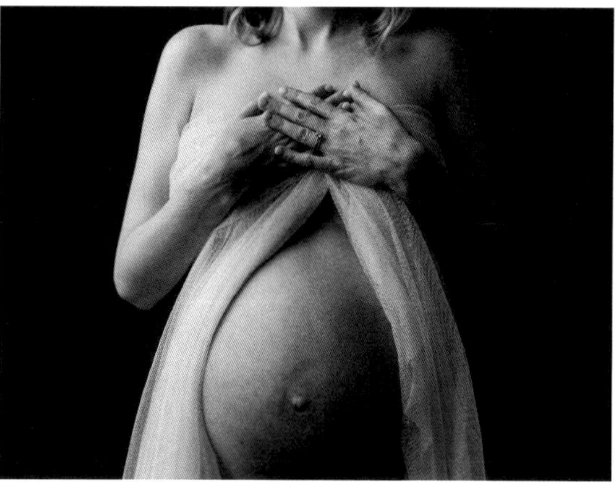
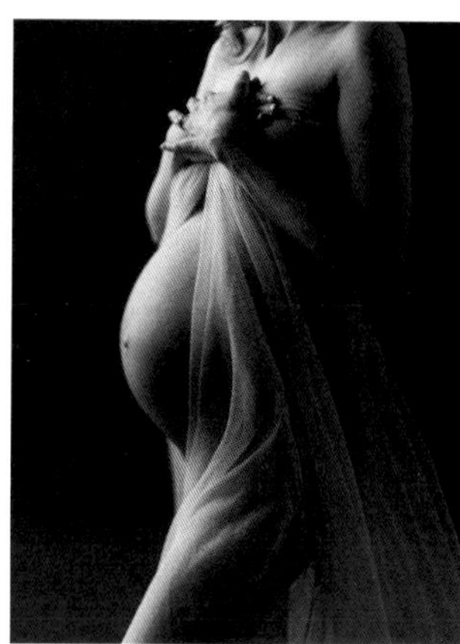

**FIGURE 10.6** My standard maternity posing flow. From left to right, my client is standing at a 3/4 profile to my right; facing the camera; and standing at a 3/4 profile to my left.

That is not the case with maternity posing. Maternity clients are adults who can follow directions and hold a position. Yay! That allows us to work within a set of guidelines to ensure that we are creating flattening images.

That said, my core poses are very simple. As I shared in Chapter 7, I always start with my client standing at a 3/4 profile to me, turned to my right. From there, I have her face the camera, and then I turn her 3/4 to my left (**FIGURE 10.6**). I make these positions interesting and flattering by making small adjustments to her posture, stance, and arm placement, and with my use of light (which we'll explore in detail in Chapter 13).

## Posture

While I'm not a fan of perfectly straight posture in family work, I do encourage it with my maternity clients. When pregnant, women are a little heavy in front, which causes a tendency for leaning slightly forward. I talk about this with my clients. When posing, I ask them to imagine that they are being pulled up by an invisible string that is attached to their sternum. This encourages them to lift their chest, roll their shoulders back, and stand up straighter.

I also advise my clients to arch their back a little to lift their belly, with the clear instruction to stop if it causes pain or contractions. Safety first!

## Body Angles in Maternity Posing

When posing a maternity client, I position them in profile at a ¾ turn toward the camera or facing the camera directly. All three can result in beautiful portraits, but there are some important things to keep in mind when directing your client's body position.

### How We See vs. How Cameras See

Our eyes see the world differently than a camera does. When we look at a three-dimensional shape—like a pregnant belly—we naturally perceive its depth. So, if a pregnant woman is standing in front of us facing directly forward, we still register the roundness of her belly because we see in three dimensions.

Cameras, however, flatten what they capture into two-dimensional images. As a result, we can lose some of the shape and depth that are visible in real life. In maternity photos, this can make a subject look wider rather than pregnant—not the look we're going for!

This is especially important to keep in mind when your client is wearing darker clothing or loose fabric. These materials tend to absorb light and reduce the highlights and shadows that help define form, making it even easier to lose the contour of the belly in the photo.

Posing your client in profile or turned ¾ is one way to solve this problem. In **FIGURE 10.7**, my client is wearing a black dress that looked amazing on her in person. But when she faced the camera directly, the black fabric absorbed light, and we lost much of the definition and shape of her pregnant belly. She ended up looking more wide than pregnant, as you can see in **FIGURE 10.7A**. In **FIGURE 10.7B**, I asked her to rotate slightly into a ¾ position. That subtle shift brought dimension back into the photo, showcasing her curves and pregnancy, and resulted in a stunning portrait.

**FIGURE 10.7** Both images were taken moments apart using the same lighting pattern.

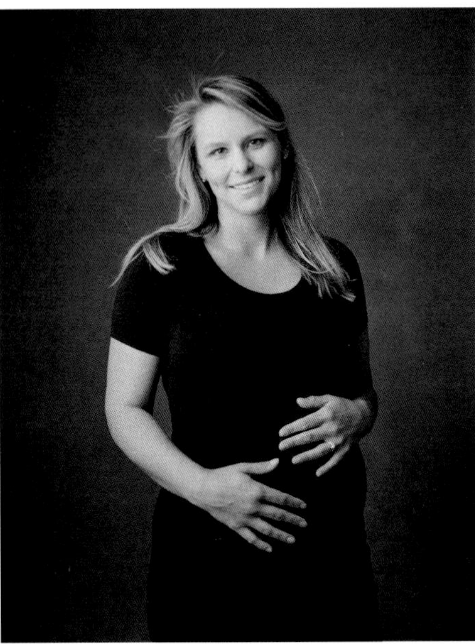

A

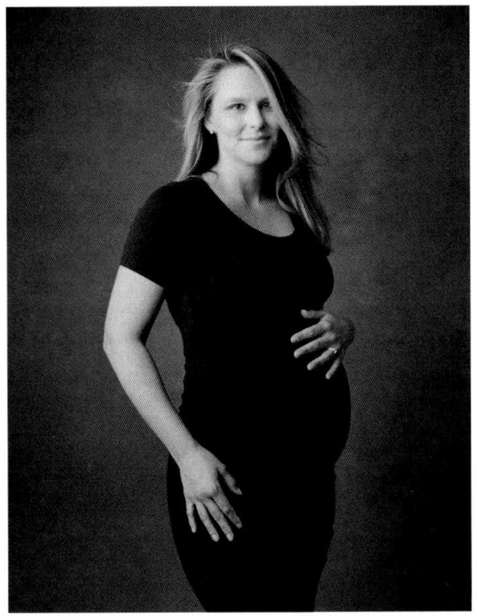

B

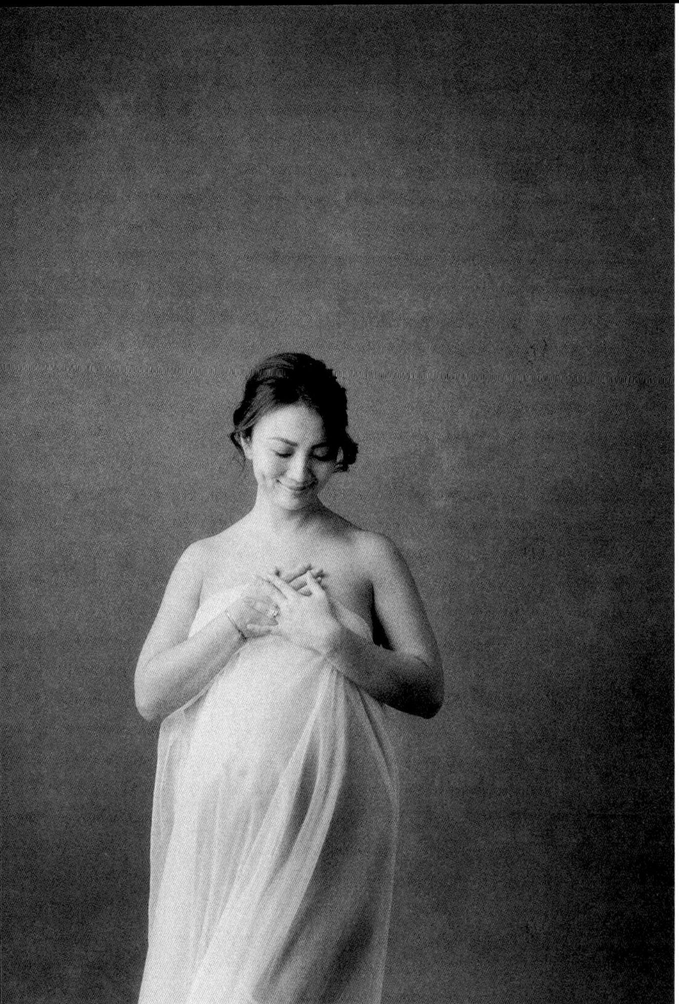

A

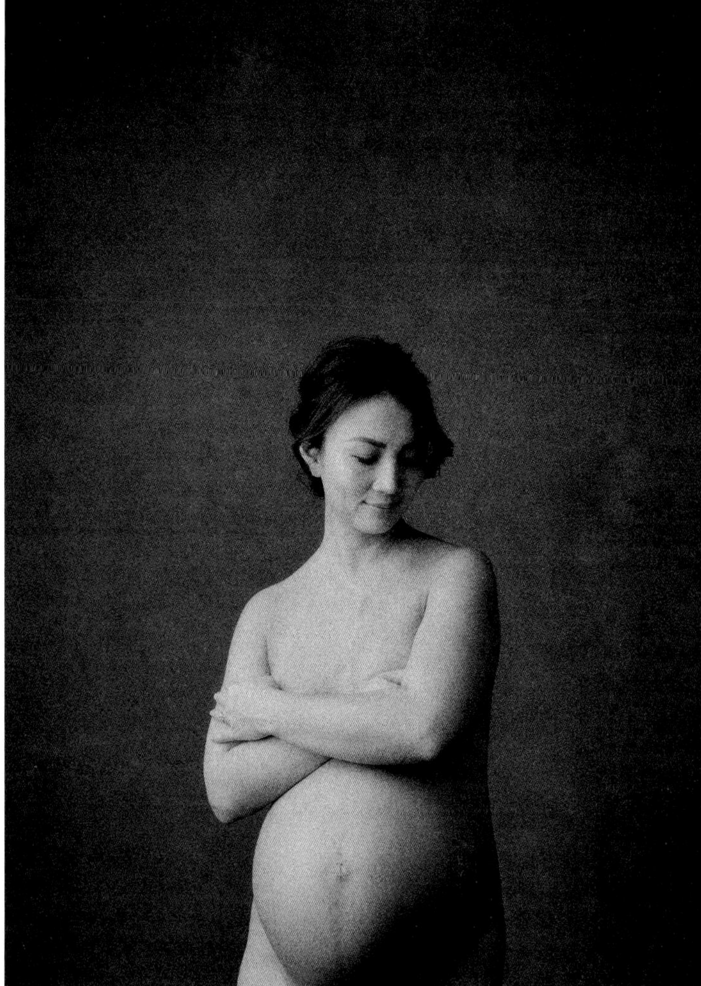

B

**FIGURE 10.8** Both images were taken moments apart using the same loop light pattern. In Figure 10.8A, my client was facing the camera, wrapped in a loose drape that covered her belly. The light reflected off the fabric rather than her skin, giving us very little play between highlight and shadow, and we lost the shape of her belly. In Figure 10.8B, I removed the drape. With her skin exposed, the light was able to wrap around her body, creating highlights and shadows that emphasized her shape—and resulted in a stunning portrait.

If you don't want to turn your client to the side, you can bring dimension back into a front-facing image by photographing your client nude or in a drape that exposes the belly. This will allow the light to reflect off the skin, adding highlights and shadows that will emphasize the shape. **FIGURE 10.8** is a great example of this. These images were taken moments apart with the same loop light pattern.

**Pro Tip:** This may be obvious, but when photographing a nude or semi-nude client who is facing the camera directly, *crop from the bottom of the belly up!* It keeps the image tasteful and focused on what you're trying to highlight.

## Client Comfort

I start my maternity sessions talking to the client about what they can expect at their photoshoot. At that time, I ask them if they are comfortable with draping and/or with nude images. Almost everyone who books a session with me has seen my work and wants the kinds of photos they see in my portfolio—which means nude or draped images. But some do share that they are not comfortable with nudes or draping, and that is fine with me! Client comfort is always my number one priority!

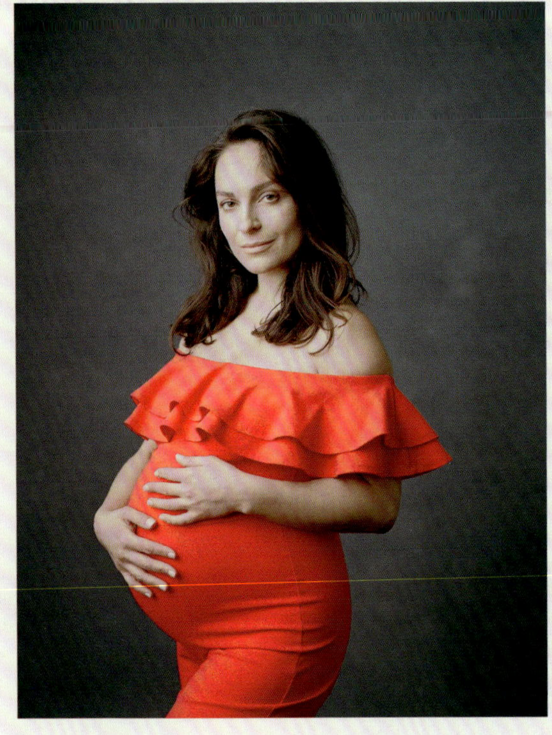

**FIGURE 10.9** Some clients prefer to be clothed for their entire session, and that is okay with me!

### Legs

Another way to highlight the pregnant form when posing is with leg and hand positioning. When a client is in a profile or ¾ pose, have them bend the knee of whichever leg is closest to the lens. This creates a pleasing shape, creating the illusion of a narrower leg, and provides additional coverage when nude or in a drape (**FIGURE 10.10**).

**Pro Tip:** I offer my clients a block to rest their feet on. This helps lift the front leg while providing stability (**FIGURE 10.11**).

When the client is facing you, have them shift most of their weight onto one leg, then bend the knee of the other leg and pull it to the center. This creates a lovely hourglass shape that accentuates the curves of pregnancy (**FIGURE 10.12**).

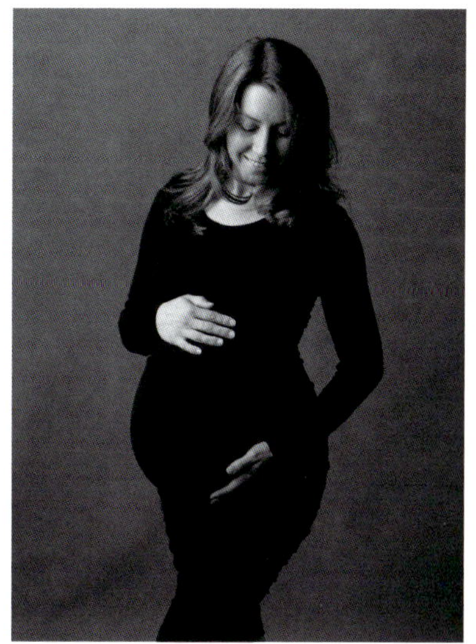

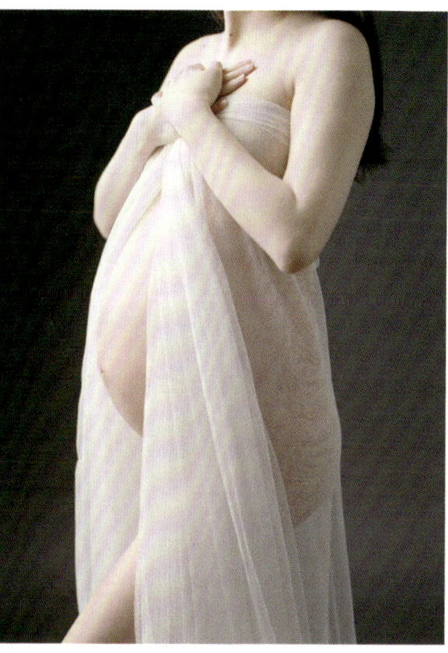

**FIGURE 10.10** In both images, the client bends the knee of the leg closest to the lens while in a profile or ¾ position.

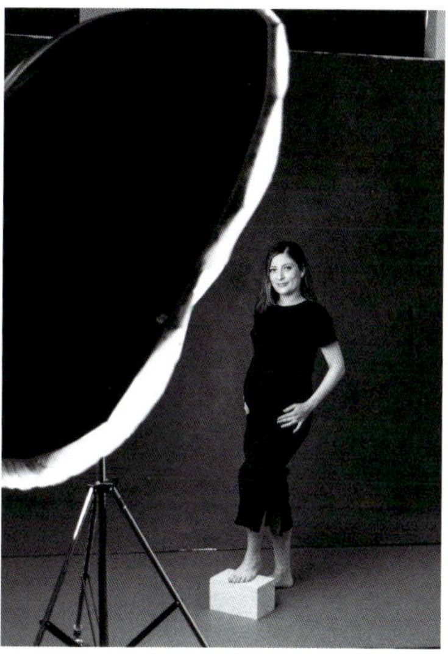

**FIGURE 10.11** Using a block for posing helps lift the front leg while providing stability.

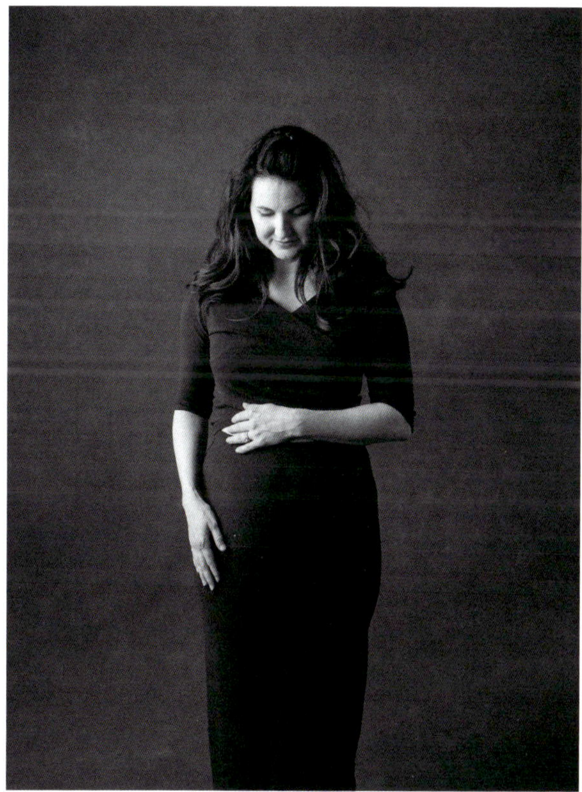

A

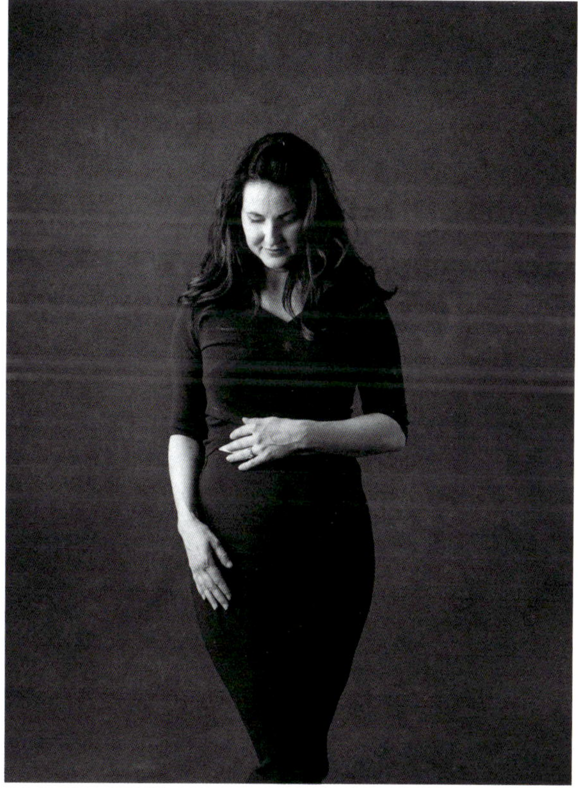

B

**FIGURE 10.12** In Figure 10.12A, both legs are straight. In Figure 10.12B, I had her shift most of her weight onto one leg, then bend the knee of the other leg and pull it to the center, creating a lovely hourglass shape.

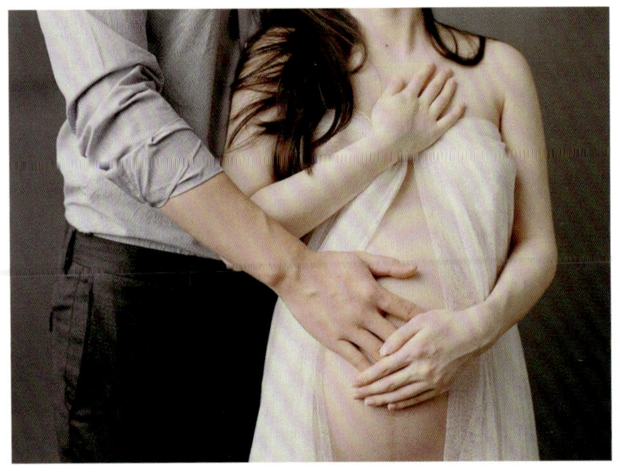

A

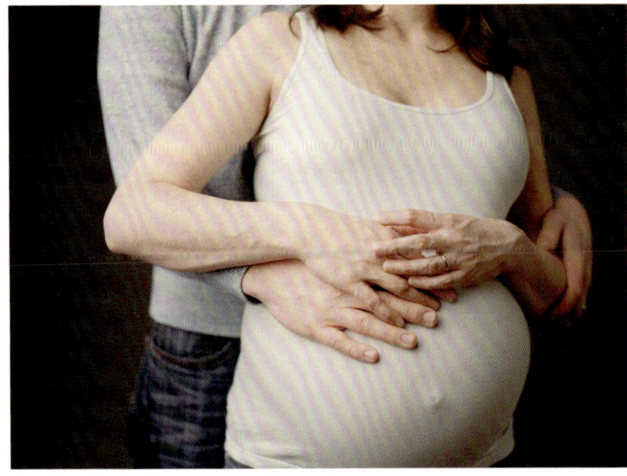

B

**FIGURE 10.13** Figure 10.13A shows stiff Barbie hands, giving the image an overly posed vibe. Figure 10.13B shows relaxed hands, resulting in a photo that looks like a candid moment.

## Hands

As you learned in Chapter 5, hands play an important role in portraiture. They tell us if a client is feeling nervous or relaxed, they can communicate nurturing and concern, and they can be used to accentuate a pose. Remember to be on the lookout for Barbie hands when posing your maternity clients (**FIGURE 10.13**).

## Arms

Like legs and hands, arms can be used to frame and draw attention to the baby bump. But arm placement can also hinder the view of the belly and diminish the impact of a pose. Because cameras flatten what they capture into a two-dimensional image, arms and hands can sometimes get "absorbed" into the shape of the body in a photo, especially when your client is standing in profile. This is important to think about, especially in the profile or ¾ position.

**FIGURE 10.14A** is a great example of this. In this image, the client was posed in profile to show off her pregnant shape, but her arms were left to hang by her side. While we can still see the silhouette of her belly, the shape of her arm was "absorbed" into her silhouette, blocking the curve of her back, and resulting in a photo where she appears thicker through her torso than she actually is.

For **FIGURE 10.14B**, I instructed her to bend the elbow of the arm closest to me and place her hand on the back of her hip. This separated her arm from her body, creating a more dynamic shape, and allows us to see the curve of her back—emphasizing the shape of her belly.

When placing your client's arms, take time to consider how they are contouring the curves of your client's body. Are they accentuating her shape or distracting from it? Slowing down to notice how small adjustments to arm placement impact an overall image is part of the work of "training" your eye (**FIGURE 10.15**). It takes some time, but the effort you put in is well worth it!

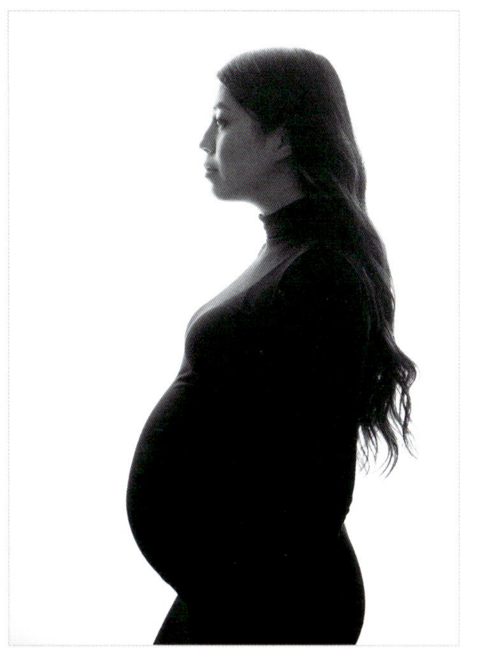

A

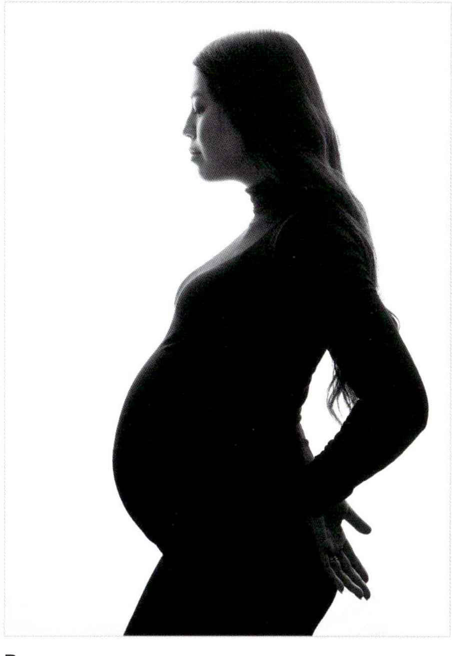

B

**FIGURE 10.14** In Figure 10.14A, the client's arm hangs by her side, blending into her silhouette. The adjustment in Figure 10.14B separates the arm from the body, reveals the curve of her back, and enhances the shape of her belly.

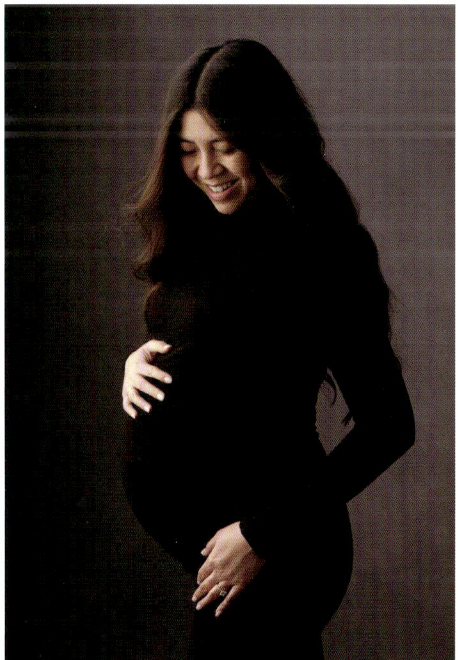

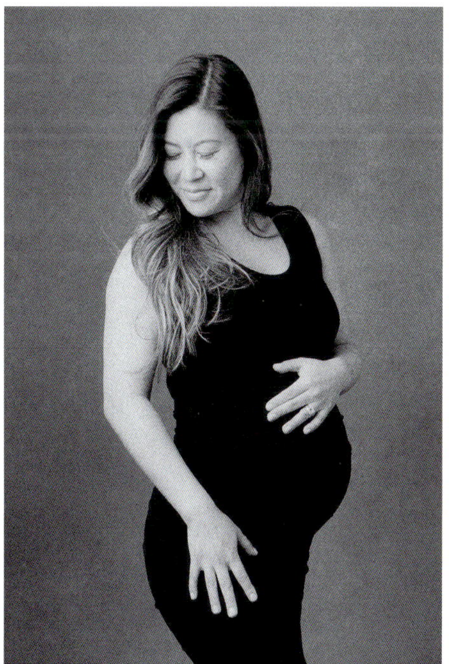

**FIGURE 10.15** In both images, the client bends the arm closest to the camera and pulls the elbow away from her body, creating space between the arm and torso. The curve of the back is visible, and the natural shape of the pregnancy is emphasized.

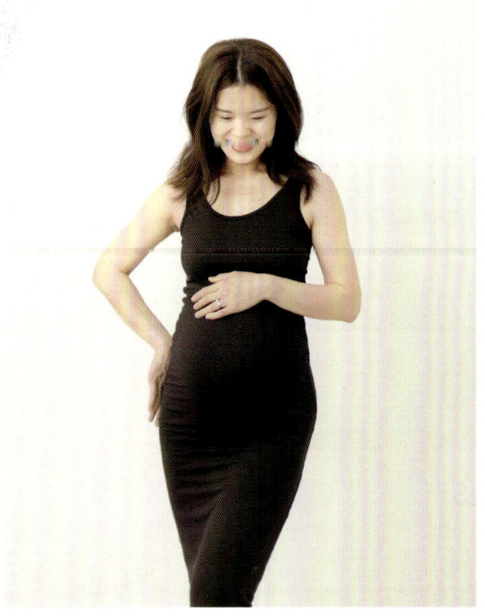

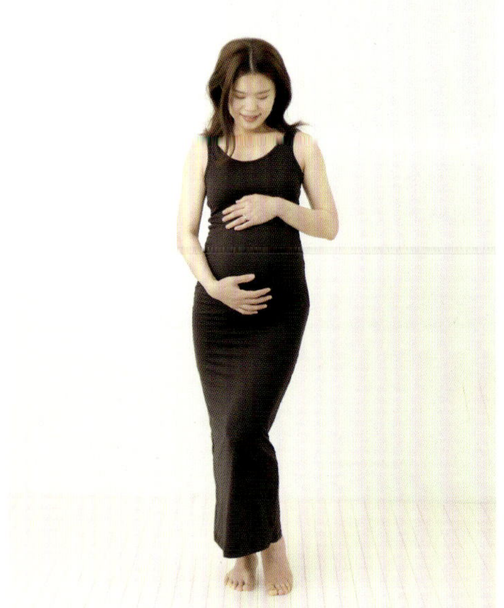

**FIGURE 10.16** When facing the camera directly, lifting the elbows slightly away from the body helps define her shape.

When working with a client that is facing you directly, directing her to lift her elbows slightly away from her body will help draw attention to the belly while also flattering the overall shape of her body (**FIGURE 10.16**).

I also recommend that once you pose your client, take the time to view your client from all angles before taking a picture. Again, this is an important step when training your eye. Not all poses look good from all angles!

For example, having a client drape one arm over the top of their belly, while the other arm cradles it from below is a very popular pose in maternity photography, but it's not flattening from all angles. The images in **FIGURE 10.17** feature this pose, but differences in camera angle dramatically changed the outcome of each image—and not all of them work.

In **FIGURE 10.17A**, my client is positioned ¾ to me. From this angle, her front arm separates slightly from her body, revealing the curve of her back and enhancing the shape of her belly. Her back arm provides separation between the darkness of her dress and the darkness of the backdrop, further accentuating her curves.

In **FIGURE 10.17B**, the hand placement is almost exactly the same as in Figure 10.17A, but from this angle, we only see the back of her hand—no fingers. Her back arm disappears into the silhouette of her body, so all we see are the tips of her finger peeking from behind her belly. From this angle, the pose is a flattened shape that lacks definition and makes the subject's torso appear thicker than it really is. And because we can't see her back arm or the fingers

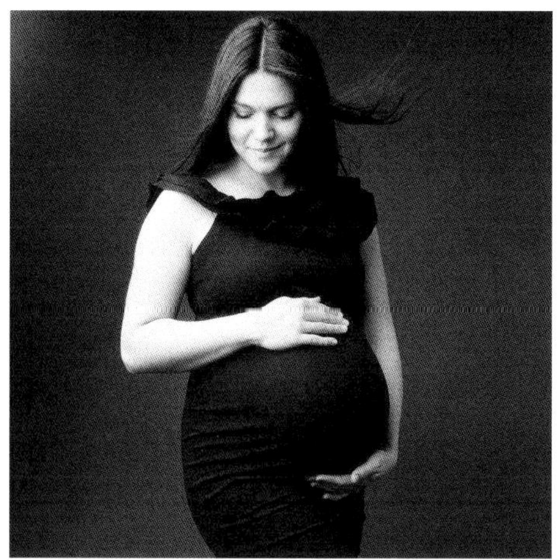

A

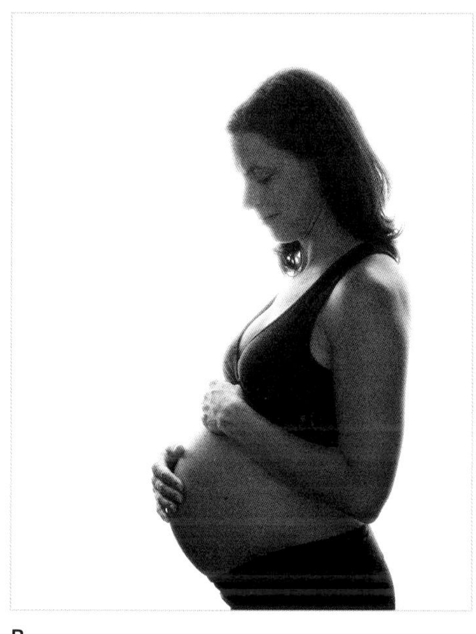

B

C

**FIGURE 10.17** All three images feature the same hand placement, but the camera angle makes a dramatic difference. In Figure 10.17A, the arm separation at a ¾ turn shows off visible curves. In Figure 10.17B, the arms blend into the body. In Figure 10.17C, keeping both arms visible achieves symmetry, balance, and a strong visual of the belly.

on her top hand, we lose the "cradling the belly" effect of the pose. It just doesn't work.

**FIGURE 10.17C** shows the client facing the camera directly—a tricky angle to pull off—but it works here beautifully. The hand placement creates balance and symmetry. Her bottom arm stays visible, running down her side, defining the curve of her belly, while the other drapes across the top, emphasizing her shape and creating a nurturing feel.

Taking the time to view a pose from all angles will help you create a "library" of poses and angles that you know work together. Then add them to your posing flow routine.

## Maximize Your Pose

Throughout the posing section of this book, I've talked about how to make the most out of each pose by changing your angles and composition, and it's no different with maternity posing. Take the time to maximize each of your poses to add variety to your client galleries!

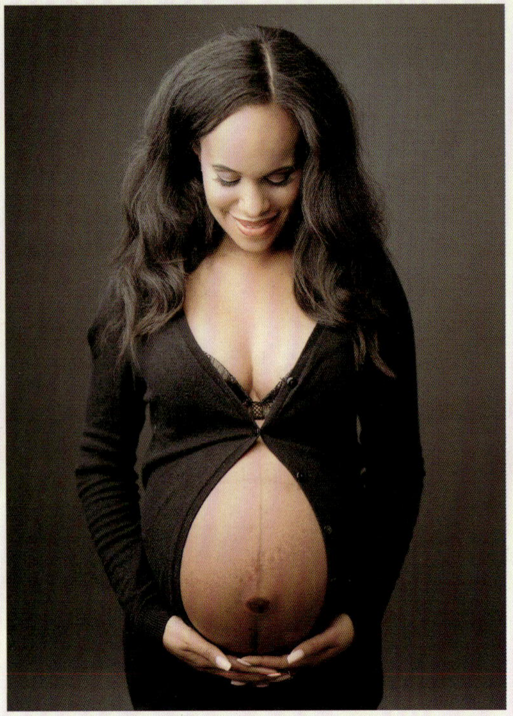

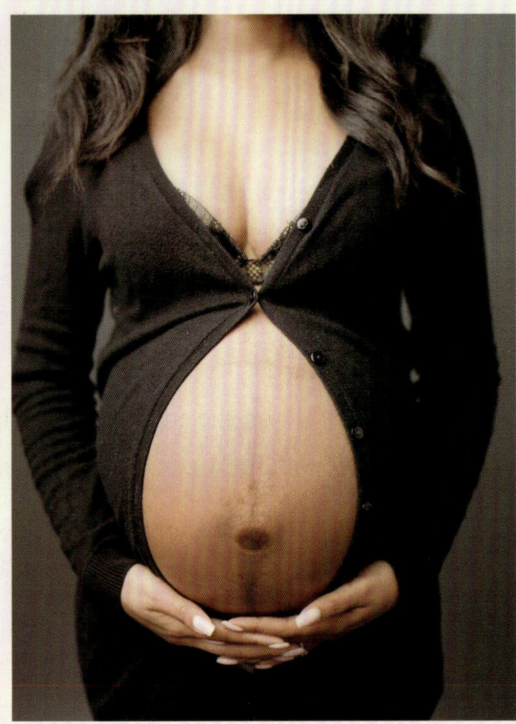

**FIGURE 10.18** Remember to make the most of each pose!

**FIGURE 10.19** Pull-back image illustrating key elements of a standing maternity pose. The client is turned 3/4 to the camera to emphasize her pregnant silhouette. Her front knee is bent to accentuate her curves, and the fingers resting on her belly are relaxed. The opposite arm is bent at the elbow and angled away from her body, allowing the curve of her back to show and further highlight her shape.

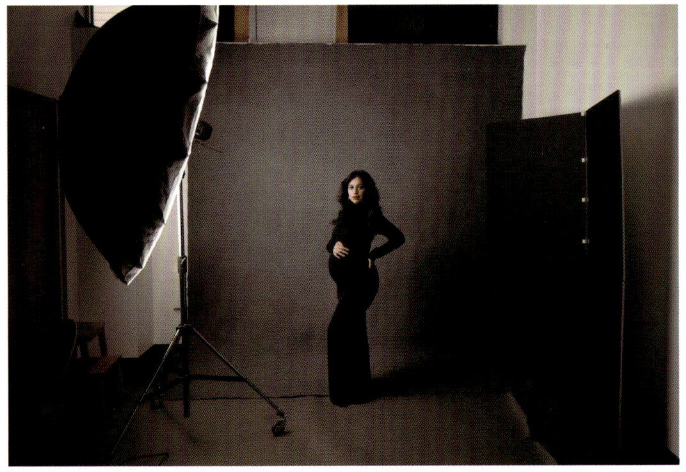

## Sitting and Lying Down

Sitting and lying down poses can be incredibly beautiful. They add variety to your client's gallery and can help your client relax—especially toward the end of a session filled with standing poses. That said, these poses can also be a bit tricky.

When sitting or lying down, the baby bump tends to be less pronounced than when the client is standing. As a result, your client can look "less pregnant" in the photos. By applying the techniques you've already learned in this chapter, you can ensure the belly remains visible and beautifully showcased.

### When Seated, Good Posture is a Must

When sitting, good posture is key. Have your client lift their chest and gently arch their lower back—this naturally elevates the belly and enhances the curve of the body. These poses tend to be most flattering when your client is positioned in profile or at a 3/4 angle to the camera.

I typically have clients sit on the edge of a stool, bench, or bed (as in **FIGURE 10.20**). This helps them maintain an upright position and makes it easier to create a soft arch in the back.

**FIGURE 10.20**
Sitting near the edge of a stool, bench, or bed helps the client maintain good posture and create a gentle arch in the lower back.

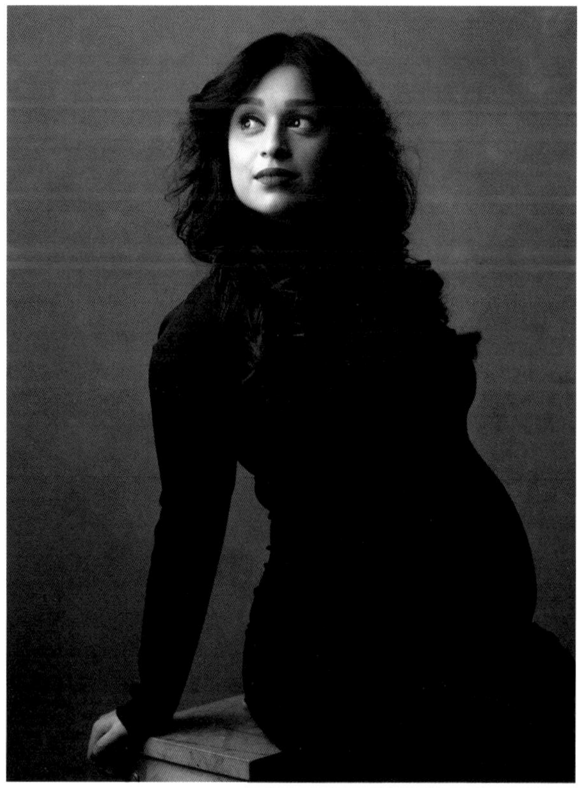

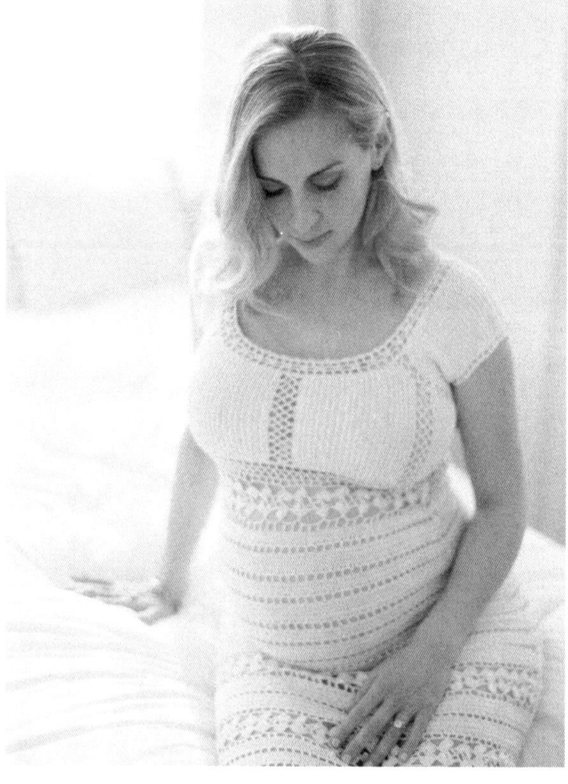

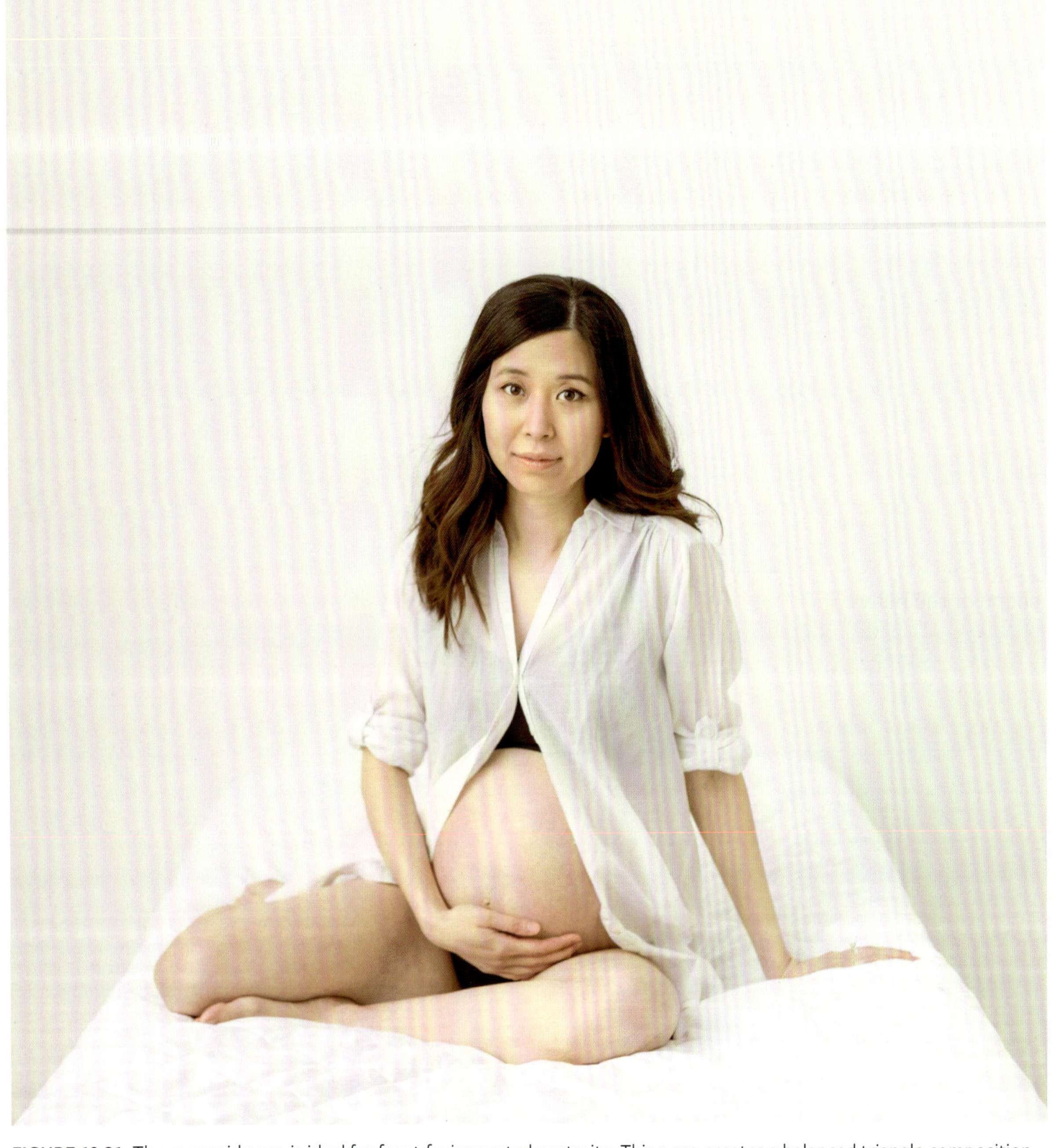

**FIGURE 10.21** The mermaid pose is ideal for front-facing seated portraits. This pose creates a balanced triangle composition that flatters the body and draws attention to the belly.

If they are facing me directly, I'll direct them into the mermaid pose and have them place one arm under their belly and one to the side. This keeps the arms from crowding the belly, helps define their shape, and creates a pleasing triangle shape (**FIGURE 10.21**).

**Pro Tip:** The classic "crisscross applesauce" pose is a popular one in maternity photography, but it's not always ideal. It can be uncomfortable for clients who are closer to their due date, and if your client isn't very far along, sitting like this may obscure the belly completely (**FIGURE 10.22**). If you do choose to use this pose, place a pillow or cushion under your client's sit bones to support better posture. Also, encourage wardrobe choices that expose some skin—this allows you to use light and shadow to emphasize the curves and make the belly more visible.

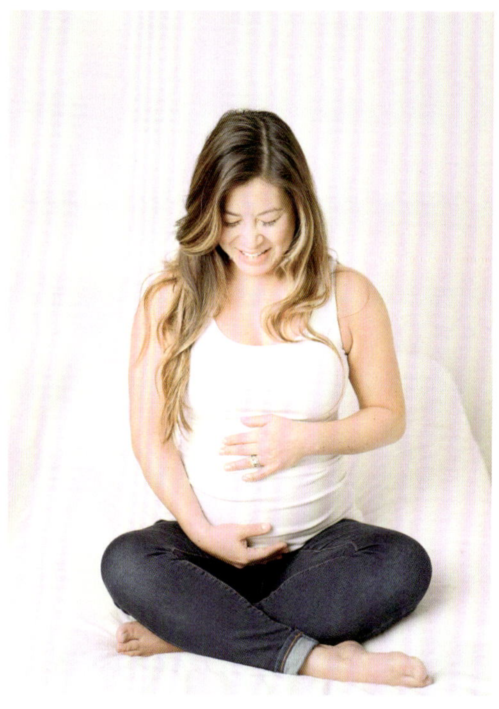

**FIGURE 10.22** Crisscross seated pose is popular in maternity photography, but it can be uncomfortable for clients who are closer to their due date, and if your client isn't very far along, it may obscure the belly completely. As you can see here, we lose a lot of the definition of her baby bump in this pose.

## Lying Down

Lying-down poses can be visually stunning, but like sitting poses, having your clients lie down has the potential of being uncomfortable and diminishing the shape of the belly.

Lying flat on one's back while pregnant creates pressure in the lower back, restricts breathing, and can cause sciatica pain. Lying on the side is often more comfortable but tends to flatten the belly, making it less ideal for showcasing pregnancy.

Because of these challenges, I use lying down poses sparingly. When I do, I have clients lie on their backs with their legs resting up on a wall. This relieves pressure from the lower back and creates a relaxed, visually appealing shape. I also tuck a small pillow under the lower back for additional support.

Once the client is in this position, I work quickly to maximize the pose—shooting from above, from the side, and over their shoulder to get a variety of flattering perspectives (**FIGURE 10.23**).

**Pro Tip:** Remember to pay attention to the details! A simple adjustment like having your client point their toes or soften their hands can elevate the image from good to stunning. These small details bring a sense of polish and intentionality to your work.

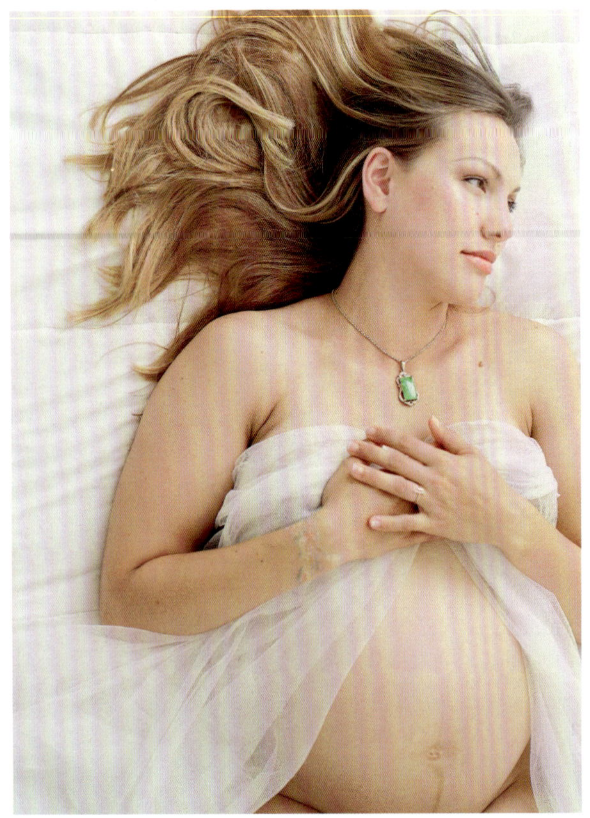

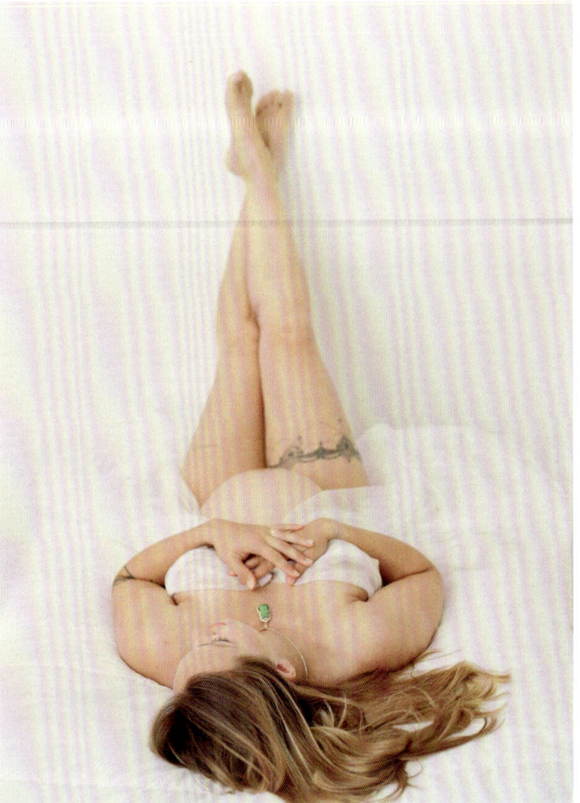

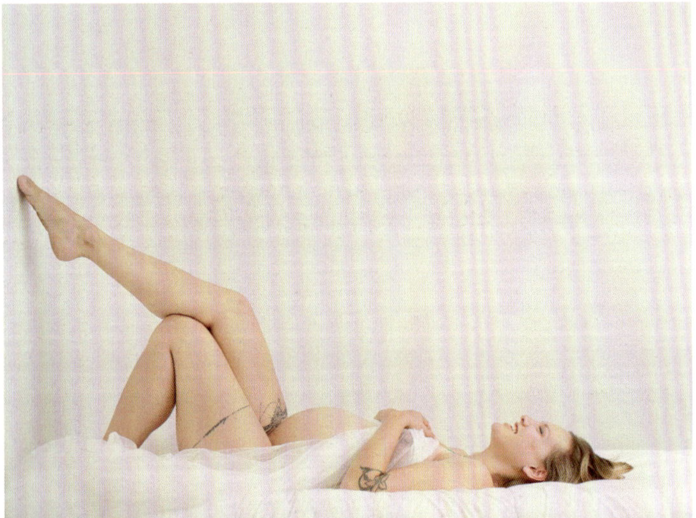

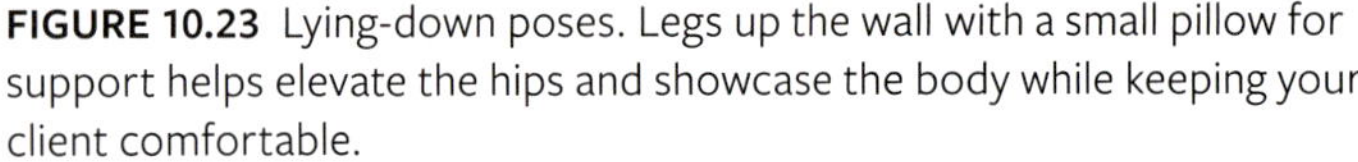

**FIGURE 10.23** Lying-down poses. Legs up the wall with a small pillow for support helps elevate the hips and showcase the body while keeping your client comfortable.

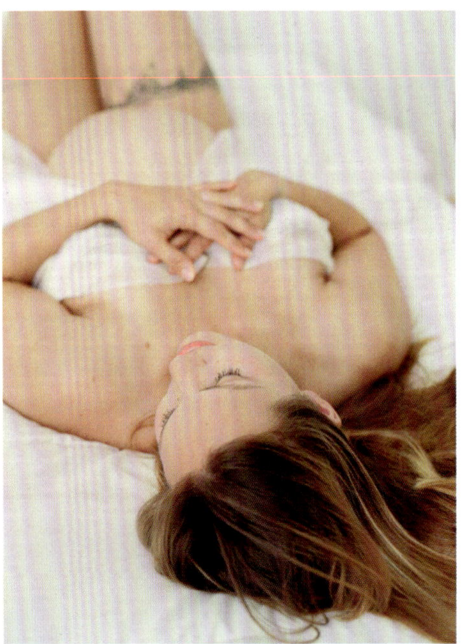

## Posing with Partners

I'm a big fan of adding partners into maternity portraits. It's a lovely opportunity to capture the couple as they begin a new chapter in their relationship. I also believe that every child deserves to have a beautiful photo of their parents joyfully awaiting their arrival. The pregnant mother, however, should remain the star of the show—always place her front and center when posing couples.

### The Senior Prom Pose

I started calling this one the "Senior Prom" pose years ago after a client's partner remarked, "Oh, like senior prom pictures," when I was explaining it. The name stuck. Now I just say Senior Prom pose and almost everyone immediately knows what I mean—which makes it super easy to explain.

To set this pose up, have your pregnant client stand ¾ to the camera. Position the partner behind her, and slightly to one side. Ask the partner to tilt their head toward their partner and place the hand that is closest to the camera on the belly. This will create a pleasing triangle shape and a sense of closeness.

Get a few pullbacks of them looking at the camera and looking down at the belly and get some close ups of their hands on the belly (**FIGURE 10.24**).

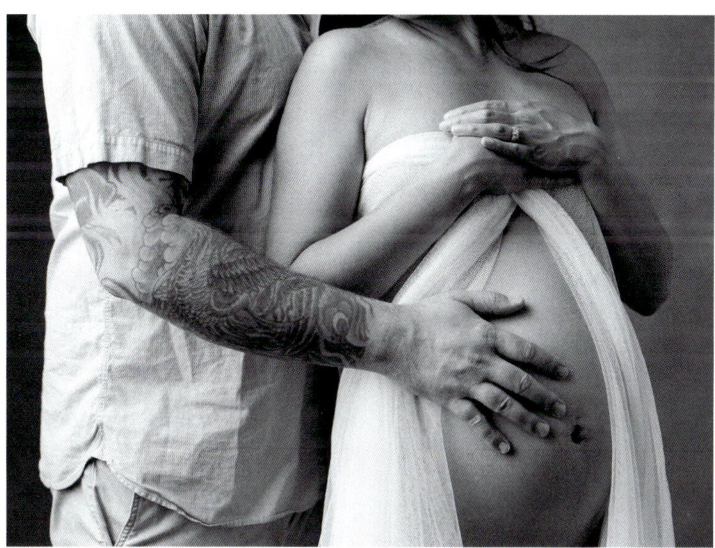

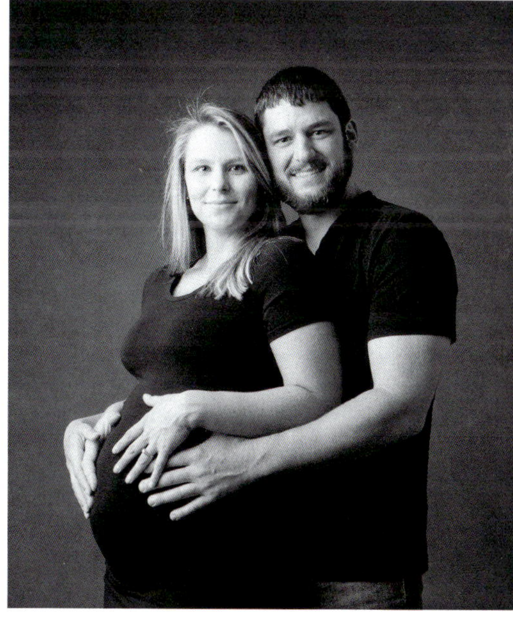

**FIGURE 10.24** Senior Prom pose. This is a timeless, flattering couple's pose.

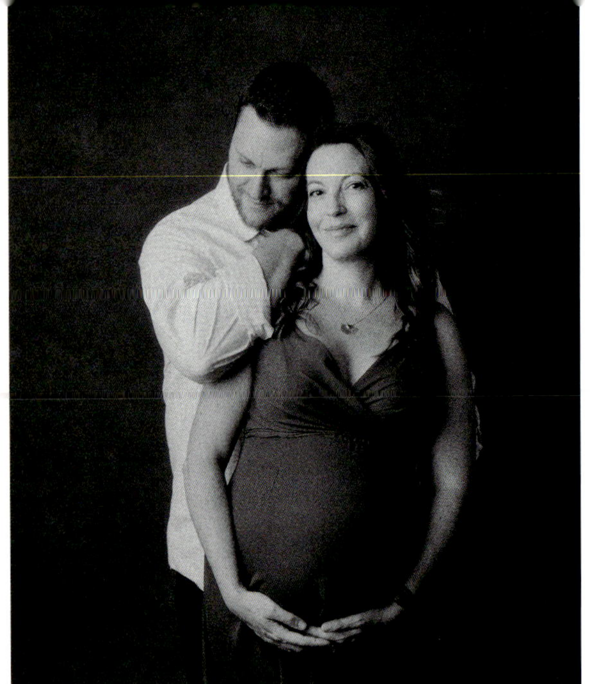

A

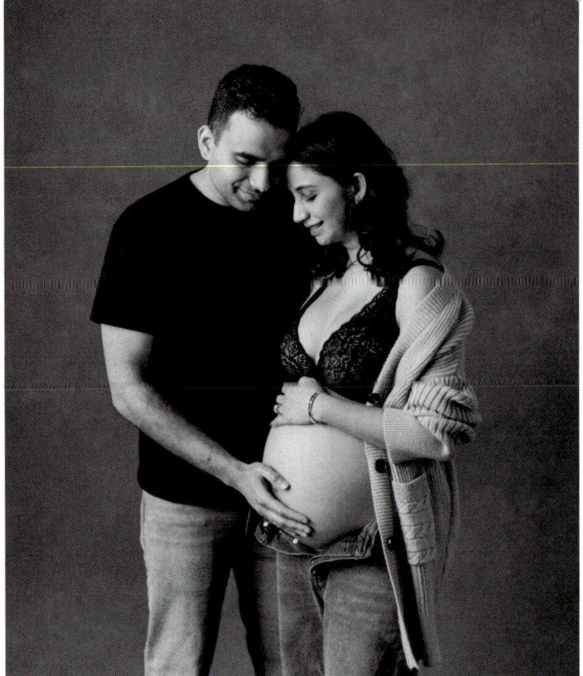

B

**FIGURE 10.25** Both variations of this pose offer a natural, affectionate feel that highlights the bond between the couple.

## Behind the Partner Pose

This is another one of my favorite partner poses. I find it very cozy and sweet. To set this up, pose your pregnant client facing the camera directly. Instruct her partner to stand slightly behind her, offset slightly to one side. If the partner is tall, have them lean slightly forward, resting their arms on their partner's shoulder, and lean into a snuggle position (**FIGURE 10.25A**). Another variation of this pose is to have your pregnant client stand in profile to you, and have her partner stand behind her, slightly off to one side as in **FIGURE 10.25B.**

You can also have the partner stand directly behind her and place a hand on each side of her belly. Zoom in to focus on their hands (**FIGURE 10.26**).

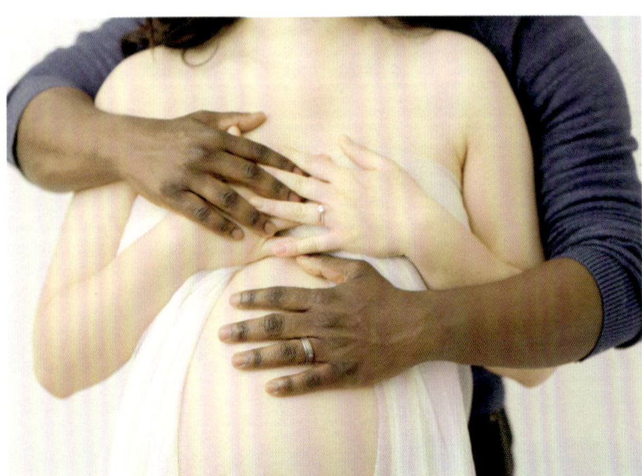

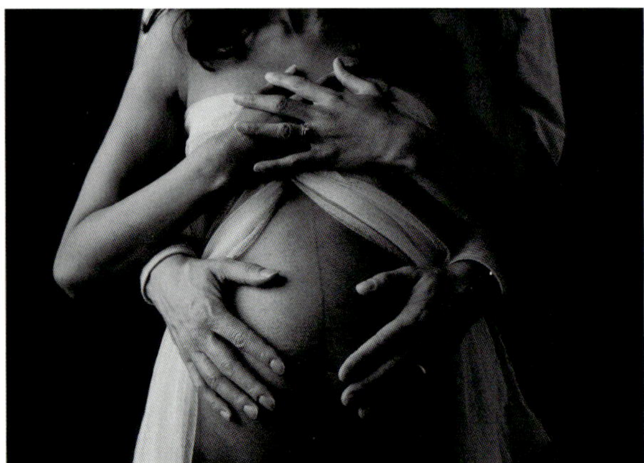

**FIGURE 10.26** Close-up belly poses featuring both parents' hands are a must for every maternity gallery.

## Belly to Belly Pose

Belly to belly is a great pose that works particularly well when using backlight. To set up this pose, stand the couple so that they are facing each other and have them hold hands. I always ask my couple to give each other a kiss when posing like this. It makes for a sweet photo and results in the triangle shape I love so much (**FIGURE 10.27**).

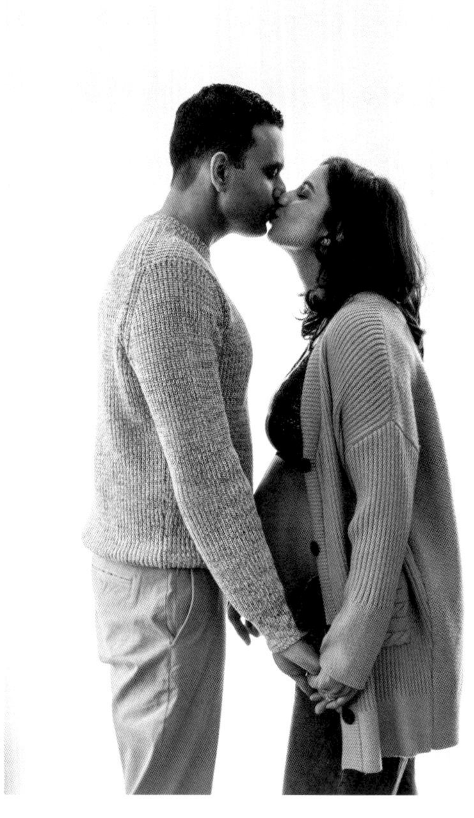

**FIGURE 10.27** Belly to belly. I always ask my couple to give each other a kiss when posing like this.

## Over the Shoulder Pose

I love this pose because it positions the partner as a strong support, highlighting the relationship while also showcases the pregnancy.

Start this pose by positioning your pregnant client facing the camera directly. Direct the partner to stand next to her, with their back to you. Direct them to drape their arm over her belly and across her torso, resting on her back or hip. Have them turn their head toward her (sometimes I'll direct the partner to kiss the top of her head). Have your client hold on to her partner with one hand and wrap the other around her belly. Pull back to get them both in the frame and crop in to showcase your pregnant client (**FIGURE 10.28**).

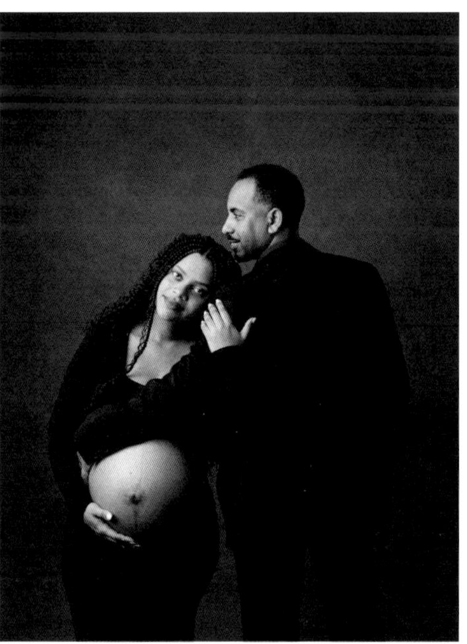

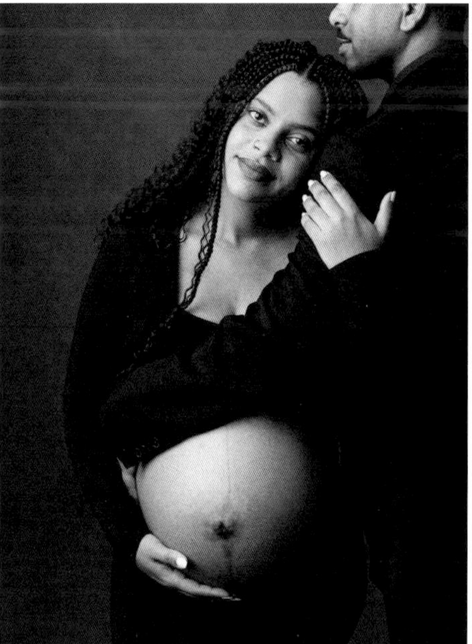

**FIGURE 10.28** Over the shoulder pose.

## Posing with Older Children

Pregnancy is a time of huge transition for the mother, of course, but also for the entire family—especially when there are other children who are about to become older brothers or sisters!

As you learned in Chapters 8 and 9, photographing children—especially young ones—requires extra flexibility. You can't expect a toddler to follow posing instructions the way an adult can. So instead of forcing a pose, I create opportunities for connection. I rely on prompts, interaction, and play to shape the photo.

I always start by posing the mother, and then I bring her child to her to shape the portrait. If your client is sitting, place the older child to one side of her, as in **FIGURE 10.29**. They may want to sit on her lap, but doing so blocks the belly. Placing them to one side provides closeness while also maintaining full view of mom's pregnant form.

If your client is standing and wants to hold their other child, the same rules apply. Ask her to hold the child to one side, as shown in **FIGURE 10.30**.

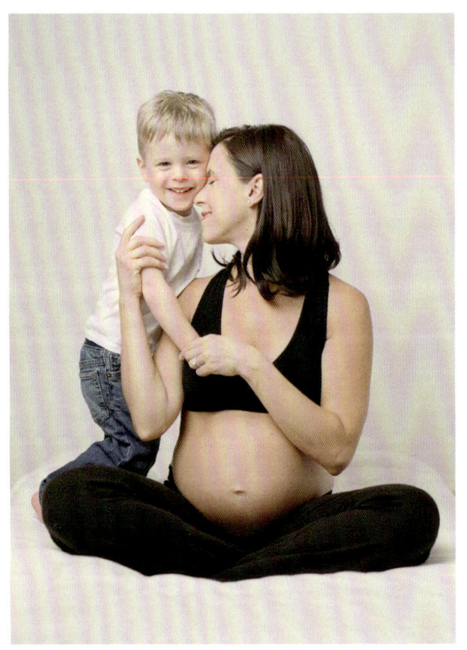

**FIGURE 10.29** Pose the mother first, then add the child into the frame, placing them to one side of her to keep the belly fully visible while still showcasing the bond between mother and child.

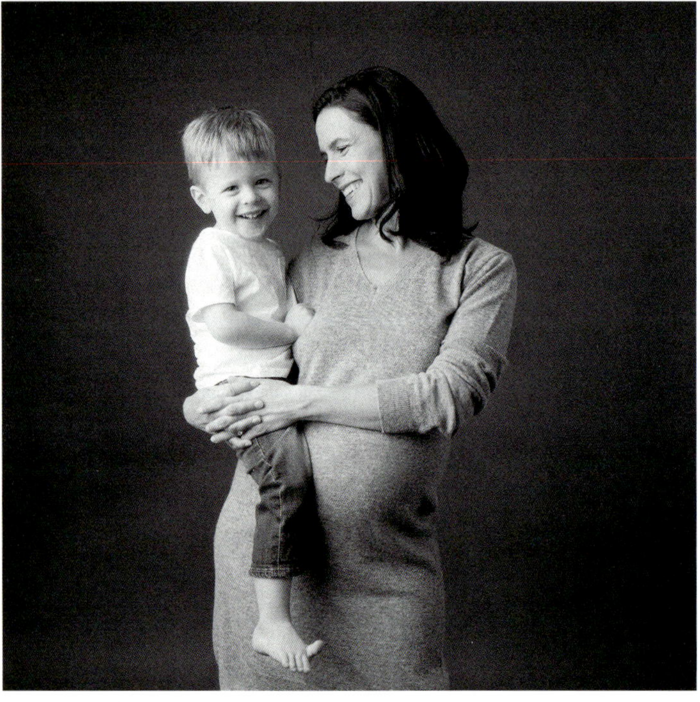

**FIGURE 10.30** The mother holds her child off to one side so her belly is still visible.

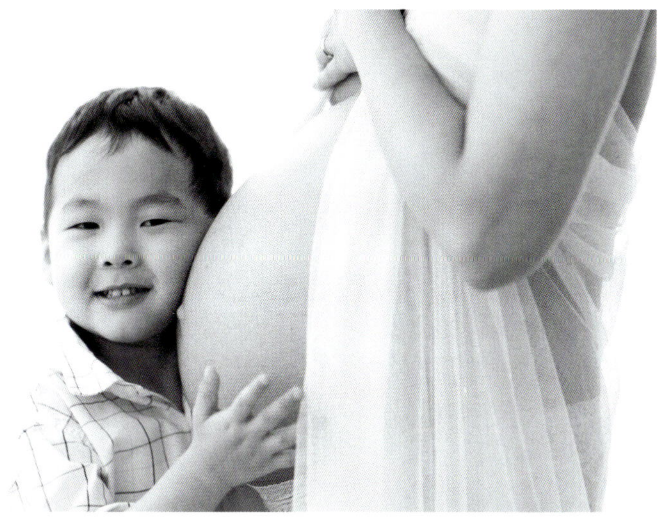

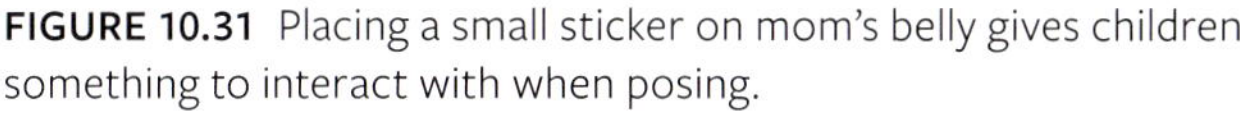

**FIGURE 10.31** Placing a small sticker on mom's belly gives children something to interact with when posing.

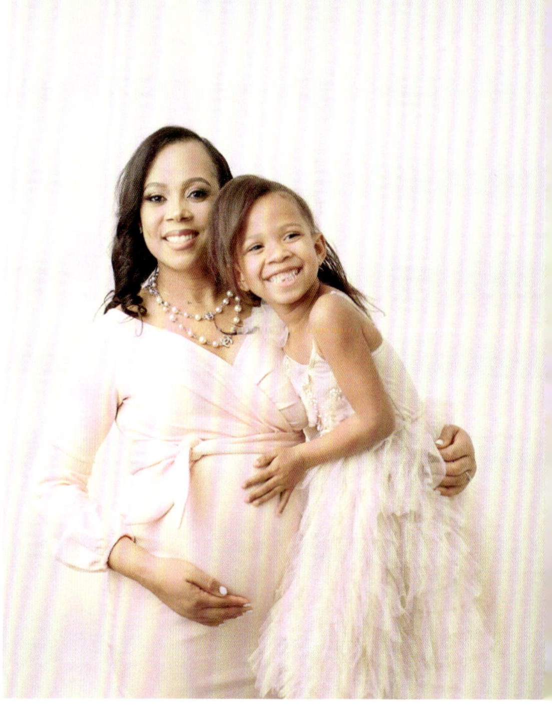

Once mom and child are positioned, direct the mom what to do and where to look. I tell them to smile, snuggle and kiss their child all they want, but avoid talking. Talking can result in awkward looking photos and will also draw the child's attention. Instead, I interact with the child, getting them to look and smile at me.

If the child is old enough to follow directions, try placing a small sticker on mom's belly and ask them to point at it, cover it with their hand, or "listen to it" by pressing their ear to the sticker (**FIGURE 10.31**). This creates the illusion that they are resting their hand or their head on their mom's pregnant belly, which makes for super cute photos.

## Final Thoughts

Maternity photography is about so much more than creating pretty pictures. It's about honoring a moment of profound change. As maternity photographers, we're not just documenting what someone looks like—we're capturing who they're becoming. Have fun with it!

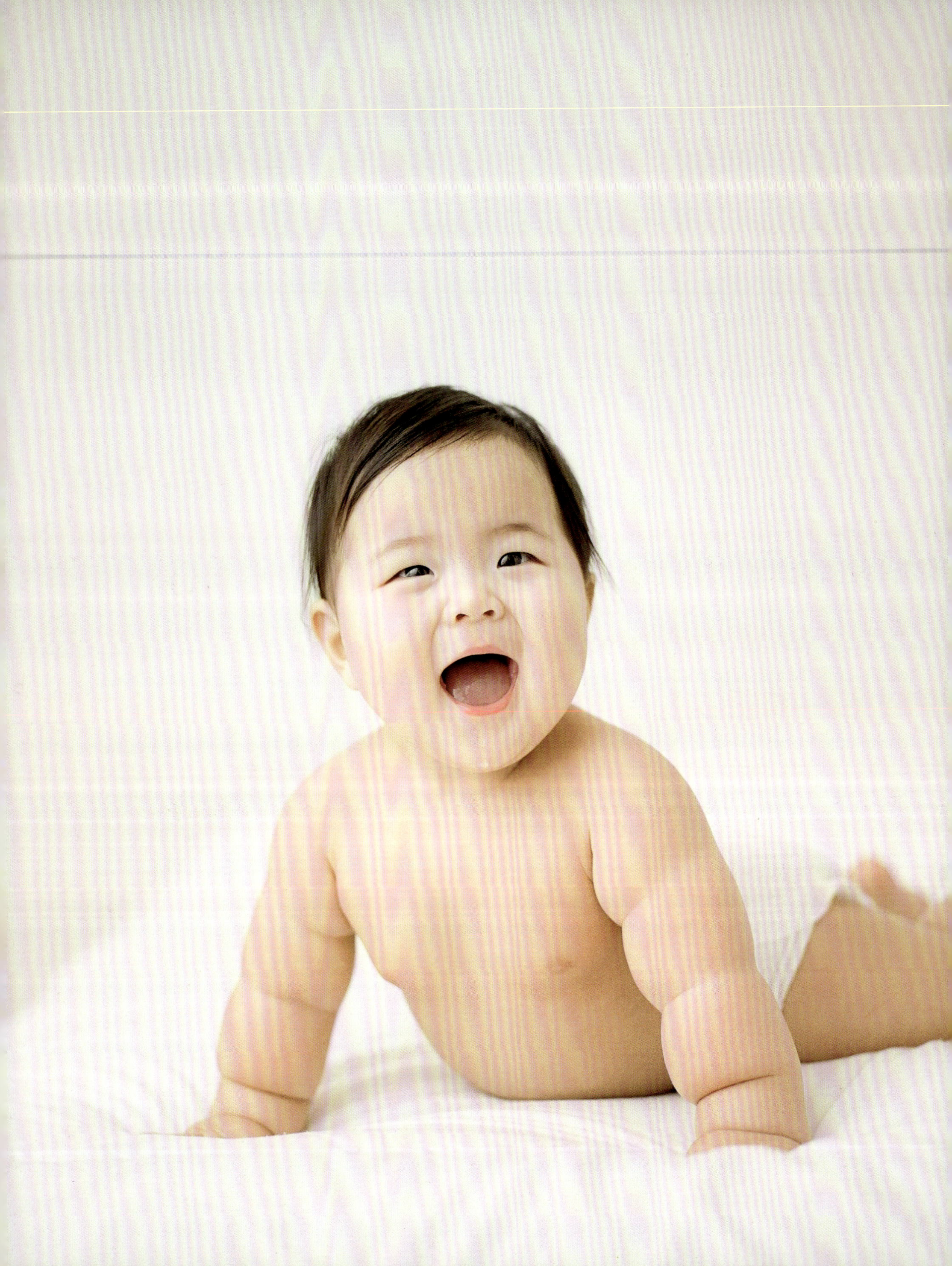

# In Real Life

By now, you know how much I love a consistent, predictable routine. I like going into each session with a clear plan for both my lighting and my posing. I stick to that plan as much as possible because I've learned that structure breeds confidence. It helps me work efficiently, create consistent results, and serve my clients well.

But I also know this: In family photography, every session is different. Kids are unpredictable. Lighting conditions shift. People have different emotions, stories, and energy. No two days—or clients—are ever exactly the same. And that's what makes this work so fun! It's also what makes flexibility essential.

My hope is that everything you've learned in this book has given you the tools you need to adapt, with intention, when needed. You've learned how to work with both natural and artificial light in the studio and on location. You've studied my approach to posing and seen how routine creates room for creativity, and hopefully you've created your own consistent, predictable routine to follow. Now, it's time to bring it all together.

This section is about taking the theory and putting it into practice. It's where we move from the "how" to the "how it actually looks." In the following real-life sessions, I'll show you how I make decisions on the spot. You'll see how I choose lighting setups, adjust my poses, and work with my clients to create connection, consistency, and beautiful photos, even in unpredictable circumstances.

You won't use every lighting technique or every pose that I've covered in this book in every session. And that's okay. What matters most is understanding your tools and knowing how to choose what serves the moment.

My hope is that seeing how I work in real life will give you the insight and inspiration to build your own flow—to adapt, respond, and create with confidence, no matter what each session throws your way.

Let's dive in.

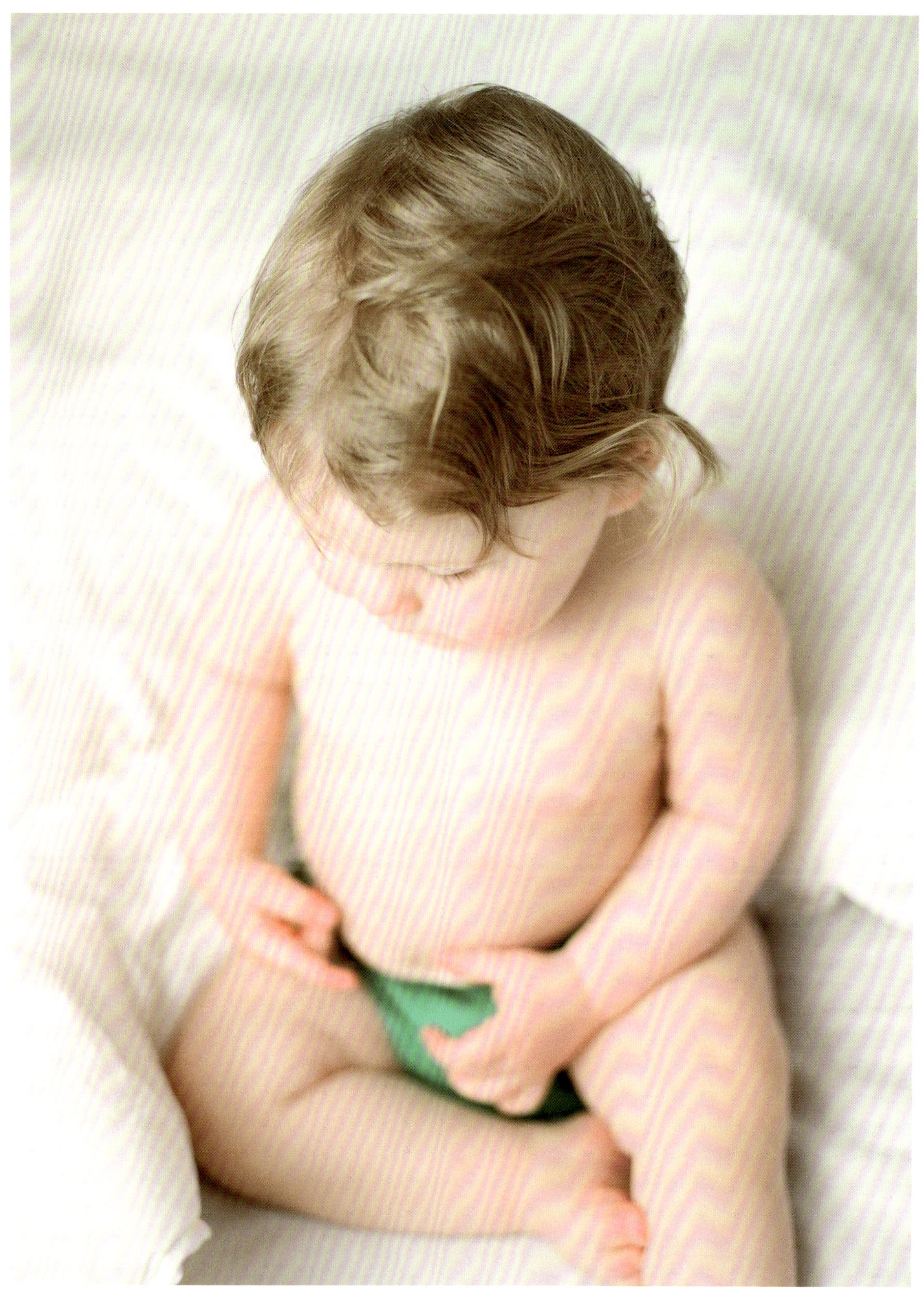

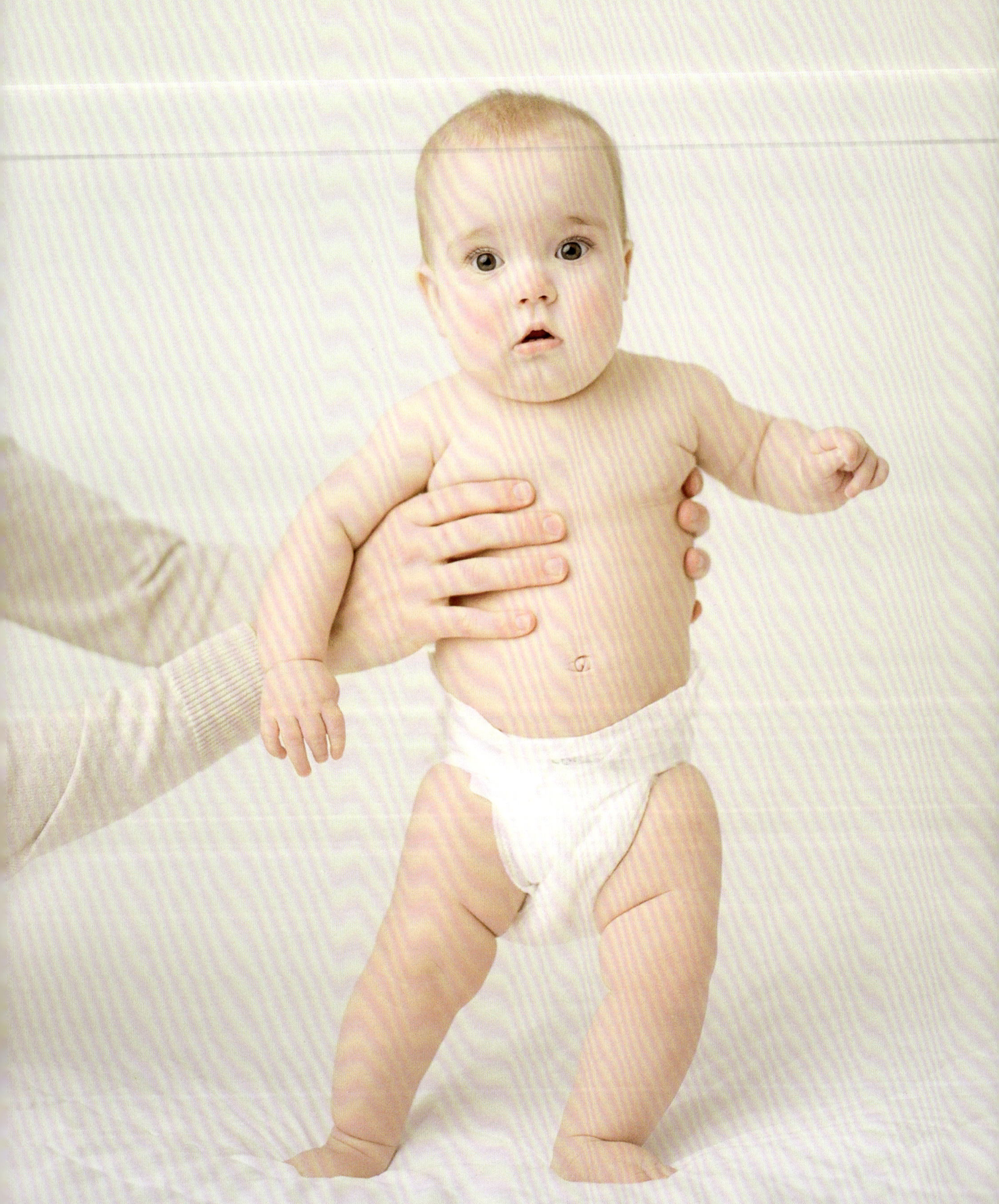

CHAPTER

# 11

# Newborn, Sitter, and Family

This is a session I'm really excited to share because it highlights the benefits of having go-to systems for both lighting and posing flow. When you have a predictable, consistent approach, your sessions run smoothly and efficiently—even when you're working with young children, short attention spans, and the unpredictability of newborns.

## Backstory: The Rosellini Family

I first met the Rosellini family when they came in for a newborn session with their first son. During that session, they shared their incredible story: After years of struggling with infertility, they had welcomed their baby with the help of a surrogate. But shortly before his birth, they discovered the wife was pregnant—a true miracle! That meant their two children would be about six to seven months apart in age.

As the mother of twins myself, I could totally relate to both the joy and the shock of this news. Having two babies at the same time is a blessing, for sure—but it also comes with a unique set of challenges. They asked me during that first session if I'd be comfortable photographing their next newborn and whether I thought I could get images of the two babies together. I said yes (absolutely!) and was thrilled to get their call seven months later.

The session I'm sharing here is from their second baby's newborn session. I chose to feature it because it's a great example of how a simple lighting setup and consistent session flow can help you work efficiently—even when the situation is uniquely challenging.

### The Challenges

Given the ages of both babies, I knew I'd need to work quickly. Babies photographed within the first 10 days of life will typically sleep through most of the session, so I wasn't too concerned about the newborn. But seven-month-olds (sitter-session babies) can tire out fast. Most of my sitter sessions last about 30 minutes, so I needed to get all the must-have images of both children and the family before the older baby became overstimulated or tired.

### Pre-Session Prep

I arrived at the studio about an hour early to prepare the space. I turned on the heat, put fresh linens on the bed, and set up my lights. I also laid out a few age-appropriate toys for the seven-month-old to play with while I worked with the newborn.

I advised the family to arrive dressed and ready to go, and to keep their outfits simple and free of logos or busy patterns. For the newborn, I recommended a front-zip or button-up onesie, which makes it easy for me to undress the baby for diaper-only images, which I prefer.

### Lighting

For lighting, I used my Westcott FJ200 strobe with a 7-foot Westcott Translucent Umbrella and a diffusion panel, set up in the bounce position at a 45-degree angle. This setup (the Sandra Coan Method) produces the soft, natural-light look that I love.

As you will see, once my light is set up, I don't have to touch it much for the rest of the session. That's the beauty of having a simple lighting system—it allows you to focus on your clients instead of fiddling with your gear.

I metered before the family arrived by sitting on the bed where the family would be placed and metering myself. I knew I would be using my digital camera for this session, so I metered for the highlights and adjusted the power on my strobe until I reached my desired aperture. My settings for this entire session were f/4, 1/125 sec., ISO 100.

## Session Flow

Despite the constraints of the session, my goal remained the same—get images of each child alone, each child with each parent, and photos of the entire family together. With that, my flow was:

Sitter alone
Sitter with mom
Sitter with newborn

Newborn alone
Newborn with mom
Newborn with family
Newborn with dad
Sitter with dad

## Sitter Alone

The seven-month-old was at the perfect "sitter" age—sitting independently but not yet crawling. I placed him on the bed with his mom sitting nearby as a spotter (**FIGURE 11.1A**). I started with some wide shots of his whole body, then moved in for tight headshots.

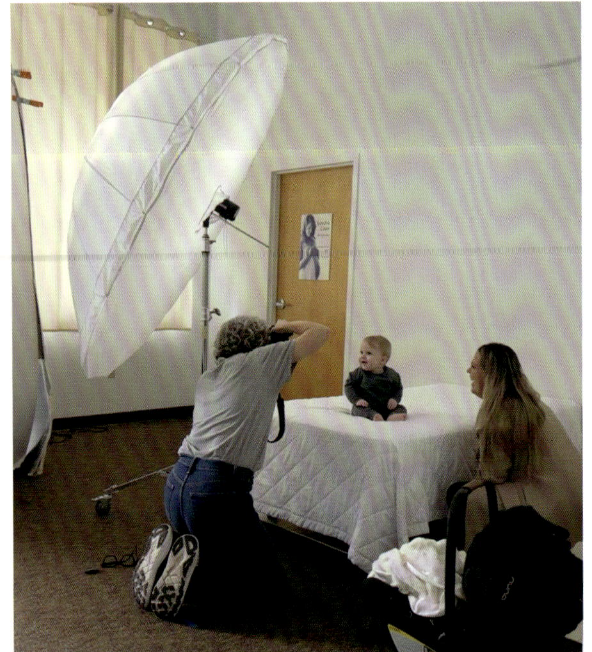

A

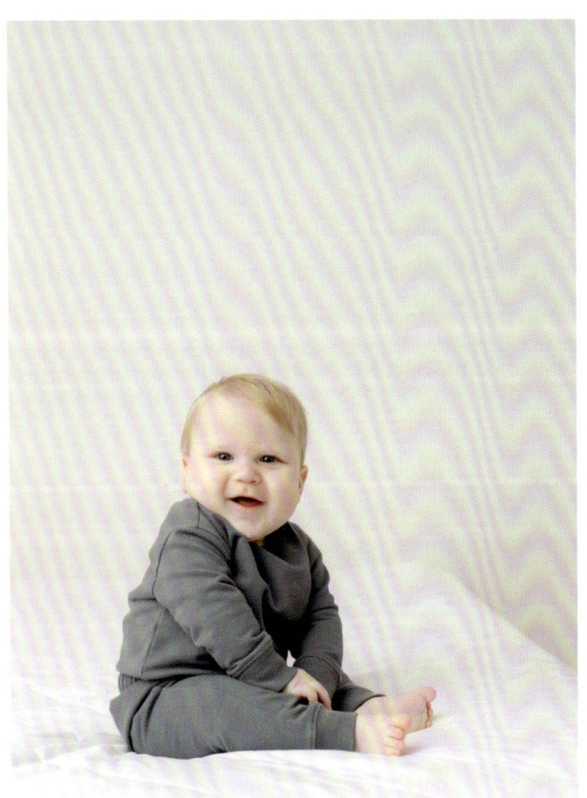

B

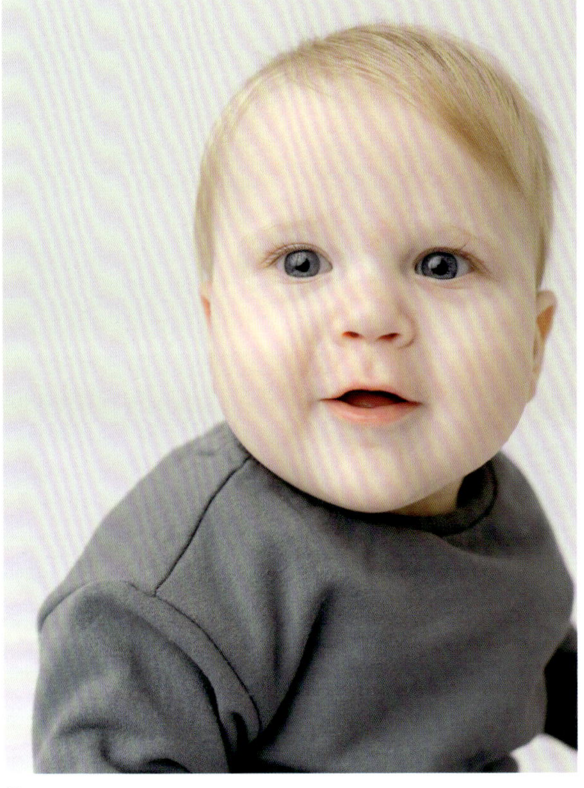

C

**FIGURE 11.1** The seven-month-old sitting independently on the bed with mom nearby as a spotter.

## Sitter with Mom

Once I had a good variety of solo images, I invited his mom to join him on the bed (**FIGURE 11.2A**). I created a mix of "candid" and posed images by directing the mom on where to look and what to do.

As you learned in Chapter 8, sitters are extremely social—and this baby was no exception. He was very engaged with me, offering lots of sweet smiles (**FIGURE 11.2B**). He also kept checking in with his mom, often looking up to make sure she was still there, which led to some incredibly endearing moments (**FIGURE 11.2C**).

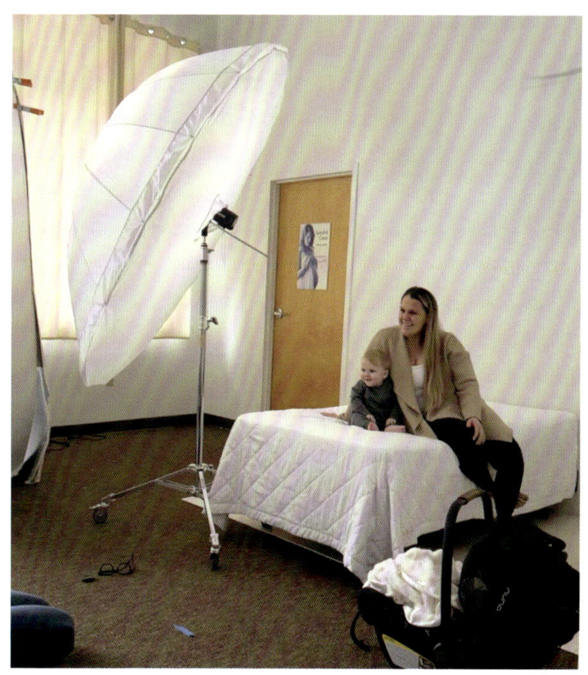

A

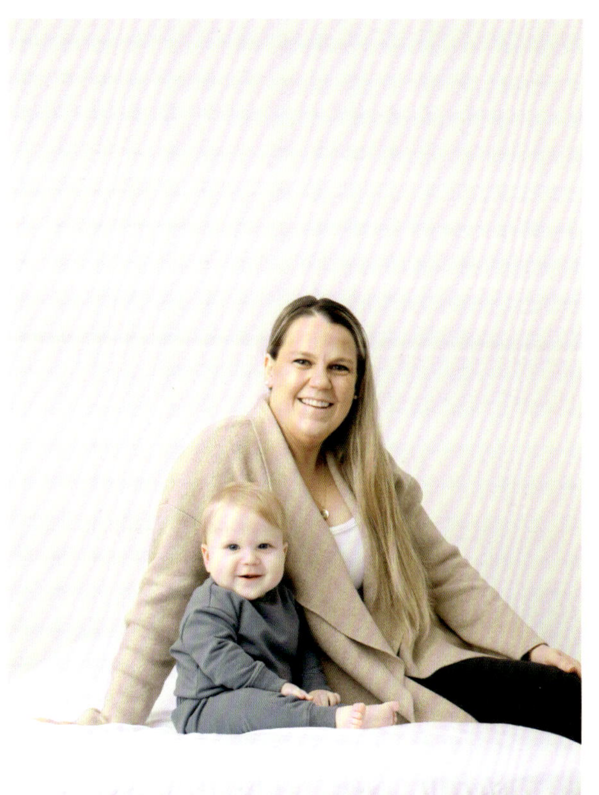

B

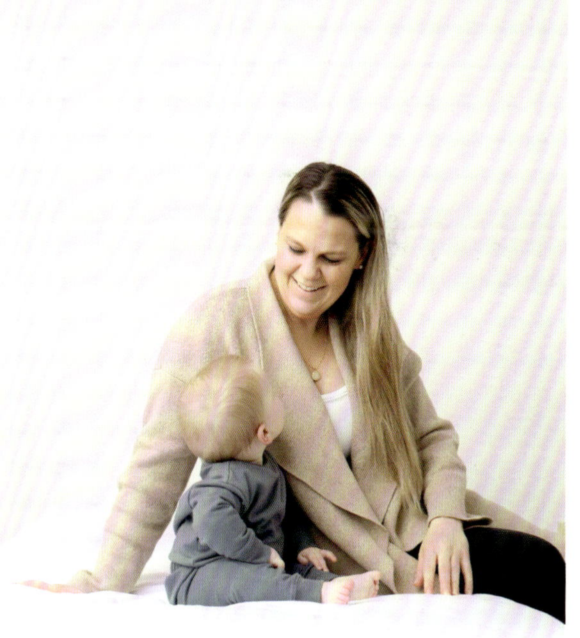

C

**FIGURE 11.2** Sitter with mom

## Sibling Photos

After the solo sitter, and sitter with mom photos were done, we took a short break while I transitioned to working with the newborn. I removed his onesie while he was still in his car seat to keep him calm and sleepy, then I gently positioned him on the bed in the Baby on Belly pose (**FIGURE 11.3**). I could have taken a few photos of him by himself at this point, but I was aware of his seven-month-old brother's timeline and wanted to make sure we got some good sibling photos, first. I grabbed an image of him sleeping peacefully (**FIGURE 11.3E**) and then invited his brother into the frame.

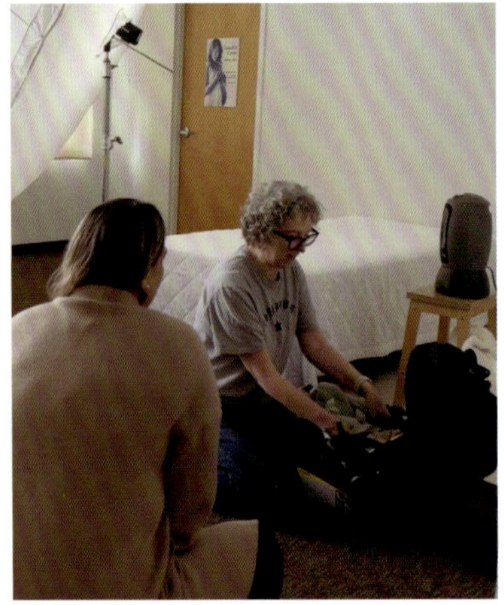

A

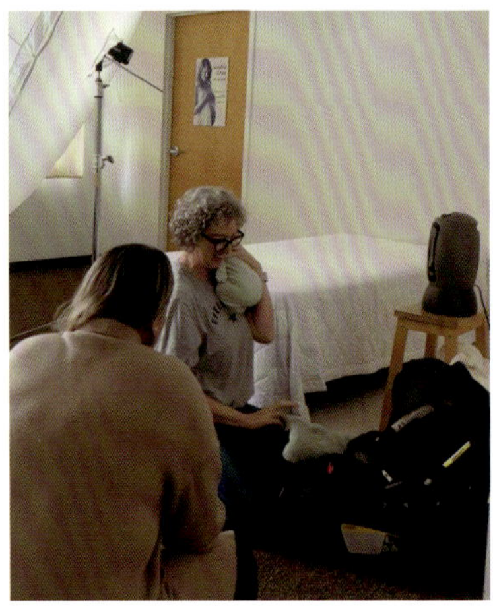

B

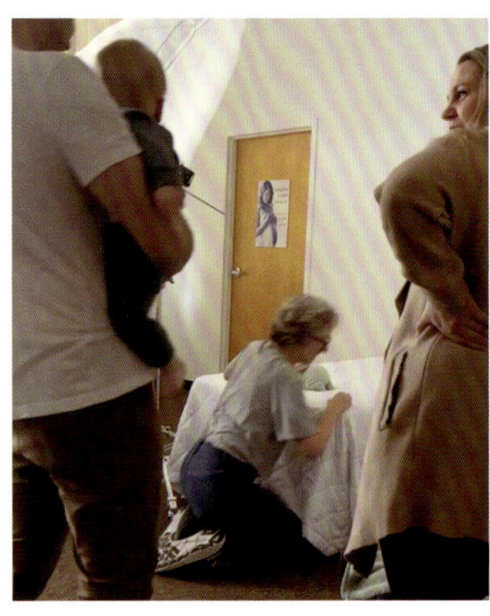

C

D

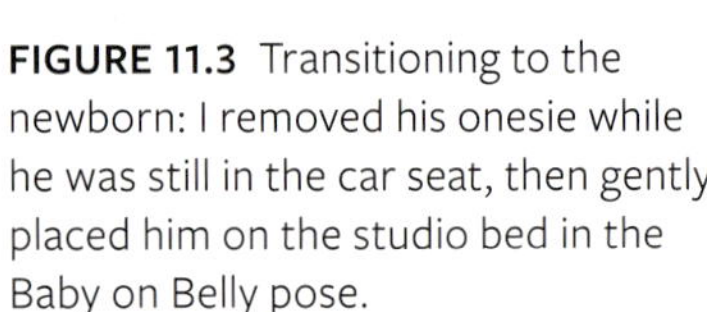

**FIGURE 11.3** Transitioning to the newborn: I removed his onesie while he was still in the car seat, then gently placed him on the studio bed in the Baby on Belly pose.

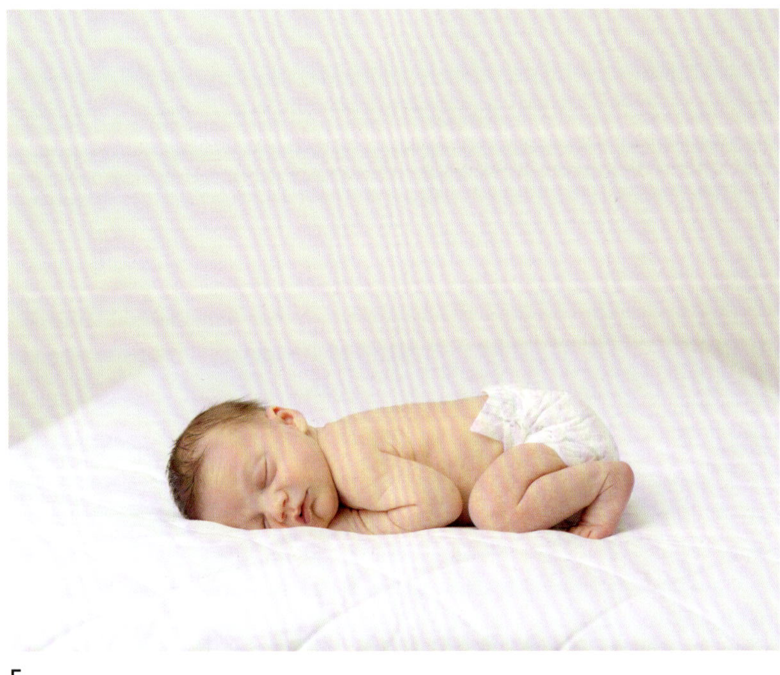

E

## How I Transition Newborns from Their Car Seat into the Pose

When I have clients coming into the studio for a newborn session, I ask that they dress the baby in something they want photos taken in, or in something that can be easily removed. If we're removing the clothing and photographing the baby in just a diaper, onesies with a front-facing zipper or front-facing buttons are ideal.

Most babies fall asleep in their car seat on the way to the studio and having them in clothing that is easy to remove allows me to undress them while they are still in their car seat. Years of experience have taught me that this is the best way to keep the baby asleep—and this is how I do it.

I start by loosening and removing the car seat straps. Then, I place my hands on the baby's feet and chest to help them relax (**FIGURE 11.4A**). I leave one hand on the baby's feet, applying light pressure, while I remove their arms from their onesie one at a time (**FIGURE 11.4B**). Then I bring the baby's arms back to their chest and reapply pressure until the baby calms (**FIGURE 11.4C**).

Once the baby is calm, I gently lift them out of the car seat and place them in the Baby on Belly position (**FIGURE 11.4D**). At this point, their arms are free from the onesie. I let them rest in this position for a minute or two, while I apply light pressure to their feet and back, or feet and head (**FIGURE 11.4E**). Once they've settled, I remove their feet from their outfit and reapply pressure to their feet and head or feet and back (**FIGURE 11.4F** and **11.4G**). I let them rest in this position for a few minutes, then slowly remove my hands and get to work (**FIGURE 11.4H**)!

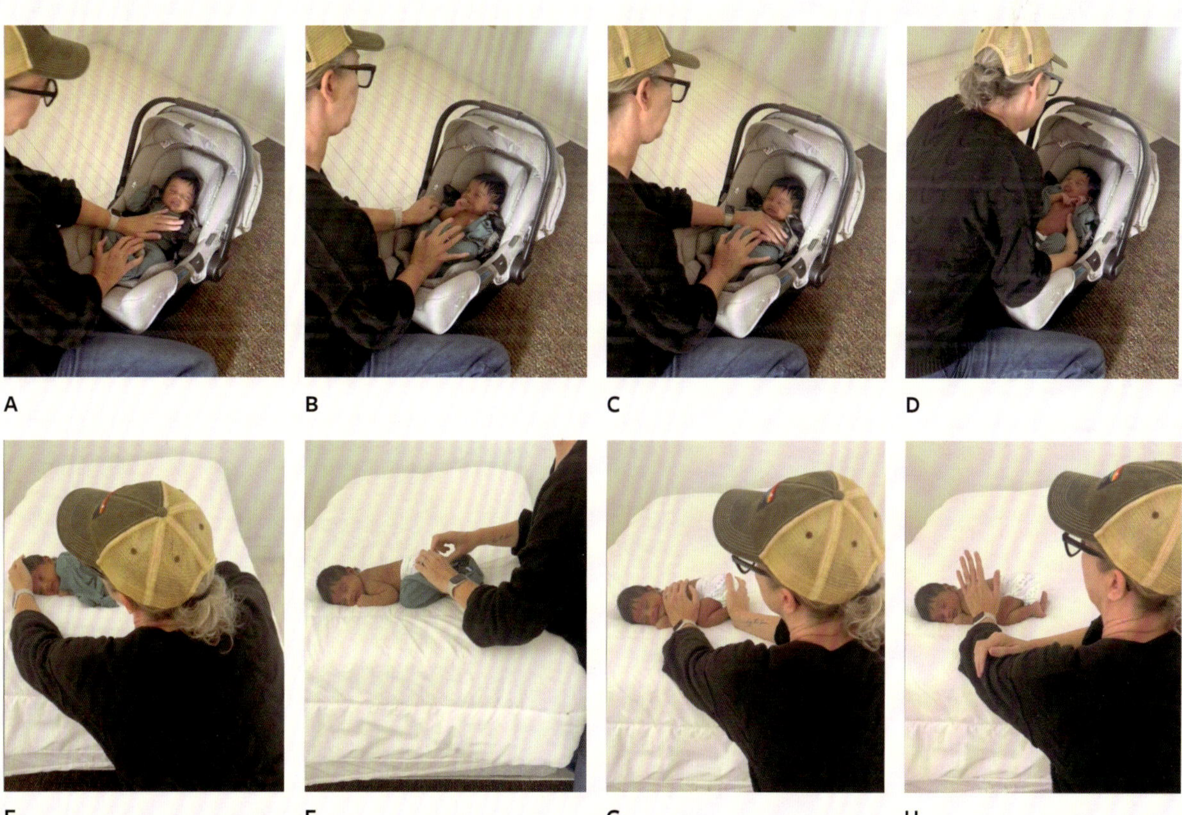


**FIGURE 11.4** A step-by-step look at how I transition sleeping babies from their car seats into the Baby on Belly position

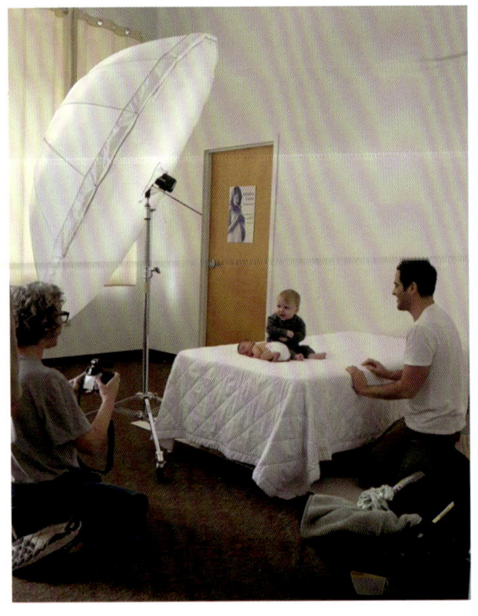

A

After the newborn was posed and comfortable, we brought the older baby back in for sibling photos, starting with the Sit and Point position. For safety, dad was positioned close by in case the older baby wobbled, tried to shift, or touched the baby too aggressively (**FIGURE 11.5A**).

Since seven-month-olds aren't developmentally able to follow directions like a toddler is, I didn't ask him to point or play any of the games that I play with toddlers in this pose. Instead, we just let his natural curiosity take over, and he reached out to touch his baby brother on his own—which made for an adorable photo, as you can see in **FIGURE 11.5B**.

Because the older baby was doing so well, and the newborn was sleeping so soundly, I decided to try a modified Safe Hold pose.

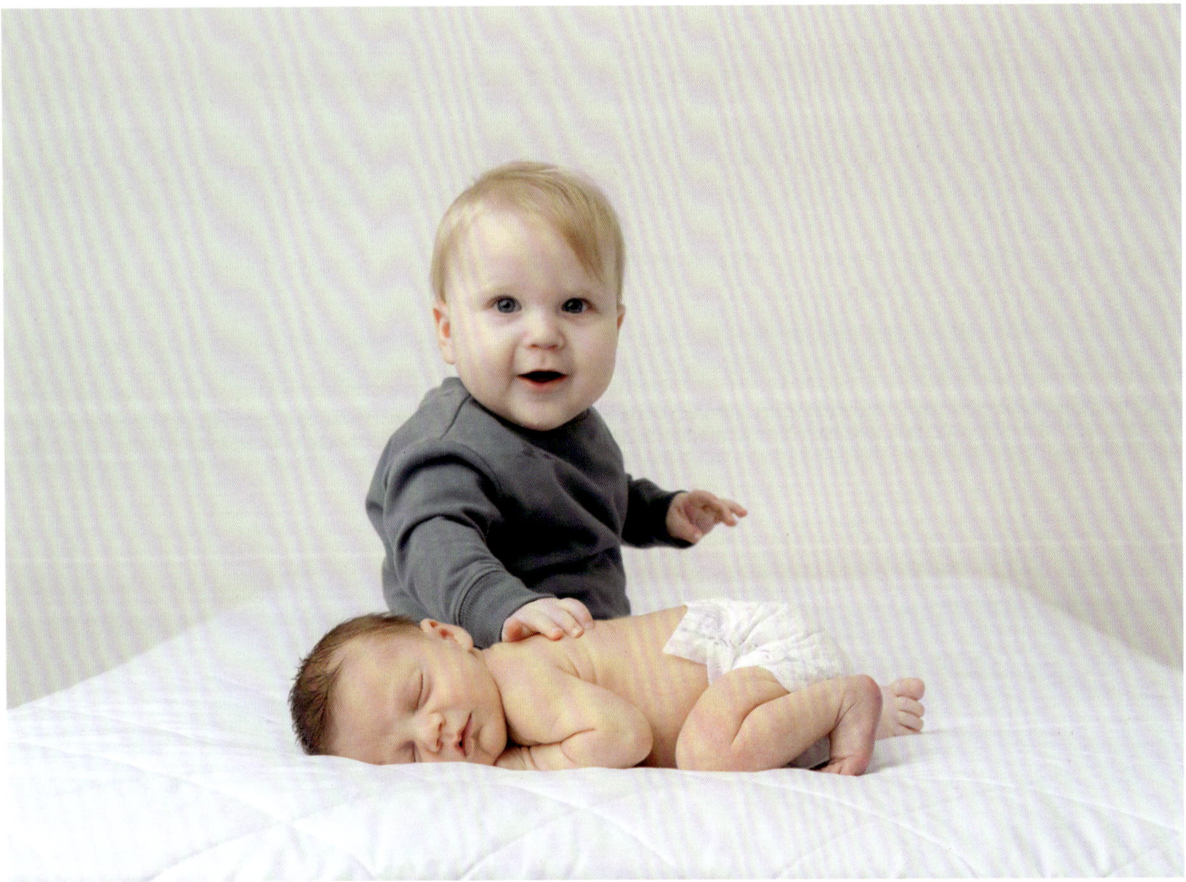

B

**FIGURE 11.5** Sibling photos in the Sit and Point pose. Dad is just out of frame for safety.

I usually set up the Safe Hold pose by asking the older child to lie on their stomach, up on their elbows, perpendicular to the end of the bed and facing the baby. I then gently lift the baby's head and place it in the crook of their sibling's arm. But that is much too complicated to attempt with a seven-month-old baby. Instead, I asked the father to turn the seven-month-old so that he was facing toward the camera. The newborn lay slightly in front of him, between his legs. From there I lifted the baby's head and rested it on his brother's leg (see **FIGURE 11.6B**).

If the older baby had refused or resisted, I would have skipped this pose—but he was calm and happy, so it worked beautifully. They were in this position for less than a minute (dad remained close for safety), and we got some truly adorable photos that the family will cherish forever.

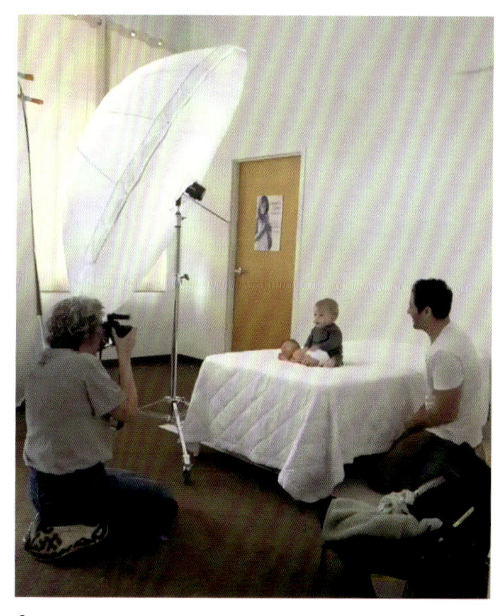

A

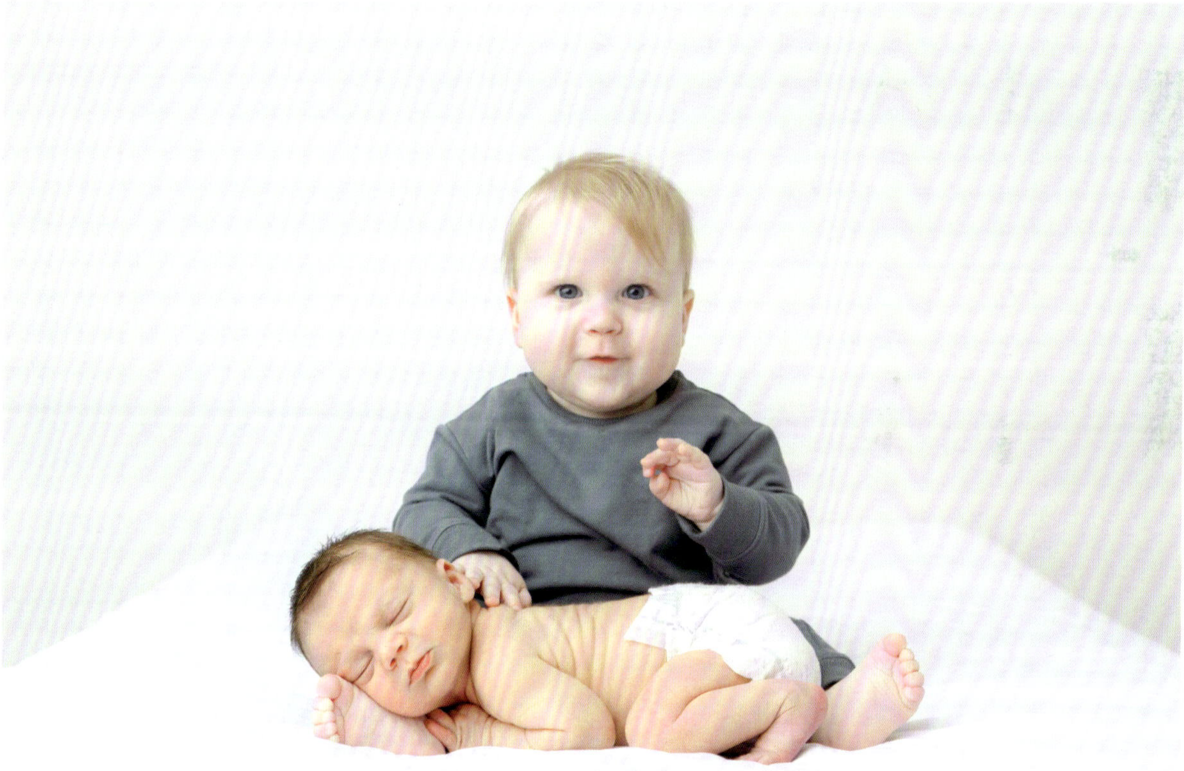

B

**FIGURE 11.6** A modified Safe Hold pose with dad sitting close by for support and safely.

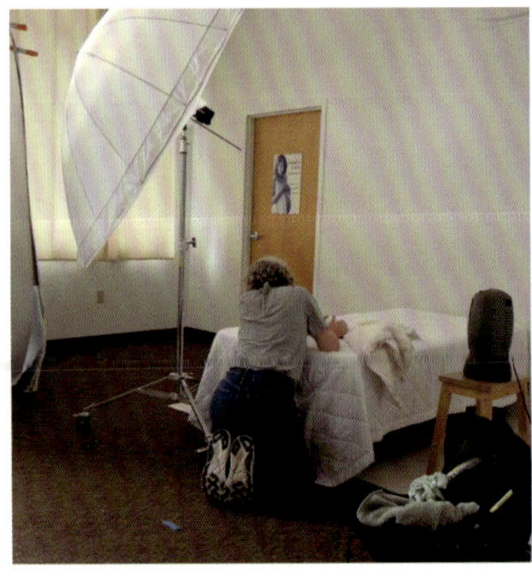
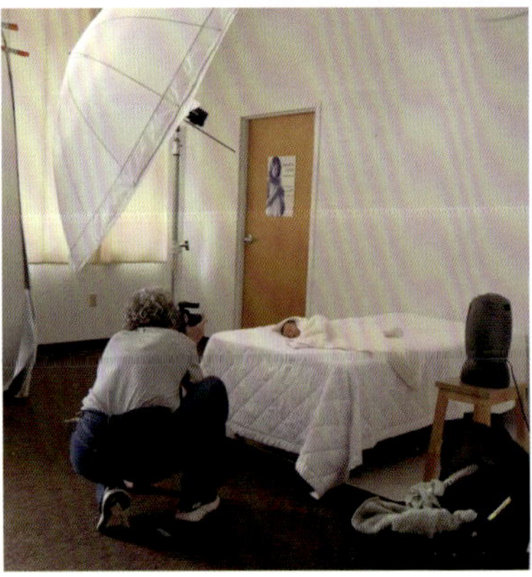
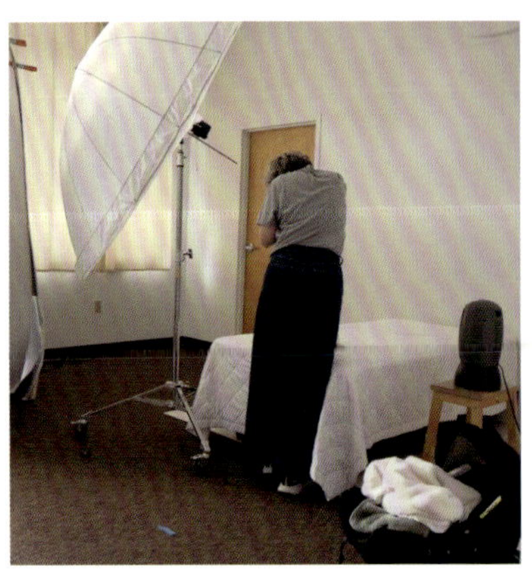
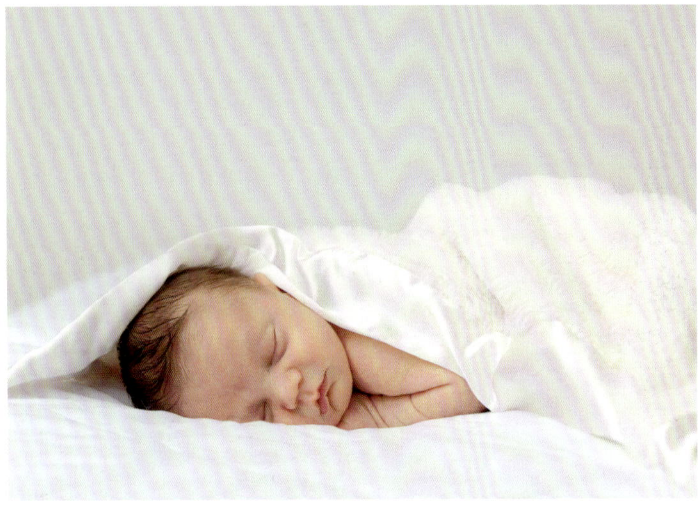
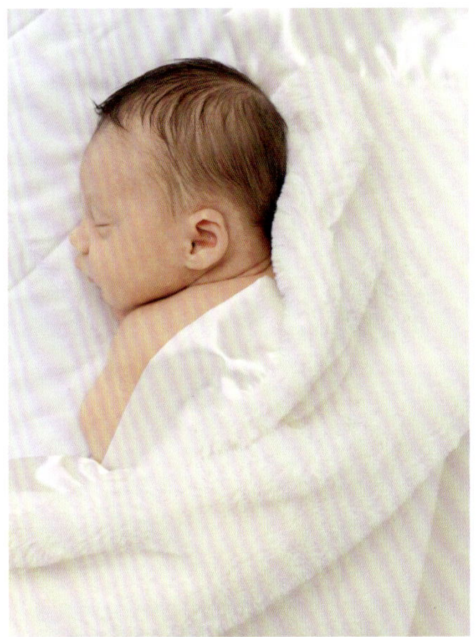
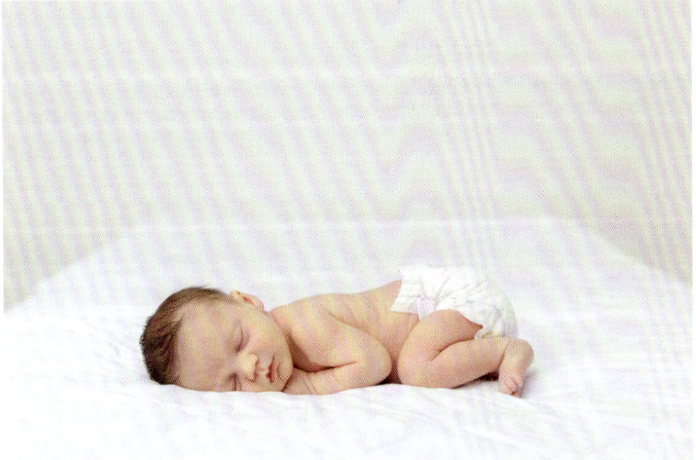
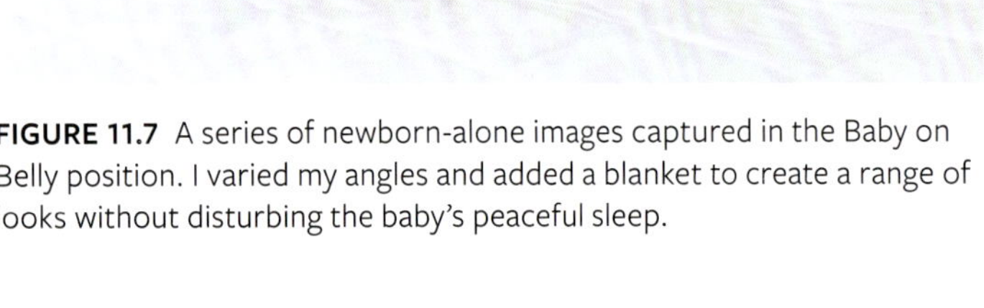

**FIGURE 11.7** A series of newborn-alone images captured in the Baby on Belly position. I varied my angles and added a blanket to create a range of looks without disturbing the baby's peaceful sleep.

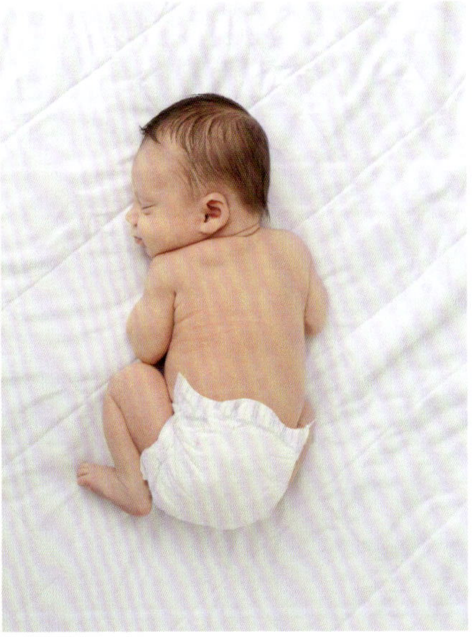

## Newborn with Mom

Once I had some solid solo images of the newborn, I had his mom join him on the bed for a few intimate mom-and-baby portraits (**FIGURE 11.8**).

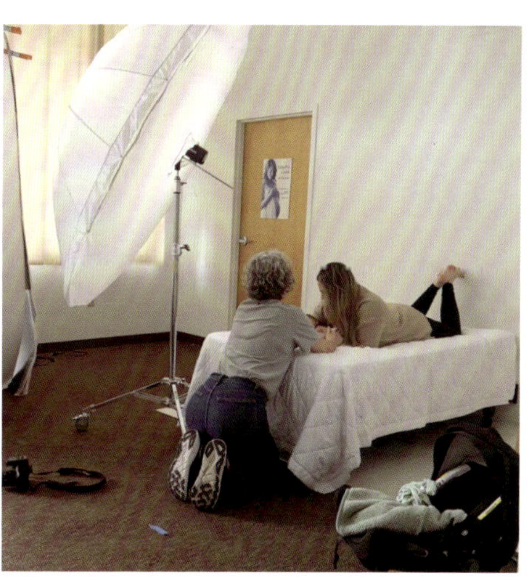

## Full Family Photos

Next, I brought in dad and the older baby to create some family portraits. As you can see in **FIGURE 11.9**, I first showed the dad where I wanted him to sit, and how to position himself and his older son. I'm a big believer in demonstrating poses as I explain them to people to cut down on confusion! Once they were positioned, I captured some photos of the four of them together (**FIGURES 11.9C** and **11.9D**).

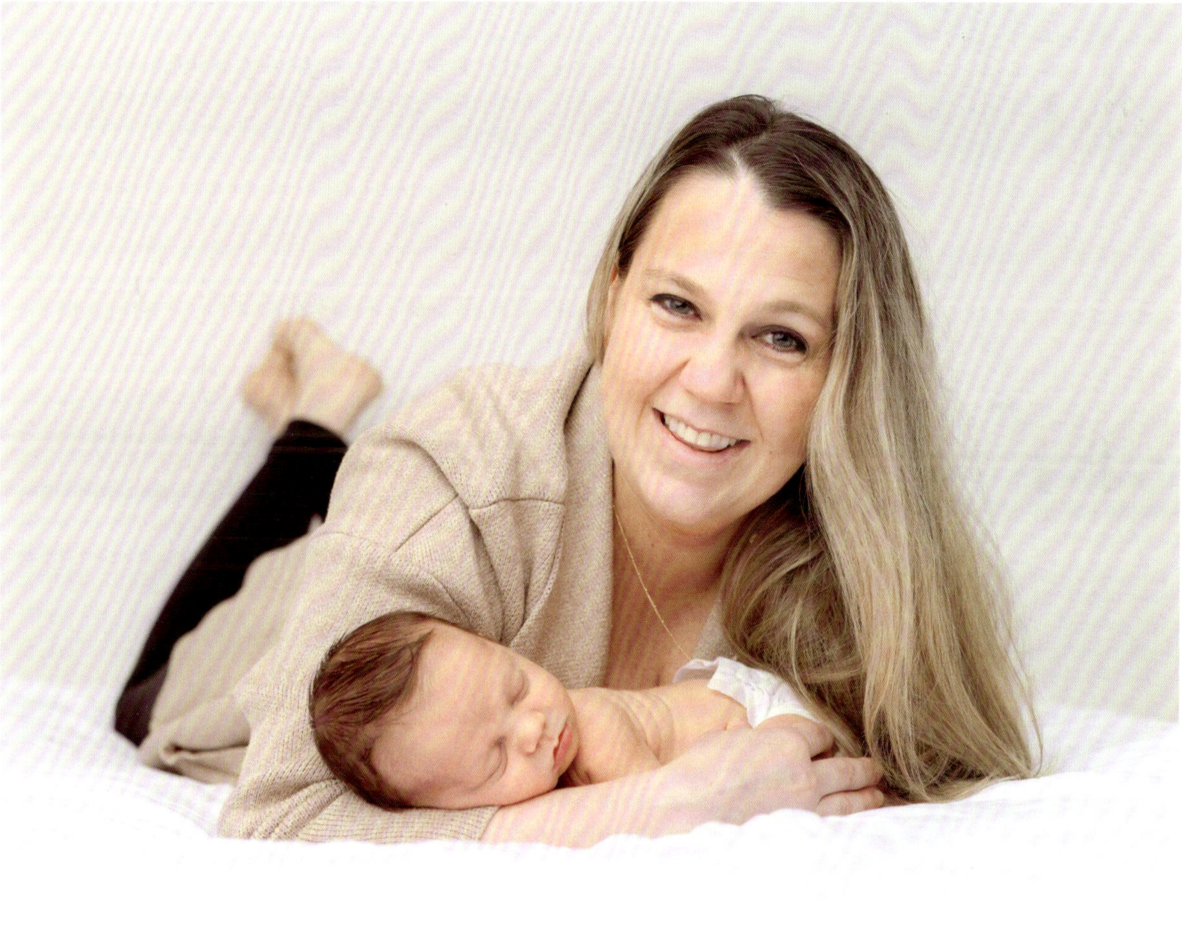

**FIGURE 11.8** Newborn with mom

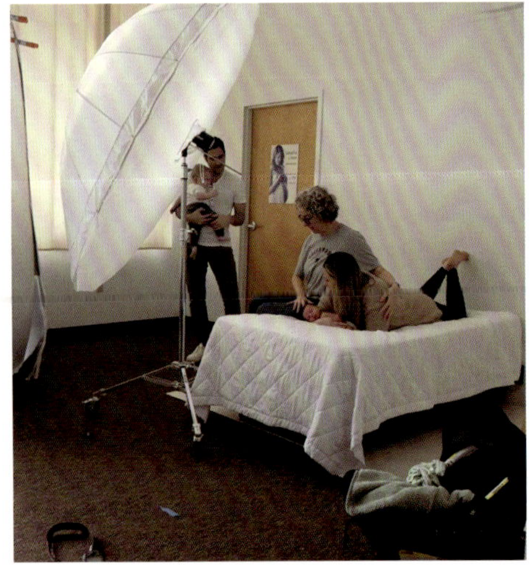

A

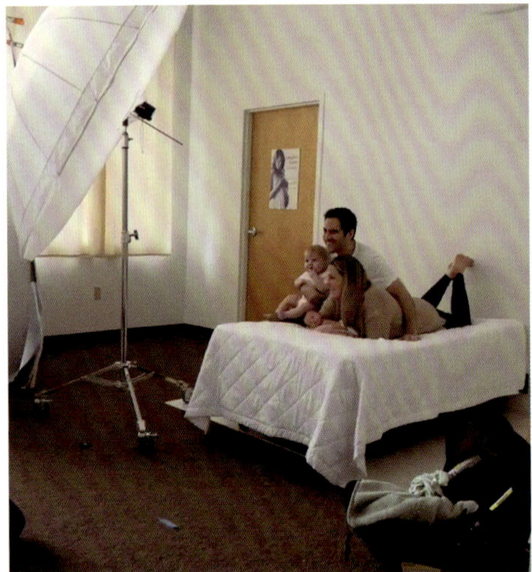

B

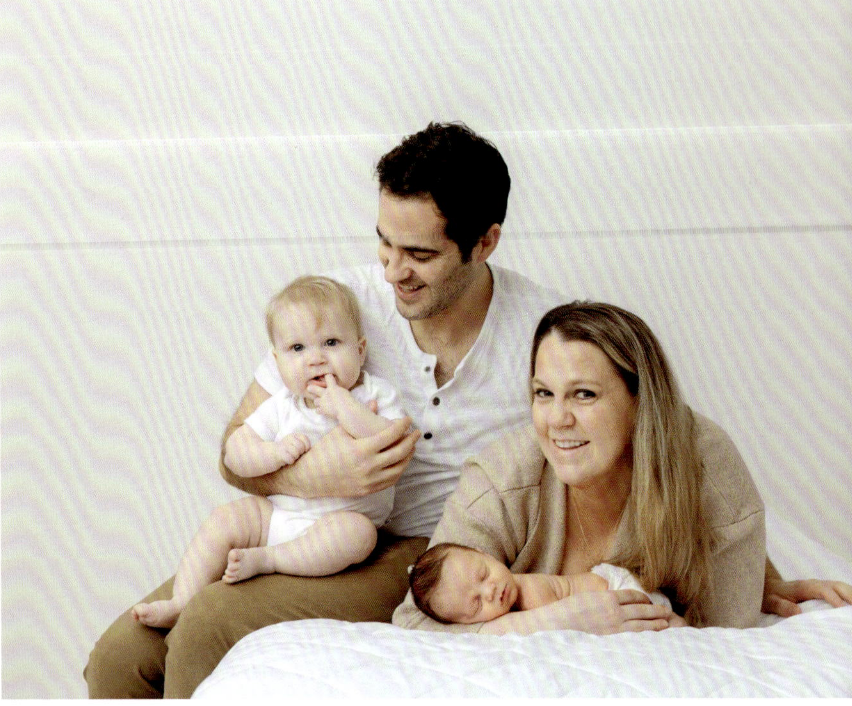

C

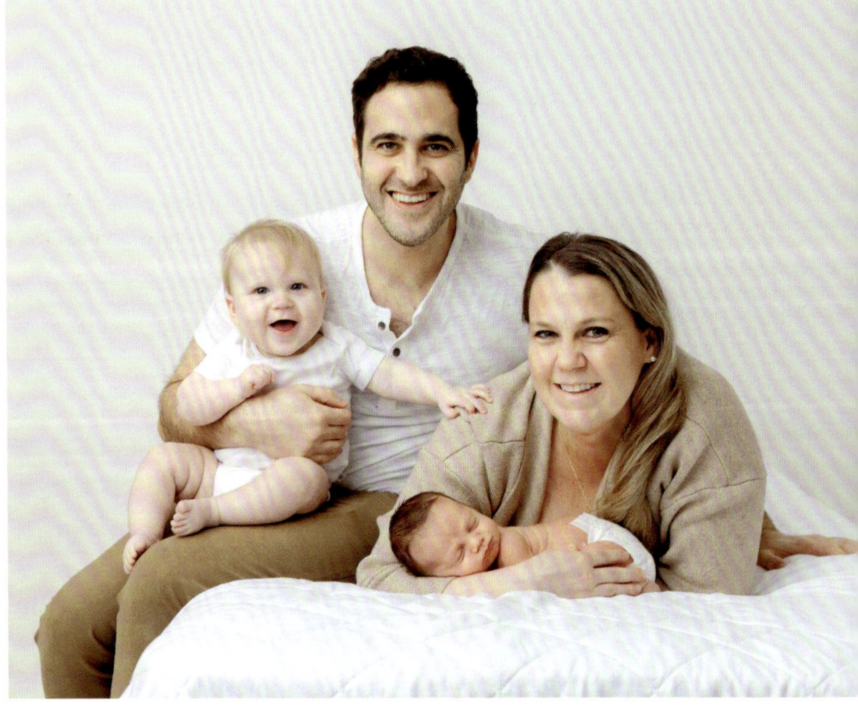

D

**FIGURE 11.9** Family portraits with all four family members. Once everyone was positioned, I photographed the full family, capturing sweet, connected moments.

## Standing Poses

After the family photos, we moved into our standing poses and captured some images of the father with both of his children. You'll notice, up to this point, all of the poses revolved around the children on the bed. I like to get them comfortable and posed first, then build out the gallery by adding in other family members. My light stayed exactly the same—no adjustments needed.

For the standing poses, however, I did make a small adjustment to my light. I lifted it up so that the bottom of the modifier was about chest level to the dad. Lifting the light up slightly ensured that the majority of the light fell from above, creating a flattering lighting pattern on his face.

### Newborn with Father

Once my light was readjusted, I positioned the father, starting with the Baby on Shoulder pose. As you can see in **FIGURE 11.10**, I demonstrated the pose for him as I was explaining what I wanted him to do. Then I lifted the baby from the bed and placed him on his father's shoulder for the photos. The final images are **FIGURE 11.10C** and **11.10D**.

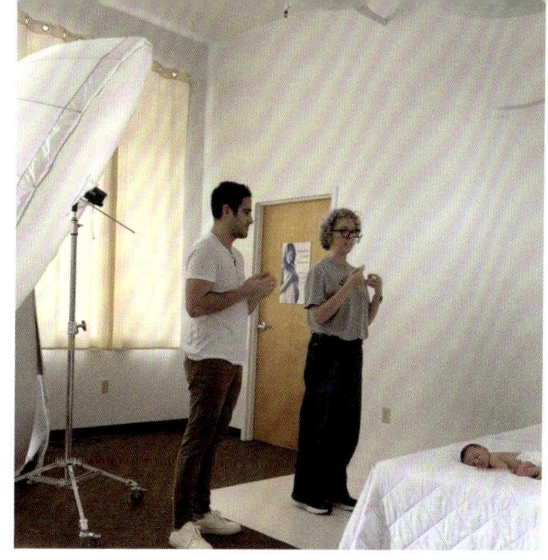

A

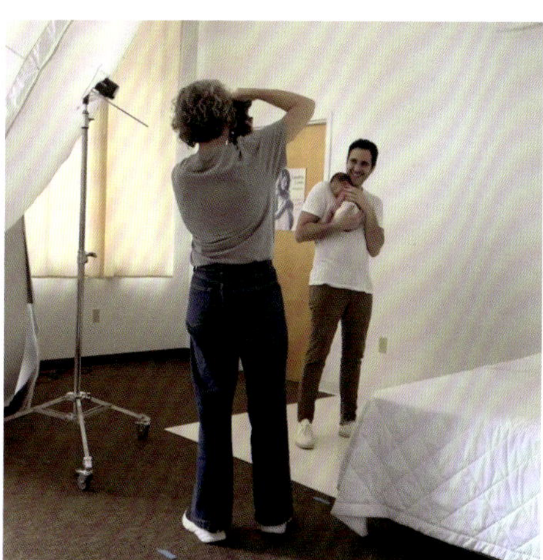

B

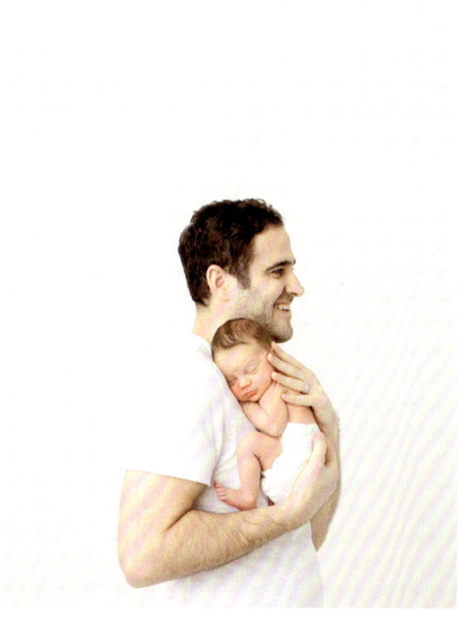

C

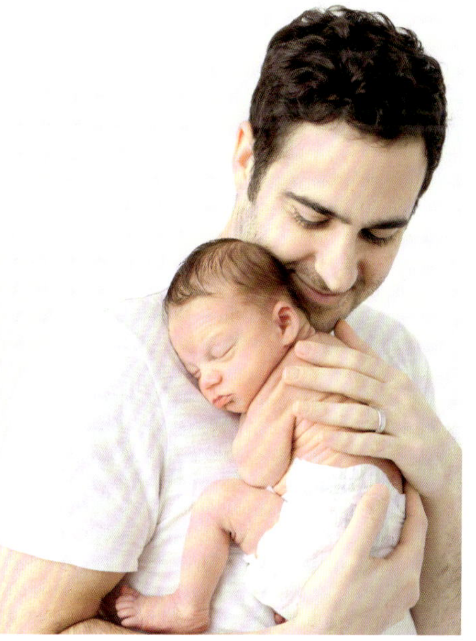

D

**FIGURE 11.10** Demonstrating the Baby on Shoulder pose for dad (Figure 11.10A), then placing the newborn gently on his shoulder for photos (Figure 11.10B). Figure 11.10C and 11.10D show the final portraits—calm, secure, and beautifully connected.

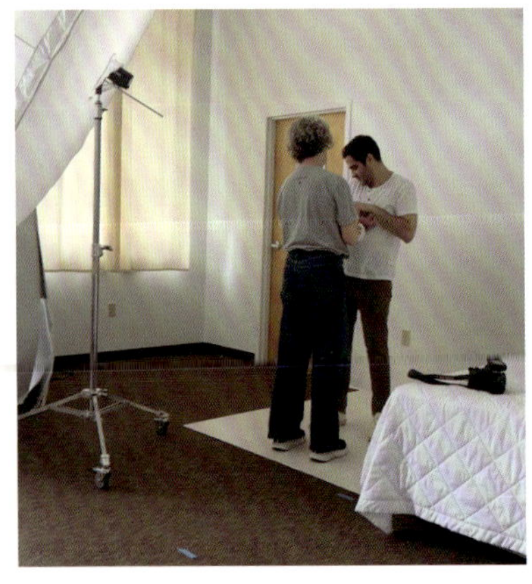

A

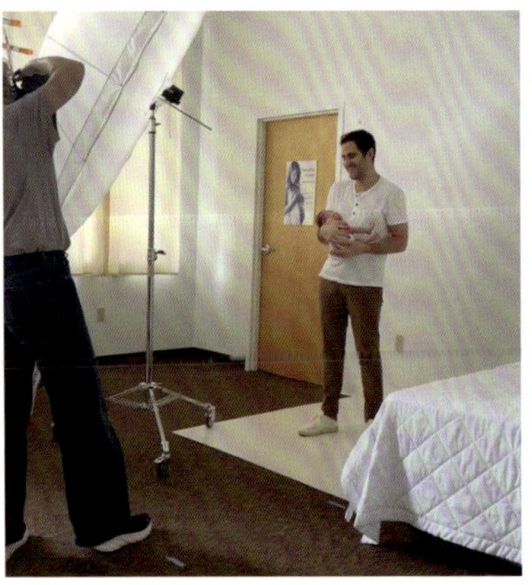

B

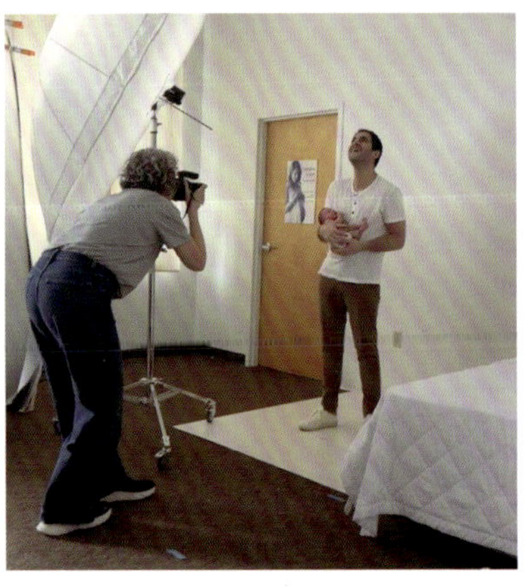

C

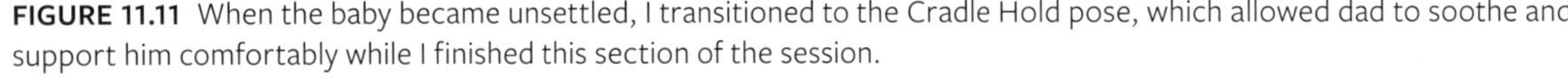

**FIGURE 11.11** When the baby became unsettled, I transitioned to the Cradle Hold pose, which allowed dad to soothe and support him comfortably while I finished this section of the session.

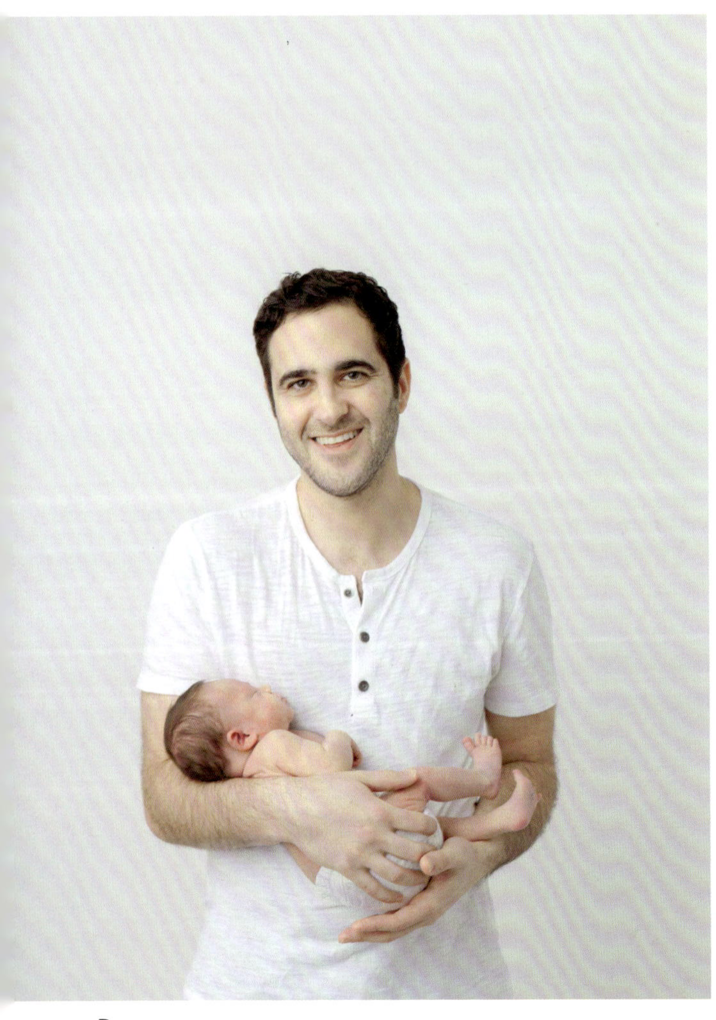

D

Babies sometimes wake when moved from the bed into the arms of a parent for standing poses—and that's exactly what happened during this session. This baby had been asleep for a while and was beginning to get hungry. As soon as we placed him on his dad's chest, he began rooting. Rather than force the Baby on Chest pose, I pivoted and moved him into the Cradle Hold position instead (**FIGURES 11.11A–C**), which helped keep him calm and comfortable while we finished the set.

**Pro Tip:** You don't have to use every pose in every session. Every baby and every family are different. For example, I skipped the Baby on Chest pose because the baby wasn't comfortable in that position. And because I was working with a sitter and a newborn at the same time, I kept things simple and didn't move the newborn out of the Baby on Belly pose for his individual photos. When you work with families, remaining flexible and ready to adjust is a must!

## Sitter with Father

Once we finished the newborn and father photos, we handed the baby to his mother for a feeding and went right into the standing poses with the sitter.

We began with the Peek-a-Boo pose (**FIGURES 11.12A** and **11.12B**), then moved into the Airplane pose (**FIGURES 11.12C** and **11.12D**).

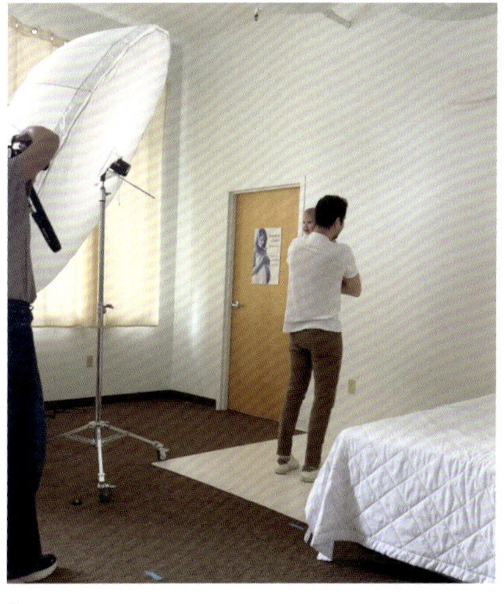

A

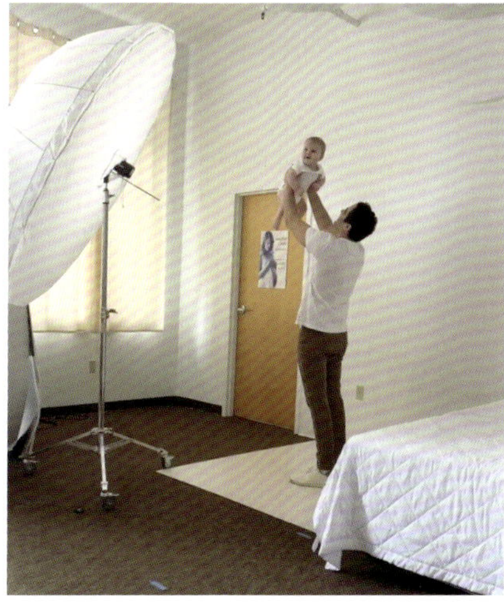

B

**FIGURE 11.12** The Peek-a-Boo pose (one of my favorites for babies this age!) and the Airplane pose (a playful favorite that captures joy and energy).

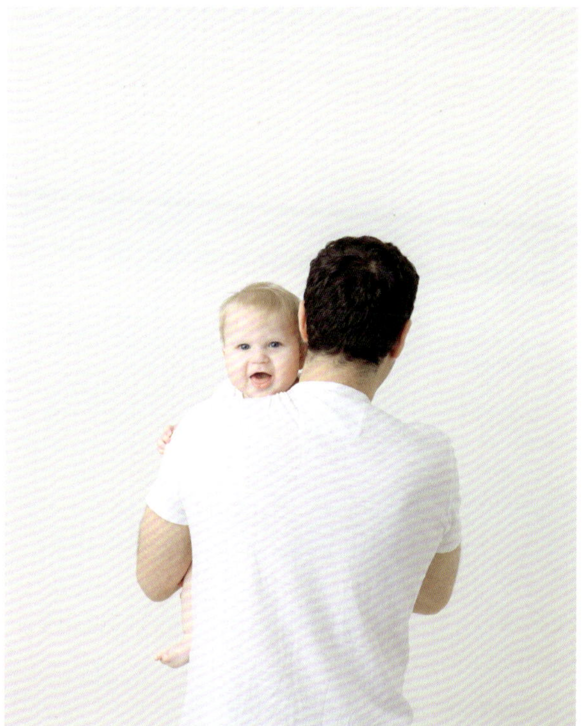

C

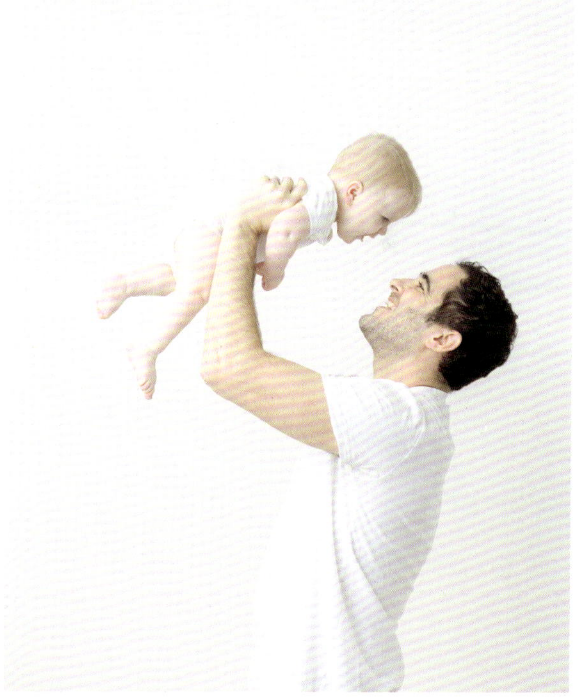

D

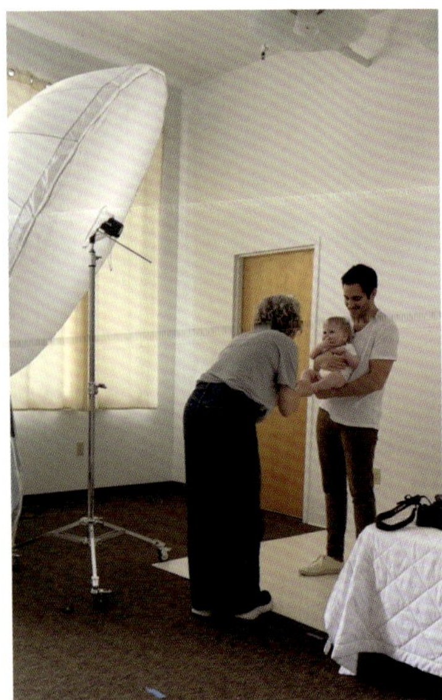

**FIGURE 11.13** Baby on chest (sitter version).

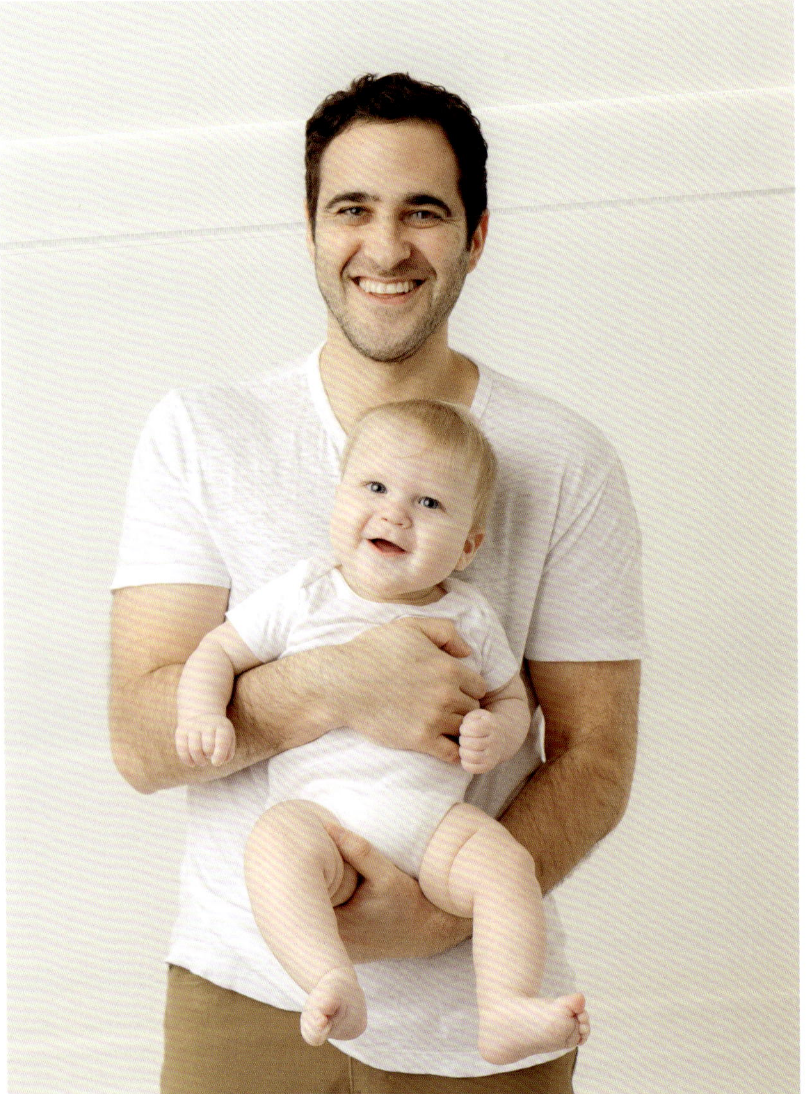

We finished this part of the session with the sitter version of Baby on Chest (**FIGURE 11.13**). Notice how the lighting stays the same throughout all of these poses—that's one of the major benefits of having a consistent lighting system in place.

By this time, our seven-month-old was clearly getting tired. He started yawning and rubbing his eyes, which let me know it was time to wrap up. I placed him on the bed one more time to capture a few images of him in his new outfit. I worked quickly, pulling back for full-body photos and moving in close for some tight headshots. This portion took less than two minutes (**FIGURE 11.14**)—and then we were done!

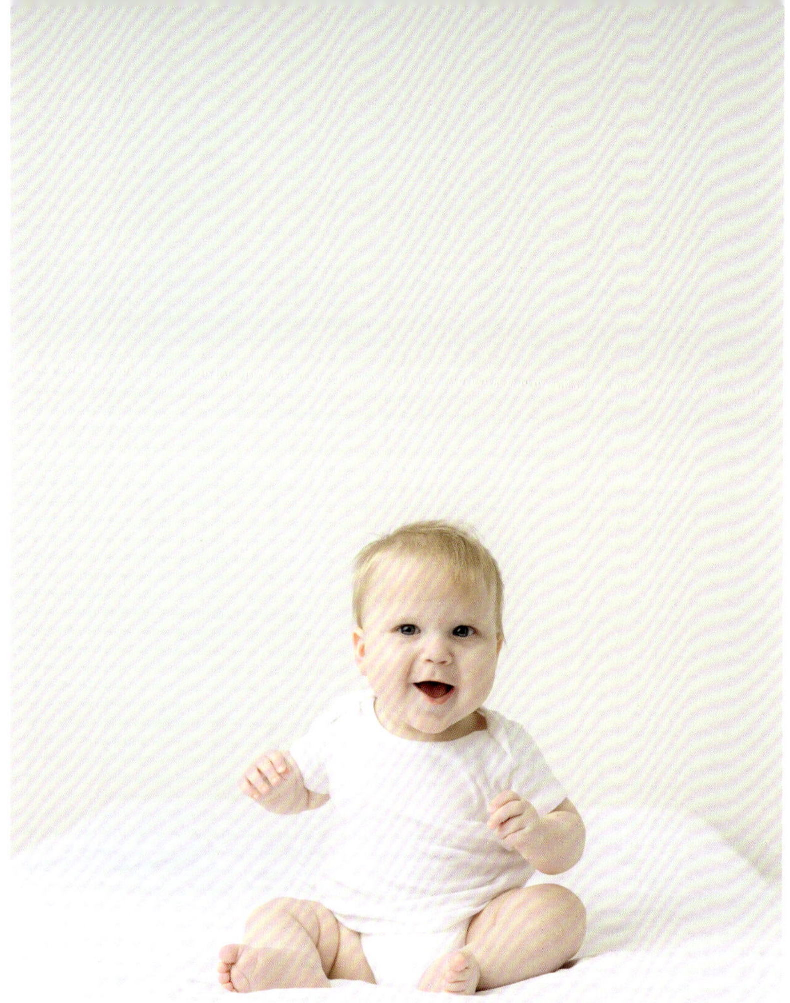

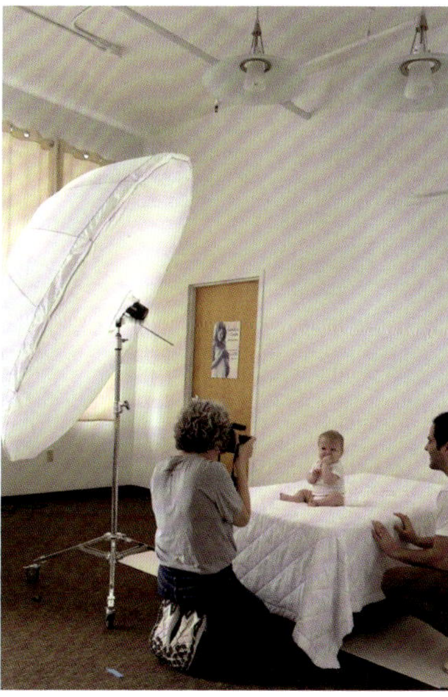

**FIGURE 11.14** Final portraits of the sitter in his new outfit.

The entire session lasted under an hour. We captured all the essential images, and both kids were calm and happy by the end. That's the power of having a solid system in place—it allows you to adapt to each session's unique needs while working quickly and confidently.

## The Takeaway

Consistency and efficiency don't just benefit you—they make the entire experience smoother and more enjoyable for everyone! Because my lighting system is simple and my posing flow is well-established, I was able to complete a full newborn session *and* a sitter session in under an hour. No rushing. No stress. Just a calm, happy family and a complete gallery of beautiful images.

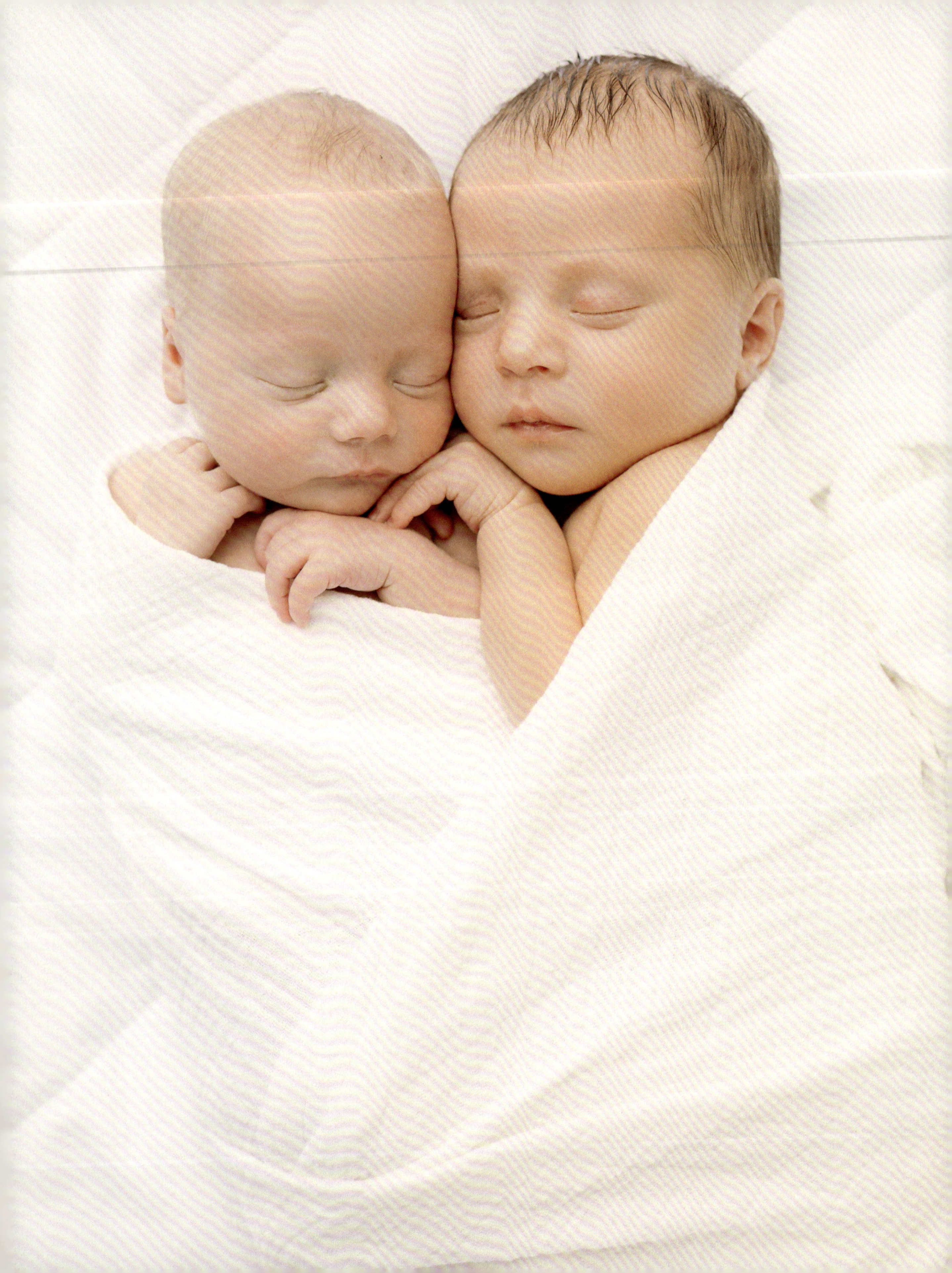

CHAPTER

# 12

# Shooting on Location

Bringing lighting into a client's home can feel intimidating, especially if it's something you've never done before. That's exactly why I've included this complete behind-the-scenes look at one of my in-home sessions—from start to finish. My goal is to show you how all the moving pieces come together, and in doing so, ease any anxiety you may have and give you the confidence to try it yourself!

## Session Prep

I never know what to expect when working on location. I don't scout the location beforehand, so I have no idea what the space (or light) will be like when I arrive. I bring everything I may need, just in case.

In addition to my camera, I bring a Westcott FJ200 strobe, a Westcott FJ80 flash, and the Westcott universal trigger that works with both lights. I also bring my 45-foot convertible umbrella with a one-stop diffusion panel and a travel stand. All the equipment easily fits into one bag.

## Who

Once I arrive at my client's home, I start by learning *who* I'll be photographing. This is a first, crucial step that helps me plan the rest of my session.

For this session, I was working with two parents (a mother and father), their five-month-old baby, and the family dog! The parents wanted solo photos of the baby, portraits of the baby with each parent, and of course, photos of the whole family together.

Since the baby was five months old—too young to be a sitter—I decided to use my go-to poses for a three-month-old. I captured her solo images while she was on her belly and on her back.

The session flow I intended to follow was my traditional flow: Baby alone; baby with mom; baby with the whole family; and baby with dad.

But, as you will see, some changes were made to accommodate the size of the room and the developmental age of the baby.

## Where

Once I knew who I was photographing, the next step was deciding *where* to photograph them. As I've shared in previous chapters, I typically start by scouting the primary bedroom. It tends to be a great location for cozy, intimate photos.

In this home, we had several wonderful spaces to work with. In addition to the primary bedroom, they had a beautiful living room filled with natural light, and a sweet nursery where the parents requested a few special images. That gave us three distinct spaces to use for the session.

## What and How

I knew I'd be using lighting in each of the rooms, but each space required a different approach. The primary bedroom and nursery were quite dark, making artificial lighting essential. The living room, on the other hand, was filled with gorgeous natural light—but tall trees outside the windows were casting a green color over everything. I used my lights there to correct the color and maintain consistency across all the images.

The size and shape of each room also varied significantly, so I had to carefully consider how I set up my lights to make the most of each space without overwhelming it.

### The Primary Bedroom

We began our session in the primary bedroom, which had two small windows facing east and south. The space had a low ceiling and not much room to work with, so instead of using an umbrella, I opted to bounce my light. Because the windows were relatively small, I chose to bounce the light off the ceiling rather than the window walls—this gave me a much larger, softer light source.

I set my strobe on a stand positioned on the side with the south-facing windows, about 45 degrees to the bed (**FIGURE 12.1**). This setup allowed me to create loop light—my favorite lighting pattern for portraits. Once my light was in place, I positioned the baby on her back, metered my exposure, and began photographing her.

**FIGURE 12.2** shows how I positioned the baby on the bed. Notice how I have the top of her head pointed toward the light to avoid accidental ghoul lighting.

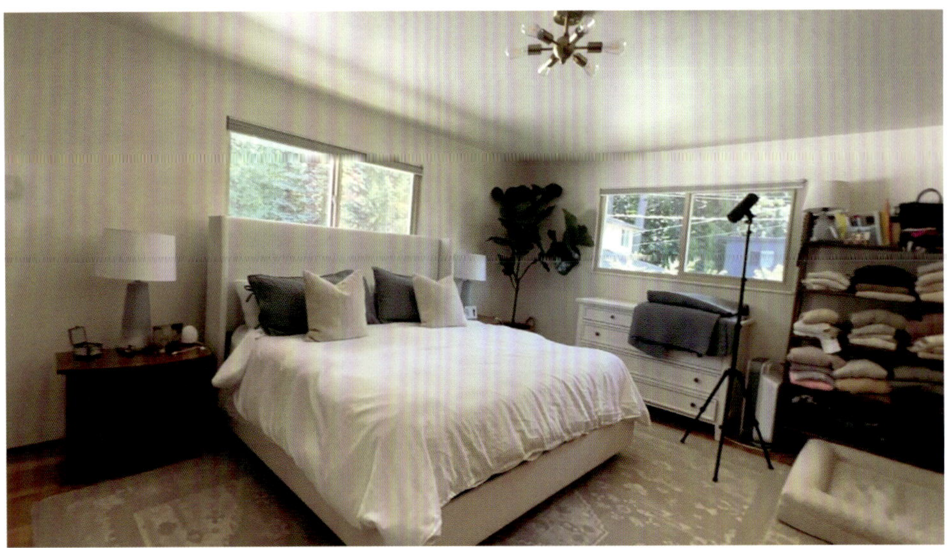

**FIGURE 12.1** Behind the scenes

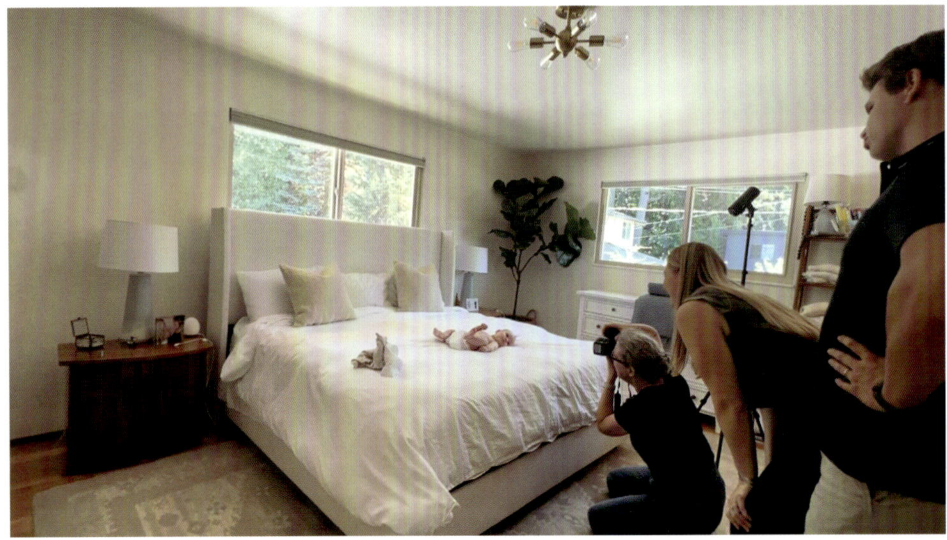

**FIGURE 12.2** Posing the baby on her back with her head oriented toward the light to maintain a visually pleasant lighting pattern.

Once the baby was positioned on her back, I worked quickly to maximize the pose, photographing her from the side and from above. **FIGURE 12.3A** shows the natural light photo. **FIGURES 12.3B**, **C**, and **D** show some of the different angles I captured with the added light.

Next, I asked her mother to gently roll her onto her belly. In doing so, I caught a sweet, candid photo of the two of them mid-transition (**FIGURE 12.4**). Remember to look for the moments that naturally occur between the poses. They often end up being some of my favorite pictures.

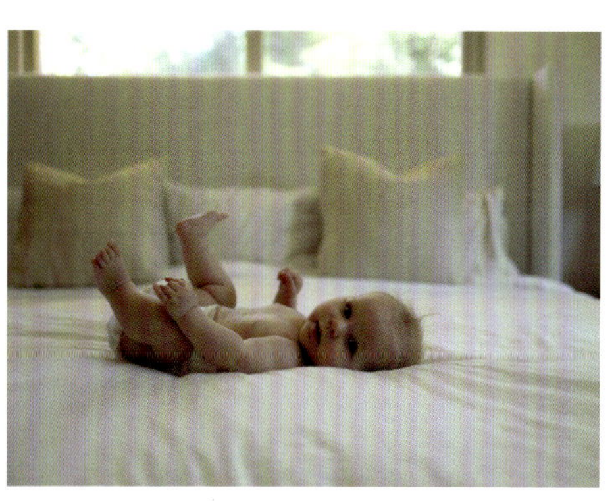

A

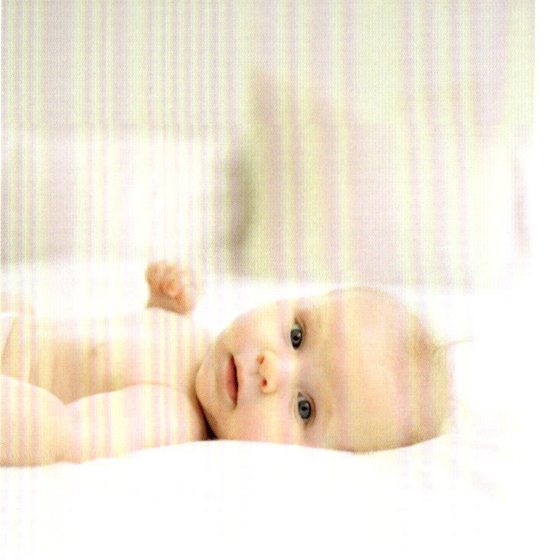

B

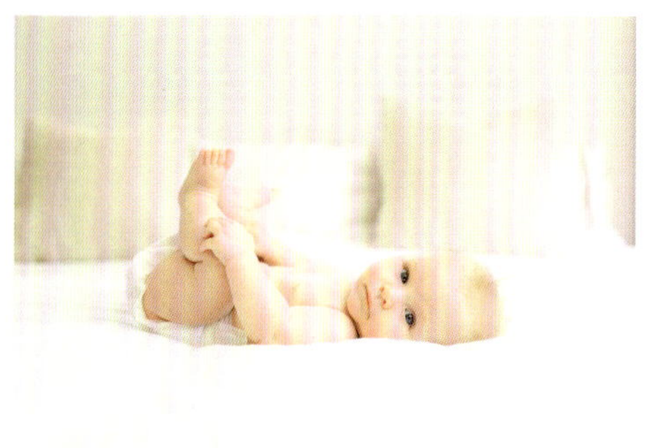

C

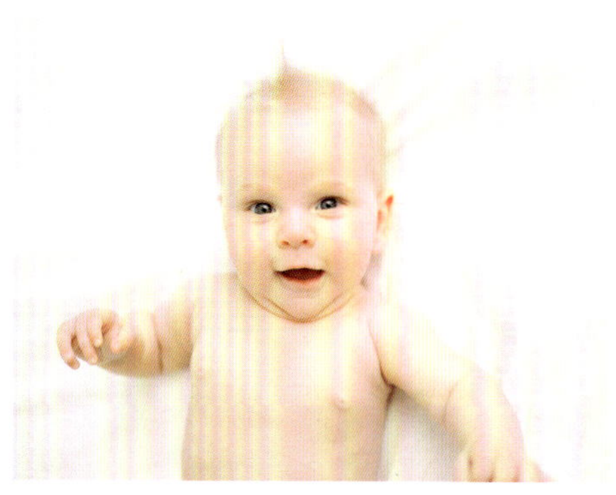

D

**FIGURE 12.3**
Figure 12.3A shows the natural-light image for reference. All photos were captured at f/1.8, 1/125 sec., ISO 100.

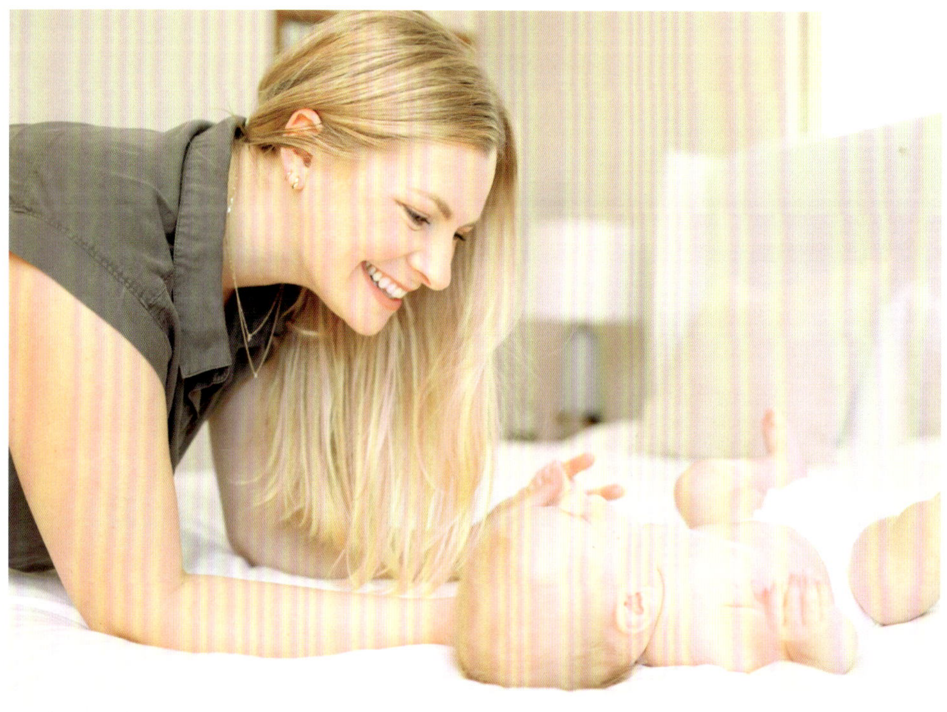

**FIGURE 12.4**
Remember to look for the moments that naturally occur between the poses!

**FIGURE 12.5A** shows the baby on her belly in the natural light and **FIGURE 12.5B** shows the photo captured with the bounced strobe light.

After finishing the solo portraits, I invited mom into the frame to get some portraits of the two of them together (**FIGURE 12.6**). For these images I used my go-to lying down pose. Due to the age of the baby, I chose to sit the baby up so she could engage with the camera.

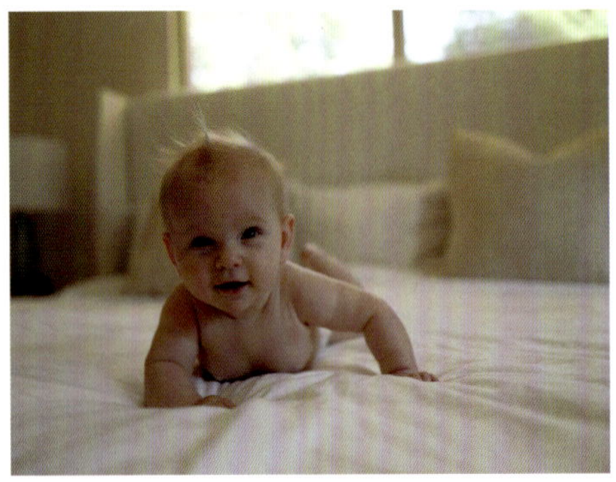

A

I did not move my light for these different shots. The only thing I did was re-meter. When photographing a baby alone, I like to work with a wide-open aperture—f/1.8 or f/2. But when working with more than one person, I will stop down to f/4 or f/5.6 (depending on the size of the family). The change in aperture means I need to increase the power of my strobe. Metering helps me determine the power I need. For these photos, I stopped down to f/4. My other settings stayed the same (1/125 sec., ISO 100).

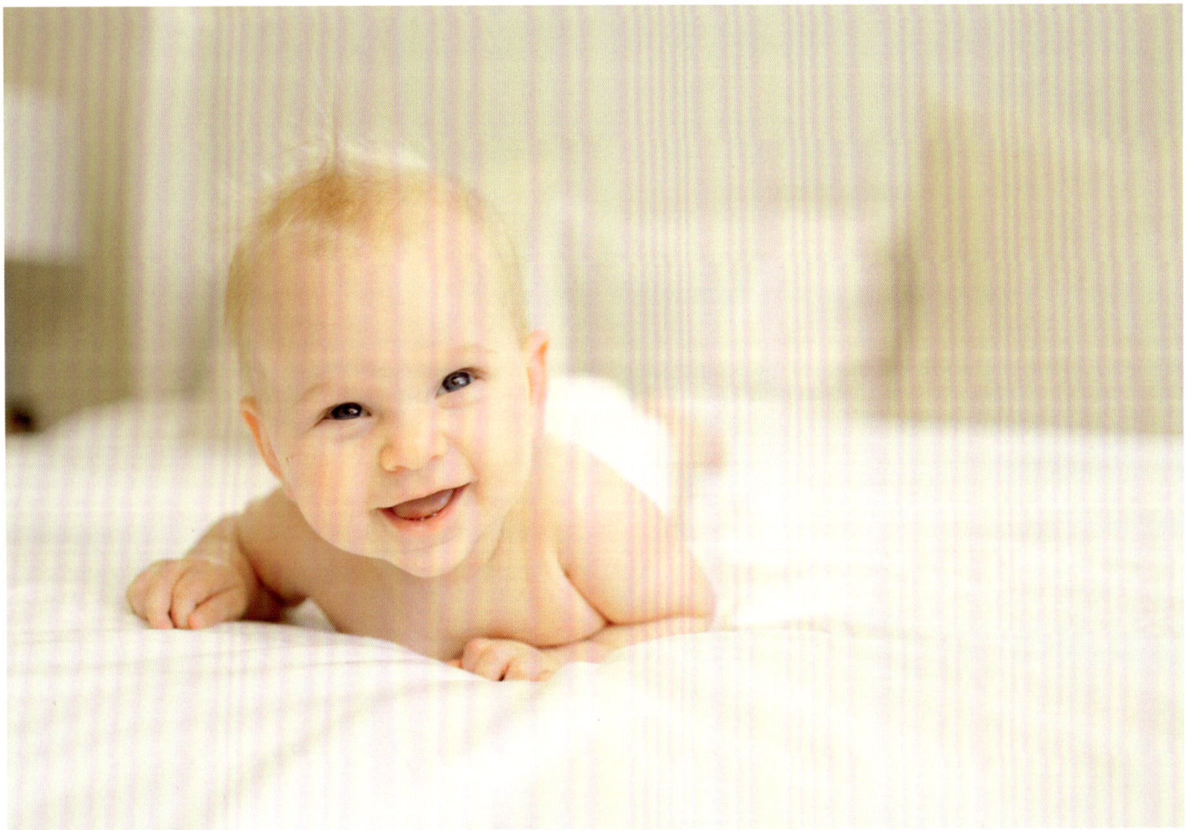

B

**FIGURE 12.5** Figure 12.5A shows the scene in natural light, whereas Figure 12.5B was taken using bounced strobe light.

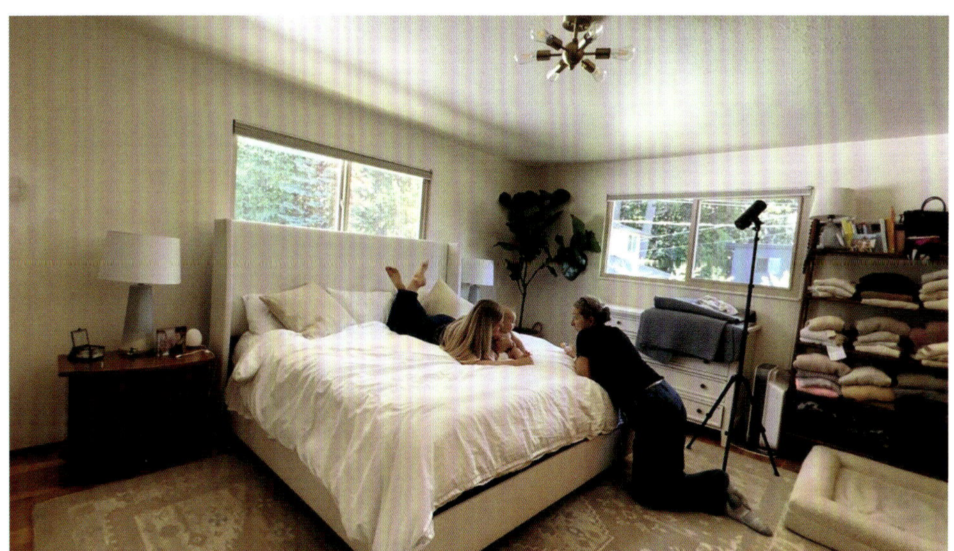

**FIGURE 12.6** My lighting setup remains unchanged for this new image, which is well-lit, intimate, and simply posed.

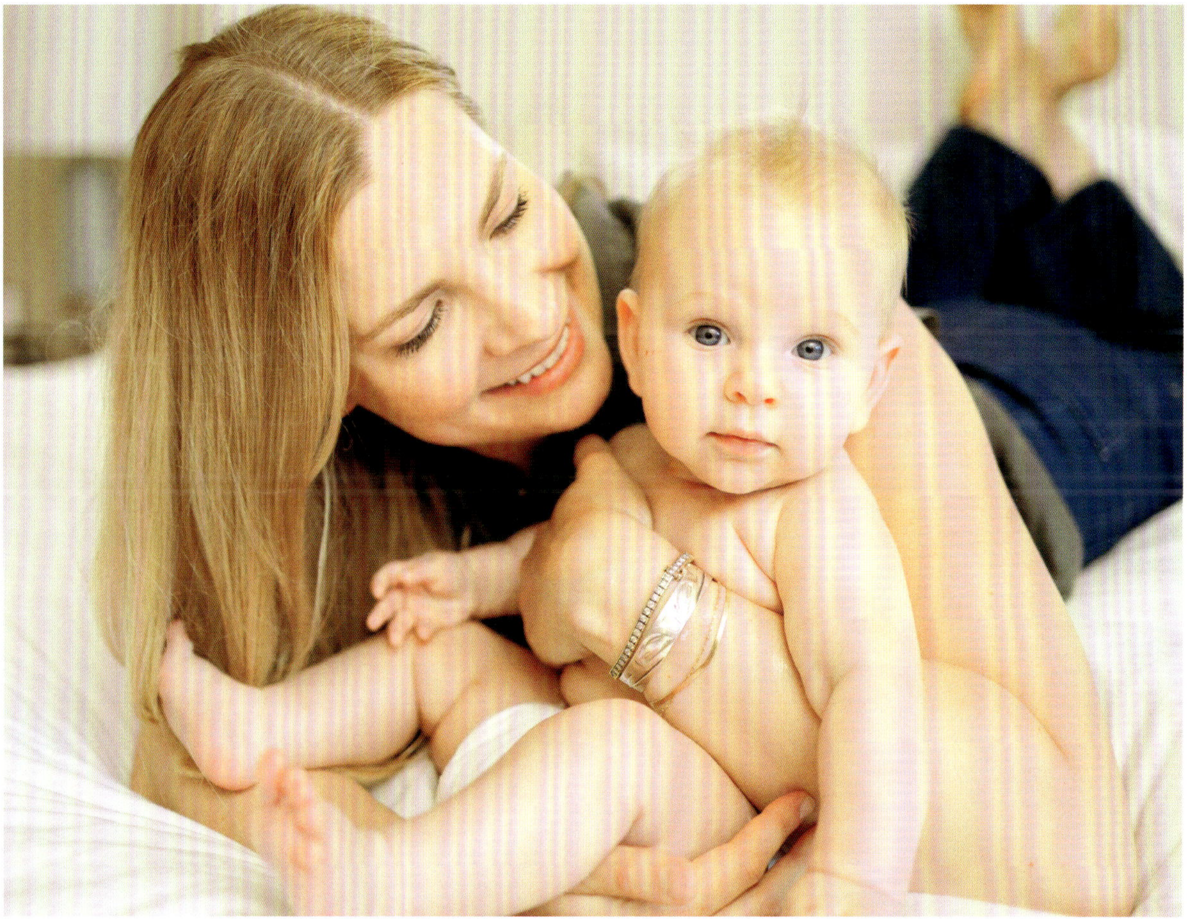

After photographing the mother and baby, I asked the father to join them on the bed for some family photos (**FIGURE 12.7**) Again, I did not move my light. Because I had already metered for the mother-and-baby photos, I did not re-meter, either.

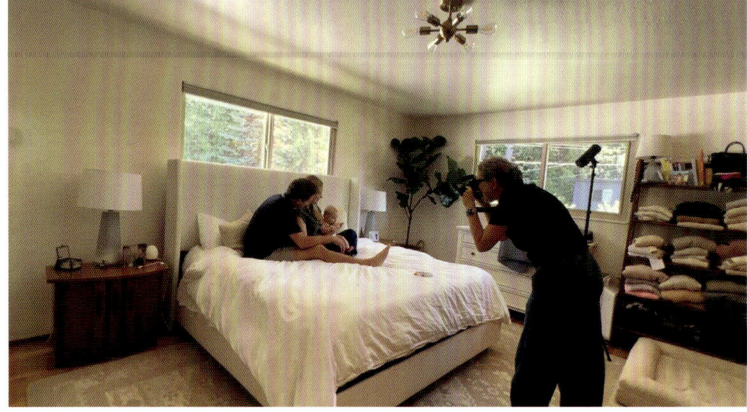

A

**FIGURE 12.7** Behind-the-scenes view of the family pose setup on the bed. Figure 12.7B is the resulting image.

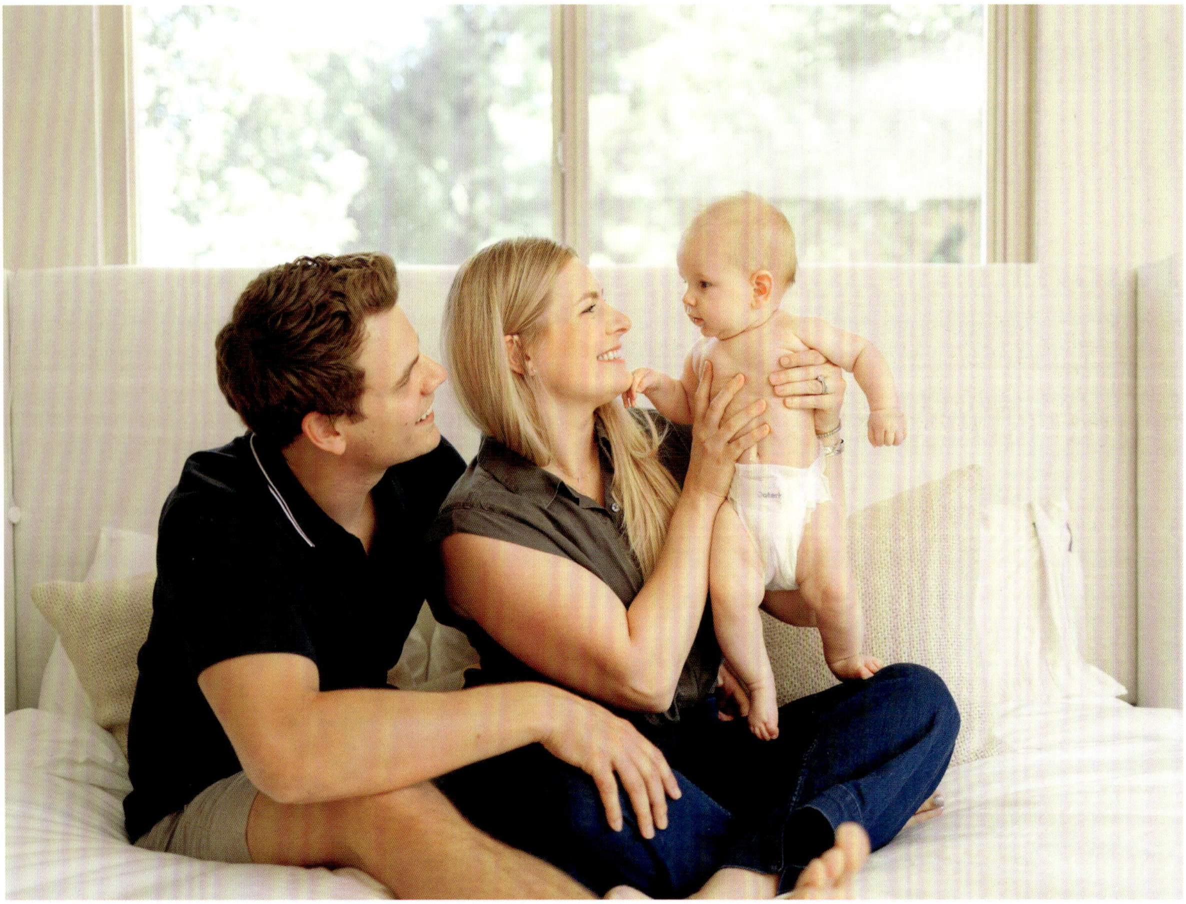

B

After family photos, I quickly took some images of the father and his baby (**FIGURE 12.8**) wrapping up our complete session flow for this room. In total, we spent about 15 minutes in the primary bedroom, including the time it took me to set up my light and meter—proof that adding light to your in-home sessions does not have to be hard or time consuming!

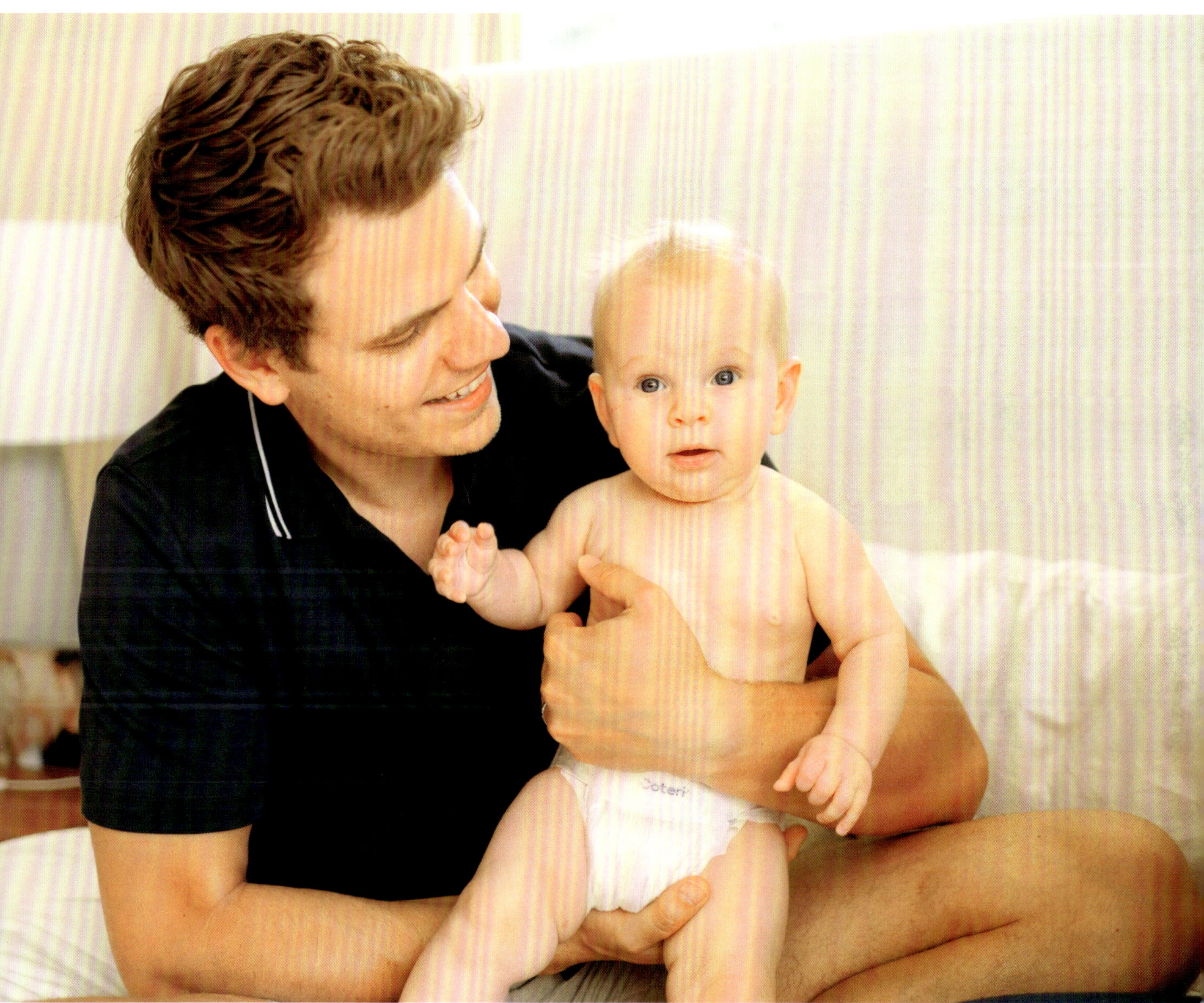

**FIGURE 12.8** Father and baby in the primary bedroom.

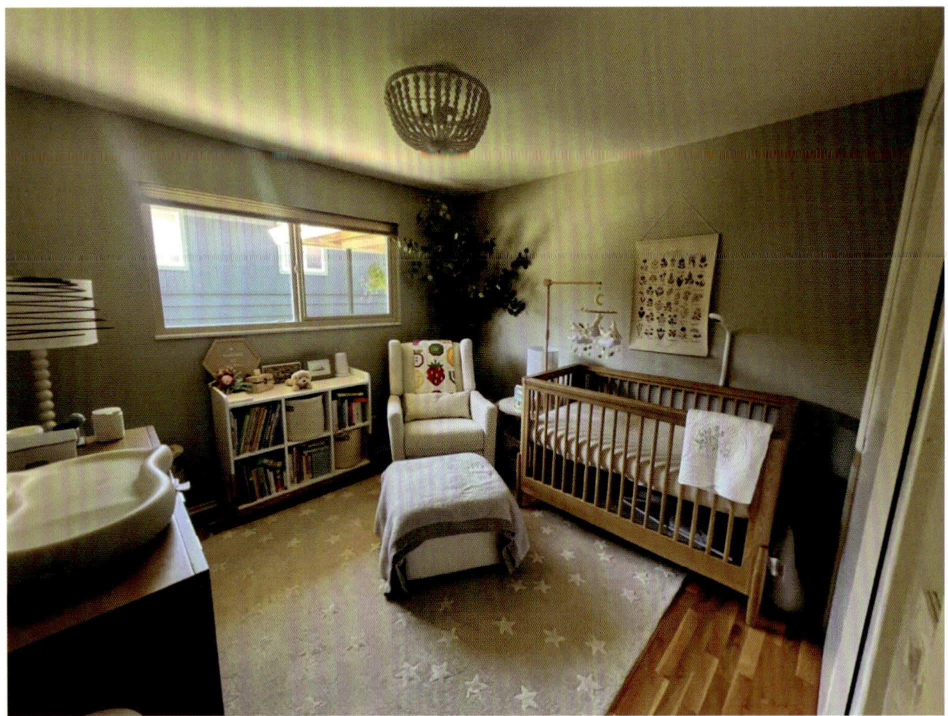

FIGURE 12.9 The nursery

## The Nursery

Next, we moved into the baby's nursery (**FIGURE 12.9**). The nursery was a more challenging location to work in due to the small space and west-facing windows. The walls were painted green and there was a color cast coming from the blue house next door, which meant that I needed to be careful with my light so I didn't bounce that green shade onto the skin of my clients.

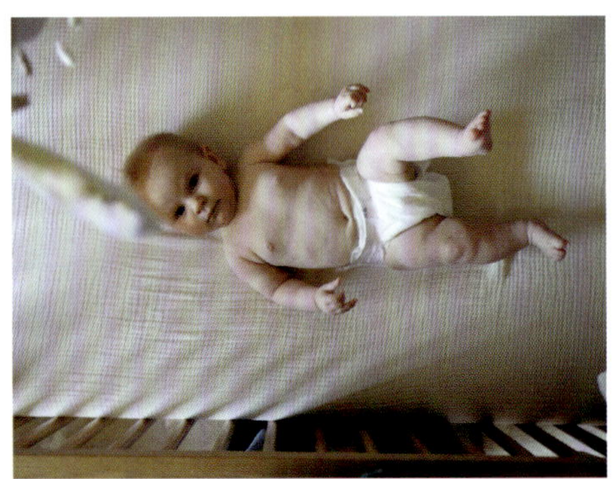

FIGURE 12.10 The unfiltered natural light coming through the west window resulted in strong, uneven shadows—not ideal for portraits.

The flow for the nursery photos was the same as the flow in the primary bedroom, only without family photos due the small size of the room.

The parents requested photos of the baby in her crib, under her mobile. In this position, her head pointed toward the window, which had the potential to create a butterfly light pattern. But it was an afternoon session, and the natural light was direct and intense due to the west-facing window. It created strong, unflattering shadows on the baby in her crib (**FIGURE 12.10**).

I knew adding a light to photograph this space was a must, so I placed the strobe and stand at 90 degrees to the crib.

I decided to bounce light off of the windows to avoid potentially bouncing green from the walls back onto my clients (**FIGURE 12.11**). This worked great for the photos of the baby in her crib.

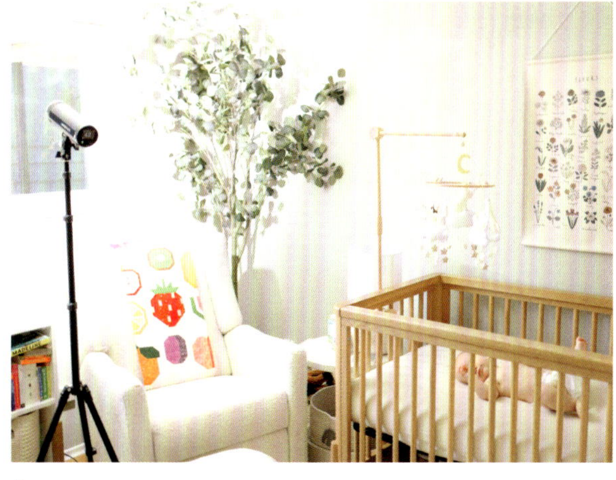

A

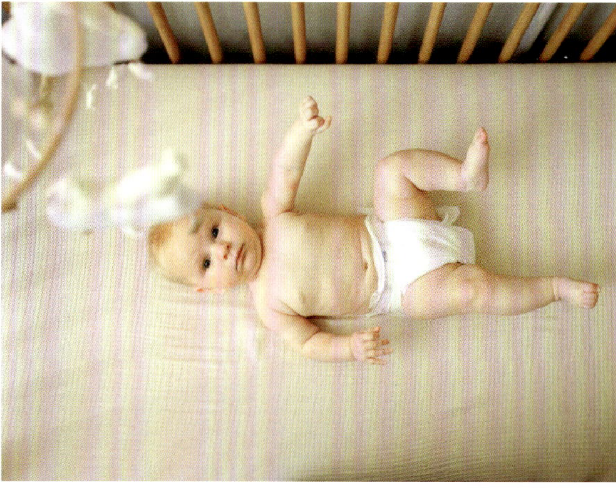

B

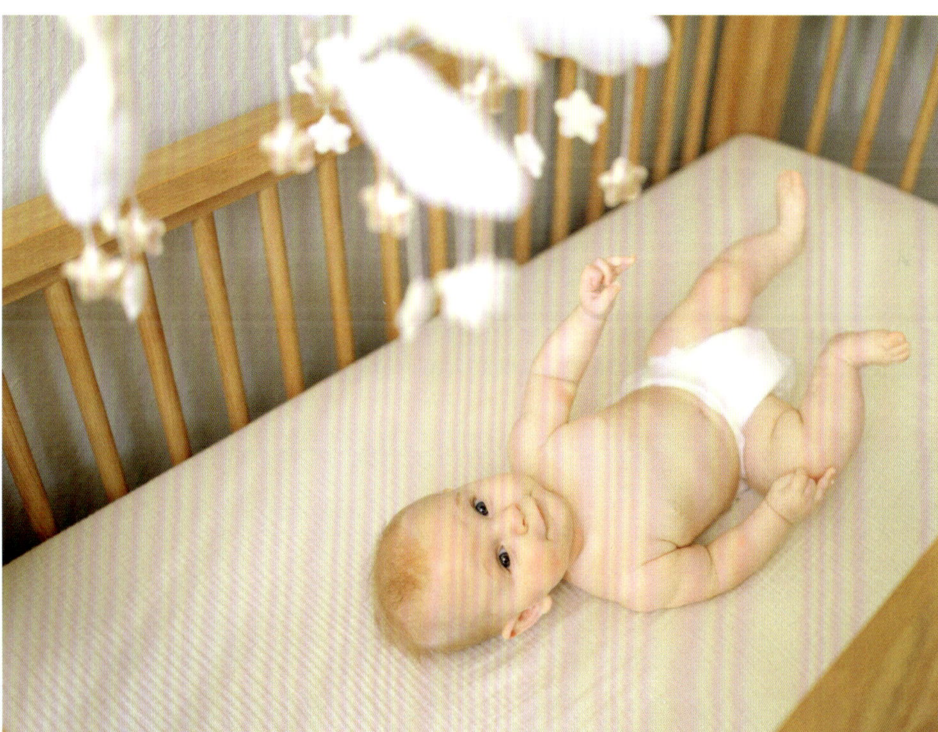

C

**FIGURE 12.11** Figure 12.11A shows the strobe positioned 90 degrees to the crib. These images were captured at f/2.8, 1.125 sec., ISO 100.

After photographing the baby, it was time for portraits with each of her parents, starting with her mom. Without moving my light, I asked the mom to pick up her baby. I quickly re-metered and adjusted the power on the strobe so that I could stop down to f/4, leaving my other two settings the same. Then I photographed the two together (**FIGURE 12.12**).

I loved the light we were getting on the two of them with the strobe in this position, but I did not like the shadows the light was creating in the background.

To fix the problem, I moved the light from its position in front of the window and instead bounced it off the ceiling opposite the crib (**FIGURE 12.13A**). This adjustment helped reduce the shadows from the tree behind the chair and created soft, flat light on my subjects (**FIGURES 12.13B**, **C**, and **D**). I re-metered after moving the light but didn't need to adjust my exposure settings for the parent-and-baby portraits. Since the nursery didn't have enough space for family photos, we moved into the living room next. A friendly reminder: it's absolutely okay to adjust your posing flow as needed based on the space and circumstances.

In total we spent 10 to 15 minutes taking photos in the nursery before moving on, including the time it took me to adjust the position of my light and meter the scene.

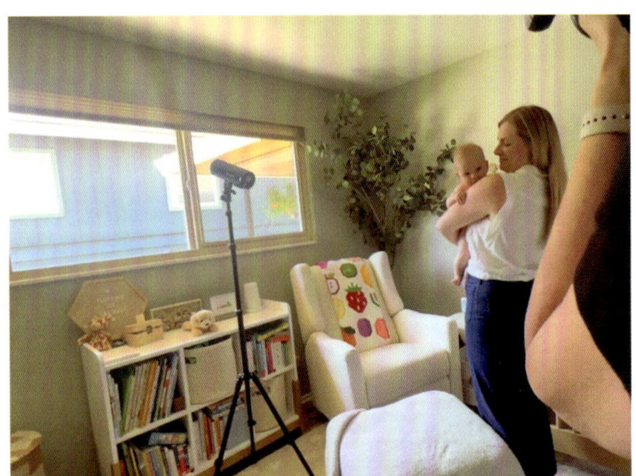

**FIGURE 12.12** Behind-the-scenes setup for the mom-and-baby portraits. Although the light is flattering on the subjects, shadows cast by the tree behind the chair are visible—and not ideal.

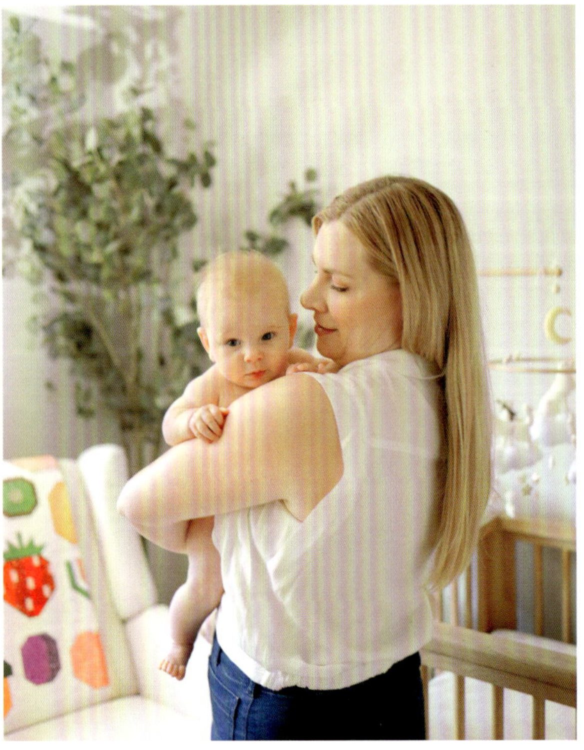

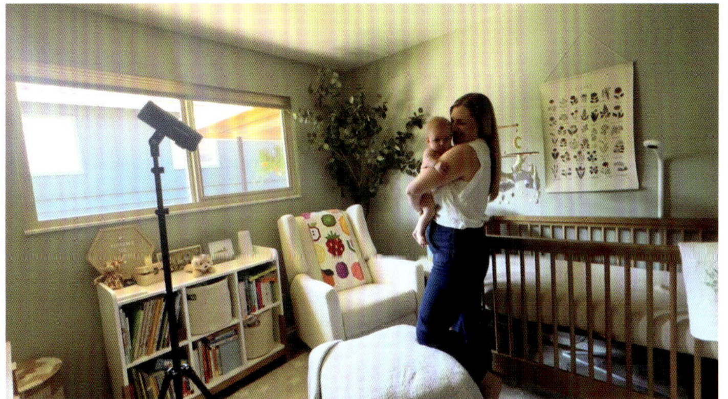

A

**FIGURE 12.13** The updated lighting setup of bouncing the strobe off the opposite ceiling for beautiful flat light and no distracting shadows in the background.

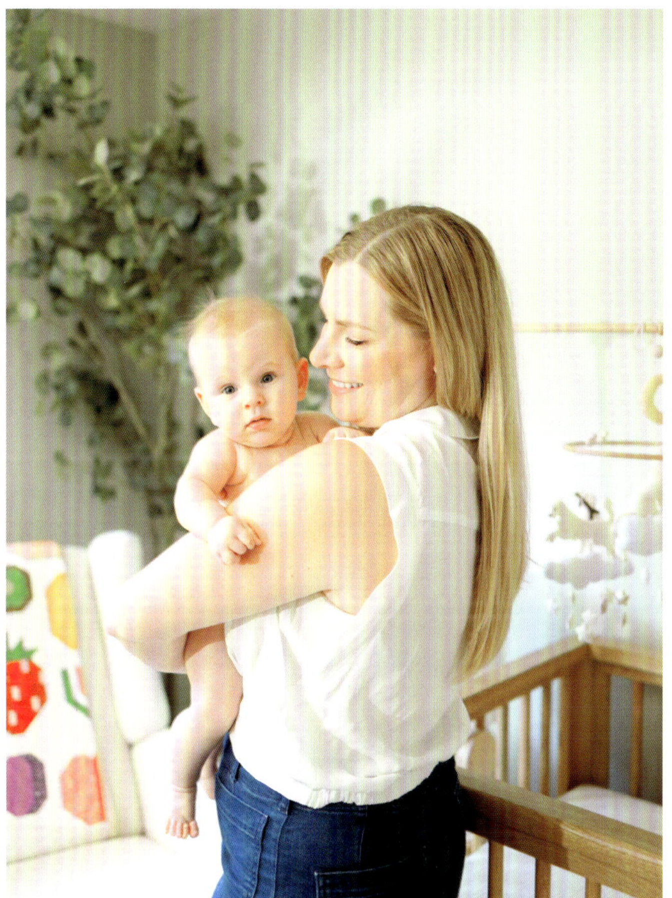

B

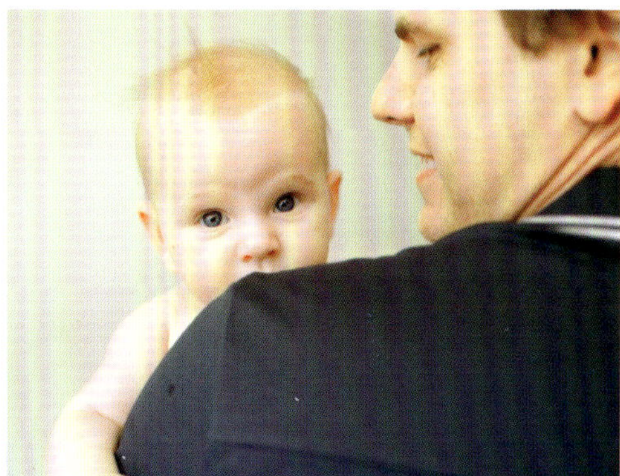

C

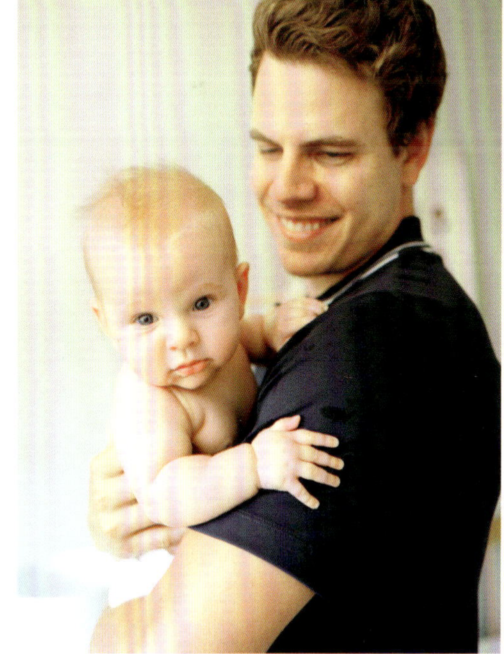

D

## Pay Attention to Shadows

When lighting your subjects, it's easy to focus solely on how the light falls on faces and skin—but don't forget to check your background. Harsh or oddly placed shadows on walls, furniture, or décor can draw attention away from your subject and make an image feel cluttered or over lit. Often, a quick reposition of your light or a subtle shift in your subject's angle is all it takes to clean things up—without sacrificing quality!

### The Living Room

The living room was our final stop during the session. By the time we got there, we had been working together for about half an hour, and the baby was starting to get tired. So I made the decision to focus only on family portraits in this space—and yes, we included the family dog!

This room was spacious and filled with beautiful natural light from large north-facing windows (**FIGURE 12.14A**). When I first arrived, I had planned to photograph in this room using only window light. But after taking a few test shots, I noticed a strong green color cast caused by a bank of trees just outside the windows (**FIGURE 12.14B**). I knew that adding artificial light would help neutralize the color and give me the clean, consistent look I wanted.

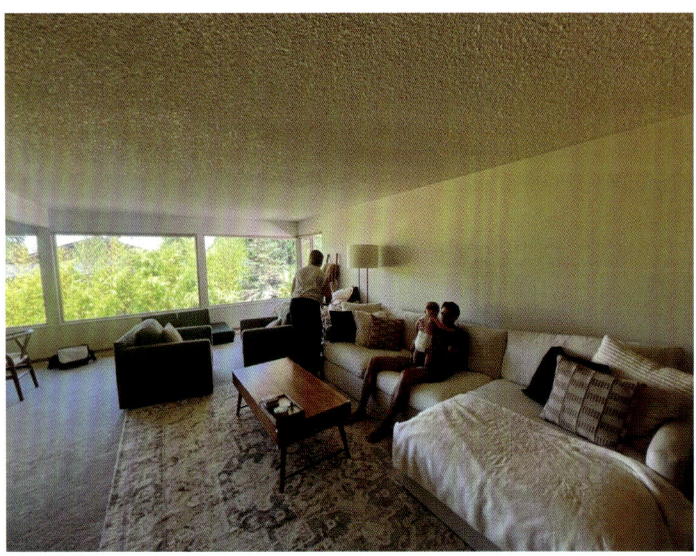

A

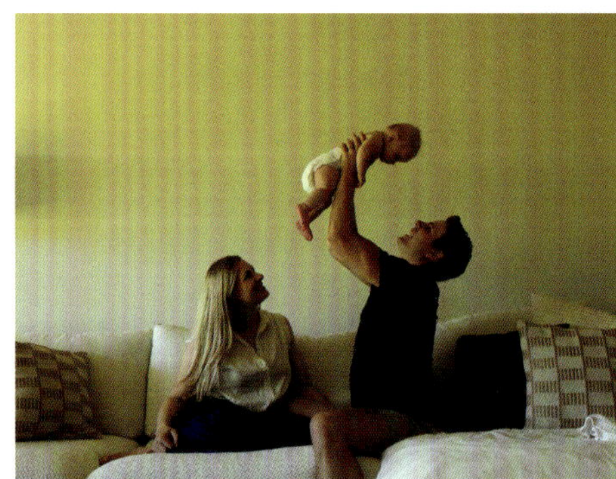

B

**FIGURE 12.14** A wide view of the spacious living room with soft natural light from large north-facing windows. Figure 12.15B is my test shot. Notice the strong green color cast from the trees outside the windows.

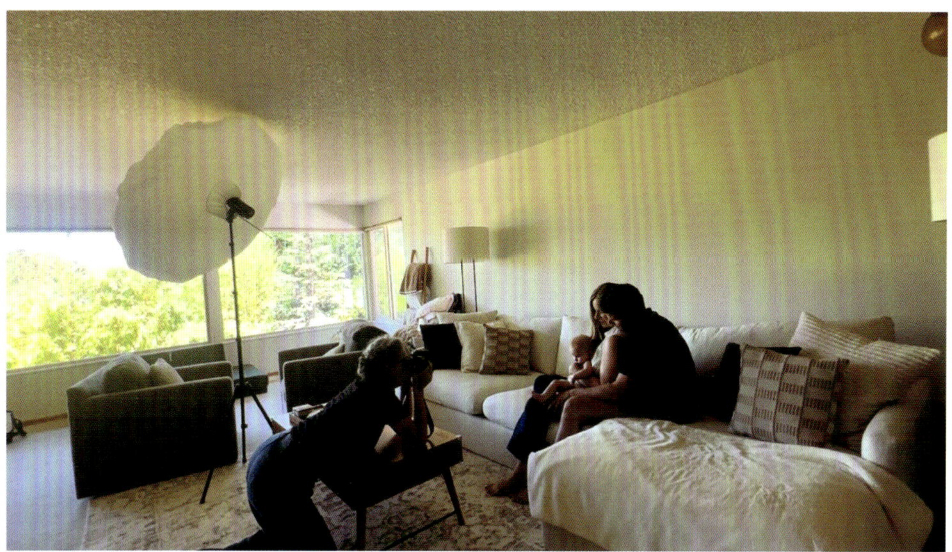

**FIGURE 12.15** Lighting setup: Strobe with a 45-inch white umbrella and diffusion panel placed close to the family in the bounce position, set at 45 degrees for soft, even lighting.

Because I had more space to work with here, I used a 45-inch all-white umbrella with a diffusion panel on my strobe and placed it in the bounce position, 45 degrees to the family seated on the couch. In **FIGURE 12.15**, you'll notice that I didn't place my light near the windows. Instead, I brought it as close to the family as I could without moving their furniture. That was intentional.

Remember: The proximity of your light source impacts its quality. The closer the light is to your subject, the softer it becomes. Since I was working with a relatively small umbrella, I wanted to get it in close to create that soft, flattering look. If I had set the light back by the windows or bounced it from across the room, the light would have become harder and less forgiving.

The images we captured in the living room ended up being sweet, relaxed, and the perfect way to wrap up the session (**FIGURE 12.16**, next pages).

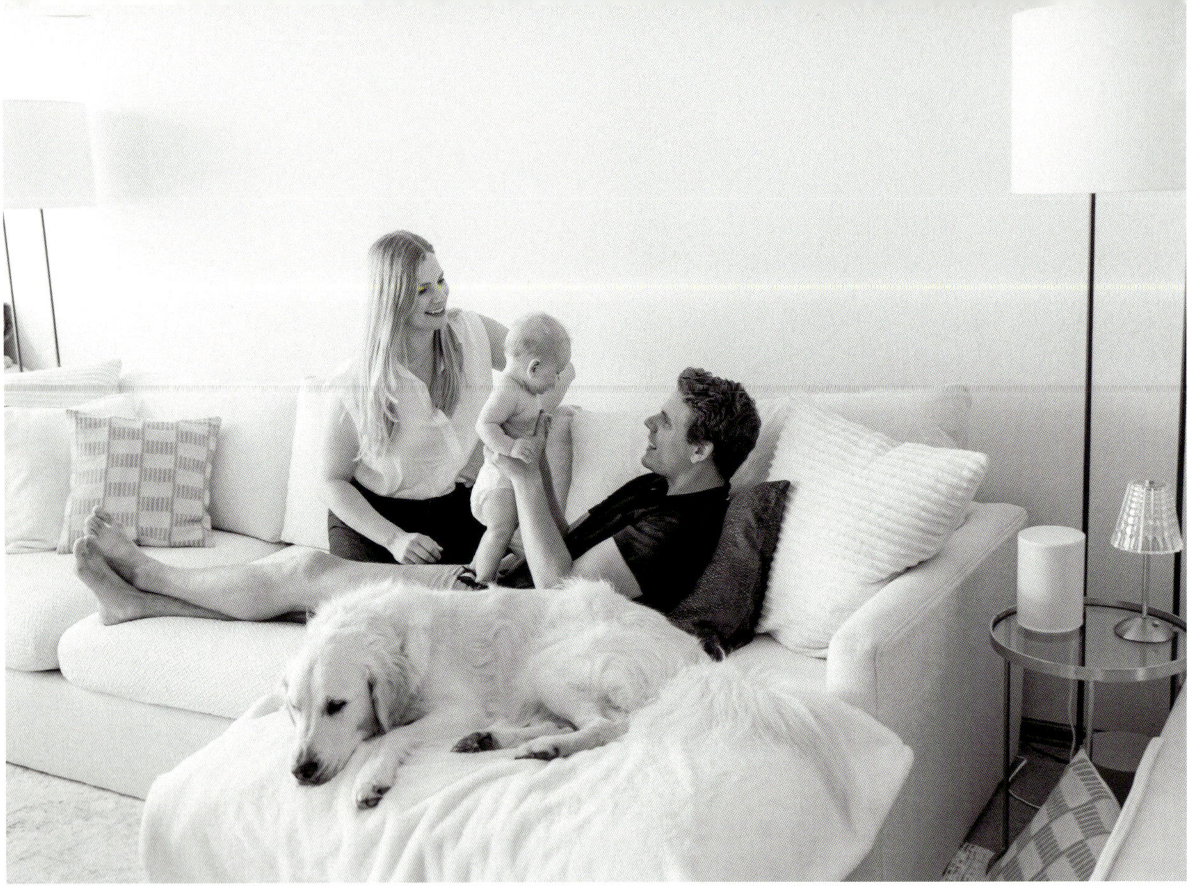

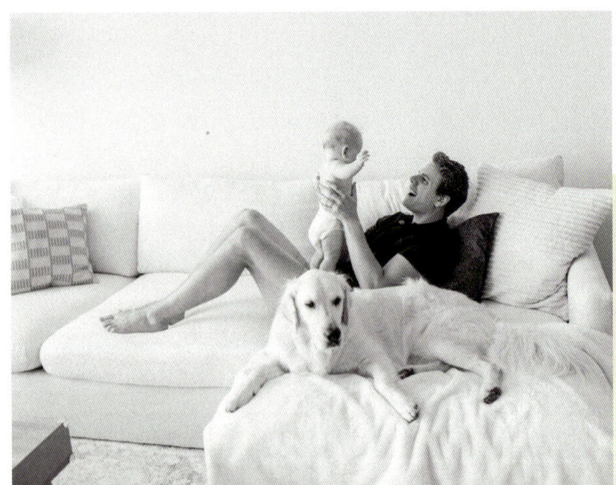

**FIGURE 12.16** The final photos

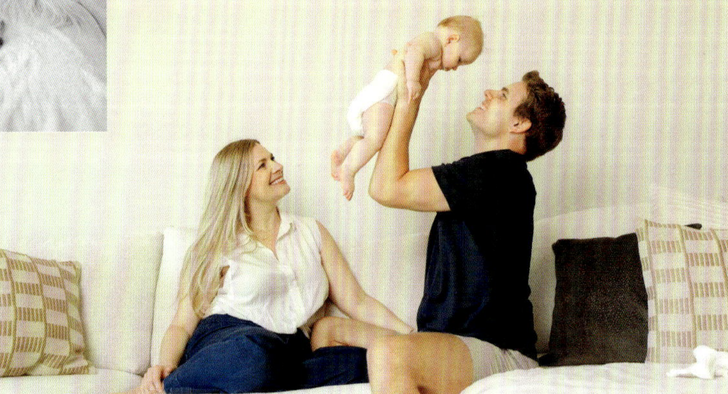

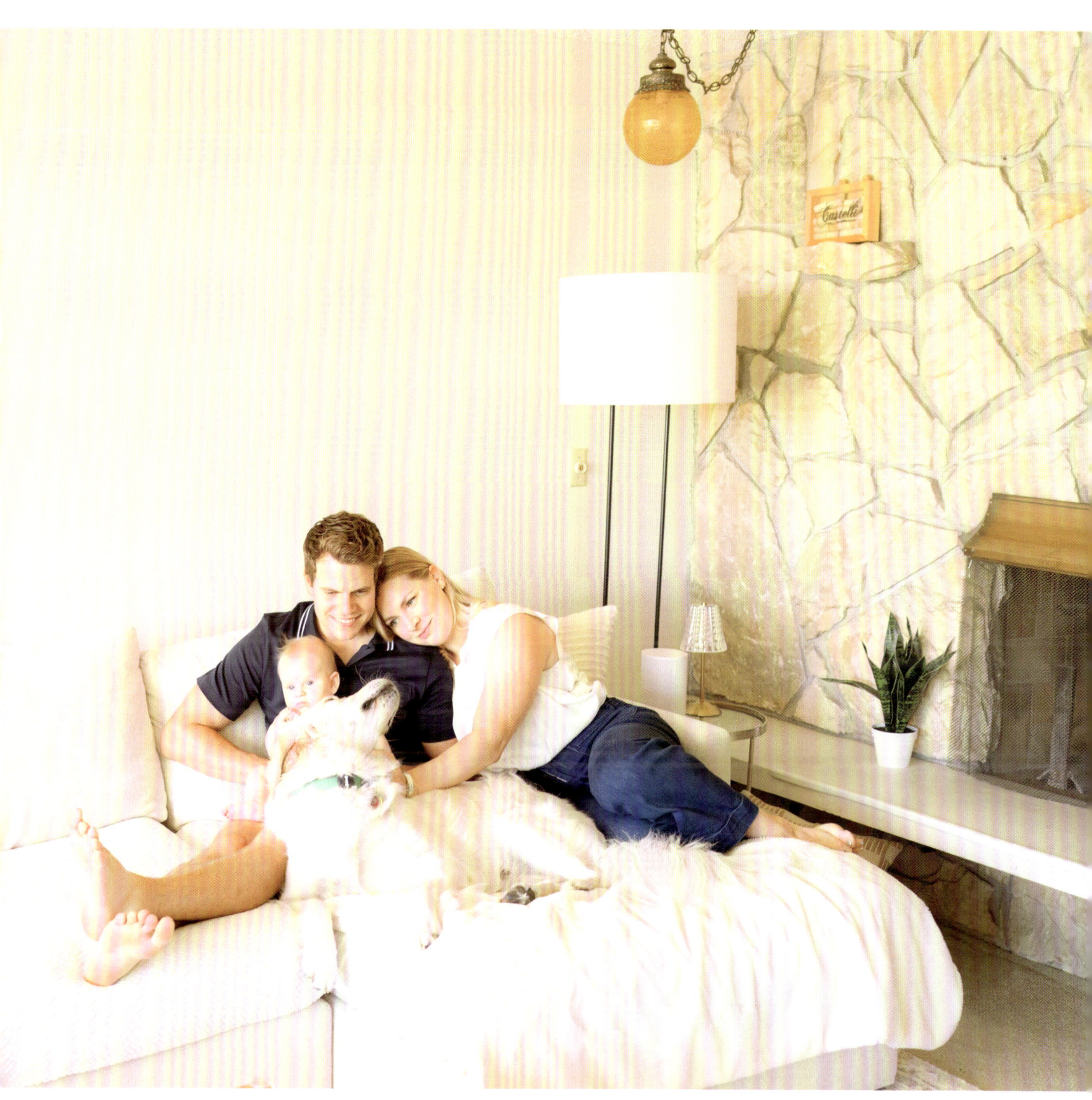

## Fresh 48 (Hospital) Session

Like all parents, I will never forget the day my children were born. It was like the world stopped, and I was in absolute awe of these little people my body had miraculously created. I'd had a hard pregnancy that ended in an emergency C-section. I was exhausted, but also in a state of total bliss. All I wanted to do was stare at my babies—their tiny faces, fingers, and toes.

I was lucky to have a photographer friend with me at the hospital that day. The photos she captured of those first precious moments are something I will cherish forever. I think of those images—how I felt that day, and how I feel when I look at them now—every time I'm asked to photograph a Fresh 48 session. They are truly something special.

A Fresh 48, or hospital session, is a photo session that takes place in the hospital or birthing center within 24 to 48 hours after a baby's birth. The goal of these sessions is to capture those special first moments and provide professional portraits while the baby is still brand new.

Offering Fresh 48 sessions is not only a gift to your clients, it's also a smart business move. These sessions fill a unique niche that traditional newborn photography doesn't cover. For families who may not want a full newborn studio session, a Fresh 48 offers the chance to have beautiful, professional photos of their baby without the need to leave the hospital. This initial hospital session allows the client to connect with you from the beginning, helping to build trust and establish a relationship. It's also an excellent way to add an additional revenue stream. A true win-win.

### Fresh 48 Cheat Sheet

Fresh 48 hospital sessions are very unique. When you're working in a studio or in a client's home, you typically have the time and space to create a robust gallery. Hospitals, on the other hand, tend to be small and busy, so your approach must adapt to fit the demands of the environment.

#### Pack Light

Hospital rooms are small, unpredictable spaces, so your equipment needs to be compact and versatile. All you need is one light, a trigger, and modifier in a stand. Lighting doesn't have to be complicated to be beautiful.

### Prepare Clients in Advance

Let clients know what to expect. Remind them they don't need to be "camera ready" after just having a baby. Their job is simply to enjoy this special time and you'll do the rest. If they don't want to be in photos, that is okay. Be mindful of the fact that the baby you are working with is brand new, and the most precious thing in the entire world to your clients. Wear a mask. Wash your hands. And keep your poses minimal and baby led.

### Be Flexible with the Flow

Come in with a plan but be ready to pivot. A tired parent, a nurse visit, or a tight space might require quick changes. The goal is to adapt without stress. A well-established posing flow will help you stay grounded and efficient.

### Remember What You've Learned About Lighting

Natural light isn't always available in hospital rooms, so it's important to know how to create your own. Set your light up on the window side of the room to mimic daylight, pay close attention to the light quality you are creating, and use flattering patterns—like butterfly or loop light—when lighting your subjects.

### Focus on Connection Over Perfection

Fresh 48 sessions are not about creating galleries full of polished poses—they're about capturing the first moments of your clients as a family. Work your angles and compositions to add variety. Allow your emphasis to be on storytelling and connection.

## Pre-Session Prep

Every hospital—and every hospital room—is different, so I prepare for these sessions the same way I prepare for in-home sessions. I pack my camera, a strobe, a flash, and a universal trigger that works with both lights. I also bring my 45-inch convertible umbrella with a one-stop diffusion panel and a lightweight travel stand. All the equipment fits into one bag so I can move through the hospital and navigate the (often) small rooms with ease. And I always bring a mask when working with newborns in the hospital as a courtesy to my clients.

## Session Flow

For this session, I was working with a family I already knew, so I was thrilled when they invited me to the hospital to photograph their baby. I arrived at the hospital in the morning, just hours after their baby had been born. Both parents

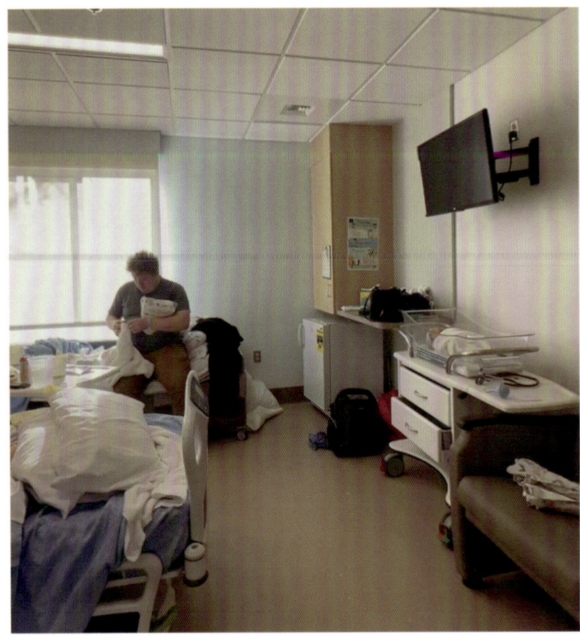

**FIGURE 12.17** Note the tight quarters and limited window light in the hospital room.

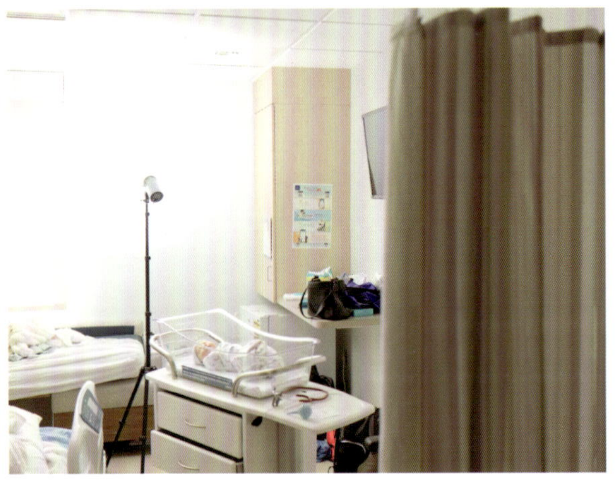

**FIGURE 12.18** My light setup in the butterfly light position.

had been up all night and were understandably exhausted. They told me they were mostly interested in photos of the baby, as they didn't feel "camera ready. No problem! I promised to check in at the end of the session in case they changed their mind.

Their room was very small and pretty dark, but it did have one east-facing window that was getting some beautiful morning light. Access to the window was blocked by dad's cot, mom was resting in her hospital bed, and the remaining space was crowded with furniture, bags and hospital equipment. The baby was up against the wall in his hospital bassinet, which left three to four feet for me to set up and work (**FIGURE 12.17**). After assessing the room, I decided that it was best to leave the baby in his bassinet for photos.

## Lighting and Posing the Newborn

I could not place the baby's bassinet close enough to the window to use natural light, so I set up my Westcott FJ200 strobe on a stand with the 45-inch white umbrella and diffusion panel on the window side of the room. I turned it 90 degrees to the bassinet to create a butterfly light pattern (**FIGURE 12.18**). I metered and got to work.

Because the bassinet was on wheels, I could easily move it to create different light patterns on the baby. Because the proximity of the light to the baby was the same in each lighting pattern, I knew my settings wouldn't change. All images of the baby alone were captured at f/2.8, 1/125 sec., ISO 100.

Because all the photos of the newborn were in his bassinet, he would be on his back for the entire session. I added variety to the gallery with different lighting patterns, by adjusting my position and use of composition, and by rotating between photographing the baby in his hat and swaddle, just his swaddle, and then just his diaper.

### Butterfly Light

This is one of my favorite lighting patterns for lighting newborns, and I used it for the majority of the photos I took at this session (**FIGURE 12.19A** shows the setup, and **FIGURES 12.19B–H** show some examples).

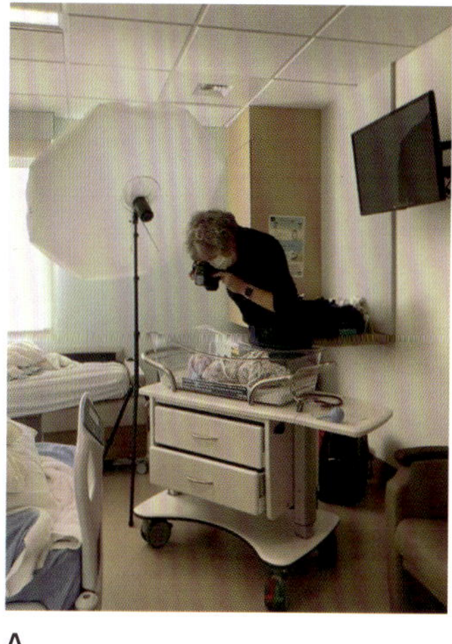

A

**FIGURE 12.19** Butterfly light setup (**A**). Images **B–H** show the finished photos.

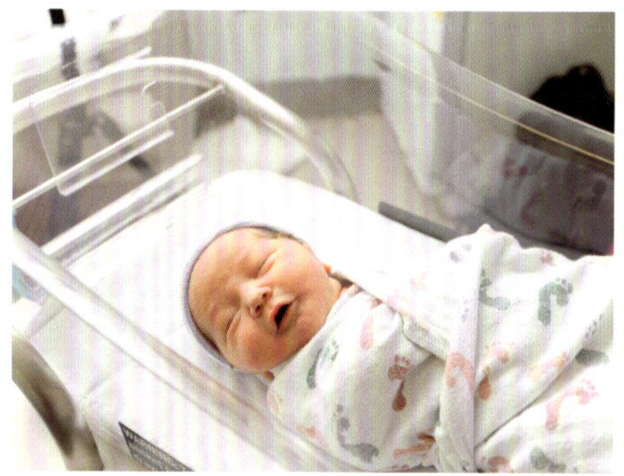

B

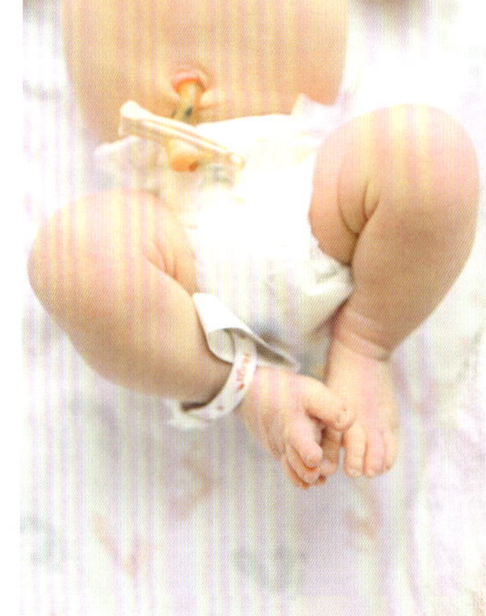

C

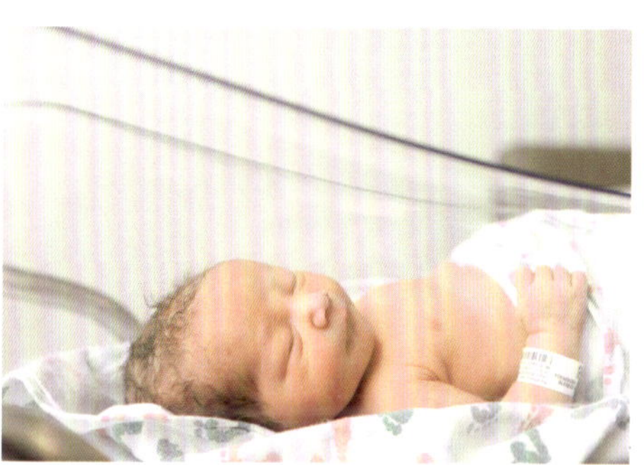

D

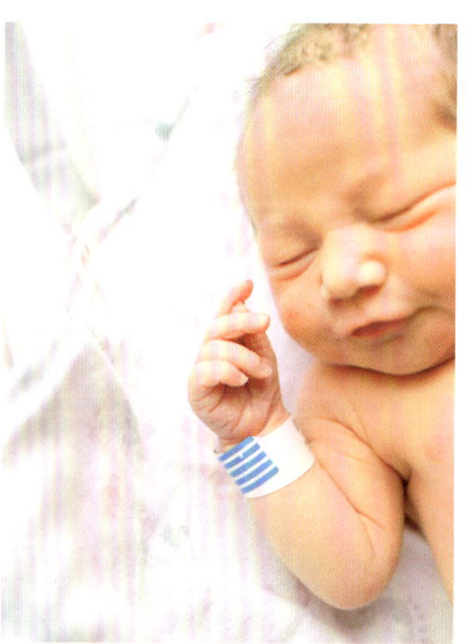

E

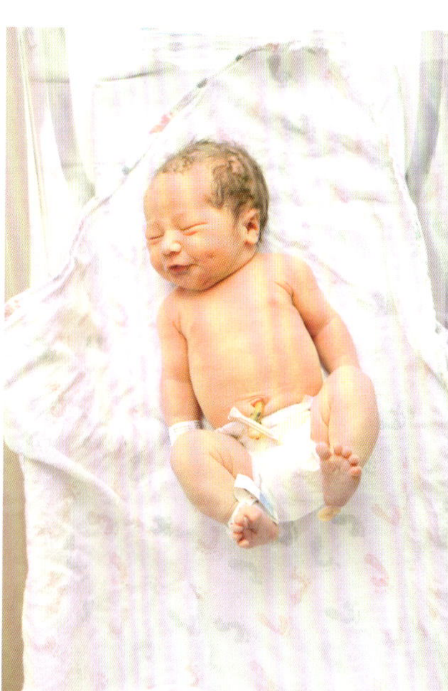

F

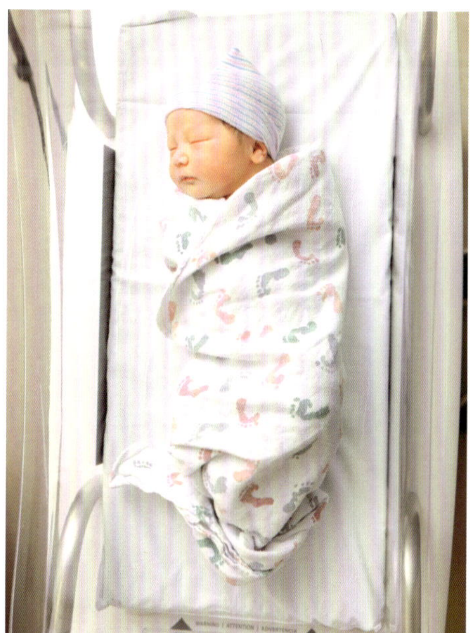

G

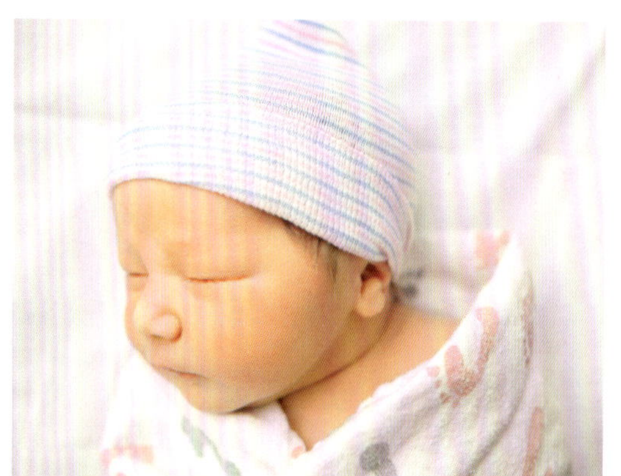

H

### Split Light

I don't often use split light with newborns in the studio, but in this session, it gave me just the contrast I needed to add a little depth to the photos. I rotated the bassinet so that the baby was lit from the side, placing my light 90 degrees to the subject (**FIGURE 12.20A**).

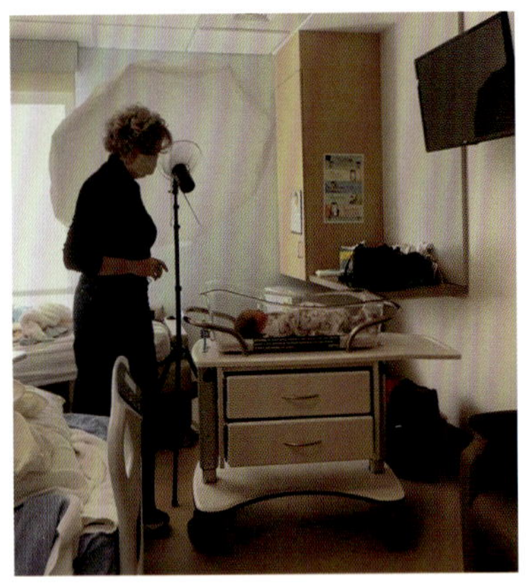

A

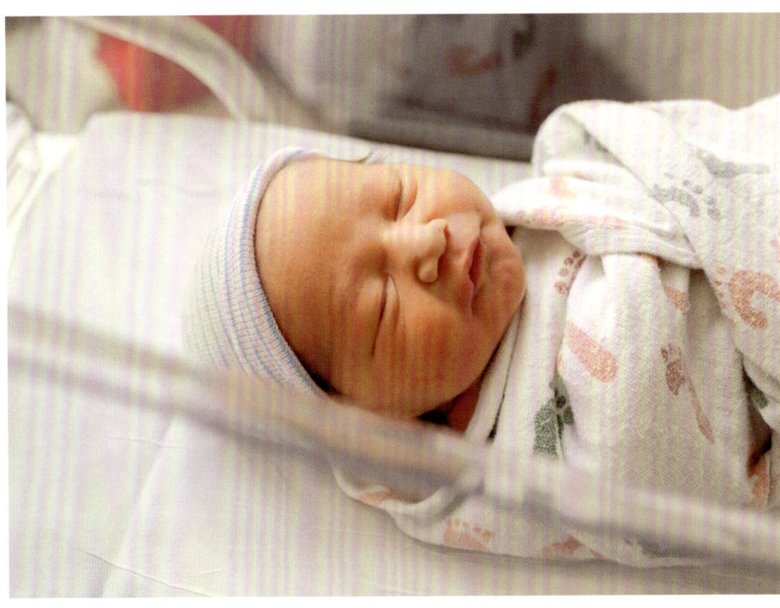

B

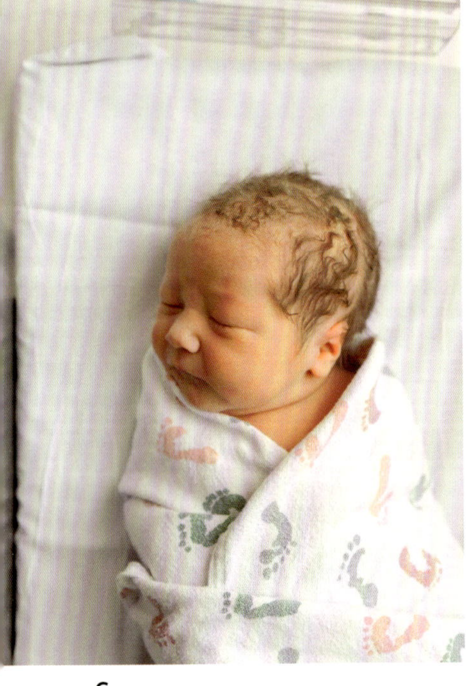

C

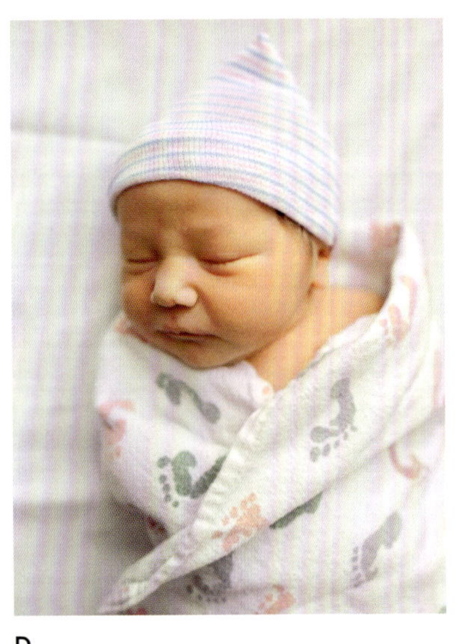

D

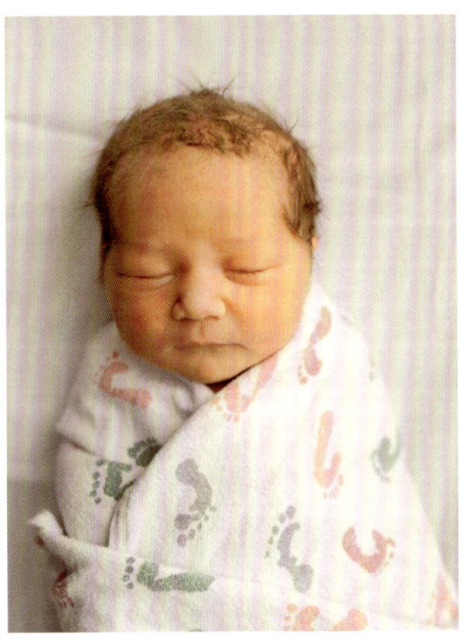

E

**FIGURE 12.20** Split light setup (**A**). Images **B–E** show the finished photos.

### Backlight

I rarely use backlight in the studio when working with newborns, but it worked beautifully here to highlight the baby's details—especially his tiny toes. **FIGURE 12.21A** shows the setup, and **FIGURES 12.21B–E** show some of the final images.

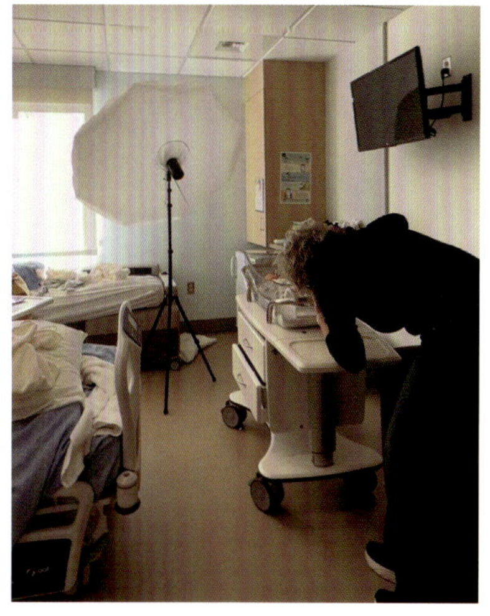

A

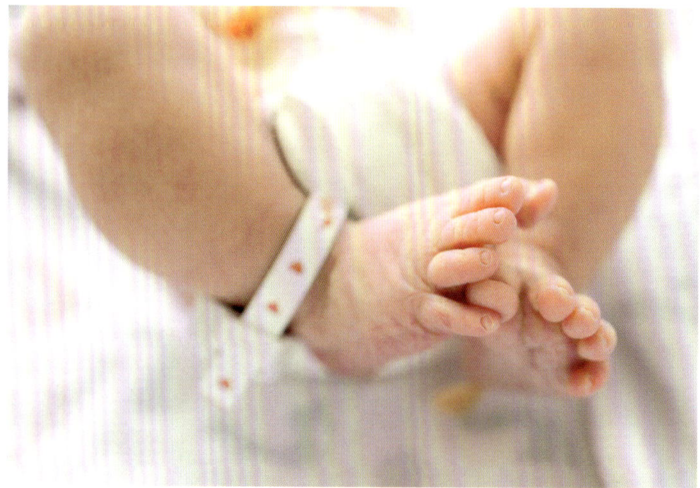

B

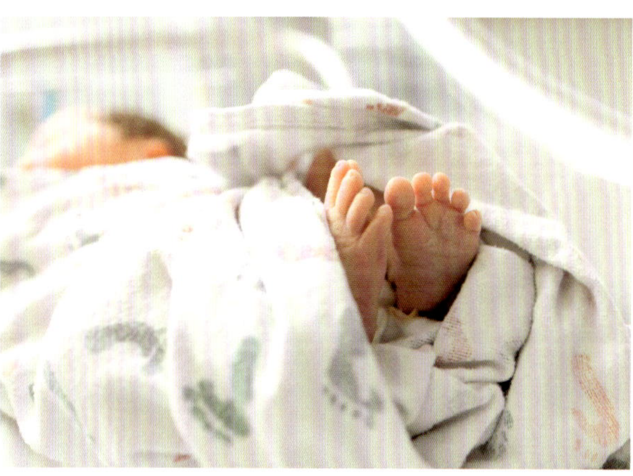

C

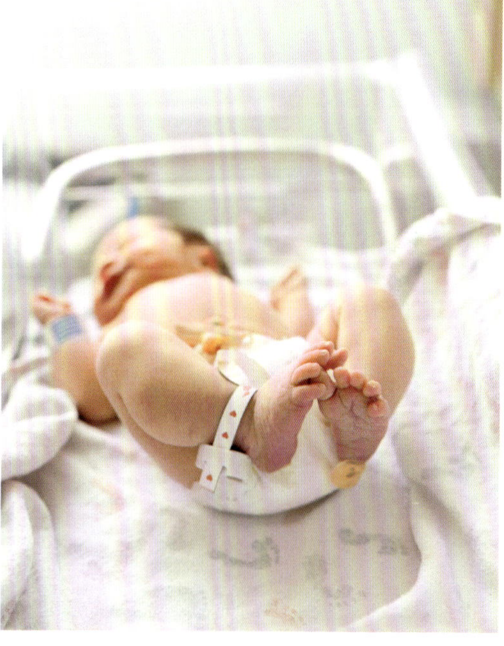

E

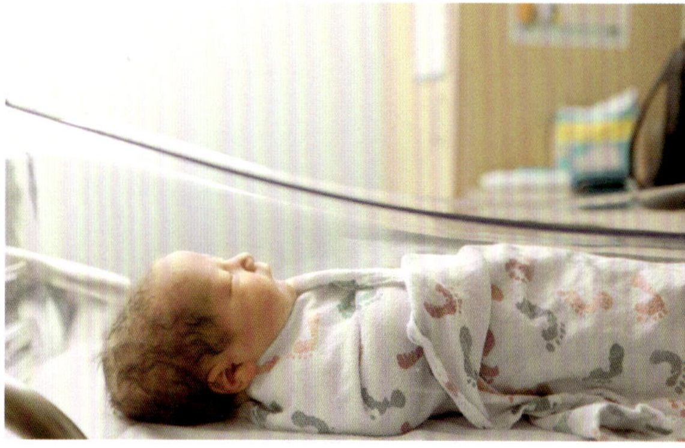

D

**FIGURE 12.21** Backlight setup (**A**). Images **B–E** show the finished photos.

Before wrapping up photos of the baby alone, I asked the dad to come over and cradle the baby's head in his hands for a couple of photos. I love taking close-ups of babies in their parent's hands to highlight just how tiny they are (**FIGURE 12.22**).

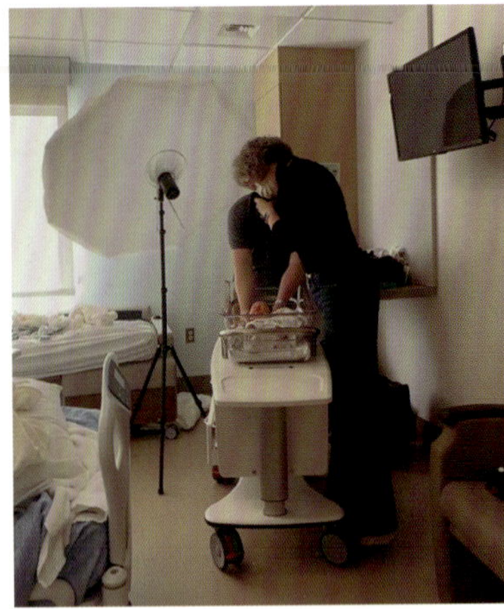

A

**FIGURE 12.22** The setup (**A**) and the finished photo (**B**).

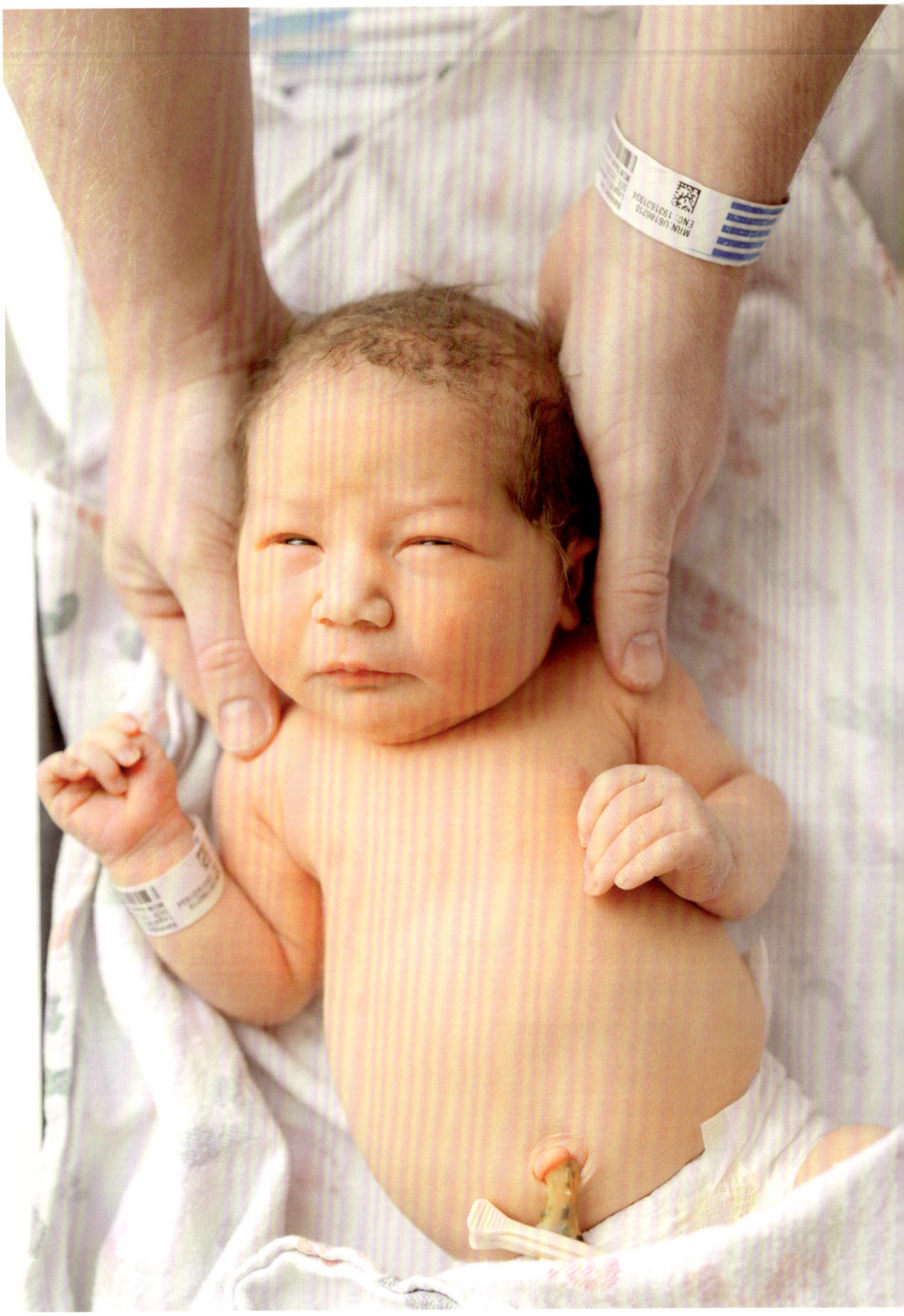

B

## Photos with Mom

After finishing my work with the baby, I checked in with the parents. They had changed their minds and decided that they would like a few photos with their baby. The room was small, so I moved the basinet out of the way. This gave us access to a blank wall that could serve as our backdrop. I positioned the mom, then placed my light in front of the window to mimic the natural light and turned it 45 Degrees to create a flattering loop light look (**FIGURE 12.23**). I handed mom her new baby, metered, adjusted the power on my strobe so that I could stop down to f/4, and got to work photographing them together. These images were captured at f/4, 1.125 sec., ISO 100.

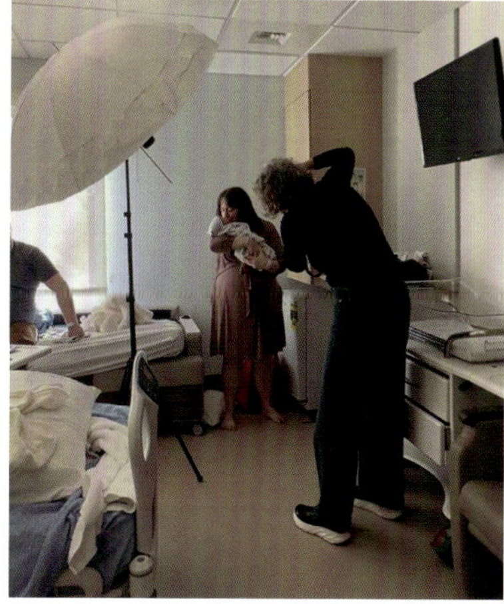

A

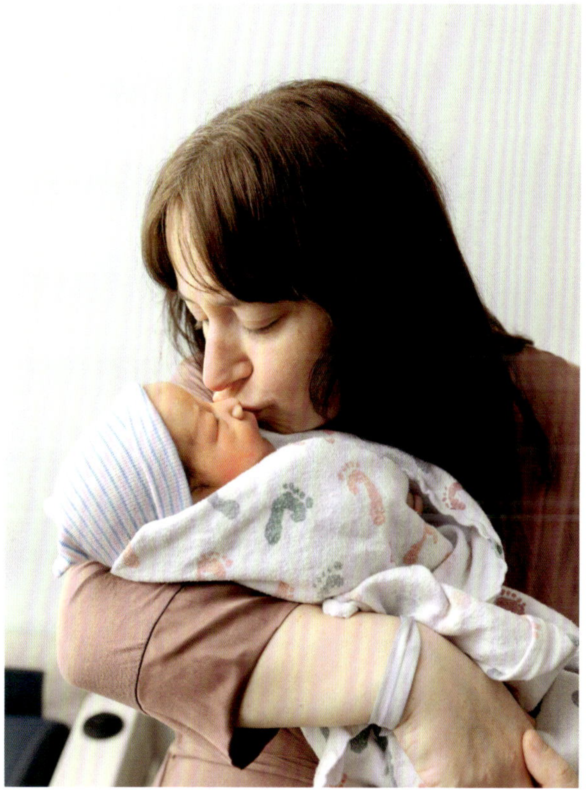

B

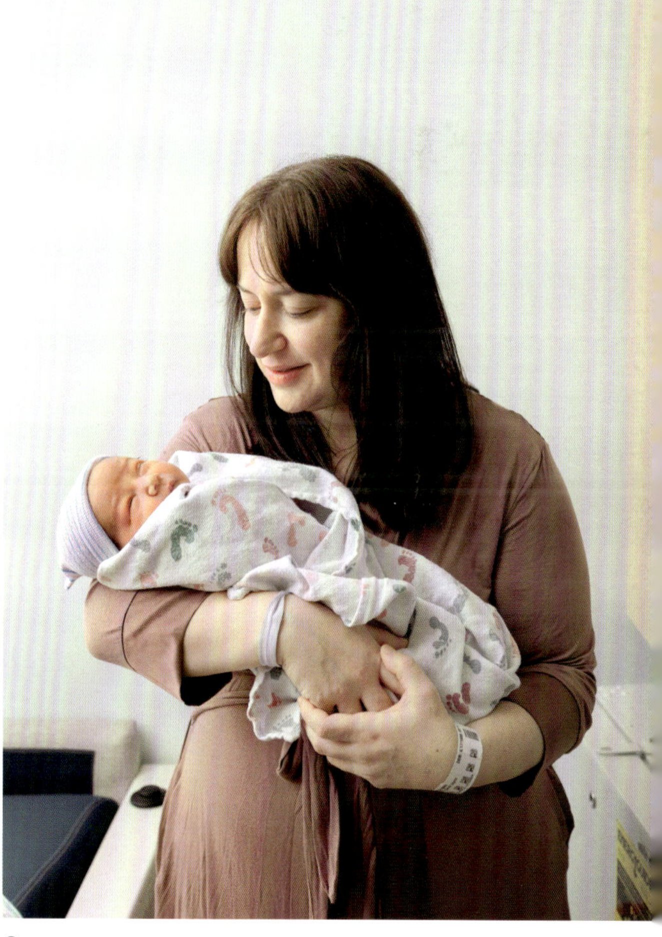

C

**FIGURE 12.23** Mother and son. Setting up my light on the window side of the room allowed me to create light that mimicked the natural light from the window.

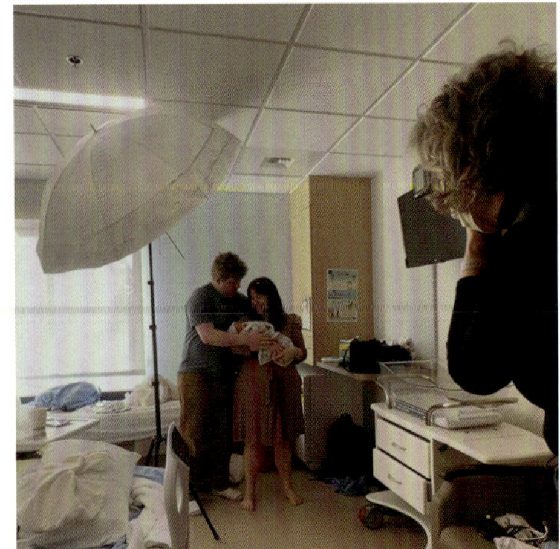

A

## Photos with Mom and Dad

After capturing some mother and son portraits, I invited dad into the frame and captured some images of the three of them together (**FIGURE 12.24**). I did not move my light or adjust my settings, and these images were also captured at f/4, 1/125 sec., ISO 100.

**FIGURE 12.24** Family photos. Figure 12.24A shows the lighting setup. Figure 12.24B shows the final image.

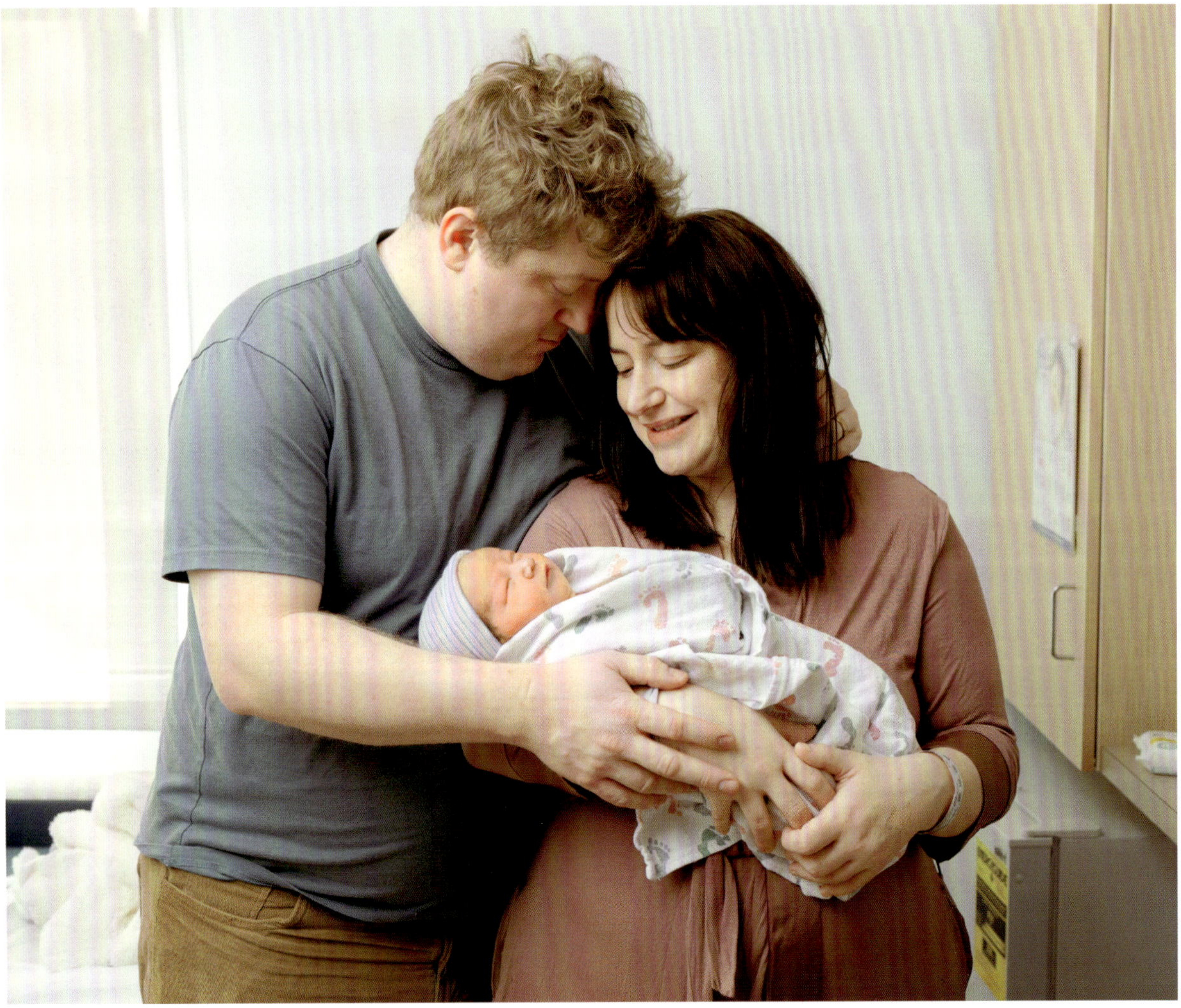

B

### Photos with Dad

We ended the session with photos of the baby and his dad. I positioned the baby so his head was facing the light to avoid uplighting (**FIGURE 12.26**). Then I captured a few final photos.

This entire session took just about an hour, including setup time, visiting, and a quick interruption from a nurse. Despite the space limitations, we created a complete gallery of beautiful images.

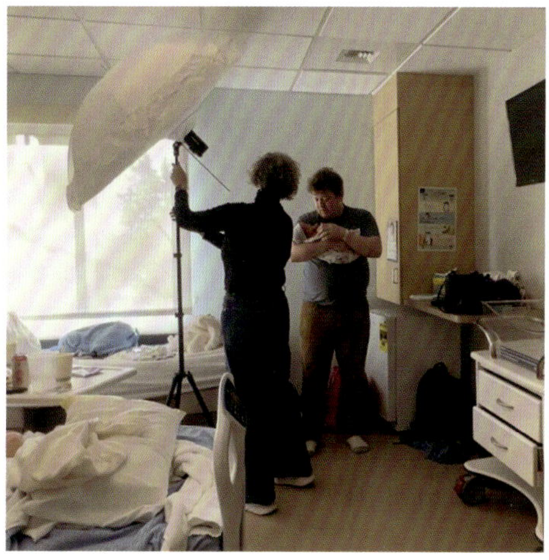

**FIGURE 12.25** Baby with dad. The baby's head is pointed toward the light to create a flattering lighting pattern.

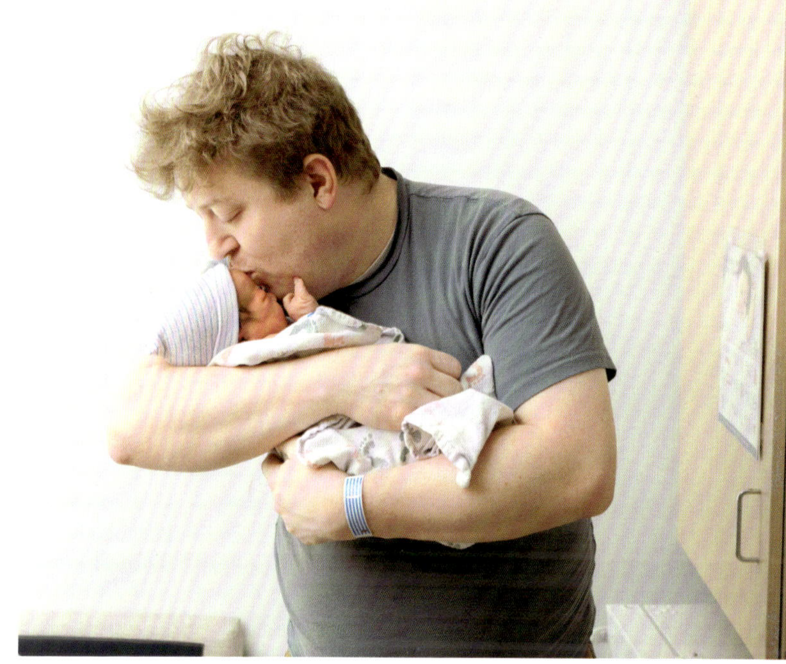

**FIGURE 12.26** Our final image, captured at f/4, 1/125 sec., ISO 100

## The Takeaway

Lighting on location doesn't have to be complicated or overwhelming. With a clear plan, a flexible mindset, and a little practice, you can create beautiful, consistent images anywhere. Trust your eye, trust your training, and remember—your job isn't to mimic natural light perfectly. It's to shape light with intention so your clients look and feel their best.

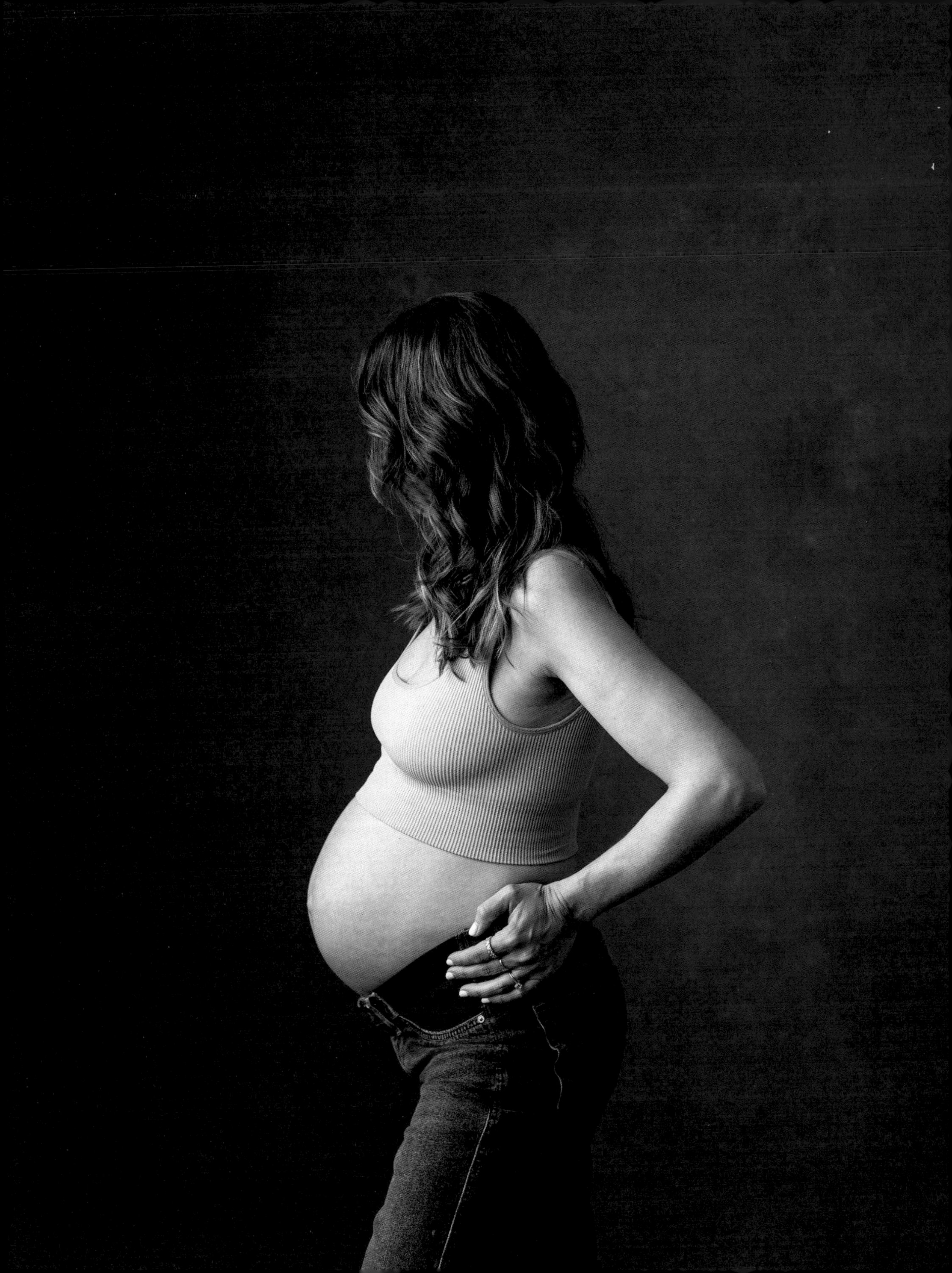

CHAPTER

# 13

# Maternity Session

As you learned in Chapter 10, the poses I use for my maternity sessions are simple and repeatable. I stick mostly to standing positions and pose my clients facing left, straight to camera, and to the right. This is a minimalist approach that I'm able to add variety to through thoughtful use of lighting and composition.

In this chapter, I'll take you behind the scenes of a real maternity session in my Seattle studio. I'll share how I prepare the space, communicate with the client, and use my posing flow and lighting to create timeless images. My goal is to show you how all the techniques we've covered in the book—lighting, posing, directing, and flow—come together in real time when working with maternity clients.

## My Philosophy

I have a somewhat old-fashioned philosophy when it comes to studio portraiture in general, but specifically in regard to my maternity work.

Once upon a time, it was common for a person to walk into a photography studio with the expectation of getting one or two great photos. Over the years, that expectation changed. Now it's more common for people to expect 50 to 100 great photos from their portrait session. And while I understand the appeal—who doesn't love seeing a ton of beautiful photos?—I believe we do our clients a disservice by trying to deliver in bulk.

When clients receive hundreds of images, the emotional impact tends to fade. Most photos end up in cloud storage. A few may be shared online or used for announcements, but many are quickly forgotten.

But when the goal is to create one or two extraordinary images, something shifts. Those photos become meaningful. They're printed, framed, and hung on walls. When we create a small collection of intentional, beautiful images, they often find a home in an album—something that can be held, revisited, and shared with future generations.

And while this is my philosophy for all the work I create, I think this is especially true in regard to maternity work. These are intimate portraits from a fleeting chapter in someone's life. My goal is to help clients walk away with *heirlooms*—not just files.

I share this with my clients. They know that at their session, I will take many photos and that I will guarantee a minimum of 25 in their gallery. But they also know my goal is to create a few *great* photos that will end up as a print or in an album.

When working with babies and families, I tend to work quickly to accommodate the needs of little ones. But when photographing maternity clients, I slow down. I pay close attention to posture, to the folds of the drape, to the way light falls, and to the composition of every frame. Everything I do in these sessions is grounded in the belief that *less is more*.

## My Look

While my newborn and family work falls into the "light-and-airy" category, I like my maternity work to be more dark and moody. To achieve that look, I do most of my maternity work in the one room at my studio that only has one very small window. This limits ambient light and gives me full control. I use a strobe paired with the Westcott 7-foot umbrella with the black backing and a diffusion panel. The size of the umbrella coupled with the diffusion panel on the front results in the beautiful soft light that I love so much. The black backing helps control light spill and results in rich shadows with depth and dimension.

My backdrop is a dark gray custom Oliphant, and I use either black-and-white film (Ilford Delta 3200 is my favorite), or, if I'm working with a digital camera, I process the images in black and white.

As mentioned in Chapter 10, the material I use for draping is a sheer curtain panel from Ikea. It's lightweight, flows beautifully, and photographs like high-end fabric, even though it's not. I also use an old box fan to add movement to the fabric and create visual interest and coverage. I always start with my clients in the drape and then move on to images in any outfits they brought with them at the end of the session.

## Full Disclosure

For this session, I had the honor of working with a returning client—someone I've photographed before and who graciously agreed to be featured in this book. I want to express my deepest gratitude to her. Maternity photography, especially in my style, is a deeply intimate experience.

While I use draping during sessions, achieving the look you see in my images often requires the client to be fully nude beneath the fabric. Knowing that behind-the-scenes photos would be included in this book, I made thoughtful adjustments to some of the poses and to the draping out of respect for her comfort and privacy. Had this been a regular client session, I would have pushed to expose more skin.

Even with those minor adjustments, what you'll see in this chapter is an honest and accurate reflection of how I approach maternity sessions.

## The Session

As mentioned earlier, I begin all my maternity sessions with the client in a drape. I always start with the "open-in-front" style because it's simple to explain, easy for the client to get into, and flattering.

Once the client has changed into the drape, I guide her to the backdrop and spend a few minutes adjusting the fabric. These early moments are about more than just styling—they're about helping the client feel comfortable, and confident. I pay close attention to how the drape falls, making sure it provides the right balance of coverage, exposure, and flow. And I talk to her about what I'll be doing and what she can expect. **FIGURE 13.1** shows a behind-the-scenes look at this part of the session.

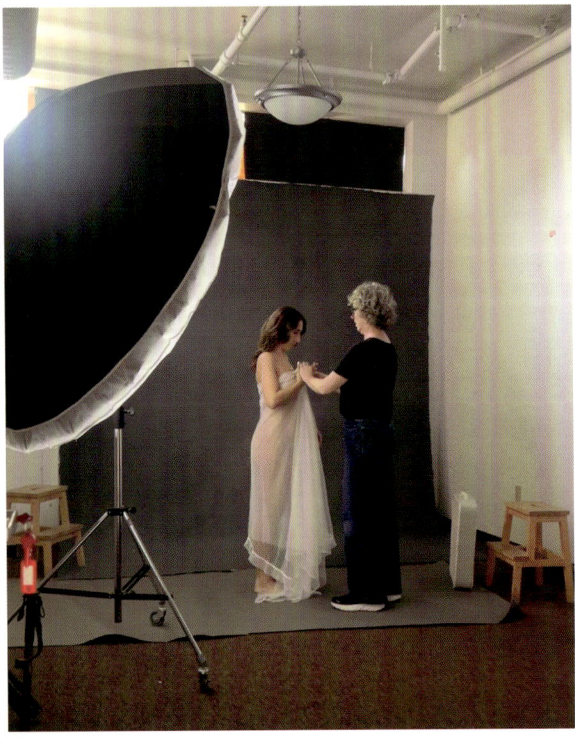

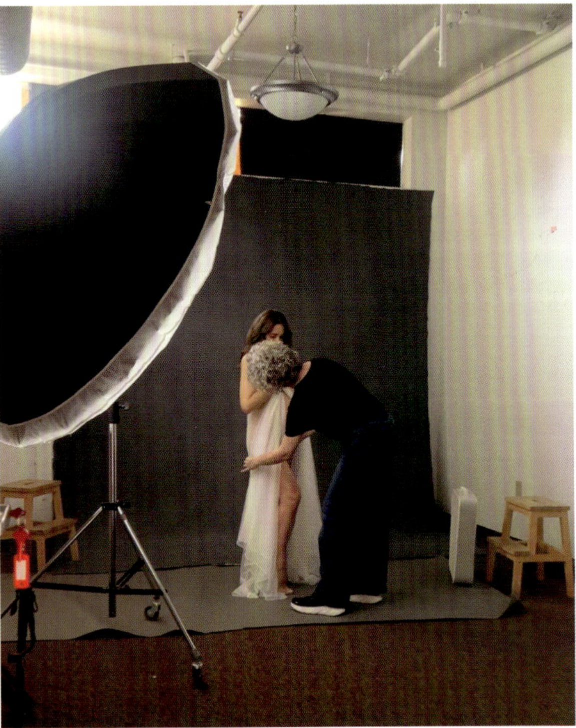

**FIGURE 13.1** Behind the scenes: Adjusting the "open-in-front" drape to create flattering lines and ensure client comfort. This process is collaborative and essential to setting the tone for the rest of the session.

## ¾ to the Right with an Open-in-Front Draping

Once the client is positioned and the drape has been adjusted, I walk her through posing fundamentals. I explain *Barbie hands* (see Chapter 5) and how to avoid them, remind her not to lock her knees, and let her know that I'll be asking her to bend her knees and arms and gently arch her back throughout the session.

I also emphasize that her comfort is the top priority. If any pose causes discomfort or triggers contractions, I tell her to let me know right away so we can pause or adjust. Then I ask her to turn slightly to my right—so she's posed ¾ to the camera. I guide her to bend the knee of the leg closest to me, and we begin. As you can see in **FIGURE 13.2**, I demonstrate the movement as I explain it, showing her exactly what I'm looking for.

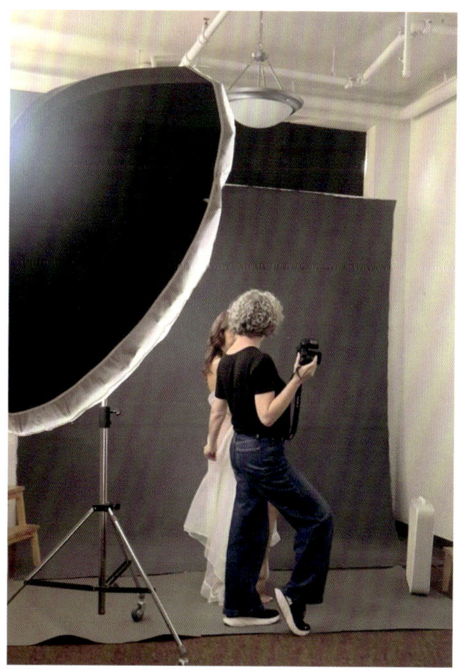

**FIGURE 13.2** Demonstrating the ¾ turn: I model the pose while explaining how to position the legs, arms, and posture—always emphasizing comfort and collaboration.

For these images, I position my light at a 45-degree angle to the client to create a classic loop light pattern—one of my go-to setups for maternity portraits. I also place a fan in front of the client to create gentle movement in the draping. The fan enhances the flow of the fabric and helps with coverage (**FIGURE 13.3**).

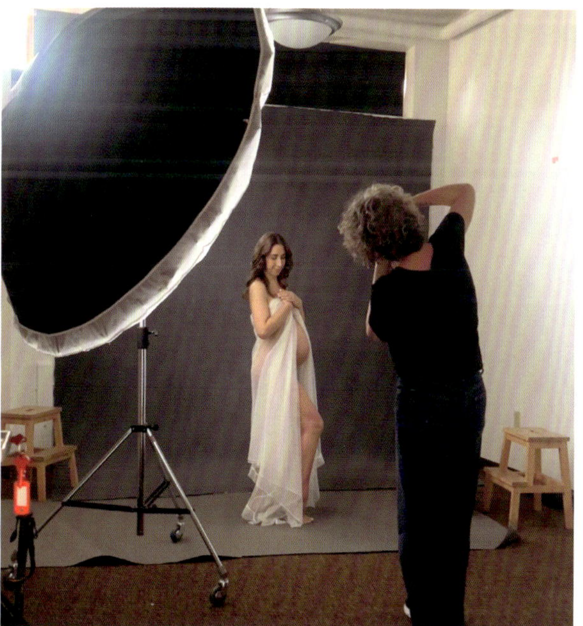

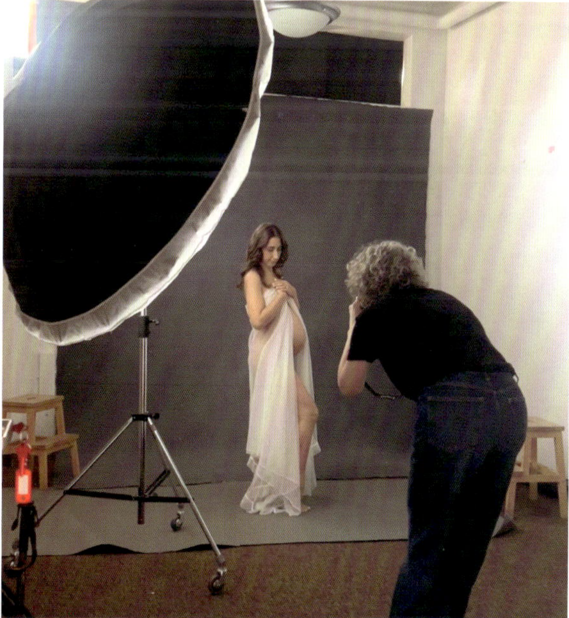

**FIGURE 13.3** My light is positioned at 45 degrees, while a fan placed just out of frame adds motion to the drape for softness and coverage.

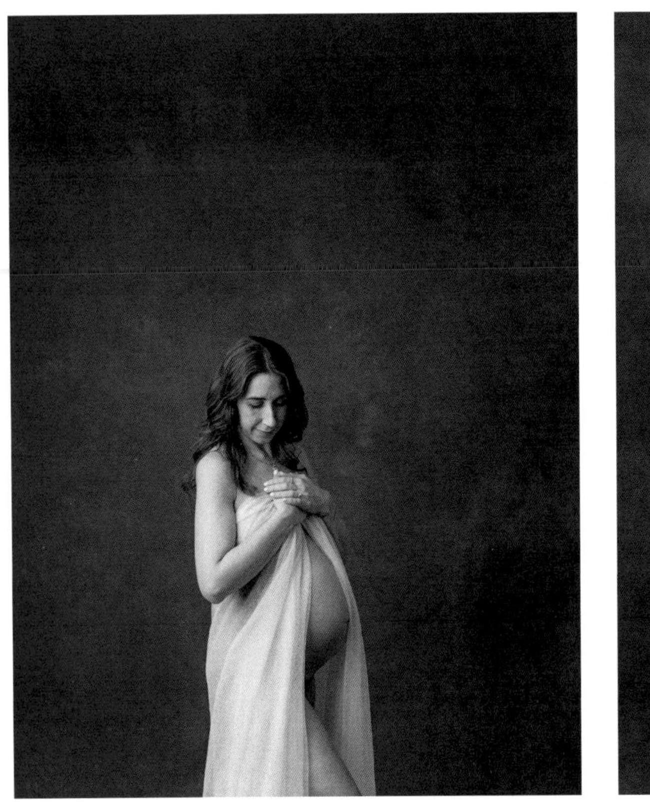

A

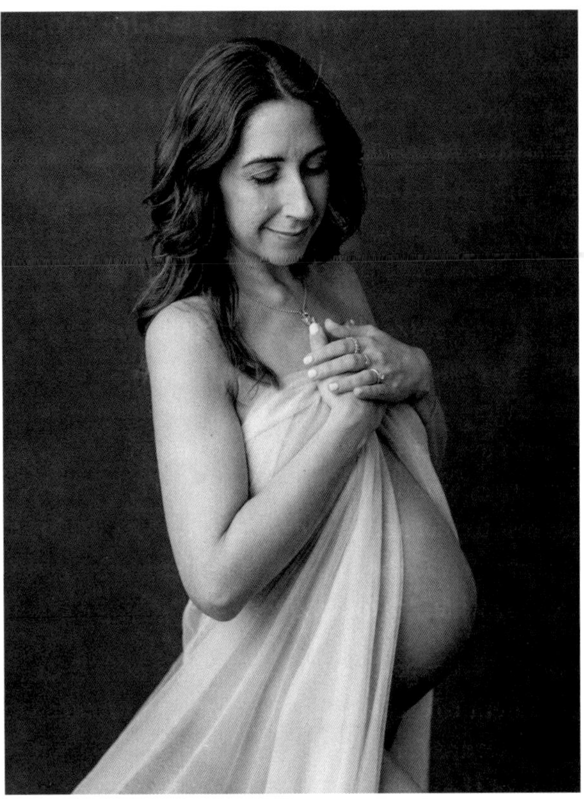

B

**FIGURE 13.4** These images were taken with the client posed at a ¾-turn to my right, using a loop light pattern and a fan to introduce subtle movement to the drape. Figure 13.4A uses negative space. Figure 13.4B, captured moments later, uses a fill-the-frame approach.

## Direct to Camera with an Open-in-Front Draping

Next, I rotate the client so that she's facing the camera directly and readjust the drape to ensure both modesty and flow. I walk her through the next pose, demonstrating how I'd like her to bend one knee and pull it slightly toward the center to create a soft curve in the body (**FIGURE 13.5**).

From there, we create a series of images: one of her gazing down at her belly, one looking directly at the camera, and a few close-ups focusing solely on her belly (**FIGURE 13.6**). My light stays at the 45-degree angle to preserve the loop light pattern throughout.

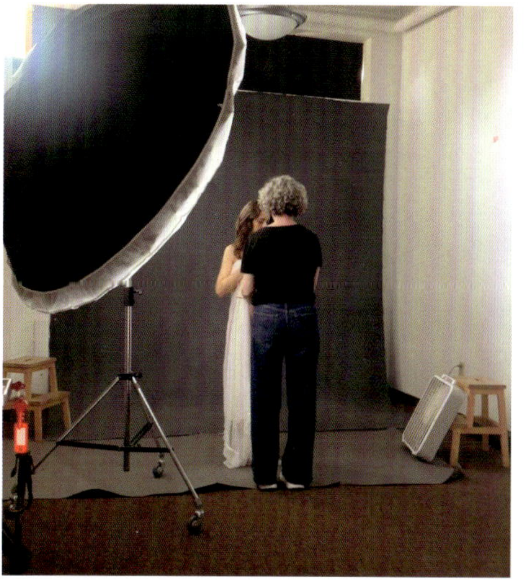

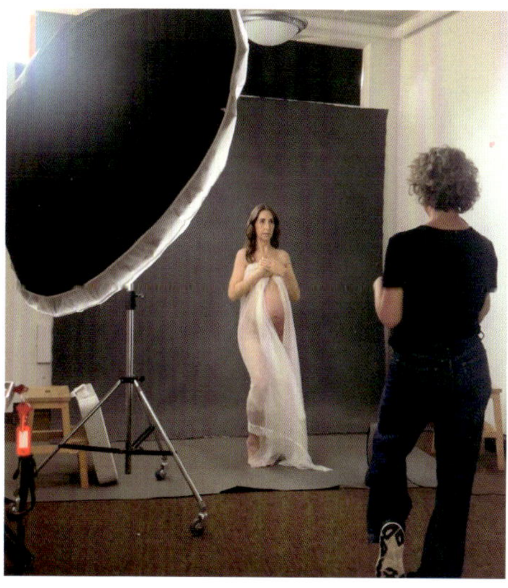

**FIGURE 13.5** Transitioning into the direct-to-camera pose. I demonstrate the desired stance while adjusting the drape for coverage and movement.

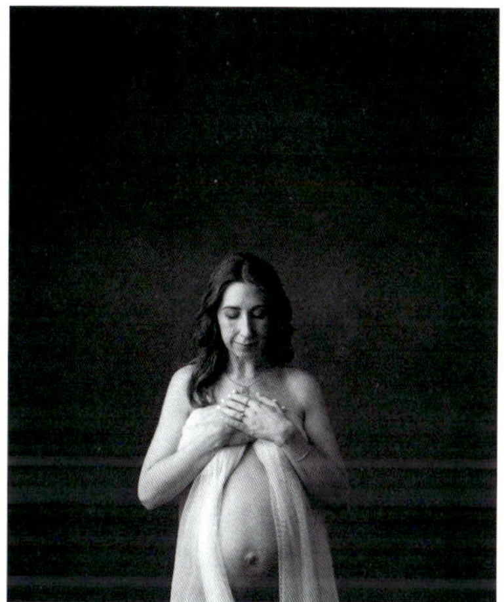

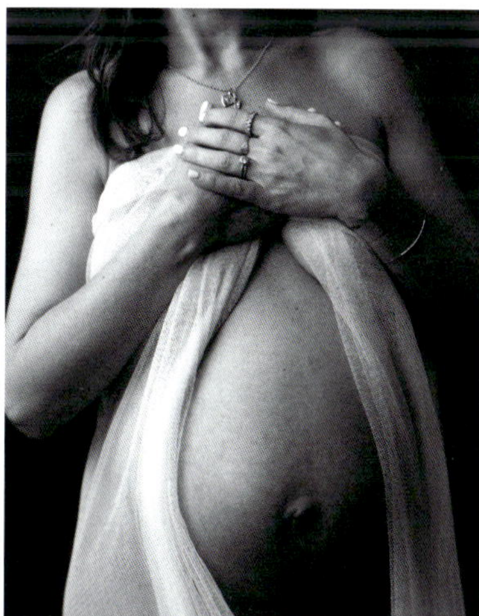

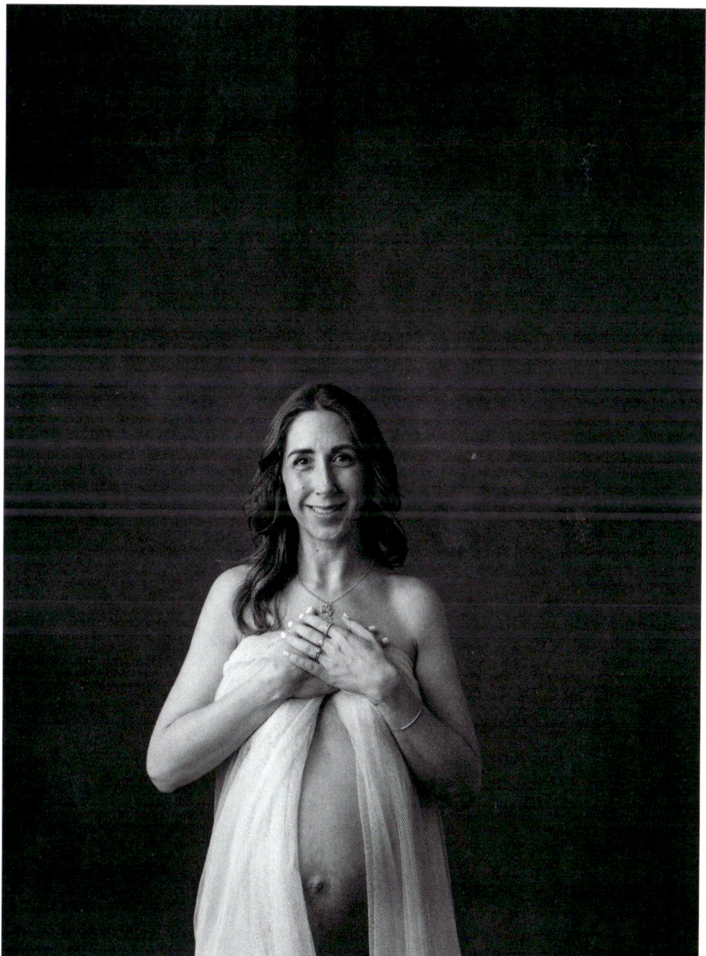

**FIGURE 13.6** A series captured from the direct-to-camera setup with loop lighting.

### ¾ and Profile to the Left with an Open-in-Front Draping

After finishing the direct-to-camera images, I ask the client to rotate ¾ to my left, bending the knee closest to me. As always, I take time to demonstrate the pose as I explain it. I begin with the same loop light setup I've been using throughout the session (**FIGURE 13.7**).

However, for the close-up images in this pose, I wanted to introduce more depth and drama—so I made a slight lighting adjustment. I moved my light from a 45-degree angle to a 90-degree angle relative to the client, shifting from loop light to a more pronounced split light pattern. The difference is subtle but impactful. In **FIGURE 13.8A**, the light is soft and even. It's beautiful—but in **FIGURE 13.8B**, the stronger shadow adds dimension and visual interest that enhances the mood of the image.

I captured both the close-up (**FIGURE 13.8B**) and pull-back images (**FIGURE 13.9B**) of this pose using the same lighting setup with the light positioned 90 degrees to the subject. **FIGURE 13.9A** shows the setup, while **FIGURE 13.9B** shows the full-body image. I composed this image using a combination of negative space and the rule of thirds to enhance visual interest.

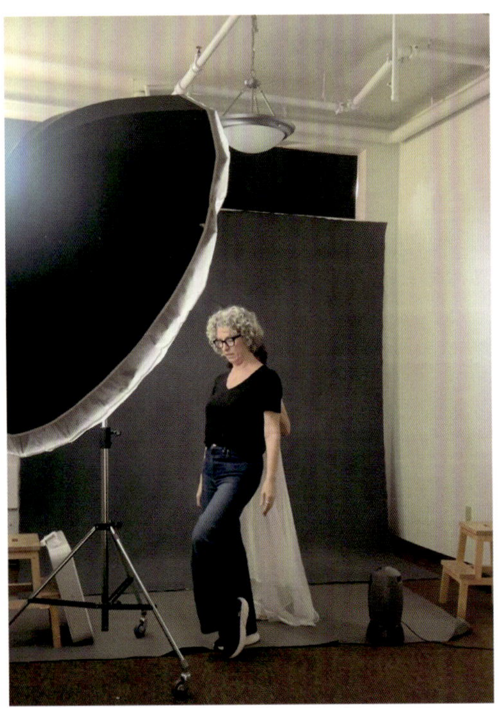

**FIGURE 13.7** Here, the client posed at a ¾- turn to my left.

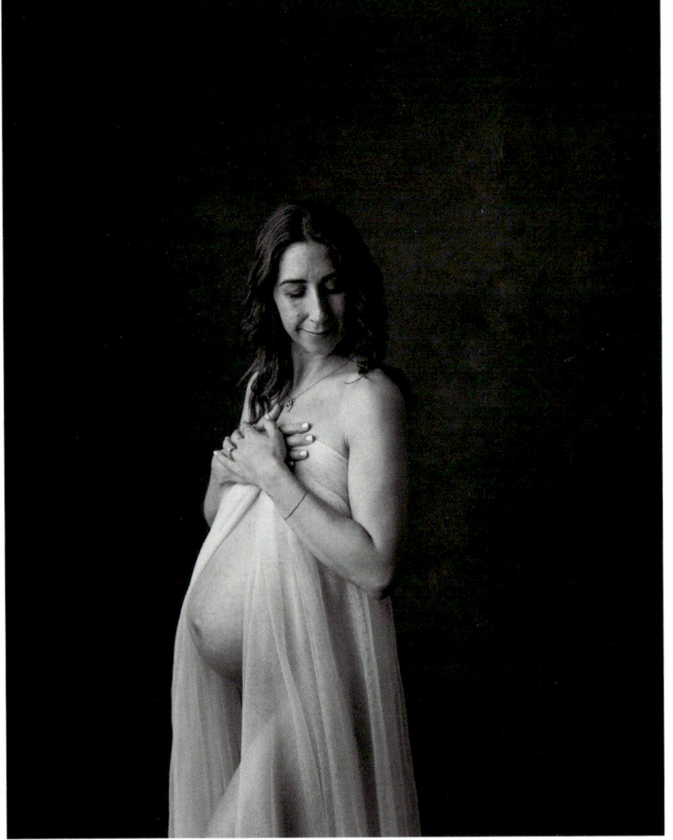

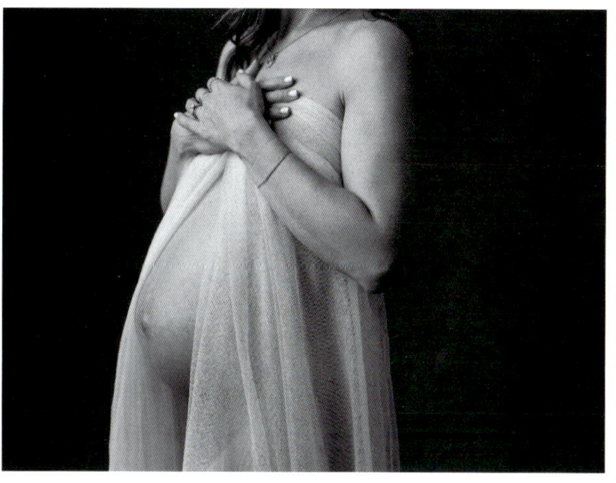

A

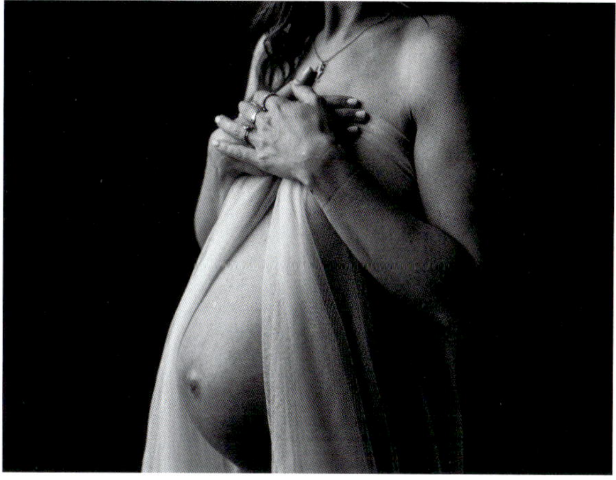

B

**FIGURE 13.8** Same pose, different lighting patterns. The image on the left uses a loop light pattern, resulting in soft, even light on my subject's belly. The image on the right uses split light.

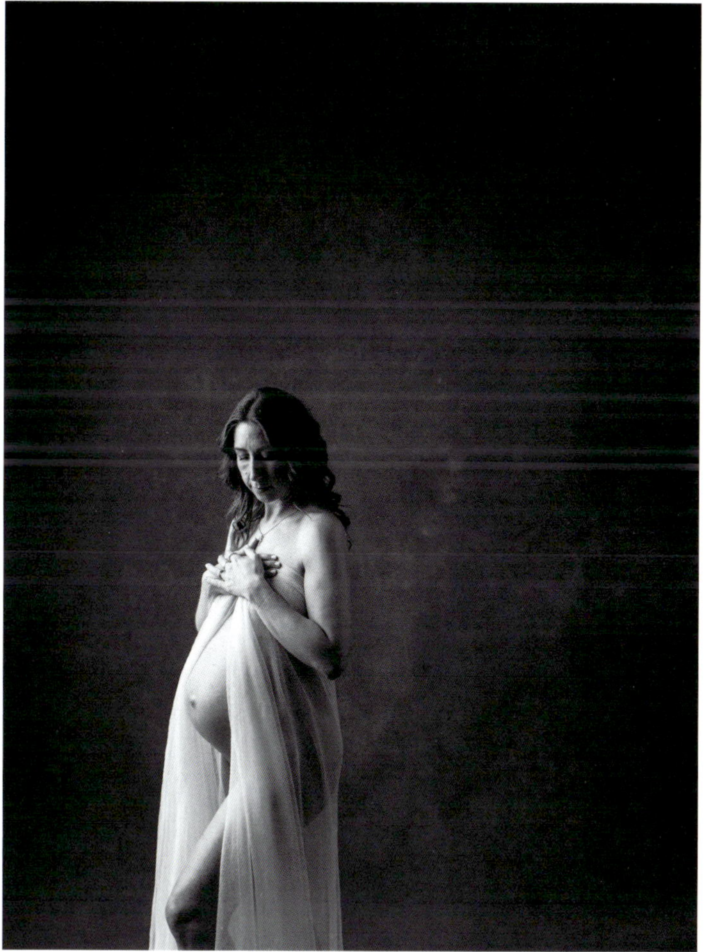

B

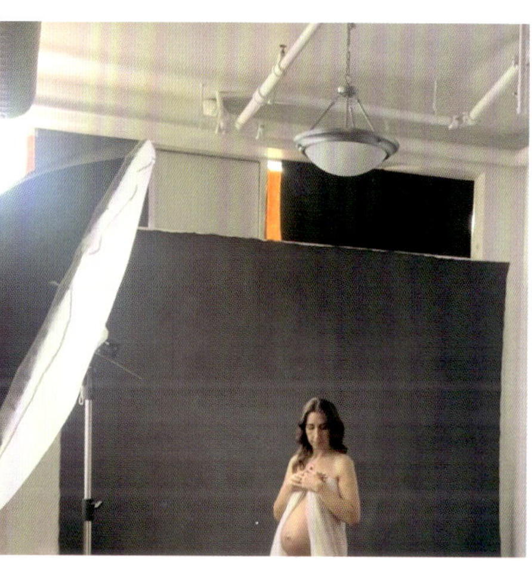

A

**FIGURE 13.9** The light is at 90 degrees to the subject to create more shadows to accentuate her curves.

Next, I shifted the light into the rim light position and moved my client into a full profile. Rim light is my favorite lighting pattern for maternity photos. I love the way it outlines the body and emphasizes the pregnant form. It also shines right through the fabric, which means careful use of posing and draping is a must for maintaining modesty. So, I took my time here, carefully adjusting the folds of the drape to provide coverage while also letting the light shape the body. This entire sequence—from the first frame to this final rim-lit portrait—took 15 to 20 minutes.

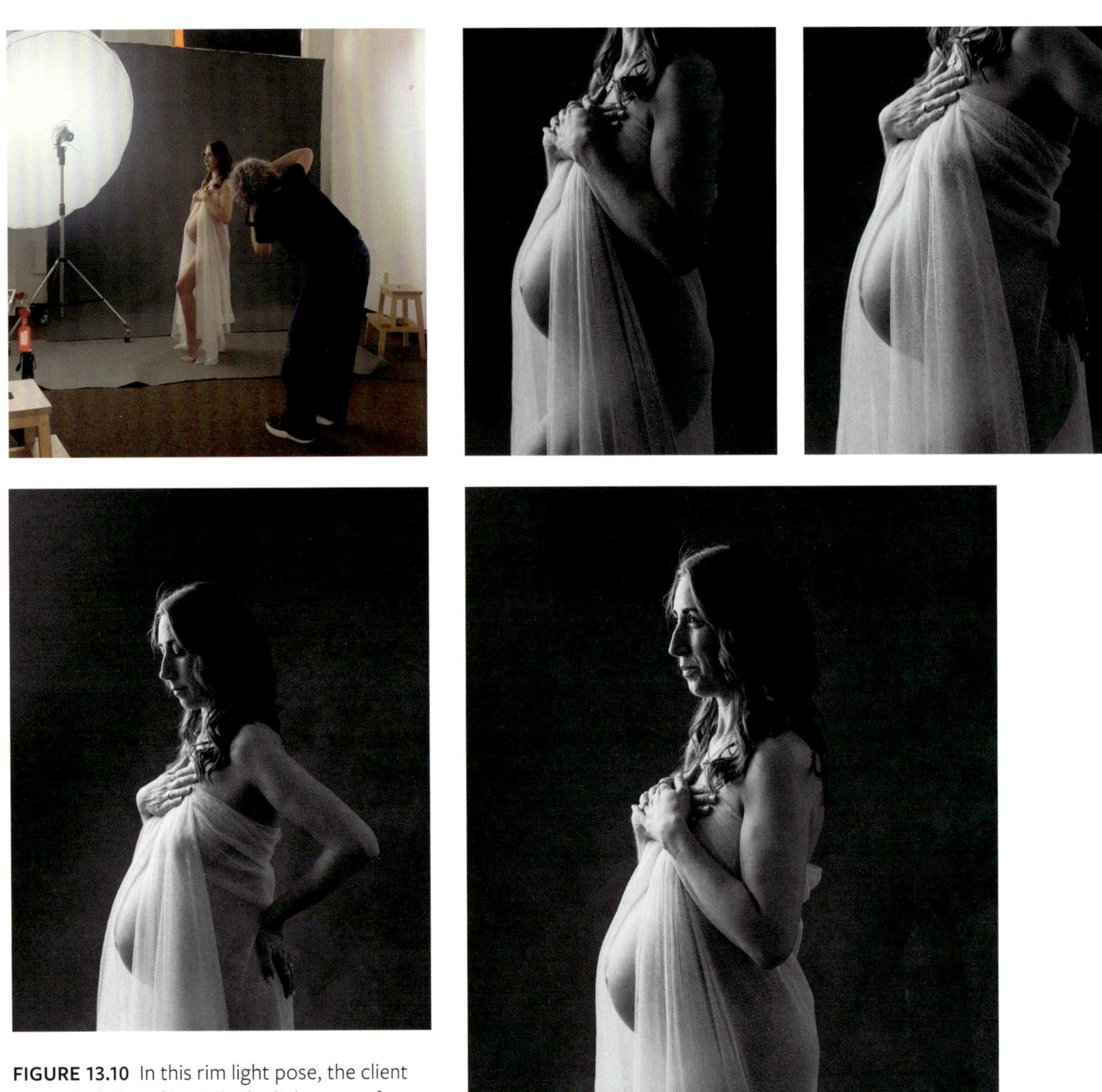

**FIGURE 13.10** In this rim light pose, the client stands in full profile while the light wraps from behind to highlight her shape.

## ¾ and Profile to the Left with an Open-in-Back Draping

At this point in the session, I transitioned the drape from the open-in-front position to the open-in-back position and repeated the posing sequence in reverse—this time starting with the client turned ¾ to my left, lit with rim light (**FIGURE 13.11A**).

I love how rim light outlines the body, and I wanted to include the top of her leg in some of the images to better emphasize her shape. But I was struggling with the drape—it wouldn't fall quite the way I needed it to, especially while still providing modesty. You can see me adjusting the fabric in **FIGURE 13.11B**.

Eventually, I grabbed the wooden posing block I keep in the studio for maternity sessions. Having the client place her foot on the block (**FIGURE 13.11C**) lifted her leg just enough to let the drape fall into place, giving me the coverage and shape I was looking for.

I spend a lot of time during maternity sessions making small adjustments like this. The results are often subtle, but they're well worth the effort. **FIGURE 13.12A** shows the image captured *before* the client placed her foot on the block. It's a lovely portrait on its own, but as you can see in **FIGURE 13.12B**, the addition of the block gave her leg just enough lift to improve the drape's coverage *and* enhance the shape of her curves.

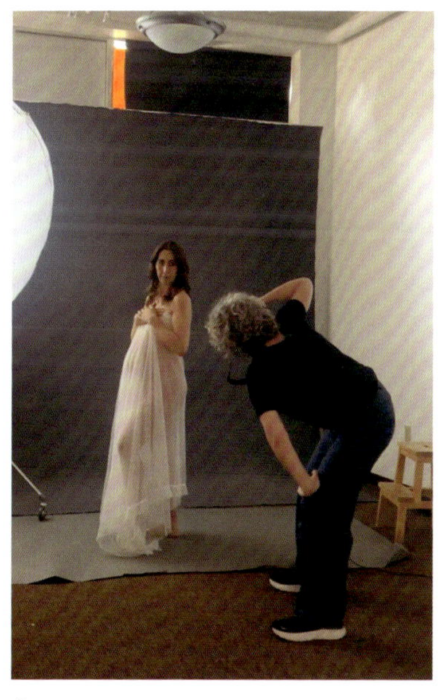

A

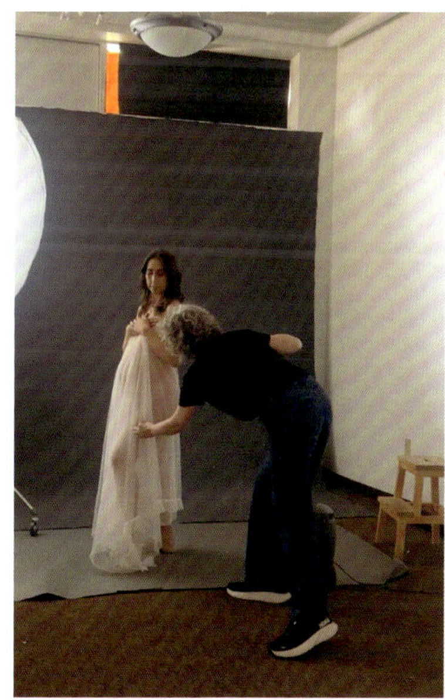

B

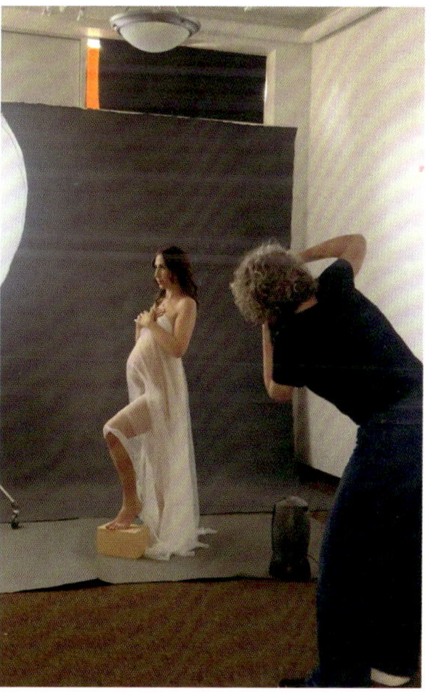

C

**FIGURE 13.11** Problem-solving with poses and props.

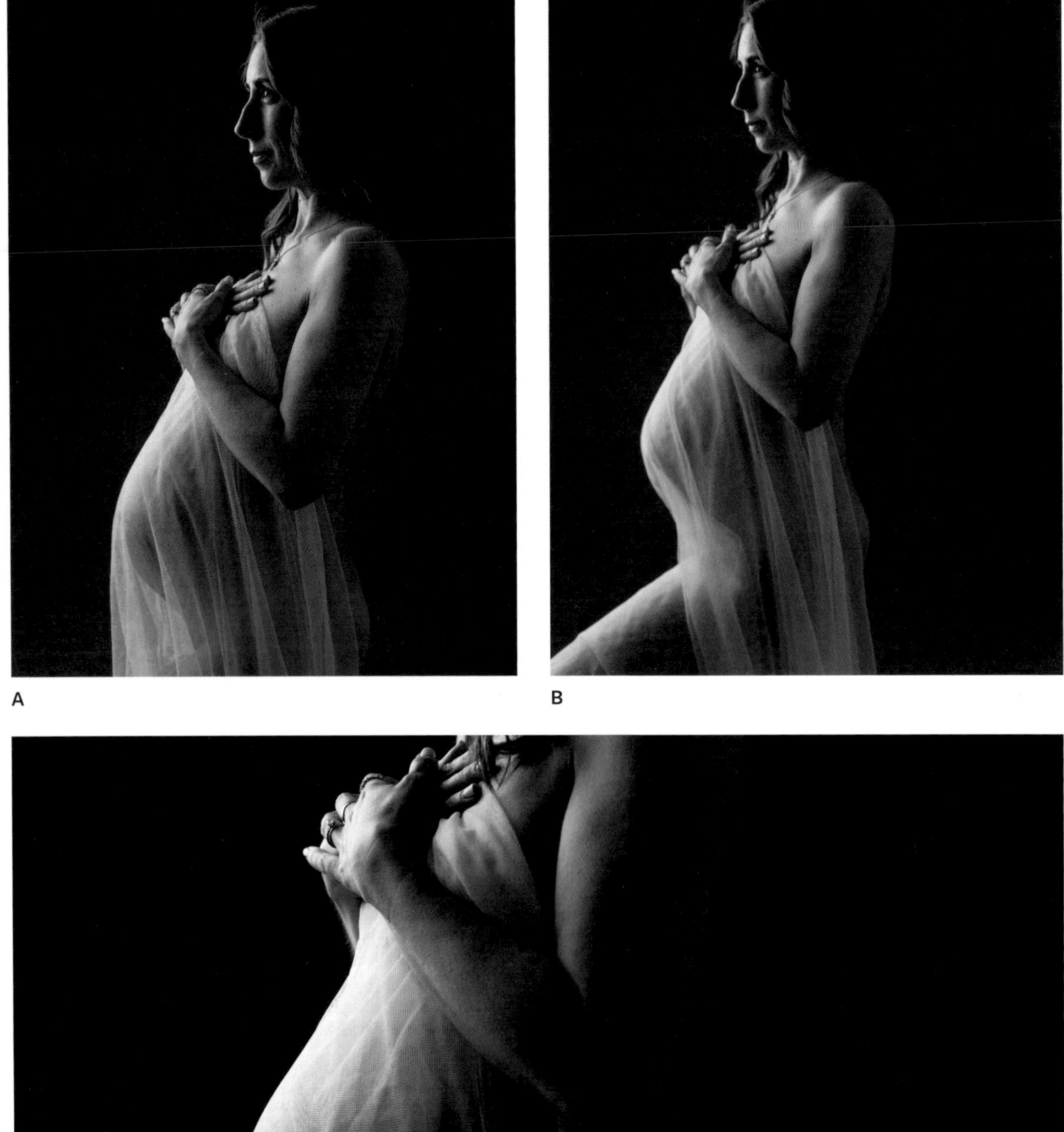

A

B

C

**FIGURE 13.12** Before and after: A small prop made a big difference! Figure 13.12C is a close-up of the profile position captured with rim light.

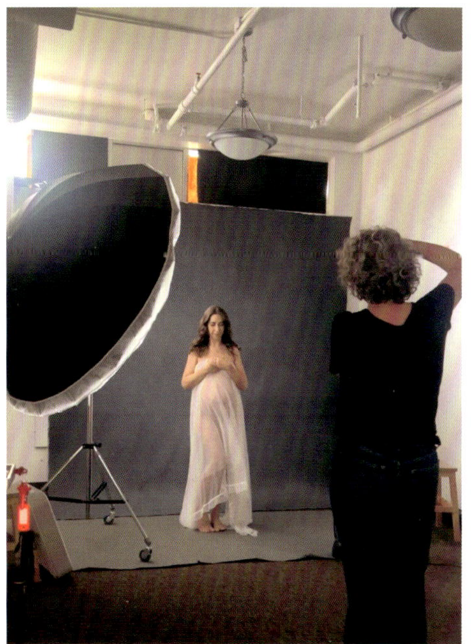

**FIGURE 13.13** Returning to loop light: A front-facing pose with the drape open in the back. The fan adds flow to the fabric, while the lighting creates dimension.

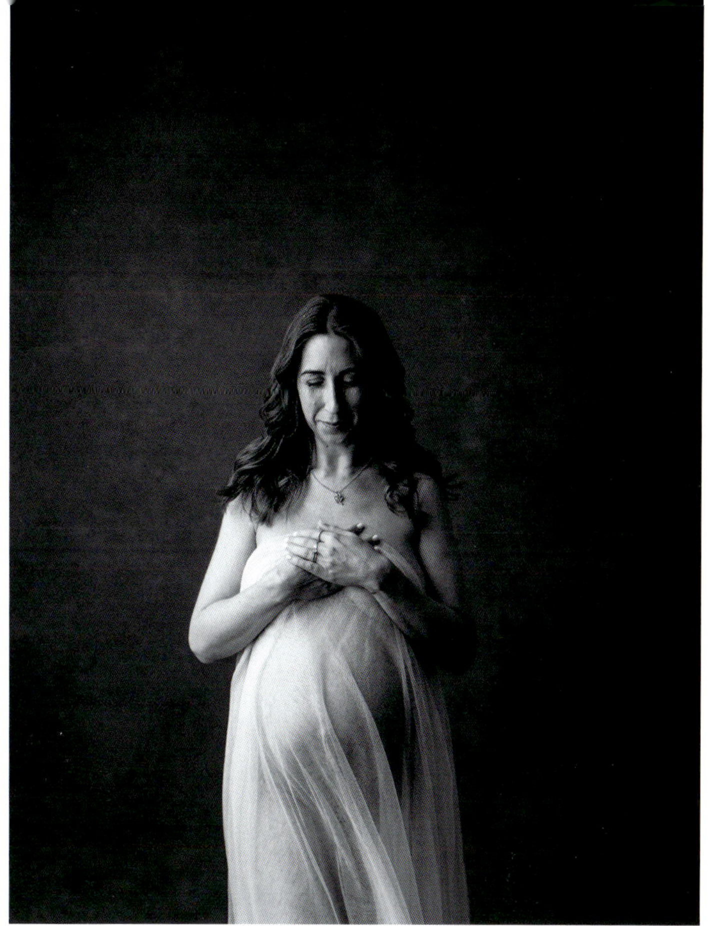

## Direct to Camera with an Open-in-Back Draping

After completing the ¾ and profile poses in rim light, I turned the client back to face the camera and repositioned the light to recreate a loop light pattern. I also placed a fan on the same side as the light to add gentle movement to the draping, which helps with both visual flow and coverage (**FIGURE 13.13**).

I chose the loop light position for these photos to create soft shadows along her belly to add dimension. As discussed in Chapter 10, when a maternity client faces the camera with fabric over her belly, it can sometimes diminish the shape.

Lighting patterns that introduce directional shadow can solve that problem, as shown in **FIGURE 13.14A**. I also wanted to soften the shadows on her face without losing the shape of her curves. To achieve that balance, I made a small adjustment: I simply had her turn her face toward the light. That one change gave the image a different look and feel (**FIGURE 13.14B**).

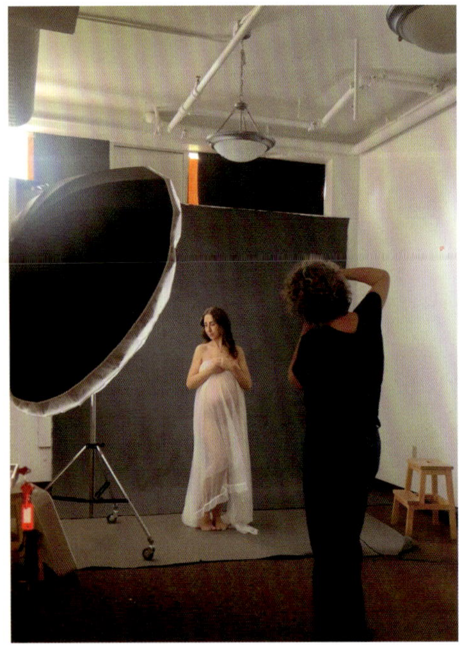

A

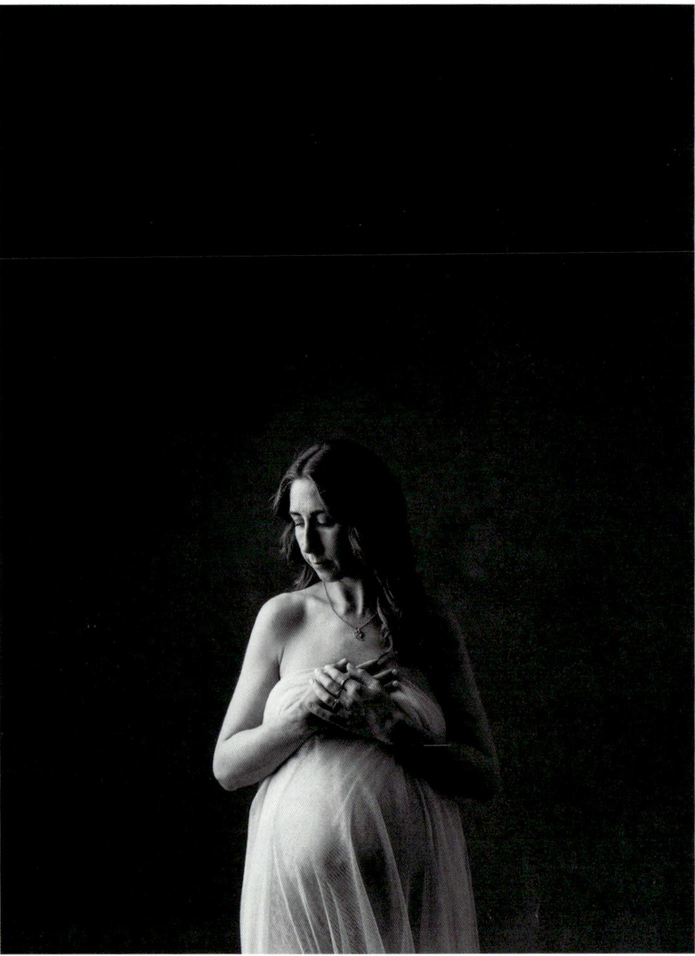

B

**FIGURE 13.14** Asking the client to turn her face toward the light changed the look and feel of this pose.

## ¾ to the Right with an Open-in-Back Draping

For the final look, I ask the client to turn ¾ to her right, with the light positioned in the classic loop light pattern. This setup mirrors how I began the session, but with the drape now open in the back. And the results were lovely (**FIGURE 13.15**).

If this posing flow seems simple, that's because it is—and that's intentional. My goal is to keep things easy and comfortable for my clients. That said, even with this gentle flow, I'm still asking the client to maintain posture, arch her back, and bend her knees—all of that is hard work when you're pregnant!

This client was 32 weeks along—right in the middle of the window I recommend for maternity sessions. And we took several breaks throughout to allow her to rest. At the beginning of the session, she shared that she practiced yoga and

Pilates and didn't think posing would be difficult. But at the end, she said, "You were right! That was a lot harder than I thought it would be." This part of the session lasted another 15 to 20 minutes.

Remember: Your clients are pregnant. Pregnancy is demanding on the body. Go slow. Keep things simple. Build in time for rest.

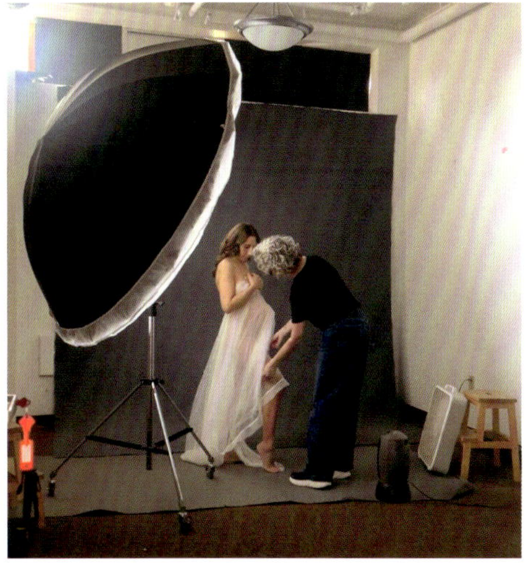

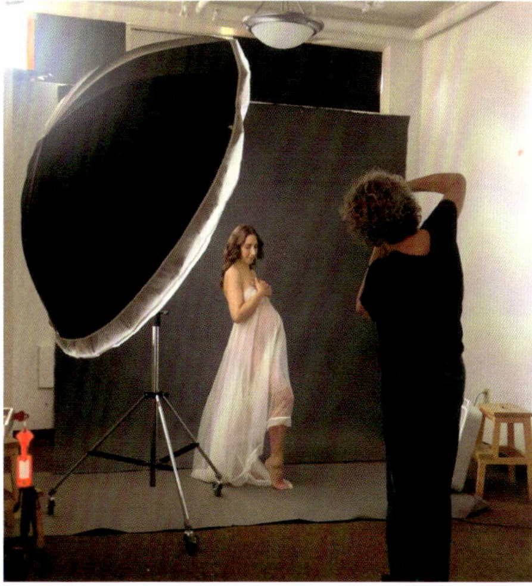

**FIGURE 13.15** Final pose in the sequence: A ¾ turn with the drape open in the back and a loop light setup.

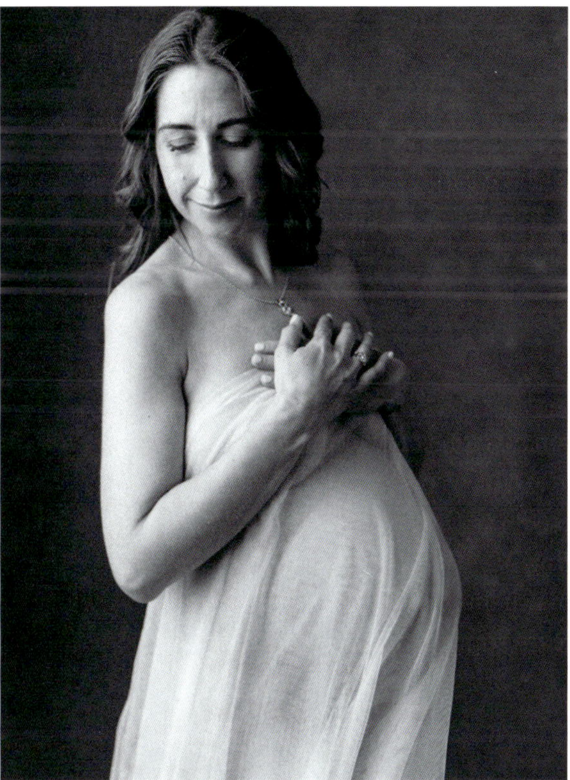

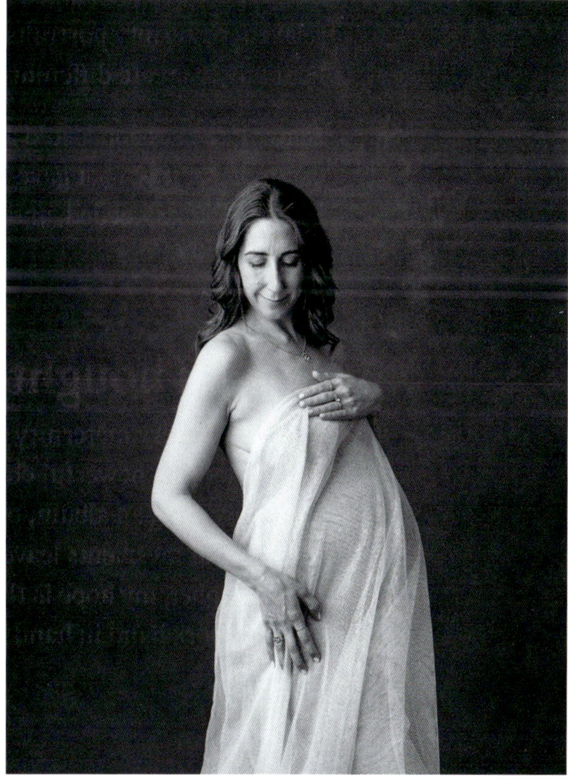

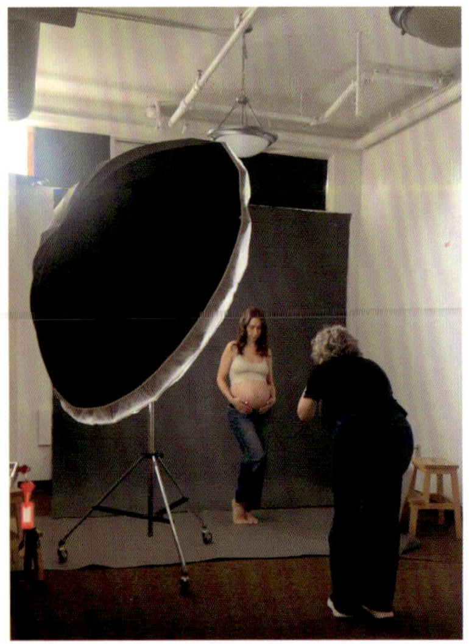
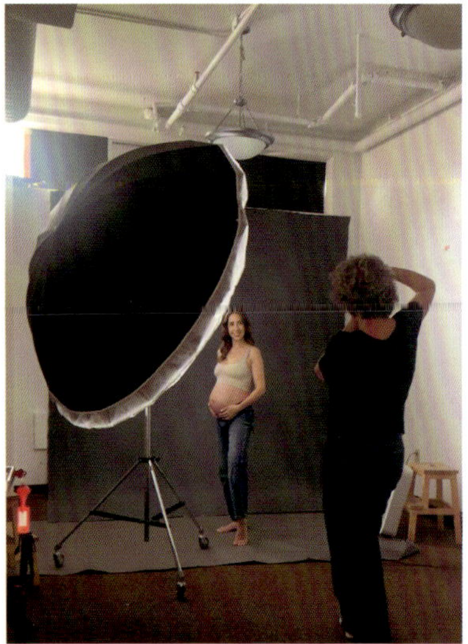
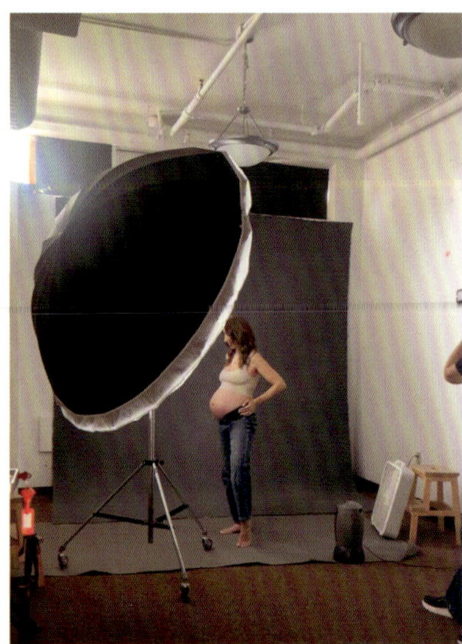

**FIGURES 13.16** Behind the scenes of our final setup: same lighting principles now applied to a casual look.

## One Last Look

We wrapped the session with something casual, just for fun. For these final images, the client changed into jeans and a sports bra, which is a great look for relaxed, maternity portraits. I left the light set at 45 degrees and had her move her body to create different lighting patterns (**FIGURE 13.16**).

In total, the session lasted about 50 minutes from start to finish, which is common for me. That gave us plenty of time to run through all the poses, make adjustments as needed, and even add in some photos just for fun at the end (**FIGURE 13.17**).

## Final Thoughts

My goal at every maternity session is to create meaningful, timeless portraits that honor this powerful chapter in a person's life. Whether the final image ends up on a wall, in an album, or tucked quietly into a drawer for the future, my hope is that my clients leave feeling beautiful and empowered. And for you, the photographer, my hope is that this chapter has helped you see how posing and lighting work hand in hand to create something beautiful.

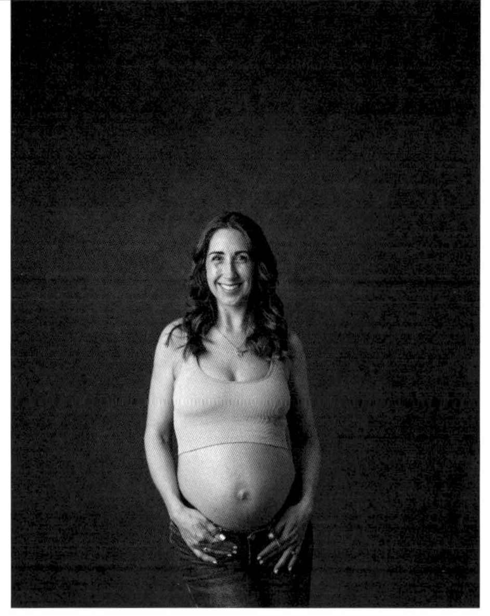

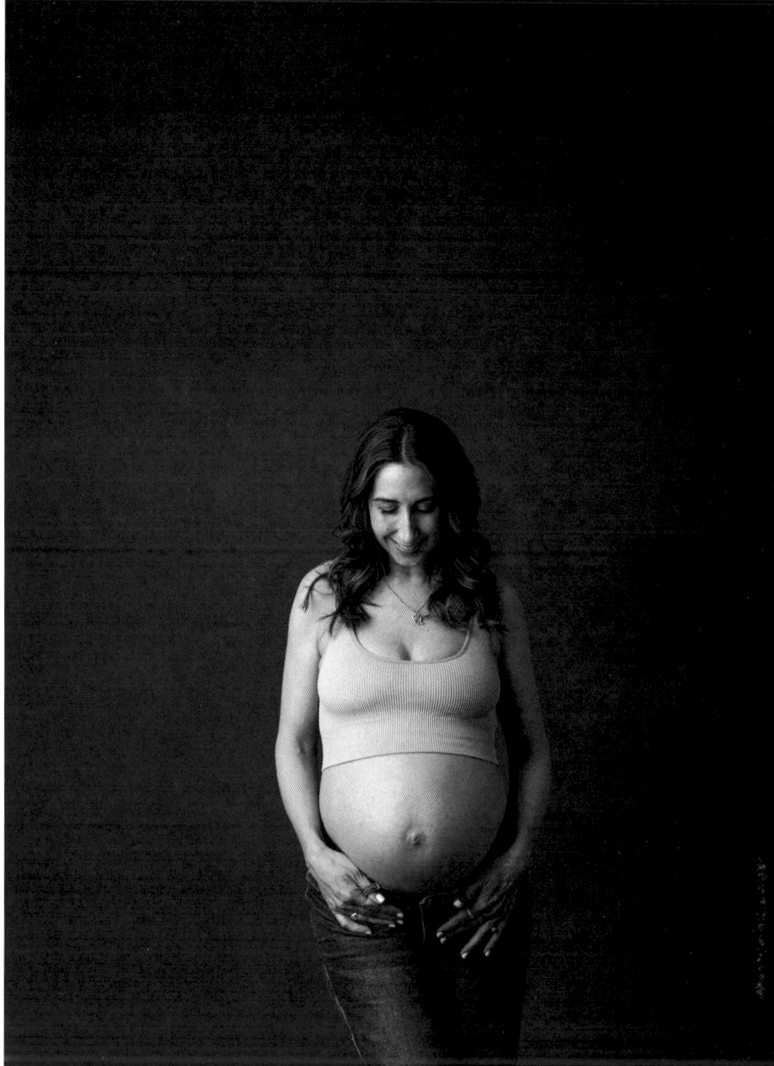

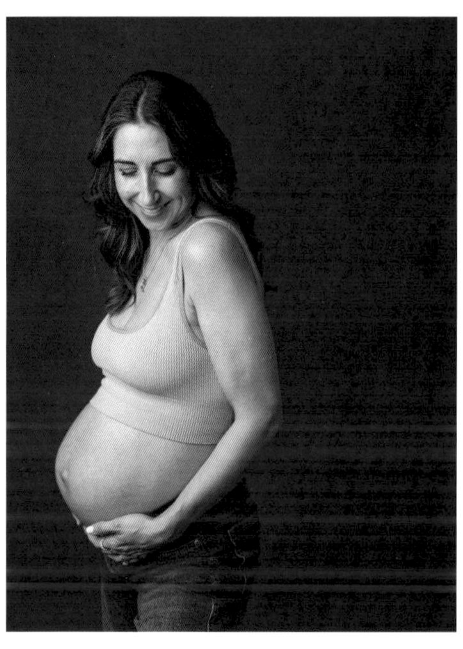

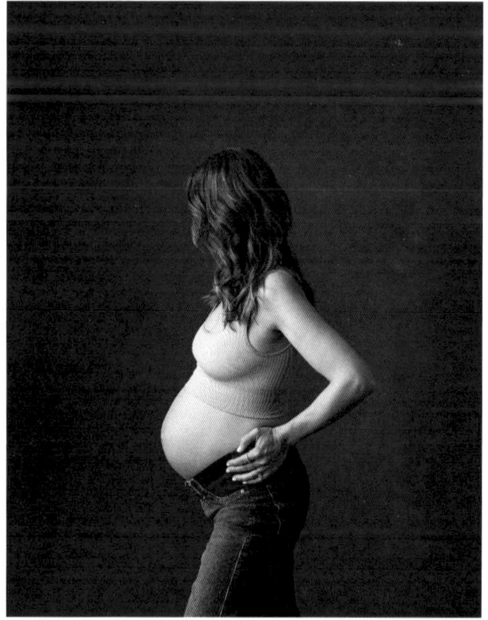

**FIGURE 13.17** The fun, final images from the session.

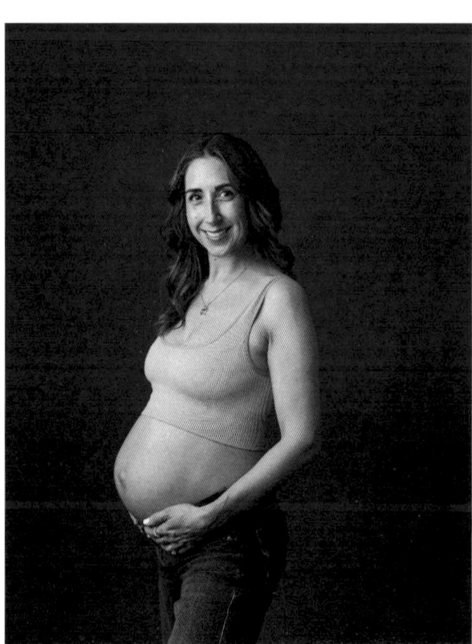

# Conclusion

This book is the culmination of almost three decades of experience and hard work. I've shared the knowledge, tools, systems, and philosophies that helped shape my signature look and my career. My hope is that you'll take what you've learned from me and make it your own.

Mastery is an evolution, and photography is a lifelong endeavor. Revisit these lessons often and practice, practice, practice! As you do, let me know how your progress is going. You can find me on Instagram at instagram.com/sandracoan and you can use #SCfamilyphotography when posting your photos so I can see your work and cheer you on.

Remember that what you do matters. As family photographers, we create the kind of work that people run into burning buildings to save. That's a big deal, so honor it.

My career as a family photographer has brought me so much joy and so many amazing opportunities! My hope is that it does the same for you.

XOXO,
Sandra

# Index

45-degree light 28, 32, 92, 351–352, 354, 362
90-degree light 29, 92, 340, 354–355

## A

accessories 223
Adams, Ansel 44
Airplane pose 258–259, 315
anchor, posing 182, 184–185, 194
aperture 37–39, 41–44, 85, 91–92
aperture priority 44
arms 159–161, 282–283, 285
artificial light 6–7, 13, 31, 48, 67–96

## B

black and white film 54–56, 91
baby-led posing 3, 128, 194, 196, 202, 337
babies 135, 140–142, 145–147, 151, 160–173, 180–184, 193–230, 238–267, 302–317, 322–345
baby asleep 196–197, 200, 210–211, 307
baby poses
  Baby on Back 200, 203–205, 211–212, 218
  Baby on Belly 196–198, 200, 208, 218, 223–225, 306–307, 310
  Baby on Chest 260–261, 314, 316
  Baby on Shoulder 260, 313342
  Baby on Side 200–201, 211
  Baby Sandwich 265–266
  sitting 214–215, 221–223, 246–247, 304
  standing 226–227, 253, 259–264, 267, 313–315
Back Snuggle pose 266
backlight 31, 58, 60–61, 113–115, 293, 341
Barbie hands 136–7, 282, 351
Behind the Partner pose 292
belly 144, 161, 164, 181, 273–275, 277–279, 282–295, 352, 355, 359
Belly to Belly pose 293
Betty (posing doll) 6–7

body language 129, 133, 151–152
bounce light 73–76, 98–101, 114–121, 123
butterfly light 24–25, 64, 337–339

## C

camera 36–38, 44–47, 68–70, 85
camera strap 198, 204, 220
candid 3, 128–129, 132, 136, 144–148, 244, 256
car seat 307
catchlight 19–25, 28–29, 78–79, 94
children 151–152, 162, 164, 166–168, 184–186, 193–194, 228–235, 238–249, 253, 257, 264–265, 294–295
chin 148
claw, the 138
clients 180–181, 274, 280, 337, 348–350
clouds 11, 18, 57, 61
cold shoe 69
color cast 100-101, 104, 109, 116
color film 51–56, 91
color of light 6, 18, 100, 104, 116–117
composition 129, 149, 157–175
consistent, predictable routine (CPRs) 178–181, 187–189, 191, 194–195, 238
continuous light 6, 11, 80–86, 91
contractions 276–277, 351
CPR *see consistent, predictable routine*
Cradle Hold pose 262–263
crawling 214, 218–220, 223–226
creating triangles *see triangles*
crotch hold 138–139

## D

dad 3, 137, 145, 155, 164, 168, 178, 182–185, 187, 243, 252, 257, 259, 303, 313–315, 320, 326–327, 344–345
daylight balance 18, 80, 82, 100
depth of field 39, 41–42, 44
diffusion 11–12, 32, 57, 72–79, 94, 102, 119, 303, 320
digital 37–40, 49–51, 53–56, 71, 90–92, 98, 111
digital noise 39–40, 44
direction of light 6, 10, 19, 57–58, 104–105
draping 189, 273–275, 279–280, 349–357, 359–361

## E

equipment 38, 68, 71, 78–82, 78, 102
exposure 14, 36–39, 41, 43–47, 49–51, 54–56, 85–87, 102
exposure indicator 46–47
exposure triangle 36–37, 47, 49, 56
eye contact 139, 144–151, 209
eye-level, shooting at 140–143, 148, 161
eyes 20–22, 24–25, 28, 64, 107, 139–141, 148–149

## F

face 149–52
family 3, 59, 102, 128, 132–133, 146–147, 168, 181–188, 237–238, 254–259, 264, 266–269, 301, 303, 311–312, 320, 344, 349
fan 232, 275, 349, 351–352, 359
father *see dad*
fill the frame 171–172
film 37–40, 49, 51–56, 90–91
film grain 39–40
flash 6, 11–12, 14, 16–18, 20–21, 32, 48, 68–71, 73, 79–93, 98–124, 303, 349
flat light 28, 61
focus 149
freeze motion 43–44, 81, 84–86, 90
Fresh 48 session 336–345

## G

gear *see equipment*
ghosting 88–90
ghoul light 24, 26–27, 64, 94, 101, 106–107, 111
ghoul light, accidental 321
Golden Hour 58–60

grain 39–40, 44, 53–55
gray card 48

## H

handheld light meter 14, 48–49, 56, 68, 71, 91–93
hands 133–138, 282, 289, 292
hard light 10–12, 16, 31–32, 57
head tilt 151–152, 154–155
head 149–152
headshot 212, 221, 225, 227–228, 231, 316
high speed sync (HSS) 89–90
highlights 49–51, 54–56, 92, 111
hospital session 336–345
hot shoe 68–70

## I

ideal light 56–57, 65
incident metering 45, 48–49, 71, 91
individuals, posing 159–161, 189
inside, photographing 11, 61
intensity, light 6, 10, 13–15, 57
internal meter 46–47, 81
Inverse Square Law 13, 16–17, 118
ISO 37, 39–40, 44, 85–88

## J

jawline 148
jumping 143, 232–234

## K

Kelvin 18, 100
kiss poses 145, 163, 239, 242–243, 256, 293

## L

labor 272, 276
leading lines 172–173
legs 280–282
light
  45-degree 28, 32, 92, 351–352, 354, 362
  90-degree 29, 92, 340, 354–355
  artificial 6–7, 13, 31, 48, 67–96
  backlight 31, 58, 60–61, 113–115, 293, 341
  bouncing 73–76, 98–101, 114–121, 123
  color 6, 18, 100, 104, 116–117
  continuous 6, 11, 80–86, 91
  direction 6, 10, 19, 57–58, 104–105
  flash 6, 11–12, 14, 16–18, 20–21, 32, 48, 68–71, 73, 79–93, 98–124, 303, 349
  fundamentals 9–32
  Golden Hour 58–60
  hard 10–12, 16, 31–32, 57
  ideal 56–57, 65
  intensity 6, 10, 13–15, 57
  midday 57, 61
  natural 7, 11–13, 31, 35–65, 68, 85, 98, 119, 303
  northern 61–63
  proximity 13, 15–16, 57, 75, 94
  quality 10–16, 31, 37, 57–58, 61, 71–72, 78, 94, 116, 337
  size 11–16, 20–22, 63–64, 71–72, 94
  soft 10–13, 61, 74–75
  south-facing 61–62, 88
  temperature 18–19, 32, 59, 100–101, 104, 109
  uplighting 24, 26, 262
  window 61–64, 87, 92, 104–107, 111, 321
light meter 48–49, 56, 65, 68, 71, 85, 91–93, 116
light modifiers 68, 71–74, 78, 94, 121, 336
light stand 71, 80–82
lighting on location 97–125
lighting pattern 19, 31
  butterfly light 24–25, 64, 337–339
  flat light 28, 61
  ghoul light 24, 26–27, 64, 94, 101, 106–107, 111
  loop light 28, 77, 95, 103, 279, 337, 343, 351–355, 359–361

Paramount light 24–25
rim light 30, 356–358
split light 29, 109, 340, 354–355
lighting system 302–303, 316–317
lollipop 166, 230, 245
loop light 28, 77, 95, 103, 279, 337, 343, 351–355, 359–361
lying down poses 235, 250–256, 287, 289–290


## M


manual mode 44–46, 81, 91
maternity 29–30, 161, 181, 189–190, 271–295, 347–362
mermaid pose 162, 167, 231, 246–251, 288
metering 31, 39, 44–48, 53–56, 81, 91, 102, 111, 116
incident 45, 48–49, 71, 91
reflective metering 45–48, 81
midday light 57, 61
middle gray 44–45, 48, 50, 53, 111
midtones 54
modifiers 11, 20, 68, 71–74, 78, 82, 94, 98, 119–122, 336, 343–344
mom 3, 135–137, 145, 151, 154, 168, 178, 182–185, 187, 250–252, 272, 291, 294–295, 303–306, 311, 320, 325–326, 330, 343
moody 56, 103, 122, 349
Moro reflex 201
Mother *see mom*
motion blur 39, 43, 84
must-have photos 181–183, 187


## N


natural light 7, 11–13, 31, 35–65, 68, 85, 98, 119, 303
negative space 170–174
newborn 128, 142, 161–164, 180–185, 193–211, 235, 239–246, 250–252, 259–260, 262, 301–303, 306–314, 336–345, 349
northern light 61–63
Northern Hemisphere 57, 61, 104


## O


outside, photographing 57–58, 61
Over the Shoulder pose 293


## P


Paramount light 24–25
parents 3, 144–145, 181–185, 209, 217, 227, 238, 243, 250–269, 291–292, 303, 314, 336, 344
patterns of light *see lighting patterns*
Peek-a-Boo pose 264, 315
perspective 141–143
perspective distortion 141–142, 229
poses
Airplane 258–259, 315
Back Snuggle 266
Behind the Partner 292
Belly to Belly 293
Cradle Hold pose 262–263
kiss 145, 163, 239, 242–243, 256, 293
lying down 235, 250–256, 287, 289–290
mermaid 162, 167, 231, 246–248, 288
Over the Shoulder 293
Peek-a-Boo 264, 315
Pretend Hold 240
Squat and Stand 264–265
standing 153, 164, 166, 226–229, 232–234, 249, 253–267, 276–278, 286–287, 291–294, 313–315, 348
Safe Hold 239–241, 308–309
Senior Prom 291
Side Snuggle 267
Sit and Point 240–241, 308
sitting 214–215, 221–223, 229, 231–232, 246–248, 253, 257, 287–289, 304

posing 127–174
- anchor 182, 184–185, 194
- babies 193–235
- baby-led 3, 128, 194, 196, 202, 337
- block 280–281, 357
- children 123, 151–153, 166–168, 173, 184–188, 194, 228, 231–235, 238–242, 244–249, 256–257, 294–295
- doll 6–7
- family 183, 185, 254–244, 255–259, 266–268, 301–303, 311–317, 344
- groups 162–163, 167–168, 182
- individuals, see one person
- newborns 128–129, 133, 140, 142, 163–164, 169–172, 183–185, 193–207, 239–245, 250–252, 259–262, 265–269
- one person 159–161, 189
- partners 181, 190, 254–256, 265–269, 291–293
- three or more people 167
- two people 162–165

posing flow 128–129, 177–178, 183–185, 302, 337
posture 153–154, 277, 287
pre-session prep 273, 302, 320, 337
Pretend Hold pose 240
proportion 141–142
proximity of light 13, 15–16, 57, 75, 94

## Q

quality of light 10–16, 31, 37, 57–58, 61, 71–72, 78, 94, 116, 337

## R

receivers 69–70, 81, 91
reflective metering 45–48, 81
reflective modifier 73
rim light 30, 356–358
rooting 200, 262
rule of thirds 169–170

## S

Safe Hold pose 239–241, 308–309
safety 198, 204, 216–218, 229, 239, 246–247, 276–277, 308–309
Sandra Coan Method 74–77, 303
school-age children *see children*
Sekonic L-358 56, 71, 85, 91, 93
Senior Prom pose 291
session flow 194–195, 302–303, 337
session prep 273, 302, 320, 337
settings, camera 36–37, 39, 44, 49, 53, 56, 81, 85
shadows 11–14, 16, 22, 49–57, 90–92, 101, 105–106, 122, 332
shape of modifier 78
shooting from below 143
shooting on location 97–125
shooting up the nose 142
shoot-through modifier 73
shutter 38–39, 68–69, 85–90
shutter drag 88
shutter shadow 90
shutter speed 37–39, 43–44, 85–91
siblings 138, 163, 166, 181, 184–186, 188, 237–249, 254–257, 268–269, 306–309
Side Snuggle pose 267
signature style 10, 32, 56–57, 128
silhouette 31, 60, 282–284
silliness 234
Sit and Point pose 240–241, 308
sitter sessions 214–215, 217–219, 253, 257, 301–309, 315–317
sitting poses 214–215, 221–223, 229, 231–232, 246–248, 253, 257, 287–289, 304
size of light, relative 11–16, 20–22, 63–64, 71–72, 94
sleep smile 197
slide film 54, 56, 91
soft light 10–13, 61, 74–75
softbox 11, 16, 31, 78–79

south-facing light 61–62, 88
Southern Hemisphere 61
split light 29, 109, 340, 354–355
spot meter 45
squat and stand pose 264–265
standing poses 153, 164, 166, 226–229, 232–234, 249, 253–267, 276–278, 286–287, 291–294, 313–315, 348
stickers 166, 226, 230, 242, 245, 295
stool 228–232
strangers 214, 217, 221
strobes *see flash*
sun 10, 18, 22, 24, 36, 57–61
swaddle 203–204, 212, 239–241
sync chord 69–70, 81
sync port 69
sync speed 53, 85–86, 89–92

## T

temperature of light 18–19, 32, 59, 100–101, 104, 109
three-month-old 208–213, 239, 242–243, 250, 252, 260, 267, 320
through the lens (TTL) 81, 91
toddlers 59, 68, 99, 116, 132, 151–152, 181, 187, 195, 228–230, 239–242, 245,
triangles 158–169, 174, 182, 231, 244, 247, 249, 254, 288, 291, 293
trigger 68–70, 80–81, 85, 911, 102, 320, 336–337
TTL *see through the lens*

## U

umbrella 11, 20, 73–76, 78–79, 82, 119–121, 349
up the nose, shooting 142
uplighting 24, 26, 262

## V

visual interest 129, 169, 354
visual interest triangle 39

## W

window light 61–64, 87, 92, 104–107, 111, 321
windows, no 99

## Z

Zone System 44–45, 111